THE HOLY FATHER, PIUS IX.

A

GENERAL HISTORY

OF THE

CATHOLIC CHURCH:

FROM THE COMMENCEMENT OF THE CHRISTIAN ERA
UNTIL THE PRESENT TIME.

BY

M. L'ABBE J. E. DARRAS.

FIRST AMERICAN FROM THE LAST FRENCH EDITION.

WITH AN

INTRODUCTION AND NOTES

BY THE MOST REV. M. J. SPALDING, D. D.,

ARCHBISHOP OF BALTIMORE.

VOL. IV

NEW YORK:
P. O'SHEA, PUBLISHER,
37 BARCLAY STREET.

CONTENTS.

SEVENTH PERIOD.

CHAPTER I.

CHAPTER II.

CHAPTER III.

CHAPTER IV

CHAPTER V.

CHAPTER VI.

CHAPTER VII.

CHAPTER VIII.

HISTORICAL REVIEW OF THE SEVENTH PERIOD.

EIGHTH PERIOD.

CHAPTER I.

Clement IX. to the refractory bishops.—25. Alliance between Jansenism and Gallicanism. Mark Anthony de Dominis. Edmond Richer. John Launoy. Baillet. The "Lives of the Fathers of the Desert," and the works of St Theresa, translated by Arnauld d'Andilly.—26. Ellie Dupin. Richard Simon. Le Courrayer.—27. The brothers Pithou. Dupuy.—28. Pascal. The *Lettres Provinciales.*—29. Antoine Arnauld. Works on "Frequent Communion" and the "Perpetuity of the Faith." Nicole. The *Essais de Morale.*—30. Victory of St. Gothard, won by Montecuculii over the Turks.—31. Capture of Candia by the Grand-Vizier, Achmet. Death of Clement IX..............Page 298

CHAPTER II.

§ I. PONTIFICATE OF CLEMENT X. (April 29, A. D. 1670—July 22, 1676). 1. Cardinal Bona. His works.—2. Election and government of Clement X.—3. The *Regale* in France. Death of Clement X.—4. Spinoza. His pantheistic system. —5. Descartes. His philosophy.—6. Dangers of the Cartesian system pointed out by Bossuet.—7. Malebranche. § II. PONTIFICATE OF INNOCENT XI. (September 21, A. D. 1676—August 12, 1689). 8. Election and first acts of Innocent XI. His character and antecedents.—9. Splendor of France under Louis XIV.—10. Fleury's "History of the Church."—11. The two fundamental maxims of Gallicanism, according to Fleury.—12. Fleury's reasoning against the exercise of the Pontifical power in the middle-ages, drawn from the "False Decretals."—13. Value of the maxim: "The king, as such, is not subject to the judgment of the Pope."—14. Difficulties between Louis IV. and Innocent XI., concerning the *Regale.*—15. Bossuet.—16. Bossuet's letter to the Pope in the name of the French clergy. Reply of Innocent XI.—17. Convocation of the General Assembly of the clergy of France, in 1682. Louis XIV. arranges the matter of their deliberations.—18. Sessions of the Assembly. —19. Declaration of the 19th of March, 1682. The *Four Articles.*—20. Letters patent of Louis XIV., requiring all the universities of the kingdom to teach the *Four Articles.*—21. The Pope condemns the "Declaration of the Clergy of France," and annuls all the acts of the Assembly of 1682.—22. Protest of the Catholic world against the Declaration.—23. Bossuet's "Defence of the Declaration of the Clergy of France."—24. Innocent XI. refuses the bulls of canonical institution to the bishops appointed by Louis XIV.—25. The "Franchises." They are suppressed by the Pope. All the Catholic powers except France submit to the measure.—26. Innocent refuses to receive Lavardin as ambassador from the court of France. The parliament appeals from the Pope to a council.—27. Louis XIV. seizes upon Avignon, and interferes in the nomination of the archbishop-elector of Cologne.—28. Revocation of the Edict of Nantes.—29. Invasion of Austria by the Turks. Mahomet IV. Kara Mustapha. Innocent XI. effects the conclusion of a treaty, offensive and defensive, between Leopold I., emperor of Austria, and John Sobieski, king of Poland.—30. Siege of Vienna by the Turks. Rescue of the city by Sobieski. —31. Condemnation of Molinos, of the "New Testament of Mons" and other works.—32. Death of Innocent XI. § III. PONTIFICATE OF ALEXANDER VIII. October 6, A. D. 1689—February 1, 1691). 33. Election of Alexander VIII.

CHAPTER III.

CHAPTER IV.

CHAPTER V.

CHAPTER VI.

CHAPTER VII

GENERAL HISTORY OF THE CHURCH.

SEVENTH PERIOD.

From Luther to the Treaty of Westphalia (A. D. 1517–1648).

CHAPTER I.

SUMMARY.

PONTIFICATE OF LEO X. (March 11, A. D. 1513—December 1, 1521).

1. General view of the seventh period.—2. State of the world at the death of Julius II.—3. Election of Leo X.—4. Reinstatement of the Cardinals Carvajal and St. Severinus.—5. Reformatory canons of the Lateran Council.—6. Decree of the council concerning the press.—7. Decree on the *Monts-de-piété.*—8. Decrees for the pacification of Christian princes, and against the errors of Pomponatius on the immortality of the soul.—9. Peace between Louis XII. and the Holy See.—10. Death of Louis XII.—11. Accession of Francis I. His policy. Policy of Leo X.—12. Cardinal Matthew Schinner. Battle of Marignan.—13. Treaty of peace between Leo X. and Francis I.—14. Question of the kingdom of Naples.—15. The *Concordat of Leo X.* between the Holy See and France.—16. Review of the concordat.—17. Last session of the seventh general council.—18. League against France. Prudence of Leo X.—19. Theologians. Cajetan. Adrian of Utrecht, etc.—20. Linguistics. The exact sciences.—21. Historians. Machiavelli.—22. Paolo Giovio. Guicciardini.—23. Poets. Ariosto. Vida. Sannazaro.—24. Michael Angelo. Raphael.—25. Conspiracy among the cardinals against the life of the Holy Father.—26. Luther. The cause of his success.—27. Luther's first years.—28. Catholic doctrine of indulgences.—29. Luther's sermon at Wittenberg against indulgences.—30. Luther's theses posted upon the doors of the church at Wittenberg.—13. Reply of Tetzel.

PONTIFICATE OF LEO X.* (March 11, A. D. 1513—Dec. 1, 1521).

1. THE disorders, factions and intrigues which followed in
the train of the Great Schism of the West, had opened the
way for revolt against the authority of the Church. The
seventh period witnessed, in the rise of Lutheranism, the fiercest
storm which had yet tried the strength of St. Peter's chair.
Heresy was introduced in various parts of Christendom, became
a powerful party in France, Switzerland, the Netherlands
and Poland, and even the established religion of the State
in England, Sweden, Denmark and in several States of the
German empire. Its establishment was the signal for a fierce
struggle between the Catholics and the so-called Reformers,
which overturned the order of all Europe until the treaty of
Westphalia. As we treat of the disturbances which ruined
the peace of the world, and compromised the future destinies
of empires and of human society itself, at the voice of a seditious Saxon monk, we shall take occasion to show that Protestantism was not the work of one man. It owed its destructive power to the combined force of every hostile passion, of
every evil instinct, of every element of hatred and cupidity
The dogmatic question was but a pretext; it was made use
of to mislead the multitude; material interest was the true
and the only motive which led secular princes to throw off the
authority of the Church. The world had reached a state in

* For this period of the history of the Church, we are largely indebted to the writings of
M. Aud n, the distinguished author whose recent and untimely death is wept by the Church
and the literary world. Audin's Histories of Leo X. of Luther, Calvin and Henry VIII.,
reflect honor upon an epoch, and adorn his name

which the names of liberty and independence seemed to present
to the over-excited imaginations new fields and boundless enjoyment.   Luther's doctrine of private interpretation and his
principle of spiritual independence responded to the instincts
of the sixteenth century ; and hence his words exercised so
great an influence, his blasphemies were so widely repeated,
his insults so loudly applauded ; his quarrels found so many
soldiers, his proselytism so many neophytes, his license so
many imitators.   From the very outset, Protestantism was
broken up into fragments and sects ; unity, which is strength,
belongs to the true Church alone.   Luther would not recognize
his own work as it exists at the present time.   The perpetual
mobility of error, its ceaseless changes, may, for a moment,
satisfy the natural restlessness of the human heart; but they
leave nothing solid or lasting.   This is the secret of the innate
weakness of Protestantism.   It stands, indeed, as a political
medium ; as a religion, it is dead.   It moves, but in a circle,
and the bounds of its conquests are not widened.   It has
wealth, honors and armies ; it has not the faith which gives
life ; it never had, it never will have a Francis Xavier, to subject new empires, to win all hearts to its sway   Circumstances
favored its first steps.   The newly-discovered art of printing
carried its anti-catholic works, by thousands, to the most obscure
hovels ; the invention of gunpowder, by changing the ancient
mode of warfare, furnished it with armies ; the light of literature, rekindled at the torch of pagan antiquity, diffused over
the learned world a kind of atmosphere of inherent freedom, of
individual independence, and—it must be said—of general unbelief, which favored its propagation.   Amid these new storms,
the Church, ever great, ever glorious, ever fruitful, found, in the
new world opened to its zeal by the genius of Christopher
Columbus, a spiritual harvest which repaired the losses experienced in Europe.   She was consoled, by prodigies of holiness,
fidelity and devotedness, for the scandals and disorders of Germany and England ; the spirit of God had not ceased to abide
within her.

2. When the death of Julius II. left the throne of St. Peter vacant, Catholic Europe had for her rulers—in France, Louis XII., whose attempts upon Italy we have already had occasion to mention ; in England, Henry VIII., the second king of the house of Tudor, who was to cover his name with the triple dis-- grace of apostasy, adultery, and barbarous cruelty, though his gay and chivalric youth gave no presage of his future ignominy ; in Germany, the Emperor Maximilian I., who had shown him- self the faithful ally of the Holy See, and who was soon to leave his crown to the heroic Charles V ; in Spain, Ferdinand the Catholic and Isabella of Castile were closing their glorious career in unclouded prosperity and in the practice of virtues equally admirable. The kingdoms of the North were, as yet, but little occupied with the general concerns of Europe. Italy, France and England were the centres of political interest. The later accession of Charles V., bringing an immense com- bination of power into the hands of one ruler, and two worlds under the same sceptre, soon ushered Germany and all Europe into a new sphere of action. Francis I., in setting himself up as a rival to Charles V., inaugurated the system, followed in France until the reign of Louis XIV., of opposing the exces- sive predominance of the empire. The germ of war was lurk- ing under the smiling exterior of peace, at the moment when the death of Julius II. caused a lull in the storm which had shaken his Pontificate.

3. On the 4th of March, A. D. 1513, the cardinals met in con- clave in the chapel of St. Andrew. The youngest among them, John de Medici, who was but thirty-six years of age, was appointed to collect the ballots. His family had lately been restored to its rights and possessions in Florence, where its power was signalized by countless benefits and a noble patronage of letters and the arts. After a conclave of seven days, on the 11th of March, the illustrious cardinal read his own name on nearly every ballot he had collected. He was Pope. When he had examined the votes, John de Medici betrayed not the least emotion. The cardinals approached to pay their homage, and

he affectionately embraced them all. The youthful Pontiff took the name of Leo X. The tidings of his election awakened universal enthusiasm in the Catholic world, which seemed to foreknow the great deeds that were to illustrate the new Pontificate. Leo X. was to give his name to a whole age. The world had spoken, until then, of the age of Pericles, the age of Augustus; it was soon to hear of the age of Leo X., and later, of the age of Louis XIV. The great men to whom Providence gives the glory of concentrating upon themselves the splendor of an entire period, belong to the whole world. Each individual renown is, so to speak, but a tributary pouring itself into their powerful personality; they do not, in themselves, possess every kind of talent or of merit; but they know how to discern, to foster and to bring them to light; they are not the diamonds, but they give the diamonds their high polish and brilliant lustre. We must, then, consider in Leo X. two simultaneous personalities and lines of action: that of the Vicar of Jesus Christ, the spiritual head of Christianity; and that of the sovereign who constitutes himself the enlightened patron of letters, art and science, who gathers round his throne painters, sculptors and architects, such as Raphael, Michael Angelo, Bramante; men of letters, like Bembo, Sadolet and Bibiena.

4. On entering upon his new dignity, the Pope found the seventeenth general council assembled, though its sessions had been interrupted by the death of Julius II. The Pragmatic Sanction had been discussed in the preceding sessions and condemned by the late Pope. Leo X. desired that the question should not be resumed, as it would only tend to increase the ill-will of the French monarch; whereas he hoped to effect a peaceful settlement. His end was identical with that of Julius II., but he sought to reach it by different means. He was naturally of a mild and peaceable disposition, as he soon had occasion to prove by an act of signal generosity. Cardinal Carvajal and the Cardinal of St. Severinus had taken a leading part in the factious proceedings of the Council of Pisa, against Julius II. On his death-bed, Julius said of them: "As a

Christian, I forgive them, but, as head of the Universal Church, I think that justice should have its course." On learning the promotion of Leo, the two culprits felt that the time had come to seek forgiveness for their fault. Besides, the sincerity of their repentance redeemed the scandal of their schism. They accordingly came to Rome under the protection of a safe-conduct from Leo. Their appearance before the council was most impressive. The two cardinals, stripped of all the emblems of their rank, were ushered into the council-hall, approached, and prostrated themselves before the successor of the Pontiff they had so deeply injured. After remaining some moments in this position, they arose; and Carvajal addressed the Sovereign Pontiff: " Holy Father, forgive our fault; pity our tears and penance; look not upon our sins, which outnumber the sands of the sea-shore." After a moment of deep silence, in which all eyes were fixed upon the suppliants, the Pope replied: " The Church is a tender mother and receives with open arms all who return to her; still, she would not, by a weak indulgence, encourage the sinner to fall again. In order, then, that you may not glory in your fault, I have determined to inflict a punishment upon you. Have you not, by the blackest ingratitude, pained the heart of your master, your benefactor, your father, Pope Julius II., of glorious memory? Did you not publish a sentence of deposition against the Vicar of Jesus Christ? Now, pronounce your own judgment." The two cardinals, covered with confusion, made no reply " Well, then," resumed the Pope, "if you consent to sign this declaration, you are pardoned by the Holy See." The document which the Pope handed them was a full disavowal of all their proceedings against Julius II. When the cardinals had signed it, Leo came down from his throne, and, approaching Carvajal, said to him: " Now you are our brother, since you have submitted to our authority. You are the lost sheep of the gospel, brought back to the fold; let us rejoice in the Lord." With the same affectionate kindness, he spoke to the Cardinal of St. Severinus, and both were restored to their dignity The world might now augur the future career of a Pontiff who could so well combine the high attributes of majesty and mercy.

5. The council carried on its work under the inspiration of the Pope. Rome had long needed a sacerdotal reform. The Lateran Council, obedient to the wish of the Sovereign Pontiff, appointed a commission, charged to determine the means, not only of reforming the morals of the clergy, but of bringing them back to the purity of the early ages of the Church. This design had been foremost in the mind of Julius II.; Leo. X. would not allow a thought so holy to fail of execution. The ordinances published for that end are a monument of ecclesiastical wisdom and prudence. " No candidate shall be raised to the priesthood who is not of mature age, of exemplary conduct, and well versed in the learning of the schools. Theology, the *Mistress of Learning,* has been too much neglected. Henceforth, no one shall be admitted to the ministry of the altar, without having made a serious study of the Fathers and the canons. But theological learning is not alone sufficient for a priest. He must also display the virtues belonging to his divine calling; he must live in the constant practice of piety and chastity; his life must shine as a lamp before men, that God may be honored by his works. In proportion to the elevation of the dignity, is the binding force of its obligations. The cardinals should be models of regularity and ecclesiastical perfection. Their abodes should be open to all men of worth and of learning, to indigent nobles, and to every person of virtuous life. The table of a prelate should be simple, frugal and modest; his house should be ruled neither by luxury nor by avarice; his servants should be few, and always under the direction of his own active vigilance; let their faults be punished, and their good behavior rewarded. He shall never give his support to the claims of ambition; but he must lend an attentive ear to the petitions of the oppressed who seek justice at his hands. He must be ever ready to plead the cause of the poor, the friendless and the orphan. If he has poor relations, justice requires that he shall assist them, but never at the

expense of the Church." Each line of the decree concerning the cardinals is an anticipative reply to the calumnies which Luther is soon to utter against the luxury of the Roman prelates. "The field of the Lord," said Leo, "must be thoroughly upturned, in order to produce new fruits." The legitimate and peaceful reform to which this expression gave rise reached every degree of the hierarchy. The methods of teaching were examined by the council with peculiar care. In Florence, in Rome, and, indeed, in all Italy, at the period of the literary revival, it was generally considered that enough had been done for the cultivation of the mind, when the student had been taught to read Virgil or Theocritus, been made acquainted with the gods of Ovid, or translated the works of Plato. Leo X., while encouraging the study of Greek and Latin antiquity, still perceived the danger of this exclusive system of education. He was unwilling that the soul should be satisfied with an entirely sensual nourishment. It must draw, from purer sources, the knowledge of the higher truths revealed by faith. "The Christian youth must be taught that he was created by God to love and serve Him; and that he must practise the teachings of the law of Jesus Christ; let the voices of the young join in the sacred psalmody of our churches; let them chant, at vespers, the psalms of the Royal Prophet; let them read, every night, the history of those Christian heroes whose names the Church inscribes among the doctors, the martyrs and the holy anchorets. The Christian child should know the Decalogue—the commandments of God—the articles of the Creed; and, under the care of their masters, the students, both lay and clerical, should hear mass, vespers, sermons, and spend the Sundays and Festivals of the Church in singing the praises of the Lord."

6. It was essential to the preservation of the faith and of morality, that they should be carefully guarded against the influence of licentious and irreligious writings. "By multiplying the literary master-pieces of classical antiquity," says a contemporary writer, "the art of printing has so

materially lowered their value, that a work formerly worth a hundred gold crowns now costs hardly twenty Moreover, it is well printed and cleared of the gross errors which disgraced it in the manuscript." This marvellous invention, however, did not only facilitate the diffusion of useful and virtuous works. The danger was as much increased as the advantage; and it was felt even at this early date. Vitalis of Thebes, a professor of law, complains, in the year 1500, of the boldness of those typographers who yielded to the attraction of dishonorable gain, and did not blush to print the books of authors " who spoke in a strain unheard even in the old Lupercalia." The council was therefore obliged, in its care of faith and morals, to treat the great subject of the press, which has never ceased to agitate and disturb the world. The decree published by Leo X., with the consent of the Fathers, is too important not to be quoted entire. " Among the multiplied cares which weigh upon Us, one of the first and most unceasing is to recall to the way of truth, those minds which have been led astray, and to win them back to God, by the help of His holy grace. This is truly the object of Our most heartfelt desires, of Our tenderest affections, of our most active vigilance. Now, We have learned, by the complaints which reach Us from all directions, that the art of printing—which, by the divine goodness, has been constantly perfecting itself in our age, although well calculated, by the great number of books which it places, at a reduced value, in the hands of all, to advance the cause of literature and science, and to form scholars in all languages, whom We would wish to see, in great numbers, in the Roman Church, since they are enabled to convert the unbelievers, to instruct them, and to bring them by holy teachings into the true fold—has, nevertheless, become a source of evil, by the bold undertakings of the masters of the art ; that in all parts of the world, these masters have not hesitated to print works translated from the Greek, Hebrew, Arabic, or Chaldean tongue into Latin, or originally written in Latin or in the vulgar tongue; containing errors against faith, dangerous teachings contrary to Christian morality, attacks upon the reputation of individuals, even upon persons in the highest dignities; and that the reading of such works, far from improving the mind, leads to the most fatal errors in matters of faith and public morality, thus giving rise to a train of scandals, and threatening the world with yet greater woes. Wherefore, lest an art so happily invented for the glory of God, the spread of the faith and the diffusion of useful knowledge, should be turned to a contrary use, and become an obstacle to the salvation of the faithful of Christ's flock, We deem it Our duty to watch carefully over the printing of books, in order that cockle may not grow up with the wheat, that poison be not mingled with the healing draught. Earnestly desiring to provide against the evil in due time, in order that the typographical art may prosper in proportion to the care and watchfulness bestowed upon it, with the advice and consent of the Sacred College, We decree and ordain that henceforth, and for all future time, no one shall print or cause to be printed any book in Our city, or in any other city or diocese whatever, until it shall have been carefully examined, approved and signed in Rome, by Our vicar, and in the various dioceses by the bishop or by any person of his appointment, who must be competent to judge of the matter treated in the work; this We decree under pain of excommunication." This decree was an important measure of social and religious order. The censorship of an ecclesiastical tribunal in Rome and in each diocese, if always respected, would have saved the world an incalculable amount of evil. The measure was perfectly warrantable in fact and in law. What government is willing to bear the insults of its subjects, to cover its administration with disgrace? But if in this instance the crime resides in the words, shall printing, which is but the multiplication, the reproduction and even the perpetuation of these words, alone escape the check? Or, viewing the question in another light, can the pastors of souls allow the flock intrusted to their care, to be depraved by the free circulation of impious doctrines, tending to overthrow all order? With the mission to act as our guides and fathers, did they not likewise receive the power to guard us against all the sources of corruption, license and impiety? In taking these precautionary measures against the abuse of the press, Leo X. and the Lateran Council proved themselves the guardians of faith and morals, of the public peace and order. They had deserved well of mankind. The decree we have just cited was a remote preparation for the establishment of the tribunal of the Index, definitively constituted by the Council of Trent, and which has since, like a watchful sentinel, stood guard over the public morals, giving timely warning of the shoals to be avoided, the dangerous errors to be branded, the false teachings and criminal theories to be condemned. While thus regulating the use of printing, for the benefit of the Catholic world, the Pope was erecting in Rome the College of the Sapiénza, which was to become the model of all universities, and to gather within its walls the most eminent representatives of literature and science from all parts of Italy

7 The Lateran Council overlooked nothing that concerned the general good. Usury had been the plague of the middle-ages. The needy were sacrificed to the rapacity of the Jews, who lent money, at exorbitant rates, and thus succeeded in almost draining the wealth of Christendom. More than once, especially in the days of the Crusades, princes had pledged their ostates or their provinces to raise the means necessary for those expeditions. But the poor were the greatest sufferers by these exactions of the children of Israel. The first effort to deliver the world from the rapacity of these usurers was made at Perugia, in the latter half of the fifteenth century, by Barnabas of Terni, a Recollet, or Minor of the strict observance. He proposed to make a general collection through the city, and to apply the proceeds to the establishment of a bank for the relief of the needy God lent a winning power to his words, for he had hardly exposed his design, when all the inhabitants of Perugia brought their jewels, gems and gold, with large sums of money as a capital for the charitable institution which was called the Mont-de-piété. The institution of the poor monk was soon known in all

the cities of Italy. The laborer, when in want, was no longer obliged to have recourse to a Jew. By pledging some article of his poor furniture, he received a certain amount of money, which he was to return at a stated time, with no other interest than a small sum to cover the indispensable expenses of the bank. Still this institution, like every other truly useful invention, was subject to detraction. Some theologians thought that it possessed all the essential properties of usury, under another form. A violent discussion ensued, but without any definite result; and the question was brought before the general council. The Fathers to whom the matter was thus referred were well known for their learning and charity After a long and serious deliberation, in the course of which the numerous writings of both parties were carefully examined, the judgment was pronounced in a Papal decree. Leo, after a brief review of the whole debate, acknowledges that a sincere love of justice, an enlightened zeal for the truth and an ardent charity, actuated both the opponents and the defenders of the Mont-de-piété; but he adds that it is time, for the interest of religion, to put an end to the disputes which jeopard the peace of the Christian world. He to whom Christ has intrusted the care of souls, the guardian of the interests of the poor, the comforter of the suffering, forbids any one to tax with usury the institutions founded and approved by the authority of the Apostolic See, and which require from the borrower but a trifling sum to cover the necessary expenses of their administration. He approves them as real institutions of charity, which it is well to protect and to propagate.

8. The general peace of Christendom was the object which Leo X. had most at heart, and he submitted to the council a decree bearing upon this point. Nuncios were sent to the various European courts, to present these views and to secure their adoption by the different sovereigns. True to the traditions of his predecessors, Leo meditated a formidable expedition against the Turks; but, as in the case of the former Pontiffs, the glorious project, worthy of the head of Christendom, was thwarted

by the disgraceful indifference of the European sovereigns. The exclusive study of Latin and Greek authors, with the predominance of Platonism, fostered by the revival of letters, had introduced into the learned world, and even among theologians, a pagan error on the nature of the soul. Virgil's *mens agitat molem* misled the humanists of the day; they held that the soul of the world, one and universal, gave life to all beings, and was the same for all men, transforming itself in each individual, and undergoing the modifications inherent in different natures. Beside this general soul, common to all, they admitted the existence of another, which they called the *intellective*, and which, according to their theory, was mortal and perished with the body A special decree was promulgated by the council, condemning these errors. The decree of the council may have been provoked by certain works from the pen of Peter Pomponatius (A. D. 1462–1526), a doctor of Mantua. In his treatise on the *Immortality of the Soul*, the author asserts that unaided reason would tend to reject that dogma, and that we can know it only by revelation. It seems to us, on the contrary, that reason rather leads us to admit the immortality of the soul. If its light is not sufficient to afford it a dogmatic certitude of this truth, still reason would rather confirm than deny it. However, Pomponatius, whom the philosophers of the eighteenth century would have claimed as one of their forerunners, always showed himself a docile child of the Church. He submitted his work to the tribunal of the Inquisition, and published it anew with the corrections pointed out by the examiners. The posthumous reputation of atheism, which it has been attempted to fix upon his name, is but a historical fiction. Pomponatius died, as most philosophers died at that time, in sentiments of the liveliest faith and most edifying piety

9. During the sessions of the Lateran Council, political events had followed on in the course of time, and called for the Pontiff's undivided attention. Louis XII., made wiser by reverses, had consented to make peace with the court of Rome. His ambassadors came to the council, and, in their master's

name, disavowed the schismatical proceedings of the false Council of Pisa. Leo received the advances of the Most Chris tian King with the joy of an affectionate father, and absolved Louis from the censures pronounced against him by Julius II. Every thing seemed to favor the hopes of the Sovereign Pontiff. Italy was freed, by the victorious arms of Hungary and Poland, from the attacks of the Turks. Emanuel the Great, king of Portugal, immensely enriched by his commerce with the Indies, sent splendid and costly presents to Rome. Leo conferred upon him the investiture of all the lands lately won by the Portuguese navigators, and ruled with equal wisdom and cou rage by the Christian hero Affonso d'Albuquerque, surnamed the Great and the Portuguese Mars. This succession of pros perous events was celebrated, in Rome, with splendid festivities, while the seventeenth general council steadily carried on its work of salutary reform, and Leo X. surrounded his throne with all the splendors of art, the glories of literature, and the grandeur of genius.

10. But the ambition of Louis XII. was not satisfied, and he was planning a new attempt upon Italy, when he was stricken down by a violent disease of which he died, on the 1st of January, A. D. 1515, in his palace of Tournelles, at Paris. The name of Louis XII. might have been recorded among those of the wisest kings, had he not been led away, by a pas sion for distant expeditions and military laurels, into a path beset with difficulties and danger. At the very time when Italy, streaming with the blood shed by his arms, looked upon him as one of those scourges sent by Providence for the chas tisement of nations, France was heaping benedictions upon his name. The public criers proclaimed his death with the words : "Our good king Louis, the father of his people, is dead !" And the whole nation was filled with mourning. Few princes, indeed, ever deserved better of their subjects. Not withstanding his many wars, he would never raise their taxes always finding means to supply his wants, by a strict and pru dent economy. "I would rather see my courtiers laughing

at my avarice," he used to say, "than my subjects weeping for my prodigality " After the example of his illustrious predecessor, St. Louis, he often went in person, without escort or attendants, to administer justice and to dictate his decrees. He shortened the formalities of trials, but condemned any haste in the procedure. He always kept two exact accounts : the one, of the favors at his disposal ; the other, of the most worthy persons in each province. When any benefice or dignity became vacant, it was always filled by the most worthy candidate. The effects of so wise an administration did not fail soon to appear. " The reigns of his predecessors seemed forgotten," says the quaint old chronicler St. Gelais, "in the happy days he gave to France."* When he travelled through the country, the people left their work, thronged the roads which they had decked with green, and filled the air with repeated acclamations of joy, as he passed. "He is indeed our father," they cried, "he stints himself for us."

11. Louis XII. left no male heir to the crown, which thus passed to Francis I., the great-grandson of the Duke of Orleans, brother to Charles VI., and Valentina Visconti of Milan. The young monarch loved to surround his throne with men of letters, artists and scholars. He was called the *Father of letters*, and was a worthy contemporary of Leo X. History presents him to us with all the qualities which command love and admiration—he was frank, honorable, kind, generous and brave. Finding his kingdom disposed by the wars of Charles VIII. and Louis XII. to undertake Italian expeditions, he prepared to assert his right to the Milanese, as heir of Valentina Visconti. Were it fair to judge, from a point so far removed, the traditional policy of the French kings at this period, we might be inclined to censure the persevering ambition which cost torrents of blood, drained the royal treasury, revolutionized Italy and disturbed the peace of the world ; and all for a result so utterly barren. But the rights they asserted, and which, to us,

* Il ne courut oncques au règne de nul des autres, si bon temps qu'il a fait durant le sien."

seem questionable enough, were doubtless far more just and well grounded, in their estimation. However this may be, when the new King of France openly proclaimed his hostile intention, the duchy of Milan was in the hands of Maximilian Sforza and defended by an auxiliary body of Swiss troops in the pay of the duke. The policy of Leo X., in this critical juncture, had been already determined. The Pope loved peace and would have wished to see it reign over the whole of Europe, but especially in Italy, for which he was planning a brilliant destiny But finding himself placed in the necessity of choosing between the contending parties, and of throwing his authority into the scales in favor of one or the other, he was bound to uphold the cause of Italian independence, so nobly defended by Julius II. The possession of Lombardy by the French would have endangered the patrimony of the Holy See ; and their pretensions to the throne of Naples would have made the Pontifical States a constant thoroughfare for their armies. The exigencies of his position explain why Leo X., though drawn toward Francis by a natural conformity of tastes and by a common love of art and letters, still felt bound to sacrifice his personal sympathies to considerations of a higher order. As head of Italy, to which position he was raised by the influence of his exalted rank and high personal character, he could not be French, he must remain Italian. This political necessity has been wholly disregarded or overlooked by some historians, who tax the conduct of the great Pontiff with partiality and injustice. It is our conviction, and, though a Frenchman, we do not fear to say it, that the first and highest duty of every people is to defend its nationality, even against the arms of France, if France invade it. Such was the course of Leo X. ; and those who are so ready with their censure, would have been the first to blame him had he acted otherwise.

12. Francis concluded an alliance with the Venetians ; he was master of Genoa ; the Italian waters were thus in his power. Leo, on the other hand, joined a league against him, with Maximilian, Ferdinand the Catholic, and the Swiss. The

Swiss were led by a cardinal who combined the military talent
of Albornoz, the valor of William Tell and the eloquence of St.
Bernard.   This was Matthew Schinner, bishop of Sion, of whom
his contemporaries said that "since the great Abbot of Clair-
vaux, such resistless eloquence had never been known as that
of the Bishop of Sion."   Julius II. had raised him to the
Roman purple.   Schinner's heroic nature displayed at once
the most opposite extremes.   He was found almost simultaneously at the advance posts, in the centre, or with the rear-
guard; a soldier in the fray, a bishop when the departing soul
was to be reconciled with its God.   Like the least of his men
at arms, he made the snow his couch, and lived, in the camp,
like an anchoret, fasting several days in the week, abstaining
wholly from meat, using no beverage but water, reciting his
office, and spending long hours in prayer on the eve of a battle.
As we have already observed, the habits of the age explain the
combination which would be wholly at variance with the spirit
of our own times.   Switzerland had, in its illustrious cardinal,
a surer rampart even than its lofty mountains crowned with
eternal snows.   But both these barriers yielded before French
valor and the spirit of the chivalric monarch.   The Alps were
scaled, and in less than eight days Francis was in Italy.   At
the first tidings of his approach, Milan revolted and expelled
Maximilian.   The French troops were within a few days'
march of the city, when the Cardinal of Sion hurried to the
rescue, with his hardy mountaineers from Uri, Underwalden,
Zug and Schwitz.   On the 13th of September, A. D. 1515, the
Swiss poured down upon the French, charging with their lances,
eighteen feet long, and their huge two-handed swords; without
cavalry or artillery, using no military strategy other than mere
bodily strength, marching steadily up to the batteries which,
under the able management of Genouillac, mowed down whole
ranks of the approaching column, and bearing back more than
thirty charges of those great war-horses, covered, like their riders,
with heavy mail.   The dauntless intrepidity of the Swiss made
the battle of Marignan one of the most obstinate combats re-

corded in history The veteran Marshal Trivulce, who had fought eighteen pitched battles, said that this one was "a battle of giants, and the others mere child's play" The king was at the head of his infantry to meet the charge of the enemy, and each soldier became a hero. The fight continued a long time, by moonlight; but toward eleven o'clock the darkness became too deep and separated the combatants, or rather every man stood at the post where darkness had surprised him. Francis slept upon a gun-carriage, within fifty paces of a Swiss battalion. At daybreak the charge was sounded on both sides, and the fight was renewed with the same fury as on the preceding day. After a desperate struggle of five hours, the Swiss, hearing the battle-cry of the Venetian allies of Francis : "*Marco! Marco!*" and believing that the whole Italian army was upon them, closed their ranks and slowly retreated, but with a front so determined, that the victorious army dared not pursue. They left more than fifteen thousand dead behind. Francis, at his own request, was knighted on the field of battle by the hand of Bayard. The Swiss, so gloriously defeated, withdrew to Milan. Their leaders spoke of peace; but Schinner, like another Hannibal, preferred voluntary exile to a treaty with the French. He accordingly left Milan and retired to Innspruck. Francis said of him to the historian Paolo Giovio : "What an unbending man is that Schinner! His fearless freedom of speech has done me more harm than all his mountain-spears."

13. The victory of Marignano opened the way for the king into Italy Leo's policy had failed; he was obliged to bow to necessity William Budé, the first Greek scholar in France, was sent by Francis I. as ambassador to Rome. The selection of the envoy was eminently suited to win the good graces of a Pope who loved and patronized learning; and Leo, in return, appointed Louis Canossa, another distinguished scholar, to represent him at the court of France. These negotiations soon resulted in a treaty of peace. The Pope gave up Parma and Piacenza, which were annexed to the Milanese; Francis recognized the

authority of the Medici in Florence, gave back Bologna to the Holy See, and pledged himself for the independence of the Pontifical States. On his return to Rome, with the treaty he had just concluded with Francis I., Canossa did not forget to represent to the Pope the deference, respect and love which the king had always shown toward the Holy See, in the course of the negotiation. The Pontiff returned his thanks for these good dispositions, by a letter in which he alluded to the many eminent qualities Heaven had bestowed upon the youthful monarch. Francis had more than once expressed a desire for a personal interview with the Pope. Leo gladly assented to the desired conference, which took place at Bologna, December 11, A. D. 1515. Francis knelt and kissed the slipper of the Pope, who raised him up and presented his cheek. The king then took his place on a splendid throne at the right hand of the Pope; and his chancellor, Duprat, made the profession of obedience. "Most Holy Father," said the chancellor, "the army of the Most Christian King is yours; dispose of it as you please; the forces of France are yours; her standards are yours. Here is your obedient son; he is ever ready to devote himself to the defence of your sacred rights by word and by the sword."

14. The Pope and the king had two important questions to decide; the French possession of Naples and the Pragmatic Sanction. Francis, once in possession of Milan, wished to drive the Spaniards from Italy and to seize the kingdom of Naples. Since neither of these two ends could be gained without the help of Rome, he solicited the armed intervention of the Pope. Leo understood that, for him, to gain time was to conquer; he accordingly represented to the king the old age and infirmities of Ferdinand, the probability of his speedy dissolution, which would free the Pope from his obligations to the house of Aragon, and promised in that event to consider whether his position would authorize him to help France in the conquest of Naples, or not. The king understood the motives of the Sovereign Pontiff, and the question was reserved.

15. The question of the Pragmatic Sanction had, under various forms, continually occupied the attention of the Roman and French courts. Louis XII., in his disputes with Julius II., had made it an occasion of displaying his resentment against the Pope, by giving force to its hostile prescriptions. In the Lateran Council, Julius had retorted by laying the French kingdom under interdict. Francis held a different position in regard to Leo X. Even before the interview at Bologna, both sovereigns entertained the same view concerning the necessity of annulling the decree; but the matter was one of too much importance to be settled within the few days they had passed together. When they separated, after the interview of Bologna, the Pope left the Cardinals of Ancona and of Santi-Quatri, and the king his chancellor, Duprat, with full powers to conclude, by a concordat, an amicable settlement of the difficulties which had so long divided the Church and France. The negotiations between the cardinals and the chancellor lasted until the 18th of August, A. D. 1517, when the agreement known as the Concordat of Leo X. was published in Rome with the approbation of the Holy See, and continued to govern the church of France until the Concordat of 1802. It brought considerable changes into the existing system of elections. We quote a few of the most important clauses : By the fourth and tenth articles, the cathedral and metropolitan churches are deprived of the right of election.—" Within six months after the vacancy of any charge, the king shall name a doctor or a licentiate in theology or law, possessing all the necessary qualifications ; the choice to be confirmed by the Pope." The same law holds for abbeys and conventual priories.—" In every cathedral a prebend shall be reserved for a doctor, or licentiate, or bachelor of theology, who must have studied ten years in a university The prebendary, with the title of *Theologal*, shall lecture at least once a week, and may absent himself from choir duty without losing any of the emoluments attached to personal residence. A third of the benefices, of whatever kind, shall be hereafter reserved for those who have taken degrees in the University." The con-

cordat regulated the period for studies; ten years for doctors and licentiates in theology; seven years for doctors in law or medicine; five years for licentiates and masters-of-arts; five years for bachelors-of-laws.—" In the collation of a benefice, the preference shall be given to the oldest or highest in degrees, in any one faculty, or to one who has taken degrees in a higher faculty   A doctor shall take precedence of a licentiate, a licentiate of a bachelor; theology must rank above law, law above medicine; and, as a mark of honor to sacred studies, bachelors in theology shall be preferred to licentiates of inferior faculties. The cure of city or suburban parishes shall be granted only to graduates, or to those who have studied at least three years in the schools of theology or law, or to masters-of-arts.   Scandalous clerics shall be punished by suspension from their benefices and then by the loss of the benefices and disqualification for Holy Orders."

16. We have given the substance of the concordat to which Leo X. has attached his name; a work of which the Papacy may justly be proud.   In speaking of the Pragmatic Sanction, the Pope remarked, that it gave up the Church of France to intrigue, violence and simony   "It is an unquestionable fact," says a late French writer, "that the elections reëstablished by the Council of Basle were but a fiction.   In each province the nobles made themselves masters of at least the highest dignities; they had, to a certain extent, some right to the nomination, as patrons of the churches, or as descendants of the pious founders."*   To put an end to such a state of things was a real benefit.   Still, passion, animosity and hate leagued together to oppose the work of Leo X.   The partisans of what were so improperly called the *Gallican liberties* pretended that the Pope had overstepped the bounds of his authority in this radical change of the system of ecclesiastical elections.   The same absurd outcry has ever been raised against each great act of the Papacy.   The Church, like every other

* Essay on Æneas Sylvius, by M VERDIERE. 8vo, Paris, 1843, p. 81

social body, has its crises, when particular evils require the
application of extraordinary remedies.   Jesus Christ, in constituting His Church to last for all ages, must have provided for all
the necessities of its future existence ; and this He did by giving to Peter and to his successors the authority to *bind and to
loose, to confirm his brethren* in the faith.   Besides, in the case
in question, abstracting from all idea of lawful authority, the
step taken by Leo X. is abundantly justified by motives of
present necessity   Doubtless it was a good and holy custom
that allowed the clergy to choose their own pastor in the days
of faith, piety and peace.   But when morality becomes corrupted, when sacred studies are neglected and the minds of
men are disordered, then scandals more readily make their way
into the sanctuary.   It is no longer worth, but wealth, that gives
the best claim to preferment ; learning and virtue, without the
appanage of wealth, must yield to the influence of riches, which
are often the fruit of dishonesty or sin.   The sovereign's choice,
confirmed by the Holy See, put an end to all abuses, to domestic rivalry and hate, and gave to the successful candidate the
twofold support of the spiritual and temporal authority, in their
highest expression.   " The bull of Leo X.," it is urged, " destroyed a system of discipline long in force in the Church of
France."   But it must be admitted that there are circumstances in which a departure from the ordinary rule becomes a
necessity   And who is to decide when that necessity exists ?
Is it the priest, who has not the fulness of the priesthood, but
is " a branch," says Thomassin, " of that divine tree of which
the bishop is the trunk ?"   Is it the bishop, whose jurisdiction,
though divine, can only be exercised within the limits and on
the subjects prescribed by the Sovereign Pontiff, " to whom it
belongs to extend or to retrench them ?" as the Cardinal of
Lorraine proclaimed in the Council of Trent ?   " Since the Primacy was given to St. Peter to remove all occasion of schism,"
says St. Jerome, " the Pope alone has the right to make laws
that shall bind the Church ; but these laws, being, by then
nature, variable, cannot bind him so far that he may not dero-

gate from them for just reasons, of which he alone is to be the judge."

17 The concordat was read in the Lateran Council before being made public. The last act of the Fathers was the formal approval of the agreement. On the 16th of March, A. D. 1517, Leo X. presided at the last session, which numbered one hundred and ten prelates. The questions which had occasioned their convocation were happily resolved. Peace was restored among Christian princes, a reform effected in morals and in the Roman court, the schism and the false Council of Pisa were abolished, and the Pragmatic Sanction annulled. Leo once more confirmed all the acts of the preceding sessions. He also prescribed the collection of tithes, and exhorted all beneficiaries to allow this collection on their benefices to be used in the war against the Turks. The Cardinal of St. Eustathius then pronounced the usual formula of dismissal: "Domini ite in pace." A solemn Te Deum was chanted in thanksgiving, and the Lateran Council, which had lasted nearly five years, was at an end.

18. The alliance between the Pope and Francis I. was viewed with apprehension by Austria and Spain. The Emperor Maximilian and Ferdinand the Catholic both sought an alliance with Henry VIII. of England. The favor of Henry's prime minister, Cardinal Wolsey, gave them every hope of success when the death of Ferdinand, in January, A. D. 1516, caused a complete revolution in European politics. The youthful Charles of Austria, afterward so famous under the title of Charles V., then sovereign of the Netherlands, having succeeded his grandfather, Ferdinand, upon the throne of Spain, needed a season of peace to establish himself firmly in his new possessions. Francis I. determined to seize upon the kingdom of Naples. The reserved question of the conference at Bologna was thus, by the force of circumstances, once more revived to trouble the peace of the world. Maximilian, hearing of the intended expedition, found all his youthful vigor and energy returning. He led an army into the Milanese, at the same time urging

his ally, Henry VIII., to invade the French coast; but the king failed to coöperate. Milan was defended for the French monarch, by the Constable of Bourbon, who had not yet disgraced his name by the infamous stain of treachery. The imperial forces were repulsed in spite of the valor of Cardinal Schinner, who led his faithful mountaineers under the standard of Maximilian. The bearing of Leo X. amid the confusion of war was such as it should have been. The treaty of alliance concluded by the Holy See with Francis was faithfully observed; and still the Pope has been accused of displaying duplicity and bad faith in this conjuncture. On learning the part taken by the Swiss, in the war, the Sovereign Pontiff at once wrote to the Cardinal of Sion: "As soon as you receive my letter, give up your undertaking; remain quiet, and do not disturb the peace of your mountains. There is nothing that a wise and prudent man should more studiously avoid than to bring trouble into a peaceful republic, and to rouse to revolt the land of his birth; this is not to serve the true interests of Christendom." These words must have seemed hard to the cardinal; but if the soldier might have felt stung to the quick, the priest was there to pour oil and wine into the wound.* The bishop obeyed the voice of the Sovereign Pontiff, bade adieu to his followers, and withdrew to await the moment when the Church should need his services. Leo wrote, at the same time, to Ennio, bishop of Veruli, his legate in the Swiss cantons: "As I already warned you—immediately after signing the treaty of friendship with Francis I.—be very careful, in your dealings with the Swiss, never, directly or indirectly, to offend his Majesty; I rely upon your prudence. You are aware that the court of France is not yet very favorable to you, it will therefore be of the utmost importance that you take no part in the diets which are announced in Switzerland; keep aloof from all popular proceedings, showing that you have not the remotest intention of doing any thing that might displease the King of

* M. AUDIN, *Histoire de Léon X.*, t. II., p. 158.

France." We are at a loss to discover, in these sentiments of the Sovereign Pontiff, the ground for a charge of faithlessness and perjury.

19. Amid these political concerns which necessarily consumed so much of Leo's time and attention, he still managed to give to literature, science and art the support, encouragement and patronage that might have been expected from a sovereign as enlightened as he was liberal. The science of theology was represented in the Roman court by the celebrated Dominican, Cardinal Cajetan (Tommaso de Vio). Cajetan was passionately devoted to St. Thomas Aquinas, whose works are too little studied in our own day, and whose *Summa* should be the manual of every theologian. It was generally said that "if the works of the Angelic Doctor could ever have been lost, they would have been found again in the memory of Cajetan;" and indeed he had learned the *Summa* almost by heart. He taught theology at Padua with distinguished success. He was heard with the same attention and pleasure by cardinals, universities, the clergy, nobility and people. His spirited, logical and manly eloquence subjugated all minds. During the sessions of the false Council of Pisa, he appeared in that city, and, with a courage equal to his eloquence, openly reproved the disobedience of the schismatical cardinals, overwhelmed them by his triumphant arguments, and branded their rebellion in its very stronghold. It was then that he wrote his celebrated treatise on *The authority of the Pope and of the Council*, in which he so ably defends the monarchical supremacy of the Sovereign Pontiff. Cajetan afterward deserved, from Clement VII., the title of Lamp of the Church. In raising him to the purple, Pope Leo X. was rewarding both talent and virtue. Another promotion, at the same time, placed among the princes of the Church the son of a poor weaver of Utrecht, destined by Providence to succeed the Pope who conferred the honor Adrian of Utrecht, for whom this glorious future was in store, had opened his way to greatness by a youth of deep and laborious study in the University of Louvain. His learning was dis-

played in the treatise *De Rebus Theologicis*, which won him the esteem and favor of Maximilian I., who made him preceptor to his son, the youthful Charles of Austria. The distinguished theologian was thus to form one of the greatest princes of the sixteenth century. His care was not lost; and when, afterward, from the chair of St. Peter, he turned his eyes upon his former scholar, now king of Spain and of the Netherlands, emperor of Germany and master of half the New World, the preceptor had no occasion to blush for his pupil. Leo had discerned the merit of the theologian of Utrecht, and in calling him to Rome, to clothe him with the purple, he placed him upon an eminence which he was worthy to hold. The Sacred College numbered other distinguished theologians. Alexander Cesarino was regarded by Paul Manutius as one of the best read men of his day in the Sacred Writings. Jacobatio, who was made a cardinal at the same period, has all the weight of a doctor, in questions of dogma. His work, *De Concilio*, received the distinguished honor of being included in the acts of the Lateran Council. It would almost seem that a vague presentiment of the coming struggles of the Church, or the illumination of a ray of divine light, had warned Leo X. to surround the Holy See with the power of virtue and learning, to meet the assaults of the Lutheran revolt. Prierias, whom he had appointed to the office of Master of the Sacred Palace, was a man most deeply versed in ecclesiastical knowledge; the professors of the Roman Gymnasium, Nicholas de Luna and Cyprian Benedetti, were eminently qualified to lead the youthful ecclesiastics into the highest walks of theological science. The groundless calumny, repeated by Protestant historians, that Leo X., in his exclusive zeal for the encouragement of literary and artistic merit, neglected to foster that divine science which is queen, mistress and mother of all the others, is abundantly refuted by facts. To what influence is the Church indebted for the great number of illustrious doctors who, twenty years later, shone with such splendor in the Council of Trent, if not to the schools founded by Leo X. ?

20. The great Pontiff appreciated the advantages to be derived from the study of languages, in clearing up disputed passages in the Sacred Writings, in settling their doubtful meaning, and in opening to the theologian the hitherto unknown field of the Eastern dialects. The efforts of the Sovereign Pontiff toward this end, caused a real scientific revolution in Europe. The Greek Fathers were studied from the original text. Lascaris and Favorino, the most celebrated Hellenists of the day, illustrated the chair of Greek, erected for them in the Roman Gymnasium. The Oriental languages were taught in Rome and in Bologna by the distinguished philologist, Theseus Ambrogio, a canon of St. John-Lateran, who spoke nearly every known idiom. Leo offered him the cardinal's hat, which he declined, preferring the obscurity of a life of study to the brilliant honors of the cardinalate. He translated the liturgy of the Eastern Church from Chaldean into Latin, and published a polyglot grammar in Chaldaic, Syriac, Armenian, &c., a splendid work, which Mazuchelli pronounces the first attempt of the kind ever made in Italy Another great Orientalist, Pagnini, a Dominican religious, conceived the project of giving a Latin version of the Bible, from the Hebrew text. He devoted twenty-five years to this great work, carefully collating all the manuscripts within his reach, and then took the result of his labors to Rome. There was but one sovereign who could then undertake the publication of so expensive a work; and Pagnini found in Leo X. an enlightened judge and liberal patron. The Pope ordered the manuscript to be re-copied and printed at his own expense. In the following year, the Psalter, with the rabbinical commentaries, was issued from the Pontifical press. The death of Leo delayed the publication of the remainder of the work, though it was afterward completed at Lyons, under the patronage of Adrian V and Clement VII. Luther soon afterward proclaimed that the Church kept the Bible from the light, whereas the Popes encouraged the publication of Pagnini's version. Leo X., Adrian VI., and Clement VII., generously patronized the author and his work. What is Luther's

assertion worth when opposed to this fact? The impulse given by Leo X., to the study of languages was soon felt throughout Europe. It was then that Cardinal Ximenes published his Polyglot Bible; the Calabrian Guidaccerio, his Hebrew grammar, a noble work which he afterward revised, in Paris, where he then held a professorship, while Francis Rossi, of Ravenna, contributed the mystic philosophy of Aristotle, translated from the Arabic. These three works bear, on the title-page, the name of Leo X., to whom they were dedicated. This serious study of the dead languages was of great service to the exact sciences. In Rome, were translated the elements of Euclid and some arithmetical works received from the Arabians. Mathematics were in high esteem in the Italian universities. It is certain that, before the Pontificate of Leo X., there was a special chair of Mathematics in the Roman Gymnasium. Copernicus taught the science at Rome, about the year 1500, but Leo X. was the first to attach any honorable emoluments to its professorship. The hieroglyphics of the Egyptian obelisks also drew the attention of the learned men whom Leo had gathered about his throne. The resuscitation of the sacred language of the Egyptians, of which the honor is claimed by the scientific men of our own day, really belongs to the sixteenth century. Pierio Valeriano, one of the early preceptors of Leo X., wrote the first scientific work giving any special information on this symbolical writing. The value of his system may be questioned, but it cannot be denied that he has displayed a high degree of learning, sagacity and talent in this kind of research.

21. If there be one department of human learning which, above all others, requires power of reflection, varied acquirements, solid judgment, a deep acquaintance with the human heart, profound erudition and an easy style, it is undoubtedly the study of history Great poets and great painters are more numerous than great historians. Leo X. had the glory of gathering about his throne every variety of talent. Historians were not wanting to this brilliant galaxy of learning. Machiavelli's History of Florence, dedicated to Leo X., is one of the finest

monuments of the Italian language and one of the deepest works ever written in any language. " Machiavelli," says M. Audin, "must more than once have awakened Tacitus while writing this work." Like his severe Roman model, the historian of Florence is grave, solemn, sober in style. No writer has ever shown a deeper insight into the most hidden folds of the human heart. The secret cause of every action is always displayed by the side of the apparent motive. His flexible style adapts itself to all subjects; it is close and concise in his political works; in history, abundant and picturesque; easy, flowing and natural in his correspondence. Machiavelli, the republican conspirator, the declared enemy of the Medici, found in Leo X. a patron and protector; he is the most complete personification of two diametrically opposite periods. He seems to possess a twofold personality, that of the ancient Roman who has, in his inmost heart, raised altars to liberty, dreaming impossible republics, whose citizens should recognize no distinction but that conferred by superior virtue, and branding tyranny and crime with the energy of indignation. But side by side with this character, equally absolute in affection and hate, appears the Italian courtier, pliant, intriguing, restless, ambitious of honors and power. Machiavelli did not appear to equal advantage in both phases of his character. The courtier was inferior to the historian, and, until the accession of Leo X., his life was little better than a long period of disgrace. The work upon which his reputation is chiefly founded, is the *Prince*. Its origin is directly connected with the history of Leo X. At the death of his brother, Julian de Medici, Leo, unable to take into his own hands the administration of the Florentine republic, was at a loss for a constitution to give to his native State. Machiavelli, the former Secretary of the Republic, was the very last man to whom the Pope might have been expected to apply for a solution of the difficulty. But Leo X., like all great men, could appreciate real talent, even in an enemy, and Machiavelli was consulted. This is the first instance of a prince seeking political counsel from a conspirator once banished from his States for conspiring against his own life. The Florentine answered the Pontiff's confidence, by the production of a master-piece. " The Prince" gave existence to the modern political system and raised it upon a truly scientific basis; it must be taken only as a series of formulas for the use of governments. The principle of self-interest becomes, in the hands of the publicist, the spring of the world and the ruler of society   Machiavelli is the advocate of brute force, cunning, fraud and deceit, when power needs the help of bad passions for success; of clemency, generosity and all the noblest inspirations, when virtue is to be called into action.   In a moral point of view, that system cannot be too severely condemned which makes of hypocrisy, fraud and perjury a governmental necessity

22. The genius of the historian always draws its inspirations from contemporaneous circumstances and events.   It cannot be denied that the expedition of Charles VIII. into Italy was favorable to the development of historical studies.   Before this period, some attempts had, indeed, been made to revive that science.   John Villani, in Florence, Æneas Sylvius, whose talents raised him to the Papacy, Poggio and Leonardo d'Arezzo, have all left some works not wholly without merit.   Yet these attempts, however laudable, were not crowned with success. With these writers, history becomes, at times, a mere collection of legends, sometimes a mere journal or a simple summary of events, recorded without method, criticism, or spirit.   The appearance of Charles VIII. converted Italy into a vast battlefield, on which the most powerful nations of the world struggled for supremacy   Paolo Giovio undertook to write the history of the great expedition, and as soon as he had finished the first book, he went to Rome, to read some portions of it to Pope Leo X.   He presented himself at the Pontifical court without introduction or recommendation; he had but to make known his name and the object of his visit, to obtain an audience. Had he been an ambassador, the master of ceremonies might perhaps have made him wait; but all the doors of the Vatican were open to one who came in the name of the Muses.

He was accordingly received in the Pope's apartments. He read several pages of his history, and the Pope affirmed that, with the exception of Livy, no historian seemed to him more eloquent than Giovio. The successful historian was speedily rewarded with the title of Roman Knight, a yearly pension and the chair of Philosophy in the gymnasium established by the Pope. Paolo Giovio was a philosophical historian, not contenting himself, as his predecessors had done, with a mere detail of facts, but likewise studying and explaining them; he correctly appreciates the manners, customs, and institutions of the various nations of which he writes; and those nations are the whole world. In the description of the glorious victories won by the French arms, his style warms into new life and color, and seems to join in the spirited charges of our soldiers. We have to regret the loss of five books of his annals, the richest in great events. To the grave recital of the historian, Giovio adds the portraits of the great men of every time and country, drawn with the pen of a faithful biographer. The patronage of Leo X. was of signal service to him; Clement VII. afterward raised him to the see of Nocera. The revenues of the bishopric, in which he never resided, together with the Pontifical liberality, enabled him to purchase a delightful retreat on the shores of Lake Como, where he wrote his work on the " Praises of Great Men," a real gallery, into which he introduces celebrated captains and philosophers, theologians and poets, orators and physicians, emperors and doges, monks and queens. When it became known that Giovio had planned the composition of such a work, all were at once anxious to appear in his gallery Hercules Gonzaga sent him the portraits of the Mantuan and of Pomponatius; from Vasari he received busts of the heroes of Roman antiquity; from Cortes, an emerald in the shape of a heart, and Aretino contributed a picture of himself, painted by Titian, that the historian might spare at least the face of him who was styled the scourge of princes. They all knew that the only true immortality on earth, exclusive of that conferred by religion, is given by history.—Beside Giovio,

Guicciardini has also chronicled the events which took place in Italy since the expedition of Charles VIII., but he has many advantages over his rival; in the first place, he was an eye-witness of most of the facts which he relates; again, he wrote in the vernacular idiom, whereas Paolo Giovio made use of Latin, the language of the learned, and hence unknown to the great mass of the people; and the offices of political trust which he held must have given him access to secrets which no other could have learned. Like Machiavelli, Guicciardini was a Florentine, and, like him, he had a grave and severe turn, professed republican principles and served the party opposed to the Medici; he had also been initiated by personal experience into the knowledge of men and their dealings. He had hardly reached his thirtieth year when the Republic sent him as ambassador to Spain. He was deputed to present its congratulations to Pope Leo X., on his accession, and when the Pontiff passed through Florence, in 1515, on his way to the conference of Bologna, it was through Guicciardini that the republic again addressed him. True to his habit of impartial liberality toward real talent, in whatever political party it might exist, Leo named Guicciardini governor of Modena and Reggio. The historian filled the post with distinguished success; he succeeded in commanding equal respect and esteem for his twofold authority as military governor and civil administrator. Adrian VI. kept him in office and Clement VII. placed him in charge of the Romagna. It was by thus · generously rewarding literary worth that the Papacy made itself the centre of the literary revival. Still, Guicciardini is not irreproachable. He sometimes displays hostile sentiments toward the Pontifical power to which he was so deeply indebted; his style is often diffuse; an overstrained patriotism blinds him to the real qualities and noble magnanimity of Charles VIII. But these stains are unnoticed amid the beauties which adorn his history. No writer, among the ancients, abounds in deeper reflections; he appeals to reason rather than to the imagination. The study of the law gave him a tone of calmness and austerity   He attributes all human events to the direction of Providence. Having lived in the camp and in the senate, among the nobles and with the people, he has an incontestible advantage over his rivals, and speaks with the certainty of experience on all the events of his time. He had drunk largely at the sources of ancient literature, especially from Livy, and shows too much fondness for harangues; some of those which he ascribes to his characters are perfect models. The address of Gaston de Foix before the battle of Ravenna is quoted with special praise. However, these amenities of style, foreign to historic truth, were but imitations of antiquity In this respect, the literary revival was but a copy, a species of perpetual reproduction of a bygone age; its writers, historians and poets all lack originality

23. The poetic art, under Leo X., numbers many illustrious names, and the great Pontiff deserves the highest praise for the impartial patronage bestowed upon every variety and expression of talent in this branch. The fact that Ariosto's " Orlando Furioso " appeared with a special privilege and a Pontifical bull authorizing the sale of the work for the profit of the poet, shows how far Leo meant to carry the indulgence and the prerogatives of a crowned Mæcenas. We do not hesitate to assert our belief that, notwithstanding all the brilliancy and splendor of the period in which the gods of Homer and Virgil returned with the almost divine language in which they were celebrated, the world was fast hurrying astray into the ways of error. It disowned its traditions, habits and Christian thoughts, it rejected the inspirations of the middle-ages, though without denying the faith; hence the strange anomalies found mingled with the most sacred names in religion. Vida, in compliance with Pope Leo's wish for a poem on the birth of Christ, and Sannazaro, treating the same subject in harmonious verse, fall into the error of peopling the groves and valleys about Jerusalem with fauns, nymphs and dryads. The genius of Christian poets was thus misled by the passion for Greek antiquity, and the influence was too powerful to die out soon; it ruled the age of Louis XIV., and has, even until our own

day, confined the human intellect to the walks of heathen Olympus. If it be true that literature is at once, in respect to public opinion, a mirror and a focus, it cannot be denied that the pagan tendencies of the revival have contributed to the philosophical wanderings of the eighteenth century Still, it would be the height of injustice to charge Pope Leo X. with the results of the literary movement of his age. A man, however great, can avail himself only of the resources furnished by his epoch. Leo X. took the age as he found it; but he raised it to the height of his own lofty views. He hailed the discovery of heathen antiquities with an enthusiasm equal to that which hailed the discovery of the New World; he could not suspect that its flowers but served to hide a deep abyss; or we should rather say that his work shared the lot of all human works, and was afterward drawn into a fatal extreme which was preparing the way for unforeseen catastrophes.

24. The originality wanting to the writers of this period appeared in the works of its artists. The age which can present, at once, two such men as Michael Angelo and Raphael is worthy to attract the attention of all posterity Buonarotti, the sculptor, painter and architect, is the type of majesty and grandeur; his name is a synonyme for every variety of talent; his genius would have sufficed to illustrate three great men. His every inspiration was a master-piece, received by the world with an enthusiastic welcome; his pencil gave to coming generations the awful scene of the *Last Judgment;* his chisel shaped, in immortal marble, the sublime figure of Moses, while his daring hand reared aloft the great dome of St. Peter's. He had reached the zenith of his glory, when he found his palm disputed by a mere youth, who overcame him in the most glorious struggle ever known. Michael Angelo, with his austere forms and the majestic severity of his compositions, had been the favorite artist of Julius II.; Raphael, whose divine pencil has idealized matter and colored his canvas with something of the tints of Heaven, was the privileged artist of Leo X.; he has remained the inimitable model, the painter by excel-

lence, peerless in the past, and most probably in the future. While heathen models were reproduced in every work of art, Raphael felt that painting should, above all things, represent the life of the soul, the leading element of Christianity. Every object in nature spoke to him of the Creator; he never fell into the error of obscuring, by excessive ornament, the beauty of its divine origin, which dwells in every created object. No artist ever more affectionately represented the Immaculate Virgin. Raphael seemed desirous to consecrate his genius to the Mother of God. In whatever form we meet his representations of that blessed Mother, whether with her eyes cast down upon the Divine Child in her arms, at the foot of the cross, or crowned in heaven by the Blessed Trinity; whether borne upward above the clouds of heaven by choirs of angels, or gazing upon the entombment of Jesus—there is not one before which we do not feel almost compelled to kneel. Men speak of the different styles of Raphael; in our opinion, he had but one; what is called a change, is but a new step forward; it is the progress of genius from its dawn, through the various stages of development, to its zenith; but it is always genius. A few months after his accession, Leo X. wrote to his favorite artist: " Raffaello d'Urbino, it is not in painting only that you have won undying glory among men; Bramante, before his death, proclaimed your talent in architecture, and named you to carry out the work he had so gloriously begun. Your plans, which have been presented to Us, attest your eminent capacity, and as Our greatest desire is to finish the temple of the holy Apostles Peter and Paul with all possible splendor, we appoint you to take charge of the work. Remember that, in this undertaking, you have a reputation to support, a growing name to illustrate for future time, a worthy return to make for the paternal affection We feel toward you, to support the renown of the great temple you are about to erect, and to show Our veneration for the Prince of the Apostles." Raphael had not time to carry out his plans for the rebuilding of St. Peter's, which many prefer to those of Michael Angelo, because they partake more of the

severity of ancient art. The gigantic plan on which it was
designed to rebuild the Basilica would require mountains of
marble, and, accordingly, Julius II. had authorized the Romans
to use the remains of the ancient monuments and to make new
excavations. Sometimes a sacrilegious mallet would shamefully
deface some master-piece of pagan art. Leo X. accordingly
wrote to Raphael : "Since it is proper that the temple dedicated to the Prince of the Apostles should be built of marble
drawn from the soil of Rome itself, where it is found in great
quantities, and as want of skill in its use threatens the destruction of the most precious monuments of antiquity, We place in
your charge all work in the ruins and excavations about the
Pontifical city We hear that some workmen, in their ignorance, deface marbles bearing inscriptions worthy of preservation in the interest of literature and elegant Latinity **We,**
therefore, ordain that none of those old remains shall henceforth be used without your express permission." This brief
saved a number of statues, inscriptions and bas-reliefs, which
now enrich the Roman museums. Leo directed him, likewise,
to complete his frescoes begun in the halls of the Vatican, under
Julius II. The subject proposed to the artist was to represent,
in a succession of great scenes, the history of the Papacy in
the world. The illustrious painter performed his task in a
manner worthy of the noble design, and the work of Raphael
has stood through succeeding ages, honored by the enthusiastic
admiration of the world. But the splendid reputation of Raphael was a source of alarm to Michael Angelo. Buonarotti
resolved to enter the arena against the painter of Urbino, and
to insure his success in the trial by securing the coöperation of
Sebastian del Piombo. Sebastian colored the canvas upon
which Michael Angelo had sketched the " Raising of Lazarus;"
Raphael's inspired pencil drew one of the most sublime scenes
of the New Testament : the "Transfiguration of Christ." When
the two paintings were finished, they were brought together in
the Hall of the Consistory The decision did not long remain
doubtful; Sebastian was a skilful master ; his brilliant coloring

could delight the eye, but could not speak to the soul. Rome, with one voice, awarded the palm to Raphael. The Trans-figuration is the master-piece in every school; the highest effort of human power, in painting; the limit between the human and the angelic, in art. This was Raphael's last triumph; genius is a slow poison, which wastes the vital powers, and which has sent many great men to an untimely grave. During Raphael's illness, which lasted fifteen days, Leo often sent to inquire after the health of his favorite artist, upon whom he was preparing to confer unwonted honors; it is said that he even intended to raise him to the purple. But, whatever may have been his projects, they were thwarted by death; Raphael died at the age of thirty-seven years, having already won immortality, at an age when most men have hardly begun to build the the edifice of their glory

25. We have hitherto shown Leo X. surrounded by the writers, historians and artists who have made his reign one of the brightest periods in history Side by side with this picture, in which the Papacy appears as queen of the world, controlling the intellectual movements, directing genius and guiding science, we shall now present the Sovereign Pontiff struggling with unwearied energy against foes both interior and exterior. We shall find parricides even in the Sacred College, and we may need to recall to mind that among the twelve Apostles there was found a traitor to sell the blood of the Just One. Motives of private revenge and the rage of disappointed ambition were the causes of the scandal which filled the Catholic world with the deepest horror. Leo X. had intrusted the government of Sienna to the Bishop of Grossetto. Cardinal Alphonso Petrucci, of the family of the Borghese, whose ancestors had long held the sovereign authority in Sienna, thought his claim superior. Being naturally of a vain and fiery disposition and excessively intemperate in his speech, he broke out into violent-complaints against the Pope, sparing neither his person nor his character. He even spoke openly of assassination. Bapt st Vercelli, a most skilful surgeon, who was then

attending the Pope, was induced to lend his aid to the cardinal's plans of revenge. A liquid poison, skilfully introduced into a tumor, with which the Pope was then afflicted, must inevitably destroy the august patient. Every thing was prepared. But Petrucci, blinded by his passion, could not keep the secret upon which depended his honor and his life. He wrote from Florence, where he was then residing, to his friends in Rome, informing them of his criminal designs and execrable hopes. The letters were intercepted; Leo could not doubt the reality of the plot. Vercelli was arrested, and the cardinal, summoned to Rome on some ostensible business, came without the least suspicion; but immediately upon his arrival, he was seized and conveyed under a strong escort to the castle of St. Angelo. Here he confessed his crime, denounced all his accomplices, declared that his aim was to rid Rome of a tyrant, and to bestow the tiara to the aged Cardinal Riario. The cardinals implicated by his confession were, Riario, Francis Soderini, Adrian Corneto, and Bandinello de Sauli. It is not easy to conceive the anguish that filled the mild and merciful heart of Leo X., at this sad occurrence. On the 3d of June, A. D. 1517, he called a consistory, and, after reviewing the many benefits he had heaped upon the cardinals, he complained of the black ingratitude of those princes of the Church. Then raising his voice, he exclaimed: "There are some among you who have betrayed their sovereign. But, before this image of Jesus crucified, I promise them pardon, if they will but confess their crime." The guilty cardinals were silent; then began a general examination, and each cardinal was called upon to declare, on oath and before Christ, whether he was guilty or not. When Soderini approached, he at first hesitated, stammered some protest, but on being more closely questioned, threw himself upon his knees, raised his hands in supplication to his judge, and with streaming eyes acknowledged his crime and begged for mercy Leo was not yet satisfied. "There is yet another," he said. "In the name of God, then, let him come forward." All eyes were at once turned toward Adrian Corneto. The cardinal drew himself up and looked haughtily at the Pope; but his assurance soon gave way; he suddenly lost color, threw himself, with his colleague, at the Pontiff's feet, and confessed his guilt. Leo kept his word; Soderini and Adrian were condemned to pay a fine; but, moved by remorse, they inflicted justice upon themselves by a voluntary exile from Rome. The Cardinals Petrucci, de Sauli, and Riario, being more deeply implicated, were solemnly degraded. The Pontifical secretary, Bembo, read the sentence before the Sacred College, and on the following night Petrucci was executed in prison; Vercelli, the surgeon, was put to the torture and then quartered. This was more than enough of blood for the aching heart of the mild Pontiff; the punishment of Cardinal de Sauli was commuted to imprisonment for life, and this sentence was at length reduced to a mere fine. The cardinal wished to return his personal thanks to Leo for this almost miraculous release. The Pope, whose countenance bore the traces of the deep pain that filled his heart, replied to the cardinal's expressions of devoted attachment: "We are willing to believe you sincere; God grant that your heart prove true to the promises now made by your lips." Riario was treated with equal indulgence. He had formerly entertained relations of close intimacy with the Pope, and was received with more indulgent mercy In the course of a Pontifical mass, Leo turned from the altar, and approaching the cardinal, thus addressed him: "Before the body and blood of Jesus Christ, I bring you peace; in the name of Almighty God, I forgive any offence you may have committed against me, and, in return, I entreat you to forget all your own feelings of resentment." Then extending his arms, he embraced the cardinal with the affection of a father.

26. But a new storm now arose, threatening not only the life of the Pope, but the very existence of the Church. At the voice of a single monk, Germany was shaken to its very centre; the ignorant and ignoble, misled by the cry of liberty; princes and nobles, by the hope of throwing off the authority of bishops and clergy; relaxed religious, hoping to escape the obligations

which had become a burden to them;—all classes of society
flocked to the standard of revolt, and the name of Luther was
repeated by every voice, as that of a liberator and a father.
Never, since the establishment of Christianity in Europe, had
any name been so widely hailed; never had the popular mind
been so deeply moved, or revolt been attended with equally
alarming signs of universality and violence. However powerful, for evil, may have been the genius of Luther, it would be
an error to ascribe to him alone the melancholy glory of the
general conflagration. His success is due to a combination of
many influences, springing from the elements of which German
society was then composed. The imperial power was as much
concerned as the Pontifical, in silencing the rebellious monk;
but it lacked the necessary means. The power of the German
emperors was neither as extensive nor as firmly established
then, as it is now The subordinate princes did, indeed,
recognize the imperial authority, but they might appeal from its
judgment to a council of their peers. The nobles, who formed
a prominent part of the state, lived by spoliation; the bishops,
compelled to defend the rights of their sees by armed force, too
often forgot the holiness of their ministry and the duties of
their high calling; the people, but half instructed in the truths
of religion, scandalized by those who should have been their
models and their guides, had become accustomed to slight the
voice and the authority of the Church. The great wealth of the
clergy had long kept alive the cupidity of the German princes
and nobles; whoever could suggest the means of adding these
possessions to their estates was sure to be heard with favor.
The cry of *reform*, uttered in the Lateran Council, was the pretext under which the German princes cloaked their grasping
designs. This word became the rallying-cry; no one thought
of studying its precise bearing or signification; it was enough
that it was popular and helped to fill the ranks of the army
that was preparing to invade the treasures of the Church.
The same phenomenon has been witnessed at a later date,
when, in the name of liberty, revolution carried its ravages

through the blood-stained fields of Europe. The word *liberty* was never even defined; and, doubtless, those who proclaimed it with the most ferocious enthusiasm never took the trouble to study its meaning. So the reform, proclaimed a necessity by the council, bore no resemblance to the movement inaugurated by the over-excited mind of Germany, in the sixteenth century. The reform designed by the Church was the restoration of morals to their primitive purity, the suppression of the abuses which had crept into the administration of church property, during the middle-ages. But there could never have been a thought of touching the dogmas or the faith which had been handed down unchanged through successive ages. The administrative reform was itself attended with complicated difficulties; for if the State charged abuses upon the Church, the Church could, with equal right, throw back the same charge upon the State. With a view in some sort to counterbalance contradictory propositions, the Papacy opposed premature innovations, and this caution afforded the ground upon which heated imaginations built the charge of the Church's opposition to the general welfare. These impatient spirits, always anxious to hasten the course of events, and believing themselves of a superior cast, whereas they were but over-rash, never took into account the real obstacles against which the Church had to struggle, and styled her moderation weakness; but thinking men, who understood that the government of the world should show something of the patience which characterizes the Divine rule, appreciated the moderation of the Papacy, and looked for greater results from its action, in proportion as it was more reserved, more mild and merciful in its perseverance. A man, nevertheless, arose with no genius but that of evil, who availed himself of the passions of all, of the cupidity of the great, of the gross instincts of the masses, respectively flattering and justifying them under the name of reform; who claimed to be the restorer of pure morality, while authorizing license by his writings and his example; who, under the specious pretext of reformation, did away with all subordination to ecclesiastical authority, with all idea of absti-nence, austerity, self-denial and continence; enriching princes with the spoils of the clergy; freeing conscience from every moral obligation, to subject it to the caprice of private judgment, that is, to disorder; this man, thus wielding all the power of hell, on earth, whose only greatness was the general perversion of which he made himself the centre, the representa-tive and the reflector, was Martin Luther.* The *Reformation* to which he attached his name was a religious and political revo-lution. At his entrance upon the scene of action, he found the elements of this twofold movement which was to shake the world, already prepared ; he did not create, but only used them. The germ of Protestantism already existed before he came to foster it with his passionate language, by turns biting or insinua-ting, polished or rude, harmonious or insulting, eloquent or vulgar, soothing like a melody or poisoning like the serpent's fang. There had been reformers before the great Reformation Luther was a name, a leader, a standard ; but he had disciples, soldiers, echoes, an army—all ready to hail and to follow, to defend and to applaud.

27 Martin Luther was born in 1483, of a poor family, of Eisleben. His boyhood was adventurous, and he was early called to struggle against adversity and want. While pursuing his studies under the most discouraging difficulties at the Latin school of Eisenach, he attracted the attention and sympathy of a pious and liberal lady, Ursula Cotta, who furnished him with means for his support, cared for him with a mother's inter-est and affection, and opened to his talent the schools to which his poverty might otherwise have made him a stranger Though favored thus by Providence, he soon forgot its favors, and looked only to the difficulties of the way before him ; his heart, deaf to the calls of gratitude, heard only the promptings of an unjust and ever-growing anger against humanity At Eisenach, Luther studied grammar, rhetoric and poetry, under

* M. BLANC, *Histoire ecclésiastique*, t. III., passim.

the celebrated teacher, Trebonius, rector of the monastery of barefooted Carmelites. The young student soon attracted attention by his acute mind, natural eloquence, rare flow of language, and his facility in composing, both in verse and prose ; he had nc rival among his fellow-students. Eisenach soon became too narrow to limit that eager intellect, which aimed at reaching the highest walks of science. He went to Erfurth, where he gave himself up, with all the fervor of passion, to the difficult study of logic, which he afterward forsook to commune with the great minds of antiquity—Cicero, Virgil and Livy He read their works, not as a student who merely seeks to understand their verbal meaning, but with an inquiring judgment, that sought to extract from them information, advice and principles for his future guidance. He had, in two years, taken his degrees in philosophy, when an unexpected event suddenly turned his thoughts into a different channel. One of his most intimate friends, the companion of his youthful toils and pleasures, was struck dead at his side, by lightning. Terrified by this warning from Heaven, the young student, on the following night, entered the Augustinian convent at Erfurth, and sent back to the university the insignia of the Master's degrees which it had conferred upon him. He now subjected himself to the most severe monastic discipline. The thought of his friend, hurried away without warning or preparation into the hands of the living God, harassed his sleepless nights. Luther fasted and tortured himself like an anchoret of Thebais, and Staupitz, the Superior of the Augustinians, was often obliged to restrain the excessive fervor of the neophyte. He soon discerned, within the hidden folds of his passionate soul, a boundless pride and an unyielding obstinacy, which he subjected to the sternest trials. At length, after a long and severe noviceship, Luther was allowed to pronounce the usual vows, and in the same year received Holy Orders (A. D. 1507). "To-day," he wrote to one of his friends, "I say my first mass; come and hear it. Unworthy sinner as I am, God has been pleased to choose me in the abundance of His mercy ; I shall strive to make myself worthy of His goodness,

and, in so far as it is possible for such a vile mass of dust, to fulfil
His designs. Pray that my holocaust may be pleasing in His
sight." The youthful priest continued to devote himself, with un-
diminished ardor, to the pursuit of the highest mysticism. He
took for heavenly communications the hallucinations of a delirious
brain. His superiors sent him to Rome, in the hope that the
change might prove beneficial by varying the train of his
thoughts, and that faith would speak more soothingly to the
heart of Luther, in the midst of the Eternal City But the
austere monk understood nothing of the splendors of Italy, of
the brilliant lustre of the Papacy He left Rome with an anathema on his lips; he was not yet, but he was soon to become
an open rebel. His faith had begun to waver, and the spirit
of the future Reformer was struggling within him. " My life,"
wrote Luther, at about this time, " is a daily advance toward
the pit of hell; for I am every day becoming more wicked and
more wretched." Still his mind was improving itself amid
these interior struggles and storms which harassed his soul.
Luther was called to the chair of philosophy in the University
of Wittenberg, by its founder, Frederick the Wise, elector of
Saxony, a patron of literature and art, an accomplished musician,
and thoroughly conversant with the writings of the classical poets
of antiquity Frederick had heard and admired the preaching of
Luther, and soon after obtained his appointment to the pulpit of
Wittenberg. The youth of the city thronged to hear his lec-
tures; they were captivated by his clear, pointed and sarcastic
style. But older and more sensible men were unfavorably
impressed by his proneness to disparage his predecessors, whose
renown was still high in the schools; " Echoes of the past," he
styled them, "giving but human sounds, like all the foolish
philosophers who seek in man the explanation of moral phe-
nomena, instead of tracing them to their source, that is to God
and to His Word." His success as a preacher was attended
with the same character of impulsive oratory and unrestrained
passion. His voice was full and sonorous, his gestures free and
noble. He had, at the very outset, announced his intention

of not imitating his predecessors ; and he was true to his word.
Turning from the beaten track of the Schools, he affected to
draw his inspirations, texts and figures, exclusively from the
Sacred Writings. The applause of his hearers, who were
pleased with his innovation, encouraged him in the dangerous
course upon which he had entered. "Luther," said a religious
after hearing one of his sermons, "has deep penetration and an
admirable command of figures; he will yet give the doctors
much trouble and raise great storms." His discourses already
betrayed the latent germ of the doctrines which he was soon to
profess publicly, in giving the last developments to Protestantism. He had already taught that faith alone obtains what the
law requires. Without directly preaching against fasts, pil-
grimages and prayer, he exalted the doctrine of faith alone in
such terms as to depreciate good works. He asserted that the
worship of God had been disfigured by superstitious practices,
calculated to kill the soul, and though he allowed some efficacy
to the indulgences of the Church, he still refused them the
title of spiritual remedies. We now find in his discourses the
constantly recurring formula : *Salvation by faith.*

28. Such was the position of the professor of Wittenberg
when Leo X., following the example of several of his predecessors, granted certain indulgences to all the faithful who
should contribute, by their alms, toward the completion of the
Basilica of St. Peter, begun by Julius II., and for the expedition
against the Turks, which the Pope still hoped to carry out.
The Archbishop of Mentz, who was intrusted with the promulgation of the Pontifical decree in Germany, charged John
Tetzel, a Dominican and inquisitor of the faith, to publish the
indulgences in Saxony The Augustinians, thinking themselves
entitled to that privilege, were hurt by what they deemed a
show of partiality toward Tetzel. Luther warmly advocated
the claim, and thus a monkish rivalry gave rise to the most
fearful storms. Before entering upon a narrative of the facts in
the case, it is important to establish the Catholic teaching concerning indulgences, which were made the subject of such bitter

controversy "Theology," in the words of the Fathers of Trent, "distinguishes in sin the *guilt* and the *punishment*. The guilt is the offence done to God; the punishment is the chastisement deserved by the offence, whether temporal or eternal. The Church having received, with the keys, the power of binding and loosing, exercises that power in regard to sins committed after baptism, both in the sacrament of penance and in the granting of indulgences; in the sacrament of penance. the Church remits the sin as to the guilt and the eternal punishment, but not always the whole of the temporal punishment. By an indulgence, the Church releases wholly, or in part, from the temporal punishment which was to be undergone for sin, in this world, by works of satisfaction; in the other, by the pains of Purgatory The indulgence, then, remits the punishment, not the guilt. The treasure of indulgences, which can be dispensed only by the Popes and bishops, is supplied from the superabundant satisfaction of Jesus Christ; a single drop of the sacred blood of the God-man would have been a thousand times sufficient to redeem thousands of worlds. To these exhaustless springs of merit are added—as agreeable to God and meritorious, because of their union with the satisfaction of the Saviour, and as applied in virtue of the communion of saints— the abounding merits of Mary, the Mother of Sorrows, who never had a fault to expiate, with those of numberless saints who have suffered for justice' sake and practised long-continued penances to atone for slight imperfections." The doctrine of indulgences is closely allied to that of Purgatory Faith teaches us that beyond the bounds of this life there is a place of purification where the soul is cleansed from the last stains of sin, that, when the time prescribed by the divine mercy and justice shall be accomplished, it may go to take its place among the blessed, "for nothing defiled can enter into the kingdom of Heaven." Faith tells us, again, that those hours of trial and punishment, of which we know not the number or extent, may be shortened and mitigated by works of satisfaction. Not that such works have any power of themselves; but when offered

by our divine Mediator to His Father, they disarm and appease
a God of charity and of mercy   So, indulgences, like prayers or
alms-deeds, do, by the application of the merits of Jesus Christ,
alleviate the temporary sufferings of the souls of our brethren.
The Church has the power to shorten these satisfactory sufferings, in virtue of the words spoken by our Lórd Himself:
" Whatsoever you shall bind upon earth, it shall be bound also
in Heaven ; and whatsoever you shall loose upon earth, it shall
be loosed also in Heaven."

29. The Dominican Tetzel, in publishing the indulgences
granted to the whole Catholic world by Leo X., was in the
right and did no more than his duty   Notwithstanding the
disorder and license of public morals, the spirit of faith and
piety was not yet wholly dead in the hearts of the people.   The
preaching of the Dominican religious was eminently successful
in Germany.   In the latter end of 1517, Tetzel went to Juter-
bock, a small town in the principality of Magdeburg and eight
miles from Wittenberg, which city was soon deserted by its
inhabitants, all flocking to hear the preacher.   Luther in vain
strove to restrain his penitents, who eagerly crowded around
the dispenser of the spiritual treasures which the Papacy was
bestowing upon the world.   In a first impulse of anger, he wrote
to the Bishop of Misnia an urgent letter, imploring him to put
a stop to what he called a scandalous traffic.   As deeply
wounded in his self-love as in his attachment to his order, he
announced that he would preach upon indulgences, and for
several days, closely shut up in his cell, he labored earnestly to
collect into a body all the anti-Catholic ideas which had been so
long developing themselves in his mind.   The Church was
crowded, and in this first open expression of his thoughts, the
preacher exposed the whole substance of the system which he
afterward established.   The whole of Luther's doctrine is contained in that religious instruction, which is clear, condensed,
and divided into paragraphs forming so many maxims or propositions.   The opinon of the Saxon monk is not mantled in
obscurity ; it appeals to the understanding, just as it was

conceived, innovating, hostile to all hitherto received doctrines, insolent against tradition, disdaining moderation, and haughty ; such as it appeared in all the after-life of the Reformer. It may not be out of place to quote some of the formulas which best display the boldness of the new doctrines—" I maintain that it is impossible to prove from the Scriptures, that divine justice requires from the sinner any other penance or satisfaction than amendment of heart; and that it nowhere enjoins the concurrence of acts or works, for we read in Ezechiel : ' The Lord will not impute sin to him who repents, or who does good.' We are told that indulgences, applied to the soul suffering in Purgatory, are imputed to it and counted in the remission of the punishment which it may still have to suffer : this is an utterly groundless opinion. Indulgences, instead of expiating, leave the Christian in the filth of his sin. Give first to your needy brother, and then, if you have means, bestow them upon the Basilica of St. Peter. If you have more than you need, and your charity finds no poor brethren in your own country, upon whom to exercise itself, then, if you are so disposed, give to churches, adorn altars, and, if any remains, give to St. Peter's at Rome, which stands in less need of it. Indulgences are neither of divine precept nor counsel ; it is not a commandment, a work affecting salvation. That souls can be freed from Purgatory by the efficacy of indulgences, I do not believe, although the doctrine is held by some new teachers. But they cannot prove it ; the Church says nothing about it. In truth, it is better to pray for them. Though some accuse me of heresy for having told them truths which will damage their traffic, what care I for their prating ? They are crack-brained dolts, who have never studied the Bible, who know nothing of the doctrines of Christ, do not understand themselves and are buried in the depth of their darkness."

30. Luther was now fairly started in his career; he had begun by an open attack upon indulgences ; he had set forth his doctrine of justification by faith, without works, the groundwork of his whole system. One month later, he posted up in

Wittenberg a famous thesis, comprising all the points of the discourse just quoted, and which, like a firebrand, wrapped the whole of Germany in the flames of religious strife. The Augustinians were thrown into consternation by the boldness of their preacher ; they begged him to use moderation and prudence. But the youthful monk was intoxicated by the renown which already attached to his name. " Dear Fathers," he replied to their warnings, " if it proceeds from God, let my work alone, it will run its course ; if it does not proceed from His Holy Name, it will fall to the ground." His theses, a true programme of rebellion, were posted upon one of the columns of the cathedral at Wittenberg (October 31, A. D. 1517). Luther's first intention was to publish them in German, that the people might also take part in the discussion ; the only concession that could be wrung from him was, that he should write them in Latin They comprised ninety-five propositions against indulgences and the Pontifical authority ; and on the following day, one of great solemnity in the Catholic Church, every one in Wittenberg who understood Latin, might read : " That the Pope has no more power than a simple village curate.—That they will be lost who rely upon a letter of indulgence for their salvation.—That the gospel treasures are nets whereby, formerly, souls of men were caught ; while the treasures of indulgences are nets in which, now, the wealth of men is caught."

31. Tetzel answered this bold tirade by a real theological thesis, analyzing the propositions, one by one, and showing wherein they were opposed to the received doctrine of the Church. Eight hundred copies of this Catholic treatise, calm in the consciousness of truth, plain, clear, logical and powerful, were sent to Wittenberg to counterbalance the effects of Luther's insolent sophisms. But the students, carried away by the impious eloquence of their teacher, seized the freshly-printed sheets, and proclaimed through the streets that they were about to burn, in the public square, the propositions of Master Tetzel, inquisitor of the faith, bachelor of theology and priest of the Order of St. Dominic. A fire was, accordingly, lighted in the

university square, and a student threw the theses into the flames, exclaiming; "Vivat Luther! Pereat Tetzel!" These tidings, and the troubles to which they gave rise throughout all Germany, soon crossed the Alps and startled the ears of the Papacy   Luther thought it prudent to anticipate the judgment of this supreme tribunal, and he addressed Pope Leo X. in terms of the deepest humility and filial submission: "Most Holy Father, I cast myself at the feet of Your Holiness, with all that I am and all that I have.   Give life, take it away; call, recall; approve, reprove; your voice is that of Christ, who dwells in you and speaks by your lips.   If I have deserved death, I am ready to die."   Leo yielded to the merciful promptings of his great soul, and allowed himself to be deceived by these hypocritical professions.   Before pronouncing a judgment, he wished the Saxon friar to be examined on the spot, and the duty was intrusted to Cardinal Cajetan, the theological light of Italy, who was then acting as Apostolic legate in Germany   "If Luther repents," wrote the Pope to his ambassador, "forgive him; if he persists, he must be silenced." Luther renewed the protestations already addressed to the Pope, but with as little sincerity.   He threw himself at the feet of the nuncio, declaring that he was prepared to disown the offensive words used by him, if he were told wherein they were reprehensible.   "My son," replied Cajetan, "I have not come to discuss the question.   I only ask you, in the name of His Holiness, to retract your errors."   Luther refused, and asked, at least, to have his erroneous propositions pointed out to him.   Cajetan quoted two, which the monk endeavored to defend.   The interview lasted more than an hour; in spite of his resolution, the cardinal was engaged in a discussion.   At length Luther asked three days to determine the course he ought to pursue; the cardinal granted the delay   Before the expiration of the term, he asked to be allowed to defend himself in writing, which request was also granted, and on the following day Luther presented a thesis in which he maintained that, in matters of dogma, a simple layman, if he rests upon authority and reason, is superior to the Pope. The nuncio endeavored, by conciliatory words, to recall the proud spirit to the path of obedience. Luther made an angry reply "Brother," said Cajetan, holding both hands of the monk in his own, "it is still time ; I am ready to intercede for you with our common Fa ther; only retract." Luther was silent, his obstinacy was unbending. One month later, appeared the bull of Leo X., which defined the teaching of the Church concerning indulgences, and condemned the new errors without even mentioning the name of Luther. The rebellious monk now threw off the mask, and gave way to the most furious invectives against the Pope. "Indeed," he wrote, "I can hardly believe that any thing so monstrous could come from a Pope, and especially from Leo X.; the ignoramus, who, under the name of Leo, tries to frighten me with this brief, shall speedily learn that I see through his idle sport, and that I shall easily counfound his wickedness and ignorance."

32. Once fairly started, Luther now pushed on in this new path, with rapid strides ; he began by publishing his appeal to a future council. "Far be it from me," he said, "to attack the authority of the Holy Father and much less to separate myself from the Church; but is not the Pope of the same flesh and nature as other men, peccable and weak like them; as likely to err and fall as was St. Peter?" The new teaching was making rapid progress; it not only disturbed the whole of Germany but also counted many followers. Among its most fervent apostles were Melancthon and Carlstadt. Melancthon, though but twenty-two years of age, already held the chair of Greek in the University of Wittenberg. He was of a pensive disposition, with a heart prone to mystical effusions of tender piety, and a mind richly stored with the wealth of classic antiquity He was seduced and controlled by the warm and brilliant eloquence of Luther. Carlstadt had studied both in Germany and Italy While dean of the University of Wittenberg, where he held the professorship of philosophy, he had given Luther the Doctor's cap. He was one of those minds as unsteady as the sand which is shifted

about by every wind.   These two disciples were most valuable
to Luther, as they won over to his interest the more unlearned
with whom the names of Melancthon and Carlstadt were an
authority ; still, to tell the truth, it was not the question of religion which brought most of its partisans to the Reformation.
Ambitious princes witnessed, with a secret pleasure, the factious
stand taken by Luther against ecclesiastical authority; they
hoped that their power would gain what that of the clergy might
lose.   Their blindness was undeceived when Luther's teaching
armed a hundred thousand German peasants against the authority of the nobles and rulers.   The peace and prosperity of
nations is always in proportion to the flourishing state of religion, the princes who are so unhappy as to forget or overlook
this truth are always the first victims of their own imprudence.

   33. Leo X. cherished the hope that the German monk
would return to the way of submission and repentance.   In the
year 1519, a second negotiator was appointed to continue the conferences begun by Cardinal Cajetan.   The Pontiff's choice fell
upon Charles Miltitz, a Saxon theologian.   Luther did not even
attempt to dispute with him, but assured him that the Pope
had not, in all Christendom, a more respectful, devoted and
obedient son than himself, and that he was ready to retract all
the errors imputed to him.   Miltitz was deceived by these false
promises, and returned to Rome, where Leo X. heard, with
transports of joy, the false professions of the Reformer.   " It
will give us unspeakable happiness," said the Pope, " to see the
Church at peace, before We die."   This joy was short-lived ;
the letter in which Luther was to make his abjuration to the
Sovereign Pontiff was far different from what had been expected.   It was but a violent attack upon the authority of the
Pope, in which the Saxon monk seems to be trying his powers
of insulting epithet and coarse imagery   Leo had exhausted
the treasures of his paternal indulgence.   But, he still hesitated ; " he loved this brother Martin," he would say, " endowed
with such a beautiful intellect.   It is only a quarrel of the

monks." Yet it was necessary to act; Germany was in commotion and threatened to throw off the yoke of the Church, all eyes were turned toward the chair of St. Peter, the whole world was waiting to hear the sentence of Christ's Vicar. At length, on the 15th of June, A. D. 1520, the bull was published. It compared Luther to the heretic, Porphyry, because, like him, he dares to insult the majesty of the Roman Pontiff, and does not hesitate to use invectives when he lacks arguments. "We see with heartfelt grief," said the Pope, "that some bold teachers, blinded and misled by the father of lies, are wresting the words of Holy Writ to a false and dangerous interpretation, so that it is no longer the gospel of Christ, but the gospel of man, and too often even the gospel of the demon." He adds that, in Germany are renewed the errors of the Greeks and Bohemians, already condemned by the councils and by the constitutions of his predecessors; and that he feels this more painfully from Germany, since the Popes, and himself in particular, have always felt a peculiar affection for the German nation, to which the Holy See is under great obligations, for its princes have been the protectors of the Church, of her doctrine and her liberties. "Still," he continues, "the duty of Our pastoral charge will not allow Us to dissemble : We must, therefore, condemn forty-one propositions contained in the writings of Luther. The unanimous voice of the cardinals, heads of orders, theologians and canonists pronounces them worthy of censure; We condemn them as respectively heretical, scandalous, false, shocking to pious ears, calculated to mislead the faithful, and contrary to Catholic faith. We forbid all persons, on pain of excommunication and privation of all ecclesiastical dignities, incurred *ipso facto*, to believe, maintain, or defend these propositions, to favor their publication, to preach them, or to suffer others to teach them, directly or indirectly, in public or in private." The Pope then recalls the fact that he had exhausted all the resources of conciliation, mildness and charity to bring back the innovator into the path of obedience. "We might," he adds in conclusion, "proceed directly against his person and visit him with a nominal sentence of excommunication. Yet, following rather the example of meekness given by our Redeemer, and with the advice of Our beloved brethren, the cardinals, We are willing to grant him a delay of sixty days, to retract his errors and burn his impious books. If, at the expiration of that time, he and his adherents have not complied with the condition, We declare that they have incurred the penalties due to heretics and are cut off from the communion of the faithful."

34. This sentence threw Luther into a rage bordering on madness. He immediately published a virulent pamphlet against the *execrable bull.* "I hold the author of this bull," he writes, "to be anti-Christ, I curse it as an insult and a blasphemy against Christ, the Son of God. But tell me, ignorant anti-Christ, were you then so senseless as to believe that men would allow themselves to be frightened? What! did you not blush thus to oppose your words of smoke to the thunders of the divine word!" Such was the style of the Saxon monk! Such the language of the father of Protestantism! And still we are obliged, in quoting him, to soften the coarseness of his expressions and images, not to soil, with his sacrilegious blasphemies and gross licentiousness, the pages of a book destined to record the triumphs and struggles of the Church, the immaculate spouse of the Holy Ghost. Luther was not satisfied with words. On the 10th of December, A.D. 1520, he publicly burned the Pope's bull at Wittenberg. On the next day he ascended the pulpit. His revolt against the Holy See found a number of fanatical admirers, and, amid bursts of enthusiastic applause from his misguided hearers, Luther exclaimed: "Yesterday I burned, in the public square, the satanical work of the Pope. I could wish it had rather been the Pope himself, I mean the Papal See. Let every Christian seriously reflect that in communicating with the Papists he renounces eternal life. Abomination to Babylon! So long as I have breath I shall exclaim: Abomination!" War was declared. The schism was effected

From that day, there was no longer any hope of coming to terms
with Luther.

35. Meanwhile the attention of Europe had been, for a
moment, called away from the seditious movements of the self
styled Reformer, by political events which threatened the public
peace; the Emperor Maximilian was dead (A. D. 1519). Charles
of Austria had already received, through his parents, the Archduke Philip, and Joanna, daughter of Ferdinand the Catholic,
the sovereignty of Spain, with the conquests and treasures of
America; the two Sicilies, the Netherlands and Franche-Comte;
beside the title of King of the Romans, which he owed to the
care of Ferdinand. He was active, industrious, prudent and
brave; his vast intellect had been improved by study and by
the lessons of Cardinal Ximenes, who still governed Spain
under the heir of Ferdinand and Isabella. His ambition was
proportioned to the development of his mind, and the young
prince, though but twenty years of age, became a candidate for
the empire. Francis I., older by six years, more renowned for
his exploits, also entered the lists for the imperial prize. The
power of either of the two competitors was a source of just
anxiety to the Germans, who were jealously watchful of their
freedom. The electors of the Holy Empire were assembled
at Nuremberg, according to the terms of the Golden Bull, to
adjudge the imperial crown. Europe watched the proceedings
of the assembly with the most intense interest. The policy of
the court of Rome was clearly marked out and steadily followed.
Leo foresaw that the success of either competitor would jeopard
the liberty of Europe, the independence of the Holy See and
the peace of Italy If Francis I. obtained the crown, there
were no more barriers of ice between France and Italy; if
Charles, already sovereign of Spain and Naples, became emperor, there was no longer a sea between the States of the Church
and the realm of that prince. Cajetan was instructed by the
Sovereign Pontiff to remind the electors of the constitution
which excluded the kings of Naples from the imperial throne, and
of the danger which would accrue from bestowing the empire

and the title of King of the Romans upon a youthful prince, like Francis I., already master of the Milanese and of Lombardy. It seemed for a moment that the neutral policy suggested by Leo X. would prevail; for the electors, justly alarmed at the dangers pointed out by the nuncio, offered the crown to Frederick of Saxony But, whether from disinterested motives, or through fear of being crushed by two formidable competitors, Frederick refused it. The electors, in admiration of his generosity, unanimously requested him to decide the question between the rival candidates. He voted in favor of the Spanish prince; and on the 5th of July, 1519, in the church of St. Bartholomew, the Archbishop of Mentz, in the name of the Electoral College, proclaimed Charles of Austria emperor of Germany. On learning this result, Leo determined at least to turn to the best account, for the Church, an election which he had been unable to prevent. It was necessary, for the peace of the world, that Charles should assist in suppressing the nascent heresy There never was a time when the union of the empire and the Holy See was more necessary. The Papal nuncio was instructed to confer upon the subject with Charles, who speedily set all Leo's anxiety at rest. On the day of the emperor's coronation at Aix-la-Chapelle, the Archbishop of Cologne, in full pontificals, approached him and asked: " Do you promise to labor for the triumph of the Catholic faith, to defend and protect the churches of Germany, to uphold the interests of the empire, to be the father and the guardian of the widow and orphan, and to render the required obedience to the Supreme Pontiff?" To each of the former questions, Charles had simply bowed assent; but at the last he raised his hand, and laying it upon the gospel side of the altar pronounced the oath: "I will; and I rely, for strength to keep my promise, upon God and the prayers of the faithful; may God and His saints assist me."

36. The youthful monarch turned his thoughts to the most extensive projects, and determined to make Francis I. repent of having been his rival in the contest for the German throne. The King of France had won great renown at Marignano,

Charles would not remain behind in the race for glory. The disorders caused by the Reformation could not but displease him at a time when he was preparing to use all the power of his empire against a formidable enemy. Even human policy urged him to pacify his new States and to check the progress of heresy; a general diet was accordingly convoked at Worms to adopt some decisive measures against it. Luther had availed himself of the interval of truce afforded by the election, to spread his doctrines and strengthen his party. His weapons against the Catholic dogmas were not confined to libels and insults. In his work on "Christian Liberty," a grave treatise of high theological pretensions, the heresiarch had clearly laid down his doctrine. He carries out his principles to their last consequences, and maintains, as truths founded on the gospel text, not only justification without works, but the impossibility of faith with works, which he regards as so many sins; also the subjection of the creature to the devil, even when it endeavors to escape from him. By the side of these cheerless doctrines, he presents as a dogma the impeccability of the soul which has never ceased to believe; "for if I have sinned," he says, "Christ has not sinned, Who is in me, in Whom I believe, Who operates, thinks, acts and lives with me, and Who alone fulfils the law." He then tries to establish the doctrine that the character of the priesthood is, in some sort, infused into all mankind, as the soul into the body; that it belongs to every one who believes, because Christ having joined Himself to humanity by a wholly mystical union, the soul has become His spouse and enjoys all the gifts which the spouse bestows upon His beloved; that all those words, priest, cleric and ecclesiastic, signify nothing, are an outrage upon the word of God, for we are all equally His children, His stewards and His ministers, and so all the outward pomp of dress and ceremonial are but vain figures, but human forms, which the spirit of Christ should banish from among Christians.

37 Nothing can be more full, clear and dogmatic. If Luther is right, the Papacy, the priesthood, Catholicism, are mere human inventions; Rome is, indeed, as he styles it,

empurpled Babylon. Champions were not wanting to defend
he outraged honor of the faith ; theologians and doctors came
from all directions to give battle to this new theology Eck,
chancellor of the University of Ingolstadt, a man of mind and
erudition, whose name was known in all the learned circles of
Germany, was first in the field. In his work entitled "The
Obelisks," he opposes the Reformer with the constant tradition
of the Church, with arguments from the Fathers and Catholic
theologians. Every honest and unprejudiced reader must see
that Eck is supported by reason, justice and truth. But the
works of Christian apologists have all, in the eyes of the
masses, precisely the defect of being too solidly right. The
heated imagination of the people requires something new and
exciting. The multitude applauded Luther, who replied to the
Catholic doctor only by the repetition of such epithets as " servant of Satan," " notorious enemy of Christ," " theologaster " and
" wretched sophist." Emser, a Leipsic professor, was not more
successful in his polemical tilt with the Augustinian monk.
" You are but a miserable Romanist," said Luther, in answer
to his arguments. " And now I say : Farewell, Rome, city of
scandals ! The wrath of my Master in Heaven will soon be
poured upon thee. Farewell, abode of dragons ; nest of
vultures, owls and bats !" The Dominican Prierias, master of
the Sacred Palace, who had grown gray in the study of theology
and the contests of the schools, now came forward to take part
in the defence of the insulted honor of Rome and the Papacy
Luther gave but two days to the composition of his pamphlet
in reply to the dialogue of Prierias. " That old monk," says
the heresiarch, " held the pen while Satan dictated. He would
do well, another time, to seek some better inspiration for the
Thomas he brings against me." It will be easily seen that
sarcasm and ridicule were the favorite weapons of the Father
of the Reformation. When his opponents think to crush him
with the mighty voice of constant tradition, he maintains that
a single man may be right against Popes, councils, doctors, the
past and the present. The Angel of the Schools, whose very

name is an authority, was represented by Luther as "a college pedant, stringing words together, like beads, wallowing in the mire and trying to reach Heaven by a road strewn with thorns and briers." Luther, now in the full career of skepticism, heaped denial upon denial. He sent forth his work on *The Captivity of the Church in Babylon*, in which he pretends, by a single stroke of the pen, to suppress the Sacraments of Order, Extreme Unction and Penance, with the doctrine of Indulgences, Purgatory and the Papacy.

38. The Wittenberg Reformer was now opposed by a crowned apologist, who rose up with all the majesty of royal power and all the logic of a disciple of St. Thomas. Henry VIII. of England had in his youth been passionately devoted to the study of theology The "angelic doctor" was his favorite author; and the royal disciple had profited by the teachings of so great a master. He did not disdain to enter the lists as a champion of Catholic truth, and his admirable work, *Assertio Septem Sacramentorum*, won for him from Leo X. the title of "Defender of the Faith," which he was afterward to forfeit by his own sad and scandalous defection. "There was a time of happy memory," wrote Henry, "when the Church needed no defenders, because she had no enemies. But now she is attacked by one who hides the wicked instincts of the demon under an outward show of earnest zeal for the truth, and who, under the influence of anger and hatred, vomits forth his viperous venom against the Church. It is time to tear off his mask. Let every soul regenerated by the waters of baptism, and redeemed by the blood of Jesus Christ, let the aged and the young, the priest and the king rise up against the ungrateful and the impious wretch." Then turning to the heresiarch himself, the royal apologist thus addresses him: "Deny, if you dare, that the whole Christian world hails Rome as its spiritual mother! Even to the remotest ends of the earth, all that bears the Christian name, on the sea and in the wilderness, bows before Rome! If this power is neither from God nor from men, the Papacy must then have usurped it; Rome must have stolen

it. But when? Can you tell us the time of this usurpation?
But if the power be of immemorial date, going far back into the
twilight of ages, then you must know that it is a received principle in human laws, that all immemorial possession is, by the
very fact, legitimate; and that the unanimous consent of mankind forbids us to touch what time has consolidated." Luther
taught, in his "Captivity of the Church in Babylon," that the
words of the Redeemer, "Whatsoever you shall bind upon
earth, it shall be bound also in Heaven," were addressed, not
to the Apostles represented by their successors in every age,
but to the faithful generally, to every man or woman who
had received baptism; thus creating a priesthood of which
every infant became a member as soon as it opened its eyes
to the light. Henry VIII. thus answers his assertion: "Luther says that the words of the institution apply to laymen as
well as to priests, and Bede says that they do not; whom are
we to believe?" Luther denied the sacrament of confirmation,
because he could not, he said, find any mention of its institution in the sacred text. "How!" replied Henry, "if you had
only the gospel of St. John, would you therefore deny the
Eucharist, because St. John does not record the institution of
that sacrament? Without tradition you would not know that
there are gospels. Had not the Church taught us the authen-
ticity of St. John's gospel, how could we have discovered it?
Why, then, will you not believe the Church when she says to
you: 'This is what Jesus Christ did for us; these sacraments
He instituted; these things have been handed down to us by
the Apostles;' just as you believe her when she tells you:
'These are the writings of St. Mark or of St. Matthew'?"
The work closes with a train of reasoning in perfect keeping
with the solid and powerful arguments which characterize it
throughout. "It is idle now," says the royal champion, "to
reason with Luther, who is of no one's opinion; who does not
seem to understand himself; who denies what he had at first
affirmed, or affirms with equal readiness what he before denied.
If you meet him with the arms of faith, he will put on the

buckler of reason; or if you appeal to reason, he will hear of nothing but faith; quote the philosophers, and he appeals to the Scriptures; turn upon him the light of the sacred writings, and he veils himself in the sophistry of the schools. The shameless innovator puts himself above all law, despises our doctors, and from the height of his notoriety laughs at the living lights of our Church; he insults the majesty of our Pontiffs, outrages tradition, dogma, morality, the canons, the faith and even the Church itself." Henry's work was presented by the English ambassadors to Leo X., who received it with transports of joy, and by a special bull bestowed upon the English monarch the official title of " DEFENSOR FIDEI." Henry, at the same time, received the congratulations of all the Catholic doctors; Germany, Italy, France, the Netherlands and Spain—all vied with each other in showering praises and congratulations upon him. This unanimous salutation drowned the voice of Luther, who made a vain attempt to overwhelm, by a torrent of invectives, the masterly work of the English monarch. " That a king of England should have written against me," said Luther, " is not surprising, since even the Pope, who calls himself the master of kings, princes, schools and churches, has taken up his pen to attack me. But what care I for their assaults? It is from Heaven that I have, by the grace of God, received my doctrine; from Heaven and from Him, whose little finger is more powerful than a thousand Popes, kings, princes and doctors. Now, if I handle Henry VIII. rather roughly, let him blame himself for it; it is his own fault. If a king of England flings his insolent lies in my face, I think that I have a right, on my part, to cram them down his throat; if he casts mire on the crown of my Master and my Christ, how can he be astonished if he finds it thrown back upon his own diadem, or if I cry out from the house-tops: 'The King of England is a liar and a varlet?' But to have done with these Papists, once for all, I answer them through the King of England: 'If age constituted right, the devil would be the most righteous creature on this earth, for he is more than five thousand years old.'"

39. Such was the attitude of Luther in respect to Catholic Europe, at the opening of the Diet of Worms, convoked by Charles V. (A. D. 1521). Aleandro attended as Papal nuncio; Luther was cited to appear, and, having received an imperial safe-conduct guaranteeing his personal safety, he set out from Wittenberg in the beginning of April. The debates were solemnly opened by the nuncio, followed by the Catholic doctors, against Luther and his adherents. The faith, so shamefully insulted by the Saxon monk, was vigorously defended. With this illustrious assembly, the abuse, of which Luther always commanded a ready supply, could not pass for argument. Aleandro obtained from Charles V a decree, commanding that all the Reformer's works should be publicly burned, if found within his States, and forbidding their reading or circulation. Luther saw that he should make nothing of an assembly so serious and enlightened. He quitted Worms, in great haste, as if fearing for his personal safety, and, under cover of a disguise, sought shelter in the castle of Wartburg, belonging to the Elector of Saxony Wartburg was an old feudal manor, perched, like an eagle's eyry, on the summit of an isolated mountain, "in the region of birds, who sing upon the trees and praise the Lord by day and by night." Here Luther had no cause to fear the observation of his enemies. In this "new Patmos," as he was pleased to style his retreat, under the name of the *Ecclesiastes* of Wittenberg, he recorded the visions of his excited imagination and awaited a more favorable turn of events. Since the Diet of Worms, Leo X. had issued a second bull against Luther. After a brief historical review of the whole question, the Pope again excommunicates Luther and all his adherents, lays an interdict upon all places which afford them an asylum, and uses every available means to check the progress of a heresy which had already grown to such formidable proportions. But these stern measures came too late to stay the destructive career of the heresiarch. He continued, with increased boldness, to strike at the dogmas of faith, to sap the very foundations of Catholicity. His daring increased with his sense of

security, and his fiery words, borne upon the wings of the press
and the voice of his disciples, to palace and hovel alike, kindled
the fire of passion and prepared the way for fresh storms.   The
progress of Lutheranism was indirectly favored by the equivo-
cal course of the distinguished scholar, Erasmus of Rotterdam.
The talented humanist had won universal admiration by the
ease and purity with which he spoke and wrote the languages
of Virgil and Homer.   Before yielding to Aleandro's earnest
endeavors to withdraw him from the cause of Luther, Frederick
of Saxony wished to obtain the advice of Erasmus.   The illustrious scholar, yielding to miserable views of personal interest
and to the fear of offending the Lutherans, returned an evasive
answer, which Frederick interpreted according to his wishes,
and continued to protect Luther.*   The fame of the great
scholar of Rotterdam will always bear the reproach of having,
by his weakness and want of decision, encouraged the first steps
of Protestantism.   He afterward, though too late, tried to repair the scandal and to measure his graceful Ciceronian pen
with the blunt speech and volcanic eloquence of Luther.   But
the odds were no longer equal, and the monk of Wittenberg
easily crushed under his thundering sarcasm the harmonious
and cadenced periods of Erasmus.   One happy hit of the theologian of Rotterdam has, however, survived : " Protestantism,"
says he, " is a tragedy which winds up like most comedies ; all
ends in a marriage."

40. Luther's mind was overheated at Wartburg, by the excitement which his novelties were creating in the world, and of
which the echoes reached him from every quarter, to stir up his
ardent soul to renewed action ; his ceaseless discussions with
Catholic theologians threw him into new errors, and, when it
became necessary to reduce his teachings to a system, he found
that he had successively attacked all the dogmas of faith.   The
sum of his teaching is, very nearly, a complete negation of
Catholicity.   The following rapid sketch may give some idea

* PALMA, *Prælectiones Historiæ Ecclesiasticæ,* t. III., p. 207.

of their bearing : 1. Luther denied all dogmatic authority in the Church; every individual was thus made a judge in matters of faith, depending only upon his own conscience and private interpretation of the Sacred Text. This was destroying, at a single blow, tradition, councils, the Fathers and canon law; sacrificing all the past to throw open to coming generations a boundless field for the unbridled excesses of heresy. This fundamental error was, moreover, to lead Protestantism into all the contradictions and doctrinal variations which have since divided it into so many different sects. 2. He rejected the Catholic priesthood, by abolishing the sacrament of Holy Orders and ascribing the priestly ministry to every one of the faithful. The Church thus became a republic, of which every member was a leader in equal authority This was formally giving the lie to all Church history, every page of which bears witness to the divine origin of the distinction between the clergy and the faithful. 3. He denied the primacy of the Pope and the authority of the Holy See; and this error is but the necessary corollary of the preceding one, for, in his eyes, the Pope was the anti- Christ, and Rome the Babylon of the Apocalypse. 4. He denied free-will, and, even outdoing the repeatedly condemned errors of Pelagianism, taught that, since the commission of the original sin, every action, even though a meritorious one, is necessarily a sin. Faith in Jesus Christ is alone available for sanctification, without any coöperation on our part. This was a proclamation of the most unbridled license, the ruin of all morality, and gave free scope to every disorder, to every prompting of passion. 5. He denied the efficacy of the Sacraments as means of sanctification. Since he refused to admit the merit of good works, the means established by Christ to increase grace within us and to bear up the soul in the practice of virtue became useless. He acknowledged but three Sacraments : Baptism, Penance and the Eucharist, in which he recognized, however, but sensible signs which excite us to faith in the merits of Christ, without communicating any other grace to our souls. 6. He denied the divine origin of sacramental Confession, and ɹeduced the sacrament of penance to individual faith in the re-mission of sins through the merits of Jesus Christ. 7 He de-nied transubstantiation, and substituted, instead of the Mass, the Lord's Supper, a mere formality, in which the words of con-secration operate in the bread and wine only a figurative pres-ence, thus destroying the Eucharistic Sacrifice, the centre and life of Catholic worship. 8. His work of destruction was crowned by the exclusion, from all Lutheran temples, of the invocation of saints and reverence for their images, which the heresiarch styled idolatry. Religious ceremonies were to him but the pomps of Satan. Until then the Catholic priesthood had preserved its dignity and maintained the high character of its august mission by means of the law of celibacy, so repeat-edly attacked by heretics, but always guarded with equal vigi-lance by the Holy See. Luther abolished celibacy, religious vows and monastic orders, thus making a wide breach in the dike which Divine Wisdom had set against the impetuous tor-rent of evil passions. Such is the appearance presented to us by the work of destruction to which Luther devoted his whole life. All the theological notions, all the institutions, the whole discipline of the Church, were thrown into disorder. Luther concentrated in one nearly universal denial all the errors which former heresies had successively opposed to each separate dog-ma of our faith. Strictly speaking, he was not inventing a system of errors, but merely collecting all past heresies into the great pandemonium called Protestantism.

41. Luther's naturally aggressive and domineering spirit would have subjected his disciples to his own personal authority, while, in his anti-Catholic theses, he proclaimed the principle of the absolute freedom and independence of the human mind. He wished to direct, according to his own notions, the work of ruin in which he had taken the lead. " He was holding con ferences," as he says himself, " with infernal spirits, in his solitude at Wartburg, for the abolition of the Mass," when he learned that his disciple Carlstadt, without waiting for the signal, was dogmatizing at Wittenberg, where he revived the

age of the Iconoclasts, destroying holy images, profaning altars, proscribing science and letters as means of perdition. Luther immediately hurried to Wittenberg and attempted to silence Carlstadt, who refused to submit. Lutheranism was thus attended by domestic discord, in its very first steps; and the infallibility which the Father of Protestantism refused to the Pope, to the Church and to tradition, was now refused to himself. The seeds of independence which he had sown in the minds of his hearers now sprang up on all sides with a vigor which he was powerless to master. He had unchained the winds, and storms sprang up beneath his feet at every step. Zwingli, curate of Einsideln, in Switzerland, had already become a party-leader In imitation of the Saxon monk, he rose up against the doctrine of indulgences, but, beside supporting the errors of Luther, he rejected the dogma of original sin, and substituted the figurative in the place of the real presence. Hatred for the Papacy, the rock against which all heresies have successively dashed themselves to pieces, was also the power that actuated Zwingli.

42. The Pontificate of Leo X., troubled by so much domestic strife, drew to a close amid the din of arms with which the ambition of Charles V and Francis I. made all Europe resound. Both monarchs strove to form alliances offensive and defensive with the other European sovereigns. The friendship of Henry VIII. was equally desirable to either of the rival princes, and they spared no pains to win it. Francis met the English king on the famous *Field of the Cloth of Gold*, where the knights, says Du Bellay, an eye-witness, " carried their forests, their meadows and their mills upon their backs." Francis had hoped by this ruinous magnificence to dazzle his English neighbor. But the more wily and successful policy of Charles had already prepossessed the mind of Henry in his favor. He had gone, almost unattended, to meet him at Dover, promised the tiara to Cardinal Wolsey, the king's favorite minister, and paid him the first instalment of a truly imperial pension, which he promised to continue if the minister served his interests faithfully with his royal master. The ambitious cardinal, who was already receiving a

similar bribe from the French court, could not resist the elo
quent reasoning of Charles, and promised him his assistance
The position of Leo was not without difficulty   The hope of
freeing Italy from the French troops was opposed, in his mind,
by the fear of seeing it all in the hands of Charles, already
master of Sicily   Italy was indeed to be the battle-field, in the
coming struggle.   Lautrec returned to take possession of the
Milanese in the name of Francis; he was attacked by Prospero
Colonna, with the imperial troops, and in a moment the conflagration became general.   Leo X. did not witness the end of
these troubles; he was snatched away by an insidious fever
from the love of his subjects and the admiration of the world.
He died on the 1st of December, A. D. 1521, at the premature age
of forty-four years, after a Pontificate of eigh; years and nine
months.

CHAPTER II.

§ I. Pontificate of Adrian VI. (January 9, a. d. 1522—September 24, 1523).

1. Election and character of Adrian VI.—2 Efforts of the Pope to reform the Roman court.—3. A new manifesto from Luther.—4. Diet of Nuremberg. —5. Adrian sends missionaries to America.—6. Religious orders. Theatines Congregation of Somascha. Barnabites. Regular Clerks of the Good Jesus. St. John of God. Ben Fratelli. Discalced Franciscans, or Minors of the Strict Observance of St. Peter of Alcantara.

§ II. Pontificate of Clement VII. (November 19, a. d. 1523—September 25, 1534).

7. Election of Clement VII. His intricate position.—8. Death of Bayard. Pavia. Treaty of Madrid.—9. The Holy League.—10. Capture of Rome by the Imperialists.—11. Treaty of peace between the Pope, Francis I. and Charles V.—12. Disturbances caused at Wittenberg by Carlstadt. The Anabaptists.—13. Luther preaches against monastic vows, and labors to abolish the Mass in the church of Wittenberg.—14. Insurrection of the peasants.—15. Luther incites the German princes to suppress the revolt.— 16. Diet of Spires (1526–1529).—17. Dispute of the Sacramentarians with Zwingli, Œcolampadius and Luther.—18. Diet and Confession of Augsburg. —19. Peace of Nuremberg.—20. First attempt of Henry VIII. to annul his marriage with Catharine of Aragon.—21. Reply of Clement VII. to his request.—22. Cromwell.—23. Discussion in the English court, on the statutes of Præmunire.—24. Henry VIII. marries Anne Boleyn. Thomas Cranmer, archbishop of Canterbury.—25. Clement VII. annuls the marriage of Henry VIII. and Anne Boleyn.—26. Death of Clement VII.

§ 1. Pontificate of Adrian VI. (January 9, a. d. 1522--September 24, 1523).

1. The throne left vacant by Leo X. was not an easy heritage to secure. There are periods in the life of the world when empires are borne onward in a plain and well-defined pathway. All things seem tending to the same splendid and glorious end, when the most unlooked-for circumstance sud-

denly turns the smoothly-flowing course of events. It would almost seem that God is making sport of the designs of men ; He shows them the goal almost within their reach, and with His all-powerful hand suddenly blots them· out from the land of the living. So it was with Leo X. He had surrounded the Papacy with an unprecedented degree of brilliancy and grandeur ; he dies, and the crown of the most brilliant of the Medici is bestowed upon an unknown scholar, Adrian of Utrecht, the early preceptor of Charles V., who now lived in studious retirement at Vittoria, in Biscay His imperial disciple was, at first, desirous to intrust him with the regency of Spain ; but Adrian thought himself unequal to the task of ruling men. His highest ambition was to spend his days in the peace and quiet of private life. Words cannot convey his painful astonishment when two deputies from the Sacred College brought him the tidings of his election to the Sovereign Pontificate. The cardinals had given him their votes because they hoped that his credit with Charles would place him in a better position than any other to combat the formidable heresy which was desolating Germany The new Pope left Spain with tears of heartfelt grief, and was solemnly crowned in Rome, on the 29th of August, A. D. 1522. Contrary to the time-honored custom of the Roman Pontiffs, he kept the name by which he had been known as cardinal and professor, and reigned as Adrian VI. On entering the Eternal City, he perceived that the Romans were preparing to erect a splendid triumphal arch for the ceremony of his installation. He at once interrupted their labors. "These displays," he said, "are more suitable for pagan princes than for Christians and religious." These words are a sufficient index to the character of the Pontificate inaugurated with such a spirit of pious austerity, and which he wished to devote to salutary reforms, thus to remove all ground for the hostile declamations of Luther and his adherents. "Adrian," says Ranke, "was of a most spotless fame ; upright, pious, industrious ; of such gravity that nothing more than a faint smile was ever seen upon his lips, yet full of benevolent, pure intentions ; a true minister of religion." When he took the helm of Peter's bark, the situation of Catholic Europe was one of intricate dangers. The King of France and Charles V vere carrying on bloody hostilities ; Soliman II., the son of Selim, was leading all the powers of Islam against Hungary; the religious anarchy created by the heresiarch of Wittenberg was spreading over the whole of Germany, and threatening the peace of all the Christian States. Adrian made every effort to remedy these three evils, but unhappily failed in all his endeavors. The ambition of Francis and Charles would listen to no proposition for peace. It was impossible for the Pope to turn against the common enemy of Christendom the weapons which the rival monarchs were using against each other. Soliman, after making himself master of Belgrade (1521), laid siege, in the following year, to the city of Rhodes, which the Grand Master of the Hospitallers, for want of a sufficient defensive force, was compelled to surrender by capitulation, together with the whole island. Charles V afterward bestowed upon the order the island of Malta (1530), where they resided, under the name of Knights of Malta, until the extinction of the order.

2. Finding his influence powerless upon the general policy of Europe, Adrian determined to signalize his Pontificate at least by a domestic reform of the clergy and of the Roman court, a reform which had long been needed and for which the leading men of the Catholic world had been earnestly laboring. Struck with horror at the evils to which the publication of indulgences had given rise, he attempted to check the abuse. He forbade the sale of the offices and dignities of the Roman court, lowered the rates of the chancery, abolished coadjutorships, and omitted nothing that could insure the bestowal of offices upon the most worthy It was a frequent expression of Adrian's that " he wished to adorn the churches with priests and not the priests with churches."

3. After the death of Leo X., Luther came forth from his retreat at Wartburg, more eager than ever for the struggle. Charles on his return from Spain, was too busy with his prepara-

tions for war against Francis to check this new flight, and no one else in Germany was powerful enough to carry into effect the edict of Worms. The Saxon monk was thus left in undisputed possession of the field; he made frequent appeals to popular passion and his powerful words found hearers everywhere. He is no longer a mere heretical monk; he is now a very tribune. "Catholic princes," he exclaimed, "the hand of God is uplifted over your heads; utter destruction shall come upon you, you shall die, even were your power greater than that of the Turk himself. You have already received your reward; you are looked upon as knaves and impostors; you shall be judged by the part you have acted; the people know you; the fearful punishment which Holy Writ calls the mockery of God shall encompass you on all sides, and you cannot avert it. The people are weary of your tyranny and iniquity and will no longer bear it; God will have no more of it. The world is not what it was when you hunted men like wild beasts."

4. Shortly after the appearance of this new manifesto, another diet was opened at Nuremburg (November, A. D. 1522). The Pope sent, as his nuncio, Francis Cheregat, bishop of Teramo, and in his instructions to the envoy, Adrian did not dissemble the abuses which afflicted the Church. He speaks as a vigilant and severe Pontiff who does not fear to point out the evil, because he has the will and the energy necessary to correct it. "We know," said the Pope to his nuncio, "that abuses have existed; that the profanation of holy things, arrogance of power and deplorable scandals have, at times, compromised the honor of the Holy See; We are sensible of the evil, nor shall We leave it unpunished." This frank confession should have won for the Pope the cordial sympathy of every honest heart. But a majority of the diet were ruled by the influence and the sarcasms of Luther. They only saw, in this frank and generous avowal, the confirmation of the grievances and calumnies heaped by the heresiarch upon the Holy See. The diet saw only one way of obtaining peace for Germany; it was

to convoke a national synod, in which every party should be represented. Meanwhile, it promised to do what it could for the maintenance of order, though it was at the same time occupied in drawing up a list of grievances against the Holy See. They were rather harsh remonstrances and unreasonable pretensions than complaints, a hundred in number, and drawn up in a spirit of hostility which betrayed itself in every line. The Pope could not satisfy these demands without encroaching upon his own authority, or ecclesiastical discipline, and on the most revered traditions. The diet refused to review what it had done, and Cheregat withdrew, crushed by his defeat. Luther had triumphed. Adrian died of a broken heart, after the return of Cheregat. He was sixty-four years old at the time of his death (September 14, 1523).

5. Adrian's pastoral care was not confined to the provinces of Catholic Europe. Hearing that missionaries were needed in America, he sent to the New World a body of Franciscan religious, full of devoted zeal for the propagation of the faith; and to encourage these zealous apostles, he gave them a proof of his confidence and Apostolic solicitude by a Pontifical bull directing that, in the Indies—by which name the whole of the New World was then known—wherever there existed no episcopal see, or in those places which the bishops or their vicars could not easily visit, the episcopal jurisdiction might be exercised by religious, especially delegated by the superiors for the purpose, except in those cases in which the episcopal character was absolutely indispensable. A similar privilege had already been granted to the missionaries of the order by John XXII.

6. While Germany harbored a rebellious monk whose fanatical declamations against the doctrines of free will, the efficacy of good works, the sacraments, and the spiritual and temporal power, were undermining every moral, religious and social principle, God raised up, in Italy, several apostolic men, whose zeal, and yet more whose example, rekindled, in the hearts of both clergy and faithful, a love of piety, pure morality and the

practice of every virtue. St. Cajetan of Thienna, of an illustrious Italian family, after bringing back to their first fervor the confraternities of the Love of God, in Rome, and of St. Jerome, at Vicenza, founded the Order of Theatines, so called because its first general, Peter Caraffa, still retained his title of archbishop of Theate after his election. The chief ends which the Theatines proposed to themselves were, to preach to the people, to assist the sick, to oppose errors in faith, to restore among the laity the frequent and devout use of the sacraments, and among the clergy a spirit of disinterestedness, regularity and fervor, a love for sacred studies, the most religious respect for holy things, and strict ecclesiastical discipline. St. Jerome Æmiliani, a noble Venetian, was at the same time engaged in erecting charitable institutions in all the cities of Lombardy; he endowed numerous hospitals and became the Francis of Paula of the sixteenth century At Somascha, a village on the frontiers of the Venetian territory, he founded a congregation named, from the place of its origin, the congregation of the Somasques. The members devoted themselves to the instruction of youth, and especially of young men destined for the ministry of the altar. A similar institution was established at Milan by three Italian noblemen: Antonio Maria Zacharia, Bartolomeo Ferrari and Antonio Morigia. They were called Barnabites, from the church of St. Barnabas which was assigned to their use. BB. Margaret and Gentilla of Ravenna at this time instituted in their native city the Regular Clerks of the Good Jesus. But holiness and good works were not peculiar to Italy alone. In Spain, an old soldier, born a poor shepherd, became, by the force of his example alone, the founder of an order of charity which has since spread throughout all the Catholic world. St. John, surnamed of God, was led to this change of life by the saintly eloquence of the illustrious Father John d'Avila, who well deserved his title of Apostle of Andalusia. Under the direction of this holy priest, John began to gather the sick poor into his modest dwelling, where he served them and provided for their wants with a zeal and charity which attracted universal admiration. The example of charity is always contagious; it awakes the noblest instincts of every generous heart. The inhabitants of Granada vied with each other in contributing to the support of his poor patients. In the distribution of his alms, the saint was ignorant of those odious distinctions too often established upon the conduct and character of the poor. The Archbishop of Granada one day sent for him and told him that he was charged with receiving vagabonds and persons of bad character; the man of God threw himself at the feet of the archbishop and replied : " The Son of God came to save sinners; we are obliged also to promote their conversion by our sighs, our tears and exhortations. I am unfaithful to my vocation, because I neglect this duty; and I acknowledge, to my confusion, that I know no other bad person in my hospital but myself, who am a most wretched sinner, unworthy to eat the bread of the poor." The saint was joined by some pious imitators, and thus began the Order of Charity or Brothers of St. John of God. They are popularly known in Italy under the name of *Fate ben Fratelli*, abbreviated into Ben Fratelli, from their original custom of begging alms, after the example of their holy founder, with the words : " Brethren, do us good for the love of God." Another prodigy of holiness and penance was at the same period given to the world by the Order of St. Francis. St. Peter of Alcantara entered the Order of Minors at an early age, and was soon distinguished among the religious by the practice of the greatest humiliations, most rigorous fasts, incredible watchings and painful austerities. The constant union of his soul with God suffered no interruption from any external employment. He told St. Theresa that he had once lived in a house three years without knowing any of his religious brethren except by the sound of their voices. Love of retirement was, if we may use the expression, his predominant passion; and he begged his superiors that he might be placed in some solitary convent, where he could give himself up to the sweet practice of contemplation. He was sent to the convent of St. Onuphrius, situated in the frightful mountain solitude of Lapa. In this retreat he com posed his golden book "On Mental Prayer," justly esteemed a master-piece by St. Theresa, Louis of Granada, St. Francis of Sales, Pope Gregory XV., and other competent judges. This work was soon followed by another no less excellent treatise on "The Peace of the Soul, or an Interior Life," in which the saint, with the pen of a proficient, lays down the rules of the contemplative life and of the highest perfection. After a long practice of the severest austerities of penance, he drew up the plan of a religious order, which should follow the rule of St. Francis in all its primitive rigor. The religious who embraced this pious institute were called Discalced Franciscans, or of the strict observance of St. Peter of Alcantara. Later, while spiritual directo of St. Theresa, he greatly encouraged her in her project of reforming the Carmelite Order, and supported her through the troubles and obstacles of every description against which she had to struggle, in accomplishing the will of God. The Order of Ursuline Nuns was established at about this time, by B. Angela de Merici, of Brescia, for the virtuous education of young ladies, and was soon spread over all Catholic Europe, winning universal esteem by the virtue and fidelity of its members to their duty Such was, in the beginning of the sixteenth century, the interior life of the Catholic Church, against which Luther and his followers poured forth their blasphemous calumnies.

§ II. PONTIFICATE OF CLEMENT VII. (November 19, A. D. 1523— September 25, 1534).

7 At the death of Adrian VI., Giulio de Medici, a cousin of Leo X., was raised to the Pontifical throne. He inaugurated his Pontificate by restoring to favor Cardinal Soderini, whose base treachery we have already mentioned. "On this occasion, to quote contemporary authors, "he proved himself *Clement* in deed as well as in name." His position was a difficult one. and God had heavy trials in store for the great soul of the merciful Pontiff. Italy was cruelly scourged by war; the Reformation was making daily progress. The orders assembled

again at Nuremburg in 1524, with unmistakable evidences of sympathy for Luther's novelties. The Papal nuncio was a man of determined will and an able theologian; he soon perceived the hostile stand of the majority, and could only oppose the decisions of the diet with protestations which were unheeded. The Catholic princes of Germany were alarmed and felt that they should need all their power to resist. Three of them, Duke Wilhelm, Duke Louis of Bavaria, and Ferdinand, archduke of Austria, met at Ratisbon, where they were soon joined by several bishops and archbishops; they concluded a treaty for the defence of the Catholic doctrine and worship against Lutheranism. But these unaided efforts were destined to remained fruitless. Before entering upon an uninterrupted narrative of the troubles caused by the Reformation, it will be well to acquaint the reader with the succession of political events that hurried the afflicted Pontiff, Clement VII., into disasters which he could not avert.

8. Since the year 1521, Italy had been the battle-field on which Charles V and Francis I. contended for the empire of the world. The French admiral, Bonnivet, a man better suited to the court than to the field, was sent against the Imperialists under the notorious Constable of Bourbon, whom a personal injury had made a traitor to his king and country. Next in command to the admiral, was Bayard, the *chevalier sans peur et sans reproche*, whose precious life paid the forfeit of his commander's incapacity, at the battle of Romagnano on the Sesia (A. D. 1521). The Constable of Bourbon approached the dying hero and said to him: "I truly feel great pity at seeing you in this sad condition; for you were so worthy a knight." "My lord," replied the fearless and faithful captain, "it is not I who am to be pitied, but you, who are in arms against your country, your king and your faith." A few moments after, the hero expired, his eyes fixed upon the cross-hilt of his sword, which recalled to him the august symbol of the religion to whose laws he had ever been faithful amid all the chances and dangers of a soldier's life. The constable withdrew with

tearful eyes. "Happy the prince," he cried, "who has such a servant' France little knows the loss she suffers to-day !" The sight of this unswerving fidelity to God and to the king, in the very arms of death, moved, but did not change the constable. Revenge is a passion that will not be sated. Bourbon fell upon Provence, which the wily emperor had flattered him with the hope of ruling in person. Aix and Toulon were soon in his power, and he laid siege to Marseilles, without the least expectation of resistance. " The third discharge of the imperial cannon," said Bourbon, " will bring those frightened burghers to our feet, with halters about their necks and the keys of the city in their hands." He was soon, however, compelled to change his tone. The garrison, the private citizens, and even the women of the town, vied with one another in constancy and daring. Francis assembled a large army under the walls of Avignon, but when he advanced upon Marseilles, the Imperialists, already exhausted by the labors of a siege of forty days, weakened by disease and want, hastily retreated into Italy. But Francis was before them; Milan opened its gates to the French king, and the whole duchy, with the single exception of Pavia, submitted to his rule. Clement VII., alarmed by the ever-growing power of Charles, thought it his duty to favor the cause of his opponent. The tidings of the French king's success were accordingly received with joy at the Roman court; but they were destined to be short-lived, and Rome was doomed to suffer, more than any other city, from the reverses of France Bonnivet advised the king to lay siege to Pavia. But Bourbon was now advancing with a reënforcement of twelve thousand Germans, levied at his own expense. Ordinary prudence would nave required the French to retreat; but the chivalric Francis deemed it a disgrace to fly before the traitor Bourbon; he accordingly determined to await his approach. This proud determination resulted in one of the most lamentable defeats ever experienced by the arms of France; the royal army was cut to pieces, the king himself remained a prisoner in the hands of the enemy After the battle, Francis wrote to his mother

" Madame, all is lost but honor" (Madame, tout est perdu, fors l'honneur)   The royal prisoner was taken to Madrid, and only obtained his release after signing a treaty by which he renounced his claims upon Italy, gave up the duchy of Burgundy to the, empire, promised to deliver up his two eldest sons as hostages for the performance of these conditions, to return his estates and rights to the Duke of Bourbon, and to bind himself, by a matrimonial alliance, to the family of Charles.

9. After signing this disgraceful treaty, Francis was set at liberty; he left his prison with the firm determination not to fulfil the terms imposed by force, and to which necessity alone could have made him subscribe.   The estates of Burgundy, which had met to deliberate upon the treaty of Madrid, thus addressed the king: " Should your majesty persist in the intention of giving us over to a foreign domination, we shall defend our own province to the last breath, and die Frenchmen." This noble sentiment was received with universal applause. Pope Clement VII., Henry VIII., the republics of Venice, Genoa, Florence, and Milan, entered into an alliance with France against Charles V ; this coalition received, from the Pope's participation, the name of the *Holy League*.   True to the traditions of Italian policy, the Sovereign Pontiff saw that the liberty of the Peninsula was lost if the youthful emperor, already master of Naples, gained possession also of the Milanese, which was yielded by the treaty   This consideration decided his policy under the circumstances.

10. The rage of the Imperialists first vented itself upon Italy   During ten whole months, Milan was given up to the barbarous fury of the Spaniards.   As soon as it became known in Germany that these rich provinces were given up to pillage, sixteen thousand German landsknechts crossed the Alps, led by a furious Lutheran, named George Freundsberg, who wore about his neck a golden chain, " with which," as he said, " he meant to strangle the Pope."   This host of brigands was led, or, perhaps, rather followed, by Bourbon and Leyva.   Its ranks were swelled, as it advanced, by numerous adventurers.   Marching

through Ferrara and Bologna, the Lutherans were about to turn into Tuscany, and many were now in the habit of swearing only by the *glorious sack of Florence;* but their heretical spirit urged them on to Rome, where the constable assured them that they should find ample booty The city was fiercely assaulted. Bourbon fell in the attack, but his soldiers avenged his loss only too well. They gave no quarter, and on the very day of their entrance, eight thousand Romans were butchered while imploring mercy on their knees. "Never, perhaps, in the history of the world," says Sismondi, "had a greater capital been given up to a more atrocious abuse of victory; never had a powerful army been made up of more barbarous elements; never had the restraints of discipline been more fearfully cast aside. It was not enough for these rapacious plunderers to seize upon the rich stores of sacred and profane wealth which the piety or industry of the people had gathered into the capital of the Christian world; the wretched inhabitants themselves became the victims of the fierce and brutal soldiery; those who were suspected of having hidden their wealth, were put to the torture. Some were forced, by these tortures, to sign promissory notes, and to drain the purses of their friends in other countries. A great number of prelates fell under these sufferings. Many others, after having paid their ransom, and while rejoicing to think themselves free from further attacks, were obliged to redeem themselves again, and died from grief or terror, caused by these acts of violence. The German troops were seen, drunk at once with wine and blood, leading about bishops in full pontifical attire, seated upon mules, or dragging cardinals through the streets, loading them with blows and outrages. In their eagerness for plunder, they broke in the doors of the tabernacles, and destroyed master-pieces of art. The Vatican library was sacked; the public squares and churches of Rome were converted into market-places, where the conquerors sold, as promiscuous booty, the Roman ladies and horses; and these brutal excesses were committed even in the basilicas of St. Peter and St. Paul, he'd by Alaric as sacred asylums

the pillage which, under Genseric, had lasted but fourteen days, lasted now two months without interruption." The wardrobe of the Sovereign Pontiffs fell into the hands of these madmen. Clothed in the sacred vestments, they assembled in the hall of conclave and proceeded to a mock election. After declaring Clement VII. deposed from the Papacy, they solemnly elected the apostate monk Luther as Vicar of Jesus Christ. Strange contradiction! They knew no better way of honoring the author of the Reformation than by conferring upon him, in derision, a dignity which he had made the chief butt of his ridicule.

11. While these scenes of desolation and horror were enacted in Rome, Clement VII. was besieged in the castle of St. Angelo, his last asylum. Here he soon found himself so closely pressed that he was forced to capitulate. On the 5th of June (A. D. 1527), the Archbishop of Capua, on behalf of the unfortunate Pontiff, signed a treaty, by which Clement was bound: 1. To pay down a hundred thousand gold ducats. 2. To place the castle of St. Angelo, as a pledge, in the hands of the emperor's officers; 3. To give up to the Imperialists the cities of Ostia, Civita-Vecchia, Citta di Castello, Parma, and Piacenza; 4. To remain a prisoner until the promised sum should have been paid. Clement found it impossible to fulfil these conditions. The governors refused to give up the cities placed in their charge. The Pontifical treasury was completely drained, and the Pope was forced to remain a prisoner. A fearful plague crowned this series of disasters; from Rimini it came even into the castle of St. Angelo, and Clement was exposed to the danger of this scourge, more fearful even than war. He managed to escape from his prison in the disguise of a travelling merchant. All seemed to conspire at once against the Pontiff. The enemies of the Medici seized the occasion offered by the confusion of the moment to drive out the family of the Pope from Florence. Clement was deeply affected by the defection of his native city; he saw that the only means of avoiding greater disasters was to renew the alliance with the victorious

Imperialists. On June 26th, 1529, he arranged terms of accommodation with Hugo Hunniades, the Imperialist commander. The power of Charles, lately confirmed by the treaty concluded with Francis, at Cambray, and known as the *Ladies' Treaty,** was now at its zenith; beside the provinces of the German empire, he ruled the Italian Peninsula from the Alps to the Mediterranean. On the 24th of February, 1530, the Pope crowned him emperor at Bologna. But Clement could not look with indifference upon the rapid growth of the imperial sway which threatened to destroy the balance of power in Europe, and especially to injure the interests of the Church. He wished to make one more effort to throw his political influence into the scales. Turning to France, he met the king at Marseilles. This return to the policy of his predecessors, under circumstances so full of peril, was heroic. But Charles was too powerful an adversary; beside, the Lutheran schism was daily assuming a more threatening attitude, and Clement VII. was powerless to stem the destructive torrent.

12. While the Catholic princes were forming their league at Ratisbon, a meeting of the Lutheran princes was held at Torgau (A. D. 1526) Philip, landgrave of Hesse, John, the new elector of Saxony, the duchies of Mecklenburg and Anhalt, Prussia, the cities of Brunswick and Magdeburg, entered into an alliance to support the cause of the Reform. Luther's principles led to consequences which their author would have wished to disavow. We have already mentioned the excesses of Carlstadt at Wittenberg. The fanatical preacher with his own hand set fire to the text-books brought to him by the students from all quarters, under pretext that the Bible must thenceforth furnish the only reading for all mankind. The people applauded these digraceful scenes, worthy of the Vandals, and followed the sectary to the plunder of churches and monasteries. Similar scenes were enacted at Zwickau by a

* The treaty of Cambray received this popular appellation from the fact that it was concluded through the mediation of the two princesses Louise of Savoy, mother of Francis I., and Margaret of Austria, aunt of Charles V.—Tr.

band of fanatics, under the guidance of Nicholas Storch; they
rejected the authority of Luther, thus putting into practice the
theories of independence which they had learned from the
Saxon monk himself, by throwing off the yoke he sought to im-
pose upon them.   They denied the validity of infant baptism,
for which, they said, they could find no warrant in Scripture.
Their leader took them to Wittenberg, where he maintained
his doctrine that infant baptism was useless; that hence it was
indispensably necessary to rebaptize adults, upon whom the
Church could not confer a valid sacrament before they had
attained the age of reason.   Their doctrine obtained for them
the name of Anabaptists, to which their disorders gave a most
bloody renown.   Melancthon, Luther's cherished disciple, wa-
vered for some time between the authority of his master and
that of the new sectaries.   Storch's objections had weight
enough with him to lead him into a serious study of the question of infant baptism; the text of Holy Writ did not supply the light he sought, and he would then have become an
Anabaptist too, had not the excesses of the fanatics given him
a disgust for their doctrines.   Luther was unable to restore
order in his divided camp.   In vain he wrote to the leaders
of the new sect, urging moderation, and reminding them of the
necessity, as he said, "of trying the spirits."   Finding his
words unheeded, he thought himself entitled to "rap these
visionaries upon the snout;" and he tried against them the violent abuse and popular preaching he had found so successful
against Catholicity.   But it is easier to start the minds of men
in the way of revolution, than to check their headlong course
when they have once begun to move on the steep descent.
When Luther tried to enforce his own opinions, he was told
that he had himself taught the sole authority of the Bible.   If
he leaned his arguments upon the Gospel, he was met with the
reply that they had learned from him their right to interpret
the Sacred Text for themselves.   The religious freedom which
he claimed to have given to the world, now turned its power
against its author.   Still he did not allow himself to be dis-

couraged, and, finding it impossible to check the movement he had rashly provoked, he did not hesitate to place himself at its head. With a view to change the current of popular ideas, and doubtless, too, to satisfy the passions which burned within his own breast, he began to preach with vehemence against monastic vows. The sermons, letters and pamphlets which soon flooded the whole of Germany were all written under this insp,.ration, to flatter the lowest instincts and stir up the ignorant populace. The arguments with which he attacked the vow of chastity and the law of ecclesiastical celibacy do not admit of quotation. It will not be hard to understand the success of Luther's doctrines, if we consider that they were supported by every bad passion, by every form of cupidity and vice. " The time has come," wrote Luther, " to do away forever with these vows against nature ; the time has come when those who make them should be treated with the greatest rigor of the law ; now is the time to destroy convents, abbeys, priories and monasteries, that such vows may never be uttered more." The Reformation was evidently intended to be a radical one. The lower instincts of man are little disposed to reason with the power that opposes their workings.

13. At all times, there have been found, even in religious orders, men unworthy of their vocation, whom a continued abuse of grace has gradually led to apostasy ; rotten branches that should be speedily lopped off from the trunk, which they injure by their misconduct and immorality Luther's preaching awaked an echo in every depraved heart; the scandal was carried out to its fullest extent. The religious deserted their convents to contract sacrilegious unions. Carlstadt was solemnly married at Wittenberg, and the Reformers loudly applauded the shameless act as a heroic deed which restored human freedom. Passions, once aroused, never stop to reason. Among his familiar friends, Luther confessed that this overflow of the sensual appetite " singularly corrupted the good odor of the gospel." But, as he meant to profit by it himself, at a later date, he was careful not to struggle too violently against it,

and continued to direct his attacks against the Catholic priesthood. "These priests, these mass-mumblers, deserve death as
truly as a blasphemer who should curse God and His saints in
the public streets." We might almost believe that in such
words we hear, by anticipation, the cries of the revolutionists
of 1793.

14. The time was far distant when Pope Leo X., misled as
to the character of the Reformer, could treat the question as a
"quarrel of monks." Minds had been working onward, since
then, and the people began to take an active share in the
scandalous disputes. The name of liberty, which seems to have
been sent on earth only to breed revolutions, was throwing all
Germany into a state of disorder. Erasmus has left us a
striking picture of the appearance of the sectaries. "I see
them," he writes, "as they come from the sermons, with rage
depicted in every feature, their eyes on fire, as if intoxicated
by the bloodthirsty harangues which they have just heard.
This evangelical race breathes but combats, seeks no other
argument than armed force." The fairest provinces of Germany,
the Rhine country, Saxony, Thuringia and Suabia, were desolated with fire and sword. A new name suddenly appeared
amid the general fermentation; a name written in letters of
blood upon the ruins of castles, churches and monasteries; it
was that of Thomas Münzer, the leader of the sect of *Conquering* Anabaptists. Luther's work on "Christian Liberty," scattered throughout the whole land, had prepared all minds for
revolt; the new prophet placed arms in the hands of the revolters and organized the rebellion as a holy war. Münzer
was born at Zwickau, in the decline of the fifteenth century.
He was successively vicar in his native town and curate at
Mülhausen, and disguised, under an outward show of austere
penance, a boundless ambition and a bitter hatred against all
superiority, hierarchical or social. At the first cry raised by
Luther against the Holy See and the Catholic Church, Münzer
distinguished himself by the fanatical ardor with which he supported the new doctrines. He soon even outstripped his master

and labored to destroy the order of society, by preaching a system of political equality and freedom, much more intelligible to the uneducated peasantry than the spiritual equality and freedom taught by the Saxon monk. The overthrow of all power, the destruction of every form of government—such was his doctrine in the widest interpretation given to it by the most ardent modern socialists. A cry of indignation went up from every court in Germany at the announcement of these revolutionary theories. The nobles were very willing to support the Lutheran crusade against the clergy, the convents and ecclesiastical property, so long as it was to redound to their own profit. They were quite ready to gather the spoils and to enrich themselves with the wealth of the altars. But when the tide of revolution threatened to sweep them along in its destructive course, when thirty thousand armed peasants rose up against their authority, demolished their strongholds, broke down their ramparts, destroyed their troops, plundered their treasure and proclaimed the downfall of all the sovereignties of the world to make way for what they called the *Kingdom of God*, they were struck with fear, and their councils called upon Luther to stem the torrent which his inflamed harangues had let loose. The Reformer at first tried the counsels of moderation and prudence, which were not even heard. His voice was drowned by the storm; like all revolutionary leaders, he possessed an immense influence for destruction, but was powerless to pacify   The banishment and proscription of Münzer, to which he contributed in concert with the German princes, only added new force to the insurrection. The furious anabaptist was looked upon as a martyr to liberty and a victim of the tyranny of princes. In his place of exile he drew up a document consisting of thirty articles, to be presented by the peasants to the princes of the empire, by which they demanded exemption from all taxes, the abolition of seigneural courts, the suppression of tithes and of all other dues, and the right for every parish to choose and to remove at will the ministers of the divine word. To give additional weight to his demands,

Münzer took care to support them all by texts drawn from the writings of Luther himself. In a few weeks, the incendiary memorial was spread through every province and received the approval of the excited multitude. It was finally handed to Luther, with the request that he would have it signed by the princes. As might have been foreseen, this proceeding was fruitless, and the hypocritical flattery with which the Reformer endeavored to satisfy the peasants gave a fresh proof of his impotence. His empty declamations were answered by the fierce war-cry of the fanatical sectaries. Münzer assumed the appellation of " Gideon, sent of God to reëstablish with the sword the kingdom of Jesus Christ." At his voice, the popu- lace of Mülhausen, in Franconia, drove out their magistrates and set up a kind of republic, of which the prophet became the chief. He had soon collected an army of thirty thousand sectaries; their numbers were fast increased by the accession of many adventurers who sought, in these times of trouble, impunity for past crimes and the opportunity of committing fresh ones. Under his command they carried on a war of bloodshed and rapine, in which the most horrible acts of cruelty, the most unheard of barbarity, were the order of the day Luther no longer hesitated to invoke the most vigorous chas- tisement upon these madmen, whose guilty hopes he had him- self excited. He wrote to the German princes, urging them to check the disorder and to lay aside the gentle means they had hitherto used. " While there remains a drop of blood in your veins," said Luther to them, " hunt these rebellious peasants like wild beasts ; kill them like mad dogs ; they are sold, body and soul, to Satan." Luther's action, in this case, was, perhaps, profoundly politic, but it was as disgraceful as it was skilful, and every drop of blood shed in that disastrous warfare must fall upon the memory of the Reformer, who gave up to the public vengeance the multitude of fanatics he had armed himself.

15. The evil was pressing; any attempt at negotiation was sure to fail against the popular movement which agitated the

masses in Germany, equally hard to arouse and to pacify   The nobles availed themselves of Luther's mistake, to throw upon him all the odium of the war they were about to undertake with the fixed purpose of effecting the utter extermination of the revolted peasants.   In looking back over the long list of evils inflicted upon the world by the Lutheran heresy, the most disastrous, perhaps, recorded in the annals of the Church; when we see its cradle stained with blood, its birth attended with so many crimes, its progress marked by numberless ruins; if we follow, step by step, the conduct of its author, if we consider the duplicity, the results of which deluged his country in blood, the boundless pride and ambition which could sacrifice the peace of the world to an unholy thirst for glory; if we look into the depths of that heart which had become the abode of evil passions, of shamelessness and base desires—it is hard to understand the blindness of those minds for which Luther is still a prophet, an apostle sent from God.   With the page of history open before us, doubt or hesitation seems to us an impossibility; none of these characteristics savor of the Gospel, though that sacred name was ever profaned by the sectaries who sought to cover their shameful disorders by the authority of the Divine Book.   Luther wrote thus in 1522: " The people are rising everywhere; they have at length opened their eyes and will no longer allow themselves to be crushed by violence."   In 1526, the man of the people, the hero of the multitudes, had changed his tone :   " The people are tigers that must be chained, wild beasts that must be destroyed without pity or restraint."   It was the singular destiny of the apostate monk that his very inconsistencies were so many mournful triumphs.   In 1522, the people obeyed the voice that urged them to revolt; in 1526, the nobles answered his appeal by rising up to crush the rebellion which he had himself proclaimed.   But if his insatiable pride could, in his own day, gloat over these bloody triumphs, history and posterity can view them only as so many subjects of opprobrium which time cannot efface.   A powerful army unde the Landgrave Philip of Hesse, the Dukes

Henry of Brunswick and George of Saxony, attacked Münzer at Mülhausen. The desperate resistance of the peasants, and the fanatical madness with which they refused to give any quarter, drew upon them the most fearful reprisals; the battle was one of the bloodiest for the numbers engaged. Toward evening the peasants were routed and fled in all directions, leaving their leader nearly alone upon the field (May 15, A. D. 1525). Münzer fled to Frankenhausen, where he remained concealed for some time; but his retreat having been discovered, he was taken and brought to Mülhausen, where he was tried and sentenced to be beheaded. In the immediate presence of death and of the awful judgments of God, the Catholic faith, which he had forsaken, once more revived within his breast. The remembrance of his crimes and the terrors of eternity opened his heart to remorse. He abjured the perverse doctrine which had made his life so miserable, and protested that he wished to die a submissive and repentant son of the Church he had so violently assailed. In these dispositions he mounted the scaffold (December, 1525), trusting in the unfailing mercy of the God Whose dying words were a prayer for His executioners.

16. Luther's popularity perished with Münzer upon the scaffold at Mülhausen. Henceforth, we shall find him among princes, literary men and the familiar friends who form a kind of court around him; his part is reversed; he no longer wields that immediate influence over the multitudes which had marked the first years of the Reformation. This new phase in the life of the apostate monk is revealed by repeated attempts at pacification. The camp into which he was now entering needed order, and he was called upon to establish it. The Catholic clergy was ruined; its property was in the hands of the nobles; episcopal jurisdiction was abolished, every form of belief was tolerated, every religious law annulled. Unless he was ready to open the door to every form of anarchy, to every shape of extravagance and disorder, it was necessary to reëstablish an authority of some kind; and the Reformer's theories were now to

receive, in practice, a formal refutation. Luther had built up his whole doctrine on the fundamental principle of individual liberty, in the widest acceptation of the term; he had, consequently, destroyed the Catholic priesthood, as a sacrilegious usurpation of the sacred ministry of religion, to the profit of a few, whereas, in his system, it belonged equally to all. Now, he was condemned himself to constitute Lutheran ministers, upon whom he must confer a kind of priestly character. He had, in the first days of his revolt against the Church, solemnly burned, in the public square of Wittenberg, a copy of the canon law, by way of strong protest that he regarded the legislation of the Church as a despotic sway from which the consciences of men must be freed, a galling yoke which had too long weighed down the people and which it should be his glory to break forever. Now he was condemned to substitute his own laws in the place of those which the antiquity of tradition and the authority of the holiest Pontiffs, the twofold consecration of time and virtue, had made equally dear and venerable. He must now frame arbitrary laws wholly devoid of authority, institutions which have no foundation on the past and no power of resistance against the dangers of the future. Finally, in obedience to the secret promptings of the vilest passions, Luther had shaken the very foundation of society, by attacking the sacred institution of marriage. It became necessary to stay the progress of these impure doctrines which threatened Europe with the foul disgrace of Mussulman polygamy The Landgrave Philip of Hesse, the victor of Mülhausen, summoned the Lutherans to meet at Homburg (October, A. D. 1526), that they might discuss these questions in concert and come to a speedy determination. Luther did not appear in the synod, but left the direction of it to one of his most ardent disciples, the apostate Lambert of Avignon, one of the first who left the Order of Minims, in which he had made his religious profession, to follow the German Reformer. It was in this assembly that Lutheranism received a definitive organization, which it has, in most respects, since preserved. The landgrave, who simply asked for a legislation and hierarchy of some kind. without any regard to their real merits, unconditionally accepted whatever was offered, only declaring that when they were once promulgated, he should strictly enforce their observance. Luther himself, urged on by the constant need of action which preyed upon his soul, put forth all the energy of his mind, all the eloquence of his impetuous nature, for the support and the propagation of the doctrines laid down at Homburg. He filled the country with *evangelical preachers*, as he called them, whose mission it was to withdraw the people from the yoke of the Church. They scattered around them printed copies of a formula composed by Melancthon, containing, in a few pages, all the new doctrines, and, as a more efficient means of spreading his teachings, Luther himself composed a *small* and a *large catechism*, which were to be placed in the hands of children. These measures had thrown Germany into a state of complete revolution. An imperial diet was convened at Spires (1526). Charles V was engaged in his protracted war with France. His brother, the Archduke Ferdinand, who commanded the imperial troops in Hungary, was hardly able to defend those rich provinces against the victorious arms of Soliman. The position of affairs was favorable to the Lutheran princes; they profited by it in the assembly, and the public calamities which were afflicting the empire helped on their exorbitant pretensions. The authorities had neither the power nor the will to deal with domestic troubles, while so many foreign enemies threatened the empire from without. With a view to cut short all recriminations, it was agreed to leave matters as they then stood, and to refer to a future time the settlement of difficulties which it was plainly impossible to remove under existing circumstances. Such was the import of the famous concession made by the Diet of Spires, in these terms: " Until the meeting of the ecumenical council, each power shall do, as regards the decree of Worms, what it deems best, and shall be answerable, for its conduct, to God and to the emperor." The next subject of attention was the defensive league to be formed against the Turks. The fairest promises were readily made; but they all proved useless, for tidings were brought, at the same time, of the defeat and death of Louis, king of Hungary, whose army had been cut to pieces by Soliman in the marshes of Mohacs (August 29, 1526). The disaster aroused in the heart of Germany the old instincts of nationality and faith which had given birth to the Crusades. But Luther and Melancthon had declared that they would rather have the sul tan than the Pope; and they accordingly labored with all their power to stifle this noble impulse. " The word of God and His work," they said, "need no armed defenders; they are strong enough of themselves to meet all the attacks of their enemies." The Turks availed themselves of the inaction of the Christian princes and of the secret sympathies held out to them by Lutheranism. Soliman laid siege to Vienna, with a formidable army The garrison and citizens of the German capital, now thrown upon their own resources, performed prodigies of valor, and succeeded for the time, in turning off from Europe the torrent of Mussulman invasion. Still the danger was threatening. Another diet met at Spires (1529); but the Lutheran princes showed far more eagerness to support the prerogatives of their new sect, than to take measures for repelling the common enemy Party spirit, always blind and selfish, is never willing to hear of terms. The Catholics, with the genuine patriotism which rises above paltry considerations of self-love and personal vanity, proposed a middle course which should, according to them, unite all the suffrages. It was very nearly the same as the declaration admitted, two years before, by the preceding diet. " The edict of Worms," said the proposal, " shall be observed in the States in which it has already been received. The others shall be free to continue in the new doctrines until the meeting of the next general council. However, to prevent all domestic troubles, no one shall preach in public against the Sacrament of the altar; the Mass shall not be abolished; and no one shall be hindered from celebrating or hearing it." These words, which certainly breathe a spirit of unquestionable moderation and justice, aroused the whole Lutheran party, which *protested*, with one voice, that freedom of conscience and evangelical truth were threatened. " The Mass is an act of idolatry, condemned by a thousand passages of Sacred Scripture. It is our duty and our right to overthrow the altars of Baal." This written protest, duly signed, was immediately sent to Bologna, to be pre sented to Charles V It was on this occasion that the Lutherans first took the name of Protestants, which they have since kept. The victories of Charles in France and Italy had just resulted in the treaty of Cambrai with Pope Clement VII. and Francis I. The emperor could now dictate terms, and he used his power. The Lutheran deputation met with a very unfavorable reception; the emperor refused to receive their protest. " The Catholics have no more idea than yourselves," said Charles, " of acting against their conscience or their faith. We expect a peaceful and regular settlement of the difficulties in Germany, from the decision of a general council, which will meet as soon as circumstances permit. Until then, it is our wish that the States strictly observe the decisions of the diet." The deputies, proud to display their independence before the most powerful monarch in Europe, drew up a formal protest against the imperial decision. Charles, in reply, ordered them to be thrown into prison. He soon afterward, however, set them at liberty, and summoned another diet to meet at Augsburg, in the following year, promising to be present in person.

17 The interval was taken up by the *Sacramentarian* discussion between Zwingli, Œcolampadius, and Luther. Zwingli, in explaining the terms of the Eucharistic institution, pretended that the words: " Hoc est corpus meum," meant: " This *signifies* my body " Œcolampadius would have the word *corpus* understood in a figurative sense, and **not** as indicating a real presence. The teaching of the Catholic Church is that the words of Jesus Christ are to be understood literally, and that they really effect what they say; so that after the consecration of the bread by the words: " Hoc

est corpus meum" (*This is my body*), there is no longer bread upon the altar, but the body of Jesus Christ, under the form and appearance of bread. This is what theologians call the dogma of *Transubstantiation*. Luther rejected the Catholic doctrine, though he was equally unwilling to admit the arbitrary interpretations of Zwingli and Œcolampadius. He accordingly wrote, with his usual vehemence, in support of his intermediate system of *Consubstantiation*. He maintained that the body of Christ is with the bread in the sacrament of the Eucharist (*In vane, sub pane, cum pane*). Zwingli retorted by demonstrating that if the literal interpretation must be received, the Catholic dogma of Transubstantiation was the only admissible one; and that if, with Luther, they admitted a figurative sense (*This is my body*, signifying : *This contains my body*, or *This bread is united with my body*), he asked in what his metonymy was less solid than Luther's synecdoche. "You call us heretics," said Zwingli, "who should be put to silence; you lay an interdict upon our works, you urge the authorities to oppose our doctrines. In what did the Pope's conduct differ from yours, when truth first tried to raise its voice?" The ecclesiastic of Wittenberg could find but little to reply to this argument. He had declaimed against tradition; he was now obliged to fall back upon it, in spite of his theories of private interpretation. "Consubstantiation," he wrote to Albert of Prussia, "is not a doctrine of human invention; it is founded upon the gospel, upon plain, unquestionable words; it has been uniformly believed and preserved throughout the whole world, from the foundation of the Christian Church until the present hour; this is proved by the works of the Holy Fathers, both Greek and Latin, as well as by daily usage and continued experience. Were it a new doctrine, had it been less uniformly kept in all the churches, throughout all Christendom, it would not be so fearful, nor so dangerous to doubt and to discuss it. Whoever doubts it might as well deny the Christian Church, and condemn, as heretical, not only the holy Church, but Christ Himself and the Apostles and Prophets, who have established it with promises of endless duration! The Church of God is the pillar and ground of truth." These words could hardly be attributed to the same pen which five years before had written : "All the Fathers have erred in the faith, and, if they did not repent before death, they are damned for all eternity St. Gregory invented purgatory and masses for the dead Augustine often erred, and it is not safe to trust him. Jerome, I look upon as a heretic who has written many impious things. I know none of the Fathers whom I hate as I do him ; he is always uttering absurdities about fasting and virginity I make little account of Chrysostom ; he is an empty declaimer. Basil is good for nothing—he is a real monk. Thomas Aquinas is a mere theological abortion, a sink of error, a compound of all kinds of heresies which destroy the gospel."* Yet these inconsistencies gave Luther no trouble. His words were adapted to the interests of his cause, hostile or flattering, according to circumstances.

18. The emperor's arrival at Augsburg was delayed until the 15th of June. It was the eve of the Feast of the Blessed Sacrament, which gave rise at once to new difficulties. Charles V called upon the Protestant princes to lay before him a written formula of their belief and of the abuses they claimed to reject. Melancthon was charged to draw up the document, which was called the Augsburg Confession, or Formula of Faith (*Confessio Augustana*). Luther received it without restriction. "I am well enough pleased," he writes, "with this document, and I see no need of change or improvement in it. Besides, I could not undertake it; I could not act with so much calmness and gentleness." The Augsburg Confession contained a preamble in two parts, the first, in twelve articles, rested upon the Apostles' Creed and that of Nice, and the second, in seven articles, exposed the abuses to be rejected. Among the abuses, Melancthon enumerated communion under one kind, private masses, celibacy, monastic vows, the distinction of meats for days of abstinence, auricular confession and ecclesiastical

* Vid. Alzog, t. III., pp. 46, 65.

government. The first part, composed with great art and moderation, contained Luther's doctrine under a softened and disguised form; still, it recognized the leading errors of the Saxon monk: 1st. On original sin, as causing an absolute incapacity for good; 2d. On justification by faith alone; 3d. On free will, faith and good works; 4th. On the worship and invocation of saints; 5th. On the presence of Jesus Christ in the Sacrament of the altar: as we have already stated, Luther admitted no change of substance. The confession was publicly read before the diet, after which the emperor submitted it to the Catholic theologians present in the assembly— Eck, Cochlæus, Conrad Wimpina, Faber and others. They pointed out the errors and showed, moreover, from Luther's writings, that he had himself, at various times, taught directly opposite doctrines. In the presence of the crying evils already caused by the Reformed doctrines, it was not easy for devoted sons of the Church to master their indignation. The first report of the Catholic doctors, drawn up under the influence of this feeling, seemed to the emperor somewhat too harsh. He pointed this out to the theologians, who recognized the necessity of keeping within the bounds of prudence and moderation. Truth must be calm and reserved; passion is suited only to the defence of error. With this view they drew up a new refutation of the confession (Confutatio Confessionis Augustanæ). Each article was calmly discussed in accordance with the rules of strict logic. The Lutheran errors were compared with Catholic tradition; it was shown wherein they diverged from the truth and by what alluring baits they had misled unthinking minds. The refutation was read, by command of the emperor, to the assembled orders. Charles had relied upon the good faith of the Protestant princes. After this precise and clear exposition of the Catholic dogmas, he did not doubt that they would at once abandon the cause of the Reformation. He accordingly addressed the assembly, expressing the desire that all divisions should thenceforth cease: " Otherwise," he added, " we shall be compelled to act, in conscience, in accordance with our coronation oath, as protector of the Holy Church." This declaration aroused all the hatred of the Protestant faction. Philip of Hesse, to the general consternation, abruptly closed the discussion opened between the princes and bishops, and quitted Augsburg. Charles then decided that a public controversy should be held in his presence, on the disputed points. Eck, the Catholic doctor, and Melancthon, the disciple of Luther, were appointed to defend their respective theses. The question of communion under both kinds was first discussed. The Catholic theologians, relying upon an analogous precedent in the case of the Hussites, promised to obtain this concession for Germany, in the event of their coming to an understanding upon the other disputed questions. Melancthon was certainly the most honest and upright of all the Reformers. He could not impugn the known truth, and he soon fell into disrepute with his own party for his moderation in carrying on the discussion. Luther did not appear at the diet; he remained at Coburg, always ready to give his advice in matters of importance. In the course of the debate, Melancthon acknowledged the authority of bishops. "Under what pretext," he said to his partisans, "can we deprive the bishops of their authority, if they teach sound doctrine? If I must say what I think, not only would I strengthen their authority, but I would even wish to restore to them full episcopal power and spiritual administration. Without a governing power, we shall languish under a tyranny more cruel than any that has yet existed!" In terms even more explicit, he wrote to the legate, Campeggio, on the power of the Sovereign Pontiff : "We have no other doctrine than that of the Roman Church. We are ready to obey her if she dispenses to us the treasures of kindness which she lavishes on her other children, and consents to overlook certain points of minor importance, which we could not now change even though we wished it. We honor the Pope of Rome and all the constitutions of the Church, provided the Pope do not repel us. But why should we tremble? Why should he reject the prayer of suppliants, when unity can be so easily restored? There are but insignificant differences in the usages which seem to oppose a sincere reconciliation. The canons themselves admit that we may differ on such matters without being cut off from the union of the Church." When Luther heard of this letter, his rage knew no bounds. " I will not hear of unity in doctrine," he wrote to Melancthon, " since it is an utter impossibility unless the Pope will lay aside all his Papal insignia. The affair will be lengthened out by continual quibbling and endless concessions. The wily Catholics have set us a snare which we must carefully avoid." Melancthon now saw clearly that the Reformer had no intention of entering upon the discussion with any degree of good faith. " All these fault-finders," said he, " plainly show that they are contending, not for the gospel, but for their own personal interest." Had Melancthon been gifted with a courage equal to his uprightness, he would have seized this occasion to break with Protestantism. But Luther swayed his timid nature with all the power which a superior mind knows how to exercise over a weak imagination. The victim passively submitted to all that was required of him. Instead of following out his projects of reconciliation, he published an " Apology for the Augsburg Confession," in opposition to the Refutation of the Catholic theologians. The Lutheran nobles presented it to Charles, who rejected it as well as the confession itself; but among the Protestants it obtained an authority equal to that of the Formula. On the other hand, the four cities which held the doctrines of Zwingli, viz.: Strasburg, Lindau, Constance and Memmingen, had published a common confession of faith, the " Confessio Tetrapolitana." Zwingli himself presented a special one of his own, in which he brings out the points of divergence between his doctrine and Luther's, in the question of the Eucharist. All was discord and confusion in the Protestant mp, and Melancthon, in despair, could not forbear exclaiming: Zwingli must have lost his senses!" The emperor, hopeless of ffecting a union now becoming daily more impracticable, at length published an edict which put an end to the disputes. " The Protestants," said he, " have been refuted by sound principles drawn from sacred Scripture. They may decide upon the course they will pursue, before the 15th of April of next year." Another edict, issued soon after, closed the proceedings of the diet. In it the emperor positively declared that he felt bound in conscience to defend the ancient Catholic faith, " and the princes promised to second his endeavors with all their power."

19. Peace could not last long with enemies who showed respect for no authority. When Charles wished to carry out the decrees of the diet, he received no support from the Catholic princes of Germany, who dreaded the consequences of a civil war in the present hostile state of the German mind. On the other hand, the emperor felt that he must conciliate the Lutheran States, to secure their help against the Turks, whose advance still continued to alarm the whole of Europe. The Protestants would come to no agreement until the imperial decree of Augsburg should have been revoked. They met at Smalcald (Schmalkalden), on the 29th of March, A. D. 1531, and concluded an offensive league of six years. They proceeded with greater assurance and daring in their new course since Luther and Melancthon, recalling their former opposition, now authorized the use of arms for the maintenance of Protestantism. Thus, in many respects, the Turkish sultan became the natural ally of the Protestant princes, since his design of profiting by the divisions in Germany gave an opportunity to those who were rending it to make head against the emperor. Charles V was obliged to enter into negotiations with them at Frankfort, and the conference ended at Nuremberg (July 23d, 1532) There it was agreed that, until the meeting of the general council, no steps should be taken against any of the princes ; that every thing should remain as it was, for the time being ; that only those, however, who had already received the Confession of Augsburg should be included in the treaty of peace. Luther had triumphed.

20. While these complicated difficulties in Germany so fearfully agitated the Pontificate of Clement VII., his attention was

called to England by events no less deplorable. Henry VIII., whose elegant apology for the Catholic faith, against the "Ecclesiastes of Wittenberg," had been so splendidly and appropriately rewarded by Leo X. with the title of "Defender of the Faith," remained for a time true to the character which he had taken upon himself. He wrote a second treatise against Luther, taking up his line of argument against the Reformer with no less vigor and logic than in the first These two works won an immense celebrity Satisfied with his success, the monarch's pride should have kept him in his course of fidelity to the Church whose cause he had so nobly defended. His minister, Cardinal Wolsey, had thrown about his reign a halo of glory and splendor. His most intimate counsellors were two men whose talent and virtue were the admiration of all Europe—Fisher, bishop of Rochester, and Thomas More, whom he had raised to the dignity of chancellor. At the age of nineteen, Henry, in virtue of a dispensation from Pope Julius II., had married Catharine of Aragon, the widow of his brother Arthur, and aunt of Charles V ; Catharine was an accomplished princess, and for twenty years Henry boasted of his happiness in possessing so amiable and virtuous a consort. If ever an exalted position could have seemed secure, it was certainly that of the queen so nearly allied to the imperial throne, whose mild and modest virtues were in benediction throughout England, and won the love and esteem of Henry himself. This happy existence was at length disturbed by a criminal passion of most disastrous consequences. Yielding up his heart to the sway of an unholy affection, the king was unable to resist the charms of Anne Boleyn. Anne was as ambitious as beautiful ; she aimed at royalty and succeeded in her design. Henry's passion was too powerful to admit of calculation. He sacrificed a lawful consort, a faithful minister, his honor, his conscience, his religion, and his faith. Cardinal Wolsey tried to oppose the influence of the royal favorite; he was disgraced and had not strength of mind to survive the loss of his fortune. On his death-bed the fallen minister uttered the memorable words :

"Had I but served God as diligently as I have served the king, He would not have given me over in my gray hairs" (A. D. 1530). Henry applied to Clement VII. for a divorce. The Pope's position was extremely embarrassing. Catharine of Aragon was an aunt of Charles V., whose troops had lately sacked Rome and seized upon the States of the Church. To act against Catharine, even supposing that the canons could have allowed such a course, would have drawn upon him the displeasure of the emperor. On the other hand, Henry urged his request with an eagerness which gave occasion for the most serious apprehensions. In the heat of his passion he might plunge into the Lutheran heresy and drag all England with him into the abyss of error. Catharine had also appealed to the Sovereign Pontiff, and Clement took the occasion to call the whole matter before his tribunal. He hoped that the time which must necessarily elapse between the opening of a long and intricate trial and the final sentence, would bring some favorable event to his assistance; but his hopes were doomed to disappointment.

21. Henry immediately dispatched a commission to Rome. His ambassadors were instructed to seek and to follow the advice of the most distinguished Italian canonists. He secretly requested their opinion upon the following points:— 1. "Whether, if a wife were to make a vow of chastity and enter a convent, the Pope could not, of the fulness of his power, authorize the husband to marry again; 2. Whether, if the husband were to enter into a religious order, that he might induce his wife to do the same, he might not be afterward released from his vow, and at liberty to marry again; 3. And whether, for reasons of state, the Pope could not allow a prince to have, like the ancient Patriarchs, two wives, of whom one only should be publicly acknowledged and enjoy the honors of royalty" Henry's agents were meanwhile busy in every part of Europe, buying up the opinions of theologians and universities in favor of the divorce; these were to be laid before the Pope as the expression of their general opinion. But the

number of these decisions was, of necessity, very limited, and the Pope was not ignorant of the measures used to obtain them. To all their urgent entreaties, Clement returned the same answer, " that he was ready to take the question into immediate consideration, and to gratify the king in any manner conformable with honor and justice. We ask but one thing in return," he added, " it is, that, under pretext of the gratitude due from the Holy Church to Henry VIII., we may not be asked to violate the unchangeable commandments of God."

22. This reply crushed the hopes of Henry He saw that it would render useless all the expedients by which he had thought to reach the end he so ardently desired. The advocates of Anne Boleyn began to despair of success, and to waver in her support, when they were rescued from danger by the boldness and ingenuity of Thomas Cromwell, a man of intriguing mind, covetous heart, and servile disposition. His father was a fuller in the neighborhood of the capital. Thomas, in his early youth, served as a trooper in the wars of Italy; from the army he passed to the office of a Venetian merchant, and, after some time, returning to England, exchanged the counter for the study of the law. His pliant mind, fruitful in expedients, recommended him to the service of Wolsey When his patron was disgraced, Cromwell forsook the fallen favorite and hastened back to court. Gratitude was never the virtue of ambitious minds. Seeing the intricate position into which the king had been led by his ardent passion, Cromwell, knowing that his fortune would be made if he found an expedient to satisfy the royal will, solicited and obtained an audience. An expedient was not hard to find for a man who " had learned, from Machiavelli, that vice and virtue were but names fit, indeed, to amuse the leisure of the learned in their colleges, but pernicious to the man who seeks to rise in the courts of princes The great art of a politician was, in his judgment, to penetrate through the disguise which sovereigns are accustomed to throw over their real inclinations, and to devise the most specious expedients to gratify their appetites, without appearing to out

rage morality or religion." Such was the man who was destined to lead Henry VIII. into new paths, and England into a schism from which she has not yet emerged. "The learned and the universities," he urged, "have pronounced in favor of the divorce. Nothing is now wanting but the Sovereign Pontiff's approval. Such a measure on the part of the Pope might, indeed, arouse the emperor's resentment. But if it cannot be obtained, is the king, therefore, to give up his rights? Why not, rather, imitate the German princes, who had thrown off the yoke of Rome? Could he not, by the authority of Parliament, declare himself the head of the Church within his own realm? England was, at present, a monster with two heads; but if the king would at once take into his own hands the authority usurped by the Pope, all anomaly would disappear, the existing difficulties would vanish, and churchmen, through attachment to their lives and fortunes, would become the most obsequious ministers of his will." Henry listened with surprise, but with ill-disguised pleasure, to a discourse which flattered at once his guilty passion, his thirst for wealth, and his greediness of power, the three concupiscences which, by their union, constitute the spirit of the world. He thanked Cromwell, and ordered him to be immediately sworn of his privy council.

23. The king now entered upon a totally new line of policy. In the archives of English legislation, there had long lain an old and now rusty weapon, but yet, in the king's estimation, wonderfully fitted to strike the blow which he was preparing to aim at the Church. Certain almost forgotten statutes, of ancient and very questionable origin, known as the statutes of *Praemunire*, made it high treason to carry out, within the realm, certain provisions or decrees of the head of the Universal Church, without the royal sanction. All the members of the English hierarchy had received their bulls of nomination and exercised spiritual jurisdiction in the kingdom, without taking out any such royal license. The whole English episcopate was, therefore, according to the statutes of praemu-

nire, guilty of high treason.   Such was the singular charge brought against the whole body of the clergy in the beginning of the year 1531, at the instigation of Cromwell.   The case was opened and sentence pronounced against the whole episcopate.   A deputation from the clergy offered a present of one hundred thousand pounds in return for a full pardon.   But the king was not to be satisfied with money   He refused the proposal, unless, in the preamble to the grant, a clause were inserted acknowledging the king "as the protector and only supreme head of the church and clergy of England."   Much time was wasted in fruitless discussions.   Warham, archbishop of Canterbury, moved an amendment in the following terms :— "We acknowledge His Majesty to be the chief protector, the only and supreme lord, and, *as far as the law of Christ will allow*, the supreme head of the church and clergy of England." The restriction contained in the words "as far as the law of Christ will allow" was the only ground on which the Catholic bishops could conscientiously sign the proposition.   They understood their position, and as a more precise definition of the sense in which they gave their signatures, the Archbishop of Canterbury and the Bishop of Durham added to their names a more explicit declaration, in these words :— "If this clause mean only that the king is the head in temporals, why all this formality, since every one grants it already ?   If it mean that he is the head in spirituals, it is contrary to the doctrine of the Catholic Church, out of which there is no salvation.   I, therefore, protest against the latter sense, and submit all to the judgment of our Holy Mother the Church; I call upon all present to witness my dissent from it, and demand that this protest be entered among the acts of the convocation."

24.   But Henry was yet wavering and irresolute ; he sought to intimidate the court of Rome, but had not determined to separate from its communion.   Finding that he could not terrify the Pope into the approbation of the divorce, he now took a decidedly hostile stand.   On the 25th of January, A. D 1533, at an early hour, Dr. Rowland Lee, one of the royal

chaplains, received orders to celebrate Mass in a retired apartment at the western end of the palace of Whitehall; the
purpose was to unite Henry VIII. and Anne Boleyn; the fear
of an illegitimate birth hastened the time of this ceremony
The chaplain, when he discovered the object for which he had
been called, made some opposition; but Henry calmed his
scruples by the assurance that the Pope had pronounced in his
favor, and that the Papal instrument was safely deposited in
his closet.   Meanwhile, the death of Warham had left the see
of Canterbury vacant; it was in the interest of Henry that
the see should be filled by a creature of his own.   With this
view, he bestowed the bishopric upon Thomas Cranmer, a priest
of more than questionable morality, who, after his entrance
into Holy Orders, had married a granddaughter of the Lutheran
Osiander, in Germany   This union was kept secret, and Cranmer had taken the greatest precaution to hide his immorality
from the public.   Still he had a secret leaning toward the
Protestant doctrines, and had signalized himself among the
English theologians who wrote in favor of the divorce.   When
Cranmer was named to the vacant archbishopric, the nomination was approved by the Pope, who was ignorant of his
scandalous antecedents, and thus he was placed in possession
of the first see in England.   The new primate inaugurated his
power by a letter to the king concerning his " incestuous
union " with Catharine of Aragon, " a union," he wrote, " which
has given great scandal, and which we have also resolved, for
the peace of our own conscience, to break off by every canonical means in our power."   The king *most graciously* consented
to receive this admonition from the *pious primate* of his kingdom.   "We deem it necessary," said he, " for the good of our
soul, to yield without delay to the representations of our spiritual father, the Archbishop of Canterbury "   Cranmer asked
to be allowed at once to institute an ecclesiastical procedure
against Catharine.   The injured queen was then residing at
Ampthill, near Dunstable.   Cranmer opened his court at Dunstable and summoned the king and queen to appear before him.

Catharine paid no heed to the iniquitous summons. The archbishop pronounced her contumacious; and, in consequence, judgment was given against her, stating that the marriage between her and Henry was null and invalid; this judgment he pronounced in virtue of his apostolic authority as legate of the Holy See, which he claimed as tributary of the primatial see of Canterbury This decision was communicated to the king by the primate, who, with much gravity, exhorted him to submit to the will of God, made known to him by a sentence given *conformably to the laws of the Holy Church*. Henry then officially announced his marriage with Anne Boleyn, and the hypocritical prelate confirmed the adultery " in virtue of the authority which he held from the successor of the Apostles."

25. It was time to put an end to these scandalous proceedings, and to inform the Catholic world that the Holy See was not disposed to become accessory by its silence. On the 23d of March, A. D. 1534, Clement VII. held a solemn consistory, in which he clearly explained the question of the divorce and the negotiations to which it had given rise. Of the twenty-two cardinals, nineteen pronounced in favor of the validity of the union with Catharine of Aragon; only three were in favor of a further delay. According to the opinion of so numerous a majority, Clement VII. pronounced a definitive sentence, declaring the marriage of Henry VIII. and Catharine of Aragon lawful and valid, condemning the proceedings against Catharine as unjust and tyrannical, and ordering the king to take her back as his legitimate wife. Before the Pontifical bull reached England, Henry had already sent to both Houses a bill abolishing the power of the Pope within the English realm, and the schism, fruit of impurity, avarice and ambition, was consummated.

26. This sad intelligence reached Rome simultaneously with that which announced the defection of Switzerland, under the leadership of Calvin. The remedy for such an accumulation of evils would have been a general council, which was now called f~ by the united voice of the whole Catholic world.

Clement had taken measures to convoke it, but the ceaseless wars between Charles V and Francis I. made his efforts use less. Broken down by multiplied reverses, discouraged by the struggles of his stormy Pontificate, filled with fear for the present and apprehension for the future, he was seized by a deep and settled melancholy, which took him to the grave (September 25, A. D. 1534). "From his dying couch, he was doomed to see the Vatican fallen from its ancient glory and political influence, the kingdoms of the west wrested from the Catholic faith, and Switzerland torn from the Holy See." The august diadem which he had worthily borne through a career of troubles and vicissitudes was indeed, to him, a crown of thorns.

CHAPTER III.

PONTIFICATE OF PAUL III. (October 15, A. D. 1534—November 10, 1549).

PONTIFICATE OF PAUL III. (Oct. 15, A. D. 1534—Nov. 10, 1549).

1. CLEMENT VII. bequeathed to his successor an immense and a difficult mission. It must aim at a threefold object : to pacify the hostile powers; to stay the torrent of heresy; to crush the schismatical attempts of England; in a word, to restore, on a firm basis, the Catholic unity which seemed to be on the point of dissolution. A man was found with a mind to plan and the courage to execute these great undertakings. Paul III. was of the noble Tuscan house of Farnese, a name already illustrious in the decline of the thirteenth century. His studies identified him with the literary movement of his age; he always showed a decided passion for the ancient classics and for the fine arts made popular by the late revival. At the age of twenty-two he was made a cardinal by Alexander VI., and from that time he was always occupied in political concerns, filling the highest posts with signal success. When Charles VIII. entered Italy, he was sent as Apostolic legate, to meet the king at Viterbo. Honored with the confidence of Julius II., Leo X. and their successors, the tiara was bestowed upon him by the unanimous vote of the Sacred College. Clement VII. had even said upon his death-bed : "If the Papacy were hereditary, we would bequeath the tiara to Cardinal Farnese." The Sovereign Pontificate was indeed a fearful burden. Paul III. met its difficulties with noble intrepidity; but before beginning his task he took the precaution to surround himself with men distinguished for merit and virtue. These ministers, who shed additional lustre on his Pontificate, were the Venetian Contarini, Caraffa, Sadolet, whose name illustrated the reign of Leo X., Pole, Giberto and Fregoso—all commanding universal esteem and respect. With them, he began to lay the foundation of a peaceful reform in the Church, to meet the unbridled radicalism of the Lutherans. His first step was to appoint commissioners for the execution of reforms

in the Chancery, the Penitentiary and the Apostolic Chamber. Under his active influence, the Camaldoli, the Franciscans and the Capuchins at once entered upon a course of strict reform.

2. To second the Pontiff in the arduous and difficult task which he had undertaken, Providence was preparing a powerful army of new auxiliaries, armed with a zeal proportionate to every want, a self-devotion equal to every enterprise, a courage fearless of every danger; who should ever display, in weal or woe, the same fidelity to duty, the same submission to the Holy See, the same ardor for the salvation of souls; who, in exile or on the steps of the throne; in the Christian pulpits of European capitals, or in the distant missions of India, China, and Japan; in literary institutions, or in the lowliest cabins; in the most enlightened cities, or the most obscure hamlets, should, always and everywhere, with the same forgetfulness and the same success, carry on the work of God. We mean the Jesuits, whose institution dates from the period when Paul III. was inaugurating his new reign. Don Iñigo Lopez de Recalde, better known as Ignatius of Loyola, the youngest son of the house of Loyola, was born in the castle of that name, in the province Guipuscoa, where his family held the first rank amongst the nobility He was reared at the court of Ferdinand the Catholic, and in the suite of the Duke of Najara. His position opened to him a splendid prospect in the profession of arms, but the hand of God checked his high career at the very outset; He had reserved that great soul for His own service. In the defence of Pampeluna against the French, in 1521, Ignatius received wounds in both legs, which obliged him to give up the military profession. The leisure hours of a long convalescence he devoted to reading romances of chivalry. These romantic narratives aroused his ardent imagination; but unable now to follow his natural inclination, he fell into a deep melancholy. He felt within himself an inexpressible longing which nothing could satisfy, and in this frame of mind he began to study the lives of the Saints, and to medi-

tate upon the Scriptures. A new world was suddenly opened
out before him ; a world of which he had never before known
the extent. The spiritual life was revealed to him with all its
charms and attractions, its sweet radiance flooded his soul, and
Ignatius arose a new man. Such is the admirable power of divine grace, displaying, at every stage of the Church's history,
its marvellous fecundity for the salvation of the world ; striking
down St. Paul on the road to Damascus, transforming Augustine in a garden at Milan, converting Ignatius on his bed of
pain in a solitary castle. The young Spaniard obeyed the
voice of God; he tore himself away from his home and kindred, and withdrew into a solitude near Manresa.* The desire
of a more active life soon turned his thoughts toward Jerusalem and the conversion of the Unbelievers. Failing in this
project, he returned to Spain, whence he passed over into
France, to attend the course of the University, and devote
himself to the study of theology The relations which he here
contracted with Peter Faber, a Savoyard, and with Francis
Xavier, decided his vocation. The three friends, together
with several other young men whom they had won, repaired
one day to the church of Montmartre. Faber, who was
already in holy orders, said Mass, after which they all took a
vow of chastity and poverty, and swore to devote their lives
to the care of the Christians and to the conversion of the Sara-
cens. The order of the Jesuits dates from that memorable
day (August 15, A. D. 1534). In 1537, we find Loyola at Venice,
with some of his companions ; here he received the order of
priesthood, and preached, with them, the truths of salvation.
A year after, they set out for Rome, the centre of all that is
great, the focus of all the living works of Catholicity ; but,
before separating, they drew up certain rules for their common
observance. It was then that Ignatius gave them the name of
Company or Society of Jesus. At Rome, they had to contend

---

* Manresa is a small town three leagues distant from Montserrat, celebrated as the
retreat of St. Ignatius, where he composed the admirable work of the Spiritual Exercises
and as a place of pilgrimage for multitudes of pious souls.

against almost insurmountable obstacles to obtain the recog
nition of the new institute; but their intrepid zeal, patience,
and humility, triumphed over every difficulty. Paul III. at
first gave them a verbal approbation, which he renewed in
1543 by a solemn bull, definitively constituting the Society of
Jesus as a religious order. These opening difficulties once
overcome, they were enabled to increase their number. To the
two vows by which they had already bound themselves, they
now joined a third, that of obedience, and added the strict obligation to *do whatsoever the Pope should command; to go into
every country where he chose to send them, to preach to the Turks,
heathens, infidels, or heretics, instantly, without discussion, condition, or reward.* " What an admirable contrast to the tendency hitherto manifested by that age!" says Ranke. " While
the Pope experienced opposition or desertion from every side,
a society of men was formed, volunteers, full of zeal and enthusiasm, with the express purpose of devoting themselves
exclusively to his service."

3. The course of events was hurrying on in England
Henry no longer set any bounds to his tyranny, or to his rebellion against the Church. The Parliament, after having abolished the Pope's jurisdiction, pronounced the king's marriage
with Catharine of Aragon illegal and invalid, confirmed his
union with Anne Boleyn, and declared the children that might
spring from it lawful heirs to the throne, to the exclusion of
the Princess Mary, daughter of the injured Catharine. It was
also enjoined upon every English subject to swear obedience
to this act, under pain of being deemed guilty of high treason.
This clause was yet to cost torrents of blood. The Bishop of
Rochester, the virtuous Fisher, and his illustrious friend, Sir
Thomas More, had been, from the outset, opposed to the
divorce. When called upon to take the oath required by the
new constitution, they refused and were thrown into the dun
geons of the Tower. Cromwell and Cranmer were appointed
their judges. " You should grant," said some one to the late
chancellor, " that your conscience has erred, since it is op-

posed to the council of the whole nation." " I might believe it," replied More, " had I not in my favor a far greater council, the whole of Christendom." While confined in the Tower, he was subjected to a harder trial than that which he had undergone with so much firmness and dignity before an iniquitous tribunal. Margaret, his wife, whom he tenderly loved, was admitted to visit him. She threw herself upon her knees before him, weeping bitterly, and begged him to submit to the will of the king, for the sake of his children. " Margaret," replied More, with the heroism of a martyr, "would you have me exchange my hopes of eternity for the few years of life that still remain to me." When notified of his sentence, he was told that the king, as a special favor, had commuted his punishment from hanging to decapitation; "God preserve all my friends," he replied, " from such favors. I trust that none of my children may ever need them." As he ascended the steps of the scaffold, he said to one of the executioner's attendants : " Let me lean on your arm to mount these steps, I shall not need it to come down." After a few moments spent in prayer, and having recited the psalm *Miserere*, he declared that he died in the faith of the Catholic, Apostolic, and Roman Church. One blow of the axe severed from its trunk that head worthy of a crown in heaven (July 6, A. D. 1535).

4. More had been preceded to martyrdom by his friend, the Bishop of Rochester. The pious prelate, who had reached the venerable age of eighty years, was arrested in 1534, and confined in a damp dungeon of the Tower. A year of strict and painful imprisonment was unable to shake his patience or his faith. Paul III., wishing to give a signal proof of the esteem and sympathy felt for the generous confessor, named him to the purple on the 12th of May, A. D. 1535, and all Europe applauded a favor so well deserved. But it only served to hasten the fate of the bishop, for Henry, as soon as he received the intelligence, exclaimed, "Paul may send him the hat, but I will take care that he have never a head to wear it on." The Roman purple was indeed to be dyed in the blood of a martyr.

He was condemned to death, June 17th, 1535, as guilty of high treason, for having maliciously and traitorously said that the king was not the head of the Church. His execution took place on the 22d of the same month. Not content with the execution of Fisher, Henry ordered the dead body to be stripped, exposed for some hours to the gaze of the populace, and thrown into the grave without coffin or shroud. The religious orders in England imitated the courageous bearing of Fisher and More. By the tyrant's order, all the friars observants were ejected from their monasteries and dispersed, partly in different prisons, partly in the houses of the friars conventuals, whose cowardly compliance saved them from the fury of the apostate king. More than fifty perished from the rigor of their confinement, the rest were banished to France and Scotland. The sons of St. Bruno showed the same constancy as the faithful disciples of St. Francis. The priors of the three charter-houses of London, Axiholm and Belleval, when summoned to take the oath, waited on Cromwell to explain their conscientious objections to the recognition of the king's supremacy. From his house he committed them to the Tower, and on the 5th of May, 1535, they were executed at Tyburn, with four other monks and a secular clergyman, who had asked leave to bring the last consolations of religion to their condemned brethren. On all these the sentence of the law was executed with the most barbarous rigor. They were hanged, cut down alive, embowelled and dismembered, and their mangled limbs scattered upon the public highway.

5. After these bloody scenes, which struck terror into the heart of England, the clergy seemed to have surrendered all sense of honor and faith. A general apostasy followed. Another question now arose respecting the manner in which the royal supremacy was to be exercised. Henry found it necessary to name a vicar for the conduct of ecclesiastical affairs. His choice fell upon the man whose counsels had first suggested the attempt and whose industry had brought it to a successful termination. Cromwell inaugurated this sacrilegious assump-

tion of power by a general visitation of all the monasteries of the kingdom, "whose wealth," he said, "was a source of great scandal to all the faithful." To give some show of system to this wholesale plunder, an act of Parliament (A. D. 1536) suppressed about three hundred and seventy-three religious houses, "for the glory of Almighty God and the honor of the realm," and added their property to the revenue of the crown. The first attempt having been attended with some disorders and opposition, it was found necessary to proceed with more caution and cunning. The religious communities were accused of taking part in the disorders and of opposing the royal prerogatives. But this process of spoliation was too slow, and violent means were resumed. In 1540, the secularization of the monasteries was accomplished. Henry's will had been executed in a disgraceful spirit of Vandalism, that spared neither masterpieces of art nor monuments of learning. The blind and senseless rage of the royal ministers had attacked even the tombs of the saints. Not even St. Augustine, the Apostle of Britain, nor the illustrious martyr of Canterbury, nor the founder of England's power, Alfred the Great, could find favor with the brutal barbarity of these revolutionists. Their ashes were scattered to the winds. Thus did Cromwell win the title given him by Fox, of "valiant soldier of the Reformation." With the wealth accruing from this pillage, Henry founded six new bishoprics and fourteen cathedral and collegiate churches. But the principal gain was to the royal visitors and favorites. This dispersion of the church property is the real source of pauperism in England. The intelligence of the king's excesses was received throughout Europe with loud and general execration, and Paul III. launched a second excommunication against Henry VIII.; but the tyrant paid no heed to the sentence and persisted in declaring himself an obedient son of the Catholic Church. He continued the use of holy water and ashes, and the invocation of saints; a royal decree provided for the preservation of the dogma of transubstantiation as an article of faith, and enjoined clerical celibacy as an indispensable obligation, "founded," said the pontiff-king, "upon a commandment of Christ." But images and relics found no favor in his eyes ; he ordered them to be burnt wherever they might be found ; the reign of the Iconoclasts seemed once more restored.

6. The murderer of Fisher and Thomas More had still another victim to immolate to his revenge. The ranks of the English clergy were honored by a man as illustrious by his birth as by his talents and virtues—Cardinal Pole. His mother, the venerable Countess of Salisbury, was the last, in a direct line, of the Plantagenets, a family which had swayed the English sceptre through so many generations. The cardinal was thus nearly allied by blood to Henry, who had hitherto loaded him with favors and seemed proud of his friendship. When the question of the divorce was proposed to the House of Lords, Pole openly pronounced against the act of injustice. This opposition was viewed as a crime of high-treason, and the cardinal deemed it prudent to withdraw from the pursuit of Crom·well's emissaries. The king visited upon the mother the revenge he cherished against the son. The Countess of Salisbury, though more than seventy years of age, and bowed down by the weight of misfortune rather than of years, was kept in the Tower, " as a hostage," said the king, " for the behavior of her son the cardinal." At length the barbarous sentence of decapitation was pronounced against her　When the executioner bade her lay her head upon the block, " No," she replied, " my head shall never bow to tyranny ; if you will have it, you must get it as you can." At these words the executioner struck a violent blow at her neck with his axe, but the stroke was not fatal. The unhappy countess, distracted by pain, ran wildly about the scaffold, with her long gray hair streaming about her shoulders ; the executioner followed her, but only succeeded, after several attempts, in striking off her head. " What a fearful scene !" exclaims the Protestant writer Cobbett. " What Englishman does not blush when he remembers that it was enacted in his own country ?"

7　From this period, the reign of Henry VIII. is but a succession of cruel acts and bloody executions. Anne Boleyn, the first cause of so many crimes, soon excited the anger and felt the vengeance of her terrible consort. Her levity and indiscretion had doubtless given rise to many unfavorable reports against her; but the severity of the punishment to which she was condemned was chiefly due to the new passion of Henry for Jane Seymour. Anne was beheaded, nor was England astonished to learn that on the very next morning its lustful monarch had married Jane Seymour, with unwonted pomp. Jane, in the following year bore him a male child, afterward Edward VI., and in less than a fortnight expired. Anne of Cleves appeared for a moment on the fatal throne; but Henry repudiated her on ignoble grounds, and doubtless thought it generous enough to spare her life. Less fortunate than her predecessor, Catharine Howard was soon led to the block still red with the blood of Anne Boleyn. Cromwell, the infamous minister of so many deeds of blood, was himself disgraced and imprisoned in 1540, on the twofold charge of heresy and treason. He proved as abject in misfortune as he had been cruel in prosperity, and was led to execution in spite of all his pathetic appeals for mercy The royal widower of five queens, of whom two had been repudiated and two beheaded, still thought of contracting another matrimonial allince. We are naturally inclined to ask, if there could have been found a woman willing to risk such a union. The prospect of a crown is an irresistible attraction for an ambitious mind, and Catharine Parr was proud to ascend the blood-stained throne. She was fortunate enough to escape the axe of the headsman, but her death-warrant had already been signed, and she would perhaps have been the third of Henry's queens to grace the scaffold, but for the early death of the king (A. D. 1547). In a reign of thirty-eight years, Henry had ordered the execution of two queens, a cardinal, two archbishops, eighteen bishops, thirteen abbots, five hundred priors and monks, thirty-eight doctors, twelve dukes and counts, one hundred and sixty-four noblemen of various ranks, one hundred and twenty-four private citizens, and one hundred and ten females. The modern Nero should have another Tacitus. That such a monster should have become the head of a religion adopted by England, the land of high and noble intelligence, where minds are accustomed to appreciate men and events with coolness and deliberation; where history is studied, understood, compared and judged; where national honor is a truly popular sentiment of so much power and vitality—is a fact which defies all the calculations of human prudence, sets at naught all the laws of probability, confounds the mind and compels it to bow before one of those fathomless abysses of divine justice, "Whose judgments are incomprehensible and unsearchable His ways." Would to Heaven that the English people, who want only the possession of Catholic truth to make them perhaps the greatest nation in the world, might at length open their eyes to the shame, the barbarity, the cruel and beastly lust from which sprang the schism that tore them from the bosom of Roman unity! Why will they not throw off the ignominious heritage of Henry VIII. to become once more the true children of St. Peter? What glory awaits them in this, the only character worthy of their noble race! Their ships, which triumphantly plough the waters of every sea, would bear the standard of the true faith to the farthest shores. Their wide-spread power would then, in some degree, share the promise of immortality made by God to His Church. But if, on the other hand, they persist in following the path of error, what assurance have we that theirs shall not be the fate of the Carthaginians; that they shall not meet the same end as did the ancient mistress of the seas? The Rome of the Popes, though it command not the troops of the Rome of Scipio, is not the less invincible.

3. The religious state of England was not improved by the death of Henry VIII. Edward VI., the son of Jane Seymour, ascended the throne in virtue of his father's will, and to the prejudice of Mary, the daughter of Catharine of Aragon. The Duke of Somerset, the young king's uncle, was at the head of

the council of regency, and trained up his ward in a spirit of hatred toward the Catholic Church. Cranmer, who had been made spiritual vicar of the kingdom, published, " by the aid of the Holy Ghost," a collection of Homilies, an Anglican Catechism, a liturgy in the English language, the Book of Common Prayer, and Administration of the Sacraments (A. D. 1549). The sacrifice of the Mass was abolished, the marriage of priests authorized, and the vulgar tongue introduced into the celebration of the divine office ; all that remained of the ancient rite was destroyed—pictures, statues, altars, sacred vestments, and private chapels. The bishops who refused to conform were dispossessed, their property was confiscated, and the new church, the " Church by law established," was definitively constituted by the aid of foreign troops. Instead of the liberal alms which the monasteries, of their wealth, distributed among the poor, severe penalties were now enacted against beggars ; they were liable to be imprisoned or branded with a red-hot iron upon the breast and forehead. Somerset was, like Henry VIII., completely under the influence of Cranmer. He ordered the execution of his own brother, whom he soon followed to the scaffold, on an indictment of treason, and was succeeded by Dudley, earl of Norwich and duke of Northumberland. At the end of three years, Cranmer's liturgy was revised, and established by an act of Parliament, which decreed the severest penalties, and even imprisonment for life, against those who refused to conform to the liturgy Forty-two new articles, approved by Parliament, were substituted for the six articles of Henry VIII.*

9. We return now to the history of other events of the same period, which we have overlooked in order to give a continued narrative of the rise and progress of Protestantism in England. The Reformer, Luther, had meanwhile been carrying on in Germany his work of destruction and ruin. In 1525, after having prepared the world for this fresh scandal, by the obscene writings in which he loaded ecclesiastical celibacy with

* ALZOG, t. III., p. 132.

insults and epithets inspired by the spirit of darkness, he publicly married Catharine Bora, a former nun, who had been perverted by his doctrines. It is probable that Luther would have married sooner, had he not feared to incur the displeasure of the Elector Frederick, who had lately expressed himself in public on the marriage of priests and monks, which he called a "concealed concubinage." He dreaded the railleries of Erasmus, who had laughed so heartily at Carlstadt. The death of the elector gave Luther courage, and his action was so prompt that he thought it necessary to explain to his friends the motives of his sudden determination. "It is the Lord," he writes, "who inspired the resolution. In marrying Catharine Bora, I have made the angels rejoice and the demons weep." These last words are an allusion to the principle, which he had for some time held, of the divine and imprescriptible obligation of marriage for all men. Catholic Europe heard the infamous act with a new cry of indignation; but Luther listened only to the voice of his passions, which spoke louder in his heart than all the world beside. Yielding without shame or remorse to their tyrannical sway, he gathered his friends about the family board, and gave free rein to all the sallies of his impure mind against the Roman Church, which he had once called his mother, but now loaded with the grossest insults. His "TABLE-TALK "— "TISCH-REDEN"—collected by zealous admirers and carried to all parts of Protestant Germany, to propagate his work of scandal and immorality, is the most disgraceful monument of the Reformation.

10. Bad example is contagious. The Landgrave, Philip of Hesse, the most zealous and powerful protector of Protestantism, formed the design of profiting, after his own taste, by the Reformer's marriage. Though already married, he had, for a long time, been living in a state of concubinage, and now determined to take a second wife, and to have the bigamy legalized. He accordingly wrote to Luther and Melancthon, stating that though he had been for sixteen years married to Christina, the daughter of Duke George of Saxony, and was the father

of eight children, yet he wished to obtain their authorization for a second and simultaneous union with Margaret Saal, a maid of honor to his sister Elizabeth. The motives on which he grounds his petition are not such as may be reproduced by a respectable pen. Luther and Melancthon were in a state of great perplexity, for Philip threatened, in the event of their refusal, to return to the Catholic Church. Still it seemed to them a serious undertaking, after the formal expression in Scripture of the unity of marriage, to bring back the world to the polygamy of the Patriarchal times. After some deliberation, the Reformers consented to grant the landgrave's request, and signed the act, " to enable him," as they said, " to promote the advantage of both body and soul, and the greater glory of God. Still," they suggested, " as it is not now a usual thing to have two wives at once, we judge that the ceremony should be performed privately, and in the presence of a few necessary witnesses (March 3, A. D. 1540)." The intelligence of this new infamy caused the greatest scandal in Europe. There was but one opinion; with one voice Catholics and Protestants alike stigmatized the shameless conduct of the landgrave, and the cowardice of Luther and Melancthon in pandering to his base passion. The Reformer thought to justify himself by an appeal to his supreme authority, which empowered him, under certain circumstances, to rise above the ordinary laws and to decide in opposition to received customs. This was to proclaim his own authority while denying that of the Church; it was a solemn acknowledgment that he had rejected the supremacy of the Pope only to set up his own. But all these inconsistencies gave very little trouble to Luther and his adherents. Catholic theologians might point them out, but they hardly ever met with a reply

11. Westphalia was made the field of new struggles and new excesses. In the beginning of 1533, the city of Münster was disturbed by two men, in a strange dress, who went through the streets, crying aloud: "Do penance; the vengeance of the Heavenly Father is at hand!" These new

prophets were an innkeeper, named John Bockelson, who became famous as John of Leyden, and the executioner Knipper Dolling. The two fanatics had first been led away by Luther's Reform, but had afterward embraced the tenets of the Anabaptists, and were now striving to raise up the standard torn from the hands of the peasants on the bloody field of Frankhausen. Their teaching would seem to have been based upon the doctrines of illuminism; they affected to preach mortification and penance, while practising polygamy; they rejected the authority, the laws, institutions and dogmas of the Church, pretending that the Holy Ghost Himself taught them in ecstasies and heavenly visions. The people were terrified at their threats and mournful cries, and the number of their adherents rapidly increased. John of Leyden was daily surrounded by an immense throng, asking for baptism. The prophet soon made himself the minister of the wrath which he had announced. When he thought his party strong enough to warrant the attempt, he took up arms against the Prince of Waldeck, bishop of Münster, and succeeded in capturing the city His victory was celebrated by the plunder and burning of churches and monasteries. All books and manuscripts, other than the Bible, with paintings and statues of the saints, were brought to the prophet, who ordered the " instruments of Popish idolatry " to be destroyed. They were burnt amid profane dances and the excesses of an unbridled and shameless libertinism. On this day of profanation, Münster was styled the " City of Zion," and John of Leyden received the title of its king. Mathiesen, a baker of the city, took the official title of prophet, and Knipper Dolling was named generalissimo of the *hosts of the Lord.* John of Leyden surrounded his ephemeral royalty with all the splendors of an Eastern reign; he had guards, a brilliant court and a seraglio. This last innovation excited some murmurs; one unfortunate wretch, whose remarks on the subject were reported to the king, paid for his freedom of speech at the block. Meanwhile, the prince-bishop, having raised a Catholic force at his own expense, was pressing the siege of the rebellious city   After a resistance of six months, the prophet at length fell into the hands of the besiegers. His execution and that of his adherents delivered Münster from his tyranny and was the just punishment of so many monstrous crimes (January 23, A. D. 1536).

12. Protestantism, like a destructive torrent, was rapidly spreading over the whole of Germany   The excesses of the fanatical peasantry and the extravagant folly of the Anabaptists should have withheld the princes in a course so dangerous to their authority; but they were guided by other views. Frederick, elector of Saxony, Philip, landgrave of Hesse, and the Prince of Anhalt, were the first to declare themselves openly   The cause of the Reformation was then successively embraced by the States of the North and by Prussia (A. D. 1523), through the apostasy of Albert of Brandenburg, grand-master of the Teutonic Order, who consented to purchase a crown at the price of a sacrilege.   His defection drew on that of Livonia, Courland and Silesia.   Sweden, perverted by its king, Gustavus Vasa, and Denmark, by Christiern II. and his successor, Frederick I. (1523), successively joined the ranks of the Reformers.   Norway soon followed their example, and, a few years later, Iceland also received the new heresy   The sovereigns were easily led to join the Lutheran cause, by the hope of sharing the spoils of the clergy, which the Reformation placed in their hands.   The nobles looked upon the step as a means to free themselves from the restraint of episcopal au. thority, and to appropriate the wealth of monasteries, which they had long beheld with a covetous eye; ecclesiastics and religious, unworthy of their vocation, longed for freedom to follow the bent of their natural inclinations.   The multitude, stupefied by the sight of so many scandals, allowed themselves to be carried on by the impulse which was leading the world to general corruption and immorality.   It is necessary to state that the nations of the North, but lately converted to Christianity, and whose religious instruction was too often neglected by pastors untrue to their high charge, were thus laid open, by their very

ignorance, to all the seductions of the sectaries. These general causes were much helped by others of a local character, such as rivalries, political or personal motives, or even lighter reasons, which often decided these religious revolutions. Notwithstanding all these combined or separately acting causes, the Reformation often met a vigorous resistance which checked for a time its triumphant career. In some States it was only after a struggle of several years that it was definitively established and enabled to maintain itself by the oppression of the Catholics.

13. The Reformers had sent their emissaries into France; but the vigilance of the government and the strong attachment of the people to the faith of their fathers baffled all their endeavors. Francis I., at the head of his court, and surrounded by all the clergy of Paris, went, in solemn procession, to restore a statue of the Blessed Virgin, which had been shamefully mutilated by a Protestant. He declared that, as "Most Christian King, he should not allow, in his kingdom, the establishment of a sect which aimed at nothing less than the overthrow of the Church." Francis, after another war conducted with glory by Marshal, afterward Constable, Anne de Montmorency (A. D. 1536) against Charles V., at length, through the intervention of Paul III., signed, at Nice, a truce of ten years with his rival. The Pope came in person to this celebrated conference, wishing to follow up the negotiations himself in order to insure their success. After the signing of the treaty, he insisted upon a meeting of the two monarchs at Aigues-Mortes. These seemingly irreconcilable enemies, who had hitherto acted toward each other with the fiercest hostility, now exchanged assurances of a fraternal friendship (1538) In the following year (1539), Europe received a proof of their sincerity in the truly royal reception given by Francis I., in Paris, to the emperor, who was on his way to suppress a revolt in Flanders. The king availed himself of the season of truce to repair the disorders brought into his States by long and disastrous wars. Age and experience had ripened his character;

his prodigality was exchanged for a prudent economy ; an assid
uous attention to business took the place of his former youthful follies.   After the example of Leo X. and the Medici, he
encouraged science, letters and arts, by a liberal patronge, " unwilling," he said " that letters should remain undowered."   He
made his kingdom an asylum for learned foreigners, enriched the
royal library with a number of valuable manuscripts, established
the Royal Printing Presses, and the College of France for the
study of Latin, Greek, Hebrew, mathematics, medicine and
philosophy   A taste for science and letters began to form part
of the national character, and was displayed by the movement
in France known as the *Renaissance.*

14. Unhappily, in the midst of this intellectual life now
springing up on all sides, and fostered by the material prosperity which peace had restored to the kingdom, France had
also her Luther.   John Calvin (his real name was Cauvin) was
born at Noyon, in Picardy, in the year 1509.   His father was a
cooper, and subsequently held the offices of Apostolical notary
and secretary to the bishop.   Through the liberality of the
noble family of Montmaurs, he was enabled to devote himself
to the study of literature and canon law in the Universities of
Paris, Orleans and Bourges.   Except, perhaps, in theology, to
which he gave less attention, the young student was generally
successful.   But his character was bad and his morals infamous.*   At Bourges he became intimate with a young man
whose licentious poems had already obtained a scandalous renown at that period.   This was Theodore Beza, a native of
Vezelai, in Burgundy, and destined to become one of the patriarchs of Protestantism in France.   Minds of such mould would
easily receive the new doctrines which the Lutherans were at
that time disseminating from Germany   They imbibed these
novelties from Wolmar, one of the professors at Bourges, and
Calvin had soon become a zealous partisan of the Reformation.
His mind dwelt chiefly upon the doctrine of justification.   The

* M. BLANC, t. II., p. 273.

freedom with which he professed his Reformatory principles, obliged him, on a requisition from the Sorbonne, to quit Paris. After a considerable time spent in various wanderings, he at length came to Basle (A. D. 1534), where he attempted to establish his new system of religion as set forth in his great work, "The Christian Institutes." Calvin's mind was following the path marked out by Luther and Zwingli;* yet its tone is everywhere more gloomy and severe. Calvin, however, begins to diverge from Luther, when he allows to man a species of liberty which the Wittenberg Reformer refuses him entirely Still he subjects this little remnant of liberty to divine predestination, even more formally than Luther and Zwingli; for the predominant characteristic of Calvin's system is the doctrine of absolute predestination, carried out with a fanatical rigor, even to absurd consequences. While Luther saw in original sin but a simple privation of strength (*privatio virium*), Calvin recognized in it a forced and predominant depravation, bending all the human faculties to evil so that they can never, in spite of all their efforts, rise again to the practice of good deeds. According to Calvin, God, the *primordial author of good and evil*, has, from all eternity, cast off a portion of His creatures and doomed them to eternal punishment, in order to show His justice in them. To give just motives for wrath and punishment, He caused the first man to fall by sin, and involved the whole of Adam's posterity in the revolt. Actual sins are imposed upon men by the Divine will, which excites to the commission of crime those whom it has predestined to eternal loss. Such is the sense of the gloomy theory known as the doctrine of *compulsory decrees*. Free-will is no more. Man is unavoidably doomed to acts for which he must suffer punishment and which it is not in his own power to commit or not to commit. The tyranny of a God who punishes sins of which He is the first author did not terrify Calvin. He clearly and openly professed his belief. "Among men," said he, "some are created for everlasting life, others for

* ALZOG, t. III., p. 92

eternal death. Their doom is irrevocably fixed, whatever be their conduct in life." By a strict parallelism, Calvin followed the same reasoning in an opposite direction to explain the doctrine of justification. Man is saved, just as he is lost, in spite of himself. There is no more merit in being a saint than in being a reprobate; both are passive instruments of a will which they must obey without being able to modify it. Now we can understand the excessive pride of the Calvinist who thinks himself one of the elect, and the unbridled license of the Calvinist who believes himself doomed. Notwithstanding the exclusive rigor of his opinions, and his unbending character, Calvin seems to have adopted neither of the Protestant views on the Eucharist. "I maintain," says Calvin, "that it is no less absurd to place the body of Christ *under* the bread than to unite it *with* the bread, than to *transubstantiate* the bread into His body" In a word, Calvin was the inveterate enemy of forms, of all outward ceremonial, the bitter opponent of all that embellishes divine worship, raises the mind and speaks to the heart.

15. The cheerless doctrine of Calvin seemed fitted only to repel. But error needs some specious appearances to allure. The apparent austerity of the new teacher was precisely the feature by which ·he attracted followers. Moreover, Calvin supported his doctrines by a close logic and a degree of learning which easily deluded weak minds. Instead of imitating the Saxon Reformers, by inveighing against all antiquity, or striving to banish from the Christian world classic literature and Greek philosophy, he acknowledged all the treasures of learning, eloquence and logic, displayed by the Fathers of the Church and theologians of the schools; he showed esteem for the authors, philosophers and poets of Greece and Rome, always displaying great prudence and sagacity If he was not altogether original, and borrowed some ideas from Luther, he at least developed them with precision and method. Still, he was too often, like Luther, guilty of rude, abusive and blasphemous language. The same spirit of intolerance and hatred of Catholicity animated them both. His opponents were al-

ways rogues, knaves, asses, &c., and his discussions are continually interspersed with such epithets.

16. After a considerable sojourn at Basle, Calvin repaired to Geneva, which became thenceforth the great field of his schismatical operations. He was persuaded to remain by William Farel and Peter Viret, two Lutheran preachers, who were spreading the new doctrines in the French cantons of Switzerland, and especially among the people of Vaud. The Duke of Savoy attempted to assert his rights over Geneva, but the inhabitants, strengthening themselves by an alliance with the canton of Berne, succeeded in throwing off his authority But this alliance would open the way for Protestantism; and the bishop pronounced a sentence of excommunication against the rebellious city This was the signal for a violent reaction against Catholicity The altars were overturned, paintings and statues destroyed, the faithful imprisoned or banished; and thus the new religion was inaugurated amid and upon the ruins of churches. Calvin, on his arrival at Geneva (A. D. 1536), finished what Farel and Viret had begun. He caused the publication of a decree requiring every citizen to abjure the Catholic faith. He forbade all amusements, dances and noisy games, " as unworthy," said he, " of the gravity of a Christian." Even ordinary conversation was subjected to a strict censorship. This stern rule was beginning to alienate the minds of his followers. A difference had arisen between Calvin and the church of Berne, concerning the use of leavened bread, which the French Reformer wished to introduce into the celebration of the Lord's Supper, and touching the abolition of all the festivals, which he had lately decreed, keeping only the Sundays. His tyrannical rule brought upon him a storm of popular indignation, and he was banished with Farel and Viret. Retiring to Strasburg, Calvin continued his war against the Church. Surrounded by French Protestant refugees,* he imbued them with the venom of his doctrines,

* These refugees were sectaries who had fled to escape the penalties decreed by the king and the parliaments against the new doctrines.

and thus furnished error with emissaries, who should perpetuate it in the bosom of our beautiful land. He gradually gathered around him a community in accordance with his religious views, and married the widow of an Anabaptist. But Calvin had left many partisans in Geneva; he was recalled to that city in 1541, and from that period became truly its civil and ecclesiastical dictator. He established a consistory, to judge all cases of misdemeanor in morals. His interdict upon dances and games was once more enforced. Domiciliary visits and inquisitorial measures were organized throughout the city, to watch the conduct of each citizen. The Genevese, and especially the Libertines, or followers of Evangelical liberty, rose up against this moral constraint. But Calvin's cruelty, his active and fertile mind, succeeded in crushing the germs of revolt. Every word uttered against him was punished with fearful severity. Thus, the translator of the Bible, Castalio, was banished, together with the physician Bolsec. Ameaux, a member of the Council of Twenty-five, was thrown into prison. Jacob Grünet was executed (1548), for having written some words in a threatening tone to the dictator, who, in open council, had called him a *dog*. Gentilis, condemned to death for saying that Calvin had erred in the doctrine of the Trinity, escaped capital punishment only by making a retraction and an apology. Michael Servetus, a native of Aragon, and a great anatomist, while passing through Geneva, was seized and burned by order of the dictator, for having published some heretical propositions on the dogma of the Trinity, which Calvin himself so poorly explained (1553). From the stain of this cruel and iniquitous execution the memory of the French Reformer can never be cleansed in the eyes of posterity. These acts of cruelty were not with him, as with Luther, the effects of a sudden and short-lived passion, but the result of a cold, unfeeling, calculating anger. Once in possession of the political power, Calvin soon replaced the doctrines of Zwingli by his own, in the Helvetic cantons. The ecclesiastical organization of Geneva

became the model of the Reformed churches in France and
the Netherlands. After a life of tireless activity, Calvin died
(May 27th, 1563,) leaving, in Theodore Beza, a devoted biographer, and a disciple capable of carrying on the work begun
by his policy By continued contact with the Reformer of
Noyon, Beza had gradually put off his youthful levity, and assumed something of the strained gravity of his master. The combination of these two elements resulted in a disposition at once
mild and severe, which gained him many partisans among the
Calvinistic communities, of which he became the true founder.

17 Such was Calvin, the French Reformer, who has often
been compared with the German Reformer. Luther appeared
in Calvin without his vehement boldness, but with the addition
of cunning, calculating ability, and cold, unfeeling cruelty
These two leaders shared the work of the Reformation ; they
contended for it as for an empire, by a war of pride and abuse.
Their followers continued to form two camps—the Lutherans
being known as Protestants, the Calvinists as the Reformed,
which name they particularly affect ; but among Catholics both
names are applied indifferently to either body, and with reason.
Both parties have, in fact, *protested* against the authority of the
Church, by revolt, and both have dishonored the name of *Reformation* by applying it to the destruction of every law as well
of faith as of morality *

18. The course of events hurries on more rapidly than the
pen of the historian, in this century of political and religious
agitation. During the invasion of Calvinism in Switzerland
and France, to detail which we have encroached upon the chronological order of facts, Pope Paul III. gave his whole attention to Germany and the schism by which it was ravaged. The
Catholics still cherished the delusive hope that an ecumenical
ssembly of the bishops would dispel the last efforts of the revolt. Luther continued to appeal to the council. Again and
again, since his famous theses, he had proclaimed before his

* M. Blanc, t. II, p. 275

whole country that he was ready to give an account of his faith to a general council.   Paul III. resolved at length to convoke the great assizes of Christendom, in order to end so many disputes, scandals and bloody struggles.   Every act of his Pontificate had in view this great design; it was the motive of his intervention to effect a truce between Charles V and Francis I.   In the year 1535, the Papal legate, Vergerio, was sent to Germany to announce to Charles V and to the princes of Christendom that the general council, which had been so long and so anxiously expected, was to meet at Mantua.   Vergerio, having occasion to visit Wittenberg, expressed an earnest desire to converse with Luther.   The Saxon monk, in this interview, spared neither rudeness nor abuse, but he could not overcome the grave and serene patience of the legate.   The conversation between Vergerio and Luther is one of the most striking pages in the history of Protestantism.   It clearly displays the perversity of the leader of the Reformation.   " Your council," said Luther, " will be a mockery   If the Pope holds one, it will be to treat of cowls, of monks, of clerical tonsure, of meat and wine, and other follies of the same kind; but of faith, penance, of the bond of charity which should unite all Christians—these grave and solemn subjects which the Reformation, enlightened from above, has hitherto been occupied in teaching—not a word will be said.   What need, then, have we of your council, which is only good for the poor nations you hold in bondage ?   You Papists do not even know what you believe.   Go on, then; assemble your council; I shall be present, I promise you, though I knew that the stake or the gibbet were awaiting me there."   The legate indulged in no retort. " Tell me, doctor," he asked, " where would you wish the council to be held ?"   " I," replied the Saxon, laughing; " wherever you wish, at Mantua, at Florence, at Padua.   It matters little where."   " And what of Bologna ?" added the legate.   " To whom does that city belong ?" asked Luther.   " To the Pope," replied Vergerio.   " Good God !" cried Luther, " and this is another city which the Pope has stolen ! Bologna, then, let it be !

I will go, and I will bring my head on my shoulders." The whole interview was but a continued insult.

19. Meanwhile, the Protestant nobles had met at Smalcald to oppose all the attempts of Rome to restore peace and union. At the instigation of the Elector of Saxony, Luther, Melancthon and the other leaders of the Reformation, in a series of conferences held at Wittenberg, drew up a new profession of faith in twenty-four articles. Melancthon, whose heart was better than his head, and who still hoped for a final re-union, signed the formula with this express reservation, that "if the Pope would recognize the *Gospel* (so the Lutherans styled their new system), he would, on his part, admit the Papal supremacy over the bishops." It required some courage in the professor to acknowledge, even in these terms, the spiritual jurisdiction of the Pope, whom his most moderate colleagues regarded as Antichrist. The Diet of Smalcald was well attended. Among the Protestant nobles were the Elector of Saxony, the Landgrave of Hesse, Dukes Ernest and Frantz of Luneburg, Duke Ulric of Wurtemberg, the Princes Wolf, George and Joachim of Anhalt, Counts Gebhard and Albert of Mansfeld, the Counts of Nassau and Reichlingen, Duke Henry of Mecklenburg, Prince Rupert and Philip of Grubenhagen. Luther, Melancthon and Bucer were also present. In vain the vice-chancellor of the empire, Mathias Held, endeavored to speak of peace and conciliation. His efforts were useless; he dismissed the diet, ordering that the truce of Nuremburg should be observed until the meeting of the next general council, at which the emperor intended to be present in person. But the Protestant nobles did not wish a council, and they multiplied their objections to the places mentioned for its convocation. Luther, who before Vergerio had affected a hypocritical indifference on the subject, now gave unrestrained expression to his hostile feelings. From his death-bed he sent forth his last pamphlet against " THE HELL-BORN PAPACY."* " A council,"

---

* *Contra Pontificatum Romanum, a Diabolo fundatum. Op. Luth*, t. VIII., *Jenæ.*

writes the dying Reformer; "what do you mean! Idiots, you know not what a bishop is, nor Cæsar, nor God Himself, nor His Word!—Pope, thou art but an ass, and wilt ever remain an ass."

20. The Protestant league of Smalcald had become a formidable power. It had equipped a force of one hundred thousand men, who made themselves masters of the Danube and formed a rampart too strong to be broken down by even the whole power of the empire. "It is surprising," says Monsignore Palma, "that a prince usually so clear sighted as Charles V and commanding such vast resources, should have neglected, at the outset, the measures necessary to avert the fatal results of the league of Smalcald and to hinder the hostile preparations which it was easier to check in the beginning than to overcome at a later period. But, yielding to the promptings of ambition, he lost the time in military expeditions against France, thus giving the Lutheran nobles time to concentrate their forces. When, at length, he had resolved to attack them, he no longer possessed the health and vigor of his youthful days. His exhausted treasury was unequal to the demands of a new war. Still his arms were not unfrequently crowned with glorious successes. At Mühlberg (A. D. 1547) he cut to pieces the army of Frederick, elector of Saxony, the avowed protector of the Protestant cause, and compelled him to abdicate the electoral dignity both for himself and for his descendants. This act of energetic authority strengthened the power of Charles V in Germany, and checked for a time the growing influence of heresy"

21. Luther died in the midst of the bloody struggles to which his doctrines had given rise. His last words were a blasphemy against the Church. "Glory to God," he exclaimed, "I have proved that the Pope, who pretends to be the visible head of the Church, the vicar of Christ, is but the prince of the accursed church, the vicar of Satan, the enemy of God, the adversary of Christ, a teacher of lies and idolatry, a regicide, a man of sin, Antichrist. So help me God Amen." Such was

the testament of the Saxon Reformer, who died at Eisleben (A. D. 1546) and was buried at Wittenberg. Never was the Church called to meet a more formidable opponent. "The tumult and agitation attending nearly the whole of Luther's life," says Alzog, "make him one of the most remarkable men of any age. His undeniable courage easily degenerated into audacity. His activity was untiring; his eloquence popular and captivating; his mind quick and rich in good sayings. He was of a disinterested character and of a deeply religious turn, and this imperious sentiment of religion which controls all his thoughts contrasts strangely with his habitually blasphemous and sarcastic language." But all these natural qualities which he so lamentably abused can never efface the shame of apostasy, the crime of rebellion, the coarse and often dishonorable features which disgrace his conduct and his writings, but especially the evils he has brought upon the Church, upon souls, upon all mankind. "Sometimes," said Erasmus, "he writes like an Apostle, sometimes he speaks like a buffoon whose coarse jests exceed all bounds, seemingly forgetful of the spectacle he is giving to the world, of the important part he is playing in it himself." While prohibiting the use of arms in matters of religion, he lays down principles and uses language which would do honor to the most furious Jacobin of the present time. He sneers like Voltaire and strikes like Couthon and Marat. The most unbounded evangelical liberty, the widest and most arbitrary right of interpretation, he loudly claims and uses for his own benefit; but upon his partisans he exercises the harshest and most shameful despotism. How great must be the blindness which can recognize an apostolic mission in the ungoverned transports, the tumultuous movements, the passionate struggles and the bitter controversies that make up the Reformer's life! "The most vulgar mind," says Erasmus, "must see that the man who raised such fearful storms in the world, who delighted only in cutting or indecent remarks, was not doing the work of God. An arrogance, like Luther's, which is without an equal, argues madness; and a spirit of buffoonery, like his, has nothing in common with the work of God." Yet the Lutherans gave to the memory of their father the honor which the Church reserves for the saints, and which they had condemned as a scandalous impiety in the Catholics. Cardinal Pallavicini correctly enough compares Luther to a giant, but a giant-abortion. In fact, there is nothing complete in his display of genius; there is greatness, but it is unformed; his energy is savage; his learning undigested; his power rash and blind, seeking only to destroy, and afterward furious at the ruins which its own violence has caused.

22. At the very time when he was leaving Germany, overwhelmed by the general desolation which his words had produced, the Church was at length gathering together in a general council all its bishops, doctors and theologians, to strengthen, by their united power, its foundations shaken by the sectaries, to restore its powerful unity threatened by the schism, to throw around its impugned dogmas the splendid lustre of their faith and learning. Mantua and Bologna had been successively named by the Sovereign Pontiff as the places of meeting. Through the influence of the Protestant princes, they were rejected. At length the Pope and the emperor definitely fixed upon the city of Trent, which, being situated on the boundary between Germany and Italy, afforded the advantage of a political neutrality favorable to all parties. The negotiations on the subject had involved a delay of several years, and it was not until the 13th of December, A. D. 1545, that the Papal legates opened the eighteenth and last general council. Its task was immense. The Lutheran reform had assailed every institution, undermined every dogma. The Council of Trent, in the name of the Universal Church, of which it was the representative, under the presidence of the Apostolic legates, during its session of eighteen years, the longest of all the ecumenical councils, triumphantly vindicated the truth of every dogma, and raised, to the glory of the Catholic faith, the most complete, the most victorious, the most unassailable monument that was ever reared (1545–1563) During s period, four Sovereign Pontiffs successively held the

See of St. Peter. But the spirit of God, which they transmitted to each other as a glorious heritage, inspired all their actions and presided over every stage of that immortal assembly The council was opened in the name of Pope Paul III., by his legates, Giammaria del Monte, cardinal-bishop of Palestrina, Marcello Cervini, cardinal-priest of the title of Santa Croce, and Reginald Pole, cardinal-priest of the title of Santa Maria-in-Cosmedin, whose generous opposition to the despotic fury of Henry VIII. we have already had occasion to notice. In the first session there were, beside the cardinals, but four archbishops, twenty-two bishops, five or six heads of orders, with a great number of doctors both secular and regular The archbishops alone represented the principal nations of Christian Europe. Olaus the Great, archbishop of Upsal, banished from his see by triumphant heresy, came to breathe out upon the bosom of the council the last sigh of Catholic Scandinavia. Robert Wanshop, archbishop of Armagh and primate of Ireland, came to bear witness in favor of the ancient faith which unhappy Ireland, more faithful and generous than Scandinavia, was to cherish unimpaired through three centuries of cruel persecution from powerful England. The Archbishop of Aix was there to confess the faith of St. Louis, which Catholic France was to uphold as its noblest heritage amid so many threatening storms. Peter Tagliavia, archbishop of Palermo, represented Italy, still faithful and condemning, by her example, the infidelity of Greece, of Asia Minor and Syria. Spain and Portugal, which, after having driven out the Moors from the Peninsula, were now laboring to plant the Christian faith in the New World, in Mexico, Peru, Brazil, India and Japan, were represented at Trent by several bishops. Catholic Germany had sent to the council the Cardinal-bishop of Trent and the substitute of the Archbishop of Mentz. Protestant Germany soon after sent deputies, who brought with them but obstinacy and bad faith.

23. Before entering upon an account of the labors of the council, it will be useful to decide the relative merits of the

two historians who have given us a detailed narrative of them; being members of two diametrically opposite parties, their narration presents the same divergence as their principles. The Venetian, Pietro Sarpi, better known as the servite religious Fra Paolo, was the first who wrote a " History of the Council of Trent;" he published it in London, in 1619, under the assumed name of Pietro-Soave-Polano, an anagram upon his name, Paolo Sarpi Veneto. Fra Paolo was one of those hypocritical characters, who, under a specious exterior, hide a dangerous and corrupt spirit. He had been captivated by the Lutheran doctrines; he paid them a hidden worship though still outwardly conforming to his original state. The republic of Venice appointed him theological consulter in its disputes with Pope Paul V " Fra Paolo," says Bossuet, " a Protestant under a religious habit, who said Mass without believing in it, remaining in a Church whose worship was to him idolatry, aimed only at leading the republic of Venice *to a complete separation, not only from the court but even from the Church of Rome.*" His history of the Council of Trent, which he ventured neither to sign with his own name nor to publish in his own country, betrayed the hostile principles which the author held against the true faith. It provoked a general outcry among the Catholics of Europe. The Protestants, on the other hand, received it with enthusiasm. In Rome, the Congregation of the Index condemned the work, with the severest comments, France was alarmed at the tendencies of a writer who was the more dangerous, as his religious profession gave him a more honorable character. Henry IV expressed his displeasure to the Venetian Senate, and the Doge enjoined Fra Paolo *to be more guarded for the future.* Fearful of the evil consequences which might result to himself from such a scandal, Fra Paolo wrote to Casaubon, to secure him an asylum in England, in case of need.

24. The Catholics could not leave unanswered a work in which the truth was so shamelessly outraged. In the year 1655, an authentic " History of the Council of Trent " was published from original documents preserved in the archives

of the castle of St. Angelo. Its author, the Jesuit Father Pallavicini, born in 1607 of one of the first families of Rome, was rewarded with the cardinal's hat.* With a judicious mind, a clear understanding, a firm and sure character, Pallavicini has all the qualities of a good historian. His thoughts are always rendered by expressions equally correct and happy. The complete documents which he had at hand are all analyzed in his work with the most conscientious exactness. The necessarily complicated discussions of a deliberative assembly as numerous as the Council of Trent are clearly and distinctly unfolded. The errors of Fra Paolo are all exposed with triumphant clearness, with a precision, vigor and abundance of proof which leave no room for reply. The learned Jesuit gives, at the end of his work, a list of three hundred and sixty-one matters of fact in which Fra Paolo is evidently convicted of having altered or misrepresented the truth, beside a host of other errors which cannot be included in a simple enumeration, but which result from the consideration of the whole work. Pallavicini's history is one of the finest monuments of human genius. It will be our guide in this brief narrative of the labors of the Council of Trent.

25. Ten sessions of this glorious council were held during the Pontificate of Paul III. In the interval of the first three, Charles V., not content with his part of armed protector of the Church, thought to enforce religious convictions as he enforced his laws, by force. The same idea misled Zeno and the Greek emperors, who had hoped, in their time, to settle religious dissensions by the mere exercise of their authority. Charles issued a formula of faith, under the form of a decree, granting to Protestants the privilege of receiving under both kinds and allowing the marriage of priests until the general council should have definitively pronounced upon all the controverted questions which were disturbing the peace of the Church. This last

---

* The Abbé MIGNE, in his Universal Collection of ecclesiastical writers, has given a French translation of Pallavicini's great work, in which the author of this History has had the satisfaction of taking some part. (3 vols., 4to, Paris.)

clause obtained for the imperial edict the name of the *Interim*. As might have been easily anticipated, the proposed mean satisfied no one. The Catholics maintained, with reason, that the emperor had no power to make such concessions. The Protestants were unwilling to admit that Charles could set bounds which they might not overstep. The Interim, therefore, met the same fate as the Henoticon; it was rejected by all parties. But Charles V was more powerful than Zeno. He was equally unconcerned at the protest of the Catholics, the condemnation of the Interim by the Roman court, the complaints of the Council of Trent, and the Lutheran recriminations. He pressed the execution of his edict and used force against the Protestants who refused to receive it. Constance and Magdeburg, which had distinguished themselves by their earnest opposition, were treated with a severity which might serve as an example to the other cities.

26. The first point to be determined by the council was, the manner of setting about the great task presented to its zeal. It was agreed that both faith and discipline should be treated together and be made to proceed uniformly with each other. Before the fourth session, two imperial ambassadors, Diego de Mendoza and Francis of Toledo, arrived at Trent. They requested, in their master's name, that exclusive attention should be given to the question of ecclesiastical reform, as the promulgation of dogmatic decisions would be likely to awake the animosity of the Protestants in Germany But the council proceeded, in spite of their protests, to promulgate its decree on the sacred writings. The canon of scripture was fixed as it now stands : the council approved, as authentic, the old edition known as the Vulgate, and "consecrated," said the Fathers, "by the usage of so many centuries." "In order," continues the decree, "to restrain petulant spirits, the holy ecumenical council decrees that, in matters of faith and morals, no one, relying upon his own private judgment, shall rashly presume to interpret the sacred scriptures in a sense either contrary to that of the Church, to which alone it belongs

to judge of the true sense of scripture, or contrary to the unanimous consent of the Fathers and of Catholic tradition." This was a condemnation of Protestantism in its very first principle, for the Lutheran Reformation was started in the name of individual liberty of interpretation, and each one of the new sectaries thought himself possessed of the right and the mission of judging of the sense of scripture according to his own fancy As a corollary of this dogmatic decision, a reformatory decree enforces the obligation of establishing chairs of theology in all the principal churches, and enjoins that "archpriests, curates, and all those who in any manner soever are charged with the care of souls, shall, at least on all Sundays and solemn feasts, either personally, or, if they be lawfully hindered, by others who are competent, feed the people committed to them, teaching them the things which every Christian must know to be saved, by announcing to them, briefly and plainly, the vices which they must avoid, and the virtues which they must follow " The bishops are admonished to watch with pastoral solicitude over the execution of these decrees in their respective dioceses, that it may not be said of Christ's flock, " The little ones have asked for bread, and there was none to break it unto them."*

27 The interval between the fourth and fifth sessions was marked by a deplorable apostasy. Vergerio, the Papal legate whose interview with Luther was related above, had yielded to the influence of the Reformation instead of combating it. He no longer concealed his sympathies with the heresy It was not without the deepest grief that Charles V and the Catholic nobles witnessed this dangerous example given by a man invested with the Pontifical confidence. The emperor wrote to Paul III., entreating him to recall his legate, while Vergerio sought a refuge in the midst of the council, hoping that the protection of the Cardinal of Trent would save him from the rigorous judgment which awaited him at Rome. Failing in this expectation, he, however, obtained from the

* Lament. iv. 4.

legates letters of recommendation sufficiently influential to dispense him from appearing for trial before a Roman court. At his own request, his case was brought before the tribunal of the nuncio and of the Patriarch of Venice. But Vergerio, sensible of the gravity of his position, at length broke openly with the Church and joined the heretics : he withdrew among the Grisons, whence he issued pamphlets, in the style of Luther, against religion, against the council, and against the Pope, whose representative he had so lately had the honor to be. A few years earlier (A. D. 1542), a scandal of the same kind had caused deep emotion in the Catholic world. Ochino, the general of the Capuchins, a man of unbounded ambition, and displaying a spirit of independence strangely at variance with the holy state into which he had entered, joined the Zwinglian branch of the Reformation. His apostasy was one of the most bitter strokes which afflicted Paul III. amid the difficult trials of his Pontificate. The apostate did not stop at this shameful defection. He was publicly married, visited England, Germany, and Poland, everywhere receiving an enthusiastic welcome from the sectaries, and everywhere spreading hatred against Rome and the Catholic faith. The Sovereign Pontiff thought of abolishing the Capuchin order, fearing that it might have been infected with the errors of its head. A secret consistory was called to deliberate upon the important measure. The Sacred College was about to confirm the intention of the Holy Father, when Cardinal Antonio San-Severino, in an eloquent and generous discourse, urged the importance of acting with perfect justice in such a matter. He enumerated the services rendered by the Capuchins, eulogized their learning, their zeal in the pulpit, the courage with which they underwent the rigors of poverty, even making it their glory. Cardinal Carpi was instructed to inquire into the conduct and the faith of the order ; and after an investigation, which resulted in their complete vindication, the useful religious, so dear to the people, so simple and submissive, were maintained in their privileges. The Pope, satisfied that Ochino's fault was altogether personal, restored his full confidence to the Capuchins, and bestowed upon their order the most ample spiritual favors.

28. After the disastrous issue of the affair of Vergerio, the Council of Trent was enabled to continue its sessions. The number of the Fathers had, meanwhile, increased. There were now nine archbishops, among others the Greek archbishop of Paros and Naxos, and about fifty bishops, among whom was Jerome Vida, bishop of Alba, in Tuscany, of whom we had occasion to speak under the Pontificate of Leo X., and Louis Lippomani, bishop of Motula and coadjutor of Verona. The latter prelate was of a noble Venetian family, and had early devoted himself to the study of letters and philosophy with the most brilliant success. His merit raised him to the highest ecclesiastical honors. He had successively held the dignities of coadjutor of Bergamo, bishop of Motula, coadjutor and bishop of Verona, and finally of bishop of Bergamo, and been intrusted with various negotiations in Portugal, Germany, and Poland. We shall find him, under Julius III., presiding as Apostolic legate in the Council of Trent. He was equally illustrious for his learning and holiness of life. Several works left by him attest his erudition and the purity of his doctrine. The principal of these are, his Commentaries on Genesis, Exodus and the Psalms, written in Latin ; the Lives of the Saints, some synodal statutes, and sermons.

29. The question of original sin was one of those which the Lutheran controversy had most obscured. Did the fall of Adam affect all his posterity? Zwingli denied it. He maintained that man is as strong to-day as he was in the beginning. "If he has preserved his free-will," said he, "it is enough, without any other resources, to bring him to heaven." Luther, taking the very opposite view, said that not only man had fallen, but that his fall was irretrievable. His free-will gives him power only for evil; his best actions are sinful; he is justified only because Jesus Christ imputes His own justice to him." Against these contradictions of error, the Fathers, in their decree on original sin, established the Catholic truth in

all its precision :—" 1. If any one denieth that the first man by
his transgression incurred the wrath and indignation of God,
and consequently death, with which God had previously
threatened him, and, together with death, captivity under his
power, who thenceforth *had the empire of death, that is to say,
the devil ;** let him be anathema. 2. If any one asserts that
the sin of Adam injured himself alone and not his posterit ;
that he, being defiled by the sin of disobedience, has transm.
ted to the whole human race only death and pains of the
body, and not sin also, which is the death of the soul ; let him
be anathema. 3. If any one asserts that this sin of Adam,
which in its origin is one, and is transmitted to all men by propagation, can be taken away either by the powers of human
nature or by any other remedy than by the merits of our Lord
Jesus Christ; or if he denies that the said merits of Jesus
Christ are applied both to adults and to infants by the sacrament of baptism, rightly administered in the form of the
Church; let him be anathema. 4. If any one denies the
necessity and efficacy of baptism conferred upon infants ; let
him be anathema." The decree closes with the words : " This
same holy council doth, nevertheless, declare, that it is not its
intention to include, in this decree—where the universality of
original sin is treated of as extending to all men—the Blessed
and Immaculate Virgin Mary, Mother of God.

30. The sixth session was held on the 13th of January, A. D.
1547 The ambassador of Charles V had received orders to
withdraw from Trent, the emperor being irritated by the determination of the council to proceed, in spite of his objection, to the
consideration of dogmatic questions. The deputies of the other
Christian princes also refused to appear in the session, through
fear of increasing the emperor's displeasure. Difficulties were
thus multiplying around the Fathers, who felt bound, at the
same time to show some consideration for political susceptibilities, so easily wounded, and to carry on the work of
God, which they had so nobly begun. It remained to

* Hebr. ii. 14.

declare the Catholic belief on justification, the great dogma which had called forth the energies of the greatest minds, and was now so much disfigured by Protestantism. This was the most delicate of the questions in debate. The discussion was stormy; some theologians even spoke of modifying the decree in favor of the Lutheran error. But the majority of the Fathers emphatically urged the declaration of the Catholic doctrine of justification by works joined to the merits of our Lord Jesus Christ. The council therefore adopted this conclusion : " The sinner is justified, when the love of God, coming down into the heart, abides in it, in virtue of the merits of the Saviour's passion, and by the illumination of the Holy Ghost. Man, thus made the friend of God, goes forward daily from virtue to virtue ; he is changed by the constant observance of the commandments of God and of the Church ; he increases,—faith coöperating with good-works,—in that justice which he has received through the merits of our Lord Jesus Christ." This doctrine presupposed the existence of free-will, which was denied by Luther. The council, therefore, utters its anathema against " whoever saith that, since Adam's sin, the free-will of man is lost and extinguished." The condemnation extended to the whole Protestant system, since its fundamental errors, as we have remarked, related to the dogma of justification. The Fathers continue : " If any one saith that without the preventing inspiration of the Holy Ghost, and without His help, man can produce acts of faith, hope, charity, and contrition, as he ought ; let him be anathema. If any one saith that man's free-will is a purely passive instrument, which can nowise coöperate toward salvation ; let him be anathema. If any one saith that all works done before justification, whatsoever be their nature, are all sins ; let him be anathema. If any one saith that by faith alone the impious is justified ; let him be anathema." The council next turned its attention to the reformatory decree obliging to the duty of residence all prelates, pastors, and abbots intrusted with the care of souls. It also provided for the visitation of churches by the bishops, and decreed that

the episcopal functions should thenceforth be exercised only by
the ordinaries, or with their special permission. The Pope, at
the same time, published a bull obliging the cardinals to residence. as well as the other prelates, and forbidding them to
govern more than one church at a time. The Pontifical rescript
was received with great applause by the council.

The question of the Sacraments followed that of Justification,
as a necessary consequence ; it was treated in the seventh session (March 3, A. D. 1547). "As the work of justification
gradually develops itself in man," says the council, " it cannot
do without the Sacraments. Through them it begins, and being
begun is increased, or being lost is recovered. All the seven
Sacraments must be preserved such as they now exist; their
institution is to be referred to the Author of our faith, because
all the institutions of the Church of Christ are made known to
us not only by the scriptures, but also by tradition. The seven
Sacraments embrace, as we know, all life and all the degrees of
its development. They are the foundation-stone of every
hierarchy ; they make known and communicate grace ; in
fine, they complete the mystical relation which approximates
man to God.—If any one saith that the Sacraments of the New
Law were not all instituted by Jesus Christ, our Lord ; or that
they are more or less than seven, to wit: Baptism, Confirmation, the Eucharist, Penance, Extreme Unction, Holy Orders and
Matrimony ; or, that any one of these seven is not truly and
properly a Sacrament ; let him be anathema.—If any one saith
that the Sacraments of the New Law are not necessary unto
salvation, but superfluous ; and that without them, or without
the desire thereof, men can obtain of God, through faith alone,
the grace of justification—though all the sacraments are not
indeed necessary for every individual ; let him be anathema.
—If any one saith that, by the Sacraments of the New Law,
grace is not conferred through the act performed,* but that faith
alone in the divine promise suffices for the obtaining of grace ;

* " Ex opere operato."

let him be anathema." The council was able, in this session, to promulgate only the decrees relative to the Sacraments of baptism and confirmation. They were followed, as usual, by a decree of discipline, establishing the rules for the conferring of bishoprics and ecclesiastical benefices.—" No one shall be raised to the government of cathedral churches, but one that is born of a lawful wedlock, of ripe age, gravity of manners, good morals and skill in letters, agreeably to the constitution of Alexander III. : *Cum in cunctis*, promulgated in the Lateran Council" (Eleventh ecumenical, 1181).—" No one shall hold, at the same time, several cathedral churches ; but those who now hold several churches shall be bound, retaining the one which they may prefer, to resign the others, within six months if they are at the free disposal of the Apostolic See ; in other cases, within a year ; otherwise, those churches, the one last obtained only excepted, shall be from that moment deemed vacant. Inferior ecclesiastical benefices, especially such as have the cure of souls, shall be conferred only on persons worthy and capable , a collation, or provision made otherwise, shall be wholly annulled. The council, however, reserves the right of the Apostolic See to allow a plurality of benefices, when it may deem it necessary "

31. Events of a serious nature interrupted the sessions of the council. The plague appeared in Trent with symptoms which warranted the most alarming fears. The majority of the Fathers decreed the translation of the council to Bologna (March 11, A. D. 1547). But Charles V., availing himself of the circumstance, showed his displeasure against a council which had not followed the system laid down by himself, and ordered the Spanish bishops not to depart from Trent, though they had been officially summoned by the legates to Bologna. Such a course might have been expected from an emperor of Byzantium. It exposed the Catholic Church to the danger of a schism. "The obstinacy of Paul III.," said Charles to the nuncio Veralli, " will ruin Christendom. But councils will not be wanting to satisfy every necessity and to remedy all disorders.

The Pope does violence to the prelates by thus obliging them to a useless removal."—" The prelates who have gone to Bologna," answered the legate, " are there by their own free will ; those, on the contrary, who remain at Trent, are there by your Majesty's order. They are the ones who are really without liberty " Under this show of displeasure lurked a political and financial scheme. To hinder the Protestant league of Smalcald from overthrowing the empire and the Church, the Pope had entered into a Catholic league with Charles, but only for a term of six months. The alliance was successful; its fruit was the victory of Mühlberg. The emperor, finding it admirably suited to further his own interests, would have wished it prolonged. But Paul III. was not the man thus to lavish subsidies upon a prince who was much more likely to use them against his rival, the King of France, than against the heretics. Moreover the promulgation of the Interim had created an incipient coolness between the emperor and the court of Rome.

32. Meanwhile, Francis I. had died at the castle of Rambouillet (March 31, A. D. 1547). Had he been more fortunate, he would have been the first prince of his day ; but fortune cannot disgrace monarchs. They are disgraced only by their own acts. Unhappily, the private life of Francis I. was but too far from honorable ; and this is the only stain upon his character The scandal given by those in high station is always dangerous for the people. The morals of France were corrupted by the example of royal license. This degradation was displayed in two French writers of that period : Marot and Rabelais. The former was a Protestant, the author of a metrical translation of the Psalms, and a licentious poet ; the latter after some years spent successively among the Franciscans and the Benedictines, at length abandoned the religious life, became a secular priest, and was made pastor of Mendon. He is known as the author of ludicrous and obscene romances. " Marot and Rabelais," says Labruyere, "are inexcusable for disfiguring their works by obscenity ; both possessed enough mind and talent to have discarded such helps, even for the sake of those who read

an author rather for amusement than for instruction. Rabelais, especially, is incomprehensible. His work is an inexplicable enigma, whatever may be said of it; it is a monster, the face of a beautiful woman with the feet and the tail of a serpent; it is a monstrous compound of subtle and ingenious morality combined with the most disgusting corruption." The crown of Francis I. passed to his son Henry II.

33. Hitherto the Council of Trent had been received without contradiction in France. But the last reformatory decrees on residence and the accumulation of benefices, were received with great displeasure. Most of the French bishops were deeply involved in these two abuses. The decrees seemed to them intolerably severe, and they refused to receive them. Thus the first sign of opposition to the Council of Trent, in France, came from those who stood most in need of reform. The case was similar in other States. The bishops highly approved of reforming the Roman court, the cardinals, abbots, priests and monks; but to require that court bishops, instead of holding two or three bishoprics at the same time, without residing in any one of them, should be limited to one see, with the obligation of residing in it, was asking too much and encroaching upon one of the "liberties of the Gallican Church." So, also, laymen, princes and kings thought it very proper to reform the clergy; but when the council speaks of reforming the rulers themselves, in order to make the reform of the clergy more complete and lasting, by withdrawing it from the pernicious influence of the world, we shall find all the princes arrayed in opposition. Such is, in truth, the only cause of the opposition against which the Council of Trent had then, and still has, to contend.

34. These difficulties embittered the last moments of Paul III. The power of Charles V seemed to him too threatening to be allowed to go unchecked. Events of a more personal nature were added to these general troubles, and contributed to increase the Pontiff's grief. Paul III. had been married before entering the ecclesiastical state. From this union there remained to him a son, Pier Luigi, and a grandson, Ottavo.

Upon his son he had bestowed Parma and Piacenza, and restored, as an indemnification to the Church, Camerino and Nepi,
which he had before given to Ottavo. The arrangement was
displeasing to the emperor, and he refused to grant to the Farnese the investiture of Parma and Piacenza, which depended
upon the duchy of Milan, as a fief of the empire. Pier Luigi,
however, did not long enjoy his power; he was assassinated
at Piacenza, and the Imperialists took possession of the city
Paul III., whose heart was still bleeding at this cruel disaster,
soon after learned that his grandson, Ottavo, had just entered into a league against the Holy See. The aged Pontiff
was crushed by this accumulation of misfortunes. On his death-
bed he repeated, in a tone of bitter grief, the words of the
Psalmist: " Si mei non fuerint dominati, tunc immaculatus ero,
et emundabor a delicto maximo." Paul III. was a man of rare
talent and of lofty views; at the time of his Pontificate, there
was need of a real superiority to resist the general restlessness
which agitated the world. To find a prominent place beside
Charles V and Francis I., required the energy of a Julius II.,
and the prudence of a Leo X. Paul III. was happily endowed
with these two different qualities. The Council of Trent, which
he succeeded in assembling, amid countless opposing difficulties, will ever be his highest claim to glory in the eyes of posterity

35. In the midst of her grief at the defection of so many
Christian kingdoms, under the Pontificate of Paul III., the
Church was still enabled to repair her losses by the progress of
the faith in America. New Christian communities were rapidly
springing up under the care of the Dominicans and Franciscans,
in Brazil, Jamaica and the other lately-discovered lands of the
West. The most illustrious of these evangelical laborers was the
celebrated Las Casas, a former companion of Columbus, afterward
a Dominican and bishop of Chiappa.* For fifty years he labored
with untiring energy to convert the Indians and to protect

---

* Chiappa-de-los-Españoles, or Ciudad-Real, a city of the Mexican Republic.

them from the oppression of the Spanish governors.   The discovery of Mexico opened a new field to the preachers of the
gospel.   Martin of Valencia, with a band of twelve Franciscans,
was sent by the Sovereign Pontiff to gather in this new harvest
of souls already ripe for the garners of the Heavenly Husband
man. The zeal of these missionaries, seconded by the celebrated
Hernando Cortez, was so successful among these idolatrous nations, that, in the year 1524, we hear of a synod meeting in Mexico, with all the canonical forms, to regulate the affairs of the
missions and provide for the spiritual interests of the neophytes.
The conquest of Mexico by Cortez and of Peru by Francis Pizarro
has furnished the disciples of the Voltarian school with subjects
for the most violent declamations.   Under the specious pretext
of defending the liberty and nationality of the Indians, they have
too freely indulged in calumnies upon the genius and courage of
these two illustrious men, whose energy, valor and heroism are
beyond question.   A conquest is never achieved without bloodshed.   The enemies of the Church have sought to make her out
a party to all the cruelties and bloodshed attending these expeditions.   It will suffice, in refutation, to quote a testimony which
cannot be suspected of undue bias in our favor—that of the
Protestant historian, Robertson.   " With great injustice," says
the historian, " have many authors represented the intolerant
spirit of the Roman Catholic religion, as the cause of exterminat-
ing the Americans, and have accused the Spanish ecclesiastics of
animating their countrymen to the slaughter of that innocent
people, as idolaters and enemies of God.   But the first missionaries who visited America were pious men.   They early
espoused the defence of the natives and vindicated their character from the aspersions of their conquerors, who, describing
them as being incapable of being formed to the offices of civil
life, or of comprehending the doctrines of religion, contended
that they were a subordinate race of men on whom the hand of
nature had set the mark of servitude.   From the accounts
which I have given of the humane and persevering zeal of the
Spanish missionaries, in protecting the helpless flock committed

to their charge, they appear in a light which reflects lustre upon
their function. They were ministers of peace who endeavored
to wrest the rod from the hand of the oppressor. To their
powerful interposition the Americans were indebted for every
regulation tending to mitigate the rigor of their fate. The
clergy in the Spanish settlements, regular as well as secular,
are still considered by the Indians as their natural guardians,
to whom they have recourse under the hardships and exactions
to which they are too often exposed. This title is, moreover,
secured to them by law. By an ordinance of Charles V., not
only bishops, but all ecclesiastics are authorized to inform and
to warn the civil magistrates, when any Indian is deprived of
liberty. Some of the Spanish priests have even refused absolution to those among their countrymen who held the natives in
slavery and employed them in the work of mining."*

36. The empire of Japan saw the missions of St. Paul renewed within its own bounds by an Apostolic man who, with
no other arms than his zeal and heroism, subjected whole
countries to the faith. St. Francis Xavier, one of the first companions of St. Ignatius, was thus, by numberless prodigies,
opening the field of distant missions, which his brethren of the
Society of Jesus were to till through the course of ages with
so much glory and to fertilize with the blood of so many
martyrs. The life of St. Francis Xavier is one of the most
wonderful in modern annals. The world seemed too limited for
the zeal which devoured this heroic Alexander of souls. India,
Japan, Corea, heard his tireless voice and witnessed the miracles wrought through his intercession, by the true God Whom
he preached. Xavier, who thought nothing done so long as
there remained any thing more to accomplish, turned his triumphant steps toward China. But his strength proved unequal to his courage. Like Moses, he died within sight of the
land which he had promised himself to win, but which it was
not given him to enter. The ship which had borne him thus

* History of America, Lib. VIII.

far, left him in a dying condition upon the shore (December 2, A. D. 1552). Here he was left, at his own request, exposed to all the inclemencies of the weather, but at length, George Alvarez, his companion, touched by his sufferings, removed him to a deserted hovel open to every wind. The heroic spirit of the dying apostle was calm and serene. His eyes, bathed in tears, gazed tenderly upon the crucifix in his hand, while he uttered the words of the Psalm : " In Thee, O Lord, have I hoped, let me never be confounded ;" and while his countenance glowed with the heavenly joy that filled his soul, he calmly breathed out his soul into the hands of the God he had served so well. St. Francis Xavier was beatified by Pope Paul V in 1619, and canonized in 1621 by Gregory XV ; in 1747 a brief of Gregory XVI. directed that he should be honored as the patron and protector of all the countries known as the East Indies.

37 While divine Providence thus sent apostles to the heathen, He was also raising up in Europe theologians and doctors to meet the encroachments of heresy. Salmeron, Laynez, Alphonso Rodriguez, Peter Faber and Bobadilla, the first companions of St. Ignatius, devoted themselves to theological and ascetic studies, in which they afterward won such high renown, while their colleague, St. Francis Xavier, bore to distant strands the faith which they ably defended by their writings. At the same period, the Spanish Dominican, Melchior Cano, born in the diocese of Toledo in the first years of the sixteenth century, was publishing his great work " De Locis Theologicis," to which words cannot do justice. The work is written in elegant Latin, without any of the pedantic affectation of pagan turns, so common to the authors who wrote at the time of the literary revival. The excellence of the matter even surpasses the beauty of the style. It is a model of good sense raised to its highest power by Christian learning, which blends, in one harmonious combination, nature and grace, humanity and the Church, reason and faith, philosophy and theology. To every subject he assigns the limits which God has

given it; he scatters the darkness and the errors with which Luther's teachings had clouded them. Melchior Cano enumerates ten *loci theologici* or sources from which the theologian may draw arguments either to prove his own conclusions or to refute opposite contradictory propositions. They are : 1st. The Sacred Writings. 2d. The Divine and Apostolic Traditions. 3d. The Universal Church. 4th. The Councils, and chiefly the General Councils. 5th. The Roman Church. 6th. The Holy Fathers. 7th. The Scholastic Theologians and the Canonists. 8th. Natural Reason. 9th. The Philosophers and Jurists. 10th. Human History The first seven authorities belong to the domain of theology proper; the remaining three it has in common with other sciences. The learned Dominican defines them, shows their force and value, and teaches the manner of using them. His work, together with the *Summa* of St. Thomas, must form the groundwork of any serious study of theology.

CHAPTER IV.

ins nephews from Rome.—23. Death of Paul IV. and of St. Ignatius.—24
First measures of Queen Elizabeth against the Catholic religion in England
—25. Acts of Parliament to reëstablish the schism in England.—26. Violence
of Elizabeth against the Catholic bishops. Intrusion of Matthew Parker,
former chaplain of Anne Boleyn, into the see of Canterbury.—27. Death
of Henry II., king of France. Is succeeded by Francis II.—28. Calvinism
in France. Assembly of the Pré-aux-clercs. Assassination of President
Minard. Execution of the apostate priest Anne Dubourg.

§ I. Pontificate of Julius III. (February 8, a. d. 1550-- March 23, 1555).

1. The interested views of political parties made the election of a successor to Paul III. a complicated and difficult matter. The Sacred College was divided between three factions :
the Cæsarians, who were for acceding to all the wishes of
Charles V ; the French, who desired a Pope favorable to
France ; the Farnesians, attached to the family of the late
Pontiff, and who hoped that the tiara might pass to one of his
nephews. The Spirit of God, which is wont to confound the
calculations of human passion and to turn them to the glory of
His Church, deceived all these different hopes. After an inter-
regnum of more than two months, the suffrages met upon Cardinal del Monte, who had been one of the Apostolic legates at the
Council of Trent. No one would have ventured the smallest bet
on his chance, and most of the cardinals had written his name
on their ballots, perhaps, with the intention of throwing away
the vote (February 8, a. d. 1550). He was thus unanimously
elected, and took the name of Julius III. When the cardinals
came forward to do the customary homage, he affectionately embraced those who had formerly given him cause of complaint,
and who had personally opposed him in the Council of Trent.
By the generous liberality of his favors, he soon satisfied them
that the Pope had forgotten the injuries done to the legate.
The time of his election coincided with that of the centennial
jubilee ; and two days after his coronation Julius III. opened
it with the usual ceremonies. One of the doors of St. Peter's

church, called the *Porta Sancta*, is opened only on this occasion, remaining walled at all other times.   The Pope strikes
upon it thrice with a hammer of gold, at the same time pronouncing the words : " Aperite mihi portas justitiæ ; ingressus
in eas confitebor Domino ; hæc porta Domini, justi intrabunt in
eam." *   The wall is immediately removed : the Pontiff kneels
while the Penitentiaries of St. Peter's sprinkle the door with
holy water ; then, bearing a cross in his right hand, he intones
the Te Deum and enters the Basilica, followed by the cardinals
and prelates.

2.   One of the first cares of the new Pope was to enter into
communication with Charles V and the King of France, Henry
II., about resuming the Council of Trent.   Since their removal
to Bologna, the Fathers had held only one session, in which
they decided upon the prorogation of the session until the hostile dispositions of Charles V should have given place to more
favorable sentiments.   The death of Paul III. greatly facilitated negotiations with the emperor.   The King of France,
though bound by an alliance with Ottavio Farnese, who was in
arms against the Holy See, did not oppose the re-opening of
the council.   Julius III., therefore, on the 14th of November
(A. D. 1550), published a bull calling upon the Fathers to meet
anew at Trent, in the following year.   Charles V caused the
bull to be received in the Diet of Augsburg, and the Protestants promised to send their deputies to Trent.   The peace of
Europe had, meanwhile, been threatened for a moment by an
attempt of the Turks, under Soliman II., upon the island of
Malta.   But a happy stratagem, devised by a high officer of the
order, averted the danger.   He wrote from Messina to the
grand master, then at Rhodes, stating that the admiral, Andrew
Doria, the terror of the infidels, had gathered a considerable
fleet, with which he would speedily sail to the relief of Malta.
The letter was intercepted by the Turks, as the writer had intended.   These false tidings, and the very name of Doria,

* Ps. cxvii. 19

alarmed the Turks. They raised the siege, and, by way of indemnification, seized Tripoli, which Charles had bestowed upon the knights, when he established them in Malta.

3. The council was thus enabled to meet at the time appointed by the Sovereign Pontiff. In the eleventh session, under the presidence of the legates named by Julius III., Cardinal Marcello Crescenzio, Sebastian Pighino, archbishop of Manfredonia (Siponte), and Louis Lippomani, Bishop of Verona, the Fathers declared the council resumed and lawfully assembled. The imperial ambassador, Francis of Toledo, the German bishops, and especially the Electors of Mentz and Treves, had now arrived at Trent, where they were received with the greatest rejoicings. On the 1st day of September, the twelfth session was held to announce to the Fathers that they would at once proceed to discuss the decree on the Sacrament of the Eucharist. But, as if it were decreed that this glorious council must be clogged at every step by new difficulties, an unexpected but bitter dispute now threatened once more to break off its continuance. Henry II. had sent troops into Italy to the help of his ally, Ottavio Farnese. The French flag soon floated over Parma and Mirandola. The emperor declared himself in favor of immediate and forcible measures for driving the French and their adherents out of Italy. The united Papal and imperial troops soon took the field; they laid waste the whole country about Parma and completely surrounded Mirandola. These hostilities agitated all Europe; it was still the eternal quarrel between the King of France and the emperor, always revived in the same terms; but now followed the most formidable attack that Charles had ever sustained. In Italy, the French joined the Farnese, while at the same time they appeared upon the Rhine in alliance with the German Protestants. Meanwhile Henry II. had sent to the council the celebrated James Amyot, preceptor of the royal children, afterward grand almoner of the king and bishop of Auxerre. The translator of Plutarch had not come on a mission of peace. He was charged to announce, in his master's name, that the alliance between the

Pope and the emperor against France, would prevent the French bishops from appearing at the council, which must thenceforth cease to be ecumenical and could be deemed only a particular council. The king threatened, moreover, to reëstablish the Pragmatic Sanction, which had been abolished since the concordat of Leo X. and Francis I. He had already issued an edict ordering that no subsidy whatever should be sent to Rome, because, he urged, " the Pope, by entering upon an unjust system of hostility against the King of France, prevents *the Gallican Church, one of the most important parts of the Universal Church,* from assisting at the council." The Fathers replied that the mission of the council was wholly foreign to the disputes which divided Christian princes, and that the neutrality observed at Trent was quite sufficient to guarantee the safety of the French bishops. The reëstablishment of the Pragmatic Sanction would be unworthy of the most Christian king. His predecessors had, with just reason, annulled it. By pursuing the opposite course, Henry would display a gratuitous hostility which would do little honor to his character. This reply did not produce the effect which might have been expected. The king persisted in his first resolve, and no French bishops appeared in the second period of the council. The Fathers were not to be overcome by this opposition, and rejected the Gallican doctrine, which claimed, by the mere absence of the French prelates, to destroy the ecumenical character of the council.

4. The thirteenth session was opened on the 11th of October, A. D. 1551. The council first promulgated the dogmatic decree on the Eucharist, which had been elaborated in the intervening congregations, where the Pope's theologians, James Laynez and Alphonso Salmeron, of the Society of Jesus, and those of the emperor, Melchior Cano, of the order of Friars Preachers, and John Ortega, of the Minors, displayed their brilliant and solid learning. The various systems of the Lutheran heresy on the presence of Jesus Christ, *figuratively* and by *impanation*, in the Sacrament of our altars, were discussed and condemned.—" If any one denieth," decreed the council, " that, in the

Sacrament of the most holy Eucharist, are contained truly, really, and substantially, the body and blood, together with the soul and divinity of our Lord Jesus Christ, and consequently the whole Christ; but saith that He is only therein as in a sign, or in figure, or virtue; let him be anathema.—If any one saith, that, in the sacred and holy Sacrament of the Eucharist, the substance of the bread and wine remains conjointly with the body and blood of our Lord Jesus Christ, and denieth that wonderful and singular conversion of the whole substance of the bread into the Body, and of the whole substance of the wine into the Blood—the species or appearance only of the bread and wine remaining—which conversion the Catholic Church most aptly calls Transubstantiation; let him be anathema.—If any one saith, that Christ, given* in the Eucharist, is eaten spiritually only, and not also sacramentally and really; let him be anathema.—If any one denieth, that all and each of Christ's faithful of both sexes are bound, when they have attained the years of discretion, to communicate every year, at least at Easter, in accordance with the precept of holy Mother Church; let him be anathema.—If any one saith, that faith alone is a sufficient preparation for receiving the Sacrament of the most holy Eucharist; let him be anathema. And for fear lest so great a Sacrament may be received unworthily, and so unto death and condemnation, this holy synod ordains and declares, that sacramental confession, when a confessor can be had, is of necessity to be made beforehand, by those whose conscience is burdened with mortal sin, how contrite even soever they may think themselves. But if any one shall presume to teach, preach, or obstinately to assert, or even in public disputation to defend the contrary, he shall be thereupon † excommunicated."—These canons were followed by eight chapters on Reform, relating to the authority of bishops and their jurisdiction over the clergy of their respective dioceses.—There shall be no appeal before the definitive sentence, from the judgment of the bishop.

* *Exhibitum*—presented.   † *Eo ipso*—by

A case of appeal from the sentence of the bishop shall be referred to the metropolitan.   In criminal matters it shall be lawful for a bishop to proceed against a cleric, even to his condemnation, as also to his verbal deposition.—And because it sometimes happens that, under false pleas, certain persons fraudulently obtain graces or absolutions, the bishop, as the delegate of the Apostolic See, shall take cognizance, even summarily, of the subreption or obreption of any grace, obtained under false pretences, for the absolution of any public crime or delinquency, or for the remission of a punishment to which he has himself condemned the criminal.—The causes of bishops shall be carried before the Sovereign Pontiff, and be by him alone decided.

5. On the 25th of November, A. D. 1551, the fourteenth session published the decrees and canons relating to the Sacraments of Penance and Extreme Unction.   Luther's errors on these two Sacraments were reduced to sixteen articles, which were delivered, for examination, to different theologians ; their debates on the articles were presided over by the Bishop of Verona.   Nine chapters were promulgated on the Sacrament of Penance.   They establish its necessity, the divine origin of the institution, its character, its effects, the obligation of auricular confession, the qualities of contrition and satisfaction.—" If any one saith, that, in the Catholic Church, Penance is not truly and properly a Sacrament instituted by Christ our Lord for reconciling the faithful unto God, as often as they fall into sin after baptism; let him be anathema.—If any one saith, that those words of the Saviour : ' *Receive ye the Holy Ghost, whose sins you shall forgive, they are forgiven them, and whose sins you shall retain, they are retained,*' are not to be understood of the power of forgiving and of retaining sins in the Sacrament of Penance, as the Catholic Church has always from the beginning understood them ; but wrests them, contrary to the institution of this Sacrament, to the power of preaching the gospel ; let him be anathema.—If any one denieth, either that sacramental confession was instituted, or is necessary, for salvation, of divine

right; or saith that the manner of confessing secretly to a priest alone, which the Church hath ever observed from the beginning, and doth observe, is not in conformity with the institution and command of Christ, and is a human invention; let him be anathema. —If any one saith, that, in the Sacrament of Penance, it is not necessary, of divine right, for the remission of sins, to confess all and each of the mortal sins which, after due and diligent examination are remembered, even those which are secret, and those which are opposed to the two last commandments of the Decalogue; let him be anathema. — If any one saith, that priests, who are in mortal sin, have not the power of binding and loosing; or, that not priests alone are the ministers of absolution, but that to all and each of the faithful of Christ the words of the institution are addressed; let him be anathema.—If any one saith, that bishops have not the right of reserving certain particular cases to themselves, except as regards external polity, and that therefore the reservation of cases hinders not but that a priest may truly absolve from reserved cases; let him be anathema.—If any one saith that God always remits the whole punishment together with the guilt, and that the satisfaction of penitents is no other than the faith whereby they apprehend that Christ has satisfied for them; let him be anathema.—If any one saith that the satisfactions, by which penitents redeem their sins through Jesus Christ, are not a worship of God, but traditions of men, which obscure the doctrine of grace, the true worship of God, and the benefit itself of the death of Christ; let him be anathema." The canons relating to the Sacrament of Extreme Unction are no less precise and explicit. " If any one saith that Extreme Unction is not truly and properly a sacrament, instituted by Christ our Lord and promulgated by the blessed Apostle, St. James, but is only a rite received from the Fathers, or a human invention; let him be anathema. —If any one saith that the sacred unction of the sick does not confer grace, nor remit sin, nor comfort the sick; but that now it should cease to be used because it was of old only the grace of working cures ; let him be anathema.—If any one saith, that the right and usage of Extreme Unction, which the holy Roman Church observes, is repugnant to the sentiments of the blessed Apostle St. James, and that it is therefore to be changed, and may, without sin, be contemned by Christians ; let him be anathema.—If any one saith, that the *Presbyteri* of the Church, whom St. James exhorts to be brought to anoint the sick, are not priests who have been ordained by a bishop, but the elders in each community, and that for this cause a priest alone is not the proper minister of Extreme Unction ; let him be anathema." The decrees on Reformation, as usual, followed the dogmatic decisions.—Those who enter into Holy Orders, notwithstanding a prohibition, interdict, or suspension from the ordinary, shall suffer punishment.—Bishops *in partibus* are forbidden to confer orders upon any cleric without the permission of his bishop. —The bishop may suspend his clerics, who have been improperly promoted by another, if he find them incompetent. Penalties are decreed against clerics who, being in sacred orders or holding benefices, do not wear a dress beseeming their state.—Voluntary homicides are never to be ordained.— The Protestants complained that the council had not awaited their arrival to promulgate its decrees. Their complaints were examined in the fifteenth session, held on the 19th of March, 1551. It was agreed to accede to their wishes, and the sixteenth session was prorogued to the 1st of May, to give them time to repair to Trent. Safe-conducts, as explicit as could be desired, were sent for their deputies ; but the sequel was soon to prove their bad faith.

6. A Lutheran army had, in the mean time, been threatening Innspruck, a city not far from Trent. Some of the prelates fled from Trent, and in a consistory, held on the 15th of April (A.D. 1552), the Pope, learning that the city was not safe from the assaults of the heretics, forwarded the order for the suspension of the council. The Imperialists opposed the execution of the order. But the Fathers still remaining at Trent determined, in a congregation held on the 24th of April, to suspend the

council during two years. In a session held on the 28th of April, 1552, the decree for the conditional suspension was read and approved by all present, except twelve Spanish bishops, who entered their protest against it. These prelates, however, soon found it necessary to act against their own protest, and to provide for their safety by flight.

7 Charles V remained at Innspruck, in spite of the attempts made by the Protestants upon that city His vigor had left him with his youth, and even his powerful mind seemed to feel the effects of age. By a blind presumption, he thought that he might without danger scatter his forces, sending some into Italy against the French, others to Hungary to meet the Turks. This feeling of security respecting the Protestants arose from the fact that he had loaded Maurice, the new elector of Saxony, with favors, hoping thus to bind him to his interests by the ties of gratitude. But the ungrateful man was secretly betraying his benefactor, though repeatedly professing his grateful attachment, and had already joined in a powerful league against him, with the other Protestant nobles of Germany and the King of France. During the night of the 22d of May, A.D. 1552, it was announced to the emperor that Maurice was approaching Innspruck, at the head of all his forces. Charles was confined to his bed by a painful attack of the gout. He was removed in a litter, and carried through mountain by-ways to Villach, in Carinthia, being lighted on his way by torches of straw, and followed by a few faithful attendants, who had not fled at the approach of danger. Meanwhile Maurice entered Innspruck, which was plundered by his soldiers.

8. Charles V., so badly served by fortune, and betrayed by the man upon whom he thought himself most entitled to lean, now found it necessary to resort to negotiations for the re-establishment of his tottering power. Conferences were held at Passau between the Imperial ambassadors and the deputies of the Lutheran princes. They resulted in an agreement known as the *Treaty of the Public Peace*. It was concluded in spite of the earn

est and repeated protests of Julius III., who strongly objected to the conditions of the treaty. The chief clauses were as follows: " The landgrave, Frederick of Hesse, a prisoner in the hands of the emperor, shall be restored to instant freedom. A diet of the empire shall be assembled within six months, to determine the means of settling all differences in religious matters, either by a general or national council, or by conferences between the two parties, or by an ordinary diet. The deliberations of the diet shall be received according to the judgment of a commission, composed equally of Catholics and Protestants. Until the complete pacification, both religions shall keep their former rights, an entire freedom of conscience and a perfect equality. Ferdinand, brother to the emperor and king of the Romans, and his son Maximilian, shall solemnly pledge themselves to give due weight to all the complaints of the German nation against the violation of its liberties." All the troops, on both sides, were to be at once disbanded, and a general amnesty proclaimed. The King of France, who had helped to restore religious liberty—or, in other words, the triumph of heresy—in Germany, was requested to make known his complaints against the emperor, that he might afterward share in the general peace.

9. Charles could not sign this treaty without a feeling of deep sorrow. Reverses seemed to crowd upon him now to outweigh the splendid success which had so long crowned his arms. The victor of Francis I., the destroyer of the Algerine corsairs, the terror of the Mussulmans, the illustrious emperor who had filled the last half century with the renown of his triumphs, was now but an aged monarch, sinking under the weight of years and misfortunes. His dreams of greatness were no longer realized. He wished to leave to his son, Philip II., the Empire, his hereditary States, Spain, the Netherlands, Burgundy, the Milanese, the kingdom of Naples, Sicily and the New World, an immense empire " upon which the sun never set." For this it was necessary that Ferdinand, his brother, long since invested with the title of King of the

Romans, with the right of succession to the empire, should yield his claims and his rights to his nephew. But Ferdinand was by no means prepared to make the sacrifice. Meanwhile, Henry II. of France, helped by his alliance with the German Protestants, had seized the imperial cities of Toul, Metz and Verdun, known as the Three Bishoprics. Charles made an unsuccessful attempt to retake them. Fortune likewise played him false in Italy, and he lost Sienna by a revolt. Defeated by his enemies, racked by a disease which left him no moment of peace, oppressed by grief at his reverses, the emperor withdrew to Brussels; here he allowed himself to sink into a state of deep dejection, and lived for some months in such perfect retirement, that the report of his death soon spread over all Europe. The Diet of Augsburg, in 1555, confirmed the treaty of Passau. This last disgrace brought the emperor to a definitive resolution. The States of the Netherlands met, by his order, in the month of October, A. D. 1555. The emperor addressed them, recalling, in a pompous discourse, all the phases of his laborious and agitated career, his frequent expeditions into Italy, Germany and Africa, the wars he had waged, the triumphs he had won: he dwelt especially upon the sacrifice he had made of his time, his pleasures and his health, to defend religion and secure public peace. " So long as my strength allowed," he continued, " I have borne the weight of these heavy cares; but now, broken down by the ravages of an incurable disease, my infirmities require that I should seek repose. The happiness of my people is dearer to me than the ambition of reigning. Instead of an old man, already sinking into the grave, I give you a prince in the flower of his age; a prince endowed with sagacity, energy and enterprise. For myself, if I have committed faults, if I have fallen into errors, in the course of so long a reign, charge them to my weakness alone. Your former emperor entreats you to forgive them. I shall ever cherish a lively gratitude for your fidelity; your happiness shall ever be the first object of my fervent prayers to Almighty God, to Whom I devote the rest of my life." Then turning to

Philip, who had fallen upon his knees and kissed his father's hand, Charles spoke to him, in the most touching strain, upon the duties of princes, and conjured him to labor with the most untiring care for the happiness of his subjects. At the close of his address he blessed the young prince and pressed him affectionately to his bosom; overcome by fatigue and deeply moved by the tears of the assembly, he fell back exhausted upon the throne he had just abdicated. A few months later he sent the imperial crown and sceptre, by the Prince of Orange, to his brother Ferdinand I.; then sailing to the coast of Biscay, he buried himself in the monastic seclusion of Yuste, in Estremadura (1556). Here Charles would hide, in solitude and silence, the greatness, the ambition and all the vast projects which for half a century had kept Europe in a state of agitation and alarm. His pastimes were limited to occasional rides on horseback, the cultivation of a garden and mechanical occupations. He had a passion for horology, and the inability to make two timepieces exactly agree is said to have drawn from him the reflection: "How absurd was it, then, to attempt the establishment of uniformity among men and empires, since I cannot even succeed in making two clocks agree." His melancholy degenerated into a gloomy and intolerant severity, and he gave up even the most innocent amusements furnished by his retreat. Regret for his abdicated throne may have had some share in producing this bitter melancholy. He was seized with a strange fancy to witness his own funeral obsequies. A tomb was erected at his request in the chapel of the monastery, to which his attendants and the monks proceeded in procession, bearing funeral tapers; Charles followed wrapped in a shroud. A coffin had been prepared, in which he was solemnly laid, and the office of the dead was chanted. He joined his voice, he mingled his tears and prayers, with those of the religious. At the end of the ceremony the coffin was sprinkled with holy water, the crowd departed and the doors of the chapel were closed upon him. Charles then rose from his coffin and withdrew to his room full of gloomy and funereal impressions. The effect of the ceremony proved fatal; on the following day he was seized with a fever, and died on the 21st of September, 1558, at the age of fifty-nine years.

10. Charles V was one of the greatest sovereigns of modern times. Educated by men of a naturally peaceful disposition, his first years showed a greater talent for administration and politics than for war. But his contest with Francis I. and the German Protestants proved him as great in the field as in council. More capable of reflection than of resolution, he was better fitted to plan than to execute. If he sometimes failed in his political schemes, it was because he allowed too little weight to moral forces, and did not believe in the possibility of disinterested heroism. The success of his arms made him bold to excess. He was deeply acquainted with human nature, and knew how to choose his ministers and generals, whom he bound to him by kindness and benefits. Thucydides and Tacitus furnished his favorite reading, but amid the tumult of passions and events he disregarded or forgot their teaching. A dissembler himself, he saw in history but a long lesson in dissimulation, and made State policy consist in the art of deceiving allies as well as enemies. Naturally distrustful, he had few confidants. Reverses and bodily sufferings made him obstinate, irritable and revengeful. His ambition knew no bounds. He is said to have entertained the idea of a *Universal Monarchy;* and if, by this expression, is meant not an immediate domination, but only a general supremacy, over the States of Europe, the idea, far from appearing to be a mere chimera, would naturally grow out of his very situation. His manner of life, like that of most of the great conquerors, was very simple. Charles spoke five languages—the Flemish, Spanish, Italian, French, and German; he was but slightly acquainted with Latin. His whole life was taken up by the design of re-uniting the two religious parties; it was the delusion of his policy His absolute character led him to throw off the restraint imposed by the constitutions of his States; but if he some-

times allowed himself to exercise an arbitrary sway, still there is no just ground for the epithets "despot" and "tyrant" lavished by partisan malice.

11. While Protestantism, favored by events, was growing into fearful proportions in Germany, a happy revolution, productive of results but too short-lived, restored the Catholic faith to England. The youthful Edward VI. died in 1553, after a reign of six years, which was devoted to the establishment in his kingdom of the schism introduced by his despotic parent. The Princess Mary, daughter of Henry VIII. and Catharine of Aragon, ascended the throne. Her arrival in London was a triumph. She had been brought up in sentiments of the purest faith. The Parliament, as prompt now to second a Catholic administration as it had before been servile under princes who favored the schism, speedily revoked all the laws passed under Edward VI. It annulled the divorce formerly pronounced between Catharine of Aragon and Henry VIII., declaring that union alone lawful and valid. With a view to secure the succession in her family, Mary determined to marry, and gave her hand to Philip II., son and heir of Charles V., who had already been once married and was the father of several children. This union was a stroke of skilful policy It would bring under the same domination the greater part of the Christian world and consolidate Mary's throne, which had already been disputed by Lady Jane Grey, the great granddaughter of Henry VII. Lady Jane subsequently suffered capital punishment. The marriage of Philip II. and Mary was celebrated with a magnificence which has seldom been surpassed. Mary, on ascending the throne, gave her first thoughts to "the restoration of that religion," says the Protestant writer Cobbett, "under the influence of which the kingdom had been so happy and so great for so many ages, and since the abolition of which it had known nothing but discord, disgrace and misery." The chief obstacle to this great work came from the holders of Church property, who had been enriched by the plunder of the bishoprics and monasteries. Eighteen years

had elapsed since this property had been wrested from its rightful owners, and during that period it had undergone numberless divisions and subdivisions. But some compromise must be made with the holders; and the peaceable settlement of the matter succeeded much better than might have been expected. "Now," adds the writer whom we have just quoted, "it was fully proved to all the world, and now this plundered nation who had been reduced to the greatest misery by the so-called Reformation, saw as clearly as they saw the light of day, that all those who had abetted the Reformation; that all the railings against the Pope; that all the accusations against the monks and nuns; that all the pretences of abuses in the Catholic Church; that all the confiscations, sackings and bloodshed; that all these, from first to last, had proceeded from the love of plunder. For now the two Houses of Parliament, who had only about three or four years before established CRANMER'S CHURCH, and declared it to be 'the work of the Holy Ghost;' now these pious 'Reformation' men, having first made a firm bargain to keep the plunder, confessed '*that they had been guilty of a most horrible defection from the true Church,* professed their sincere repentance for their past transgressions, and declared their resolution to repeal all laws enacted in prejudice of the Pope's authority" The churches were once more given back to the Catholic worship. The married priests were removed from their livings, to the great satisfaction of the people, who had witnessed with pain the abolition of ecclesiastical celibacy The bishops deposed by Cranmer were restored to their sees. The apostate prelate himself was imprisoned on a charge of high treason, and soon after condemned to the scaffold, which he deserved for his numerous crimes (A. D. 1556). The sacrifice of the Mass was again celebrated throughout the whole extent of the kingdom; while the needy and wretched were no longer condemned to the brand of infamy and servitude for their misfortune, according to the barbarous laws of Henry VIII. All seemed to promise that the abyss of revolution was now closed up, that England would be England again, and that hospitality and charity would return.*

12. Cardinal Pole, who had presided at the opening of the Council of Trent, and whose heroic mother had shed her blood for the faith, was still on the continent at the time of Mary's accession. Pope Julius III., judging that he might now return to his country in perfect safety, named him Apostolic legate in England. "The session of Parliament which was to consecrate the official reëstablishment of the Catholic religion, was opened in the month of November, A. D. 1554, with a most splendid procession of the two Houses, closed by the king on horseback and the queen in a litter. Their first act was a repeal of the attainder of Cardinal Pole, passed in the reign of Henry VIII. While this was going on, many noblemen and gentlemen had gone to Brussels to conduct the cardinal to England. On the 29th of November, the two Houses addressed a petition to the king and queen. In this petition they expressed their leep regret at having been guilty of defection from the Church, and prayed their majesties, who had not participated in the sin, to intercede with the Holy Father for their forgiveness and for their re-admission into the fold of Christ. The next day, the queen being seated on the throne, with the king on her left, the legate, though at a greater distance, on her right, the Lord High Chancellor, Bishop Gardiner, read the petition. The king and the queen then spoke to the legate, and he, after a speech of some duration, gave, in the name of the Pope, to the two Houses, and to the whole nation, ABSOLUTION, in the name of the Father, Son, and Holy Ghost; at which words, the members of the two Houses, being on their knees, made the hall resound with AMEN! Thus was England once more a Catholic country; she was restored to the fold of Christ. Julius III. hesitated a long while before consenting to countenance, by silence, the plunder of Church property; Cardinal Pole only yielded to the necessity with heartfelt grief; but Gardiner, who was now the queen's

* COBBETT'S "Reformation," Letter VIII.

prime minister, and indeed all her council, were for the compromise. Mary, however, proceeded to restore all the Church and abbey lands in her own possession. Her intention was to apply the revenues, as nearly as possible, to their original purposes. She restored Westminster Abbey, the monastery at Greenwich, the Black-Friars in London, and a number of hospitals, which she liberally endowed."*

13. Such was the queen, according to the Protestant historian Cobbett, upon whom so many English writers have bestowed the now almost historic epithet of *bloody*. "The truth is," continues Cobbett, whose authority is of great weight here, "that the executions ordered during the reign of Mary, in virtue of existing laws, and after regular form of trial, generally reached a set of most wicked wretches, who sought to destroy the queen and her government, and, under the pretence of *freedom of conscience*, to obtain the means of again preying upon the people."

In the midst of this season of consoling triumph for the Church, Julius III. expired, on the 23d of March, A. D. 1555, after a Pontificate of five years.

§ II. Pontificate of Marcellus II. (April 9, A. D. 1555—May 1, 1555).

14. The votes of the Sacred College bestowed the tiara upon Cardinal Marcello Cervini, who took the name of Marcellus II. (April 9, A. D. 1555). His firmness, zeal and virtue inspired the world with hope. To save his administration from even the suspicion of nepotism, Marcellus would not suffer his relations to come to Rome after his elevation; he introduced numerous reductions in the expenditure of his court, and turned his whole attention to the resuming of the Council of Trent, which had now been two years adjourned, for the great work of pacification and reform. "Reformation," said the Pope to the

---

* COBBETT, *ubi sup.*

Cardinal of Mantua, " is the only means, not only of increasing but even of preserving the Pontifical authority   It will abolish only what is superfluous and onerous—luxury, pomp, retinues, with other excessive and useless expense, which bring the Papacy into contempt, instead of making it venerable and majestic.   By putting an end to all these vanities, we shall really increase its power, its reputation and finances, which are the sinews of a government ; but what is more, the measure will call down upon the Popes the divine help, which they may hope to receive who strive to do their duty "   Death did not allow Marcellus to execute his generous designs.   He was stricken down by apoplexy on the twenty-second day of his Pontificate. His contemporaries apply to him the words of Virgil, uttered of another Marcellus :

"Ostendent terris hunc tantum fata."

§ III. Pontificate of Paul IV   (May 23, a. d. 1555—August 18, 1559).

15. An administration so short as that of Marcellus II. seems hardly calculated to produce a serious effect upon ecclesiastical affairs.   Still it was important in its influence upon the spirit of the Roman court, to which it gave a tendency that appeared in the next conclave.   Cardinal Caraffa, first superior-general of the Theatines, founded by St. Cajetan of Thienna, was elected Pope on the 23d of May, a. d. 1555, and took the name of Paul IV   The new Pope had already reached the advanced age of seventy-nine years, but he had lost none of his youthful zeal and vigor.   He was one of the most earnest advocates of the reform.   He combined all the qualities which give a man the right and the power to command others.   To an ardent nature and a strong will, he joined deep convictions. He was born in time to behold Italy in the freedom of the fifteenth century, and his whole soul was bent on restoring those fading glories.   " He was wont to compare the Italy of

that age to a well-tuned instrument, of which Naples, Milan, the States of the Church and Venice, were the four strings." Full of this project, Paul IV could not view without pain the predominant power of Spain, which had disturbed this Italian harmony; and he now brought all his power to bear upon that foreign domination.

16. By the abdication of Charles V., as we have seen, the imperial crown passed to Ferdinand I., and the hereditary States—Spain, the Netherlands, Burgundy, Naples, the Milanese and the New World—to Philip II., already king of England by his marriage with Mary Tudor. Ferdinand I. assumed the imperial title and insignia without asking the usual confirmation of the Holy See. This step inaugurated a complete revolution. The Empire of the West had been reëstablished by Pope St. Leo III., in the person of Charlemagne. The emperor, by the very origin of the institution, became of necessity the armed defender of the Roman Church. The Pope had, and was naturally entitled to, a principal part in his election, either by making the choice himself or by approving the choice of the electors who were to make it. For several centuries the electors were seven in number, and, according to the old constitutions of the empire, which constitutions were common to all Christian nations, they must be Catholics and in communion with the successor of St. Peter. Charles V had indeed abdicated the imperial throne; but his abdication had not been ratified, as it should have been, by the Sovereign Pontiff; the throne was not canonically vacant, and Ferdinand could not aspire to it. The abdication of Charles and the succession of Ferdinand had been ratified by the seven electors; but this confirmation could not, on any ground, dispense with the consent of the Holy See. Beside, three of the electors were heretics, and were accordingly, by the constitutions of the Holy Empire, disqualified for the office. Thus, when Ferdinand's ambassador appeared before Paul IV to notify him of his master's accession, the Pope, in concert with the cardinals, replied by laying down the principles just

quoted. " The only way to remove all difficulties," continued the Pope, " would be for Ferdinand to apply to the Holy See, which would supply what was wanting in the mode of election." Diplomatic negotiations were opened on the subject; but Ferdinand finally recalled his ambassador and determined to do without the Pope's confirmation. His successors have followed his example. From that time there has remained of the Holy Roman Empire only the name; it is now, in truth, but the secular Empire of Germany

17 The relations of Paul IV with Philip II., as heir to the Italian possessions of Charles V., were not more happy The Pope made a wide distinction between Philip II., king of Spain, of Naples and of the Milanese, and Philip II., the consort of the queen of England. Charles V., Philip II. and Ferdinand I. had all opposed the election of Paul IV., with whose political opinions they were well acquainted. "If God wills that I should be Sovereign Pontiff," said the aged cardinal, "the emperor cannot hinder my election. I shall thus be much better satisfied with it, since I shall be indebted for it only to God." The new Pope had hardly ascended the throne of St. Peter, when he received a deputation, consisting of a bishop and two noblemen, from England ; they came in the name of the king and queen, to make the act of submission to the Pontifical authority. They were charged, moreover, to request, in the name of their sovereigns, the erection of Ireland into a kingdom, to which petition Paul readily acceded. An Apostolic bull, dated June 7, A. D. 1557, officially recognized the title of Sovereigns of Ireland, which Philip and Mary wished to assume. The ambassadors were then admitted to an audience with the Pope, and in the name of their nation acknowledged him as head of the Universal Church. They presented him a copy of the act recognizing his authority, begged that he would ratify the absolution pronounced by the legate, and confirm the bishoprics established during the schism. The Pope willingly granted all these just requests.

18. All these marks of good-will toward the royal consort

of the English queen did not in the least involve a change in the Pope's determination to destroy the Spanish influence in Italy To insure success in such an undertaking, he needed the support of France. He hoped, by the help of that nation, so dear to the Holy See, to recover the independence of Italy " If, in this sacred cause," said Paul, " I am neither heard nor helped, posterity will at least bear witness that an aged Italian, even at the gates of death, instead of seeking repose and preparing himself in peace to die, alone conceived the noble designs which should give back to his country its existence and its nationality " During the course of the formalities attending the abdication of Charles V., the truce of Vauxelles (February 5, A. D. 1556), between France and Spain, gave a season of quiet to the exhausted people; but the truce, dictated rather by necessity than by a desire for peace, was broken almost as soon as signed. Henry II., urged on by the Guises, whose influence was then all-powerful, soon violated the treaty The Pope entered into a league, offensive and defensive, with the King of France against Philip II. (December 15, 1556). To place himself in a position for beginning hostilities, the Pope felt the need of energetic men. His family shared all his antipathy for the Spanish domination ; and, feeling sure of its coöperation, he naturally turned to it for support. This all-absorbing thought blinded him in regard to his nephews and betrayed him into an error which he afterward had occasion most bitterly to deplore. He raised to the cardinalate his nephew, Charles Caraffa, whose hostility to the Spaniards was well known. Unfortunately, this youth had none of the qualities which become a prince of the Church. He had been trained in the rude and licentious life of the camp; and his uncle committed a grave error by intrusting to him the conduct, not only of secular, but of spiritual affairs. The Pontiff's other nephews, seeing by what route they could most easily reach his favor, were not slow to adopt his anti-Spanish feelings ; they also received dignities and offices of trust. The elder was made Duke of Palliano; the younger, Marquis of Montebello; they all aspired to the highest honors. Thus Paul IV., whose whole mind seemed taken up with projects of reform, was indirectly favoring one of the most crying abuses— nepotism. Though he eventually repaired his fault with a courage and resolution which became for him an occasion of new merit before God and of true glory in the eyes of men.

19. Hostilities had now fairly begun in Italy The Duke of Guise hastened toward Milan with a formidable army; but, hampered by court intrigues, he tarnished his reputation by a fruitless campaign, and was obliged to return to France without having effected anything in behalf of his ally, the Pope. Philip and Mary had sent a large force to the Netherlands, under Emmanuel-Philibert, duke of Savoy, a great general and the mortal enemy of Henry II., who had seized his States. In spite of the heroic efforts of the Constable of Montmorency, of the Prince of Condé, and Admiral Coligny, the Duke of Savoy defeated the French in the bloody battle of St. Quentin (August 18, A. D. 1557), comparable in its disastrous results to the fields of Crécy, Poitiers and Agincourt. The road to the capital was open. "Is my son in Paris?" inquired Charles V., when he heard, in his retirement, of the defeat of the French. But Philip had not his father's genius. He knew not how to avail himself of a victory that might have placed the whole of France in his power. His officers urged him to march at once upon Paris. "No, no," replied Philip, "we should never drive an enemy to desperation." While he wasted his time in reducing the chief fortresses in Picardy, Henry II. was organizing a powerful army, of which the Duke of Guise took command on his return from Italy

20. The departure of Guise from Italy left the Pope to his own resources, before the Duke of Alva, the greatest captain that Spain, then so fruitful in warriors, had sent forth, since Gonsalvo of Cordova. He was at this period viceroy of Naples. His troops marched upon Rome, which was defended by a few troops, unaccustomed to the art of war. The Pope felt the need of other defenders, and he took into his pay the undisci-

plined bands of Peter Strozzi, an Italian chief. The two hostile armies presented a strange anomaly. The Duke of Alva was a fervent Catholic; he imposed upon his troops the greatest moderation in the attack, and a deep respect for the Holy See. The force of Strozzi, on the other hand, levied for the most part in Germany, was composed almost entirely of Lutherans, and revelled in all the license and excess of war without care or remorse. The situation of the Pope was extremely critical, but, happily for him, the struggle was to end on another field. The Duke of Guise had been made lieutenant-general of the kingdom, by Henry II. He was now to uphold the national honor, and he did not deceive the hopes which were entertained of his talent. In mid-winter he pitched his camp before that of the Spaniards and the English, in the very heart of Picardy. By a skilful manœuver, he succeeded in deceiving the enemy as to his real intention, and fell suddenly upon Calais, where he was not expected. During two hundred and ten years, the possession of this port had left France in the power of the English. After the disaster of Crécy, Edward III. had taken it only after a siege of eleven months. Within ten days the Duke of Guise took it by storm (January 10, A. D. 1558). Guines, Ham, and Câtelet fell in quick succession, and the English domination disappeared entirely from the soil of France. Queen Mary felt this blow most severely. It hastened her death, which occurred on the 17th of November, 1558. On her death-bed she declared that, if her breast were opened, the word "Calais" would be found engraven on her heart. In the following spring the Duke of Guise seemed to surpass himself in the capture of Thionville, the strongest place held by the Spaniards; while in Piedmont, Marshal de Brissac, with a handful of troops, nobly sustained the honor of the French arms, and made a diversion in favor of the Pope, by obliging the Duke of Alva to leave the Roman territory to oppose his march. Both monarchs were equally desirous of peace; Philip, because he had no inclination for war; Henry, because he saw the necessity of repairing the misfortunes of France, and of arresting

the progress of Calvinism in his States. The Constable of
Bourbon was charged to enter into arrangements with the King
of Spain, and on the 2d of April, 1559, the treaty of Cateau-
Cambrésis was signed by both parties. This peace was known
as the "Unfortunate Peace," because, by the terms of the
treaty, Henry gave up one hundred and eighty-nine fortified towns which he had taken in Italy and the Netherlands; but it has not been noted that, by preserving the
"Three Bishoprics"—Metz, Toul and Verdun—France once
more held her natural limits, which is the greatest security
of a State.

21. The terms of the treaty of Cateau-Cambrésis, in relation
to the Pope, were more honorable than might have been anticipated. It was agreed "that the Duke of Alva should repair to
Rome and do homage to Paul IV., in the name of the Catholic
king, his master. The Sovereign Pontiff should thenceforth
enter into friendly relations with the Catholic king, and renounce the league with France. Philip was to return to the
Pope all the places in the Roman States, taken during the war.
The fortifications erected there were to be razed; and all property, of whatsoever nature, taken from the Pope in the course
of the war, was also to be restored. A general amnesty secured
the safety of all who had taken up arms on either side." After
the ratification of these conditions, the Duke of Alva came to
Rome, and made the profession of homage which had been
agreed upon. The issue of the war, though relatively favorable
to the Sovereign Pontiff, yet ruined his most cherished hopes.
The Spanish domination at Naples and Milan was now fixed
upon a firmer foundation than ever. Philip II. was enjoying
the preponderance won by Charles V The Pope's personal
enemies, the Colonnas and Sforzas, once more took a brilliant
position; the check in this respect was complete. But men of
such energy do not quail before a difficult position; they are
either crushed by events, or they meet and master them, and
then turn the powers of their strong will to other combats. So
it was with Paul IV He bore his defeat with courage, and

turned his whole attention to the second part of his great design—ecclesiastical reform.

22. The Pope, one day, in a consistory of the cardinals, repeated the words "Reform, reform!" One of the cardinals replied : "Holy Father, we must begin the reform among ourselves." Paul understood that these words referred to the disorders of his nephews, which had long been a subject of loud complaint with the Romans. The Sovereign Pontiff did not hesitate; he made diligent inquiries, which revealed the whole truth. With the proofs of the charges in his hand, the Pope met the cardinals in an extraordinary consistory, made known this family misfortune, and decreed that his nephews, with their families and servants, should quit Rome within twelve days. The same decree deprived them of the power and the dignities they had so long abused. Cardinal Caraffa was banished to Civita Lavinia. John Caraffa, duke of Palliano, general of the Pontifical States and prefect of the galleys, lost these two high offices, and was exiled to Gallese. Antonio, marquis of Montebello, was required to confine himself to his marquisate, situated in the Romagna. All three were warned that they should be tried for treason if they quitted their place of exile. Several of the cardinals would have interceded in behalf of the nephews, but the Pope forbade any one even to mention their names in his presence. When he had struck this blow and the three exiles had left Rome, Paul exclaimed : "Now We can, We must say : Of Our Pontificate, the first year."—"An event now occurred, forever memorable," says Ranke; "a Pope, by a sort of self-violence, emancipated himself from all partiality to his kindred."

23. He now gave himself up without reserve to the work of reformation, and he allowed no day to pass without doing something for that great end. Time only was wanting to him to resume the Council of Trent, which the ceaseless wars that filled his Pontificate had made it impossible to convoke. But, if he could not resume the council, he at least prepared, by wise regulations, the reforms which the council afterward promul

gated. The administration of temporal concerns, ecclesiastical discipline, religious orders, public and private morals—nothing escaped his watchful control. To reach the end proposed, he displayed an energetic severity which gained him some honorable enmities. He restored the Inquisition in Rome and fixed the limits of its jurisdiction. These multiplied cares, responsibilities and troubles, added to the weight and infirmities of advanced age, soon prostrated the Pope and led him to the grave. The year which he had styled the first was likewise to be the last of his Pontificate. Calling the cardinals around his death-bed, he begged their forgiveness for the faults and negligences of which he might have been guilty in the course of his reign, exhorted them to remain in perfect union, and to choose a successor capable of guarding the interests of the Church. A few days later (August 18, A. D. 1559), he expired, while repeating the words of the fifty-first Psalm : " Lætatus sum in his quæ dicta sunt mihi; iu domum domini ibimus." The popularity which is so often achieved at the expense of honor and conscience, had no value in the eyes of Paul IV   The people repaid his contempt of their favor by heaping insults upon his memory   They burned the palace of the Inquisition and destroyed the statues raised in his honor, in the beginning of his reign. The same year was marked by the death of St. Ignatius, rich in virtues and merits. He was succeeded in the government of his order by James Laynez.

24. The death of Mary was followed in England by a new revolution, which placed upon the throne her sister Elizabeth, the fruit of Henry's adulterous union with Anne Boleyn. In the preceding reign, Elizabeth, who had been trained in the principles and prejudices of Protestantism, gave great edification by her zeal for the Catholic faith. Not only did she appear with affected regularity at the celebration of Mass, but she even kept, in her private apartments, an elegant chapel, attended by a Roman Catholic chaplain; she even had a confessor officially attached to her person. Mary had always doubted the sincerity of this outward conformity ; and on her death-bed

her solicitude prompted her to require from her sister an avowal of her real sentiments. The hypocritical princess replied to this touching mark of attachment, by " praying Almighty God that the earth might open and swallow her up alive, if she were not, in heart and soul, a *true Roman Catholic*." This was a horrible perjury The first act of the new queen was to recall to court the partisans of the Protestant religion, who had been removed by Mary Those who had been confined for religious causes were released. The Bishop of Winchester was thrown into prison for his sermon at the funeral of Queen Mary, in which he maintained the necessity of reëstablishing Catholicity in England. Every thing seemed to augur a coming defection ; but that which cleared away every doubt was a proclamation, forbidding the Catholic clergy to preach in public, and ordering the established worship to be observed " until consultation might be had in Parliament by the queen and the three estates."

25. Paul IV had refused to recognize the legitimacy of Elizabeth, declaring that, by right of inheritance, the English throne should have descended to Mary Stuart, queen of Scotland, as the nearest lawful heir of Henry VIII. Mary had married, in 1558, the Dauphin of France, afterward Francis II. She was a sincere Catholic, and would have carried out the religious policy of Mary Tudor, while her union with the heir to the French throne would have put an end to the hostilities which had so long divided the two kingdoms. But Mary Stuart found in England only a cruel death upon the scaffold. The bishops, alarmed at the tendencies of the new government, assembled in London and determined to officiate at the coronation of the queen, only on the express condition that she should take the accustomed oath to maintain the liberties of the Catholic Church. Elizabeth took the oath ; a perjury cost her but little. A few months later, the statutes " passed in the late reign for the support of the ancient faith" were repealed, and the schismatical acts of Henry VIII., in derogation of the Papal authority, and consequently breaking off all connection not only with the Church and the whole Christian world, but also with

the thousand years of Catholic England, were in a great measure revived. It was enacted that the book of Common Prayer should alone be used by the ministers in all churches, under the penalties of forfeiture, deprivation and death; that the spiritual authority of every foreign prelate within the realm should be utterly abolished; that the jurisdiction necessary for the correction of errors, heresies, schisms, and abuses, should be annexed to the crown, with the power of delegating such jurisdiction to any person or persons whatsoever, at the pleasure of the sovereign; that the penalty of asserting the Papal authority should ascend, on the repetition of the offence, from the forfeiture of real and personal property to perpetual imprisonment; and from perpetual imprisonment to death, as was inflicted in cases of high treason: and that all clergymen taking orders, or in possession of livings; all magistrates and inferior officers having fees or wages from the crown; all laymen suing out the livery of their lands, or about to do homage to the queen, should, under pain of deprivation and incapacity, take an oath, declaring her to be supreme governor in all ecclesiastical and spiritual things or causes, as well as temporal, and renouncing all foreign ecclesiastical or spiritual jurisdiction or authority whatsoever within the realm.

26. The English clergy opposed these bills with a most vigorous but fruitless resistance, which, however, does them honor, and gives us the hope that God may one day remember His mercies upon the land of so many confessors and martyrs. They presented to the House of Lords a declaration of their belief in the real presence, transubstantiation, the sacrifice of the Mass, and the supremacy of the Pope; with a protestation that to decide on doctrine, sacraments and discipline, belonged not to any lay assembly, but to the lawful pastors of the Church. Both universities, Cambridge and Oxford, signed the confession of the clergy, and the bishops unanimously seized every opportunity to speak and to vote against the measure. To dissolve or neutralize this opposition, the Bishops of Winchester and Lincoln were committed to the Tower.

Elizabeth, soon after, sent for the other bishops, required tnem to conform to the new statutes, and, on their refusal, drove them from her presence with expressions of contempt and resentment. The oath of supremacy was tendered to each in succession; but all, with the exception of Landaff, sacrificed their situations and their liberty to the dictates of their conscience. Tunstal, of Durham; Morgan, of St. David's; Ogilthorpe, of Carlisle; White, of Winchester, and Bangs, of Coventry, died under the infamous treatment to which they were subjected. A few succeeded in escaping from prison, and reaching the continent. Bonner, bishop of London, died in a dungeon, after an imprisonment of ten years. Watson, of Lincoln, languished during thirty-three years in a dungeon of the Tower. At the head of the intruded hierarchy was placed Matthew Parker, formerly chaplain to Anne Boleyn; the new primate thus succeeded, not the glorious archbishops of Canterbury, St. Augustine, St. Dunstan, St. Anselm, and St. Thomas, whose see he was usurping, but the perjured apostate Cranmer. But an unexpected impediment arose from the refusal of the Catholic prelates to consecrate the new metropolitan, who was obliged to receive that rite from Barlow and Scory, two bishops who had conformed under Edward VI. Since the consecration was performed according to the altered ritual, it may certainly be doubted that he received the episcopal character, and that he could validly confer it upon others. However this may be, the schism was again actually established in England. "After requiring all her subjects to take the oath of supremacy," says Cobbett, " offering them the alternative of torture or apostasy, this worthy daughter of Henry VIII. decreed the penalties of high treason against any priest who should celebrate the Holy Sacrifice within the limits of the kingdom. The executioners were too few for the number of victims, and my pen refuses to record all the atrocities which filled the world with horror. Having overturned the altars and set up the tables, she compelled her Catholic subjects to attend in the churches of the new worship, under enormous penalties. Thus were the sincere and conscientious Catholics in the kingdom incessantly harassed,

ruined by enormous fines, brought to the gallows, or compelled to flee from their native country " Such was the queen
upon whom Protestant writers have bestowed the title of
" great" and " good," and whom the Voltairian school would
exalt to the dignity of a heroine.

27 The year in which Pope Paul IV died at Rome witnessed the close of Henry's reign in France (A. D. 1559). Amid
the brilliant festivities by which the treaty of Cateau-Cambrésis was celebrated in Paris, the king wished to take part in a
" passage at arms." The Count of Montgommery, captain of
the guards, and the most skilful tilter of the court, in breaking
lances with the king, had the misfortune to wound him mortally
They broke their lances with dexterity, but Montgommery
having neglected to throw away the stock of his as soon as it
broke, it accidentally struck the king in the face, forced up the
visor of the helmet, and entered above the right eye so deeply
as to touch the brain. The king forbade that any thing should
be done to his innocent but unfortunate adversary, and died fifteen days after, leaving four sons, of whom three reigned during
the troubles of the Reformation. The throne immediately
passed to the Dauphin, Francis II., husband of Mary Stuart,
the unhappy queen, whose career, then so brilliant and promising, was soon to meet with such a tragic end.

28. The progress of Calvinism in France, under the zealous
care of Theodore Beza, was slow but sure, and was preparing
lamentable disasters for the kingdom. The first meetings of
the Calvinists were held secretly at Paris, in a house in the
Rue Saint Jacques (A. D. 1555–1557). It is a remarkable fact,
that, whether it come in the name of religion or under the mask
of philosophy, revolutionary anarchy, which threatens to grind
royal thrones and human greatness into dust, has always
sprung into being under the shadow of the throne; its most
zealous propagators have been the great lords most interested
in struggling against it. The first French soldier who gave the
example of apostasy was a descendant of St. Louis, a member
of the royal house of Bourbon; the Prince of Condé. A prize
so noble and so unexpected emboldened the sectaries. During

the spring of the year 1558, the Calvinists or *Huguenots*, as
they were called, began to hold regular evening meetings in
the Pré-aux-Clercs in Paris, often to the number of five or six
thousand, singing the psalms of Marot, which they had adopted
in their meetings for public worship.   Antoine de Bourbon,
king of Navarre, to please his wife, Jeanne d'Albret, a zealous
Protestant, was often present at these assemblies.   Francis of
Châtillon, called Dandelot, a brother of Admiral Coligny, had
also joined the new sect, and encouraged the preachers in his
territory   On the 14th of June, 1559, the Parliament assembled
to take measures against the invasion of Calvinism.   The president, Minard, and the first president Lemaître, were in favor of
the rigorous application of the laws made by Philip Augustus
against innovators.   Several counsellors, on the other hand,
undertook to defend the heretics, and gave way to recriminations
and abuse against the court of Rome.   The most violent of these
declaimers was an apostate priest named Anne Dubourg.   He
was arrested as he left the hall; the Bishop of Paris declared
him a heretic, deposed him from the priesthood, and gave him
over to the secular arm.   Dubourg appealed to the Archbishop
of Sens, who was the metropolitan of Paris.   The death of
Henry II., which occurred in the interval, did not interrupt
the trial; it was continued by order of Francis II., who was
guided by his uncles, the princes of Lorraine.   Seeing President
Minard among his judges, Dubourg said to him, in a threatening tone : "You shall not long be my judge."   The Reformers
took care to insure the fulfilment of this prophecy ; Minard was
assassinated on the same evening, as he was entering his abode.
It was afterward discovered that Lemaître and Marshal Saint-
André, both strong opponents of the new doctrines, would have
met the same fate had they been at the palace: Three days
later, the apostate priest, Dubourg, was condemned, hanged,
and burnt (1559).   The Calvinists, secretly encouraged by
Elizabeth of England, turned their thoughts to the organization
of an open revolt.   The wars of *religion*, as they have been
styled, were now, for half a century, to cover France with terror, bloodshed and ruins.

CHAPTER V.

Carlos, son of Philip II. of Spain.—22. Battle of Lepanto.—23. St. Pius V publishes the catechism of the Council of Trent, the Roman breviary and missal. Palestrina.—24. Socinianism.—25. Heresy of Baius.—26. Death of St. Pius V Saints and scholars of his epoch. St. Theresa. Carmelitc Reform.

§ I. PONTIFICATE OF PIUS IV (December 26, A. D. 1559—December 9, 1565).

1. While Cardinal Giovan-Angelo Medici was taking possession of the chair of St. Peter, under the title of Pius IV., the Lutheran and Calvinist heresies were committing fearful ravages in Europe. England, under the rule of the daughter of Henry VIII. and Anne Boleyn, was wading through torrents of blood in the way of schism. In Scotland, the fierce zealot, Knox, was setting up the most intolerant Calvinism, throwing both Church and State into utter disorder. This sect was also making progress in the Netherlands, under favor of the popular hatred of the Spanish rule. Philip II. appreciated the political importance of opposing the advance of these doctrinal novelties. At his request, Paul IV had erected three new metropolitan sees : Utrecht, Mechlin and Cambrai, beside several bishoprics. The German Protestants, availing themselves of the liberty granted them by the treaty of Passau, began the publication of a new ecclesiastical history, known as that of the *Centuriators of Magdeburg*, under' the direction of Flaccus Illyricus. The first volumes appeared in 1559. An uncompromising hatred of Catholicity and a constant aim to connect the heresies of every time and country with the predominant ideas of Luther's novelties, thus to form a kind of tradition of error through the course of ages, is the characteristic feature of this collection, which has served as the groundwork and model of all attempts of the same kind since made, whether singly or collectively, by the writers of the so-called Reformation. The Waldenses, aroused by the tumult of religious insurrection, began to move in the valleys of Piedmont and Savoy Just as the Lutheran branch had absorbed the scattered

remains of the Hussites in Germany, so the remaining Walden-ses, dwelling among the mountains, naturally fell into the ranks of the Calvinists. Their number amounted to about three or four thousand in Provence, Merindol, Cabrières, and the neigh-boring country. They caused great troubles, and brought upon themselves some very severe treatment from the royal forces (A. D. 1545–1559).*

2. The court of Francis II. was divided between three fac-tions, headed by the three principal families of France—the houses of Bourbon, Montmorency and Lorraine. At the head of the Bourbons was Antoine, king of Navarre and duke of Vendôme, the husband of Jeanne d'Albret, by whom he had Henry IV. Of a weak and vacillating disposition, he long hesitated between the faith of his fathers, the faith of St. Louis and Charlemagne, the old religion of France, and the novelties of an apostate German monk. But yielding at length to the influence of his wife, who had already been misled by the new errors, he gave his name, without ever really giving his heart, to the cause of the Reformation. The Prince of Condé, Louis de Bourbon, declared his sentiments more openly, and thus be-came the leader of the Lutherans and Calvinists in the kingdom. The house of Lorraine, divided into two branches, the Lorraines and the Guises, was represented by three heroes—Charles III., duke of Lorraine, whose descendants still sit upon the thrones of Austria, Hungary and Bohemia; Francis of Lorraine, duke of Guise, the hero of Calais and Thionville, and the savior of France; and the great Cardinal of Lorraine, the all-powerful minister of Francis II. They had pledged themselves, at any price, to maintain the Catholic faith in France. In this determi-nation they were supported by the clergy, the parliament, and the mass of the people, with all the energy of devoted attach-ment to the faith. The third party, which hoped to restore peace between the other two, and, by this reconciliation, to spare the bloodshed which must otherwise ensue, was that of Montmorency. It was called the party of the "Politics," or

* M. BLANC, t. II., p. 300.

the " Mixed Party " The Montmorencies, the " First Christian
Barons," are one of the glories of France and of the Church,
by their hereditary fidelity to God and to their country   Their
origin is, on respectable authority, referred to the foundation of
the French monarchy * The claim of antiquity would give but
little glory to the house of Montmorency, had not its members,
from the earliest days of our history, given it additional lustre
by an uninterrupted discharge of the highest offices of State, by
a display of splendid talents, heroic virtue, and the most valuable services to the monarchy and to the nation.   This illustrious house has given to France six constables and eleven marshals.   Henry IV used to say that " if the house of Bourbon
ever became extinct in France, none was more worthy to take
its place than that of Montmorency " Anne de Montmorency,
constable of France, under Francis I., Henry II., Francis II.,
and Charles IX., joined an exemplary piety to fearless valor.
He was a great captain, a great diplomatist, a great minister—
but what is more, a true Christian.   He never omitted to perform his devotions, even when leading the armies of the king,
and if the provost happened to come to him while thus engaged,
to report some case of disorder, he only interrupted his prayer
to order a severe punishment, and then resumed his Pater or
Credo with the greatest composure ; this gave rise, among his
soldiers, to the expression, " God save us from the constable's
Pater-nosters." From his early youth, Anne de Montmorency
gloried in the surname of " Christian Cato," which had been bestowed upon him in the brilliant court of Francis I.   His presence had more effect there than that of the king himself, and
vice was silent at his approach.   The " Politics," like all other
compromising parties, could hope for very little success amid
the general conflagration of minds ; and the constable, true to

---

* Some authors ascribe the foundation of the house of Montmorency to Liseius, one of
the most powerful among the Frankish nobles who received baptism with Clovis. Others
draw their descent from Lisbius or Lisbeius, who gave hospitality to St. Denis, was converted by the apostle to the Christian religion, and shared with him the glory of martyrdom.

the last, remained unshaken in his attachment to the royal cause.

3. The Calvinists were bitterly incensed at the punishment of Dubourg, nor was their irritation appeased by the active watchfulness of the Cardinal of Lorraine; but they deemed themselves skilful enough to set it at fault. A conspiracy was formed by Admiral Coligny and Dandelot to murder the Guises and seize the person of the youthful monarch, then at Amboise. The apparent leader of the conspiracy was Bari de la Renaudie, a gentleman of Périgord, bold and intelligent; but the plot could not be kept so secret as not to reach the ears of the Regent, Catherine de Medici, and of the princes of Lorraine, who composed her council. By a stroke of skilful policy, they obtained the publication of an edict giving to every subject the liberty of coming in person to lay his complaints before the king. The conspirators either did not see the plan, or thought themselves strong enough to turn it against its authors. They came, armed and in strong force, to the neighborhood of Amboise, where the court was then held. La Renaudie was slain in a wood, near the castle; nearly all his companions were surprised, killed in the action, or executed. Such was the end of the conspiracy of Amboise, in which the Reformation measured weapons, for the first time, with the royal authority (A. D. 1560). The Prince of Condé was deeply implicated by the confession of La Renaudie's secretary; he was accordingly summoned to appear before the court. Upon his denial of all connection with the conspiracy, the king pardoned him. The Cardinal of Lorraine pursued the sectaries with the greatest energy, and even thought of establishing against them a royal tribunal of inquisition similar to that of Spain, when his plans were changed by the appearance, in the political arena, of one of those virtuous but short-sighted men who, in seasons of revolutionary agitation, wish to do good without cutting away the roots of the evil, and waste all their energies in struggling against effects, without ever attacking the cause. This was the chancellor, Michel de l'Hôpitai. In the generous delusion of his patriotism, he

thought that the influence of the parliaments would alone suffice to check the disorders which were hurrying on his country
to destruction. He would have resumed, for the salvation of
his country, monarchical institutions at the point where Louis
XII. had left them, and have carried out a social progress, of
which all the elements and conditions no longer existed.
L'Hôpital was the sport of the revolutionists of his day, who
made use of his virtue only to increase the disorders he had
hoped to check ; so true it is that, in seasons of social disor-
ganization, evil profits even by the good intentions of honest
men, as, in periods of amelioration, good is often accomplished
even by means of the vices of the wicked. L'Hôpital opposed
all his influence to the establishment of the Inquisition, and,
with this object in view, obtained the publication of the edict
of Romorantin (May, 1560), which transferred the cognizance
of heresies from the parliament to the bishops. To put an end
to religious dissensions, he imagined a kind of assembly of the
notables in which the Huguenot leaders should explain their
doctrine before the Catholic doctors. This conference ended
only in a challenge to civil war. Admiral Coligny, declaring
himself the leader of the new sect, presented a petition in the
name of the Protestants, promising that it would soon be signed
by ten thousand persons. "And I," exclaimed the Duke of
Guise, "shall present one of an opposite nature, which a
hundred thousand men, who own me as their chief, will sign with
their blood to-morrow." Shortly after, the Prince of Condé,
whose religious fanaticism knew no bounds, was arrested, tried
by the royal commissioners, and condemned to death. "The
head of heresy and rebellion," said the Duke of Guise, "must
be struck off at one blow." (December 10th, 1560.) The scaffold of the prince was to be erected in front of their place of
meeting, as a terrible warning to the Huguenots. The death
of Francis II. saved Condé.

Charles IX., a boy of eleven years, succeeded to the crown
and to the difficult task of governing France amid so many
storms.

4. Pius IV., who had now held the Papal throne for a year, determined to carry on the work of reform, begun by his predecessor. These two Pontiffs differed in every point, in character, habits and education. Paul IV belonged to a noble house of Naples, and had been brought up in a spirit of hatred for Austria, which his energetic character had afterward more fully developed. Pius IV was born an Austrian subject, and he was bound by ties of affection to the Austrian rule. Paul IV. was energetic, resolute and enterprising; Pius IV was of a mild, simple and kind disposition. Notwithstanding this difference of character, Pius IV. adopted the line of conduct marked out by Paul IV It is no rare thing in the history of the Popes, to find examples of intelligent succession, in which one Sovereign Pontiff continues the work of another, by applying different or opposite qualities to the same end. Pius IV was helped in the government of the Church by his nephew, St. Charles Borromeo, the model of bishops and the restorer of ecclesiastical discipline. St. Charles was born in 1538, in the castle of Arona, on Lake Maggiore, of the noble family of the counts of Borromeo; he was early remarkable for his fervent piety and a wisdom beyond his years. On entering the ecclesiastical career, he was presented with several rich benefices; but he respectfully represented to his father that what remained of his revenues, after deducting the amount necessary for his education and the service of the Church, belonged to the poor, and that any other use of them would be unlawful. The count wept with joy at this display of virtue in his youthful son. Charles had just finished his studies in canon law, at Milan, when he received tidings of the election of his uncle, Cardinal de Medici, to the Papal throne, and an order to repair at once to Rome. He was immediately made a cardinal and archbishop of Milan, though but twenty-three years old, and in spite of all his earnest endeavors to avoid these dignities; but the Pope wished to honor his virtue, and to avail himself of his great zeal and talents in the government of the Church. Cardinal Borromeo gave his unvarying attention to public

affairs, managing them with rare penetration, discussing them with the greatest wisdom, and always facilitating the decision of whatever was brought before him. The honors which had sought him out, at an age when most other men still have need of guidance, by a happy privilege were, if we may so speak, below his merit, and Rome, which had loudly condemned the nepotism of Paul IV., applauded the elevation of the present Pontiff's nephew. The glory of God was the chief end which Charles kept in view, in every action and undertaking. His impartiality and disinterestedness were truly admirable. His judgments were never biased by any considerations, however powerful; in the exalted dignities which his modesty would gladly have avoided, he consoled himself with the thought that they placed him in a position to labor for the good of the Church.

5. His first care was to enter, by order of Pius IV., into negotiations for the re-opening of the Council of Trent, interrupted since the Pontificate of Julius III. The bull of indiction was published on the 29th of November, A. D. 1560. "Immediately upon being called to the government of the Church," said the Pope, "We were sensible that the only means of successfully opposing the spread of schism, heresy and moral corruption, was to resume the ecumenical council already convoked by Paul III., and by Julius III., his successor of happy memory The Lord having at length vouchsafed to grant peace and unity among Christian kings and princes, it seemed to Us that nothing now stands in the way of its celebration." Apostolic nuncios were sent to bear the bull to all the European courts. The patriarchs of the East, of Ethiopia, and of Russia, were summoned. The cardinals of Mantua, Hercules Gonzaga and James Puteo, to whom the Pope soon joined Seripando, general of the Augustinians and archbishop of Salerno; Osio (Hosius), bishop of Culm; Simonetta, bishop of Pesaro, and Mark Altemps, bishop of Constance, were appointed legates to the council. In thus choosing them from among the different nations of Europe, Pius hoped to secure their greater unanimity,

and to give to their deliberations a character of universality more striking in the eyes of the world.

On the 18th of January, A. D. 1562, the seventeenth session was held, which re-opened the Council of Trent; there were present one hundred and twelve prelates. On the 26th of February, the Fathers met in the eighteenth session, to arrange the order of matters to be examined. Still the political troubles which had so long delayed the progress of the great assembly were now renewed with greater intensity, as the council seemed to draw near to its close. The pretensions of princes, questions of precedence between the ambassadors of the different courts, the claims put forward by the Protestants, the various aims of Catholic princes who wished to secure the ascendency of their own views, interests, and personal ambition, were the obstacles to be overcome. The nineteenth and twentieth sessions were spent in settling these difficulties. At length, on the 16th of July, the twenty-first session resumed the series of dogmatic and disciplinary canons, promulgated by the council. The grave question of communion, under both kinds, so loudly claimed by the Lutheran and Calvinist Reformers, was decided. " If any one saith," decrees the council, " that each and every one of the faithful of Christ is obliged, by divine precept or by necessity of salvation,* to receive the most holy sacrament of the Eucharist under both species; let him be anathema.—If any one saith, that the Holy Catholic Church was not induced by just causes and reasons to communicate, under the species of bread only, laymen, and also clerics when not consecrating; let him be anathema.—If any one saith, that the communion of the Eucharist is necessary for little children before they have reached the age of discretion; let him be anathema.— As to the two questions before proposed, but not yet discussed, viz.: whether the reasons by which the Holy Catholic Church was led to give communion, under the one species of bread only, to laymen, and also to priests when not consecrating, are so to

---

* *Necessitate salutis;* as necessary for salvation.

be observed, that on no account is the use of the chalice to be allowed to any one soever; and whether, in case that, for just reasons, founded on Christian charity, it were judged proper to grant the use of the chalice to any nation or kingdom, this concession should be made under certain conditions; and what those conditions should be, this same holy synod reserves them to another time—the earliest opportunity that shall present itself—to be examined and defined." The council afterward referred the decision, on this point, to the Sovereign Pontiff, to be regulated by him according to circumstances and conjunctures. The decree on Reform comprised nine chapters.—Bishops shall both confer orders, and give dimissorial letters and testimonials gratis.—No cleric shall be promoted to holy orders, unless he holds some ecclesiastical benefice or patrimony, sufficient for his honest livelihood.—Daily distributions are to be made among the canons who are present at the divine service.—Bishops are empowered to establish new parishes, and to make unions of several benefices, according to the spiritual wants of their respective dioceses.—Bishops are to visit all the churches of their diocese, even those which have before enjoyed the privilege of exemption.—In all cases of reform, if met by claims of exemption or other privileges, they may act as delegates of the Holy See.

6. In the interval between the twenty-first and twenty-second sessions, the Fathers of Trent received an oath of adherence to their decrees, from Abdisu, Catholic patriarch of Eastern Assyria, who had come to Rome to obtain the confirmation of his title by the vicar of Jesus Christ. Thus, while the provinces of Europe, invaded by Protestantism, were struggling with sacrilegious efforts to break away from Catholic unity, and rush into the blood-stained path of interminable anarchy, the scattered remnants of the ancient churches of Mesopotamia and Chaldea, mournfully seated upon the banks of the Euphrates and the Tigris, amid the forgotten ruins of Babylon and Nineveh, sent their patriarch to the Eternal City, to bind them closer to the centre of Catholic unity and to draw

from its breast new life and spiritual strength. In the meantime, Pius IV had erected new bishoprics in America and the Indies, to receive the new nations that were thronging into the doors of the Church. Japan opened its eyes to the light of faith, and China was looking out for the companions of St. Francis Xavier.

7 On the 17th of September, A. D. 1562, the twenty-second session was opened, with six cardinals, three patriarchs, one hundred and forty-two bishops, and seven generals of orders. Nine canons were promulgated on the holy Sacrifice of the Mass : " If any one saith, that in the Mass a true and proper sacrifice is not offered to God; let him be anathema.—If any one saith, that by these words, *Do this for a commemoration of me* (Luke, xxii. 19), Christ did not institute the Apostles priests, or did not ordain that they and other priests should offer His own body and blood; let him be anathema.—If any one saith, that it is an imposture to celebrate Masses in honor of the saints, and for obtaining their intercession with God, as the Church intends ; let him be anathema.—If any one saith, that the ceremonies, vestments, and outward signs, which the Catholic Church makes use of in the celebration of Masses, are incentives to impiety rather than to devotion; let him be anathema.—If any one saith, that Masses, in which the priest alone communicates sacramentally, are unlawful, and therefore to be abrogated ; let him be anathema.—If any one saith, that the rite of the Roman Church, according to which a part of the canon and the words of consecration are pronounced in a low tone, is to be condemned ; or that the Mass ought to be celebrated in the vulgar tongue only ; or that water ought not to be mixed with the wine that is to be offered in the chalice, on the ground that it is contrary to the institution of Christ; let him be anathema." Each one of these canons, it will be seen, meets some of the errors which Protestantism was laboring to popularize in Germany The decree of reformation regarding the morals of the clergy comprised eleven chapters.—Bishops are admonished to watch over the life, propriety of conduct.

and learning of clerics.—The council lays down the qualifications necessary for those priests who are to be promoted to the cure of cathedral churches.—Dispensations expedited out of the Roman court must be committed to the bishop to whom it belongs to make them public.—Bishops are appointed the executors of all pious bequests, and visitors to all manner of hospitals not under the immediate protection of kings.—Administrators of church property, of what kind soever, shall give in their accounts to the ordinary, unless it be otherwise specified in the deed of foundation. In fine, severe penalties were decreed against the spoilers of churches and the usurpers of ecclesiastical property or revenues.

8. The expected arrival of the Cardinal of Lorraine, as the ambassador of Charles IX., induced the Fathers to delay the next session until his appearance at Trent. The council had reached a period of crisis. The question of the sacrament of Holy Orders gave rise to a discussion on the institution of bishops; it was to be determined whether the institution is divine, or whether bishops hold their mission mediately from the Pope. No preceding article had ever excited more lively discussions, or more animated expressions of opinion. " So violent was the storm," says Pallavicini, " that the hopes hitherto entertained of peace in the Church were changed into despair." It needed all the tact and the virtue of St. Charles Borromeo, his patience, his united gentleness and firmness, his ascendant over the mind of the Pope, his uncle, and his winning influence exerted upon the legates and the Fathers of the council, to restore the opposite parties to harmony The discussion was for a moment interrupted by the arrival of the Cardinal of Lorraine, who was received with extraordinary honors. He was met by all the Fathers, and, in a general congregation, delivered an eloquent, spirited, and profound discourse on the duties of the council and the hopes which its convocation had awakened in the heart of Catholic Europe. The deliberations on the institution of bishops were then resumed. All agreed that the power of Order is given to them immediately

from Jesus Christ; but opinions were divided upon the origin of their jurisdiction. By some it was referred immediately to Christ; while others maintained that it is communicated to them only mediately, through the Sovereign Pontiff. The Cardinal of Lorraine succeeded in silencing these purely speculative debates, which but indirectly concerned the practical question at stake. " The heretics," said he, " profit by your intestine dissensions to extend their ravages. They maintain that the prelates instituted by the Pope are not true and lawful bishops; this is what must be directly condemned, instead of raising idle and endless discussions." This was the wisest course, and it was finally adopted. The death of the Cardinal of Mantua, closely followed by that of Cardinal Seripando, both legates and presidents of the council, caused another delay in the proceedings. Pius IV immediately appointed Cardinals Morone and Navagero in their stead. The new legates were as remarkable for their prudence and thorough knowledge of men, as for devotion to the interests of the Holy See, and they fully justified the confidence placed in them by the Holy Father. They brought to a happy conclusion the dispute which had arisen between the ambassadors of France and Spain, concerning the precedence of their respective sovereigns, and were enabled at length to hold the twenty-third session.

9. The long-delayed session was celebrated on the 15th of July, A. D. 1563. The council promulgated the decree on the sacrament of Holy Orders, which had given occasion to so much discussion: "Whereas the ministry of the priesthood is a thing altogether divine," says the council, " to the end that it might be exercised in a more worthy manner, and with greater veneration, it was suitable that there should be several orders of ministers attached to the service of the altar; so that those already marked with the clerical tonsure should then ascend through the minor to the higher orders. For the sacred text makes open mention not only of priests, but also of deacons, and lays great stress upon the manner of their ordination. And from the very beginning of the Church, the names of the fol

lowing orders, and the ministry proper to each one of them. are known to have been in use; viz.: those of subdeacon, acolyth, exorcist, lector, and porter; though these were not of equal rank; for the subdeaconship is classed among the higher orders by the Fathers and sacred councils, wherein also we very often read of the other inferior orders. If any one saith, that there is not in the New Testament a visible and external priesthood; or that there is not any power of consecrating and offering the true body and blood of the Lord, and of forgiving and retaining sins; but only a commission and bare ministry of preaching the gospel; or that those who do not preach are not priests at all; let him be anathema.—If any one saith, that, beside the priesthood, there are not in the Catholic Church other orders, both greater and minor, by which, as by certain steps, advance is made unto the priesthood;* let him be anathema.—If any one saith, that Holy Orders or sacred ordination are not truly and properly a sacrament instituted by Christ our Lord; or that it is a human invention; or that it is only a kind of rite for choosing ministers of the word of God and of the sacraments; let him be anathema.—If any one saith, that in the Catholic Church there is not a hierarchy by divine ordinance instituted, and consisting of bishops,. priests, and ministers; let him be anathema.—If any one saith, that bishops are not superior to priests; or that they have not the power of confirming and ordaining; or that the power which they possess is common to them and to priests; or that orders conferred by them, without the consent or intervention of the people or of the secular power, are invalid; or that those who have neither been rightly (*rite*) ordained, nor sent, by ecclesiastical and canonical power, but come from elsewhere, are lawful ministers of the word and of the sacraments; let him be anathema. —If any one saith that the bishops established by authority of the Roman Pontiff are not true and lawful bishops, but that their institution is a human invention; let him be anathema." Thus the holy Church of God, ever living, from St. Peter to

* Per quos, velut per gradus quosdam, in sacerdotium tendatur.

Pius IV., embracing within herself all ages, all generations, all promises, and all graces, now showed forth, at Trent, the divinity of her priesthood and hierarchy. The decree on reformation, promulgated with the canons, on the sacrament of Holy Orders, was designed, by regulating the conditions for admission into the priesthood, to preserve the ecclesiastical hierarchy in all its primitive purity and splendor. The most important chapter of the decree, the one which has been most serviceable to the Church, and which alone would have sufficed for the glory of the Council of Trent, is that which ordains the establishment of seminaries in every diocese; this institution was, even then, deemed so beneficial, that the prelates exclaimed from all sides, "that they would feel amply rewarded for all their labors even should they obtain no other fruit from the council." The Pope was the first to give the example by founding the Roman Seminary, which he placed in charge of the Jesuits. We give the leading features of this memorable chapter, which may be regarded as the living and practical summary of the holy Council of Trent, as the perpetual reformation of the Church by herself. "Youth," said the decree, "unless trained in religious principles, is prone to follow after the pleasures and dissipation of the world. Unless it be formed, from its tender years, unto piety and religion, before vicious habits have perverted the heart, it cannot constantly persevere in ecclesiastical discipline, without the special help of Almighty God. The holy synod therefore ordains, that all cathedral and metropolitan churches shall be bound, each according to its means and the extent of the diocese, to maintain, to educate religiously, and to train in ecclesiastical discipline, a certain number of youths of their city and diocese, or, if that number cannot be met with there, of that province, in a college, to be chosen by the bishop for this purpose, near the said churches or in some other suitable place. Into this college only those shall be received who are at least twelve years old, born in lawful wedlock, who can read and write passably, and whose character and inclination afford a hope that they will always serve in the ecclesiastical ministry The holy council wishes that the children of the poor be *principally* chosen ; without, however, excluding those of the more wealthy, provided they be maintained at their own expense, and manifest a desire of serving God and the Church. The bishop, having divided these youths into as many classes as he shall think fit, according to their number, age, and progress in ecclesiastical discipline, shall, when it seems to him expedient, assign some of them to the ministry of the churches, keeping the others in the college to be instructed ; always supplying the place of those who have been withdrawn, by others ; that so this college may be a perpetual *seminary* of ministers, for the service of God. That they may more easily be trained in ecclesiastical discipline, they shall, immediately on entering, receive the tonsure, and always wear the clerical dress ; they shall learn grammar, singing, ecclesiastical computation, and the other liberal arts ; they shall devote themselves to the study of sacred Scripture, ecclesiastical works, the homilies of the saints, the manner of administering the sacraments, especially those things which seem adapted to enable them to hear confessions ; in fine, they shall learn all the ceremonies and rites of the Church. The bishop shall take care that they be present every day at the sacrifice of the Mass ; that they confess their sins at least once a month ; that they receive the body of our Lord Jesus Christ, according to the judgment of their confessor, and that they serve on festivals in the cathedral or other churches of the place." This decree displays, throughout, the care, the tenderness, the motherly prudence with which the Church of God labors to form seminaries. Amid tears and sorrows, her heart thrills with joy This was, in fact, a new creation of the Spirit of God, a spiritual creation which renews the face of the earth, and in which the Church herself finds the youth of the eagle, and is always renewing her existence, ever ancient and ever new With time and experience, by combining the different degrees of seminaries or ecclesiastical schools, she will be enabled to organize each diocese into a Christian academy, a Catholic university, where all knowledge shall be made to glorify God; the natural sciences, by exciting admiration for the love and wisdom displayed in His works; literary studies, by enabling His ministers to announce His word with greater dignity, to sing His praises more harmoniously; the study of sacred literature, by giving a deeper insight into the hidden meaning of the Holy Text, and by smoothing the way for those who still wander far from the truth, to return to the fold of Christ; the science of theology, and the study of the doctors and Fathers, by enabling us to draw from the sacred founts the knowledge of our dogmas, the spirit of faith, of piety, of zeal, and understanding. Fifty years ago France saw all her seminaries buried beneath the ruins of the churches and of the throne; but soon again the same churches, rising to new life, at the call of St. Peter's successor, build up, according to the admirable design of the Council of Trent, not only greater seminaries to fit the youthful Levite immediately for the ministry, but also elementary seminaries, to prepare them remotely, by literary studies, for the same great end. What a noble work of regeneration, which gladdens Heaven and earth, sends apostles and martyrs to Tonquin, to China, to the farthest wilds of America, and to the isles of the ocean!

10. After the happy close of the twenty-third session, nothing now remained to delay the course of the council. On the 11th of November, A. D. 1563, the twenty-fourth session was opened, and the decrees and canons on the sacrament of Matrimony were promulgated. The canons were twelve in number: " If any one saith, that matrimony is not truly and properly one of the seven sacraments of the evangelic law, and instituted by Christ the Lord, but that it has been invented by men in the Church, and that it does not confer grace; let him be anathema.—If any one saith, that it is lawful for Christians to have several wives at the same time, and that this is not prohibited by any divine law; let him be anathema.—If any one saith, that those degrees only of consanguinity and affinity which are set down in Leviticus (ch. 18) can hinder

matrimony from being contracted, or dissolve it when contracted; and that the Church cannot dispense in some of these degrees, or establish others that may hinder and dissolve it; let
him be anathema.—If any one saith, that the Church could not
establish impediments dissolving marriage; or that she has
erred in establishing them; let him be anathema.—If any one
saith, that clerics constituted in Holy Orders, or regulars, who
have solemnly professed chastity, are able to contract marriage;
let him be anathema." The decrees on reformation, promulgated in the same session, forbid clandestine marriages; prescribe severe penalties against abduction and concubinage, and
renew the ancient prohibitions of solemn nuptials from Advent
until the Epiphany, and from Ash-Wednesday until the octave
of Easter inclusively The other disciplinary decrees read in
the twenty-fourth session relate to the manner of proceeding
in the choice of bishops and cardinals; to the celebration of
provincial synods every third year, and of diocesan synods
every year; to the power of the bishops for dispensing in cases
of irregularity and suspension; to the institution of a grand penitentiary in cathedral churches; to the qualities required in
those who are to be promoted to the dignities and canonries of
cathedral churches, and the obligations of those so promoted;
to the duty devolving upon the chapter during the vacancy of
a see; to the abrogation of expectatives, and other favors of
the same kind, &c.

11. The labors of the council were now drawing to a close.
Every attempt that was made to bring the Protestants to Trent
fell before their bad faith; even the authority of the Emperor
Ferdinand could not induce them to attend. Such is the wont-
ed course of sects and heresies. They always appeal from the
Pope to a general council, and, in the end, refuse to receive the
judgment of either. On the 3d of December, A. D. 1563, the
twenty-fifth and last session of the Council of Trent was opened,
with the attendance of the legates and two other cardinals, three
patriarchs, twenty-one archbishops, one hundred and sixty-eight
bishops, and seven generals of orders. The Bishop of Nazian

zum, then coadjutor of Famagusta, addressed the illustrious assembly : " The day of gladness has at length dawned upon the world," he exclaimed, " when the bark of the Church, freighted with the anxious hopes of humanity, comes forth from the long and furious storms by which it has been assailed, and rides secure within the port. Would to God that they, for whom we have dared the dangerous enterprise, had been willing to share it with us ! Would that they had toiled with us to re-build the temple of the Lord ! Greater still would then be our joy ; and yet we are not accountable for their absence. We have chosen this city on the borders of Germany, and thus on the very frontier of their country ; we have come with no armed guards, that they might feel no apprehension for their personal liberty; we have given them a safe-conduct, drawn up in the very terms dictated by themselves ; but they have remained deaf to our entreaties and our prayers. Now, at the happy close of the immense task imposed upon us, we should give eternal thanks to Almighty God, whose infinite goodness has enabled us to celebrate this joyful day, amid the universal assent and approbation of the Christian world. Endless thanks, too, to Pius IV., our sovereign and holy Pontiff, who has de-voted his time and his thoughts to the accomplishment of this great work. O admirable piety and prudence of our pastor and our Father ! O supreme happiness of the Pontiff, who sees this council, so long interrupted, now peacefully closed under his authority and his auspices ' I call you to witness, too, great Pontiffs Paul and Julius, whose loss we still weep ; how earnestly did you not long to see the event which we now behold with tears of joy ! And you, holy Fathers, who have now so well served the Church by your illustrious labors, what a halo of glory will surround your names, what honors will be heaped upon you by the Christian world ! You will be hailed by all as pastors and fathers ; all will be eager to intrust you with their life and their salvation. O glad and happy day, when our peo-ple shall once more behold us, when they shall once more em-brace their pastors and their fathers !" The decrees were then read which related to the doctrines of Purgatory, the worship of saints, the veneration of relics and holy images, religious orders, the observance of fast days, the catalogue of books, the Catechism, Breviary, and Missal, to which the council wished to give uniformity in all the churches throughout the world, the revision and arrangement of which was left to the care of the Sovereign Pontiff. When the decrees had been read and approved, the secretary addressed the assembled prelates: "Most illustrious lords, and most reverend Fathers, doth it please you, that, to the praise of Almighty God, this sacred ecumenical synod be ended, and that the confirmation of each and every thing which has herein been decreed and defined, as well under the Roman Pontiffs, Paul III. and Julius III., of happy memory, as also under our most holy lord Pius IV., be requested, in the name of this most holy synod, by the presidents and legates of the Apostolic See, from the most blessed Roman Pontiff?" They answered: "It pleaseth us." Then Cardinal Morone, the first legate and president, blessing the assembled prelates, pronounced the usual closing formula: "Most Reverend Fathers, go in peace." And all answered, "Amen." Tears flowed from every eye; the Fathers, amid mutual embraces, congratulated each other upon the successful close of their labors. The eighteenth ecumenical council, the last general assembly, held by the Catholic Church, up to the present day, was at an end. Never before had the body of dogmas and discipline been so connectedly treated. The new sectaries had assailed all—dogma, worship, canon law; the Council of Trent consolidated every thing upon the immovable bases of sacred Scripture and tradition. The true faith shone forth in all its splendor, freed from the clouds of Protestant error. Catholic unity, the divine hierarchy of the Church were once more exposed to the sight and to the veneration of the world. The reformation, in the name of which the Lutherans had armed thousands of their followers, was peacefully accomplished "The reforms decreed by the Council of Trent," says Ranke, "are of the highest importance. The faithful were again sub jected to severe discipline. Seminaries were founded, in which the young clergy were carefully educated in austere habits, and in the fear of God. The parishes were regulated anew, strict rules laid down for the administration of the Sacraments and for preaching, and the coöperation of the regular clergy governed by fixed laws. The duties of their office, especially the supervision of the clergy, were strongly impressed upon the bishops. They also solemnly bound themselves by a peculiar profession of faith (which they subscribed, and to which they swore), to observe the decrees of the Council of Trent, and to render entire obedience to the Pope, a measure, the consequences of which were most important." But the Catholic princes did not second the reformatory movement in the Church, as they might justly have been expected to do. They ordered that all the dogmatic decisions should be received in their States without restriction. But the decrees on discipline met with difficulties, in some points, in Germany and France. The parliaments refused to register them. To meet badly-disposed governments, the bishops caused the decrees to be received in the particular councils which assembled from every direction. But the refusal of the judicial courts to register them remained as a weapon in the hands of Gallicanism. Pius IV at once approved all the acts of the Council of Trent, and appointed a standing commission of eight cardinals to interpret its decrees and watch over their observance. On the 25th of March, 1564, he published a special bull, confirming the *Index*, or catalogue of books condemned by the council.

12. "Had the so-called Reformers," says M. Blanc, "really desired peace and the good of the Church, they would have received ample satisfaction in the Council of Trent; but, under the specious pretext of reviving the Apostolic Age in its primitive purity, they would change every thing, and raise themselves on the ruins of the Roman Church. Intoxicated by unhoped for success they oppose but insults to the decrees of that immortal assembly; and men who could not agree among themselves, even upon the most important points, set up the

absurd claim to a more thorough knowledge of the true doctrine and a better appreciation of the most expedient laws of discipline, than was possessed by that immense number of bishops, gathered together from all parts of Christendom, and more venerable even by their virtue and learning than by age and experience." The French Calvinists had been in motion during the whole time of the Council of Trent. As intolerant as they were bold, they wished to root out what they called idolatry; and they began to overturn the altars, to burn castles, and demolish churches. In 1561, they had summoned Charles IX. and the regent, Catherine de Medici, to tear down the images of Jesus Christ and the saints. Catherine, whose favorite maxim was, "Divide and govern," and who equally dreaded both parties—the Guises, or the Catholic party, because of their influence in the government; the Huguenots, on account of their violence—placed herself between them with the professed intention of preserving the balance of power, but with the real design of destroying them by means of each other. This policy, which she thought very deep, only increased the strength of both factions, aroused a civil war and destroyed the royal authority   The states-general, which the Chancellor l'Hôpital looked upon as the only means of quieting the troubles, met at Orleans (A. D. 1561), under very unfavorable auspices. It was in vain that the too credulous chancellor, in his opening address, exhorted the members to lay aside all personal considerations, and to look only to the common good; his words were unheeded: what else could have been expected from men who came prepared to cut each other's throats? When the deputies separated, they had come to an agreement upon not one of the contested points. Francis, duke of Guise, the Constable Anne de Montmorency, and the Marshal of St. André, James d'Albon, formed an association called the *Triumvirate*, with the design of maintaining the Catholic faith in the kingdom (1561). Philip II., king of Spain, the declared enemy of the Protestants, wished to be at the head of the league. While these events were taking place, a royal edict was promulgated

(July, 1561), by Catherine, in the name of the young king. The concessions made to the Calvinists displeased the Catholics. The court, led by the advice of l'Hôpital, thought that the troubles might be quieted by conferences between the doctors of the two religions. They were opened in the month of August, 1561, and are known as the " Colloquy of Poissy " Six cardinals and forty bishops appeared on the Catholic side ; the Calvinists were represented by thirteen Reformed ministers, led by the celebrated Theodore Beza, the first disciple and the coadjutor of Calvin. The Cardinal of Lorraine, but especially Father Laynez, the general of the Jesuits, whose clearness, precision, and depth of thought and language had won a paramount authority at Trent, confounded the partisans of error. So complete was the triumph, and so striking the eloquence of Laynez, that the parliament now readily confirmed the establishment of the Jesuits in Paris. Even the King of Navarre, seeing the want of sincerity displayed by the Calvinist ministers, in the conferences, forsook their party, abjured the heresy, and joined the triumvirate.

13. The Reformers were not crushed by their defeat at Poissy Strong in the concessions which the crafty policy of the queen-mother held out to appease them, they only waited for an opportunity to act. On Sunday, the 1st of March, A. D. 1562, the Duke of Guise, passing through the little town of Vassy, in Champagne, stopped to hear Mass. The Huguenots,* who were at the same time holding their meeting in a barn near the church, began to sing psalms at the moment when the priest was ascending the altar. The duke sent one of his attendants to request that they would suspend their singing, as it distracted those who were present at the divine office ; but they refused to comply Some noblemen of the duke's suite having approached the meeting through curiosity, those who kept the door thought that they had come to insult them. From sharp

---

* The Calvinists received the appellation of Huguenots at about the time of the conspiracy of Amboise. The origin of the name is uncertain, though it is most probably derived from the German word *Eidgenossen, Confederates*.

words on both sides, they soon came to blows, and a general tumult followed. The duke, on hearing the noise, hastened from the church to restore order; while exerting himself in this attempt, he received a wound in the cheek. At the sight of his blood, his followers were exasperated beyond control; the duke strove in vain to check their fury; deaf to his cries, they rushed upon the Huguenots, killed about fifty and dispersed the remainder. This is what Protestant writers call the "Massacre of Vassy;" representing as an odious and deliberate assault an occurrence which was, in truth, purely accidental. The news of the event passed through the kingdom like an electric spark, everywhere enkindling the flame of civil war. "Cæsar has crossed the Rubicon!" exclaimed the Prince of Condé. The Calvinists flew to arms, took possession of the largest cities, Lyons, Rouen, Tours, and Orleans, everywhere committing horrible ravages and profanations. They stripped the churches, tore down the altars, seized and melted the sacred vessels; they destroyed the images and burned the relics of the saints. At Tours they did not spare even the body of St. Martin, those august remains venerated by France and by the whole world. In many places the priests and religious were massacred. In Dauphiny, the famous Baron des Adrets, the Calvinist leader (1562), distinguished himself by deeds of unparalleled ferocity. Two-thirds of France were desolated by these scenes of blood. In this first civil strife, Antoine de Bourbon, king of Navarre, whose return to the Catholic cause we have already mentioned, died of a wound received at the siege of Rouen (1562).* Condé, at the head of a body of German Lutherans, was marching upon Paris, with the intention of taking it by surprise at Dreux, he met the Catholic army under the Constable Montmorency and the Duke of Guise (December 19, 1562). The Catholics remained masters of the field. The Protestants disgraced themselves by the murder of Marshal Saint André, who had fallen into their hands, while the victorious Duke of Guise shared his table and his bed with his prisoner

* M. BLANC, t. II., pp. 305, 306

the Prince of Condé. The war was carried on by Coligny, who held Orleans, which he made the bulwark of Calvinism. The Duke of Guise, who had been appointed by Catherine lieutenant-general of the kingdom, determined to make a last effort to crush the rebels, and he accordingly hastened to invest the city defended by the admiral. He pressed the siege with his usual vigor, and was already in possession of a portion of the suburbs, when he was assassinated by a Calvinist gentleman, Jean Poltrot de Méré, and died while uttering a petition for the pardon of his murderer.* Thus fell Francis, duke of Guise (February 18, 1563), " whom his very enemies acknowledge to have been the greatest man of his age," says the celebrated historian De Thou. The forgiveness he had asked for Poltrot was not granted by the court. The assassin when examined, implicated Coligny The admiral undertook to defend himself; but the two apologies which he published have not cleared his memory from the infamous imputation. The death of Guise obliged the queen to treat with the rebels. The edict of Amboise (March 19, 1563) granted a general amnesty to the Calvinists, with freedom of conscience and the public exercise of their worship in one town of each bailiwick. Still hostilities were resumed in 1567 Coligny and Condé formed the project of seizing the king, who was then at Monceaux, in Brie. Catherine and Charles, receiving timely warning of the plot, retired first to Meaux, but on the following day they set out before daylight for the capital, with an escort of Swiss infantry These troops, under the command of Montmorency, presented so resolute an appearance that Condé feared to attack them openly, and satisfied himself with harassing them during the

* The life of the duke had already been attempted by a Calvinist at the siege of Rouen. The man was seized and brought before the duke, who asked him if he had ever unwittingly given him any ground for his hatred and this attempt upon his life. The culprit acknowledged that he had in this deed consulted only the interests of his religion. "Well," said the prince, "if your religion requires you to murder a man who, on your own admission, has never done you any harm, mine commands me to pardon you; judge for yourself which is the better of the two." And he immediately ordered his intended murderer to be released.

long and tedious march.   The young king, then but seventeen years old, remained sixteen consecutive hours in the saddle, without tasting food.   Equally careless of hunger and fatigue, he cheered on his escort.   " Courage, my friends," he exclaimed, " I would rather die with you, a king and free, than live a prisoner."   Nothing so much imbittered him against the Calvinists as this odious conspiracy against his person; and he never forgot it (Sept. 29, 1567).   The second civil war now began; the Reformers had taken their measures.   They obtained possession of Orleans, and their madness did not spare the cathedral, which had been respected in the first troubles. Negotiations were opened, but they were fruitless, and on the 25th of the following October the royal army engaged the rebels, who had posted themselves in the plain of St. Denis, as if to beard the king in his own capital.   The Catholic arms were victorious, but the triumph cost the valued life of the constable, Montmorency   Though surrounded by the enemy, the hero refused to surrender.   Unhorsed and covered with wounds, he still cried to those who were flying to his assistance: " Follow the enemy; lose not your time with me; I will die upon the field of honor."   He received the honors of royal sepulture; and France mourned his loss as that of a savior and a father.   Catherine de Medici, taking advantage of the victory of St. Denis, succeeded in negotiating a peace with the rebels. The treaty was signed at Longjumeau, March 27, 1568; but the truce was necessarily short amid the general exasperation which animated all parties.   It was popularly known as the *lame* peace (la paix boiteuse), or the *unstable* peace (la paix mal .ssise), by a humorous allusion to the two plenipotentiaries of Charles IX., Gontaut de Biron, who was lame, and De Mesme, lord of Malassise.   Amid these troubles and disorders, the Pontificate of Pius IV closed in death (December 9, 1565). God had prepared a successor worthy to carry on his work.

§ II. PONTIFICATE OF ST. PIUS V (January 7, A. D. 1566—May 1, 1572).

14. The Papacy was about to be illustrated by a name forever glorious in the annals of the Church, a memory equally dear to the hearts of the Catholic faithful and formidable to the enemies of the faith. The Council of Trent had systemized the magnificent theory of the great religious reform. St. Pius V undertook to insure its application, in its widest bearing, to public morals. "The sixteenth century," says the Count de Falloux,* "was marked throughout by three very distinct lines of policy : the Protestant policy, convulsively struggling in the midst of intellectual and social disorder ; the State policy of rulers, which argues, combats, or bends, according to the necessity or the chance of the hour ; the opposition of the Church, invoking eternal and divine principles." St. Pius V was the representative of the Catholic opposition. He devoted his whole Pontificate to the glorious task. In France, he upheld, by his counsel, his authority and his treasure, the cause of the true faith against the errors of the heretics. In England, he openly stood forth in defence of Mary Stuart, the unhappy victim of Elizabeth's bloody vengeance. In the Netherlands, he seconded the measures of order and repression decreed by Philip II. against the *Gueux*. Finally, he crowned his career of external contest by a league against the Turks and the glorious victory of Lepanto. Within, he reformed the ecclesiastical administration; restored the unity of the liturgy; condemned the errors of Baïus ; stood like a wall of brass against moral corruption, and toiled with unwearied zeal to repress abuses, disorders and crimes. His reign was one long contest; the spirit of St. Gregory VII. and of Innocent III. breathes in his whole bearing and in his every act. He once more raised up the Sovereign Pontificate to the lofty height whence it controls nations and kings, and from which Protestantism sought to hurl it down.

* *Histoire de St. Pie V.*, 2 vols., 8vo. Angers, 1844. t. I., p. 248.

15. The influence of St. Charles Borromeo was paramount in the conclave which met to elect a successor to his uncle, Pius IV "I resolved," says the saint, "to look, in this election, only to religion and faith. And as I was acquainted with the piety, the irreproachable life, and the devout spirit of the Cardinal of Alessandria, Michael Ghislieri, I was convinced that the Church could not be better governed than by him." The voice of the Sacred College ratified the choice of the saint, and Cardinal Michael Ghislieri was elected Sovereign Pontiff. His election filled him with the deepest grief, and he remained buried in mournful silence while his colleagues came forward to offer their glad congratulations. When asked the cause of his melancholy, "Alas!" he replied, "in the Dominican convent, where I lived always with God, I hoped to save my soul; when made cardinal-bishop, I began to fear; but now, as Pope, I almost despair of salvation." All good Catholics applauded his election. "God has raised up to us another Paul IV!" they cried. But the Roman people, fearing the austere morality and well-known severity of the new Pontiff, openly showed their apprehensions. St. Pius was informed of their fears. "We trust in God," he replied, "and We hope so to reign that Our people may feel more pain at Our death than they now do at Our accession."

16. His first measures were animated by that zeal for discipline, of which he gave so many proofs in the course of his Pontificate. "He banished useless luxury; converted into alms the largesses which the Sovereign Pontiffs were accustomed to bestow at their accession; reformed the public morals; obliged bishops to residence; induced the cardinals to give the example of modesty and piety; forbade the single combats which were then displayed in public games; abolished the sale of indulgences; in a word, he everywhere gave force to the discipline and principles of the Council of Trent." He was a living example of the regularity which he urged upon others, and he observed the same strict discipline as when a simple religious. Fasts, prayers and ever-increasing occupations had

nothing in them that could terrify his austerity ; with indefatigable activity he attended in person to the execution of his orders. " After so many circumstances had concurred to excite and to foster a religious spirit," says Ranke, " after so many resolutions and measures had been taken to exalt it to universal dominion, a Pope like this was needed, not only to proclaim it to the world, but also to reduce it to practice ; his zeal and his example combined produced the most powerful effect."

17 The treaty of Longjumeau was violated almost as soon as it was signed. War broke out anew. All the edicts in favor of the Reformers were annulled, and the profession of the Catholic faith was a necessary qualification in every candidate for a public office. St. Pius V encouraged Catherine de Medici and the young king, Charles IX., to oppose a strong resistance to the progress of heresy in their States. He adopted severe measures to turn off the contagion from the Comtat-Venaissin, which still belonged to the Holy See ; and furnished subsidies to the King of France to help him in his war against the Calvinists, whose numbers had lately been considerably increased by the accession of a number of English and German adventurers Thus strengthened, they were led by the Prince of Condé against the Catholic forces, under Marshal Tavannes. The armies met at Jarnac, on the Charente (March 13, A. D. 1569). The Calvinists were defeated, and their leader paid with his life for all the bloodshed he had caused while fighting against his God and his king. His death, however, did not crush the rebellion. Jeanne d'Albret, the widow of the King of Navarre, hastened to Cognac with Henry of Béarn, her son, then sixteen years old, and the young son of Condé. " My friends," said she, addressing the soldiers, " here are two new leaders whom God has sent you, and two orphans whom I intrust to your care." Henry of Béarn, afterward Henry IV., was proclaimed, notwithstanding his youth, chief of the league, and Coligny commanded under him. The Calvinists soon found themselves strong enough for another attempt; the young king of Na-

varre, who was making his first campaign, signalized the opening of his career by the victory of La Roche-Abeille; Coligny
was less happy in the siege of Poitiers, gallantly defended by
the young duke of Guise, Henry-le-Balafré, son of Francis of
Lorraine, who gave promise of being a worthy successor to his
father, and whom this exploit raised to a seat in the royal
council. Coligny fell back upon Moncontour, where he was
attacked by the Catholic army The rout of the Calvinists
was complete, and their cause would have fallen there, had not
the victorious leaders been divided among themselves. Coligny
speedily repaired this new disaster, and, for a third time, an
accommodation was proposed. The treaty was signed at St.
Germain-en-Laye, August 15, 1570. The Calvinists obtained
four places of security—La Rochelle, Cognac, Montauban,
and La Charité. They were to enjoy freedom of worship in
two cities of each province; they were made capable of holding any public office and of aspiring to any dignity, civil, administrative, or military In a word, their religious existence
was officially recognized. The Pope deplored these concessions, which were inexplicable to him, since the royal arms had
lately been crowned with unvarying success. But the policy
of Catherine de Medici prevailed over the repeated counsels of
the Sovereign Pontiff.

18. The efforts of the Pope to save Mary Stuart from the
jealous hatred of Elizabeth, queen of England, were equally
fruitless. The misfortunes of the ill-fated widow of Francis II. had so much interested the Holy See, the Popes had
given so many proofs of their affectionate sympathy, and of their
earnest wish to soothe the bitter sufferings of the hapless Queen
of Scots, that it is necessary here to speak of her, as she was
known in Rome, where there was an earnest desire to obtain
daily accounts of a life of tears and resignation, of a heroic
captivity ending in martyrdom. Mary Stuart was the daughter
of James V., king of Scotland; she never saw her father, whose
death placed her upon the throne eight days after her birth.
The regency was intrusted to James Hamilton, earl of Arran.

The young queen was betrothed, in her fifteenth year, to Francis II., and soon after left her native mountains for "that so lovely land of France," to which the untimely death of her consort soon forced her to bid a last farewell. On her return to Scotland, she was incessantly harassed by the machinations and secret plots fomented by the gold of Elizabeth. Having married her cousin, Henry Darnley, she found but a traitor in the one who should have protected her; but he soon after perished, the victim of the ambition of Bothwell, who forced the queen to accept his hand. Mary, weary of this continued succession of plots and treason, unable longer to live in a kingdom where her throne was swimming in blood, determined to take refuge in England, and accordingly placed her life and liberty in the hands of her sister-queen, Elizabeth. She had hoped that this last mark of generous confidence would awake the better instincts of Elizabeth's heart. But England gave to the persecuted princess only the cold hospitality of a prison. On learning this gross violation of international law, Pius V published a solemn sentence of excommunication against Elizabeth. "Considering that that princess," said the Pontiff, "has, throughout all England, usurped the title and authority of supreme head of the Church; that she has abolished the ancient and true worship, restored by Mary, the lawful queen; that she has forbidden the prelates, the clergy, and the people, to acknowledge the Roman Church, to obey its laws and canonical sanction; that she has imprisoned the faithful bishops and clergy, and put many of them to death by tortures, that she still persists in her course of cruel violence, refusing to receive the Apostolic nuncios sent by us to England; We, therefore, declare that she has forfeited every claim to that kingdom, and we hereby absolve her nobles, subjects and people from their allegiance." The Pope made no mention, in this document, of the disgraceful treatment of Mary Stuart, lest his words should only aggravate, instead of lessening, the sufferings of the captive queen The bull was a signal for fresh persecutions in England; the captivity of Mary Stuart became still more rigorous

Still her false cousin dared not yet perpetrate the regicide; she doubtless feared the indignation of Europe, and did not yet feel powerful enough to set it at defiance.

19. The monarch who showed the greatest zeal for the maintenance of the Catholic faith in Europe was Philip II. The Netherlands, which he had received by the will of his father, Charles V., were, by their geographical situation and their neighborhood to Germany and France, naturally exposed to the twofold contagion of Lutheranism and Calvinism. Philip had intrusted the government of these States to his sister Margaret, duchess of Parma, to whom he assigned the cele brated Cardinal Granville, bishop of Arras, as prime minister The cardinal, who was a man of untiring industry, deeply versed in business, allowed no obstacle to stand in the way of his designs. Beside, enough had been preserved of the former ad ministration, to satisfy the national pride without compromising the public peace; each province still keeping its own stadt-holder. Notwithstanding these concessions, the Calvinists, who had many partisans among the people, soon spread abroad the spirit of discord. The revolt was brooding in silence and se-crecy, when the council of regency was called upon to decide whether the acts of the Council of Trent should be promulgated in the Netherlands. Granville used all his influence to secure an affirmative decision. The Calvinists seized the occasion to display their hatred against him. William, prince of Orange, stadtholder of Holland, Zealand, and Utrecht; the Count of Eg-mont, stadtholder of Flanders and Artois; and the Count of Horn, high-admiral of the United Provinces, formed a league against the cardinal. The Protestants, at the same time, pub-lished a confession of faith, preceded by a letter, in which they represented to the king, that, as faithful subjects, they had *hitherto paid the taxes.* This was indirectly threatening the king. Meanwhile, they had begun to make open demonstra-tions against the regent. Margaret was alarmed, and requested Philip to withdraw Granville; the king refused, and the con-federates retired from the council of state, until the urgent

representations of Margaret had obtained the recall of the minister (A D. 1564). The power of the triumvirs was greatly increased by this concession. Still the majority of the council voted in favor of adopting the decrees of Trent; and Philip, to whom the votes had been sent, ordered that the penalties decreed against heretics should be carried out in all their rigor. The royal ordinance gave a new pretext to the malcontents, whom William of Orange directed with an uncommon degree of dissimulation. He was cold, reserved, timid in appearance, and spoke but little, to which habit he owed his surname of " the Silent." He was a son-in-law of Coligny, and, like him, closely bound to the cause of the Huguenots. On the 16th of February, 1565, a dozen noblemen, under his influence, signed the compact or " compromise of Breda," demanding a redress of grievances. Within a few months the league numbered four hundred gentlemen, who placed themselves and their arms at his service. The triumvirs, who were the real movers of the compact, did not sign it, as if wishing to observe a kind of neutrality The meetings held by the faction aroused the whole of the Netherlands. About the month of April, two hundred and fifty gentlemen came to Brussels, to present a petition to Margaret. The regent wrote to Philip, acquainting him with the demands of the confederates, in the mean time suspending the edicts of which they complained. It is said that one of the lords of Margaret's court, in speaking of the petitioners, applied to them the epithet of " Gueux " or " beggars." The revolters immediately seized upon it, and the word became a party appellation which they were proud to bear. Their badge was a gold medal, bearing on one side the effigy of Philip, and on the reverse, two hands holding a wallet, with the legend, "Faithful to the king, even to carrying the wallet;"—*Fidèles au roi, jusqu'à la besace.* The Calvinists began to rise in all directions; they plundered and profaned more than four hundred churches in the provinces of Brabant and Flanders alone; their error was everywhere established by force of arms (August, 1566). Margaret also raised forces, recaptured Valenciennes and Cambrai, subjected the turbulent people of Antwerp, and restored the royal authority, with the Catholic religion, in all the revolted provinces The rebels found their only safety in flight. William would have dragged along with him the Count of Egmont, who, fearful of losing his property, had made his peace with the court. The two friends persisted each in his own determination. "Adieu, landless prince," said the count to William; "Adieu, headless count," replied the prince; and, with this exchange of ill-boding titles, they parted.

20. The deepest calm now seemed to have followed the tumultuous disorders in the Netherlands; but the revolt, though suppressed for the time, was still secretly fermenting. The successive emigrations of whole communities impoverished the country Philip was satisfied that force alone could protect the majesty of religion and of the throne, openly outraged by the rebels. The Duke of Alva was made generalissimo, and ordered to the Netherlands with an army of twenty thousand men; Margaret resigned her authority into the hands of the duke. Alva entered Brussels on August 22, A. D. 1567; and soon after, Egmont and Horn were arrested and put to death (June 3, 1568). The same sentence nominally included the Prince of Orange; but he had taken the precaution to place himself without the reach of the punishment which awaited him. A royal commission, called the "Council of Tumults," was appointed to bring to punishment the authors of the late troubles. The property of the factious leaders was confiscated. William of Orange had been, in the mean time, raising troops in Germany and France, with a view to a simultaneous attack upon the Spaniards in Friesland, Guelders, and Brabant. His brother, Louis of Nassau, also led an army in his support. Alva succeeded in thwarting all their plans. Louis was defeated at Gemningen, near the Ems (July 21, 1568). With the remnants of his army he joined the forces of his brother William, and together they endeavored to effect a junction with Condé, the leader of the French Calvinists; but Alva, who saw through their design, soon forced them by fresh defeats to retreat into Ger-

many. William now changed his plan of operations, and placed all his forces on sea; he hoped thus to make himself master of the country in which a price had been set upon his head.

21. Philip was not to suffer from foreign enemies alone. He was doomed to meet them even in the bosom of his own family His affections as a father were not more spared than was his royal solicitude. On the 20th of January, A. D. 1568, he thus wrote to Pope Pius V : " Most Holy Father, I feel bound, not only by the duty which I owe, in common with all Christian princes, but especially by the filial devotion which I shall ever cherish toward your Holiness, to acquaint you with my conduct, and the serious events which trouble my reign. It is with the desire of fulfilling this duty, that I now make known to your Holiness my intention of ordering the arrest of my son, Don Carlos. Your Holiness may judge of the powerful necessity which obliges me to such a measure, by the effort it has cost me to take the resolution. It is enough to say, that I am a father, and a father deeply interested in the honor of his son. I have tried every means in my power to correct his vicious inclinations and to curb his excesses. I have exhausted gentle means, and the painful conviction has forced itself upon me, that all these efforts have failed to inspire him with any feeling of piety toward God, or with any of the qualities necessary to the presumptive heir of the many kingdoms which God has placed under my authority; I find myself compelled to secure his person, in the hope that this display of rigor may recall him to a better frame of mind. My administration is well known to your Holiness and to all Europe ; and you cannot doubt that I have taken this resolution only after mature deliberation with my council, on the importance of the motives, and finding myself driven to it by the misconduct of the prince, whose unruly disposition has perverted the good lessons of his masters, and the care bestowed upon his education. Your Holiness will, I trust, be satisfied by my conduct, that I have no other object in view than to promote the glory of God, the interests of my States, the good and the peace of my subjects, to which I sacri

fice all my natural tenderness for an only son." Don Carlos had, indeed, been acting the part of an unnatural son, and deserved the punishment which was about to be inflicted upon him. He had plotted against the life of his royal father, and all the papers relating to the conspiracy had been seized. The Pope's reply to the King of Spain was what it should have been—confiding, fatherly and consoling. If Pius V was endowed with a strong mind, he had also received a warm and generous heart. Don Carlos was arrested by the Duke of Feria, captain-general of the guards, and tried by the Council of Castile, not by the tribunal of the Inquisition, as some historians erroneously assert. The unfortunate prince was arraigned on the charge of high-treason; the judgment was pronounced conformably to the laws of the kingdom, and Don Carlos was condemned to suffer capital punishment. Some writers pretend that Philip, to avert the dishonor of such an end, caused the physicians to hasten the death of the prince. This charge, which rests upon no documentary evidence, is contradicted by the modern historian of the Inquisition, Llorente, whom no one will accuse of partiality for Philip II. "Don Carlos," he says, "when warned that his illness must prove fatal, made his confession and received the Blessed Sacrament. The king entered his room, gave him his blessing, with many tears, and in a few moments Don Carlos had ceased to live (1568)."

22. The Popes—and this constitutes one of their highest titles to glory—were the first to appreciate the fact that the destruction of the Turkish power was a question of life and death for Europe. Under Soliman II. and Selim II., his son, their progress became more alarming than ever; the Mediterranean was covered by their fleets; masters of Greece and Hungary, it now only remained for them to conquer the islands of Malta and Cyprus, and then to throw themselves upon Italy. A first attempt upon Malta (A. D. 1565) was defeated by the heroism and admirable manœuvres of the grand master, La Valette. The baffled Turks made a descent upon the island of Cyprus, where they signalized their barbarous revenge by a

most bloody slaughter. Pius V. represented their danger to the European princes, and succeeded in effecting a league between the Venetians and Spaniards, to whom he joined all the forces of Italy He himself appointed the leader of the expedition, and his choice decided the victory He named the brave and chivalric Don John of Austria, whose capacity he well knew. The Christian squadron, which had been joined by the Knights of Malta and the galleys of the Duke of Savoy, met the Turkish fleet of two hundred and forty-five galleys and eighty-seven ships of every class, in the Gulf of Lepanto (October 7, 1571). Here were to be renewed the prodigies of Charles Martel and of the hero of Rhodes and Malta. The combat lasted five hours. In the heat of the onset, the two flag-ships found themselves engaged in close quarters. The Turkish commander, Ali Pacha, was slain, and his head, displayed upon the mast of a Christian galley, completed the defeat of his followers. Twenty-five thousand infidels were slain and ten thousand captured. St. Pius, like another Moses, prayed while the Christian army fought. At the very moment when victory crowned the arms of Don John at Lepanto, the Sovereign Pontiff received a divine revelation of the event. Suddenly breaking off a council which he was then holding, he said to the cardinals: "This is not the time to talk of business; let us go and return thanks to God in His temple; our arms have just been blessed with victory" And the holy Pontiff, shedding tears of gratitude, threw himself upon his knees in his oratory Some days after, it was known that at that very hour the cross had triumphed in the Gulf of Lepanto. In gratitude for this signal victory, St. Pius decreed that throughout the Christian world the feast of the Rosary should be yearly solemnized on the first Sunday in October; and to the Litany of the Blessed Virgin he added the invocation: "Auxilium Christianorum, ora pro nobis." The victory of Lepanto crowned the work of the Crusades, the work of Charles Martel, of Charlemagne, of Godfrey de Bouillon, Tancred, and St. Louis;—the defence of Christian humanity, of Catholic society, against Mahometan barbarism.

23. The saintly Pontiff had not neglected the internal administration of the Church. In 1566, he published the "Catechism of the Council of Trent," an admirable compendium of theology, which had been compiled under the eyes of the council, in two years of assiduous labor, and finished three years later by a commission consisting of Leonard Marion, archbishop of Lunciano; Ægidius Foscarari, bishop of Modena, and Francis Foreiro, theologian of the King of Portugal, at Trent. Their work was carefully revised by St. Charles Borromeo; who steadily pursued his course of reformation in the Church and the religious orders, though often at the peril of his life. The Humiliati, whom the holy archbishop strove to bring back to their primitive regularity, hired a renegade priest to murder him. The assassin discharged a blunderbuss at him, as he knelt in prayer at the evening devotion of his household; the ball struck the cardinal, but, by a miraculous interposition of Heaven, fell harmless at his feet; the Pope punished the authors of the crime and abolished the Order of the Humiliati. With a view to establish liturgical unity throughout the Church, the Council of Trent had ordered the publication of a uniform Breviary and Missal, to be used by every member of the Catholic clergy. On the 9th of July, 1568, Pope Pius V published a constitution abolishing all particular Breviaries less than two hundred years old, and ordaining, everywhere, the form of the office contained in the Roman Breviary. The Missal appeared two years later (A. D. 1570). "In order that all," said the Pope in his bull, "may embrace and observe, in all places, the traditions of the holy Roman Church, the Mother and Mistress of all the others, We forbid, henceforth and forever, that the Mass be said or chanted otherwise than is prescribed in the Missal published by Our order; except when, in virtue of a primitive institution or of a custom dating farther back than two hundred years, certain churches have assiduously observed a particular usage in the manner of celebrating Mass." May these grave and solemn words of St. Pius V be, at length, unanimously received in every church and in every diocese!

The question of church music had also been discussed by the Council of Trent. Pope Marcellus II. thought of banishing it entirely from the divine office. But Providence had prepared, in Rome itself, a man of a deep liturgical genius, and had given him powers equal to his great mission. Louis Palestrina, afterward proclaimed the " Prince of Church Music," was then a chanter in the Papal chapel. He prevailed upon Marcellus to hear a Mass of his own composition. The Pope was delighted with the simplicity, the unction and the richness displayed in the work of Palestrina. The anathema prepared against music was revoked, and the Mass of the great composer kept its name —" the Mass of Pope Marcellus." St. Pius V continued to patronize the artist, and made him Master of the Papal chapel.

24. Lutheranism had now opened new ways of independence, into which were blindly pouring all the self-confident minds arrayed in rebellion against the Church. A thousand different sects were already springing up in the very bosom of Protestantism. Among the heretics of this period were Lælius Socinus and his nephew Faustus, whose erroneous doctrine is known by their name, as Socinianism. They taught that the sacred Scripture is the only rule of faith, and its only interpreter, the light of human reason. Thus far they agree with Luther. But the Socinians draw their own conclusions. All mysteries must be rejected, from the very fact that they are mysteries, and that, therefore, reason cannot comprehend them. They even deny creation, " for they could not conceive," they said, " how God could give being to substances by the only act of His will." They reject the dogmas of original sin, of the divinity of Christ, and of the Redemption. The only sacraments they receive are Baptism and the Lord's Supper, though they grant them no other virtue than that of exciting faith The resurrection of the body they reject as an impossibility They do not admit the doctrine of eternal punishments; but teach that, after a greater or less duration, all created beings will return to nothing. The Socinians hold that it is not lawful to make war, to appeal to the law for the reparation of an

injury, to swear before a magistrate, to discharge the office of judge, especially in criminal cases, to kill a robber or a mur- derer, even in lawful self-defence. The two founders of this sect were natives of Vicenza, but they began to teach their error in Switzerland. Proscribed by the government of Geneva, they went to Poland, where their sect soon numbered many fol- lowers; they made their residence at Rachow, in the district of Sandomir, whence they issued their profession of faith or "Rachovian Catechism."

25. Another error, springing, like Socinianism, from the teachings of Luther, was introduced by Baïus (Michel de Bay), chancellor of the University of Louvain. The doctrine of Baïus views human nature in the three states of innocence, the fall and the reparation: 1st. The state of innocence pre- sents nature in its perfect integrity, free from concupiscence, endowed with immortality, predestined to the intuitive vision of God, gifted with hope and charity 2d. The fall, by de- stroying this beautiful harmony, deprived man of all these gifts. Nature, now subjected to concupiscence, has no other power than that of committing sin, and liberty no longer exists; man acts under the impulse of an irresistible constraint. 3d. In the state of reparation, man receives two graces, one of which communicates the Holy Ghost or grace to the soul, and raises it above concupiscence; the other is the imputation of the merits of Jesus Christ, to pay the debt of sin. The first grace establishes man in a kind of equilibrium between chastity and concupiscence, and by yielding an inevitable obedience to the one of these two powers which prevails, man does it without violence or coaction, that is, voluntarily; this is the extent of his liberty Moreover, the imputation of the merits of Christ is not made to all without distinction, but only to the predestined. In saying that the Redemption was universal, Baïus speaks of the intrinsic value of the Precious Blood, and not of a help given to all. From these principles, the chancellor concluded that, in the natural order, no action is morally good; that all the actions of infidels are sins; that God commands things

which are impossible to those who have not grace; that good works have no efficacy to save us from eternal or even from temporal punishment; which could not be without the previous imputation of the merits of Jesus Christ. This comfortless doctrine, which its advocates had the boldness to put forward as the pure teaching of St. Augustine, was comprised in seventy-six propositions condemned by a bull of Pius V (A. D. 1567).*

26. So many arduous labors exhausted the strength of St. Pius V., who died on the 1st of May, A. D. 1572. He was beatified, one century later (1672), by Clement X., and canonized by Clement XI., in 1712. His death was deeply mourned in Rome and in all the Christian world; the Turks celebrated it by public rejoicings at Constantinople. Amid the grief caused by the errors and disorders of his time, his Pontificate was consoled by a great number of saints and learned men in every rank of society St. Philip Neri and St. Camillus of Lellis founded, together, a congregation of regular clerics for the care of the sick. The learned Cardinal Baronius undertook his herculean task, the "Annals of the Church," to refute the Centuriators of Magdeburg. The Carthusian, Lawrence Surius, published his collection of "Lives of the Saints," a valuable work, but soon after surpassed by that of the "Bollandists." The two Jesuits Rosweyde and Bolland conceived the idea of raising this colossal monument, which our own age, at length, hopes to complete; and Bolland has left it his name.†All nations came forward, at once, to offer their tributes of virtue and holiness. Holland saw nineteen of her children martyred by the Calvinists at Gorcum (July 9th, 1572) St. Felix of Cantalicio, near Citta Ducale, in the States of the Church, sanctified the duties of a laborious life. St. Pascal

---

* *Vid.* BLANC, t. II., pp. 310, 311. Wo have abridged his analysis of the doctrines of Baïus.

† When Cardinal Bellarmine was informed of the plan of the work undertaken by Rosweyde, he inquired the author's age; and on learning that he was forty years old: "Is he sure," asked the cardinal, "of living two hundred years? For it will take no less than that to finish such a work properly."

Baylon was a poor shepherd of Aragon, who won the kingdom of Heaven while tending his flocks. St. Benedict of Philadelphia, an Ethiopian by birth, edified Sicily under the habit of the Minors of the Strict Observance. St. Francis Caracciolo founded the Order of Minor Clerics at Naples. St. Bartholomew of the Martyrs, archbishop of Braga, displayed in Portugal the most ardent charity and deepest humility. Florence gloried in St. Mary Magdalen of Pazzi and St. Catharine of Ricci. The Society of Jesus was, at the same time, presenting to Christian youth admirable examples of all the virtues which adorn that age, in the person of two young noblemen, respectively of Poland and Italy—St. Stanislaus Kostka and St. Aloysius Gonzaga. St. Francis Borgia also forsook the high dignities and brilliant honors lavished upon him in the court of Spain, to enter the Society of Jesus, which he afterward governed as its third general. The Order of the Jesuits, a real nursery of great men, contained, at this period, three justly celebrated theologians—Cardinal Bellarmine, the immortal author of the " Controversies," an immense arsenal in which he has arranged, with perfect method, all the weapons necessary to defend the faith of the Church and to combat against heresy; Suarez, whose theological works, remarkable for their clearness and precision, fill twenty-three folio volumes; Cardinal Tolet, whom his masters called " a prodigy of genius," and whose " Summa casuum conscientiæ," or " Instruction for Priests," deserved the eulogy of Bossuet. Louis of Granada was also writing his ascetic works, among which is the well-known " Sinner's Guide." In the midst of all these names dear to the Church, shone that of St. Theresa, who was of a noble family of Avila. Every kind of glory was in store for this chosen soul, early prevented by all divine graces. In her native country, she founded (1562) a reformed convent of Carmelites, which became the model of that order remarkable for its austerities and the practice of the highest virtues. St. Theresa not only edified the Church by her angelic life, she also wrote several works which breathe the purest love of God. " The Way of

Perfection," " The Interior Castle of the Soul," her " Lite," written by herself, and her " Poems," will always be in the hands of those who strive to ascend to the height of Christian perfection.   St. John of the Cross did for the Carmelite monks what St. Theresa had done for the nuns of the same order They are the two shining lights of Carmel.

CHAPTER VI.

§ ˅. Pontificate of Gregory XIII. (May 13, a. d. 1572—April 7, 1585)

1. Election of Gregory XIII. Massacre of St. Bartholomew.—2. Success of William the Silent, in the Netherlands. Persecutions in England.—3. Brownists. Moravian Brethren. Rodolph II., emperor of Ge many, obtains the confirmation of his election by the Holy See.—4. Cardinal Henry, king of Portugal.—5. Reformation of the Calendar, known as the *Gregorian Calendar.*—6. The Roman Martyrology. Death of Gregory XIII.

§ II. Pontificate of Sixtus V (April 24, a. d. 1585—August 27, 1590).

7. Antecedents of Sixtus V.—8. Life of Sixtus V., by Grogorio Leti.—9. Domestic administration of Rome by Sixtus.—10. Institution of the Congregations of Cardinals.—11. Death of Mary Stuart in England. Sixtus excommunicates Queen Elizabeth, and enters into a league against her with Philip II. Destruction of the *Invincible Armada.*—12. The League in France.—13. Murder of the Duke and of the Cardinal of Guise. Assassination of Henry III. by Jacques Clément. Accession of Henry IV.—14. Change in the conduct of Sixtus V toward Henry IV and the League. Death of the Pope.

§ III. Pontificate of Urban VII. (September 15, a. d. 1590—September 27, 1590).

15. Election and Death of Urban VII.

§ IV. Pontificate of Gregory XIV (December 5, a. d. 1590—October 15, 1591).

16. Election, brief Pontificate and death of Gregory XIV.

§ V. Pontificate of Innocent IX. (October 30, a. d. 1591—December 31, 1591).

17. Election and death of Innocent IX.

§ VI. Pontificate of Clement VIII. (January 29, a. d. 1592—March 3, 1605).

18. Election of Clement VIII.—19. Clement's policy in regard to France. —20. Abjuration of Henry IV at St. Denis.— 21. Clement receives the

§ I. PONTIFICATE OF GREGORY XIII. (May 13, A. D. 1572—April 7, 1585).

1. Cardinal Ugo Buoncompagno succeeded St. Pius V on the 13th of May, A. D. 1572, at the very time when France was startled by the fearful tidings of the "Massacre of St. Bartholomew." The Calvinists had obtained the royal signature to the treaty of St. Germain only through the necessity in which the court was then placed of securing peace at any cost. Still, their intrigues had not ceased. They formed a plot to murder Charles IX. and his mother during the festivities attending the marriage of the King of Navarre with Margaret, the sister of Charles. Such, at least, is the official account sent to all the foreign courts on the day following St. Bartholomew's. The royal council had been discussing the course to be followed in regard to the Huguenots. "To avert the evils which threaten the kingdom," said Catherine, "the only and the infallible expedient would be to put the admiral to death ; he is the cause and the author of all these civil wars ; the designs of the Huguenots would perish with him ; and the Catholics, satisfied with the sacrifice of one or two men, would remain true to the king's authority " All the members were in favor of the proposed measure. But Charles, going far beyond the end proposed, rose from his seat and said: " Since you think good to kill the admiral, be it so; but also let all the Huguenots in France perish with him, that there may not be one left to reproach me with his death ; give the order at once !" This violent language which the young and passionate prince might, perhaps, have been easily induced to

recall, was taken literally   At about two o'clock on the morning of St. Bartholomew's Day (August 24, 1572), the bell of
the church of St. Germain-l'Auxerrois gave the signal for the
execution of the Calvinists.   Coligny was murdered in his own
house; the tocsin sounded in all directions.   The soldiers and
the inhabitants, who were only waiting for the moment to act,
soon spread themselves throughout the whole city   The houses
inhabited by Huguenots were broken open; the destined victims, wherever they were met, were struck down, sabred, shot,
or drowned.   The King of Navarre and the Prince of Condé
owed their safety only to their title of princes of the blood;
and on the next day their abjuration, signed by their own
hands, was forwarded to the Sovereign Pontiff, with a promise
to be ever faithful to the Catholic religion.   The promise was
extorted by fear, and they soon practically revoked it.   The
proceedings against the Calvinists in the provinces was rather
the effect of a popular reaction than of any royal order.   Among
the bishops and governors, there were many who opposed these
deeds of vengeance, and their conduct, during these troubles,
will be a lasting glory to humanity   It has been said that
Rome received with public rejoicings the lamentable tidings of
St. Bartholomew's Day   The courier who brought the account,
announced to the Pope that the King of France had just escaped
a fearful conspiracy against his life.   The Cardinal of Lorraine,
who was still in Rome, where he had taken part in the conclave,
begged the Pope's permission to offer up solemn thanksgiving
to God for the protection granted to the king. When the whole
truth was afterward disclosed, the Sovereign Pontiff, by his
words and his bulls, publicly showed his horror at such a crime.
This bloody measure produced an effect quite contrary to that
which had been anticipated by Charles.   The King of Navarre
and the Prince of Condé had fled and retracted their abjuration;
this was the signal for a fourth civil war.   The Calvinists
seized several fortified places, among others La Rochelle, which
successfully stood nine assaults of the royal forces, under the
Duke of Anjou, with great loss to the besiegers. The duke

was called to the throne of Poland by the nobles of that kingdom, and left the prosecution of the siege to his generals, who were not more successful than himself. To save the honor of the royal arms, it became necessary to grant to the besieged terms of capitulation, securing to them the free exercise of their worship; the same privilege was extended to Nîmes and Montauban (July 6, 1573) This particular treaty did not check the progress of civil war in other parts of France, and it was impossible to foresee the end of the public disasters, when Charles was prostrated by a sudden illness. "His whole body was shaken by a convulsive shuddering," says Mézeray, "becoming at times stiffened with violent shocks; and the blood gushed from every avenue, even through the very pores." In this fearful torture, he died on the 30th of May, 1574. As soon as the tidings of his brother's death reached the Duke of Anjou, now Henry III., he hastily abandoned his throne in Poland to take possession of that of France, where the last of the Valois was to bury his dynasty amid the shameful scandal of the "Mignons" and the incapacity of the *sluggard* kings.

2. The Reformation was ravaging other lands as well as France. On the 23d of January, A. D. 1579, William of Orange, after a series of successful campaigns against the Duke of Alva; Don Luis de Requesens, grand commander of Castile; Don John, the illustrious hero of Lepanto, and the Archduke Matthias, who successively commanded in the Netherlands for Philip II., obtained the ratification of a "treaty of union" between the provinces of Guelders and Zutphen, of Holland, Zealand, Utrecht, Friesland and Gröningen. It was agreed that the confederated provinces should form but one inseparable body, that every means should be adopted and all forces made common for the defence of the new State; that questions of war, of peace and of taxes should be decided only by a unanimous vote, others by a plurality William did not allow his own interest to be forgotten. He secured for himself the dignities of stadtholder, admiral and generalissimo of all the forces, military and naval, to be held for life. Until this time, the rebels had headed their ordinances

with the name of the lawful monarch; after the year 1579
they ceased to observe this formality, and the oath was made
in the name of the Prince of Orange. Calvinism was thus
taking possession of the Netherlands, and this news was brought
to Rome, to sadden the heart of the Sovereign Pontiff, already
deeply moved by the religious troubles in France. Meanwhile
Elizabeth was staining the soil of England with the blood of
her Catholic subjects. Among her most illustrious victims
were Henry Percy, earl of Northumberland, and his son, the
Earl of Arundel, the first peers of the realm. But the missionaries were objects of special hatred to the cruel daughter of
Henry VIII. The prisons were almost exclusively devoted to
the confinement of religious offenders. The executions began
in 1577, and the most barbarous tortures were inflicted upon
faithful Catholics to force them into apostasy Ireland was
not spared; but nothing was ever able to shake the ancestral
faith of that heroic isle. In Ireland, the persecution has lasted
through three centuries, and still continues, with bloodshed,
proscriptions and spoliation of every kind. When history shall
have ceased to be a conspiracy against the truth; when the
passions and prejudices by which the successive governments
of England have been unwittingly swayed, shall have yielded
to cool reflection and impartiality, there will be but one voice
to brand the executioners and exalt their victims. God grant
that the day of justice and light may soon dawn for Catholic
Ireland; may her faith yet triumph over her English oppres-
sors; it is the only revenge worthy of the blood of so many
martyrs !

3. The reign of Elizabeth witnessed the rise of the sect of
Brownists or followers of Robert Brown. They were fanatical
Puritans whose only worship was inward prayer. The Anabaptists also established themselves in Elizabeth's kingdom,
while another branch of the sect was formed under the name
of " United Brethren" or "Moravians." " Two of the followers
of Storch—Hutter and Gabriel—bought a tract of land in Moravia, upon which they settled and established a kind of repub-

&c. Its members devoted themselves to agricultural pursuits, and led a community life. Being repeatedly driven from their abode and dispersed, they were weakened by their separation and by the disorders into which they fell. They finally joined the Socinians in Transylvania.* Error was thus crumbling into a multitude of different sects, in proportion as it receded from the centre of authority, the source of light and of all truth. Germany was still the scene of the most animated and lively religious dissensions. Ferdinand I. was succeeded, on the imperial throne, by Maximilian II. (A. D. 1564). Their reigns were but a succession of negotiations with the Protestants, who multiplied their confessions and formulas of faith without ever coming any nearer to unity Both emperors were successively occupied in endeavoring to maintain an equilibrium between their Catholic and Protestant subjects; they lacked both the power and the genius necessary to triumph over the difficulties of an inextricable situation. Rodolph II. succeeded his father Maximilian, in 1576. Pope Gregory XIII. admonished him to send an ambassador to Rome, for the express purpose of soliciting the confirmation of his authority by the Holy See. The new emperor seemed at first inclined to follow the example of Ferdinand and Maximilian, who had refused to ask the Sovereign Pontiff's sanction for their election. But he was convinced, at length, that the step would enhance the splendor of his crown, and that an emperor need not blush at an act of submission in which a Charlemagne could glory

4. An unexpected source of trouble was now opened in Portugal. The death of Sebastian, the late king, left the throne to his uncle, Cardinal Henry (A. D. 1578). The ministers of the new king, urged him to marry, to secure a direct succession to the crown. Henry, yielding to their representations, determined to apply to the Pope for the necessary dispensation. He was not only a cardinal, but also archbishop of Evora. Gregory fully appreciated the weight of the reasons of state

* M. Blanc, t. II., p. 316.

alleged, but he was also aware of the consequences which must result from such an unprecedented departure from every canonical rule. To grant the dispensation was, undoubtedly, within the power of the successor of St. Peter; but the precedent would be dangerous. The Church, which had maintained, amid so many perils, the indissolubility of the marriage-tie, must display the same firmness in guarding the indissolubility of the priestly vows. Such was the tenor of the Pope's reply to Henry's ambassador; and that prince, changing his design, steadily resisted all the entreaties of the Cortes to the contrary Political interests and considerations were broken upon the rock on which the Church of Christ is founded, and the world was not scandalized by the introduction of Protestant usages into the bosom of Catholicity

5. Gregory now turned his attention to a measure of immense importance, which was to illustrate his Pontificate. This was the reformation of the calendar. Rome received its first calendar from Romulus and Numa; but this production of an imperfect knowledge was full of inaccuracies and errors. It was improved by Julius Cæsar, according to the calculations of the astronomer Sosigenes, whose operations were based upon the principle that the sun moves through the ecliptic in three hundred and sixty-five days and six hours. This was a very near approach to the truth, though not perfectly correct; for in reality, the sun makes its yearly revolution in three hundred and sixty-five days, five hours and forty-nine minutes. Sosigenes thus added eleven minutes to each year, which would involve an error of one day in a hundred and thirty-four years. Thus, from the time of the Council of Nice (A. D. 325), until the reformation of the calendar in 1582, the error of computation in the ephemerides, had reached ten days; so that the vernal equinox, which, in 325, was announced for the 21st of March, fell on the 11th, in 1582, though still announced for the 21st. A reform was evidently necessary Gregory called to his aid all the lights of science, to effect it; he appointed a commission of all the most distinguished astronomers; but the

glory of having brought the great work to a successful issue is chiefly due to an Italian physician named Lilio. For the past, it was easy enough to remedy the error of the eleven minutes. It was only necessary to restore the vernal equinox to the 21st of March, as it was in 325, and this could be done by reckoning as the twenty-first day of the month the one which the calendar reckoned the eleventh. For the future, the following method was adopted to insure correctness. Since the precession of the equinoxes resulted from the accumulation of each year's excess of eleven minutes, the result was an error of one day at the end of each period of one hundred and thirty-four years. Thus, a lapse of four hundred and two years would bring in an error of three days; and, consequently, it was decided to cut out three days of every four hundred years. If the remaining two years were not taken into account, it was because it would take twenty-six thousand eight hundred years to make the difference of a day. Strictly speaking, this is a defect in the new calendar; but it will be easy to remedy it if the world sees the end of that long revolution of ages. When the suppression of three days in each four hundred years had been agreed upon, it remained to decide in which particular years it should be effected. It was agreed that it should fall upon the first three secular years of each period of four hundred years. Consequently, those years, which should all be *bissextile*, are only common years. The year 1700 was the first to feel this reduction; the year 1800 next; the same must be the case in 1900; but the year 2000 will be bissextile. From the year 1582, until 1700, the old calendar was but ten days behind the new. The suppression of a day in 1700 made the difference, for the whole of the eighteenth century, eleven days, and that of 1800 carried it to twelve. The reckoning according to the old calendar is known as the *Old Style;* the computation by the Gregorian calendar is the *New Style*. It was adopted at once by all Catholic countries; the Protestant nations hesitated more or less about receiving the benefit done to society at large, because it came from a Pope. But they

yielded at length, though England held out until the last cen·
tury   Russia is now the only country in Europe which still
preserves the *Old Style.*

6. Gregory XIII. was to complete another great work,
closely allied to the reform of the calendar—the publication of
the Roman Martyrology. The illustrious Cardinal Baronius
was intrusted with the task, and a new edition appeared by
the authority of Gregory XIII. The brief of promulgation,
dated February 14, A. D. 1584, enjoins all patriarchs, archbishops,
bishops, abbots and superiors of churches, to conform to the
new edition, in the office in choir. The saints whose feasts are
celebrated only in certain places are not to be inserted in the
Roman Martyrology ; their names are to be written in a separate
book, and afterward placed in the order prescribed. This was
the last act of Gregory's Pontificate. He died on the 7th of
April, 1585, after a reign of twelve years, entirely devoted to
the glory of God and the exaltation of the Church.

§ II. PONTIFICATE OF SIXTUS V (April 24, A. D. 1585—August
27, 1590).

7 While the modern world almost universally adopted the
method of hereditary transmission of power, the Church alone,
by her system of election, made the spiritual sovereignty attainable from every rank and every class of society   After
having placed herself under the government of men surrounded
with all the splendor of birth and fortune, she did not hesitate
to stoop to the lowliest names and to raise them to the Papal
throne. Sixtus V., who succeeded Gregory XIII. (April 24,
A. D. 1585), was of this class. His ancestor, Zanetto Peretti, a
Sclavonian by birth, fled into Italy before the successful progress of the Ottoman arms in Illyria and Dalmatia, and settled
at Montalto. He met with little good fortune in the land of
his adoption, and his descendant, Peretto Peretti, the father of
Sixtus, was obliged to quit the city on account of debt. He
removed to Grotta-Mare, near Fermo, and here was born to

him a son, who was destined to become Pope Sixtus V He
received in baptism, as if by a happy omen, the name of Felix.
The future Pontiff was too poor to enjoy even the advantages
offered by the neighboring country school, and it was only by
indomitable perseverance that he managed to acquire a knowledge of reading and writing.   He watched his father's swine ;
and it was during these long hours spent in the fields that he became his own teacher.   This promising disposition encouraged
a Franciscan religious to adopt him, and to undertake to draw
out the treasures which he discovered in the strong mind of the
youth.   Having afterward been received into the order of his
benefactor, he distinguished himself in the general chapter of
1549, by a brilliant defence of some theological theses.   His
success on this occasion won him notice and respect; Cardinal
Pio of Carpi, the patron of the Franciscans, from that time
warmly espoused his interests, and his advance was rapid.
St. Pius V raised him to the cardinalate, and consulted him in
the most difficult cases.   After the death of that Pontiff, Cardinal Montalto (so he was now called) lived a secluded, quiet,
frugal and industrious life, devoting his time exclusively to
study and meditation.   It was from this retreat that the hand
of Providence drew him forth to rule the world.

8. The new Pope possessed, in the highest degree, all the
qualities necessary to command.   His firm and resolute will
recognized no obstacle, would bend to no necessity   His history is full of examples of this unbending severity   Romance
writers, however, have seized upon the glorious name of Sixtus
V and made it that of a hero of fable, by the numberless im-
probable anecdotes with which they surround it.   The chief
author of these fables is the satirical writer, Gregorio Leti, who
was born at Milan (A. D. 1680), became a Calvinist in Geneva,
and, after a life of debauchery, was obliged to support himself
by his satirical or licentious romances.   In this spirit he wrote
his " Life of Sixtus V.," of which he said himself that "a well-
told fiction has always more charms for the reader than the
naked truth."   Serious history has nothing in common with

such works; and we must draw from other soarces the materials to erect a monument to so illustrious a memory

9. When Sixtus was reminded of the custom of distributing
money among the people on the accession of a new Pontiff,
he replied: " That custom always occasions some evils; it is
the most robust, and not the most needy, who seize the money "
He ordered the amount usually spent in largesses to be distributed in the abodes of the poor and the hospitals.   Rome soon
felt that it was ruled by a strong arm.   The peace and security
of the Pontifical States had long been disturbed by numberless banditti, remnants of the Guelph and Ghibelline contests.
Gregory XIII. had distributed strong bodies of troops through
the Roman campagna, to check their boldness.   Sixtus disbanded the greater part of the troops and diminished the
number of the sbirri by one half.   But he announced that no
pardon would be granted, during his reign, to any one guilty
of a crime against persons or property.   The threat was
speedily followed by its execution; and the fear inspired by
the stern justice of the Pope effectually put an end to all
trouble from the brigands.   Sixtus availed himself of the
public tranquillity to arouse the activity and industry of the
Romans.   " He wished to give a lasting glory to his Pontificate;
he enforced the rules, concerning the College of Cardinals,
against nepotism; he increased the Vatican library; drew forth
from amid the ruins which covered them the splendid monuments of ancient art; ordered a new edition of the Septuagint
and the revision of the Vulgate promised at Trent; re-organized
the public administration by instituting fifteen congregations to
manage all business (A. D. 1588); raised up the great obelisk
brought by order of Caligula from Egypt to Italy; and furnished
the city with a plentiful supply of water by the splendid aqueduct on the Quirinal."*

10. For the discharge of so many different duties, he
leaned upon the congregations of cardinals.   If he did not
found them all, he yet gave them such a development and

* ALZOG, t. III., p. 213.

perfection as to make them his. "The seven most important," says Ranke, "those of the Inquisition, the Index, the
affairs of the council, of the bishops, of the religious orders,
the 'segnatura,' and 'consulta,' he found already in existence.
Nor were the political affairs left wholly unprovided for in
these, for the two last mentioned had cognizance of judicial
and administrative business. Sixtus now determined to add
eight new congregations to those already existing, of which
only two, however, were to be employed on the affairs of the
Church—the one, on the founding of new bishoprics, the other,
on the direction and the renovation of ecclesiastical usages :
the remaining six were destined for separate departments of
administration; for the annona, the inspection of roads, the
abolition of oppressive taxes, the building of ships of war,
the printing-presses in the Vatican, and the University of Rome.
He established a high standard for the qualities befitting the
office of cardinal generally They were all to be 'distinguished
men, their morals unimpeachable, their words oracles, their
expressions a rule of life and thought to others; the salt of the
earth, the light set upon a candlestick.' He fixed the number
of cardinals at seventy; 'as Moses,' says he, 'chose seventy
elders out of all the people to take counsel with him.'"* Under
this strict administration, the Roman court soon wore an
appearance of severity in keeping with the authority of the
Pontiff. Cardinal Gallieno di Lomo gave his wealth to pious
foundations; the learned Rusti was distinguished by his irreproachable circumspection; Sirlet by his science. Frederick
Borromeo, the nephew and successor of St. Charles (A. D. 1584),
followed in the footsteps of his illustrious predecessor, displaying a heroic charity during the great plague at Milan.
The Cardinals Madruzzi, Valeri, and Santano, celebrated in
various departments, reflected glory upon the Roman purple.

11. While the spirit of Christianity was drawing new life
from the pure fountain-head of orthodoxy, the Lutheran and

---

* History of the Popes, vol. I., book IV., § 6.

Calvinist Reformation continued its ravages in Germany, the Netherlands and France. Elizabeth still ruled in England. The imperious queen drew her motives of hatred against Catholicity from her self-love as a woman and from her political interests. In 1582, she made it a crime of high-treason to induce any English subject to forsake the State religion for the faith of Rome. The Jesuits had established missions in the kingdom to oppose the progress of heresy Elizabeth gave them fifteen days to quit the island. Those who did not comply with the despotic order—and they were- not few—became the objects of a persecution which recalls the martyr-ages of the Church. Meanwhile an innocent and unhappy victim had been for eighteen years pining in a dungeon, anxiously awaiting the hour of justice which she was not to see. All the sovereigns of Europe had displayed a common interest in her sad fate; but their intervention could not avert the fearful vengeance that was soon to fall upon her. A commission of forty-six members, chosen from among the peers of the realm and the councillors of the crown, condemned Mary Stuart to death (A. D. 1586). Parliament confirmed the sentence and requested Elizabeth to have it carried into immediate execution. The Queen of Scots wrote a touching letter to Pope Sixtus V., declaring her fixed resolve to live and die in the Catholic faith. The Pope had not waited for this last proof of devotion to interest himself in behalf of the Scottish queen. He had urged upon Elizabeth the most pressing entreaties in her favor. It may be that his display of active solicitude helped to delay the execution which took place only on the 18th of February, 1587 The crime was at length consummated. A stain of royal blood was fixed forever upon the memory of Elizabeth. Sixtus V issued a solemn bull of excommunication against the crowned regicide. He placed England under interdict; declaring Elizabeth a usurper, deposed from all power and cut off from the communion of the Church; ordering the English to join the army to dethrone her, and promising the most extensive spiritual favors to those who should seize her person and deliver

her over to the Catholics. At the same time, he entered into a
a league with Philip II. of Spain, engaging to furnish ample
subsidies for the war. But the result did not correspond with
his anticipation. Philip raised a most imposing force; but the
"Invincible Armada," the fleet which was to conquer England,
was completely destroyed by the elements before reaching its
destined field of operations.

12. The condition of France was not improved by the
death of Charles IX. His successor, Henry III., had married
Louise de Vaudemont, a cousin of the Duke of Lorraine; this
was espousing the cause of the house of Guise, or, in other
words, the Catholic cause. But the indolent and voluptuous
prince wasted in frivolous pleasures the time which he ought
to have devoted to the difficult administration of his kingdom.
The shameless profligacy of the monarch revolted his subjects,
and thus contributed much to swell the ranks of the factious
Calvinists. The king's brother, the Duke of Alençon, quitted
the court and joined Henry of Navarre and Condé. This defection was followed by a new war. The Catholic army, commanded by the Duke of Guise, who then won his glorious surname "le Balafré," attacked the insurgents at Château-Thierry.
Victory favored the right; but Catherine, whose crafty policy
still ruled in the name of her son, thought it expedient to enter
into negotiations with the Calvinists, and the edict of Blois granted them freedom of worship, places of safety and a right to sit in
the parliaments. These concessions excited the indignation of
the Catholics, who formed themselves into a national association for the maintenance of the ancient faith in the kingdom.
This was the origin of the LEAGUE, which was also called the
Holy Union. The members of the association swore " to defend the faith of their fathers; to restore to the provinces of
the kingdom their ancient rights, franchises and liberties, such
as they were in the time of Clovis; to punish, chastise and
put down those who persecute the Union, *without any respect of
persons;* to render prompt and faithful obedience to the chief
who should be named." Had Henry III. appreciated the value

of his title of " Most Christian King," he would have wished
to be the only chief of the League; but he paid little heed to
these movements, and the confederates intrusted to Henri-le-
Balafré, an authority which made him more powerful in France
than the monarch himself. Sixtus had promised to support
the members of the League, and Philip II. openly proclaimed
himself their protector. The death of the Duke of Alençon, at
this juncture (A. D. 1584), left the succession to the throne full
of uncertainty and danger, as Henry was childless. Henry of
Navarre thus became the nearest heir; but, according to the
old constitution of the French monarchy, the throne could not
be held by a heretical prince. France now presented the sad
spectacle of a war undertaken for an inheritance not yet open.
Henry of Guise and his brother, the cardinal, declared that they
would use all their power to oppose the accession of a Huguenot to the sovereign power in the Most Christian kingdom.
The Pope sanctioned the resolution by excommunicating Henry
of Navarre. This step of Sixtus has been loudly blamed by a
certain school. A serious investigation of facts would have
spared these criticisms, which look very much like calumnies.
As Sovereign Pontiff, Sixtus V was bound to maintain, in every
Christian kingdom, the faith of which he was the depositary
But what would have become of Catholicity in France, had
Henry IV seated Calvinism upon the throne? The League,
then, in the general idea by which it was actuated, was a pre-
servative institution for the monarchy; and the Popes could
not but approve it. We have no difficulty in acknowledging
that political intrigues, personal ambition and even less honorable motives soon gained entrance into this struggle of a people
for the faith of its fathers. This was the first time that the
crown was arrayed against religion in the kingdom of France.
By this very fact, the rupture was a great scandal. Henry
IV., whom it was the object of the League to debar from the
throne, was destined to be one of the greatest kings by whom
it was ever filled. But it will be the eternal glory of the League
to have forced the conviction upon Henry that he must be a

Catholic prince who would wear the crown of St. Louis. Sixtus V., while opposing the claim of Henry of Navarre, acknowledged his brilliant qualities. Great men understand and appreciate each other. Had Sixtus lived to witness the conversion of Henry the Great, it would have been the crowning of his dearest earthly hopes; but that happiness was not to be granted him.

13. The contest known as the " War of the Three Henrys" —Henry III., Henry of Navarre, and Henry of Guise—began in 1586. The League had lately been organized in Paris under the name of " The Sixteen," from the fact that a council was formed, composed of one member from each of the sixteen divisions of the city, to guard the interests of religion. The Catholic and Calvinist armies met with varied success. At Coutras, the military genius of Henry triumphed over superior numbers; but the Huguenots were repulsed from the banks of the Loire by Henry III., and defeated at Vimori in Gâtinais, and at Auneau in Beauce, by the Duke of Guise (A. D. 1587). The duke's popularity was growing into formidable proportions. His vigilance, activity and zeal were contrasted with the habitual indolence of Henry III. Parties never stop half way The " Sixteen" caused the proposition to be maintained in the Sorbonne, that " an unworthy prince may be deprived of his authority, just as a suspected guardian may be removed from his administration." The people of Paris received the duke with the honors of a triumph ; he was hailed with the emphatic titles of " Destroyer of the Germans," "the Scourge of Heresy," "the Maccabeus of France," " the just one who is to confound the court of Herod." Under the circumstances, the king thought it necessary to quit Paris, where the Duke of Guise thenceforth ruled with sovereign power. These events were soon followed by a violent reaction. The Duke of Guise and his brother, the cardinal, were assassinated by order of the king. Sixtus was deeply moved by the account of this tragedy The murder of a prince of the Church, by order of a king of France, without the previous judgment of the Roman court, was an

unprecedented outrage. The Pope expressed his grief in a full consistory "A cardinal," he exclaimed, "has been murdered without trial, without examination, as if there were no longer a Pope on earth; nay, even as if there were no God in Heaven!" But he did not limit his indignation to these complaints; he summoned the king to appear at Rome, threatening him with excommunication unless he should justify his conduct. "We are bound to act thus," said Sixtus, "otherwise God would call us to account for our conduct as the most unprofitable of all Popes. In the discharge of a sacred duty we have nothing to fear even from the whole world. We doubt not that, if Henry III. persists in his wicked resolutions, God will visit him with the punishment of Saul." The anticipation of the Pontiff was realized. The Pope uttered his warning on the 23d of June, 1589; on the 1st of August following, Henry III. fell by the regicide dagger of Jacques Clément. This crime changed the face of events, but only added to their complication. The Apostolic nuncio had quitted France after the murder of the Cardinal of Guise. Sixtus immediately sent Cardinal Gaëtano to Paris, to acquaint him with the real state of things in France. Henry of Navarre had assumed the royal title, and was marching at the head of a brave and faithful army to win his throne. The League had invested the aged Cardinal of Bourbon with the title of king, but no one looked upon him in any other light than that of a royal shadow; the "Sixteen" still ruled Paris and received Gaëtano with enthusiasm. The Duke of Mayenne, a brother of the Duke and Cardinal of Guise, had taken the title of lieutenant-general of the crown of France, and prepared to oppose the claim of Henry, by whom he was defeated on the brilliant fields of Arques and Ivry, where Henry IV displayed both his chivalric daring and the military genius of a great captain.

14. The accession of Henry IV increased the alarm of Sixtus. The Protestant cause seemed triumphant in France. The Pope tried for a moment to avert the threatened danger by making common cause with the League and Philip II. of

Spain. Meanwhile, the republic of Venice, at the tidings of
the battle of Arques, sent in an act recognizing the government of Henry IV   The Sovereign Pontiff was much affected
by this step.   "Venice has deeply offended Us," said he to the
ambassadors.   "The King of Navarre is a heretic excommunicated by the Holy See; and yet the republic has recognized
him, in contempt of all Our remonstrances.   Is the republic
placed so far above all the kingdoms of the earth, that it is
entitled to set an example to the others?   There is still a king
of Spain; there is still an emperor.   Does the republic fear the
King of Navarre?   We will defend her with all Our might,
should it become necessary; and We have the power.   But
does the republic meditate any attempt to injure Us?   In that
case, God Himself would be Our defender."   The Pope's unshaken
determination ever to oppose the accession of a heretical prince
to the throne of France was soon made known to Henry IV.
He was already wavering in his religious convictions, but now
he understood the necessity of a definite return to the bosom
of Catholic unity   It may reasonably be believed that the
energy displayed by the Pope was not one of the least motives
of his conversion.   Henry determined to send to Rome, as his
ambassador, the Duke of Luxemburg, with the special mission
of consulting the Pope on this serious matter.   Olivares, the
Spanish ambassador, on learning the arrival of the French
commissioner, hastened to the Vatican and begged the Pope
not to grant the honor of an audience to the minister of a
Huguenot prince.   "If Your Holiness," said Olivares, " persists in admitting him, I shall be under the necessity of making a
formal protest, in the name of the king, my master."   "Protest!" replied the Pope.   "What protest will you advance?
You offend the majesty of your royal master, whose prudence
I well know.   You may retire."   Luxemburg was presented
to Sixtus, and assured him that the hero of Arques and Ivry
was ready to kneel at the feet of His Holiness to seek absolution and admittance into the Catholic Church.   "Let him come!
Let him come!" exclaimed the Pope; "that I may embrace

and console him!" Here it is evident that Sixtus V was not
acting a political part. He saw the possibility of Henry's conversion, and from that moment he could have no objection to
his sitting upon the throne; and when the ambassadors of
the League came to complain to Sixtus of the favor shown to
the envoy of Henry of Béarn; "So long," replied the Pope, "as
We believed the League to be working for religion, We assisted
it; now We are convinced that it is acting only through motives
of ambition or under a false pretence, Our protection is at an
end." The immortal Pontiff was not to witness an event which
everything concurred in promising. He died on the 27th of
August, A. D. 1590, after a reign of five years. History ranks
his name among those of the greatest men who have ever ruled
the world.

§ III. Pontificate of Urban VII. (September 15, A. D. 1590—
September 27, 1590).

15. Urban VII. was elected on the 15th of September, A D.
1590, but had hardly time to take his seat upon the Pontifical
throne. He died within twelve days after his promotion, giving
thanks to God that he was thus spared the obligation of giving
an account of a power which he had never exercised.

§ IV Pontificate of Gregory XIV (December 5, A. D. 1590
—October 15, 1591).

16. Cardinal Nicholas Sfondrati was elected Pope on the
5th of December, A. D. 1590, and took the name of Gregory
XIV. When he heard his name announced after the counting
of the votes, and saw his colleagues coming forward to salute
him with the title of *Santo Padre*, he could only exclaim: "God
forgive you! But what have you done?" This mark of
humility promised a virtuous Pontiff. Gregory XIV., in a
short reign of less than a year, justified the hopes of the world.
Henry IV., whose successes were growing in number and bril-

liancy, did not seem eager to keep the promises made to Sixtus
V The apprehension was becoming more warrantable that
triumphant Calvinism might take possession of France, with
the most popular of kings; for it was evident that the genius
of Navarre must soon overcome every obstacle. The Pope did
not hesitate to oppose a conquering prince. He declared himself in favor of the League. " Do you," he writes to the " Sixteen," " who have made so laudable a beginning, persevere to
the end, and stay not until you have reached the goal of your
course. Inspired by God, We have determined to come to your
aid. First, We send you assistance in money; We likewise
dispatch Our nuncio, Landriano, to France, in order to bring
back all deserters to the Unity of the Holy Church; lastly,
We send Our nephew, Ercole Sfondrati, duke of Montemarciano,
with horse and foot, to employ their arms in your defence.
Should you stand in need of yet more, We are ready to make
still greater sacrifices to provide you with it." This declaration
itself, the repetition of the excommunication of Henry IV.,
which was connected with it, and lastly the injunction to all the
clergy, the nobles and the third estate, to sever themselves
from him, under pain of rigorous penalties, produced a deep
impression in France. From this time may be dated the formation, among the king's adherents, of a party of Catholic royalists, who incessantly urged him to return to Catholicity. The
Pope was also laboring to reach the same end. The immense
sums collected by Pope Sixtus were now put into requisition
for this work, which was, unquestionably, one of vast importance. Gregory had always before his eyes the lot of Protestant
Germany He wished, at any cost, to save France from a like
misfortune. But death arrested him in the midst of his under
takings (October 15, 1591). Gregory XIV left his successors
to gather the fruit of his energetic labors.

§ V. Pontificate of Innocent IX. (October 30, a. d. 1591—
December 31, 1591).

17. Giovan-Antonio Fachinetti was elected on the 30th of
October, a. d. 1591, and took the name of Innocent IX. The
Romans all agreed in ascribing to this Pontiff a mature wisdom,
purity of life, liberality, magnificence, and experience in the
management of business. He was once solicited to grant a
certain favor, the petitioner at the same time presenting him
with a considerable sum of money to defray the expenses of
the Pontifical treasury, during a season of famine in the Roman States. The indignant Pope rejected the offered wealth,
and replied : " We ask not money, but obedience." These high
qualities promised a glorious reign; but Innocent died, two
months after his election, December 31, 1591.

§ VI. Pontificate of Clement VIII. (January 29, a. d. 1592—
—March 3, 1605).

18. The conclave was now re-opened, the fourth time within
fourteen months. Cardinal Ippolito Aldobrandini, who belonged
to a distinguished family of Florence, was elected and took the
name of Clement VIII. " The new Pope," says Ranke,
" brought to his office an exemplary diligence. He devoted no
less attention to the details of internal administration and to
personal affairs, than to the politics of Europe or the great
interests of the Church. He confessed every evening to Cardinal Baronius; every morning he celebrated Mass himself.
He thus raised to an extraordinary pitch the reputation he had
always enjoyed for virtue, piety and an exemplary life."
19. " Public curiosity was now universally excited, as to
the manner in which this Pope, so full of talent, activity and
energy, and moreover of such blameless life, would treat the
most momentous question of Europe—the state of France." He
must choose between two alternatives. He might, like his
predecessors, attach himself to the League and Philip II. against

Henry; or he might take part with the French monarch. The adoption of either course depended upon the conduct of Henry. Never had decision been more anxiously expected; never was decision more delicate or dangerous. When he came to the Apostolic chair, Clement VIII. found himself surrounded by elements which singularly complicated his position. The Holy See had a legate in France, attached to the Spanish party, and an army destined to oppose Henry IV ; moreover the estates of France had espoused the cause of the League. The Pope felt the necessity of moving with extreme caution amid these intricate circumstances, which, to a certain extent, paralyzed his freedom of action. He saw that he must expect the solution of so many difficulties from the course of the events themselves. And this policy he accordingly adopted.

20. The Spaniards were urging the Duke of Mayenne, lieutenant-general of the kingdom, to proceed to the election of a Catholic king. The estates met for the purpose, toward the end of January, A. D. 1593, but without result. Still, even amid the troubles of war and the din of arms, Henry IV was thinking of his return to the true faith ; and if he had hitherto resisted all the solicitations of the Catholics of his party, it was because he did not wish that the change should be, or seem to be, the result of weakness or of policy, but of a thorough conviction. At length, in the hour marked by Providence, he sought the light which he had always desired, without having yet been able to reach it, and. while conferences were opened at Suresnes, he asked for the necessary instruction. The celebrate Jacques Davy Duperron, afterward a cardinal, began the instruction of the prince, at first by simple conversations, and then by regular conferences, in which the most able prelates and doctors among the royalists and the members of the League took part. To these conferences Henry brought all that sincerity and frankness which formed the prominent characteristics of his great mind. Duperron having brought some of the doctors of the opposite party to acknowledge that salvation was attainable in the Roman Church,—"What!" exclaimed

Henry, " you agree that salvation can be attained in the religion of the Catholics; while they, on the contrary, assert that it is impossible in yours! In à matter of such importance, it is surely worth while to be sure of our course, and prudence forbids a moment of delay " From that hour the king's conversion was decided. It is impossible to describe the joy that filled the hearts of the French royalists at this announcement. Only the League, for which ambition had now become the sole motive power, betrayed its total want of disinterestedness and its bad faith. Elizabeth, the schismatical queen of England, on learning the king's conversion, felt, to use her own words. " a most poignant grief, and a deep depression of spirits." On the 25th of July, 1593, Henry IV made his abjuration in the presence of the Archbishop of Bourges, in the great church of St. Denis. Henry had said : "I wish to swear upon the tomb of the kings, my ancestors, to live and die in the faith which they professed." When he entered the church, the prelate put the usual questions according to the formula for this ceremony " Who are you? What do you wish?" " I am the king," answered Henry ; " I ask to be received into the bosom of the Catholic Church." " Do you desire it?" asked the archbishop " Yes," replied Henry, " I wish and I desire it." Then kneeling before the prelate, he made his profession of faith, in these words : " I promise and swear, in the presence of Almighty God, to live and to die in the faith of the Catholic, Apostolic and Roman Church ; to protect and defend it against all enemies, at the peril of my blood and of my life, renouncing al contrary heresies." " And I," added the archbishop, " saving the authority of the Holy See, absolve you from the crime of heresy and apostasy ; I receive you into the holy Roman Church, and admit you to its sacraments, in the name of the Father, and of the Son, and of the Holy Ghost." The ceremony was witnessed by an immense multitude. The Parisians, who had come to St. Denis in spite of the orders and the satellites of the League, blessed the hour which had removed the last barrier between the people and their king.

21. But Henry IV had been excommunicated by the Holy See; it belonged to the Holy See to remove the censures inflicted by itself. The clause, " Salva Sanctæ Sedis Apostolicæ auctoritate," used by the Archbishop of Bourges, in the ceremony of the reconciliation, reserved the final absolution, in conformity with the canonical regulation, to the Pope. The joy of Clement VIII. was deep and unbounded when he was fully satisfied of the sincerity of the king's religious change. He gladly opened the arms of his mercy to the son thus returning to his father's house. But the Spanish ministers brought into play all the resources of diplomacy and intrigue, to break off the negotiation, and to change the favorable disposition of the Pope. Happily, Henry was represented at the Roman court by a minister equally able and devoted, the celebrated D'Ossat, for whom this negotiation afterward won the cardinal's hat. D'Ossat unanswerably proved the sincerity of his royal master's conversion. He showed that ambition had no part in the step, since Henry had only taken it when victory had already opened to him the gates of his capital. The collection of D'Ossat's letters on this subject is a master-piece of modern diplomacy On the 17th of December, A. D. 1595, Duperron and D'Ossat received the Pontifical absolution in the name of the king. The Pope's throne was erected on a raised platform in front of St. Peter's; it was occupied by Clement VIII. and surrounded by all the cardinals. The two representatives of the French king threw themselves at the feet of the Pope, and promised, in the name of Henry IV., upon the Holy Gospels, that their prince would remain true to the faith of the Catholic, Apostolic and Roman Church. Conformably to the rites prescribed by the Pontifical, *Miserere* was recited, and at each verse the Pope touched the the heads of the prostrate ambassadors with a light wand. The Pontiff then stood up, and having recited the usual prayers, with uncovered head, he resumed the tiara, seated himself upon the throne, and, raising his voice, he pronounced the absolution : " By the authority of Almighty God, and of the blessed Apostles St. Peter and St. Paul, We grant to Henry of Bourbon,

king of France and Navarre, absolution from the censures incurred by the sin of heresy" Then giving his blessing to the ambassadors, he continued : "Announce to the king, your master, that We have opened to him the door of the Church militant upon earth ; it must be his to win an entrance, by lively faith and works of sincere piety, into the Church triumphant in heaven." From that day the League fell into a state of disrepute from which it never rose again ; and the Roman Pontiff blessed the divine goodness which had made him the instrument of the civil and religious pacification of the French kingdom. Henry was anointed and crowned at Chartres ; he was prayed for in all the churches, and the religious orders hastened to acknowledge him. The king, on his part, restored the Catholic worship wherever it had been abolished during the late troubles, and ever after showed himself sincerely orthodox and devoted to the Holy See.

22. The troubles of the League were followed by a famous theological discussion which, through the spirit and earnestness displayed on both sides, soon grew into a passionate contest. The celebrated Spanish Jesuit, Molina, had lately published, at Evora, his work on predestination, entitled, *Liberi arbitrii cum gratiæ donis concordantia*, or "The Concord of Grace and Free-will" (A. D. 1588). The author maintained that God pre destines men to eternal glory only in view and in consideration of their merits ; that the grace by means of which they obtain these merits is not efficacious of itself, but by the consent of the will, and that it is given in circumstances in which God foreknew that it would work its effect; in fine, that this grace is refused to no one. Molina's whole system may be reduced to the following eight propositions: 1. God, by the knowledge of simple intelligence, sees all that is possible, and consequently, infinite orders of possible things. 2. By the *scientia media*, God certainly sees what, in each order, each created will, by the use of its liberty, will do if God gives it a certain grace. 3. He wills, by an antecedent and sincere will, the salvation of all men, provided they will it themselves, and

correspond with the graces granted them. 4. He gives to all the help necessary and sufficient to work out their salvation, though He bestows upon some more than upon others, according to His good pleasure. 5. In the state of our fallen nature, there are no absolute decrees of predestination on the part of God, efficacious of themselves and antecedent to the prevision of the free consent of the human will; consequently, no pre-destination to everlasting glory before the prevision of the merits of man, no reprobation which does not suppose the fore-knowledge of the sins that will be committed. 6. God's will to save all men is real, sincere and active: it is by that will that Jesus Christ was destined to be the Saviour of the human race; it is in virtue of that will, and of the merits of Jesus Christ, that God grants to all the graces sufficient to work out their salvation. 7 God, by the *scientia media*, sees, with full certainty, what a man will do under given circumstances, and helped by a given grace; consequently He knows those who will make a good or a bad use of grace. 8. In consequence of this foreknowledge, He predestines the former to eternal glory, and the latter to reprobation.

23. This doctrine met with the most vigorous resistance from the Dominicans, who taxed it with Pelagianism and semi-Pelagianism. The Jesuits, with few exceptions, among whom Henrique and the celebrated Mariana were especially remarkable, supported Molina. The dispute grew warm and gradually spread until all the schools and universities were divided into two camps under the names of Thomists and Molinists. The teachings of Molina passed from Portugal, where he was teaching theology, into Spain, Touraine, France, and even into the midst of Germany The Dominican Bannez, alarmed at the rapid growth of Molinism, presented petition upon petition to the Papal nuncio; but his complaints only resulted in a prohibition to style Molina and his adherents heretics. Notwithstanding this order, the Dominicans still continued to make war upon the Jesuits with a violence which even the ardor of the discussion could not excuse. Clement VIII., on learning the state of

things from some Spanish bishops, forbade both parties to discuss the irritating questions then so popular. In 1597, the Pope determined to call up the whole matter before his tribunal. For its examination, he instituted the special congregation *De Auxiliis*, consisting of cardinals and theologians. The most able men of both orders appeared in defence of their respective opinions. Thirty-seven conferences were held in the Pontificate of Clement VIII., in which the celebrated Dominican, Thomas Lemos, especially distinguished himself. But the question was not settled during the lifetime of this Pontiff. The discussion of ten years was at last ended by Paul V., by the means which, it seems to us at this day, might have been adopted in the beginning. He dismissed both parties, leaving to each one the liberty of following his own opinion, with a formal prohibition to charge the opposite one with heresy or rashness.*

24. The closing years of Clement's Pontificate were signalized by two events of great importance—the addition of the duchy of Ferrara to the Ecclesiastical States, and the peace of Vervins. Alfonso II., duke of Ferrara, died without legitimate heirs. Cesare d'Este, a distant relation of the duke's, attempted to take possession of the duchy; but the Pope insisted upon the anterior rights of the Holy See, founded upon the donations of Pepin and Charlemagne, and which had been only interrupted by a kind of usurpation, since legalized. Henry IV supported the claim of Clement VIII., and the duchy of Ferrara remained definitively annexed to the States of the Church. The support given to the Pontifical power, by France, on this occasion, was rewarded by the active mediation of Clement in the conclusion of the peace between Henry IV and Philip II. of Spain. The Sovereign Pontiff drew up the preliminary articles of the treaty, which was signed at Vervins (A. D. 1598). The Spaniards were to restore Calais and the cities they had taken in Picardy Henry on his part, gave up the city of Cambrai. The treaty

---

* M. BLANC, t II., p. 321.

of Vervins effaced the last traces of the League in France. Cardinal D'Ossat was, in the mean time, opening fresh negotiations at Rome in the name of Henry IV., concerning the marriage of that prince with Margaret of Valois. This union, contracted at the time of the eventful day of St. Bartholomew, had been forced upon the young King of Navarre by the express will of Charles IX. and the policy of Catherine de Médici. The circumstances which clearly proved the constraint put upon Henry on that occasion were of public notoriety Clement accordingly pronounced the union null (1599) ; and Henry was enabled to marry the Princess Mary de Medici (1600), by whom he had one son, afterward Louis XIII.

25. The Pope now hoped to profit by the happy combination of circumstances in which he found himself placed. A Turkish war had broken out anew in Hungary; the large and lofty views of the Pontiff gave him the idea of turning the forces of the whole Catholic world against the ancient and hereditary foe of Christendom. But if, on the one hand, the Ottoman empire showed symptoms of declining strength, which justified the hopes of Clement; yet, unquestionably, the execution of such an undertaking required a more sincere and cordial union of the different States of Europe than was possible after so violent a shock of interests and passions. The time had not yet come for a new Crusade against the East. Clement was not slow to realize this truth, and he forthwith broke off the immense preparations which he had begun. He saw, with the greatest satisfaction, the reëstablishment of the Jesuits in France. Henry IV., not satisfied with checking the violence of the Huguenots toward the head of the Church, took a decided stand in favor of the illustrious sons of Loyola, which filled the Pontiff's heart with joy The Society of Jesus had been banished from France, after the attempt of John Chastel upon the life of Henry, because the regicide had studied for a time in a college of the Jesuits. In spite of Chastel's protestations, and of the manifest proofs offered by him of the innocence of the society, even to his last breath and under the most cruel tortures,

those religious were driven from the soil of France by the parliament, of which the majority, according to the president, **De Thou**, was *Huguenot.* Since the time of their banishment, the Pope had repeatedly urged upon the king that this unjust rigor, exercised against a society which had deserved so well of the Church, could rejoice only the enemies of religion, or, at most, a few prejudiced Catholics. In all his interviews with D'Ossat, the plenipotentiary of France at Rome, Clement expressed his concern at this event. The cardinal himself earnestly desired the recall of a religious order which had been made a victim of Calvinist hatred. Henry IV soon realized the wishes of the Pope and of his legate. He recalled the Jesuits and gave into their charge the college which he had lately founded at La Flèche. "I believe them better fitted than any others," said he, "to instruct youth" (A. D. 1604). From that time the royal favor was never withdrawn by Henry from the Jesuits. Clement did not long outlive this act of justice, performed at his solicitation. He died on the 3d of March, 1605. after a reign which reflected glory upon the Church.

§ VII. Pontificate of Leo XI. (April 1, A. D. 1605—April 27, 1605).

26. Clement VIII. had foretold to Cardinal Alexander-Octavian de Medici that he should be his successor ; the cardinal had acted as legate in France, and displayed the greatest ability and prudence during the troubles which agitated that kingdom. He was elected Pope on the 1st of April, A. D. 1605, and took the name of Leo XI. The Pontiff was nearly related to the Queen of France. The letters in which Duperron announces the election to Henry IV are full of exultation, and the accession of the new Pope was celebrated in France with public rejoicings. But Leo merely appeared upon the Apostolic chair; he survived his election only twenty-six days, and bore with him to the grave the regrets of the whole Christian world.

CHAPTER VII.

§ 1. PONTIFICATE OF PAUL V (May 16, A. D. 1605—January 21, 1621).

1. State of Europe at the accession of Paul V.—2. Persecution by Taiko Sama and his successors in Japan.—3. Chinese missions. Father Ricci.—4. America. St. Turribius, archbishop of Lima. St. Rose of Lima.—5. *Reductions* in Paraguay. Rome and Venice.—6. The *Gunpowder Plot.*—7. Progress of Catholicity in Europe, under Paul V.—8. Zeal of Henry IV. for the Catholic faith. His death.—9. Death of Paul V

§ II. PONTIFICATE OF GREGORY XV. (February 9, A. D. 1621—July 8, 1623).

10. Election of Gregory XV Congregation of the *Propaganda.*—11. The Jesuits expelled from Holland and called to the University of Prague by the Emperor Ferdinand II.—12. Addition of the Palatine library to that of the Vatican by Gregory XV.—13. Reform in religious orders in France. Death of Gregory XV.—14. Saints and holy works in the beginning of the seventeenth century.—15. St. Francis of Sales.

§ III. PONTIFICATE OF URBAN VIII. (August 6, A. D. 1623—June 29, 1644).

16. Election of Urban VIII. State of Europe at his accession.—17. Thirty Years' War.—18. The Italian war.—19. Capture of La Rochelle.—20. Escheat of the duchy of Urbino to the Holy See.—21. Jansenius.—22. His work entitled "Augustinus." The five erroneous propositions pointed out by Cornet, syndic of the Theological Faculty of Paris.—23. Saint Cyran. Urban VIII. forbids the reading of the "Augustinus." The University of Louvain refuses to submit to the Pope's decision.—24. The "Augustinus" condemned by the Bull, *In Eminenti.*—25. Death of Urban VIII.—26. Saints and good works of his Pontificate.

§ I. PONTIFICATE OF PAUL V. (May 16, A. D. 1605—January 21, 1621).

1. Cardinal Camillo Borghese was elected Pope on the 16th of May, A. D. 1605, and took the name of Paul V. The new

Pope was but fifty-three years old, skilled in the dispatch of business, and had acquired great experience by passing through every grade of clerical dignity   Deeply versed in canon law, he had conceived a high idea of the mission intrusted to the Papacy   To unimpeachable morals he joined great mildness and affability   On his accession, he found the imperial throne occupied by Rodolph II., successor of Maximilian ; Henry IV reigned in France, where he had just extinguished the last sparks of civil war by the " Edict of Nantes," which gave to the Calvinists freedom of worship and places of security. The too famous Elizabeth had died in 1603, leaving the English crown to James I. of Scotland, whose education and personal affections drew him toward Catholicity, while fatal circum-stances and motives of policy kept him on the Protestant course inaugurated by the daughter of Henry VIII.   Philip III. re-ceived the Spanish sceptre in 1598, from his father, Philip II., who died soon after the pacification of France and Spain by the treaty of Vervins.   The kingdoms of the north were ruled by schismatical princes.   The division inaugurated in Europe by the Lutheran Reformation was thus spreading its ravages, and the nations, wrested from the guardian authority of the Church, were holding on a course beset with shoals and tempests.

2. Christian blood was poured out to fertilize the distant shores hitherto closed to the light of the gospel. Japan had received the faith through the zeal of the missionaries, and the seed of the divine word was productive under the care of those apostolic workmen. Religion was advancing in these countries with mighty strides. An embassy of converted Japanese princes was present at the coronation of Pope Gregory XIII. and brought back to Japan the Pontifical blessing. It seemed as if God would repair, by these distant conquests of the faith, the losses suffered by the Church in Europe. But a persecu-tion, which lasted thirty-six years, was begun by the Emperor Taiko-Sama. It was inaugurated by the martyrdom of nine religious, three Jesuits and six Franciscans, whose blood was shed upon the soil to which they had brought the glad tidings

of the gospel. The Japanese Christians numbered their martyrs by thousands. The successors of Taiko-Sama were excited by the Dutch navigators, who were all Protestants, to carry out the same cruel policy toward the Catholics. Finally, in 1614, the Emperor Quixasu banished all the missionaries, destroyed the churches and ordered all the Christians in Japan to apostatize on pain of death. A body numbering more than a thousand Christians emigrated to the Philippines to escape the fury of the barbarous prince. The deserts were peopled by a multitude of confessors who there revived the austerities of Thebais and Nitria. Yet all this courage and perseverance was powerless against the intrigues of Holland and England, whose ships were the only ones then admitted to the Japanese ports for purposes of trade. This reproach must ever stain the names of both these nations upon the page of history, until, returning from their erring course, they shall have nobly atoned for it before God and men, by their zeal in bearing the only true civilization—Catholicism—to every quarter of the globe.

3. But Providence now opened the gates of China to the faith. Father Matthew Ricci, a member of the Society of Jesus, was the first to enter the empire, cut off, by its manners, habits and traditions, from the rest of the world. Having in the year 1600 gained admission, with several of his brother religious, to the court of the emperor,, he obtained permission to preach the gospel. He made his vast acquaintance with arts and sciences subsidiary to the cause of religion, by exciting the curiosity of the Chinese. In a short time, the name of Ricci * had won such renown, both in the capital and in the provinces, that the Chinese compared him to their Confucius. Glory and power came to him in equal proportion. But it was not for these earthly advantages that the Jesuit had devoted his life to the diffusion of the gospel. He had now but one ambition; to establish

---

* Ricci had assumed the Chinese name *Li*, which was the first syllable of his family name in the only form in which the Chinese could articulate it, and the surname, *Ma-teou* (Matthew). The other missionaries followed his example, and all took Chinese names formed generally in the same manner.

upon a firm foundation, throughout the whole empire, the work begun with so much labor.   A novitiate arose in Pekin; here he received the Chinese youth, trained them, in the practice of virtue, to a knowledge of letters and the study of mathematics. And, as if all these labors had been but a recreation for his old age, he wrote a detailed account of all the events that passed before his eyes; he was at every moment called upon to receive the mandarins or the lords, whom a love of science or mere curiosity brought to his abode.   Beside these many different occupations, Ricci composed works, in the Chinese language, on morals, religion and geometry, and explained to his native pupils the first six books of Euclid.   Death snatched him away in the midst of these labors; he died on the 11th of May, A. D. 1610, at the age of fifty-eight years, leaving to the Chinese the remembrance of a man whom they still revere, and to his order an example of virtue, learning, wisdom and firmness. This untimely death exposed to cruel vicissitudes the good work which Ricci had so laboriously begun.   In 1617, a violent persecution broke out against the missionaries.   They were scourged, imprisoned, banished, and sent back to the shores of Macao.   Three years later the emperor, Van-Lié, who had signed the edict of proscription, died at the moment when Thien-Min, king of the Tartars, had entered his States, cut his army to pieces, and was arousing the Chinese from the traditional torpor which seemed to be, for them, the only condition of existence.   Tien-ki, Van-Lié's successor, took measures to check the advance of the Tartars.   The Christian mandarins advised him to apply to the Portuguese for officers, who would improve the efficiency of their army   " Still," they added, " the Portuguese will give us aid, only when the Jesuits, who have been ignominiously banished, shall receive justice from the emperor."   Tien-ki annulled the edict of banishment issued by his predecessor, and restored the Fathers.   It was then that Father Adam Schall, a native of Cologne, appeared in China.   He was a thorough mathematician and astronomer, and, walking in the footsteps of Ricci, he too won a reputation for universal knowledge. Having been directed by the emperor to correct the calendar, Schall profited by the occasion to do away with lucky and unlucky days, as superstitious observances, and to help the spread of Christianity   At Sigan-Fou, he induced the pagans themselves to build a church.   At Pekin, he succeeded in obtaining a decree from the emperor, authorizing the Jesuits to preach the gospel throughout his dominions.   This mission called for chosen men, accomplished scholars.   He who devoted himself to labor in this field was a true hero ; for those distant seas had not yet been explored by navigators, and they were fruitful of shipwrecks.   Thus Father Diaz, writing to the general of the society, for a yearly supply of twenty missionaries, says : " They would not be too many even if, by a special blessing of Providence, they could all reach Macao alive ; but it is not an unusual thing for one-half of them to die on the way   It would, then, be well to send twenty, in order that we may count upon ten every year."

4. No less successful were the missions in America. The island of Cuba, the empire of Mexico, and that of Peru, had each a hierarchy canonically established.   The archiepiscopal see of Lima was then filled by St. Turribius, the Borromeo of the New World.   During his episcopate of twenty-five or twenty-six years, St. Turribius held three provincial councils with the bishops of that part of America, and fourteen diocesan synods with the principal ecclesiastics of his archbishopric. These councils and synods of the New World were not unworthy to be cited as models for the Old.   The holy archbishop labored zealously to apply to his clergy and people the salutary measures prescribed by the Fathers of Trent.   He established seminaries in which the youth of the country gave bright promise of an efficient native clergy   While the saintly prelate thus toiled for the glory of God and the salvation of souls, St. Rose of Lima was edifying her native city by the spectacle of her amiable virtues, and deserved, by the angelic purity of her life, the honors of public worship which the Church eventually decreed her.

5. But another portion of the Western World was the scene of a work which might well arrest the admiring attention of the world—whole tribes of savages become a people of saints. The Spanish conquerors of the New World had reduced the natives to slavery, and doomed them to toil in the mines. In vain did the clergy, both regular and secular, protest against an abuse as impolitic as it was barbarous. Their complaints were unheeded. There yet remained at the foot of the Cordilleras, in the plain that looks toward the Atlantic, between the Orinoco and the Rio de la Plata, a country filled with savages, where the Spaniards had not yet carried their baneful conquests. It was in the shades of these forests that the missionaries undertook to form a Christian republic, and to bestow, at least, upon a few of the natives the happiness which they were not allowed to bring to all. Yet these very tribes appeared, above all others, the least fitted to receive the truths of the gospel. Indolent, stupid and ferocious, they were the very type of primitive man degraded by his fall. There is no more striking evidence of the degeneracy of human nature, than the littleness of the savage amid the grandeur of the wilderness. On reaching Buenos Ayres, the Jesuits who had devoted themselves to that toilsome mission ascended the Rio de la Plata, and, entering the waters of the Paraguay, went in different directions, seeking the Indians in their native woods. The old accounts represent the Jesuit missionary with a breviary under the left arm, in the right hand a large cross, with no provisions other than faith and confidence in God. These apostles are described as forcing their way through the dense virgin forests, wading through vast marshes, waist deep in water, climbing steep and rugged rocks, entering into dens and precipices, at the risk of finding serpents and wild beasts instead of the human beings they sought. Many perished from hunger and fatigue; others were murdered and devoured by the savages. The first tribe that listened to the voice of the Jesuits was that of the Guaranis. They were formed into a colony under care of the Fathers Mareta and Cataldino, whose names are entitled to rank among

those of the benefactors of the human race. The colony received the name of Loretto, and, as the Indian churches successively arose, surrounded each by its little Christendom, they were all designated by the general name of " Reductions." In a few years they had reached the number of thirty, and, together, constituted that " Evangelical Republic" which has never been equalled in perfection by any government, ancient or modern. Each community or village was ruled by two missionaries, who had the direction of both spiritual and temporal matters. Public schools were opened in each one of them, for the education and instruction of the young; on leaving these schools, the young men were placed, according to their taste or particular fitness, in one of the workshops of the Reduction, to learn some useful trade. Those who showed a greater inclination for agricultural pursuits were enrolled in the class of husbandmen; while those who still retained some of the roving propensities of their former life followed the herds and flocks. There were no public market-places in the villages; on certain appointed days, every family received all the necessaries of life. The land was parcelled out, and each family cultivated a portion equal to its wants. There was, beside, a public field called the " Property of God." The fruits of this common property were set apart to supply the failures in the crops, for the support of widows, orphans and the sick. The military, civil and political offices of the Reductions were vested in a *cacique*, or war chief, a *corregidor*, for the administration of justice, with *regidores* and *alcaldes* for the police duty and the direction of the public works. The usual punishment for a first offence against the laws was a private reprimand by the missionaries; a second infraction was visited with a public penance at the door of the church, as among the first Christians; the third time the offender received a few strokes from a whip. And still, during the existence of this republic, through a space of one century and a half, hardly a single instance has been found of an Indian incurring the last-mentioned punishment. "All their faults," says Father Charlevoix, "are the faults of children; for such they remain, in many respects, during most of their lives, especially displaying all the good qualities of little ones."* Muratori paints this Christian republic in a single word, when he entitles his description of it, "Happy Christianity." Even Voltaire was obliged to confess that "the establishments formed in Paraguay by the Spanish Jesuits alone seemed to be, in some respects, the triumph of humanity"

While the heart of Pope Paul V was gladdened by these tidings from the New World, he was forced into a struggle against the obstinate resistance of an Italian State, which had always before been obedient to the Holy See. The Venetian Senate had issued a decree forbidding the alienation of secular property in favor of the churches or the clergy. It had ordered the arrest of two ecclesiastics and brought their case before a civil tribunal; at the same time prohibiting the building of churches, abbeys and hospitals, without permission from the secular authorities. Paul V protested against these measures, and the Senate refusing to consider the protest, the Pope, with the assent of the Sacred College, published a sentence of excommunication against the Republic (April 17, A. D. 1606). The Senate, far from yielding, declared the sentence unjust, decreed the severest penalties against the publication of the Papal sentence, and tried to induce the clergy to continue the public discharge of their sacred functions. The greater part of the regular clergy quitted the country, obedient to the voice of the successor of St. Peter. The Theatines, the Capuchins and the Jesuits were banished from the Venetian territory By the side of this material struggle arose one of a spiritual character. Paolo Sarpi, whom we have already had occasion to mention, was charged by the Doge and the Senate to defend the rights of the Republic. This duty he undertook to perform by attacking the Pontifical authority in aggressive pamphlets,

---

* In 1721, the Bishop of Buenos Ayres, Don Pedro Faxardo, could report to Philip V., of Spain: "Among these tribes of Indians, naturally inclined to the practice of the worst vices, innocence is so universal, that I do not believe a single mortal sin is ever committed in these Reductions."

which were distributed among the people generally. Baronius and Bellarmine met the violent attacks of the rebellious monk with an overwhelming array of learning and unanswerable argument. Paul V thought for a moment of trying the force of arms against the Venetian Republic. But he feared that the Senate might profit by that act of rigor to drag the whole State into the ranks of the Reformation. In this delicate juncture, Henry IV offered his mediation to the Sovereign Pontiff, who gladly accepted it. Preliminary negotiations were opened, and so skilfully carried on by the French king's ministers at Rome and Venice, that in 1607 the difficulty was definitively settled. The Pope consented to recall the censures he had pronounced. The Venetian Senate, on the other hand, annulled its decrees against the Holy See, restored the religious who had been expelled from Venice at the time of the interdict, except the Jesuits, who were not recalled until some time after, and withdrew the offensive laws which had given rise to the whole discussion.

6. The celebrated "Gunpowder Plot" had just been discovered in England, and the attention of the Sovereign Pontiff was attracted by the persecutions to which it gave rise against the Catholics. The king, James I., was born in the bosom of Catholicity This was enough to awake the suspicions of the schismatics, that he cherished a hidden affection for the faith of his fathers; and they left no means untried to ruin the Catholics in his estimation. The Gunpowder Plot occurred very opportunely for their purpose. Under the parliament house was a large unoccupied cellar, into which an opening had been made from beneath an adjoining house; here, on the day before the session, when the king, with all the nobility and both houses of parliament, was expected to be present, were discovered thirty-six barrels of powder and a quantity of combustible matter. The royal officers also seized a man whom they found in charge, with slow matches and a horse saddled and ready to fly as soon as the train should have been fired. The sensation to which this discovery gave rise throughout the whole king-

dom may be imagined. The chief conspirators were arrested. They were Percy and Catesby, both of noble lineage, both urged to the deed by political and personal motives entirely foreign to religion. This last point was not clearly proved in the trial; and yet the Protestants industriously spread the report that all the Catholics in the kingdom had shared in the odious conspiracy, and that its authors were the missionaries. The last assertion was aimed at the Jesuits who had come to England to combat the schism. They were accordingly persecuted with the utmost rigor, and more than thirty priests, religious and secular, Englishmen and foreigners, died under the torture. The Protestants might then exult in the success of their plans to make the Catholics odious to the king. More thorough and accurate investigation has since shown that the "Gunpowder Plot" was the work of one of James' ministers, who, with some of the courtiers, adopted this means of exciting the king's resentment against those of his subjects who had remained true to the Catholic faith. This hostility against the Catholics was likewise displayed in the parliamentary decree requiring every English subject to take the famous "Oath of Allegiance." By this oath they were bound to obey the king, notwithstanding any sentence of excommunication and deposition pronounced by the Pope, whose right to exercise any authority in England was utterly rejected. Paul V immediately dispatched two briefs to England, forbidding the Catholics, under the most severe penalties, to take the required oath (A. D. 1607). The persecution was accordingly carried on with renewed violence; the wretched victims were proscribed and cast into prison; many were driven to seek in a strange land the freedom they no longer enjoyed at home.

7 Still, amid all the serious cares of Paul V., Catholicity, under the standard of the Papacy, was steadily winning fresh triumphs. The King of Congo, lately converted to the faith, sent to the Pope a solemn request for missionaries to teach his people. In Poland, where Protestantism had ruled for a season, Sigismund III. was now following the impulse given by Catho

licity to the whole of Europe. He became king of Sweden by the death of his father, John (A. D. 1592). On his accession—though he had promised to uphold the privileges of the Reformed churches, and to leave all his subjects in the enjoyment of full freedom of conscience—all the hopes of the Catholics at once revived, while the Protestants were equally alarmed. They began a system of formidable opposition; but still Sigismund continued to favor the Catholic cause, and if he did not succeed in securing its complete triumph, he still showed the vital power of Catholicism in that period of religious reaction. It was to his influence that Poland owed the preservation of her faith; in that kingdom Protestantism was utterly annihilated (1607). In Germany, where each sovereign assumed the right of introducing into his States a religion according to his fancy, the Catholic princes felt especially bound to bring back their subjects to the Roman communion. Numerous conversions were witnessed in all parts of the land; this was the reaction against the Lutheran movement which had marked the opening of the preceding reign; Catholicity now began to make rapid progress in all directions. Switzerland, the soil in which Calvin had sown his cheerless and cruel doctrines, seemed farther removed than any other province from the influence of a return to Catholic truth. But God was preparing for her an apostolic missionary, whose mild and captivating speech, whose amiable and winning character, inexhaustible meekness and unwearied zeal, should renew among the mountains of Chablais and on the borders of Switzerland the wonders of conversion which marked the Apostolic age. We shall yet have occasion to speak more in detail of this wonder of the seventeenth century, of this saintly bishop and perfect gentleman, St. Francis of Sales, who united in his person the highest degree of virtue and learning, and who was the friend of St. Vincent de Paul.

8. But France was the field in which religion won its most splendid triumphs. Whatever Protestant writers may say to the contrary, the conversion of Henry IV was sincere, if a conversion may be judged by its visible results. Since his abju-

ration in the church of St. Denis, Henry had openly proclaimed his religious tendencies. His private instructions to the French ambassadors at Rome abound in the most unequivocal expressions of love and veneration for the Holy See. We have mentioned his efficacious mediation in the difficulty between Rome and Venice. We afterward find him seeking counsel from the Pope for the management of his political relations with Spain, confiding to him all his views, in which he displays a keen penetration and a masterly comprehension of the general condition of Europe. In the year 1598, he announced his intention of restoring the Church to a condition as flourishing as that which it enjoyed a century before. He recalled the Jesuits, and promised to support them in spite of the parliaments. The edict of Nantes, it is true, seemed to the Catholics to favor the Huguenots beyond measure. But the critical historian will perhaps find in this act of royal clemency, only a measure of pacification which should give to France a moment's calm after so many storms. Had Henry IV. known how to govern himself as he governed his people, he would unquestionably have been the greatest of kings. France, degraded and bleeding under the last of the Valois, rested at length under his paternal sceptre. Henry VI. was the monarch of his people's heart; they spoke with one voice to bless his rule. But this concert of praise was changed into a cry of grief and despair, when, on the 14th of May, A. D. 1610, Henry IV fell by the knife of the infamous Ravaillac. All Europe joined in the wail of France, and the great king had the glory of being mourned even by his enemies. Pope Paul V gave free expression to his grief. In a consistory, convoked as soon as the sad intelligence reached Rome, the Pope expressed all the anguish of his heart at an event so calamitous for the Church. He wrote to Mary de Medici, exhorting that princess to defend the faith, and to bring up her son, Louis XIII. in sentiments of true love for religion, " which has lost," said the Pope, " so powerful a protector in Henry IV "

9. Paul V continued to watch with zeal over the work of

moral reform, so happily begun in the Council of Trent. This reform was displayed by practical results and appeared in the foundation and discipline of a number of monastic institutions. No other Pope ever approved a greater number of religious orders and various congregations. The sisters of " Our Lady of Bordeaux," the " Ursulines of Paris," the Pauline Congregation, the Congregation of Priests of the Oratory, established by Cardinal De Berulle, the Nuns of the Visitation, instituted by St. Francis of Sales, all received their confirmation at his hands. This great Pontiff died on the 21st of January, A. D. 1621, after a reign of fifteen years. Paul V is one of the glories of the Catholic Church. In his Pontificate occurred the celebrated case of Galileo, which the enemies of the Church have always used as a ground of calumny against the Pope. The truth is that Paul V allowed Galileo to maintain his theory as an astronomical hypothesis ; but, at the same time, condemned the decided and peremptory tone with which the learned astronomer proclaimed his discovery, and claimed to rest it upon texts of Sacred Scripture.

§ II. Pontificate of Gregory XV (February 9, A. D. 1621—July 8, 1623).

10. Cardinal Alexander Ludovisio was elected to succeed Paul V on the 9th of February, A. D. 1621, and took the name of Gregory XV One of his first acts was to raise the bishopric of Paris to the rank of a metropolitan see, at the request of Louis XIII. The new Pope had always shown the greatest zeal for the conversion of infidels and heretics ; this zeal inspired the design of founding the College of the Propaganda (1622). The origin of the Propaganda is properly to be traced to an edict of Gregory XIII., in virtue of which a certain number of cardinals were charged with the direction of missions to the East, and catechisms were ordered to be printed in the less-known languages. But the institution was neither firmly established nor provided with the requisite funds. Gregory XV

gave it a constitution, contributed the necessary funds from his private purse, and as it met a want, the existence of which was really felt and acknowledged, its success was daily more and more brilliant. Who does not know what the Propaganda has done for philological learning ? But it chiefly labored, with admirable grandeur of conception and energy, to fulfil its great mission- -the propagation of the Catholic faith—with the most splendid results. Urban VIII., the immediate successor of Gregory XV., completed the work by the addition of the " Collegium de Propaganda Fide," where youth are trained in the study of all the foreign languages, to bear the name of Christ to every nation on the globe. The year which witnessed the establishment of the Propaganda was also signalized by the canonization of four saints, who enjoy a well-deserved celebrity in the Catholic Church—St. Ignatius of Loyola, St. Francis Xavier, St. Theresa, and St. Philip Neri.

11. But while the Sovereign Pontiff decreed that public worship should be paid to the founder of the Society of Jesus and to his illustrious disciple, the Jesuits were driven from Holland and forbidden to return, on pain of being arrested as enemies and obliged to pay a ransom (A. D. 1622). This measure was the more inexplicable, as the constitution of Holland contained an article granting freedom of conscience to all. " But it has always been the lot of the Jesuits," says a recent historian, " under every heretical government, to bear the weight of all the hatred and prejudice aimed at the Catholic Church." But from an opposite motive, the Emperor Ferdinand II., in order to root out heresy from his States, forbade the exercise of the Protestant worship at Prague, removed its ministers, and placed the university in charge of the Jesuits. The zeal of that religious prince did not stop here ; he also caused the expulsion of the Protestant ministers from the rest of Bohemia, from Moravia and part of Silesia.

12. Duke Maximilian, elector of Bavaria, and a zealous defender of Catholicity, having obtained possession of Heidelberg, presented its rich Palatine library to the Pope. Even

before the conquest of that city, Gregory XV had, through his legate, requested this favor of the duke. The elector readily promised to grant the wish of the Roman Pontiff. As soon as the news of the taking of Heidelberg reached the legate, he claimed the fulfilment of the promise. He knew that the manuscripts were of inestimable value, and he sent a special request to Tilly to protect the library from injury during the pillage. The Pope then dispatched Doctor Leone Allacci, scriptor of the Vatican, to Germany, to take possession of the literary treasure. Gregory was overjoyed; he declared that the acquisition of the Heidelberg library was one of the most fortunate events of his Pontificate; one of the most honorable and advantageous to the Holy See, to the Church and to learning generally; it was also glorious, he said, to the Bavarian name, that so precious a spoil should be preserved in Rome, the centre of the world (A. D. 1623).

13. Another fact of no less importance marked the Pontificate of Gregory XV.—the reform of the old religious orders in France. He saw considerable abuses to be corrected and the necessity of carrying out the great moral reform of Paul XV was becoming daily more evident. Louis XIII., who deserved the surname of the "Just," was convinced of this necessity He requested, and obtained, from the Pope, a brief to put an end to the disorders which scandalized the faithful, and intrusted his chief almoner, Cardinal De La Rochefoucault, with the delicate and difficult duty The virtuous prelate formed a council composed of a Benedictine, a Carthusian, a Dominican, a Minor, a Jesuit, a Cistercian, and of several others of solid and enlightened piety He met with a strong opposition, which gave a sad but convincing proof that long habits of relaxation are fearfully destructive of primitive fervor and piety. Still, by means of prudence, courage and zeal, the cardinal succeeded in restoring regular discipline to a flourishing state in all religious houses. Gregory XV., who had seconded his efforts with all the means at his command, did not live to witness the success of the glorious undertaking. The Pontiff died at the age

of seventy years, after a short but prosperous reign (July 8, A. D. 1623).

14. The first half of the seventeenth century was richly blessed with holy works and saintly characters. While in the distant Indies the blessed Peter Claver, a Jesuit, was faithfully fulfilling his vow " to be the slave of the negroes" (A. D. 1624), in Spain, St. Joseph of Calasanz was founding the regular clergy of the pious schools, *scholarum piarum* (1617), for the benefit of young men, but especially of the poor. St. Fidelis of Sigmaringen, the apostle of the Grisons, fell by the weapons of the Calvinists, a martyr to his zeal (1622). " Forgive them, Lord," he uttered as he expired, " for they know not what they do." At the same time, St. Josaphat, archbishop of Poloczk, in Lithuania, also gave his blood for the faith, and was murdered by the inhabitants of Muscovy, whom he had come to convert (November 16, 1623). Thus, at the very time when the Lutheran heresy flattered itself that it might soon witness the obsequies of the Church, that divine spouse of Christ was displaying a wonderful vitality and wealth of good works in every part of the world; in the Indies, in Japan, in China, in the New World, in Spain, in Italy, in Germany and in Poland. It was like a new outpouring of the spirit of truth which ever abides in her and which had inspired the decrees of the Council of Trent. The Carmelite nuns of St. Theresa's reform were established in Paris in 1604, and the barefooted friars of the same order, in 1611. The French clergy was illustrated, at this epoch, by a simple priest, who rose up to be its glory and a prodigy of Christian charity with which his name is synonymous. St. Vincent de Paul, born in 1576, at Poï, in the diocese of Acqs, was now laying the foundation of the truly apostolic congregation of St. Lazarus, or of the " Priests of the Mission," and giving a foretaste of his life of marvels.

15. The same period witnessed the death of St. Francis of Sales, so thoroughly French in mind, in language and in heart. Francis was born on the 21st of August, A. D. 1567, at the castle of Sales, three leagues from Annecy, and trained by a

pious mother in sentiments of the most tender piety   Entering the ecclesiastical state at an early age, he undertook the conversion of the province of Chablais, where his efforts were crowned with the most splendid success.   He was soon after placed in the episcopal see of Geneva, which he found thickly peopled with Calvinists, upon whom he at once began to exercise his disinterested zeal.   Henry IV., hearing that the income of the see of Geneva was very limited, directed that a pension of a thousand crowns should be offered to the bishop in his name.   "Tell his Majesty," replied Francis, "that I feel too much honored by his gift to refuse it, but that, not being in immediate want of money, and being utterly unable to keep it, I beg his permission to leave it in the hands of his treasurer, to be drawn as necessity shall require."   Henry, on receiving this answer, said to his ambassador: "I have never been better thanked for a pension than by the Bishop of Geneva."   The example of the holy prelate's life and the resistless unction of his words brought back the Calvinists in crowds to the true fold.   "I can convince the heretics," said Cardinal Duperron, "but it takes the Bishop of Geneva to convert them."   The affectionate piety of the saint appears in every work from his graceful pen.   Henry IV requested of him a book that should show virtue in an attractive light.   St. Francis answered the royal wish by his immortal work, the "Introduction to a Devout Life," which was received with universal applause and translated into every European language.   The King of France declared that the author had surpassed his expectation.   Mary de Medici sent a jewelled copy to James I., who, although a Protestant, read it with the greatest delight and asked his bishops "why they could not write with the same unction?"   The treatise on the "Love of God," fit sequel to the "Introduction," filled the measure of affection and love with which St. Francis was regarded by all.   The number of souls saved by these two works is known only in heaven.   The holy bishop, in concert with St. Jane Frances Frémiot, baroness of Chantal, founded the Order of the Visitation, which has preserved its fervor and regularity through every storm, and still continues to edify the Church. St. Francis of Sales died on the 28th of December, 1622, rich in glory and merits. His virtues recall those of the greatest bishops whose names the Church holds in veneration.

§ III. PONTIFICATE OF URBAN VIII. (August 6, A. D. 1623— June 29, 1644).

16. Cardinal Maffeo Barberini, sprung from an old and illustrious family of Florence, was elected Pope on the 6th of August, A. D. 1623, and took the name of Urban VIII. The new Pope, by his distinguished love of letters, his mild and amiable disposition, his patronage of scholars, and his collection of Latin hymns, in which the graces of poetry minister to the most tender outpourings of piety, had won among the learned the surname of the "Attic Bee." His election was received with universal favor, and the zeal which he displayed for the interests of religion confirmed the hopes inspired by his promotion. The Pontificate of Urban VIII. was contemporaneous with a series of events which threatened the peace of Europe. In France, Louis XIII. had intrusted the management of affairs to a man whose bold and unbending mind was to direct, with the hand of a master, the destinies of the world. Richelieu, bishop of Luçon and afterward cardinal, was about to rule for a quarter of a century, in the name of his royal master, and to prepare France for the splendid reign of Louis XIV. In England, James I. left his throne to his son Charles I. (1625), who inaugurated a reign which was to end upon the scaffold, by a blind favoritism toward the Duke of Buckingham, a frivolous, ambitious and narrow-minded minister, whose incapacity was opening a gulf beneath the throne, into which the royal power was doomed to sink. In Spain, Olivares, prime minister of Philip IV., was endeavoring to oppose his influence to that of Richelieu.

17 All these elements of dissension, which were working

in the bosom of European society, combined to give to the Thirty Years' War, which broke out in Germany, a character of fierceness and obstinacy without a parallel in history The struggle was opened by a revolt of the Bohemian Protestants, under the elector-palatine, Frederick V (A. D. 1618). The emperor, Ferdinand II., supported by the Spaniards and the Catholic League of Germany, defeated the rebels in the battle of Prague. Their leader was deprived of his electorate, which the conqueror bestowed upon Maximilian, duke of Bavaria (1620). The contest seemed to be at an end; but it was only in its first stage, called the "Palatine War." The powers of the North took part with the German Protestants. Christian IV., king of Denmark, marched against the emperor (1624–1629), and this phase of the struggle was called the "Danish period." The "Swedish period" was opened by the brilliant exploits of Gustavus Adolphus (1630–1635). At length Richelieu threw the resources of his great mind into the scales and opened the "French period" (1635–1648). It does not enter into the scope of our work to give a detailed account of the events which belong to the political history of Europe. The Thirty Years' War, which began on a religious ground, was not carried out on any determined plan, nor to the particular end for which it had been undertaken. No man, in the beginning, could foresee its extent or its real bearing. From all directions and on all occasions, it was constantly receiving new elements of agitation and revenge; every personal enmity, every political altercation, was merged in this great quarrel, and never was the truth of the axiom more truly demonstrated, that "war is fed by war."

18. Amid the general conflagration, Italy had her own private grounds of fear. The house of Austria had been growing in power since the time of Charles V., and was beginning to exercise a marked influence on the general interests of Europe. Its alliance with Spain added to its already too threatening preponderance. The Alpine passes were held by Spain; Austria seized those which lead to the German States. The minor

principalities of Italy deemed it a threat to be thus surrounded, hemmed in by the two formidable powers. Venice and Savoy concluded a treaty, offensive and defensive, with France, in virtue of which the house of Austria was to be forced, by their united power, to give up the passes and the territory of the Grisons. At the same time the Pope was chosen as mediator and supreme arbiter between the parties. The Pontifical troops garrisoned the fortified places which caused so much fear and rivalry Urban strove to keep the balance equal among so many opposing claims and to secure the triumph of peace. But Richelieu, whose foreign policy was wholly directed to the abasement of the house of Austria, refused to adopt the peaceful measures proposed by the Sovereign Pontiff. Regardless of the Pope's complaints, he began to act on the offensive in Italy, marched French troops suddenly into the Valteline, and drove the Papal garrisons out of the fortified towns. Spite of all his leaning to France, Urban VIII. possessed too much sense of his high dignity to allow the expulsion of his garrisons. He ordered troops to be raised and to march into the Milanese, for the express purpose of retaking the lost places, with the coöperation of the Spaniards. The French minister found himself in the anomalous position of a cardinal at war with the Sovereign Pontiff. He saw the danger of such a position, and hastened to get out of it. A treaty of peace was soon proclaimed between the belligerent powers.

19. All Richelieu's genius was now called to the wants of France. Buckingham had been preparing a formidable invasion to help the French Calvinists. In July, A. D. 1627, he appeared off the coast of France with a large fleet; he landed in the isle of Rhé, occupied it, and laid siege to the citadel of St. Martin. The Huguenots were soon in arms to second this movement in their favor. The centre of their power was La Rochelle, which had been granted to them by the edict of Nantes. Richelieu, whose genius unfolded its resources with redoubled vigor in moments of difficulty, took the city in October, 1628. The principal fortress of Protestantism in France

had fallen.   The Huguenots were obliged to receive terms from the conqueror : they ceased to be a power, and allowed Richelieu to act with more freedom in the general concerns of Europe. It was then that he began to take a really active share in the Thirty Years' War, which was ended by the treaty of Westphalia, in 1648, and completed the downfall of the Austrian power.

20. Urban VIII. profited by the political struggles which shook all Europe, to increase the influence of the Holy See, by making it the mediator between the contending powers.   The events of his time afforded him daily opportunities of displaying his firmness, zeal, and vigilance.   His career was vast, immense, and he was ever equal to his mission in that stormy epoch.   The duchy of Urbino, after the death of the last duke, who was childless, escheated to the Holy See, notwithstanding the jealousy of the other Italian States, which were greatly troubled at the successive additions made to the Pontifical States.

21. While the political world resounded with the clash of arms, a new struggle was shaking the religious world, and was gradually assuming the character of a heresy, the more dangerous in proportion as its partisans pretended to remain in close communion with the centre of unity   The other sects openly professed their contempt for ecclesiastical authority   Luther, Calvin and Zwingli gloried in having broken asunder the bonds which held them to the Roman communion; the Jansenists, on the contrary, wished to be of the Church, in spite of the Church, and would never acknowledge that they had separated themselves from it.   Cornelius Jansenius was born in Holland in 1585.   He began his studies at Utrecht and finished them in the University of Louvain.   He studied theology under the nephew of the famous Baïus and under James Janson, two zealous propagators of Baïanism.   The young student was so much taken up with the great question of grace, then discussed in all the schools, that he read the works of St. Augustine ten times successively, and summed up the fruit of

his reading in an enormous folio volume, which he published under the title of "Augustinus," after his promotion to the bishopric of Ypres. He died before the publication of the whole work, declaring in his will that he submitted his doctrine to the judgment of the Holy See.

22. The "Augustinus" is divided into three parts, which treat of grace, free will, original sin, and predestination. Jansenius lays down the principle, that the human will is not free According to his theory, the human will is taken captive and held in bonds by the desire after earthly things, and is unable, by its own strength, to raise itself from that condition ; grace must come to its assistance. This impotence, according to Jansenius, arises from the fact that the will is weakened by concupiscence, which draws it away from what is good into the opposite extreme, so that man can no longer will efficaciously. With this doctrine of the weakness of the will, Jansenius maintains the irresistible force of grace. Grace, he says, is always efficacious, and it is not in the power of man to avoid or to resist its action. The system contained in this work has since been summed up by Dr. Cornet, syndic of the theological faculty of Paris, in these five propositions : " 1st. Some of God's commandments are impossible to just men, spite of their good will and endeavors. 2d. In the state of fallen nature, we never resist interior grace. 3d. For merit or demerit, there is no need of a freedom exempt from the necessity of acting ; it is enough to have a liberty free from constraint. 4th. The semi-Pelagians were heretics only in so far as they maintained that man can resist interior and prevenient grace. 5th. Jesus Christ did not die and did not shed His blood for all men." Such is the doctrinal substance of the " Augustinus."

23. On its first appearance at Louvain (A. D. 1640), it excited, on one side, the most enthusiastic admiration, on the other, the most merited censure. A Frenchman, John Duvergier, of Hauranne, so well known as the Abbé de Saint-Cyran, introduced the " Augustinus" into France and labored to spread its doctrines. Saint-Cyran was an innovator imbued with the

spirit of Calvinism, but a secret and skilful innovator, who knew how to prepare remotely the elements of the sect which he wished to draw around him. He soon had as proselytes the family of Arnauld d'Andilly, whose two daughters, celebrated as Mothers Angélique and Agnes, directed the abbey of Port Royal. Whether or not there was, at this time, between Saint-Cyran, Jansenius and other believers in their doctrines, a secret association, a plan of attack against the Church, drawn up by the sectaries at Bourg-Fontaine, is one of those problems which history has not yet satisfactorily solved. However this may have been, it is certain that every thing was made ready in France for the long-continued scandals which appeared with the work of Jansenius. With a view to silencing the discussions which were daily growing more. bitter, Urban VIII. published a decree forbidding the reading of the "Augustinus." The University of Louvain refused to receive this Pontifical order. It was in vain that the Pope addressed a second brief to the refractory doctors, representing the scandal of their disobedience; the second appeal was not more effectual than the first. Leaving the rebels to follow their self-willed course, Urban determined to pronounce a solemn and decisive judgment. The work of Jansenius and the writings on both sides were placed in the charge of the holy office, that they might be examined with the utmost care and attention.

24. On the report of the consulters, and by his own personal examination, the Pope found the "Augustinus" condemnable in two points : first, because it treated the question of grace in a manner contrary to the formal prohibition of the Holy See; and in matter, since nearly every page renewed the errors already condemned in the writings of Baïus. Therefore, on the 6th of March, A. D. 1642, the Pope issued the bull, *In Eminenti*, condemning the work. "After a thorough examination of the work entitled *Augustinus*," said the Pope, "it has been found to contain a formal expression of several propositions already condemned by Our predecessors, which it teaches to the great scandal of Catholics, without any respect for the

authority of the Holy See.   With the intention of applying
a suitable remedy to this disorder which is agitating all Christian society, and which tends to the ruin of the Catholic faith,
We, of Our own accord, of Our certain knowledge and in the
fulness of the Apostolic power, do, in all things and for all time,
by this present constitution, which shall have force of perpetuity,
confirm and approve the constitutions of Our predecessors,
Popes Pius and Gregory   In virtue of the same authority,
We, by these presents, absolutely prohibit, and wish that all
hold as prohibited, the work known as the "Augustinus," as
containing and renewing, to Our certain knowledge, the articles,
opinions and sentiments censured and condemned by the said
constitutions.   Moreover, We command, on pain of incurring
all the penalties and censures contained in the constitution of
Pius, Our predecessor, that none of the faithful, of what rank
or condition soever, presume to speak, write, or dispute, concerning the articles condemned in this book.   Absolution from
the censures incurred by the refractory shall be exclusively
reserved to the Sovereign Pontiff, except in danger of death."
The judgment of the Roman Church, to which Jansenius,
on his death-bed, declared his submission, did not meet
with the same obedience from his disciples.   The University
of Louvain received the decision only after many delays and
evasions.   In France, the Archbishop of Paris, John Francis
de Gondi, had silenced both parties even before the decision of
the Holy See.   As soon as he received the bull, he ordered its
reception throughout his whole diocese.   The faculty of Paris
supported his endeavors by forbidding the condemned propositions to be maintained ; still they had many partisans, chief
among whom were Saint-Cyran and the young doctor Arnauld.
The bull *In Eminenti* had been sent to all the Catholic churches
in the world, and was everywhere received with submission
and respect.   The King of Spain, as sovereign of the Netherlands, commanded the doctors of Louvain to follow this
example and to put an end to their scandalous opposition.   But
the partisans of the new error paid as little heed to the royal

order as to the Pontifical censures. Subterfuge and discussion were multiplied and prolonged in the University of Louvain.

25. Urban VIII. was preparing again to fulminate the ecclesiastical censures against the rebel theologians ; but he was not to see the end of those troubles which were destined to disturb the whole of the seventeenth century Of all the heresies, Jansenism has shown itself the most hypocritically obstinate. Its spirit more or less pervaded society, especially in France, and the baneful error entirely disappeared only in the great storm which, at the close of the eighteenth century, convulsed France and the world. Urban VIII. died on the 29th of July, A. D. 1644. Louis XIII. had gone before him to the grave (May 16, 1643), after displaying upon the throne the example of Christian virtues. His contemporaries called him the "Just." To the most fervent prayers he owed the birth of the royal infant, Louis XIV., who was destined to raise his father's kingdom to such a height of glory In gratitude for this favor of Heaven, Louis XIII. placed his kingdom under the protection of the Blessed Virgin* (August 15, 1638). He died in the arms of St. Vincent de Paul. His minister, Richelieu, had passed away some months before him (December 4, 1642). Richelieu was born to command; he knew how to plan and to execute great things. The two great objects which he had steadily kept in view during his long administration were accomplished. The Calvinists had been crushed in France. The house of Austria, assailed, at once, in all its possessions, in Alsatia, in the Netherlands, in Italy and Catalonia, during the French period of the Thirty Years' War, had lost its paramount influence in European councils. Four years more, and the sword of Condé was to finish the great work of Richelieu, when the victories of Rocroy, Friburg, Nordlingen and Lens, had forced the Imperialists to sign the treaty of Westphalia, which put an end to the Thirty Years' War and to the prepon-

---

* To this event may be traced the origin of the yearly procession celebrated on the feast of the Assumption, and known as "Le vœu de Louis XIII."; it is still kept in many churches in France

derance of Austria (1648).   The imperial colossus which, since
the time of Charles V., threatened to crush Europe, was now,
according to the prophetic expression of Henry IV., but the
statue of Nabuchodonosor, with feet of clay and a head of gold.
Looking only at these great results, we might be inclined to
pronounce the ministry of Richelieu in every way worthy of
the eulogium of history and the admiration of posterity   But
genius, however great and lofty, always betrays some weak
point by which it pays its tribute to human nature.   Richelieu
thought that, by exaggerating the power of royalty, he was
doing his country a service.   He took upon himself the task of
crushing the power of the nobility, to aggrandize the throne
upon its ruins.   This was a deep political error.   When there
was no longer any intermediary power between the king and
the people, a question of principle was substituted for a question of persons.   Popular sovereignty stood face to face with
royal sovereignty, and its accession was signalized by the ruin
of France.   All is of a piece in that history !*   The executions
of Marshal de Marillac and of the youthful De Thou were so
many unjust and uncalled-for cruelties which all the lustre of
his glory cannot hide in oblivion.

26. While the world was pre-occupied with the movements
of belligerent powers and the grand manœuvres of politicians, Christian charity was silently working its highest wonders.   A humble priest had accepted the mission of healing
every wound, of soothing every pang caused by the war.   St.
Vincent de Paul was the support of the wasted provinces of
Lorraine, Champagne and Picardy   He sent relief to the
Catholics of England, Ireland and Scotland, who were suffering
under Protestant oppression.   In his tireless zeal, he hastened
to relieve every pain.   The treasures of charity were multiplied
in his hands.   He harbored the little ones forsaken by their
mothers *in the natural order*, and thus became their father *in*

---

* The heroic blood of the Montmorencys, which Richelieu sacrificed to a false and disastrous theory, left upon the purple of the cardinal a stain which time cannot efface.

the order of grace. He established hospitals for the sick, the aged and the incurable; and, to perpetuate for all time the many fruitful works with which he had blessed his age, he founded that admirable institution, the " Sisters of Charity," the wonder of the world, the living evidence of the divinity of the Catholic religion. The congregation of St. Lazarus, also of his foundation, was, at the same time, sending missionaries to the ʳChristian slaves in Barbary, and on the shores of India and Madagascar. The heart of St. Vincent took in the whole world. St. Francis Regis was at this period the apostle of the mountain districts of Vivarais, Cevennes, Vélay, while Michel Le Nobletz evangelized the people of Brittany Adrien Bourdoise and Claude Bernard, so widely known as the "Poor Priest," recalled the holy life and pious toil of the clergy of the first ages of the Church. The venerable pastor of St. Sulpice, Father Olier, was laying the foundation, in his parish, of the seminary which still bears its name and whose rule has become that of nearly every seminary in France. The spirit of religion still animated society, spite of the ravages of Protestantism. The Church was still the rich field of the Heavenly Husbandman, bringing forth hundredfold fruits of grace and life.

CHAPTER VIII.

HISTORICAL REVIEW OF THE SEVENTH PERIOD.

1 Protestantism. Its development favored by human passions.—2. Principies of Protestantism in their application to the political and social world.—3. Council of Trent.—4. The Jesuits.—5. Their constitution.—6. Their hic-rarchy.—7. Labors of the Jesuits.—8. Contemporaneous orders. Congre-gation of the Benedictines of St. Maurus.—9. Foreign missions.—10. The-ologians.—11. Commentaries on Sacred Scripture.—12. Ascetic works.—13 Art still subsidiary to the service of the Church.

1. The prominent and controlling feature of the seventh period of the history of the Church is Protestantism. We have sufficiently enlarged upon the circumstances which favored its development, and pointed out the nature and dangerous conse-quences of its teachings. The concurrence of the great events which changed the society of the middle-ages ; which, by the revival of letters, gave a new impulse to the human mind ; which opened, in the discovery of America, unknown paths to the ambition of adventurers and to the genius of commerce ; which gave, in the invention of printing, a medium of rapid interchange of thought between different nations ; which, by the use of fire-arms, changed the ancient mode of warfare, thus multiplying, in every quarter of Europe, those bands of merce-nary troops, ready to sell their blood to the highest bidder— these causes unquestionably helped the progress of Luther's errors. It seemed to be the impression that all must be new in an age and in a society upon which had dawned, at once, the light of so many new discoveries. In Germany, Luther appeared, in some sort, the Columbus of theology   Yet serious and reflecting minds were not misled by these deceitful appear-ances. They soon perceived that the so-called Reformation

owed its success only to the complicity of all the worst passions. " The success of the Protestants," says Bossuet, "is
not surprising, nor is it at all honorable to themselves. The
causes of that success could not have been more natural nor
more human. What wonder that heresies which favor the
inclinations of corrupt nature should have spread with great
rapidity? Why should we be surprised that, when the doors
of the cloisters were opened, when priests, monks and nuns
found themselves at liberty to marry, many allowed themselves
to fall into the snare set by concupiscence? When men were
offered full liberty to dispense with the hardest obligations of
the ecclesiastical laws, such as fasting and penance, what
miracle that carnal souls, with which the Church was at that
time filled, should have been disposed to give a willing ear to
such carnal doctrines? Is it, again, a miracle that men who
were assailing incomprehensible mysteries, which appeared
contrary to sense and reason, should have dragged along with
them, into the ways of impiety, the curious, proud, presumptuous minds, which always abound? Is it, in fine, a matter of
astonishment, that, by the excitement of an ill-regulated zeal
against the disorders which the Church was the first to mourn,
many Christians were carried even into schism and revolt. The
new Reformers having enlisted in their cause concupiscence,
pride, vanity, a spirit of independence and imprudent zeal, and
adapted their opinions to passions so natural, so common and
so powerful, their success is not more surprising than that of
Mahomet, for it displays the same characteristics."

2. Beside, to view the Reformation as a purely theological
dispute, would be to view it in too narrow a light. The political and social characters of Lutheranism equally claim the
attention of the historian. When the teachings of the monk
of Wittenberg had introduced the principle of private interpretation into religious questions, the Christian world of the middle-
ages, which had rallied around the See of Rome, as the centre
of all authority, gave place to a society in which incredulity
was substituted for the warmth of religious polemics. Ideas

of liberty were gradually transferred from the sphere of religion to that of politics. The nations of northern Europe, intoxicated with this new spirit of independence, seemed to vie with each other in seeking the most crooked by-ways of pride, license and impiety. When the saving yoke of religion was thrown off, when that curb was broken, radical ideas of liberty possessed the masses. They were inflamed by the philosophy and the Voltairian writings of the eighteenth century; the inconceivable supineness of rulers allowed the work of destruction to come to a head; and, at a given moment, every throne was seen to totter, some crumbled amid bloodshed, an unprecedented torrent of crimes deluged Europe, leaving it strewn with ruins and scaffolds. The barbarism of civilization, a thousand times more fearful than that of the ninth and tenth centuries, threatened every nation in the name of *liberty*. It seems to us that the close connection between the two fatal epochs of the Reformation and the Revolution has been too much overlooked. The one was the cradle of the other. Luther's principle, applied to the political and social world, has overturned all Europe, and thrown it into a deep and dark gulf where it rolls in continual convulsions, unable to find either peace or repose.

3. At the very moment when Protestantism thus invaded the world, under a show of restoring the Church to the primitive purity of its institution, a salutary reform was springing from the midst of the Church itself, a reform promulgated by the lawful authority, in a solemn assembly, amid the acclamations of the whole world. The crying need of a council had long been felt and its convocation was earnestly desired, but the wars between Charles V and Francis I. always placed new obstacles in its way. We have seen with what persevering energy the Papacy struggled against these ever-renewed difficulties, and finally succeeded in assembling the immortal Council of Trent. "It does not require a deep investigation into the sessions of this celebrated council," says Alzog, "to produce the conviction that never did any synod, with more prudence, clearness and precision, unfold and define so complete a body

of important questions.   Extremes met upon common ground, each tempering the other, and the result was the equilibrium necessary for Catholic truth.   The Spanish bishops and theologians distinguished themselves by the wisdom with which they managed to settle the opposition and the difficulties of all kinds which came under various forms from the different nations. No other assembly ever brought together a greater number of cardinals, bishops and theologians distinguished for sincere piety and solid learning.   What happy changes, what an immense advance would have been wrought in the Church, had all their decrees been faithfully observed, according to the desire of those virtuous representatives of Catholicity!   But personal considerations, of policy or of ambition, unhappily prevailed in some European States and prevented the adoption of the disciplinary canons of the council.   In France, the opposition proceeded from the parliaments, strongly imbued with the principles of Gallicanism.   In Spain, the decrees were always promulgated with the accompanying restriction : " Without prejudice to the royal prerogatives."   The opposition, in France, was chiefly directed against the decrees relating to fines and imprisonment, in spiritual matters to be left to the ecclesiastical power, against those forbidding duels, concubinage, and divorce; those reserving the judgment of bishops to the Pope alone, and those relating to the consent of parents deemed necessary in France for marriages, and not required by the council, &c., &c.

4. In the great struggle between Protestantism and the Church, the members of the old religious orders had not done all that might have been expected from their zeal and piety Some had stood passive spectators of the combat; others had even given the scandal of apostasy.   The Holy Ghost, ever abiding in the Church, then raised up a new order, called into being by the force of circumstances, and, therefore, fitted to meet the wants of the time.   This order, being especially destined to counterbalance the influence of Protestantism in the Church, has always appeared an object of terror to Protestant minds, which can view it only as an equally frightful and odious

ɔugbear for mankind. Even within the pale of the Catholic Church itself, truth and justice have not always shaped the judgments formed of the illustrious order of the Jesuits, which has awakened so many storms of hatred only because it has evei waged a relentless war against every evil passion. The constitution of the order, which is much clearer and stronger than that of any other, may be summed up as follows :

5. The end of this society is the greater glory of God —A. M. D. G.* its motto. Its members are to labor for the salvation of their neighbor as for their own. Their duty toward their neighbor they discharge by means of preaching, missions, catechetical instructions, conferences with the heretics, the confessional, and especially by the education of youth ; their own perfection they seek by means of mental prayer, examination of conscience, the reading of ascetical works and frequent communion. Candidates for admission are tried by a novitiate of two years, during which time all studies are laid aside, and the novices devote their time chiefly to spiritual exercises. At the end of the novitiate the novice may be admitted to the first vows, which are like those of other orders. The poverty of the members consists in their incapacity to possess, either individually or collectively, any income or property ; they are to remain satisfied with what is given them to supply their wants. The colleges, however, are endowed, in order that neither students nor teachers may be taken from their duties to provide for their own subsistence. After the novitiate they begin the course of studies—languages, belles-lettres, rhetoric, philosophy, theology, Church history, and the Sacred Scriptures. While pursuing these studies, they preserve the spirit of piety in their hearts by means of frequent examination of conscience, by approaching the Sacraments at least every eighth day, and by renewing their vows twice a year. When they go out of the house, they should generally have a companion. After the completion of his studies, the Jesuit performs a second

* Ad majorem Dei gloriam.

novitiate, lasting one year, during which he is employed in spiritual duties and lives in retirement, perfecting himself in the knowledge of the constitutions of his order. The members of the order are divided into three classes, according to their degree of learning and virtue : 1st. The *Professed*, who, beside the three monastic vows, make a fourth vow of absolute obedience to the Pope, in regard to missions. There are comparatively few *Professed*, or Jesuits of the four vows. From this class are chosen the general and the other principal superiors. Their establishments are : the *Professed houses*, directed by a *præpositus ;* the *colleges*, containing at least thirteen members, under a *rector ;* the *residences*, in charge of a *superior.* The pretended *monita secreta* of the *professed*, which have been so often charged upon the society as a reproach, are but a shameful calumny ; the same is true of the passage in the constitution of the order, which has often been and is still construed by some writers as if it gave to the superiors of the order the right of obliging their inferiors to commit a sin ; but this results from a malicious mistranslation ;* 2d. The *Spiritual Coadjutors*, who are in greater number, according to their talents and the constitutions of the order, aid the *Professed* in their ministry ; 3d. The *Temporal Coadjutors*, or lay brothers, who are received for domestic employments.

6. Each province is governed by a *provincial.* At the head of the whole order is a general, who resides at Rome, and enjoys full power within the limits of the constitution. Modifications can be introduced only by the General Congregations The general appoints nearly all the officers of the order, to

---

* The passage alluded to is the following : "Visum est nobis in Domino, excepto expresso voto quo Societas summo Pontifici, pro tempore existenti, tenetur, ac tribus aliis essentialibus paupertatis, castitatis, et obedientiæ, nullas constitutiones, declarationes vel ordinem ullum vivendi, posse obligationem ad peccatum mortale vel veniale inducere, nisi superior ea in nomine Domini Jesu Christi, vel in virtute obedientiæ, juberet." The context and the connection of the passage evidently shows the meaning to be that "the four solemn vows alone are always binding ; the other constitutions and ordinances can be binding only when the superior commands in virtue of obedience or in the name of Jesus Christ."

prevent whatever dissensions and intrigues might arise from elections by suffrage; yet these appointments are made after consultation with the provincial and the proper consulters The superiors of the various houses, at stated times, send reports to the general of the capacity and conduct of their subjects. The general has also six *assistants*, whose advice he is bound to seek; they are to be tried and able men, belonging to different nations, by the names of which they are respectively known. They are elected by the General Congregation, and form the council of the general, but without authority, except that of calling a General Congregation in extraordinary cases. The General Congregation also elects the general's *admonitor*, who must admonish him whenever he deems it necessary. Thus the society, constituted on the plan of a firmly organized constitutional monarchy, with a wise and perfect legislation, was destined, both by this organization and by the vigorous spirit which animated it, to acquire a great authority and wield an immense influence in the world. The constitution maintains the strictest unity in the system and matter of teaching, amid the most fruitful activity; it aims at repressing, with the most vigorous energy, whatever is at variance with the doctrine of the Church, leaving, at the same time, in matters of mere opinion, a freedom which favors the aspirations of genius.

7 The Society of Jesus, thus constituted, spread with wonderful rapidity Germany, the cradle of Protestantism, was opened to its zeal by the Emperor Ferdinand I. The universities, shaken by the Lutheran movement, threatened a speedy ruin. For twenty years, not a single priest had been furnished by the once flourishing University of Vienna. This state of things induced Ferdinand to call the Jesuits into his States (A. D. 1551). The most distinguished among the members who answered his call were Le Jay and Canisius. By uninterrupted courses of instructions, frequent sermons, the re-organization of the University of Vienna, the publication of a new catechism and the prudent administration of the diocese, Canisius soon restored order, and had the glory of bringing

back multitudes of Protestants to the Church.   The celebrated college of the Jesuits at Friburg, in Switzerland, also recalls the energetic zeal of Canisius (beatified, November 20, A. D. 1864). The same circumstances brought the sons of St. Ignatius to Bavaria.   At Ingolstadt, they were intrusted with the chairs of theology   Le Jay explained the Psalms, Salmeron the Epistles of St. Paul and the Gospels, while Canisius taught dogma. Their eminent success here soon opened to them the gates of Munich (1559).   They revived the taste for classical, literary and scientific studies, which the Protestants rejected in their system of teaching, as a worldly, useless and dangerous occupation.   From that time the Catholic Church of Bavaria was protected against hostile attacks.   The same benefits arose from the foundation of their colleges at Cologne (1559), Treves (1561), Mentz (1562), Augsburg and Dillingen (1563), Paderborn (1585), Wurtzburg (1586), Münster and Saltzburg (1588), Bamberg (1595), Antwerp, Prague, and Posen (1571), and in other northern countries.   Everywhere they became the support and the bulwark of the Church.   Their remarkable works in every department of theology, philosophy, grammar.and philology, were found in every quarter of the learned world. Such were the works of Tursellini (*De Particulis Linguæ Latinæ*), of Viger (*De Idiotismis Linguæ Græcæ*), of John Perpinianus, Pontanus, Vernulæus and others, on elegant latinity; of James Balde, Sarbiewski, Jouvency, Vanière and Spée, on poetry; of Clavius, Hel, Scheiner, Schall, de Bell, Poczobut, at Wilna, on mathematics and astronomy; of Kircher, Nieremberg and Raczinski, on natural philosophy and history; of Acunha, Charlevoix, Dobritzhoffer and Gerbillon, on geography; of Aquaviva, Mariana and Ribadeneira, on history, hagiography and political science.   It has been universally conceded by men of judgment, that the Jesuits' system of teaching, by the union of science and religion, by the wise and paternal guidance with which it supports the mind, is admirably suited to the education of youth.   In support of this opinion, we will only quote the words of the most just, but the most unfortunate of kings. " Government," said Louis XVI., " has always found a special support in that celebrated society, which trained up youth in obedience to the State, in the knowledge of arts, sciences and literature. Choiseul gave up the Jesuits to the persecutions of the parliaments; he gave up youth to systems of false philosophy, or to the influence of the most dangerous parliamentary opinions. By overthrowing the Jesuits, he has made, to the great prejudice of education and science, a gap which no other religious body can ever fill." It is not surprising that the ability and moral worth of the Jesuits should have often caused them to be summoned to the courts of princes. Thus they were involved in the great political events of the seventeenth century This has been brought against them as a crime, as if sovereigns were not free to use the lights and counsels of learned men, for the single reason that those men have made a vow to devote their energy and their zeal to the greater glory of God and of the Church.

8. We have successively mentioned the new religious orders which came forward with the Jesuits, to offer their services to the Papacy, in its struggle against the spirit of independence and schism awakened by the teachings of the Reformers. The Theatines, the Somasques, the Barnabites, the Oratorians and the Lazarists proved themselves worthy champions of the truth. The Carmelite nuns of St. Theresa, the Order of the Visitation, of St. Francis of Sales, the Ursulines and the Sisters of Charity, were renewing the prodigies of austerity, of holy contemplation and of heroic self-devotion which characterized the fervor of the early ages. The Benedictine order put forth a new branch destined to revive its ancient glory. This once flourishing and active order had been gradually sinking under the influence of relaxation. It had become poor in the midst of its immense wealth. After many fruitless attempts at reformation, the duty was undertaken by Didier de la Cour, prior of the monastery of St. Vannes. He was still young when this community was placed under his charge, and he determined to restore it to its former reputation for science and literature, and to introduce

the disciplinary reform which had now become indispensably necessary. The monasteries of Moyen-Moutier and of St. Hidulphus received the new rule which was confirmed by Pope Clement VIII. (A. D. 1604). It was also favorably received by many other monasteries in France. The general chapter, held in 1618, in the abbey of St. Mansuy, at Tulle, resolved to form a particular congregation of the reformed houses, under the patronage of St. Maurus, the greatest of St. Benedict's dis ciples. The congregation was approved by Pope Gregory XV It attracted the attention and lively interest of Richelieu, and soon numbered one hundred and eighty abbeys and conventual priories. Beside the rule common to all the Benedictines, the congregation had several particular statutes, and a superior-general who resided in the abbey of St. Germain, in Paris. The "Congregation of St. Maur" soon produced names which science has crowned with immortality—Mabillon, Montfaucon, Ruinart, Thuillier, Martène, Durand, D'Achery, Le Nourry, Martianay, those giants of erudition who have displayed prodigies of learn-ing and of patient toil.

9. The charity and self-devotion of the faithful ministers of the gospel were not confined to the nations which had long been folded in the Christian Church, but were displayed among the most remote and savage of the heathen tribes. No order showed a more heroic zeal than the Society of Jesus, whose members knew no higher ambition than to die in foreign mis-sions, for the love of Christ. The discoveries of the Portuguese and Spaniards afforded them the occasion and the means of satisfying their wish. We have already spoken of the labors of St. Francis Xavier in the Indies, and of his colleagues in China and Paraguay The work undertaken by these hardy missionaries was greatly encouraged and, in some sort, system-atized by the institution of the Propaganda, established by Gregory XV *Congregatio de Propaganda Fide*) This congrega-tion consisted of fifteen cardinals, three prelates and a secretary The abundant alms of the faithful thus found a sure and regular destination. The college annexed by Urban VIII. to the con-

gregation of the Propaganda became the seminary of foreign missions. The Pope's example was nobly imitated, and the work was facilitated by liberal endowments; numbers of apostolic laborers from all the Catholic nations were there prepared for their future career, and every year, on the Sunday after the feast of the Holy Trinity, Rome witnessed the renewal of the sublime spectacle of Pentecost, and heard the gospel preached in every known idiom under the sun. This feast of the Propaganda, in which the name of the Lord is praised in every tongue spoken on earth, is one of the solemnities which best realize and show forth the fundamental idea of the Catholic Church.

10. All the facts of the world's history are bound together by a living chain. Each great movement sends its echoes in all directions. Thus the great struggle against Protestantism, the discussions raised in the midst of the Church itself, and the institution of new orders, made a very marked impression upon the scientific world. The assaults of the Protestants turned general attention upon dogma, which was now seriously studied, not as formerly, in a merely speculative point of view, but especially in a historical light, the most necessary in the polemics against the so-called Reformers. The most learned theologian who has left us any of these works is unquestionably Father Denis Petau, of Orleans (A. D. 1583). His works are so solid, so complete, so full of sagacity, that every student of theology should consult them with the greatest care. Beside the publication of the writings of several Church historians and of some philosophers,* and his historical and astronomical work entitled *Rationale Temporum*, which formed an era, his *Dogmata Theologica* attracted the greatest attention. It is an exposition of the true teaching of the Catholic Church in all time, and opposed to the changeable doctrines of the heretics. This work was unfortunately left unfinished, by the death of the author (1652). It seems hardly credible that an ordinary lifetime should have sufficed for the composition of works so voluminous, so con-

---

* Epiphanius, Synesius, Nicephorus, the Emperor Julian, and Themistius.

scientiously accurate and so remarkable in every particular.
Father Petau's style is, in general, graceful and happy, his expression clear and methodical; he establishes a liberal and
ingenious alliance between history and dogma.   In the religious
polemics naturally arising from controversies with the heretics,
the most prominent names were those of Eck, Coclæus, Stanis-
las Hosius and Berthold.   But the most eminent of these theologians is certainly Robert Bellarmine, of Florence (1542).   He
was trained, with equal care, in piety and learning, and entering
the Society of Jesus in the year 1560, he distinguished himself by his indefatigable application to study   He taught the
various branches of theology, and wrote a Hebrew grammar, a
biography of ecclesiastical writers (*De Scriptoribus ecclesiasticis*),
and the celebrated controversial work entitled *Disputationes de
Controversis Christianæ fidei articulis, lib. IV*   Bellarmine was
thoroughly conversant with all the Protestant writings—the
works of Luther, Melancthon, Calvin, Beza, of the Socinians,
and, in general, of all the enemies of the Catholic Church.   He
explains the disputed points and the state of the question, with
precision and impartiality   His proofs, resting upon tradition,
are unusually full and irresistibly logical.   The promotion of
the learned Jesuit to the Roman purple, brought no change to
his simple and laborious life.   The work which he composed
in later years, the *Scala ad Deum*, shows the deep and sincere
piety, self-devotion and resignation which adorned his saintly
and beautiful soul.

11. The Catholic doctors did not, as the Protestants falsely
asserted, neglect the study of Sacred Scripture.   The works
of Bellarmine and of Pagnini, on the Hebrew tongue, exercised
a happy influence upon that department of sacred learning.
The Dominican, Sixtus of Sienna (A. D. 1569), composed an
Introduction to the Knowledge of the Sacred Writings, which is
of value in elucidating portions of the Sacred Text.   Vatable
published, under Francis I. (1540), a new translation of the
Sacred Scripture, with short notes; it is much esteemed for
clearness and conciseness.   The *Commentaries on the Bible*, by

the Jesuit, Stephen Menochius, met with great and deserved
success. Cornelius à Lapide holds the foremost rank among
the interpreters of the sublime theology of St. Paul. The
Jesuit Maldonatus and' William Estius, chancellor of the University of Douay, also immortalized their names by their
works on the Sacred Writings.

12. This display of learned and pious study was crowned
by the ascetic works then given to the world, and which were
among the last fruits of the happy influence exercised by the
middle-ages upon Catholic literature. Of this nature were the
" Spiritual Exercises" (*Exercitia Spiritualia*) of St. Ignatius;
the writings of St. Charles Borromeo, *Instructiones Confessario-
rum et Concionatorum ;* the *Rhetorica Ecclesiastica* of Valerius
Augustinus; that of the celebrated Dominican, Louis of Granada,
and especially the sermons of the great preachers of the day—
in Italy, Clarius, bishop of Fuligno ; Cornelio Musso, bishop
of Bitonto—in the kingdom of Naples (A. D. 1574), Charles
Borromeo, and the Jesuit Father, Paul Segneri (1694)—in
France, Simon Vigor, archbishop of Narbonne (1575), the Jesuit
Father, Claude de Lingendes (1666), his relative, John de
Lingendes, and Francis Ferault, of the congregation of the Oratory—in Spain, Louis of Granada—in Poland, Peter Skarga.
Finally, the spirit of piety, devotion, and religion was revived
and nourished in the hearts of the faithful, by the republication
and the new translations of the writings of St. Theresa, St. John
of the Cross, St. Francis of Sales, the pious Louis of Granada,
author of the " Sinner's Guide," of the " Memorial of a Christian Life," of a treatise " On Prayer," &c. These beneficial
reproductions remind us of the words used by Pope Gregory
XIII. in a letter to Louis of Granada : " You have done more,"
wrote the Pontiff, " for all those who shall seek for instruction
in your works, than if your prayers had obtained from Heaven
light for the blind and life for the dead."

13. Beside these works of an exclusively religious character, arts and letters still felt the inspiration of Catholicity, in
spite of all the efforts of Protestantism. Corregio, Titian, Car-

raccic, Domenichino, Guido Reni, with the artists of the Rhine and the Netherlands, still perpetuated the traditions of Michael Angelo and Raphael. Poetry took a new flight into the sphere of religion, when Tasso (A. D 1580) consecrated it to the recital of the chivalric exploits of the middle-ages, in his " Jerusalem Delivered ;" when Calderon de la Barca (1640), a priest and canon of Toledo, after a brave career in arms, sung the heroism of Christians and the immortal glory which awaits them. At the same period, Lope de Vega, who died in 1635, in the solitude of a cloister, devoted his fertile imagination, his unfailing spirit, to embellishing the deepest subjects and expressing the sublimest ideas of faith. Music too was joined to poetry and painting. The genius of Palestrina restored the true dignity of the art, and insured its eternal duration. Thus did Catholicism rule the highest intelligence at the very time when its enemies, leagued in hate, boasted that they should soon attend its obsequies.

EIGHTH PERIOD.

From the treaty of Westphalia (A. D. 1648) to the accession of
Pope Pius IX. to the Sovereign Pontificate (A. D. 1846).

CHAPTER I.

§ I. Pontificate of Innocent X. (September 15, a. d. 1644—January 7,
1655).

1. Features of the Eighth Period of the History of the Church.—2. Address of
the Marquis of St. Chamond, French ambassador at Rome, to the cardinals
in conclave. Election of Innocent X.—3. Murder of the Bishop of Castro.
Innocent orders the city of Castro to be razed to the ground. The case of
Antonio Barberini.—4. Mazaniello. John IV of Portugal, head of the
royal house of Braganza.—5. Treaty of Westphalia.—6. Charles I., king of
England. *Covenant* signed by the Puritans in Scotland.—7. Cromwell.—
8. Death of Charles I. The *Fronde.*—9. Jansenism. Bull *Cum occasione*
—*Respectful silence.*—10. Death of Innocent X.

§ II. Pontificate of Alexander VII. (April 7, a. d. 1855—May 22, 1667).

11. Election of Alexander VII.—12. Christina of Sweden.—13. Pre-Adamites
Abjuration of Isaac de la Peyrère, leader of the Pre-Adamites.—14. Mis
understanding between Alexander VII. and the court of France, concerning
the administration of the diocese of Paris, in the absence of the archbishop,
Cardinal Retz.—15. Peace of the Pyrenees, between France and Spain.—
16. Death of Cardinal Mazarin. His character.—17. Louis XIV His age
—18. Affair of the Duke of Créqui, the French ambassador at Rome.—19
Bull of Alexander VII. against Jansenism.—20. The "Formula."—21.
Ordinance of the vicars-general of the diocese of Paris, concerning the
"Formula."—22. New Formula of Alexander VII. Opposition of the
"Four Bishops." Death of Alexander VII.

§ III. Pontificate of Clement IX. (June 20, a. d. 1667—December 9, 1669).

23. Peace of Clement IX., called the *Clementine Peace,* in the affair of Jansenism.—24. Brief of Clement IX. to the refractory bishops.—25. Alliance

between Jansenism and Gallicanism. Mark Anthony de Dominis. Edmond
Richer. John Launoy. Baillet. The " Lives of the Fathers of the Desert,"
and the works of St. Theresa, translated by Arnauld d'Andilly.—26. Ellie
Dupin. Richard Simon. Le Courrayer.—27. The brothers Pithou. Du-
pey.—28. Pascal. The *Lettres Provinciales.*—29. Antoine Arnauld. Works
on " Frequent Communion" and the " Perpetuity of the Faith." Nicole.
The *Essais de Morale.*—30. Victory of St. Gothard, won by Montecuculli
over the Turks.—31. Capture of Candia by the Grand-Vizier, Achmet
Death of Clement IX.

§ I. Pontificate of Innocent X. (September 15, a. d. 1644—
January 7, 1655).

1. The eighth period of the history of the Church comprises
two very different epochs : the age of Louis XIV., and the
eighteenth century   The age of Louis XIV., the golden
age of French literature, bore a deep religious impress. In
spite of the Gallican tendencies which controlled the bishops
and the court of the " Grand Monarque" beyond measure ; spite
of the lamentable disagreements which arose between the Holy
See and France, faith was still . shedding abroad the full radiance and splendor of genius.   Bossuet and Fénelon recalled,
even amid their theological contests, the days of Augustine and
Chrysostom.   The treaty of Westphalia gave to Protestantism
the religious tolerance which it had been for thirty years trying
to win by the sword.   It might have been expected that this
concession would impart new life and power to the cause.   But
the day of its decline began precisely at the hour when it ob
tained the right to exist.   It ceased to be formidable as soon
as the contest was over.   The propagation of error needs the
factitious vitality of combat ; the victory which gives it peace
is the signal of its dissolution.   Catholicism, on the other hand,
felt itself endowed with new vigor ; a general reaction took
place in its favor.   Every kind of talent did homage to the
truth, and seemed to seek its service as an honor.   The heretics
asserted that the Roman Church had changed in her dogmas,
and that her teaching was not that of the Apostles.   Antiquity
was studied with the greatest care, under every aspect, and the

calumnies of the sectaries were proved to be groundless. From the eminence of that great century, enlightened by one belief, one feeling of respect for holy things, the eagle eye of Bossuet discerned, in the dim horizon of the future, a race of impious men who sought, in atheism, an asylum for their passions, a stronghold for their disorders. The eighteenth century verified the apprehensions of his great mind. Systems of false philosophy, as far removed from true wisdom as from the true faith, spread even to the ends of the earth. Two men of equal celebrity, though of diametrically opposite genius, Voltaire and Jean Jacques Rousseau, popularized by their writings the hatred they felt toward the Church. France, perverted by their teaching, gloried in heaping outrages upon the religion of her fathers, in holding up to public contempt the Pontiffs and the priests who had civilized the world. She presented to the universe the sad spectacle of a society without a God, without faith, without religion. But the human heart may not, with impunity, throw off the only curb strong enough to master its passions and control its evil instincts. The irreligious doctrines of the eighteenth century, while spreading among the masses, deposited the seeds of hatred and revolt. How can authority, which is from God, subsist, when the people are taught that "God is only a name"? Then France was swept by a fearful storm which swallowed up, in blood and ruins, the ancient monarchy, the ancestral religion, the old nobility, whose blood had bought the nation's glory and was now poured out in streams upon the scaffold. The demon of revolution triumphantly overran affrighted Europe. The Church of Christ seemed indeed to be in her agony   But she has promises of immortality against which all the efforts of hell shall never prevail. Providence watched over her destinies. A conqueror, whose name and glory filled the world, raises up the altars of Sion, and when, afterward, intoxicated by the splendor of his victorious career, he forgets that it is God who gives power, and that His hand, in anger, breaks the rebellious instruments of His designs; when he too would struggle with the august Pontiff who sits upon the throne of St Peter, he is struck, and the world reëchoes with the sound of his fall. His fate is a fearful warning to the proud spirits that refuse to bow under the guardian yoke of the Church. The world then enters upon the ways in which we are now walking; human policy has before it an undefined horizon; but we, children of the Church, are sure that the hand of God will not be withdrawn from us. The past is our security for the future. Already may we see the promise of a return to the faith. Ever fruitful in works of salvation, the Church has brought forth institutions, which the early ages might well envy us. The society of the "Propagation of the Faith" bears the name of Jesus and the light of the gospel to the uttermost bounds of the earth. The blood of martyrs is poured out upon distant shores, to fecundate the growth of the seeds of life. The worship of Mary is growing with wonderful rapidity, and gathers together, in powerful associations, the noblest hearts and the most enlightened minds. An irresistible religious movement is drawing the intelligence of the world to a deeper and more serious study of Christian dogmas. The press, which by its licentious and impious productions had corrupted the society of the eighteenth century, now lends its immense resources to the cause of the true faith. The clergy is equal to its sublime mission; its eloquence, its zeal, its teaching, its virtue, and its writings, have reconciled the science of our age with religion. Whatever may be the destiny which God has in store for the society of to-day, the Church will always hold in it a prominent place, and wield a powerful influence over its destinies.

2. When the cardinals had met in conclave to elect a successor to Urban VIII., they were addressed by the Marquis of Saint-Chamond, ambassador of the young king of France, Louis XIV., then but six years old. In the course of his address, the marquis uttered the following sentiments: "Our kings, deservedly styled 'Most Christian,' have done more than any other princes to increase the revenues and the authority

of the Roman Church. The Sacred College may rely upon the same assistance on the present occasion, and on all others, from my royal master, since the period of his birth was one of miracles, of victories, and of triumphs ; since he springs from the race of St. Louis, through the most devout and pious parents that ever swayed the royal sceptre. His early training is intrusted to the queen-regent, who teaches him no more ordinary lesson than that of honoring and upholding the Church, and who can set before him no higher examples, ancient or modern, than those afforded by her own royal line, and of more than sixty sovereigns, her predecessors, who have ever maintained the closest union with the Holy See." These were noble words,. uttered in the name of a youthful sovereign, whose splendor was to outshine that of all his predecessors. Happy for himself had he always professed, for the successors of St. Peter, the respect which he had been taught in childhood to bear them. On the 15th of September, A. D. 1644, Cardinal Pamfili was elected Pope, and took the name of Innocent X.

3. The new Pope signalized his accession by two acts of energetic firmness. The Bishop of Castro had been murdered before having had time to take possession of his see. As the act was perpetrated by the orders of the duke of that city, Innocent ordered his troops to march against the rebellious subject. Castro was taken and levelled with the ground ; upon its ruins was raised a pyramid bearing the Italian inscription, *Quì fù Castro !* "Here Castro once stood." Cardinal Antonio Barberini, chief treasurer of Urban VIII., was convicted of exactions and embezzlements, which compromised the Pontifical administration and aroused a general storm of dissatisfaction in Rome. Without awaiting the issue of his case, Antonio fled to France, where he found in Cardinal Mazarin, prime minister of Louis XIV., a powerful protection, due to the large sums of money which he brought to the royal treasury, and which were to serve the French arms in the war against the house of Austria. Innocent was firm in a circumstance which involved the honor of the Holy See. In 1646, he issued a bull in which he an-

nounced that any member of the Sacred College, leaving the
Roman States without the Pope's permission, should be punished by the confiscation of his property ; that unless the delin-
quent made his submission to the Pope within six months, he
should be forbidden entrance to the churches and deprived of
his benefices and offices ; in fine, that persistence in the rebellion would forfeit the cardinalate, without hope of rehabili-
tation, except by the Sovereign Pontiff in person.   This bull
met with violent opposition in France ; the parliament of Paris,
which had for two centuries past arrogated to itself the right
of overruling the Pontifical decrees, declared it null and abusive.
A decree of the royal council forbade that any more money
should be sent to Rome for the expediting of bulls ; they spoke
of seizing Avignon ; a land and naval force seemed to threaten
Italy   But Mazarin, whose position was analogous to that of
Richelieu, felt that he could not make war upon the Pope to
whom he had sworn fidelity and obedience as a cardinal.   Negotiations were accordingly opened with the court of Rome.   The
Barberini made their submission, and the Pope consented to
pardon them out of consideration for the Most Christian King,
who had honored them with his protection.   Cardinal Barberini
was subsequently raised to the archbishopric of Rheims and
made grand-almoner of France.

4. Two events of a very serious nature had lately occurred
at Naples.   In a popular outbreak against the Duke of Arcos,
viceroy of Naples for Philip IV., a fisherman of Amalfi
found himself suddenly raised to the highest power, and
hailed, by a delirious mob, sovereign of Naples.   The name
of Mazaniello was thus ranked among those of the celebrated
adventurers whom the caprice of the multitude draws, for a
moment, from obscurity, only to plunge them as rapidly into it
again.   Innocent X. refused to sanction a power which could
evidently be but ephemeral.   When advised to seize the opportunity to send troops to Naples, and thus to recover the
ancient sovereignty of the Holy See in that kingdom, the
Pontiff generously replied that it was unworthy of the common

Father of the faithful to aggravate the misfortunes of a Christian prince. He at once sent to the viceroy a sum of thirty
thousand crowns, and allowed him to levy troops in the States
of the Church, assuring him that the Holy See would faith
fully defend the interests of the Catholic king. This support,
together with the inexperience of the revolutionary leader and
the want of courage displayed by the strangers who had planned
the revolt, helped the viceroy to allay the storm. Mazaniello
was put to death by the very men who had raised him to
power. The rebels next offered the throne to the Duke of
Guise, who allowed himself to be seduced by the prospect of
a crown. The new chief defeated the Spanish troops under
Don Juan, and seized the reins of government. But he was
betrayed by the Neapolitans themselves, and fell into the
hands of the viceroy, who soon restored the authority of
Philip IV in all southern Italy (A. D. 1646–1647). A few
years earlier, a revolution of far different nature had wrested a
kingdom from the Spanish crown (December, 1640). At the
death of Cardinal Henry (1580), Philip II. attached Portugal
to his States. But a hostile administration soon excited the
discontent of his new subjects; in 1640, the Duke of Braganza
was raised to the throne and founded his dynasty   Philip IV
was despoiled of what Philip II., with impolitic derision, called
" the little kingdom of Portugal." The court of Spain made
every effort to deter the Pope from recognizing the new Portuguese monarchy   " Let John IV be disregarded," said the
Spanish ambassadors, " and let the bishops presented by him
be refused the canonical institution." But the Pope, who had
just refused his countenance to the popular outbreak in Naples,
was too wise not to discern the wide difference between the
two situations. He recognized John IV as lawful sovereign,
notwithstanding the urgent remonstrances of the Spanish court.

5. The attention of all Europe was now called to the event
which was to close the Thirty Years' War. All eyes were
anxiously turned toward the city of Münster, in Westphalia,
where the representatives of all the powers were elaborating

the famous treaty which put an end to so many and such long-continued struggles. A Papal legate was present to guard the rights of the Holy See. So bitter was the hatred of Protestantism against the Roman Church, that the Swedish ambassador quitted the city, on the legate's arrival, and withdrew to Osnabrück. It is not our intention to speak of the provisions made by this assembly, concerning political questions foreign to ecclesiastical history Yet it must be said that the Catholic sovereigns did not do for religion what might justly and fairly have been expected from their zeal. The legate strove in vain to inspire the ambassadors with higher and nobler views; the interests of heaven were sacrificed to those of earth. The Protestants were confirmed in the possession of the archbishoprics, bishoprics, monasteries and convents which they had seized. The Pope and the bishops saw themselves deprived of all active means of jurisdiction over the Catholics residing in Lutheran countries. The various sects of the Reformation all obtained the free exercise of their respective worship. It was agreed that in the countries where the Catholics and Protestants lived together, each party should keep the property, rights and revenues of which it could prove possession in the year 1625, which was called the *normal* year, except in the Palatinate, where the year 1619 was fixed as the *normal* year. But in 1624, most of the Church property was in the hands of the Reformers. The remaining clauses of the treaty belong to profane history; they are too long to be enumerated here. Pope Innocent X. protested against all the terms unfavorable to the Catholics, but he was unheard. The politicians who then governed thought that they had done much in thus separating their action from that of the Papacy Blinded indeed they must have been not to see the lowering storm-clouds of revolution gathering thick in the horizon, always bursting upon the power that presents itself to the people without the majesty of a religious character. Having thus thrown off the guardian authority of the Sovereign Pontiffs, which had, until then, presided over its destinies, Europe was yet to learn, by a sad experience, that the Church has not only the promise of everlasting life, but that she alone, by her beneficent influence, can secure peace and stability to the kingdoms of the earth.

6. England was now teaching the world how low a people can fall when they have lost the true faith, and with it all respect for lawful authority Henry VIII. had let loose against the Church of Rome all the fury of popular passion. The same fury was now turned against the royal power, and the unfortunate Charles I. became its victim. Scotland was invaded by Calvinism, which appeared under the form of the redoubtable sect of Puritans—fanatical champions of independence, who claimed to rule the public worship entirely and according to their own notions. Charles made an attempt to enforce the observance of the established Anglican liturgy; the royal edict was received with the cry of revolt: "Presbyterianism or death!" The Puritans drew up and signed a new *Covenant*, "sealed," said they, "by Heaven itself." After the announcement that the Spirit of God had revealed itself to Scotland, and that "out of the Kirk of Scotland there was no salvation;" after an almost incredible strain of invectives against Sixtus V., Paul V., Urban VIII., and against the Roman Church in general, every signer was bound to defend the *Covenant* to the death, even against the king himself. When Charles consulted his prime minister, the Earl of Strafford, about the means of crushing a rebellion so powerfully organized, the earl replied: "Your majesty should make instant prèparations for war, yet with the resolution of doing everything possible to avoid one." The answer was wise, humane, and worthy to be addressed to a king. Charles appreciated it; but his weakness prevented him from profiting by the prudent policy of his minister. He conceived the fatal design of calling a national assembly—the "Long Parliament"—which brought upon England the most disastrous of revolutions.

7 Among the ambitious men of every rank who met in that famous assembly, the name of Oliver Cromwell, the envoy of the Scotch Puritans, stands prominent. We borrow from

the pen of Bossuet a sketch of that celebrated character. "He was a man of unusual depth of mind, as refined in dissimulation as he was skilled in political management; capable alike of undertaking and of concealing any action; equally active and indefatigable in peace and in war; leaving to fortune nothing that he could take from it by counsel and foresight; but yet so watchful and ready, that he never missed the occasions thrown in his way; in a word, one of those bold and restless spirits born to change the fortunes of the world. How hazardous is the fate of such minds; how many appear in history, whose very boldness has brought them to ruin! And yet how much can they not achieve when God is pleased to use them as His instruments! To this man it was given to mislead the people and to prevail against kings. For, when he perceived that, in the countless sects which were wandering without any fixed or certain rules, the charm by which all those minds were held in error was the satisfaction of being able to dogmatize without opposition or hinderance from any secular or ecclesiastical authority, he used this weakness with a ready skill which changed the shapeless mass into a strong and formidable power. When once the multitude has been caught with the bait of liberty, it will follow blindly if it but hear the name pronounced. These men, wholly taken up with the first idea which had transported them, ran on without seeing that they were rushing into bondage; and their crafty leader—perceiving that by fighting and teaching, by assuming an infinite variety of characters, by acting the doctor and the prophet, as well as the soldier and the captain, he had so captivated the world that he was now looked upon by the whole army as a chief sent of God to protect independence—began to be convinced that he could urge them on still farther. I shall not dwell upon the details of his disastrous undertakings, of his celebrated victories, at which outraged virtue wept, nor of the long season of unmolested triumph which astonished the world. It was the design of God, to teach kings what it costs to quit His Church. He would show, by a striking example, to what lengths heresy can go; how naturally indocile and independent it is, how fatal to royalty and to all lawful authority Besides, when Almighty God has chosen a man to be the instrument of His designs, nothing can check his career; he either fetters, or blinds, or crushes all that is capable of resistance."

8. Cromwell soon made himself the master of a Parliament which wanted no master. Forced into a war with his rebellious subjects, Charles was defeated and withdrew to Scotland. He was told that "a prince hostile to the *Covenant* could not be admitted into the kingdom of the *Saints*." The Scottish *Saints* sold their king to the *Saints* of England for the sum of eight thousand pounds. The unfortunate monarch was doomed to a hard captivity Innocent X. raised his voice against the outrage; England had been too long taught to disregard it. Kings had given the first examples of contempt for the Holy See; the people, in turn, refused to hear the same Holy See, when it undertook the defence of kings. The *Independents* and the *Agitators* in London, excited by the council of fanatical leaders, called for the head of Charles. Henrietta of France, queen of England, the worthy descendant of Henry IV., displayed a heroic courage in her attempts to save her royal consort. Her efforts were vain. On the 20th of January, A. D. 1649, Charles was brought before a self-constituted court of justice. His step was firm, his countenance erect and unmoved. He did not uncover, but first seated himself, then arose, and surveyed the court with an air of superiority which abashed and irritated his enemies. A smile of contempt was seen to quiver on his lips at the passage of the charge which described him as a "tyrant, traitor, and murderer." When called on to answer, by those who dared to constitute themselves his judges, he demanded by what lawful authority he had been brought thither. "God," he continued, "has placed a trust in my keeping; God has, by a long and ancient succession, transmitted to me a mandate ; I shall never violate or betray them. I should already disown them did I reply to the new and unlawful authority by which I am questioned. When I am satis-

fied as to your title, I shall be prepared to say more." He was shown, upon the desk, the fatal axe which threatened his life. He touched it with a look of disdain, and only said, " It does not frighten me." Three times was Charles brought before the murderous tribunal. Meanwhile four of the.lords who had composed the ministry of the unhappy sovereign—Richmond, Hertford, Lindsay and Southampton, names worthy to be honorably enshrined in the remembrance of posterity—appeared before the Commons, declaring that, according to the Constitution of England, the king was not responsible; that they had advised all the measures for which Charles was now called to account; and that, to save the anointed head of their sovereign, they came to offer theirs to the executioner. In this noble, self-sacrificing protest, the Earl of Strafford would unquestionably have shared, but the Puritan fanatics had already immolated that victim of their revenge, and, to crown the deed of infamy, had compelled the king to sign the unjust warrant against his faithful servant. The self-devotion of the late ministers of Charles failed to move his rebellious subjects. The voice of religion, the claims of nature, political interests, the prayers of a sympathizing people—all were rejected. The king must prepare to die. His two children were brought to him for the last time; he blessed them, and to his daughter, the Princess Elizabeth, afterward Duchess of Orleans, he gave two valuable diamonds for her mother, as a last pledge of his affection; and then, turning away from every creature, he sought in the high thoughts of heaven, a refuge from his deep afflictions and unparalleled misfortunes. Unhappily, he had not the consolations afforded by the true faith; he had followed in the way of the Anglican schism, and the words of Bishop Juxon were.as cold as his faith and his worship. On the 30th day of January, 1649, a day of shame and of mourning for England, upon a scaffold erected on a level with the windows of his apartments in Whitehall, the head of Charles I. was struck off by the headsman's axe. The executioner seized the head, all dripping with blood, and, showing it to the people, exclaimed : " Behold the head of a traitor !"   The crime was accomplished.

Royalty, thus martyred in England, was likewise proscribed in Paris.   On the 6th of January, 1649, the queen-regent and Cardinal Mazarin were compelled to fly, taking with them the youthful Louis XIV., to save him from the fury of the Fronde. The history of those years of blood and tumult does not belong to the annals of the Church.   Beside, from the gloom of that storm was yet to rise the triumphant splendor of the Great King.

9. The question of Jansenism now re-appeared with new ardor.   The five propositions drawn from the " Augustinus" by Dr. Cornet, were submitted for examination to the Holy See. Eighty-eight French bishops signed a petition entreating Innocent X. to end the discussion by a definitive sentence.   On the other hand, eleven bishops begged the Pontiff not to pronounce judgment, and sent four doctors to Rome to plead the cause of the " Augustinus."   Innocent appointed a commission, which gave two years to the examination of the work of Jansenius and the five propositions.   At length, on the 31st of May, A. D. 1653, the bull *Cum occasione* appeared, condemning the propositions. The bull was received by the Catholics in France and the Netherlands.   But the partisans of the Bishop of Ypres tried to evade its consequences by a subterfuge.   They protested that, in the question of doctrine, they submitted to the decision of the Sovereign Pontiff; but they complained at the same time that the condemned propositions should have been ascribed to the " Augustinus."   This is the origin of the question of fact, which afterward became the leading one; for the abettors of Jansenism asserted that the Church was not infallible when it was to be decided whether a given proposition was, or was not, contained in a book, and whether the meaning it conveyed was really that of the author.   In this light the bull of Innocent X. was to be received, said the sectaries, " only with a respectful silence."   This was but an ingenious evasion meant to disguise an unpardonable insincerity   A council of bishops, held in

Paris on the 26th of March, 1654, declared that the bull *Cum occasione* condemned the five propositions as coming from Jansenius, and in the sense in which they were understood by that author; Pope Innocent, by a brief issued in the same year, confirmed the declaration.

10. This was the last act of the august Pontiff. Toward the end of December, A. D. 1654, Innocent felt an unusual weakness, and the physicians despaired of his life. Cardinal Azzolina, his confessor, was charged to communicate the intelligence to the dying Pontiff, who received it with a calmness and serenity which edified all those present. He sent for Father Paul Oliva, a Jesuit, to assist him in his last moments. Turning to Cardinal Sforza, who stood by his death-bed, " See," he said, " the end of all the splendor of the Sovereign Pontificate." He was desirous that all the faithful should profit by the lesson, and ordered that the gates of the palace should be open to all. He died in sentiments of the deepest piety, on the 7th of January, 1655, after a reign of eleven years.

§ 2. PONTIFICATE OF ALEXANDER VII. (April 7, A.D. 1655— May 22, 1667).

11. Cardinal Fabio Chigi was unanimously elected to succeed Innocent X., and took the name of Alexander VII. The new Pontiff was born at Sienna (February 15, A. D. 1599), and was distinguished even at an early age, for his remarkable talents.* He successively held the posts of Inquisitor at Malta, vice-legate at Ferrara, nuncio in Germany at the time of the treaty of Westphalia, bishop of Imola and cardinal; discharging every duty with eminent virtue and rare penetration. Still the court of France, ruled by Mazarin, saw his promotion with pain. At Münster, Fabio Chigi had defended the interests of the Holy See with a noble independence which the cardinal-

* We have a volume of poems from the pen of Alexander VII., printed at the Louvre (A. D 1656); they form a folio volume, entitled *Philomathi Musæ Juveniles*. He composed them while still a youth, and a member of the Academy of the *Philomathi* at Sienna

minister could not forget. On the other hand, the Jansenist party, whose leaders, Arnauld d'Andilly, Pascal, and Nicole, secluded in the convent of Port Royal, exercised by their talents, their austere life, and their reputation for learning, a marked influence upon the French society of that period, remembered that Fabio Chigi was the secretary of the commission appointed by Pope Innocent X. to examine the five propositions of the "Augustinus." They could not, without anxiety, see the chair of St. Peter filled by a Pope whose antecedents left no hope to heretics. This double prejudice of the court and of Jansenism was to be expressed by a twofold struggle which occupied the whole Pontificate of Alexander VII.

12. The first year of his reign was signalized by an event which gave joy to the Church. Sweden, the kingdom in which Lutheranism first changed the whole political constitution ; in which the Catholic reaction found both representatives and opponents amongst the highest classes, was the very country in which Catholicism achieved a most unlooked-for conquest; it won over to itself Queen Christina of Sweden, the daughter of Gustavus Adolphus. That princess, whose career abounds in strange and romantic episodes, renounced the throne of her fathers to embrace the true faith. After having received sound instructions in the mysteries of religion, she made her solemn abjuration at Innspruck. She hastened to Italy to receive the blessing of the Holy Father, and deposited her crown and sceptre upon the altar of our Lady of Loretto. Every preparation had been made by the cities of the Roman territory to give her a magnificent reception. Christina entered Rome in triumph, and there she ended her days, after an excursion into France, made memorable by the murder of Monaldeschi, one of her attendants, at Fontainebleau. She left her valuable collection of manuscripts to the Vatican library, that noble monument of literary and scientific wealth, raised by the Papacy to European genius.

13. The heart of Pope Alexander VII. was likewise consoled at this time by the conversion of the chief of the sect of

Pre-Adamites. This name was given to a sect of men who held that the earth had been inhabited by a generation of men anterior to Adam. A Calvinist, Isaac de la Peyrère, published a work in Holland (A. D. 1655), under the title : " Præadamitæ, sive exercitatio super versibus 12, 13, 14, cap. v., Epistolæ Pauli ad Romanos, quibus indicantur primi homines ante Adamum conditi," in which he maintained this absurd system, and undertook to support it by the authority of St. Paul. According to his theory, Moses relates the origin of the Jewish nation only, and not that of the whole human race. There were two creations of men : the first in the beginning of the world, when God placed in it a race which spread over the whole earth, and constituted the Gentiles ; the second, at a much later date, when God created Adam to be the father of the Jewish people. As these senseless speculations had little to interest human passions, they did not obtain a wide-spread influence. La Peyrère himself renounced them in 1657, at the feet of Pope Alexander VII., and embraced the Catholic religion, which he professed to the end of his life with a most edifying fervor.

14. A lamentable difference had lately arisen between the Pontifical court and the government of the King of France. The Archbishop of Paris, Jean-François-Paul de Gondi, better known as Cardinal de Retz, took a leading part in the troubles of the Fronde. When Mazarin had overcome the insurgents and reëstablished his authority, he caused the arrest of the archbishop on a charge of treason, and sent him to the prison of Vincennes. The prisoner managed to elude the vigilance of his guards and fled to Rome, where he took part in the conclave which elected Alexander VII. That Pope conferred upon him the pallium, spite of the remonstrances of the French ambassadors, and continued to treat him as archbishop of Paris. The cardinal had intrusted the administration of his diocese, during his absence, to vicars-general, who were not acceptable to the court. Mazarin entered into negotiations with the Holy See, in which he endeavored to maintain that the crime of high treason in a bishop, was enough to disqualify him from holding

any jurisdiction whatever in the kingdom. It was impossible for the Pope to sanction a doctrine which would legitimate every act of tyranny Alexander agreed that the cardinal should change his vicars-general, since they were obnoxious, but he claimed for him the right of substituting others more agreeable to the king. But Mazarin, with that stubborn and crafty persistence which formed the distinctive trait of his character, refused all accommodation. The contest between the minister and the archbishop had been too personal for the former to let it pass without being revenged. The Pope saw that the discussion would only be imbittered by further delay, and he accordingly determined to bring it to an end by the exercise of his authority; he appointed an Apostolic vicar to administer the diocese during the absence of the Ordinary All the fury of Gallicanism was let loose upon the Pontifical decree. The Assembly of the French bishops declared that it was a manifest violation of the liberties of the kingdom. The question was beginning to assume proportions which alarmed Mazarin. He was not prepared to risk a schism, and he accordingly proposed a middle course, which should insure the return of peace. The king was to name six ecclesiastics, among whom the archbishop might choose one, at his pleasure, to act as his vicar-general. The plan was adopted and put an end to the dispute.

15. Mazarin now turned his whole attention to the reëstablishing of peace between France and Spain. It was the masterpiece of his policy, and gloriously crowned an administration so full of storms and troubles. After a series of twenty-five conferences held in the Isle of Pheasants, formed by the Bidassoa, a stream on the boundary between the two kingdoms, the " Treaty of the Pyrenees" was signed by Mazarin and Don Luis de Haro, on behalf of their respective crowns. Spain ceded to France—in the Netherlands, Arras and the whole of Artois, except the town of St. Omer; in Flanders, Gravelines and several other important places; in Hainaut, Landrecies and Quesnoy; Thionville, Montmédy, Marienbourg, Philippe-

ville and Avesnes, in the duchy of Luxemburg; toward the Pyrenees, Perpignan and the whole of Roussillon with the county of Conflans. The Prince of Condé, perplexed for a moment by the troubles of the Fronde, had yielded to the fatal inspiration to place his victorious sword at the service of Spain; he was pardoned, and returned to expiate his passing weakness by unvarying fidelity and glorious feats of arms. But the most important article of the treaty was the one which concluded the union between Louis XIV and the Infanta of Spain, Maria Theresa, daughter of Philip IV The princess made a formal renunciation in her own name and in that of her descendants, of all right of succession in the Spanish realm; the clause was but an empty formality, if France proved too weak to assert such a claim, and but a useless barrier in the contrary supposition. Mazarin foresaw what these renunciations would be worth; and the event, forty years later, proved the correctness of his calculations. France now took the foremost rank among the European powers.

16. This success crowned with glory the declining years of Mazarin; though he did not long enjoy it. He died on the 9th of March, A. D. 1661, at the age of fifty-nine years. "Cardinal Mazarin," says Hénault, "was as gentle as Cardinal Richelieu was violent, one of his greatest talents consisted in knowing men thoroughly The characteristic feature of his policy was rather finesse and prudence than force. He believed that force should never be used until all other means have failed, and his mind furnished him with a courage equal to the circumstances; bold at Cassal, quiet and active in his retreat at Cologne, enterprising when princes were to be checked, but insensible to the satirical attacks of the Fronde, despising the threats of the coadjutor, and listening to the murmurs of the populace as we listen, on the beach, to the sound of the ocean's roar. There was, in Cardinal Richelieu, something greater, vaster, less studied; in Cardinal Mazarin, more address, more management, and fewer extravagances. The people hated the one and derided the other; but both were masters of the State."

17 The death of Mazarin was to change the face of affairs. The young king of France had hitherto seemed a stranger to the government of his own realm.   Each one of the surviving ministers looked for the first place.   No one thought that a prince brought up at a distance from affairs of State, would venture suddenly to take their full weight upon himself.   They did not know that he had for some time been trying his strength and his genius for reigning.   When Harlay de Chanvalon, archbishop of Rouen, and president of the Assembly of the clergy, asked him to whom he should now apply on matters of business; " To myself," replied Louis.   On the day following the death of Mazarin, having called together his ministers, he addressed the chancellor as follows: " Sir, I have called you before me, together with my ministers and secretaries of state, to inform you that hitherto I have been willing to leave the government of my affairs to the late cardinal; I shall, in future, be my own prime minister.   You will assist me with your counsels when I ask you for them.   I enjoin you to give me a daily account of every thing.   The scene is now changed," he added in a deeply impressive tone; " the government of my States, the management of my finances and foreign relations shall be guided by other principles than those of the late cardinal.   Gentlemen, you know my will; it is for you now to put it into execution."   The sovereign who uttered these words was, indeed, to change the fortunes of France, and to make her the first of nations.   His name and his glory were destined to adorn the greatest age of modern history   France, peaceful and prosperous within, victorious without, seemed to rule the world.   Louis XIV stands before the historian, surrounded by the immortal minds whose genius he had the tact to discover, aud whose efforts he encouraged and rewarded.   " That monarch," says Cardinal Maury, " had, at the head of his armies, Turenne, Condé, Luxembourg, Catinat, Créqui, Boufflers, Montesquiou, Vendôme and Villars; Château-Renault, Duquesne, Tourville, Duguay-Trouin, Jean Bart commanded his fleets. Colbert, Louvois, Torcy, were called to his council.

His first senate was headed by Molé and Lamoignon, its organs were Talon and d'Aguesseau. Vauban fortified his citadels; Riquet de Caraman opened canals; Perrault and Mansard built his palaces; Girardon, Poussin, Mignard, Le Sueur embellished them; Le Nôtre laid out his gardens; Corneille, Racine, Molière, Quinault, La Fontaine, La Bruyère, Boileau, La Rochefoucauld enlightened his mind and amused his leisure; Montausier, Bossuet, Beauvilliers, Fénelon, Huet, Fléchier, Fleury educated his children. Bossuet, Fénelon, Bourdaloue, Fléchier, Massillon spoke to him from the Christian pulpit, in their inspired accents." This splendid combination of glory, greatness and genius, laid the foundation of the moral preponderance of France.

18. Louis XIV., it must be confessed, did not always sufficiently rely upon this incontestable superiority to secure his preëminence; he sometimes displayed an excessive arrogance toward the other European sovereigns. His bearing, in a memorable difficulty with Alexander VII., will sufficiently show this trait. His ambassador at Rome was the Duke of Créqui, a man of violent and ungoverned temper. His attendants offered some insult to the Corsican troops who composed the Pontifical guard. The insulted regiment seized its arms to avenge its injured members. Without waiting for the issue of the investigation begun by the Pope, the Corsicans attacked the ambassador's residence, killed several French subjects, and fired upon the coach of the ambassador's wife, killing one of her attendants (A. D. 1662). These were certainly deplorable excesses; but, in truth, it was only a military quarrel, provoked by the insolence of the French retinue, and in which the Roman government had not the least share. The Pope's nephew, Cardinal Chigi, hastened at once to the French ambassador, made ample apologies in the name of his uncle, and offered to make any reparation he might require. The duke refused to listen to his excuses, withdrew into Tuscany, and sent to the court of Versailles a report representing the matter in the most disadvantageous light for the Holy See. Louis, on receiving this

account, immediately ordered that Piccolomini, the Papal nuncio in France, should be conveyed by a guard of fifty soldiers, to the frontier of Savoy. At the same time he seized Avignon and the Comtat-Venaissin, threatening, moreover, to march his troops into Italy. The Pope vainly offered every possible explanation of the fatal affray. Louis was inflexible. The year 1663 was spent in fruitless negotiations. At length the Pope proposed the mediation of the Catholic King, of the Grand Duke of Tuscany, of the Venetian republic and the other Italian States. It could not be denied that the French had begun the quarrel. The Corsicans had, of their own accord, resorted to arms, and thus caused all the subsequent evil. But the court of Louis XIV would not listen to reason. The king demanded that the Pope's nephew, Mario Chigi, should be exiled, that Cardinal Imperiali should come to Versailles to present the Pope's apology, and finally, that a pyramid should be erected in Rome, with an inscription to perpetuate the crime and the punishment of the Corsicans.* On these terms he was willing to make peace with the Sovereign Pontiff. This was the bearing of an absolute monarch, and not of the Most Christian King. "Every wise man," says Muratori, "condemned this arbitrary proceeding of the King of France against the vicar of Jesus Christ, on account of an accident which had happened through no fault of his." All the conditions were fulfilled, and peace was restored between the crown of France and the Holy See.

19. One of the first cares of Alexander VII., on ascending the Pontifical chair, was to decide the case of Jansenism, which the bull of Innocent X. had not brought to a close. Doctor Arnauld had lately published two letters, in which he asserted that the five propositions ascribed to the "Augustinus," were nowhere to be found in that work. The Sorbonne condemned the two letters (January 14, A. D. 1656), which did not deter the doctor from issuing other writings in which he advanced the doctrine: "That grace, without which we can do nothing, was wanting to a just man, in the person of St. Peter, on an

* This monument was removed under Clement IX., with the consent of Louis XIV

occasion in which it cannot be said that he did not sin." This was simply presenting in a historical form, the first of the five condemned propositions. A second decree of the Faculty of Paris condemned the doctrine of Arnauld (January 16, 1656). The Jansenists, however, still continued to dogmatize on the same theme. Alexander thought it his duty to interfere. In a bull dated October, 1656, he promulgated a new constitution confirming every point of the bull published by Innocent X., which he embodied, entire, in his own. He declares and defines that the five propositions in question are really taken from the work of Jansenius entitled "Augustinus," and that they are condemned in the sense intended by the author. He again condemns the "Augustinus," and every work, printed or manuscript, which has been, or may yet be, written in its support. "Precision and precaution," says a modern writer, "could hardly have been carried further; they seemed at first almost overstrained; they proved even insufficient."

20. The bull of Alexander VII. was received with submission by the General Assembly of the French clergy (A. D. 1657) They declared that the provisions of the decree, as well as of that of Innocent X., should be enforced against those who continued to profess the condemned doctrine. To secure the better execution of the Apostolic decrees, they prepared a *formula*, or profession of faith, which was to be signed by all the ecclesiastics of every diocese, within the space of a month. The formula was drawn up in these terms: "I sincerely submit to the constitution of Pope Innocent X., of the 31st of May, 1653, in its true sense, which has been defined by our Holy Father, Alexander VII., on the 16th of October, 1656. I acknowledge that I am in conscience bound to obey these constitutions; and I condemn, with my lips and in my heart, the doctrine of the five propositions of Jansenius, contained in his 'Augustinus,' which has been condemned by those two Popes and by the bishops, which doctrine is not that of St. Augustine, as Jansenius has falsely explained, contrary to the true meaning of that doctor." As soon as the decree of the General

Assembly of the clergy was published in France, and the words "formula" and "signature" were heard, the Jansenists everywhere reiterated the assertion that they were ready to submit to the decisions of the Holy See, in matters of faith, but that they could not be obliged, against their conscience, to acknowledge that a heretical doctrine was contained in the work of a pious and learned bishop, who had died in communion with the Church. Arnauld wrote several works in support of this declaration. They gave rise to scandalous discussions and disorders. Tired of all this disputing and opposition, the king summoned the presidents of the Assembly of the clergy to meet him at the Louvre (1660). He exhorted them with great earnestness to seek prompt and efficacious means for the extirpation of Jansenism, promising to support them with the full weight of his authority In consequence of this injunction and of a report of eleven commissioners appointed to carry out the royal wish, the clergy unanimously resolved that every ecclesiastic, secular and regular, in the kingdom, should be required to sign the formula. It was, moreover, decreed that all those who had written against the bulls should make a formal retraction. A decree of the council and a letter of the king to all the prelates of the kingdom, ratified the sentence of the Assembly and enforced its execution. But Jansenism had yet another deplorable scandal to add to the many by which it was already disgraced.

21. The vicars-general, who administered the diocese of Paris in the absence of Cardinal de Retz, issued an ordinance requiring all to sign the formula, but distinguishing, at the same time, between the right which they were required to acknowledge, and the fact for which only respect or a respectful silence was asked. "In the time of Innocent X.," continued the ordinance, "the question in Rome was to know whether the five propositions were true and Catholic, or false and heretical." Thus the administrators required nothing more, in regard to the question of Jansenius, than that all should profess the full and sincere respect due to the Papal constitutions, without at all prejudging the facts in the case. This

line of argument betrayed either an incurable obstinacy or a manifest insincerity. Alexander addressed to the administra tors a brief, expressive of his lively indignation, threatening them with the censures of the Church unless they made an immediate retraction. This fearful warning called forth a new decree from the administrators, in which they did, indeed, re tract their assertion, but with so much circumlocution, that it was easy to discover in it the resentment of wounded self- love. Still, the advocates of the "respectful silence" did not cease to stun the court, the city and the whole kingdom with their clamors. "The bishops assembled in Paris," they pro tested, "have acted as if they constituted a national council, whereas the object of their meeting was exclusively limited to temporal matters." This wily pretext, based upon a false and lying allegation, caused a delay of more than two years in the execution of the order in the provinces. Louis exerted his authority a second time. A decree of the royal council (May 1, A. D. 1662) enjoined all the bishops to require the signatures of every refractory ecclesiastic, without exception or explanation. The order was urgent; the monarch who gave it was accustomed to have his will respected, even by his enemies. But heresy acknowledges no authority, spiritual or temporal; and all the power of the great king was unable to compel the signature of a single Jansenist. They intrenched themselves in the "re- spectful silence," "quite prepared," they said, "to condemn the five propositions in themselves, but not to admit that they were really in the 'Augustinus.'" Deplorable blindness of partisan obstinacy! The men who could reason thus, prided themselves on their great zeal for religion and for the salvation of souls. But what benefit could result to religion from these ceaseless quarrels? What advantage were the simple faithful to draw from the scandalous resistance of a certain number of bishops, doctors, and religious, to the orders of the Sovereign Pontiff, the judge of faith, the guardian of doctrine, the lawful and incontestable head of the Church.

22. Indignant at this display of manifest insincerity, Louis

XIV called together the bishops who were then in Paris, to deliberate upon the best means of overcoming the obstinacy of the Jansenists. The Assembly held to the signing of the formula, and urged the king to use his power, in accordance with the desire of the Pope, to enforce the execution of the decree within two months. The bishops wrote to Alexander VII. that they had found the declaration of the Jansenists crafty, wicked, and concealing heresy under the deceitful appearance of obedience in words. The heretics now assailed the prelates with a storm of insulting and calumnious libels. This insolent attack was another motive which induced the king to urge, by letters-patent, the execution of the decree. Some months later he issued a still more explicit declaration, and appeared in person in the parliament to have it registered before his own eyes. He then wrote to the Pope, requesting him to send a formula himself, with orders to the bishops to sign it and to have it signed by their clergy Alexander accordingly drew up a new constitution (A. D. 1665), in which, " to take away all pretext for disobedience, and all subterfuge from heresy," he commanded the bishops, all ecclesiastics, regular and secular, all religious, doctors, licentiates and regents of universities, to sign, within three months, the following formula, very nearly the same in form as the one before issued by the Assembly of the French clergy : " I, the undersigned, submit to the Apostolic Constitution of Innocent X., given on the 31st of May, 1653, and to that of Alexander VII., of October 16th, 1656 ; and in the sincerity of my heart I reject and condemn the five propositions drawn from the work of Jansenius, called the ' Augustinus,' and in the sense in which they were understood by the author, as the Apostolic See has condemned them by the same constitutions. I swear it; so help me God and the Holy Gospels." The king immediatly issued an edict requiring all the prelates of the kingdom to sign the Pope's formula; declaring, at the same time, that if any bishop had not yet signed it at the end of three months, he should be prosecuted in accordance with the prescriptions of the Holy

Canons. Spite of this order, four prelates, the bishops of Alet, Nicholas Pavillon; of Beauvais, Nicholas Chouart de Buzenval; of Pamiers, Francis Gaulet, and of Angers, Henry Arnauld, refused to obey In the pastoral letters addressed to their respective dioceses, they protested and declared that, *concerning the act of Jansenius*, they owed to the Church only the obedience of deference, which consisted in observing a respectful silence. The king suppressed these pastoral letters on the 10th of July, 1665; and Alexander VII., by a decree of the Index, condemned them on the 18th of February, 1667 He then directed that a commission of nine bishops should open the trial of the four refractory prelates; but death did not allow him to carry out the delicate matter. Pope Alexander died on the 22d of May, 1667, with the reputation of an enlightened, firm, and energetic Pontiff, the very man that was needed to combat the most obstinate of heresies.

§ 3. PONTIFICATE OF CLEMENT IX. (June 20, A. D. 1667—December 9, 1669).

23. Cardinal Julius Rospigliosi, of Pistoja, was elected to succeed Alexander VII., and took the name of Clement IX. Nineteen French bishops had taken occasion, at the death of the late Pontiff, to side with the four refractory prelates. They published pastoral letters, teaching that the Church cannot pronounce with infallibility upon a human action, as, for example, in appreciating the doctrine of an author; * that in such a case the Church can require only a respectful silence on its decisions. All the old quarrels thus threatened to spring up again with renewed violence. Clement IX. at once confirmed the bulls of his predecessors by a brief, in which he threatened to prosecute the rebellious bishops with the greatest rigor. Louis

---

* We must be careful to distinguish between the natural (*obvious*) sense of a book and the real thought or personal meaning of the author. It is the former sense that the Church condemns, and justly calls the sense of the author, whatever may have been his secret thought, which is nothing to the reader

XIV actively coöperated with the Pontiff. The Jansenists were alarmed, and thought it prudent to ward off the threatened punishments by a hypocritical show of submission. They promised to sign the formula, without any mental reservation, if they could be spared the shame of a public retraction of their charges. Full of paternal kindness toward his erring children, the merciful Pontiff granted the favor; he accepted the proposals of peace, and the bishops signed the declaration. We shall not enter into the details of the frauds used by the Jansenists to bring the matter to a speedy conclusion, to deceive the Pope, the king, the bishops and the clergy; it is enough to have pointed them out, and to add that the captious sectaries took advantage of the reconciliation, which was known as the "Clementine Peace." They affected to infer that the Pope, by not obliging the four bishops to retract their charges, had implicitly approved their distinction between the fact and the right. In this display of fanatical obstinacy, history would almost seem to have made a backward step of three centuries, to the time when the Greeks of the Lower Empire lengthened out religious disputes by endless sophisms.

24. The insincerity of the four bishops, however, only added new lustre to the noble language and conduct of Clement IX. The following brief, which he addressed to them when they had signed the formula, we quote, as a memorable monument, which will ever proclaim the doctrinal unchangeableness of the Papacy and condemn the shameful artifices of the Jansenists: "Venerable brethren, health and Apostolic benediction. Our nuncio at the court of France has put Us in possession of letters by which you inform Us, with every mark of submission, that, agreeably to the Apostolic letters issued by Our predecessors, Innocent X. and Alexander VII., you have, in sincerity, subscribed, and caused to be subscribed, the formula contained in the letters of the same Pope Alexander. Though in consequence of certain reports which reached Our ears, We deemed it Our duty to act with deliberation in this case (for We could never have admitted, in this respect, any exception or restriction whatever,

being, as We are, inviolably attached to the constitutions of Our predecessors); yet now, in view of the renewed and considerable assurances which have come to us from France, touching the true and perfect obedience with which you have in sincerity subscribed the formula; beside, that having condemned, without exception or restriction, the five propositions, in all the senses in which they have been condemned by the Apostolic See, you are very far from wishing to renew the errors condemned by the same See ; We wished now to give you a mark of Our paternal affection, since We are sure that you will in future forget nothing that can daily give Us new proofs of the sincere obedience and submission which you have shown toward Us on this occasion." Nothing could be more clear, precise and formal than this brief. If Clement IX. was deceived by a faithlessness which defeated all calculation, eluded every condemnation, and disconcerted the most skilful measures, the whole infamy must fall upon the bishops and doctors who pretended to bring back the Church to its primitive integrity by disgraceful subtleties and pitiful evasions.

25. To form a correct notion of the power of Jansenism, and of the circumstances which fostered its prodigious growth; to account for the infatuation with which the French society of that period received a heresy, whose obscure teaching in one of the highest questions of theology, could not be within the reach of the vulgar, we must refer the history of Jansenism to the hostile movement which was displayed, in the beginning of the seventeenth century, against the Pontifical power. The Jansenists, by their subtle distinction between right and fact, came to calling in question the infallibility of the Pope ; it was this feature of their system which gave them the readiest access to minds already imbued with Gallican ideas. All the tendencies of the doctors and jurists of the seventeenth century were summed up in this one idea—to make the Pope the first of bishops, but to allow him nothing beyond that primacy of honor; to refuse him dogmatic infallibility, and to bestow it upon the Universal Church at large, or assembled in its general councils ;

therefore, to put the council above the Pope ; to deny the right of the Roman Pontiff to intervene in the temporal affairs of Europe ; in a word, to overthrow the whole religious and political system of the middle-ages, in order to draw the world into the way of lawless independence ; such had been the aim of the legists of that age. They did not perceive that they were merely underpinning the error of Luther, while disguising it under less violent forms, and preserving, at least in appearance, the outward bond of ecclesiastical communion. Marc-Antonio *de Dominis*, archbishop of Spalatro and primate of Dalmatia (1607), was the first to maintain these novelties. His work, " De Republica Christiana," destroyed all idea of a monarchy in the Church; Dominis looked upon it as an aristocratic system, in which the Pope was but the minister, and, in some sort, the delegate of the community   The Theological Faculty of Paris condemned the work, while the author went to justify himself in Rome, where he atoned for his errors in the Castle of St. Angelo.   But his teaching was not imprisoned with him. Edmund Richer, doctor and syndic of the Faculty of Paris, defended it with more subtlety, and, we may also add, with more unskilfulness.   In presenting, in a general way, his principles on the community, as the essential origin of sovereignty, he was attacking the temporal monarchy no less than the spiritual jurisdiction of the Sovereign Pontiff. Richer's treatise, " De Ecclesiastica et Politica Potestate," was condemned in the synods of Paris and Aix (A. D. 1612) as well as at Rome.   Its author was deprived of his office.   Before his death, however, Richer was persuaded by Richelieu to sign a retraction which his partisans pretend to regard as extorted, but which seems, on the contrary, to have been free and sincere.   Jean Launoy, a doctor of the Sorbonne and an avowed Jansenist, professed the same opinions in a work entitled *Puissance du roi sur le mariage*.   In the theory of Launoy, Christian marriage is made a purely civil matter ; the author takes from the Church the right of establishing the invalidating impediments, and ascribes it exclusively to princes, in opposition to the express doctrine of the Council of Trent, which anathematizes the very proposition advocated by Launoy "Independently of this end of non-acceptance," adds a late author, "the opinion of the doctor of the Sorbonne may be said to lead to the total ruin of Christian morality; for if the validity of marriages depends entirely upon the secular power, what will hinder Christians from marrying their own sisters, as did the illustrious Ptolemies, and all Egypt with them; from establishing the community of women, as the incomparable Plato would have done, and as the grave Cato actually did; or from becoming polygamists, according to the teaching of the Arab Prophet?" This work of Launoy, proscribed, by its very nature and aim, at the tribunal of every Christian reader, was condemned in Rome by a Pontifical decree. Launoy showed no more respect for the venerable traditions upon which rests the worship of the saints, than for the divine authority of the Church. He was popularly known in France by the nickname of *Dénicheur des Saints*. He erased from his calendar the name of St. Catherine, martyr, to whom all past ages had paid a marked devotion. On her feast he affected to say a mass of requiem, as if a defect of authenticity in the acts of a saint honored by the Church with public worship, could prove any thing against her existence or her sanctity This wretched system, under pretext of a more enlightened criticism, attacked the lives of the most illustrious saints. Catholic writers of undoubted learning and purity of intention, undertook to redress the injuries done to hagiology in this respect. Baillet distinguished himself by the affected rigorism with which he composed his "Lives of the Saints," rejecting all wonderful facts as apocryphal legends, and thus introducing Protestant rationalism into the appreciation of those privileged beings, the very essence of whose existence is, so to speak, miraculous. In open contradiction to this system of *a priori* negation, a professed Jansenist, Arnauld d'Andilly, brother of the celebrated Doctor Arnauld, now published his translations of the "Lives of the Fathers of the Desert, written by the Fathers of the Church," and of the "Works of St. Theresa."

every page of which abounds in facts altogether of the super
natural order, superabundantly proving that in every age of its
history, the Church has preserved, as a token of its divine
origin, the power of miracles given by Jesus Christ at the time
of its foundation.

26. The reaction against the authority of the Church was
now drawing along the majority of the French doctors. In this
spirit, Ellies Dupin wrote several works : an "Abridged History of the Church, by question and answer, from the beginning of the world to the present time ;" a "Profane History"
from its beginning to the same date ; a "Universal Library of
Historians ;" and one of "Ecclesiastical Writers." The last of
these works called forth especial opposition. The Benedictines
of St. Vannes, under the direction of Petit-Didier, abbot of
Senones, were the first to point out the errors of Dupin. They
chiefly concerned original sin, Purgatory, the canonical books,
the eternity of future punishment, the veneration of saints and
of their relics, the adoration of the cross, grace, the Pope and
the bishops, Lent, divorce, clerical celibacy, the Fathers and
tradition. Thus nearly the whole Protestant theory was embodied in the writings of a doctor who claimed to be a member
of the Catholic communion. The Benedictines of St. Vannes
published their "Remarks on the Works of Ellies Dupin," in
three volumes; but that author soon met a yet more formidable adversary Bossuet addressed to the chancellor of the
kingdom a memorial in which, with close, spirited and eloquent
reasoning, he advocates the suppression of so pernicious a work.
"In his abridgment of discipline," says Bossuet, "the author
grants to the Pope nothing more than that the Roman Church,
founded by St. Peter and St. Paul, be looked upon as the first,
and its bishop as the first among all the bishops, without attrib-
uting to the Pope any jurisdiction over them, or saying a word
about the divine institution of his primacy ; on the contrary,
he makes this a matter of discipline, which he declares to be
variable. He is not more clear in speaking of bishops, but
simply says that the bishop is above the priests, without stating

that he is so by divine right. These great critics are not very favorably disposed toward ecclesiastical superiority, and have very little more regard for that of bishops than for the Pope's. One of the highest prerogatives of the chair of St. Peter, is that it is the chair of St. Peter, the principal chair to which all the faithful must look for unity, and, as St. Cyprian styles it, ' the source of sacerdotal unity.' It is the spirit of our modern critics to condemn those who acknowledge, in the Papacy, a supreme authority established by divine right. To join all antiquity in this recognition, is, in their eyes, to flatter Rome in order to win her favor." Bossuet thus closes his memorial : " Without going farther in the examination of a work so full of errors and of rashness, it is easy to see that it manifestly tends to the overthrow of the Catholic religion; that it everywhere betrays a spirit of singularity which must be crushed; in a word, that its doctrine is intolerable." Ellies Dupin was banished by Louis XIV., and deprived of his chair in the Sorbonne. His " Universal Library " was condemned by the Archbishop of Paris, suppressed by a parliamentary decree in 1696, and branded with the anathema of the court of Rome.—Another scholar, no less dangerous, Doctor Richard Simon, wrote, in the same spirit as Dupin, 1st, a " Critical History of the Text, the Versions and the Commentaries of the Old Testament;" 2d, " Critical History of the Text of the New Testament;" 3d, " Critical History of the Principal Commentators on the New Testament." All these works were condemned at Rome. Bossuet also denounced them to the chancellor as " a mass of impious doctrines and a bulwark for libertinism." Richard Simon, in fact, announces himself as the partisan of the Socinians and the forerunner of modern free thinkers. " His real aim," says Bossuet, " is to destroy the authenticity of the Canonical Scriptures, to make a direct attack upon the inspiration of the Sacred Text, and to reject, in opposition to a formal decree of the Council of Trent, several passages as doubtful or apocryphal ; to weaken the whole teaching of the Fathers, and by a particular design, that of St. Augustine on grace." The illustrious Bishop of Meaux, with the object of refuting Doctor Simon, composed his magnificent treatise, "Defence of Tradition and of the Holy Fathers," in which he displays a triumphant array of learning, logic and eloquence. Spite of his energetic efforts, the gangrene of Jansenism continued to infect the French clergy, and, at a later period, a canon of St. Genevieve in Paris, Pierre-François Le Courrayer, scandalized the world by the spectacle of a complete apostasy. In a "Dissertation on the Validity of Anglican Ordinations," he almost unconditionally declared in favor of the Reformation of Henry VIII., and in a later work, *Declaration of my last sentiments upon religious discussions,* he rejects all the mysteries of Christian faith, the Trinity, the Incarnation, the dogma of original sin, the real presence, transubstantiation, and the infallibility of the Church. Le Courrayer quitted France for England, where he was received as a conquest by the Archbishop of Canterbury; the university of that city presented him with a doctor's diploma; the court of London gave him a pension, and he died amid the wealth and honors bought at the price of apostasy

27 Some French jurists, unhappily too faithful to the spirit of opposition which characterized the Councils of Basle and Constance, seemed altogether pre-occupied with the thought of combating the prerogatives of the Roman Church. The brothers Peter and Francis Pithou, converts from Calvinism, were particularly remarkable in this fierce contest. They worked together to produce their famous " Treatise on the Gallican Liberties," in which, under the pretext of freeing the clergy of France from the Pontifical authority, they completely subject it to the secular power.* To support the work of the brothers Pithou, another legist, Pierre Dupuy published a compilation under the title of *"The Liberties of the Gallican Church Proved."* It was censured and denounced to the Episcopate by twenty-two bishops and

---

* "The great servitude of the Gallican church," says Fleury, "is the undue extent of the secular jurisdiction." This consideration has not prevented the works of the brothers Pithou and of Dupuy from becoming the great armory of Gallicanism.

archbishops in France, "as a detestable work, full of the most poisonous propositions, and cloaking formal·heresies under the plausible name of liberties." "For," says Bossuet, "the jurists and the magistrates understood the term 'Gallican liberties,' far otherwise than the bishops; they looked upon themselves as the fathers and doctors of that church, as its natural defenders, not only against the Pope, but against the bishops." The parliament, which seemed to think itself the permanent council of Gaul, helped to strengthen the spirit of hostility against the Holy See. "Protestant in the sixteenth century," says the Count de Maistre; "with the Fronde and Jansenism in the seventeenth; philosophical, at length, and republican in the last years of its existence, the parliament but too often appeared in antagonism to the true fundamental maxims of the State. The seeds of Calvinism, fostered in that great body, became far more dangerous when its essence changed its name, and was called Jansenism. Then conscience was set at ease by a heresy which proclaimed the principle, 'I do not exist.' The poison reached even those illustrious names in the magistracy of which foreign nations envied France the possession. Then all errors, even the errors hostile to each other, being always ready to unite against the truth, the new philosophy in the parliaments leagued with Jansenism against Rome. If we take into consideration the number of magistrates in all parts of France, that of the tribunals which made it a duty and a point of honor to walk in their footsteps, the many clients of the parliament, and all that blood, friendship, or mere ascendency drew into the same gulf, we shall easily perceive that there was material enough to form in the heart of the Gallican church a formidable party against the Holy See."

28. Such were the auxiliaries of Jansenism in France. The leaders of the new sect were three men of different degrees of celebrity, and whose names were repeated by every tongue of fame. The *Lettres Provinciales* had just appeared under the title of " Letters of Louis de Montalte to a Provincial friend." Their author, a deep mathematician, had already illustrated the

name of Pascal by brilliant discoveries made at an age when
other men have hardly closed their course of scholastic studies.
He was now known in France as a first-class writer. Never
before him had the French language attained the purity, the
elegance, the choice of forms and turns of expression which
fixed it for all time. For style, the *Lettres Provinciales* were
one of the finest monuments of literature, not that they have
never since been surpassed by any other work,* but because
they were the first to appear in the highest rank, and thus acquire a simple priority of date, As to the matter of the work,
Voltaire says of it, without evasion ; " The whole work indeed
rests upon a false ground, it is very evident." Pascal's object
was to attack the Society of Jesus, of which the members
showed themselves the most determined opponents of Jansenism. For this purpose he gathered a number of texts from the
various writings of their casuists and theologians, isolated them
from their context, combining them with the greatest art, and
often with a dishonesty unworthy of his genius. In their decisions, often uncertain and doubtful, as well as in the doctrine
of some of their moralists on probabilism, authority, and mental reservations, he found ample matter for satire, and an exhaustless fund of ridicule, Moreover, he did not scruple to
unbury obscure and forgotten writings, and especially to attribute to a whole society the opinions of a few individuals. Still
the work won an immense success. It was condemned by the
court of Rome, and Louis XIV ordered that it should be examined by a commission consisting of thirteen archbishops,
bishops, doctors or professors of theology, who gave their decision in these terms : " After a careful examination of the
work entitled *Lettres Provinciales*, we certify that the heresies
of Jansenius, condemned by the Church, are maintained and
defended in it. In his insolence and malignity, the author
spares neither the Pope, nor the bishops, nor the king, nor his

---

* In style, in literary wealth, in historical and philosophical importance the *Discourse
on Universal History* and the *Funeral Orations* of Bossuet, and the *Telemachus* of Fénelon, are infinitely superior to the *Lettres Provinciales*, which are more praised than read.

chief ministers, nor the sacred Faculty of Theology of Paris, nor the religious orders. The book is therefore deserving of the penalties decreed by the laws against defamatory and heretical libels." A corresponding decree of the Council of State condemned the *Provinciales* to the flames. Pascal did not retract. It is sad to read in the immortal collection of his *Pensées* such sentiments as these : "When I saw myself condemned, I feared that I might have written amiss, but the example of so many pious writings which have met the same fate, leads me to believe the contrary. It is no longer allowable to write any thing good, so corrupt and ignorant has the Inquisition become. It is better to obey God than men. I fear nothing ; I look for nothing. Port-Royal is alarmed ; it is a bad policy When they cease to fear, they will themselves inspire greater fear. Silence is the greatest persecution. The saints never remained silent. Vocation, it is true, is necessary ; but it is not from the decrees of councils that we shall know whether we are called, but from the necessity of speaking. If my letters are condemned in Rome, what I condemn in them is condemned in Heaven. The Inquisition and the Society of Jesus are the two scourges of truth." How deplorable the blindness that led astray in the ways of error one of the noblest minds of which humanity could ever boast.

29. Antoine Arnauld had just published his work on "Frequent Communion," in which the spirit of Jansenism was openly displayed. The God of the Eucharist is no longer, in the eyes of Arnauld, the God of grace and mercy ; He is an inexorable judge, more surrounded with terrors than on the Mount of Sinai. The terrified faithful are no more to draw near to that awful majesty The effect of the work was immense. The number of communions decreased in Paris at a fearful rate.* At once the Catholics raised a general outcry

---

* St. Vincent de Paul wrote to one of his missionaries: "It may be that some have profited by reading the book on 'Frequent Communion,' but if it has served to make a hundred persons more respectful toward the Sacraments, there are at least ten thousand whom it has injured by withdrawing them altogether from them. Now we no longer see the Holy

against so dangerous a work. The book was submitted to the
Holy See, and the author was obliged to retract. In vindication of their corypheus, the Jansenists stated that Arnauld had
only aimed at combating the relaxation of confessors, who
were too ready to admit sinners to a participation in the sacred
mysteries. "That is an excess," said St. Vincent de Paul.
"which was deplored by St. Charles Borromeo himself. But
the theories of the 'Frequent Communion' go still farther
The author gives unqualified praise to the piety of those who
would put off communion until the end of their lives, as being
unworthy to approach the body of Jesus Christ. He assures
them that such humility is more pleasing to God than all
manner of good works; that it is speaking in a manner de-
rogatory to the King of Heaven to say that He is honored by
our communions. But even closing our eyes to all these considerations, we cannot help seeing that the dispositions required by the young doctor for the reception of the Holy
Mysteries are so elevated, so far above our human weakness
that no man living could flatter himself with the thought that
he is worthy   If, as he maintains without the slightest modi-
fication, they only can be allowed to receive the Holy Eucharist who are entirely purified from all the images of their past
lives by divine love, pure and unmixed, who are perfectly
united to God alone, being wholly perfect and irreproachable
then we must grant with him, that those who receive according to the practice of the Church, with the ordinary dispositions, are antichrists. No! On such principles, holy communion is now only for M. Arnauld, who, after making the
standard of the necessary dispositions one which might have
terrified a St. Paul, does not omit to proclaim several times
in the course of his apology, that he says Mass every day'
Arnauld was not more willing than Pascal to abide by the

Table frequented as it used to be, not even at Easter; many parish priests in Paris com
plain of this; at St. Sulpice the number of communicants has decreased by three thousand
at St. Nicholas du Chardonnet, fifteen hundred persons failed in this duty of religion, and
so of many others."

various censures which his work incurred. He quitted his native land, and ended at Brussels a life which might have reflected glory upon the Church. " Arnauld," says a late writer, " was gifted with great eloquence ; but he did not sufficiently regulate its impulse. His powerful logic was sometimes weakened by careless diction, a heavy and dogmatic tone, and, in his first contests, it was necessary that Pascal's charms of expression and stinging satire should set off his arguments to insure their reception. He had not at command, like that inimitable writer, the art of condensing and of being precise, without ceasing to be eloquent." Of the hundred and fifty volumes which we owe to his fruitful pen, the most important and only blameless one is the celebrated treatise on the " Perpetuity of the Faith," in which he established the dogma of the real presence against the Calvinists. In this work he was helped by Nicole, another Jansenist leader, whose early fortunes were similar to those of Arnauld. Like him, he preferred exile to submission. At a later period, however, he returned from the wanderings of his youth, and obtained permission to reside in Paris. It was then that he wrote his *Essais de morale*, a work less universally read than esteemed, in which the leading ideas of the sect are found buried in dissertations which at present seem cold and heavy Such was Jansenism in France in the Pontificate of Clement IX. Intrenched in its stronghold of Port-Royal, it spread its seductive influence over the finest intellects of the great age. The warm-hearted Racine yielded his affectionate soul to that cheerless doctrine ; the severe Boileau devoted some of his beautiful verses to its praises, and bestowed upon the " Great Arnauld" a patent of immortality. Strange is the inconsistency of the human mind! At the very time when the temporal authority was glorified in its highest impersonation, and reached its zenith under Louis XIV., men did not blush to encourage sectaries who rose up in open revolt against the highest spiritual authority, pretending to make of the Church a kind of aristocratic republic, whose head would have been such only in name

30. Public attention had been for a moment withdrawn from these lamentable contests, by a series of events which threatened the safety of Europe and the destinies of the Christian world.   In the course of the year 1662, the emperor of Austria, Leopold I., had made an armed invasion of Transylvania, a tributary province of the Porte, and had seized several strong places, among others, Szecklhyel and Serinvar.   The Turks were then ruled by the Sultan Mahomet IV., a weak and voluptuous prince, who spent his days in hunting, and would have been personally incapable of avenging the honor of his arms ; but his vizier, Achmet Kuprili, a man of eminent ability, placed himself at the head of all the Turkish forces, and carried the crescent in triumph through the kingdom of Hungary   The fall of Neuhausel, of Ujivar and of Serinvar, before the victorious arms of Achmet, was soon followed by the brilliant and decisive victory at St. Gothard, a village near the Raab, a tributary of the Danube.   On this celebrated field, the Turks met the Austrians and Hungarians, who were joined by six thousand French troops sent by Louis XIV., under the Count of Coligny and the Viscount d'Aubusson de la Feuillade, whom the Mussulmans surnamed the *man of steel ;* the illustrious Montecuculli, an Austrian field-marshal, was commander-in-chief of the allies.   The whole of the Christian artillery played at once upon the Turkish camp on the opposite bank of the Raab.   The Austrians, Hungarians and French swam the stream.   More than fifteen thousand Mussulmans were killed or drowned, and their cavalry, heedless of the commands and threats of the vizier, who would have carried on the fight, fled in disorder (August 1, A. D. 1664)   On the day after the victory of St. Gothard, Montecuculli, on horseback, sword in hand, surrounded by his battalions, intoned the Te Deum, and the great voice of the army joined that of its leader to swell the solemn anthem of praise to God.   " Let us also give thanks to Mary !" exclaimed the hero ; and the soldiers repeated with enthusiasm the august name of the Mother of God.   This religious spirit, displayed amid the terrible array of battle, recalls

the great combats of the old crusaders, and carries us back in imagination to the ages of valor, when each soldier was a hero, and every hero a martyr.

31. The defeat at St. Gothard imbittered the soul of Ach-met, but did not crush him. "I shall wrest Candia from the Venetians," said he on his return to Adrianople, "or I shall die in arms on that island which the Christians have held too long." He accordingly urged on the undertaking with a cour-age and perseverance almost unparalleled in history In the opening of the year 1667, he began the siege of Candia under the fire of the Venetian batteries. The Turks attacked with headlong daring, and the Christians, far inferior in numbers, defended their post like heroes. The gigantic struggle, now become so unequal, lasted two years. The Venetians were re-duced to six thousand fighting men. They offered Achmet a large sum of money to withdraw and leave the city of Candia to the besieged. "We are not traders," answered the vizier; "we are in no want of money We want Candia, and it shall be ours." Clement IX. sent assistance to the heroic Vene-tians. Louis XIV equipped a fleet manned by five thousand warriors, the flower of his nobility,* under the command of the Duke of Navailles and Francis de Vendôme, in whose veins flowed the blood of Henry IV., and who was to die, as became his descent, before the walls of Candia. By an inexplicable fatality, these re-enforcements, which could have secured the triumph of the Christian arms, soon afterward left the island they had come to defend. In the month of August, A. D. 1669, the Duke of Navailles returned to France with his squadron. The Pontifical galleys left at the same time. The Venetian garri-son numbered now but three thousand men, while the ranks of the besiegers were daily strengthened by fresh arrivals from Anatolia, Roumelia, Egypt and the Barbary Coast. To continue the struggle was impossible. The Venetians made

* In this auxiliary force we find the names of a Saint-Paul, a Créqui, a Beauvau, a Fénelon, related to the illustrious archbishop of Cambrai, a Castellane, the youthful de Sé vigné, and a host of others equally illustrious.

proposals of surrender, to which the grand-vizier agreed.   On
the 27th of September, 1669, he received the keys of the city
in a silver ewer, and gave a thousand ducats to those who
brought them.   He insisted upon the complete evacuation of
Candia by the Venetians, and furnished ships to take them to
the shores of the Adriatic.   They took a last tearful leave of
that island of Crete which their republic had held during a
period of four hundred and sixty-five years.   Pope Clement
IX. died of grief at the disaster which had befallen Christian
Europe (December 9th, 1669).

CHAPTER II.

§ I. Pontificate of Clement X. (April 29, a. d. 1670—July 22, 1676).

1. Cardinal Bona. His works.—2. Election and government of Clement X.—
3. The *Regale* in France. Death of Clement X.—4. Spinoza. His pantheistic system.—5. Descartes. His philosophy.—6. Dangers of the Cartesian
system pointed out by Bossuet.—7. Malebranche.

§ II. Pontificate of Innocent XI. (September 21, a. d. 1676—August 12,
1689).

8. Election and first acts of Innocent XI. His character and antecedents.—
9. Splendor of France under Louis XIV.—10. Fleury's "History of the
Church."—11. The two fundamental maxims of Gallicanism, according to
Fleury.—12. Fleury's reasoning against the exercise of the Pontifical power
in the middle-ages, drawn from the "False Decretals."—13. Value of the
maxim : "The king, as such, is not subject to the judgment of the Pope."—
14. Difficulties between Louis XIV. and Innocent XI. concerning the *Regale.*—15. Bossuet.—16. Bossuet's letter to the Pope in the name of the
French clergy. Reply of Innocent XI.—17. Convocation of the General
Assembly of the clergy of France in 1682. Louis XIV arranges the matter
of their deliberations.—18. Sessions of the Assembly.—19. Declaration of
the 19th of March, 1682. The *Four Articles.*—20. Letters patent of Louis
XIV., requiring all the universities of the kingdom to teach the *Four Articles.*—21. The Pope condemns the " Declaration of the Clergy of France,"
and annuls all the acts of the Assembly of 1682.—22. Protest of the Catholic world against the Declaration.—23. Bossuet's "Defence of the Declaration of the Clergy of France."—24. Innocent XI. refuses the bulls of canonical institution to the bishops appointed by Louis XIV.—25. The " Franchises." They are suppressed by the Pope. All the Catholic powers
except France submit to the measure.—26. Innocent refuses to receive
Lavardin as ambassador from the court of France. The parliament appeals
from the Pope to a council.—27. Louis XIV. seizes upon Avignon, and interferes in the nomination of the archbishop-elector of Cologne.—28. Revocation of the Edict of Nantes.—29. Invasion of Austria by the Turks.
Mahomet IV. Kara-Mustapha. Innocent XI. effects the conclusion of a
treaty, offensive and defensive, between Leopold I., emperor of Austria, and

John Sobieski, king of Poland.—30. Siege of Vienna by the Turks. Rescue of the city by Sobieski.—31. Condemnation of Molinos, of the "New Tes tament of Mons" and other works.—32. Death of Innocent XI.

§ III. Pontificate of Alexander VIII. (October 6. a. d. 1689—February 1. 1691).

33. Election of Alexander VIII. Louis XIV. renounces the right of the *Franchises;* restores Avignon and the Comtat-Venaissin to the Pope.— 34. Bull *Inter multiplices,* condemning the "Declaration of the Clergy of France," and annulling all the acts of the Assembly. Death of Alexander VIII.

§ I. Pontificate of Clement X. (April 29, a. d. 1670—July 22, 1676).

1. At the death of Clement IX. all Rome seemed to join in one unanimous desire to see the chair of St. Peter occupied by the pious and learned Cardinal Bona. John Bona was born (a. d. 1609) at Mondovi, in Piedmont, of a noble family allied, it was said, to the house of Bonne Lesdiguières, of Dauphiny. At the age of fifteen years he entered the Cistercian Order, in the reformed Congregation of St. Bernard, known in France under the name of Feuillants.* He was successively prior of Asti, abbot of Mondovi, in 1661 general of his order, and at length, in 1669, cardinal. His works comprise several treatises full of piety and learning; the work "De Rebus Liturgicis" displays curious and interesting researches into the rites, pray- ers and ceremonies of the Mass. Among his ascetic works, the most distinguished is the treatise "De Principiis Vitæ Christianæ," written with so much unction and simplicity, that it has been compared to the "Imitation of Christ." But the treatise in which the pious cardinal surpassed himself, "De

* This secondary order, detached from the great monastic family of Citeaux, was insti- tuted in 1577, by Jean de la Barrière, in the monastery of Feuillant, near Toulouse. His religious practised austerities which appeared superhuman. They were to go at all times bare-headed and bare-footed, to sleep on boards, eat upon their knees, and suffer extraordi- nary privations. The Feuillants took a large share in the troubles of the League, especially a certain Father Bernard de Montgaillard, called *Le Petit Feuillant,* who was remarkable for the vehemence of his sermons. In 1630, Urban VIII. made a division between the Feuil- lants of Italy, under the name of "St. Bernard's Reform," and those of France

Divina Psalmodia," is a learned explanation of the Office of the Church, and, in particular, of the Breviary. A deep and critical examination into the origin, the order, the disposition and significance of each part of the divine office, makes of this work a precious mine in which the priest may find the meaning of the prayers which he recites every day, with considerations suited to keep alive his devotion, to inflame his zeal, to raise his mind and heart. Cardinal Bona deserves to rank among the Fathers and Doctors of the Church.

2. Yet he was not elected Pope. The choice of the Sacred College fell upon a no less virtuous and worthy candidate, Cardinal Altieri, then eighty years old ; he took the name of Clement X. " This Pontiff," says a Protestant author,* " followed the governmental maxims of his predecessor. As he had no living kindred, and was unwilling to witness the extinction in his own person of the ancient line from which he sprung, he adopted the family of the Paluzzi, gave them the name of Altieri and all his hereditary estates. Though he clothed his new relations with high dignities and advantages, and usefully employed the new cardinal Altieri as his chief minister, still this was not a nepotism burdensome to the Apostolic chamber. On the contrary, he instituted a special congregation to provide means for lowering the taxes. He abolished the tithe which had been ordered during the war with the Turks. He cut off all superfluous expenses, both at court and in the State, and deposited in the *Mont-de-piété*, to be used for the public good, all the income of the Pope's private purse. That was also a wise law by which he announced, in the year 1671, that commercial pursuits, when carried out on a large scale, would not derogate from the dignity and honor of the nobility in his States, provided they did not enter into a retail trade."

3. This Pontificate witnessed the rise, in France, of the question of the *Regale*, which afterward became so celebrated and so productive of fatal consequences. To understand the

---

* SCHRÖCKH. *Kirchen-Geschichte seit der Reformation*, t. VI., p. 332

origin of the question, it is necessary to form a clear and exact idea of the position taken by Louis XIV. in regard to the Papacy. However sincere may have been the attachment which he professed for the Catholic faith, that absolute monarch could not endure that the court of Rome should pursue a policy independent of his own. He had seen with secret displeasure, that the court and dependents of Clement IX. leaned to the side of the Spaniards, with whom he was then at war. For this he revenged himself by incessant encroachments on the spiritual power. An edict, dated St. Germain-en-Laye (February 10, A. D. 1673), extended the *regale* to all the dioceses in the kingdom. The name of *regale* was given to an abusive custom introduced into France, which consisted in turning over to the royal treasury the revenues of vacant bishoprics and other benefices. Some dioceses, situated in the provinces bordering on the Alps and Pyrenees, had hitherto escaped the arbitrary measure. It was especially upon them that the new edict was intended to bear. The French clergy showed a disposition to submit, doubtless apprehending that any attempt at resistance would but give rise to greater evils. The only prelates who took a decided stand in opposition, were the Bishops of Pamiers and Aleth; their property was confiscated by the king. Nor did he stop here; he claimed the right of raising means to pay military pensions, upon the benefices of the Church, and anticipated, by an act of violence, the remonstrances which he expected from the Sovereign Pontiff, inflicting a deep wound upon the holders of the Roman funds, by subjecting the donations sent to Rome to a strict and controlling supervision. Such was the situation at the death of Clement X., after a painful illness, on the 22d of July, 1676. He bequeathed to his successor the storms which the policy of Louis XIV was conjuring up between France and the Holy See.

4. It was during the Pontificate of Clement X. that Benedict Spinoza, a Dutch philosopher, published his celebrated work, " Tractatus Theologico-politicus," in which he makes open profession of pantheism. According to his system, the Divinity

is nothing more than the soul of the universe, which thinks in men, feels in animals, vegetates in plants, and dwells in an inanimate state in the bosom of the earth. Thus there is but one substance, variously modified, infinite in all respects; since God necessarily acts from all eternity, the existence of beings is, therefore, necessary and eternal. All religion, all revelation, are human inventions. The appearance of such a theory drew a cry of indignation from a society so deeply religious as was that of the age of Louis XIV. Spinoza's work was condemned by all the learned faculties of Europe; by a decree of the States-General of France, it was suppressed throughout the whole kingdom.

5. For the better understanding of the repugnance shown by the seventeenth century to aberrations of the nature of Spinoza's, it is important to have a precise idea of the philosophical system which was then predominant. René Descartes (A. D. 1596–1650), a native of Lahaye in Touraine, dethroned the philosophy of Aristotle, which had held sovereign sway, since the middle-ages, in all the schools of Europe. His famous "universal doubt" has often been made a subject of reproach, as containing a germ of skepticism. We cannot better defend Descartes against this charge than by quoting his own words :— "When I said," wrote the philosopher, "that we can know nothing with certainty, without the previous knowledge that God exists, I also stated in express terms that I spoke only of the knowledge of those conclusions, the remembrance of which may come to mind, though we do not advert to the reasons whence we drew them. For the knowledge of first principles, or axioms, is not generally called science by dialecticians. But when we perceive that we are thinking beings, this is a primary notion which is no longer deduced from any syllogism. And when I say, ' I think, therefore, I am, or I exist,' I do not infer my existence from my thought, as if by the force of some syllogism; but as we see a thing known to us, I behold it by a simple inspection of the mind; as appears from the fact that, if I deduced it from a syllogism, I must first have known

this major; 'all that think, are or exist;' but, on the contrary, that major is taught me by what I feel within myself, that I cannot think unless I exist.   For it is the property of our mind to form general propositions from the knowledge of particulars. I assert, moreover—which may at first sight seem paradoxical— that there is nothing in all my philosophy that is not old; for as to the principles, I receive only such as have hitherto been generally known and admitted by all philosophers, and which, therefore, are the oldest of all.   And what I deduce from them seems so manifestly—as I demonstrate—to be contained and enclosed in those principles, that it appears also that the con- clusion is very old, since nature herself has engraved and im- printed it on our minds."   From these different passages it is evident that Descartes had no more intention of calling in question, even for a moment, the first principles which he even believed innate in man, than the practical and moral conclusions which flow naturally from them; but only the metaphysical judgments and conclusions which constitute science, properly so called.   The illustrious philosopher was chiefly led to follow this course, by a lively wish to prove to skeptics, atheists, and materialists, the existence of God and the immateriality of the soul.   To cure them, he inoculates himself, so to speak, with their disease.   He subjects all his scientific judgments and conclusions to doubt, examination and personal evidence.   He always holds to this capital truth : "Whether I am or am not deceived by some one, still the fact remains that I doubt, that I think; therefore I am, and I am a thinking being.   This much is, at all events, certain.   What is no less certain is, that it is not I who preserve my own existence any more than I gave it. He who gave and preserves it is, then, God, that infinitely per- fect Being, of Whom I have a clear and precise idea, as of myself, and Whose existence is implied by that very idea." Such is, in substance, the progressive reasoning of Descartes in his six *Méditations Métaphysiques.* Avoiding the long and circuitous route of the ordinary systems, he seeks, by inward evidence, to convince the materialist and the skeptic that, so long as they do not recognize the existence of God, all their science has no certitude founded upon reason. He admits. moreover, that his system must be applied only by chosen minds, free from corporeal images and practised in argumentative contests. Even though Descartes had not succeeded in his undertaking, it would suffice for his glory to have made the attempt.

6. The dangers of the Cartesian system were equal to its advantages. Bossuet pointed them out with his usual eloquence. "I see," he exclaims, "a great struggle preparing against the Church, under the name of Cartesian philosophy I see more than one heresy springing from its bosom and from its principles, which are, I think, misunderstood; and I foresee that the consequences drawn from it against the dogmas held by our fathers will make it odious, and will rob the Church of all the fruit she hoped to gain from it, to establish, in the minds of philosophers, the divinity and immortality of the soul. From the same misinterpreted principles, another fearful evil is insensibly gaining ground; for, under the pretext that we must admit nothing which we do not clearly understand, which, to a certain extent, is true enough, each one takes the liberty of saying, 'I understand this, and I do not understand that;' and upon this only ground a man may receive or reject what he pleases, without reflecting that, beside our clear and distinct ideas, we have others, confused and general, embracing truths so essential that their denial would overthrow every thing. Under this pretext, there has crept in a freedom of judgment which leads some, without any regard for tradition, rashly to advance whatever they think; and never, in my opinion, has the excess appeared to a greater extent than in this new system."

7 The followers of Descartes had given occasion to this severe criticism of the illustrious Bishop of Meaux. The Oratorian Malebranche was one of those whose philosophical speculations wandered most widely The general aim of his principal works—*De la recherche de la Vérité—Traité de la Nature*

et de la Grâce—Méditations Chrétiennes et Métaphysiques—was
to show the relation of the philosophy of Descartes to religion,
and to prove that the Cartesian system affords the demonstra-
tion of several other truths in the order of nature and in that
of grace.   In this there was nothing that was not praiseworthy
Unfortunately, the imagination of Malebranche was better suited
to poetic reveries than to the stern precision of the scholastic
teacher.   Descartes, we have seen, limited the use of his system of philosophic doubt to certain master minds; he would
not have the first principles of natural reason, which he supposed innate in man, nor their primary conclusions, subject to
it, and still less the truths of the natural order, but only the
remote and scientific conclusions of the purely natural order.
Malebranche, regardless of these distinctions, lays down the
philosophic doubt as the necessary basis of all science; he affects the greatest contempt for all the philosophers who have
gone before him, and submits every thing to interior eviden :e,
which he calls the interior master, the Word of God communicating itself to every man by natural reason.   This borders
closely upon the philosophy of a visionary   His *Traité de la
Nature et de la Grâce,* which may be said to contain and to sum
up all his errors, has been victoriously refuted in a special work
by Fénelon.   Bossuet uttered his judgment on the theory of
Malebranche in three words—*Pulchra, nova, falsa.*   It is evident, then, that, with the exception of a few purely speculative
deviations, the philosophy of the seventeenth century was
thoroughly imbued with a religious spirit; it was only in the
course of the following century that it took the anti-Catholic
stand which it has kept to our own day

§ 2. Pontificate of Innocent XI. (September 21, a. d. 1676—
August 12, 1689).

8. At the death of Clement X., the cardinals met in conclave to the number of sixty-seven.   On the evening of the
20th of September, the Sacred College, with one accord, pro-

ceeded to the chapel, and all the electors, without a single exception, pressed forward to kiss the hand of Cardinal Odescalchi. This manner of election by homage was certainly less tumultuous, and sufficed to establish the legitimate promotion of the Sovereign Pontiff. Odescalchi burst into tears and entreated to be allowed a moment for reflection. A dead silence at once followed, during which all gazed with anxiety and admiration upon the spectacle of humility and detachment from earthly dignities. Meanwhile, Odescalchi had prostrated himself before them, bathed in tears. He entreated his colleagues to choose "a more worthy subject," and not to crush him beneath a weight to which his strength was wholly inadequate. They could not yield to his wishes, and, on the morrow, a regular ballot confirmed, by unanimity of suffrage, the election of the pious and humble cardinal, who took the name of Innocent XI. On taking possession of the Vatican, the new Pontiff sent for his nephew, Livio Odescalchi. "You will make no change," said the Pope to him, "in your manner of life; you will receive neither presents nor visits, as nephew of the Pope; you will remain in the palace which We inhabited as cardinal; you can have no part in the government of the court. Such is Our formal and irrevocable intention." The young nobleman punctually obeyed the injunctions of his uncle Innocent XI. immediately gave his attention to the work of domestic reform; he admitted to his service none but persons remarkable for their modesty and good morals. A congregation of four cardinals and four prelates was instituted to examine the conduct and capacity of candidates for various benefices. Merit was the only title of admission. Cardinal Cibo once handed the Pope a list of candidates for several vacant offices, with a note of the recommendations offered by their respective patrons. Coming to one of the names, unaccompanied by a recommendation, Innocent asked the cardinal: "By whom is this one recommended?" "By nobody," replied Cibo. "In that case," rejoined the Pope, "We give him Our protection and prefer him to the others. A recommendation has very little weight with Us, when the person recommended is wanting in virtue. Dignities should be the reward of virtue, not of ambition; of true worth, not of intrigues." Such was the Pontiff whom Louis XIV was destined to meet in his career of ambition and despotism. Some authors pretend to account for the determined resistance of Innocent XI. in his struggle with Louis XIV., by the military habits which they ascribe to the younger days of the Pontiff. They say that Odescalchi, before he was made cardinal, had served in the war in Flanders. This erroneous statement has been victoriously refuted by Count Rezzonico, in a learned dissertation published at Cosmo (A. D. 1742). The mistake arose from an identity of names; a relative of the Pope's, an Odescalchi, having in fact taken an active part in the war. Innocent had entered the ecclesiastical state at an early age; and having spent nearly all his life in the sanctuary, he had never incurred reproach by the harsh and unpolished manners of a camp-life, nor by habits of violence which may be familiar to soldiers Raised to the Sovereign Pontificate, he looked for motives of action only in his duties as spiritual head of the Church and independent sovereign. "Innocent XI.," says Ranke, "was of the utmost purity of heart and life, meek and gentle, but impelled by the same conscientiousness which governed his private life, to fulfil the duties of his office with inflexible integrity"

9. Louis XIV was now at the zenith of his power and glory Abroad, his arms were everywhere victorious. Holland invaded, in spite of the heroic efforts of the brothers De Witt (A. D. 1672); Franche-Comté reunited to the French territory, spite of the confederation of Spain, Austria and Lorraine (1674); the victories of Condé at Senef and Oudenarde, over the first generals of the empire, which won for the hero that charming sentence from Louis: "Cousin, for one who is loaded as you are with laurels, it is not easy to walk;"* the astonish-

* On his return to court, as Condé, then suffering from an attack of the gout, was slowly ascending the grand staircase of the palace, at the head of which he perceived the

ing success of Turenne, who defeated the Imperialists at Seintz-heim, Ladenberg, Ensheim, Mulhausen and Türcheim (1675), though contending with forces three times as numerous as his own, and whose fall on the field of Salzbach drew from his adversary Montecuculli, the high encomium, "There fell a hero who was an honor to mankind;"—so many brilliant feats of arms, closed by the glorious peace of Nimeguen, placed Louis XIV. at the head of the world, and obtained for him the epithet of Great, bestowed by the enthusiasm of his people, and to which the nations most jealous of France have acknowledged the justice of his claim. Colbert wrote to him : " Sire, we can but be silent, admire, and daily give thanks to God that He has granted us to live in the reign of such a king as Your Majesty, whose power shall be limited only by His will." At home, the prosperity of the State, luxury, abundance, works of art and genius raised his kingdom to that degree of intellectual and moral superiority which signalizes great periods. " Louis XIV.," says Voltaire, " showed that an absolute monarch, who seeks to do good, accomplishes every thing with ease. He had but to command, and his successes in administration were as rapid as his conquests had been. It was truly admirable to behold the seaports, formerly deserted and dismantled, now surrounded with works, at once their ornament and their defence, filled with shipping and sailors, and containing already nearly sixty large vessels ready for a warlike armament. New colonies, under the protecting shadow of the French flag, sailed from all parts of the coast for America, the East Indies, and Africa; while in France, under the eyes of the monarch, thousands of men were busy in raising immense edifices, adorned by all the arts which follow in the train of architecture; and, in the interior of his court and of his capital, nobler and more elegant arts gave to France pleasures and a glory of which former ages had never dreamed." Louis XIV. could with some reason utter the words so ill interpreted or so little understood : *"L'Etat, c'est*

king waiting to meet him : "Sire," said the hero, "I beg your Majesty's pardon for my delay." To which Louis made the gracious answer we have quoted.

moi—1 am the State"—for he had made himself the impersonation of the interests of France, of the consciousness of power,
the dignity, the pride of the nation, and even of its passions
and its spirit. The French nation felt that it lived and ruled
in Louis XIV. But a power so immense has its moments of
blindness, of error and weakness. Man, however great, ever
bears the stamp of that original imperfection which leaves its
impress on all his works. The Great King, whose ministers, by
their exaggerated flattery, had impressed him with the idea
that his will was the only limit of his power, wished to im-
pose his unbridled absolutism upon all Europe. The religious
convictions which ruled his life, notwithstanding the weak
points of his nature, did not withhold him in his career of encroachments upon the Pontifical authority. We have seen him,
under Alexander VII., contending against the Holy See with
a violence unworthy of a Most Christian King, who assumed
the title of " Eldest Son of the Church ;" the Pontificate of
Innocent XI. presents a series of attempts of the same kind,
arising on the one hand from a boundless ambition and haughtiness ; borne, on the other, with a truly apostolic firmness.

10. We are coming to the time at which Gallicanism appears in its greatest obstinacy. It is important to form a correct idea of the doctrine which agitated the whole of the seventeenth century, sending the echoes of its intestine struggles
even to our own days. We may present the question in the form
in which it is given by Fleury, whose moderation is so highly
praised by the Gallicans. Fleury, successively preceptor of
the sons of the Prince of Conti, of the Count of Vermandois,
one of the natural sons of Louis XIV ; assistant-preceptor of
the Dukes of Burgundy, Anjou, and Berry, and afterward confessor of the young king Louis XV., is the author of a " History of the Church," in twenty quarto volumes, which has long
been the only classical work of the kind admitted into the
schools of France. The style is pure, easy and abundant;
the narrative clear and natural. A long and deep study of the
Fathers and Doctors had made Fleury familiar with the sub-

jects which he treats. Many minor points of detail could doubtless be found open to criticism; but, in a work of such length, it would be unjust not to recognize the difficulty overcome, or to dwell too minutely upon slight defects. Only prejudiced minds, or men who have never attempted any thing, have the easy courage to judge so severely. In our estimation, the great, the only reproach which Fleury has justly incurred, is to have set out with the fixed purpose and determination of combating, in all ages and on every favorable occasion, the authority of the Holy See and the Pontifical supremacy. To this unhappy feature his history is indebted for the injury of having been praised by nearly all the Protestant writers. Basnage thus wrote of it at the time of its publication: "To mention Fleury, is to give an idea of the highest reputation for sincerity ever deserved by any author. Yet we predict that in Italy, in Spain, and especially in any part of the States of the Pope, his work will never win the esteem enjoyed by Baronius. I am convinced, and I say it before the whole world, that there is not a single Catholic who has not been scandalized by it." The Lutheran, Gruber, writes as follows, at the same period: "Fleury is an author abounding in excellent sentiments; for he speaks of the Pontifical primacy with so much ambiguity, that he seems rather to destroy than to establish it; and we may evidently count him among *the most remarkable witnesses of the truth*, who have lived in our day" We have nothing to add to praises so significant. A system which claims to be Catholic is judged when it wins such commendations from the bitterest enemies of Catholicism. Besides, it must be said, Fleury was only displaying the tendencies of the French clergy of that period; which fact explains the prodigious success of his history in France.

11. Fleury has also left us a "Discourse on the Liberties of the Gallican Church," which he reduces to two great maxims: "The king, as such, is not subject to the judgment of the Pope. The Pope, as such, is subject to the judgment of a general council." This was the thesis of the Fathers of Basle

and of Constance. "Some politicians," says Fleury, "have endeavored to decry the doctrine of the superiority of a council by a comparison with the States-General. They will be made, it is objected, superior to the king, as the council is to the Pope, and on the same principles." He rejects the consequence by this last and principal reason: "As to France, we know that, from the time of Charlemagne, the national assemblies, though frequent and usual, were only called to advise the king, and that he alone decided." It is of little consequence to us now to see by what artifice Fleury disposed of an objection which might to some extent influence a sovereign as absolute as Louis XIV The logic of revolutions took upon itself to apply to the second successor of the Great Monarch the consequences which Fleury thought to turn aside by an argument quite contestable in itself, in a historical point of view. There had been a demand for a Church without a head; the people, in turn, wished for a government on the same model. God has his thunder-strokes by which he lowers the pride of the wise and laughs at their vain science. But it is necessary to proclaim as an incontestable principle, that the Church is really a society ruled by a head. That head has not only disciplinary power, independently of the general councils, which are not permanent, which do not govern during the period of their sessions; which cannot exist without the condition of being convoked and presided over by the authority of the supreme head of the Church; which make laws, but leave to the Pope the care of having them put into execution: he has, moreover, the sacred deposit of the dogmatic truths, expressly taught by Christ Himself in His gospel, or handed down from age to age by apostolic tradition. This deposit he faithfully keeps without ever erring; for the promise of infallibility was made to him in the person of St. Peter on the day of the foundation of the Church. The Pope, in fine, is not subject to the judgment of a general council, since there can be no general council without his authority, his concurrence and his sanction. As to the first of the Gallican maxims: "The king, as such, is not subject to the judgment of the Pope," it says too much or too little. If it refers to a Catholic king, he is subject, like all other Catholics, to the judgment of the Pope; the maxim exaggerates the independence of the king. If it refer to a prince without the Roman communion, it is a very weak expression of the liberty of the sovereign, who not only is not subject to the judgment of the Pope, but cannot even recognize the lawful existence of the Pope. It is evident that Fleury meant to speak only of a Catholic king; but really, in his heart, the king meant Louis XIV He then aims at establishing a distinction between the two qualities of king and of Catholic; as king, Louis XIV was not subject to the judgment of the Pope; he is only so as a Catholic; this is the natural meaning of Fleury's maxim. In other words, the king cannot be, according to Fleury, deposed or excommunicated by the Pope. The whole course of the history of the Church, from the conversion of the Barbarians, affords examples of the contrary. Fleury knew them; he gives them himself, in their proper place, but he weakens their force by extrinsic considerations which we deem it our duty to point out.

12. Speaking of the titles sometimes made up in the middle-ages, he adds, " But of all these false documents, the most pernicious were the *Decretals*, ascribed to the Popes of the first four centuries, which have inflicted an irreparable injury upon the discipline of the Church by the new theories they brought in, relative to the judgment of bishops and the authority of the Pope." If we must believe Fleury, the whole Church, deceived by false documents, was, during all the period of the middle-ages, granting to the Sovereign Pontiffs a right which they did not really possess. The Popes were usurping an unlawful power. We should have to strike out from ecclesiastical history eight centuries, which constitute its brightest pages. But, then, what becomes of tradition ? What of the infallibility of the Church ? Where is the promise of Christ, " to be with her *all days*, even to the consummation of the world ?" The charge is a very serious one. How does Fleury support it ?

In his *Institution au droit ecclésiastique*, after summing up the law of the first eight centuries, he thus concludes : " These few laws sufficed, during eight hundred years, for the whole Catholic Church. The Catholics of the West had fewer than the Orientals, and even these they had for the most part borrowed from them; but there were none made for the Roman Church in particular. She had, until then, so faithfully preserved the tradition of the apostolic discipline, that she had felt very little need of any reformatory regulation, and what the Popes had written on the subject was for the instruction of the other churches. The law which was in use during those eight hundred years might be called the 'Ancient ecclesiastical law' The 'New' came in force soon after that date. Toward the end of the reign of Charlemagne, a 'collection of canons' was scattered through the West, brought from Spain, and bearing the name of one Isidore, by some surnamed *Mercator*, or the *Merchant*. It has been discovered, in the last century, that these Decretals, from St. Clement I. (A. D. 100) to St. Sericius (398), did not emanate from those whose names they bear. They are all of the same style, far removed from the noble simplicity of those early ages. *They are made up of long passages from the Fathers*, who lived long after, *as St. Leo* the Great (461), St. Gregory the Great (604), and others of a later epoch; we even discover in them some of the laws of the Christian emperors; the matters which they treat do not belong to the period to which they are ascribed; the dates are false." Such are the words of Fleury On his part, the learned De Marca expressly acknowledges that those false Decretals were composed, with very little variation—*si pauca demas*—of the sentences and the very expression of the laws, of the ancient canons and of the Holy Fathers who flourished in the fourth and fifth centuries. Thus, according to Fleury himself, the false Decretals are *made up of long passages from St. Leo, St. Gregory and other Fathers*, who lived in the first eight centuries, in the ages of the *ancient ecclesiastical law*, as he calls it. Is it, then, possible to say that these extracts from the *ancient law* have formed a completely *new* and unheard-of law, which has destroyed the *ancient*, changed the government of the Church, and *inflicted an irreparable injury upon the discipline of the Church.* The charge, refuted by these proofs, is a calumny against the Church and an insult offered to God Himself, since He would have proved false to His promise of being with the Church "all days, even to the consummation of the world." And this argument of Fleury's is the soul of his history

13. What remains in practice of the axiom : " The king, as such, is not subject to the judgment of the Pope ?" The Pope can effectually exercise his judgment upon the king only by a sentence of deposition or excommunication. Fleury's maxim is thus reduced to the expression which we have already given : " The king can be neither deposed nor excommunicated by the Pope." That the king cannot be deposed by the Pope in a society which no longer looks upon the Pope as the head of its hierarchy, which no longer invokes his judgment as that of a supreme tribunal, at which all conflicts and political struggles might be settled without bloody revolutions or popular tumults, without any of those great crises which hurry nations on to ruin —we readily grant. The middle-ages were ruled by a different political law, upon which we have already dwelt at sufficient length. The seventeenth century rejected that law to flatter the pride of an absolute monarch ; and now that the appeal to the Pope has been laid aside, we are reduced to the necessity of appealing to the people. This, however, is a question of politics, and does not concern us here. But the Pope can always excommunicate a Catholic sovereign when that sovereign has the misfortune to be guilty of a serious departure from the line of his duty ; the Pope is as truly his judge as he is that of the simple faithful. The Pope can exercise this right ; the Pope has exercised it ; and we shall yet see the immortal Pius VII. fulminating against the greatest captain of modern times the sentence of which Heaven took upon itself the execution by a series of unparalleled disasters. This is, in our opinion, what remains in practice of the Gallican maxim :

"The king, as such, is not subject to the judgment of the Pope." We have established, as a principle, that throughout the whole period of the middle-ages, the public law of Europe clothed the Sovereign Pontiffs with a supreme jurisdiction over all crowns; and in that common tribunal princes and people found an assurance of peace, order and stability   We acknowledge that the European public law is now changed; that it has entered upon new paths; that it no longer grants to the Holy See that high sovereignty which grateful nations once bestowed. We also state, with the page of history open before us, that no sovereign, since the seventeenth century, the epoch of the great change in European jurisprudence, has been *deposed* by a Pope. But the right of excommunication is inherent in the very office of the Sovereign Pontiffs; it is independent of the changes of public opinion. It belongs, by his very position, to the head of the Catholic Church, to cast off unworthy members from the body of the Church. The Popes have, therefore, that right to-day as they had it eighteen hundred years ago, in all its fulness, over sovereigns as over the simple faithful. The power of the keys, conferred upon St. Peter, subsists with all its independence, with all its vigor, with its full extent and responsibility, with all its duties and all its rights, in the person of Pius IX., the august successor, in the See of Rome, of the Prince of the Apostles.   We shall now see how Gallicanism, under Louis XIV., began the contest.

14. We have said that the Bishops of Aleth and Pamiers earnestly pleaded the immunity of their churches, to which the king wished to extend the right of *regale* from which they had until then been exempt.   They grounded their protest upon a formal decree of the fourteenth general council, the second of Lyons (A. D. 1274), which, while recognizing the right of *regale* in the churches in which it was already established, forbade its extension on pain of excommunication.   "Louis XIV.," says De Villecourt, bishop of La Rochelle, " having made appointments to the vacant benefices of Pamiers and Aleth, those who, in opposition to the laws of the Church, had been put in pos-

session by *regale*, were placed by their respective bishops under ecclesiastical censure, for having presumed, on such a title, to take possession; but the Archbishops of Narbonne and Toulouse, to whom they appealed, committed the grave error of pronouncing these censures null, and of setting aside the decrees of their suffragrans. The bishops appealed from the sentence of their metropolitans to the Holy See; it was their right, and, in fact, their duty Innocent XI., in conformity with the Holy Canons, of which France, after having trampled upon them, was soon to boast herself the incorruptible guardian, annulled the decisions of the archbishops, and gave expression to bitter reproaches against the ministers of the king, who abused his confidence by giving him faithless counsels to the profit of their own interest and ambition. He declared, with energy, that nothing should prevent him from making use of his Apostolic authority against such abuses, whatever the result might be in regard to himself." He twice admonished the king not to lend an ear to flatterers, and not to touch the liberties of the Church As he received no answer, he reiterated his warnings a third time; now, however, he added, " he would write no more, he would make use of every weapon which God had placed in his hands." Unhappily, the French clergy sided with the king against the Pope, thus weakening the force of the Pontifical admonitions. " It is painful," says the learned prelate already quoted, " to reflect that all the members composing the Assembly of the clergy in 1682, instead of making common cause with the Sovereign Pontiff, who was protecting the rights of their colleagues, encouraged the king to maintain his usurped right of *regale*. They carried their weakness and adulation so far as to assure him that nothing should separate them from him; they charged the Holy See with having entered upon a vain undertaking, saying that *they wished the whole world to know their dispositions in this regard*. Could this handful of court-prelates flatter themselves that they represented the whole French clergy, and expressed its sentiments, what an idea should we have to form of that clergy? That period would unquestionably have been the most disastrous for the Church in France. The Holy Father was unyielding, as he was bound to be, in the defence of the canonical regulations; but the agents of the French clergy gave their whole attention to the means of making him repent this firmness, worthy of a successor of St Peter."*

15. The French episcopate had then at its head a prelate who, by his eloquence, recalls Tertullian and St. Chrysostom; by his learning, St. Augustine and St. Jerome; and Origen by his tireless activity   To name Bossuet, is to name the highest impersonation of human genius in letters, eloquence, theology, metaphysics and history. "Political like Thucydides," says Chateaubriand, "moral like Xenophon, eloquent like Livy, as profound and graphic as Tacitus, the Bishop of Meaux had, moreover, that solemnity and elevation of style, of which no example is to be found, except in the admirable exordium of the book of Maccabees. Bossuet is more than a historian; he is a Father of the Church.—What a survey has he taken of the earth! He passes along with the rapidity and the majesty of ages. With the rod of the law in hand, and with irresistible authority, he drives before him pell-mell both Jews and Gentiles to the grave; he brings up the rear of the funeral procession of all generations, and, supported by Isaias and Jeremias, he raises his prophetic lamentations amid the ruins and the wreck of the human race. The first part of the *Discourse on Universal History* is admirable for the narration; the second, for sublimity of style and lofty metaphysical ideas; the third, for the profundity of its moral and political views.—But what shall we say of Bossuet as an orator? To whom shall we compare him? And which of the harangues of Cicero and Demosthenes are not eclipsed by his *Funeral Orations?*--There are three things continually succeeding one another in Bossuet's

* In the history of this difficult period, we shall continue to follow the most admirable work of Mgr. de Villecourt, *La France et le Pape*, which throws so much light upon the ecclesiastical matters of the reign of Louis XIV., and which entitles the illustrious author to a high rank among historians.

discourses : the stroke of genius or of eloquence ; the quotation so admirably blended with the text as to form but one piece with it; lastly, the reflection, or the survey taken with eagle eye of the causes of the event of which he treats. Often, too, does this star of the Church throw a light upon discussions in the most abstruse metaphysics, or the most sublime theology To him nothing is obscure. He has created a language employed by himself alone, in which frequently the simplest term and the loftiest idea, the most common expression and the most tremendous image, serve, as in Scripture, to produce the most striking effect." This admirable picture, sketched by the illustrious author of the " Genius of Christianity," leaves us nothing to say. And yet Bossuet commands our admiration on many other grounds. Protestantism never recovered from the blow inflicted by the *Histoire des Variations.* The " Exposition of the Catholic Faith" won Turenne to the truth. His " Defence of Tradition" is a masterpiece of erudition and logic. His treatise " On the Knowledge of God and of one's self," and the *Politique Sacrée,* written for the instruction of the Dauphin, are inimitable models. Bossuet's genius was universal. While his fruitful pen was throwing light upon so many different subjects, in works in which lofty views and splendid style vied with logic and eloquence, he still found time to write to the nuns of his diocese frequent letters, breathing the spirit of St. Francis of Sales, and full of all that is sweetest and most delicious in Christian mysticism. In one point alone has Bossuet failed. Captivated by the absolute royalty of which Louis XIV was the radiant image, he bowed that logical mind, whose rectitude was in every other respect truly wonderful, before the splendors of the Great King. "Bossuet," says Mgr de Villecourt, " possessed a rich and brilliant imagination, noble and sublime conceptions ; he dazzled his hearers ; he dazzled his readers ; I could wish to believe that he never dazzled himself by those splendid flashes of genius which brought so many admirers from all directions. Had he, in the question of the *regale,* been less taken up with his own talents, kept within the rules of an unbending logic, as he did in most of his controversial works never would he have given the place of truth to opinions which he well knew to be admitted neither by the Roman Pontiff nor by the great majority of the bishops in communion with the Holy See; never would he have consented to make to himself friends among sectaries and men of doubtful faith. Had he never concerned himself about the *Declaration of the Clergy of France* (A. D. 1682) and its *Defence*, he would perhaps have seen the confirmation, by the Holy See, of the title of "Last of the Fathers of the Church," bestowed by the admiration of his contemporaries.

16. The part taken by Bossuet, in the difficulties between the Holy See and the court of France, was unworthy of his magnificent intellect. The clergy (A. D. 1682), led away by the advice of the Bishop of Meaux, resolved to carry out its opposition to Innocent XI. In the name of all his colleagues in the episcopate, Bossuet addressed to the Pope a letter, which was rather a lesson given to the head of the Church than a judgment respectfully submitted to the Apostolic authority The Sovereign Pontiff was reminded that there were many things which *the necessity of the times should cause to be tolerated*, that this necessity was sometimes of such a nature that it could even change the laws, especially when it became necessary to heal dissensions and to strengthen the bonds of peace between royalty and the priesthood. St. Yvo, of Chartres, and St. Augustine were made to say "that those who did not bend the rigor of the canons to the good of peace, were mere *blunderers* who filled their own eyes with the dust which they were trying to blow into those of others." The Pope was told, in conclusion, "that he should follow the promptings of his goodness in an occasion in which it was not permitted to use courage." Innocent XI. answered the letter of the French clergy with a dignity worthy of a St. Leo. He reproached the bishops of France " with having, through a most censurable weakness, forsaken the holy cause of the liberty of the Church; with not daring to utter a single word for the interests and the honor of Jesus

Christ, but of having covered themselves with eternal infamy, by a disgraceful connection with the secular magistrates. He calls upon them to repent, and concludes by annulling and condemning the acts already null in themselves, as manifestly unlawful."

17. This brief only embittered the already prejudiced minds. Le Tellier, archbishop of Rheims, proposed to *ask the king's leave* to convene a national council of the bishops then in Paris, or at least to convoke a General Assembly of all the clergy of the kingdom. Louis granted the request which he had perhaps himself provoked. But he had too much sense to consent that the Assembly should call itself a *council*. It would have been too glaring an irregularity that some bishops, displeased with the canonical decision of a Pope, should assemble in council to judge him. The king therefore declared himself in favor of a General Assembly to consist of two bishops and two deputies of the second order from each province. He expressly ordered them to decide, solemnly and lawfully, the doctrine of the Gallican church on the temporal power of the Popes, on the particular independence of the kings of France and on the infallibility of the head of the Church.

18. Every thing foreboded a fearful explosion. Minds were aroused and full of passion. It was boldly said : 'The Pope has goaded us on ; he shall repent of it." We could wish to doubt that such a deplorable expression was ever uttered ; but Fleury has been careful to record it for our sorrow.* In vain did Bossuet, in his opening discourse, a real master-piece of inspiration and eloquence, insist upon the doctrine of *the unity of the Church*. All his oratorical art was unable to disguise the feeling of hostility to the Holy See which animated all their hearts. On the 3d of February, A. D. 1682, began the operations of that famous Assembly of the Gallican clergy, composed of thirty-four archbishops and bishops and of thirty-eight ecclesiastics of the second order. They acknowledged the right of extending

* FLEURY, *Nouveaux Opuscul.*, p. 210

the *regale* to every diocese in the realm. The Bishop of Tournay, Choiseul-Praslin, was then appointed to draw up the propositions relative to the Pontifical power. His work was not received by the Assembly, and the task was intrusted to Bossuet. "The French," says Cardinal Sfondrati, "should have considered that an Assembly convened in a season of troubles and mutual dissatisfaction, as well as the propositions which might be published by that Assembly, would be ascribed, not to zeal for religion, but to a feeling of revenge, and would the more readily be interpreted unfavorably, as the bishops saw very well that it was not for himself or for his own, but for them and for the liberty of their churches, that the Pope had taken the field. Gratitude, or even the most ordinary regard for propriety, of which the French are so jealous, demanded that, while the Pope was battling for their interest with so much energy and courage, they should at least exercise no act of hostility against him. How did it become the French bishops to turn their arms against their benefactor?" But passion is a stranger to reason. On the 19th of March, 1682, appeared the celebrated *Declaration of the Clergy of France*, drawn up by Bossuet, to clothe with a melancholy renown the name of the immortal Bishop of Meaux. We give the "Declaration" and the text, as found in the works of Bossuet.

19.* "Many attempts are made to overthrow the decrees of

---

* DECLARATIO, *Die decimo nono Martii*, 1682.—"Ecclesiæ Gallicanæ decreta et libertates a majoribus nostris tanto studio propugnatas, earumque fundamenta sacris canonibus et Patrum traditione nixa, multi diruere moliuntur; nec desunt qui earum obtentu primatum beati Petri ejusque successorum romanorum Pontificum a Christo iustitutum, iisque debitam ab omnibus Christianis obedientiam, Sedisque Apostolicæ, in qua fides prædicatur, et unitas servatur Ecclesiæ, reverendam cunctis gentibus majestatem imminuere non vereantur. Hæretici quoque nil prætermittunt quo eam potestatem, qua pax Ecclesiæ continetur, invidiosam et gravem regibus et populis ostentent, eisque fraudibus simplices animas ab Ecclesiæ matris Christique adeo communione dissentiant. Quæ ut incommoda propulsemus, nos archiepiscopi et episcopi Parisiis mandato regio congregati, Ecclesiam Gallicanam repræsentantes, una cum cæteris ecclesiasticis viris nobiscum deputatis, diligente tractatu habito hæc sancienda et declaranda esse duximus:

"1. Beato Petro ejusque successoribus Christi Vicariis, ipsique Ecclesiæ, rerum spiritualium et ad æternam salutem pertinentium, non autem civilium ac temporalium, a Deo traditam potestatem, dicente Domino: 'Regnum meum non est de hoc mundo,' et iterum: Reddite ergo quæ sunt Cæsaris Cæsari, et quæ sunt Dei Deo,' ac proinde stare Apostolicum

the Gallican church, its liberties so zealously upheld by oui forefathers, and their foundations, based upon the holy canons and the tradition of the Fathers. Some there are also who, cloaking their real designs under the name of these liberties, do not fear to strike at the primacy of St. Peter and of the Roman Pontiffs, his successors, instituted by Jesus Christ; at the obedience which is due to them from every Christian, and at the majesty, so venerable in the eyes of all nations, of the Apostolic See, in which the unity of the Church is taught and preserved. The heretics, on the other hand, leave nothing undone to represent this power, which contains the peace of the Church, as intolerable to kings and people, and, by this artifice, to draw away simple souls from the communion of the Church and of Jesus Christ. It is with a view to remedy these evils that we, archbishops and bishops, assembled in

istud: 'Omnis anima potestatibus sublimioribus subdita sit; non est enim potestas nisi a Deo; quæ autem sunt, a Deo ordinatæ sunt. Itaque qui potestati resistit, Dei ordinationi resistit,' Reges ergo et principes in temporalibus nulli ecclesiasticæ potestati Dei ordinatione subjici, neque auctoritate clavium Ecclesiæ directe vel indirecte deponi aut illorum subditos eximi a fide, atque obedientia, ac præstito fidelitatis sacramento solvi posse Eamque sententiam publicæ tranquillitati necessariam, nec minus Ecclesiæ quam regno utilem, ut verbo Dei patrum traditioni, et sanctorum exemplis consonam, omnino retinendam.

"2. Sic autem inesse Apostolicæ Sedi ac Petri successoribus Christi vicariis rerum spiritualium plenam potestatem ut simul valeant, atque immota consistant sanctæ œcumenicæ synodi Constantiensis a Sede apostolica comprobata,* ipsorumque romanorum Pontificum ac totius Ecclesiæ usu confirmata, a Gallicana perpetua religione, custodita, decreta, *De auctoritate conciliorum generalium,* quæ sessione quarta et quinta continentur, nec probari a Gallicana Ecclesia, qui eorum decretorum quasi dubiæ sint auctoritatis ac minus approbata, robur infringant, aut ad solum schismatis tempus concilii dicta detorqueant.

"3. Hinc apostolicæ potestatis usum moderandum per canones Spiritu Dei conditos, et totius mundi reverentia consecratos; valere etiam regulas, mores et instituta a regno et Ecclesia Gallicana recepta, Patrumque terminos manere inconcussos, atque id pertinere ad amplitudinem apostolicæ Sedis, ut statuta et consuetudines tantæ Sedis et Ecclesiarum consensione firmata, propriam stabilitatem obtineant.

"4. In fidei quoque questionibus præcipuas Summi Pontificis esse partes ejus decreta ad omnes et singulas ecclesias pertinere; nec tamen irreformabile esse judicium, nisi consensus Ecclesiæ accesserit.

"Quæ accepta a Patribus ad omnes Ecclesias Gallicanas atque episcopos in Spiritu Sancto a ictore præsidentes, mittenda decrevimus, ut idipsum dicamus omnes, simusque in eodem sensu et in eadem sententia."

* We have seen in what terms Pius V. approved the Council of Constance.

Paris, by order of the king, together with the other ecclesias tical deputies, representing the Gallican church, have deemed it proper, after mature deliberation, to establish and declare:

"I. That St. Peter and his successors, the Vicars of Jesus Christ, and even the whole Church, have received power from God, only over things spiritual and which concern salvation, and not in temporal and civil matters, since Jesus Christ Him self teaches us that His kingdom is not of this world; and again, that we are to render unto Cæsar the things that are Cæsar's, and to God the things that are God's; and that accordingly these words of the Apostle cannot be altered or shaken 'Let every soul be subject to higher powers: for there is no power but from God; and those that are, are ordained of God. Therefore he that resisteth the power, resisteth the ordinance of God. We therefore declare that kings and rulers are not subject to any ecclesiastical power by the order of God, in temporal matters; that they cannot be directly or indirectly deposed by the authority of the head of the Church; that their subjects cannot be released from the submission or the obedience which they owe them, or absolved from their oath of fidelity; and that this doctrine, necessary for the public tranquillity, and not less profitable to the Church than to the State, must be inviolably observed as conformable to the word of God, to the tradition of the holy Fathers and to the examples of the saints

"II. That the fulness of power possessed by the Holy Apostolic See and the successors of St. Peter, the Vicars of Jesus Christ, in spiritual matters, is such that the decrees published in the fourth and fifth sessions of the holy ecumenical Council of Constance, approved by the Holy Apostolic See, confirmed by the practice of the whole Church and of the Roman Pontiffs, and always observed by the Gallican church, remain in full force and efficiency; and that the church of France does not approve the opinion of those who assail these decrees, or weaken them, by asserting that their authority is not well established, that they are not approved, or that they concern only the period of the schism.

" III. That thus the use of the Apostolic power must be regulated according to the canons dictated by the Spirit of God and consecrated by universal respect, that the rules, the customs and the constitutions received in the kingdom, are to be maintained, and the bounds set by our fathers to remain inviolable ; that it even concerns the dignity of the Holy Apostolic See that the laws and customs established by the consent of that most venerable See and of the churches, should subsist unchanged.

" IV That although the Pope has the principal voice in matters of faith, and that his decrees reach all the churches and each church in particular, yet his decisions are not irrevocable, unless confirmed by the consent of the Church.

" We have resolved to send to all the churches of France, and to the bishops who govern them by the authority of the Holy Ghost, these maxims which we have received from our fathers, that we may all say the same thing, that we may all hold the same sentiments and follow the same doctrine."

A circular letter conveyed this Declaration of the Assembly to all the French bishops.

20. On the 23d of March, letters patent of Louis XIV made it binding upon all the universities of the kingdom to teach these doctrines. " We forbid all our subjects," said the king, "and strangers residing in our kingdom, seculars and regulars of what order soever, to teach in their houses, colleges, or seminaries, or to write, any thing opposed to the doctrine contained in this Declaration. We ordain that all those who may hereafter be chosen to teach theology in all the colleges of each university, secular or regular, shall subscribe the Declaration before entering upon such function ; that they shall consent to teach the doctrine therein contained, and that the syndics of the theological faculties shall present to the ordinary of the diocese and to our solicitor-general, copies of the said submissions signed by the clerks of the said faculties. That in all the colleges and houses of the said universities, where there are several professors regular or secular, one of them shall be ap-

pointed every year to teach the doctrine contained in the said Declaration; and in colleges where there is but one professor, he shall be obliged to teach it during one of the three consecutive years. We ordain that no bachelor shall henceforth be admitted to the degree of licentiate in theology, nor in canon law, nor receive the degree of doctor, without having defended the said doctrine in one of his theses." Soon after, the solicitor-general of the parliament went to the Sorbonne to have the famous Declaration registered. On the refusal of the doctors, he ordered the registers to be brought to him by force, had the Declaration entered in his presence, and all in virtue of the " Liberties of the Gallican Church !"

21. Innocent XI. against whom the whole fury of the storm was directed, was not slow in standing forth to meet it. In a brief dated April 11, A.D. 1682, he thus addressed the bishops who had taken part in the General Assembly : " In virtue of the authority intrusted to Us by Almighty God, We condemn, annul and abrogate all that was done in your Assembly concerning the *regale,* with all that resulted from it, and all that may hereafter be attempted in consequence; and We declare the whole proceeding, forever, null and void." " We ask, in all sincerity," says a late writer, " if an act, so odious in its origin, as was that of the Four Articles, so open to suspicion, in the object of its authors, so hurtful to the Pontifical authority, could be received by the head of the Church, the guardian and moderator of the canons, the teacher of all the Christians, the shepherd of the sheep as well as of the lambs ? Is it for the superior to bend before his inferiors ? Instead of favoring the power of brute force, the heirs and usurpers of which were one day to strip the church of France, was it not the duty of the bishops to consult their head, to obey his fatherly voice, to give to their people an example of submission to his judgment?"

22. The Assembly of 1682, was therefore an evil, says Mgr. de Villecourt; it was the fatal germ of what afterward appeared as the " Civil Constitution" of the clergy of France. The *Declaration* was received with indignation by all Catholic Europe

The two articles which first appeared against it, came from the University of Louvain. A national council of the Hungarian prelates, headed by their primate, branded the acts of the Assembly of France. Rome spoke by her Pontiffs; Spain by her Aguirre, her Gonzalez and her Roccaberti; Austria by her Sfondrati; the Netherlands by Schelestrate; France herself, whose real sentiments were suppressed by the civil power, found a worthy representative of her doctrine in the theologian Char las, whose learned pen and close logic won the admiration of Bossuet himself. This unanimous concert of voices coming at once from every part of Christendom, must have been a fearful thunder-clap in the ears of the Bishop of Meaux. A kind of logic more imposing than any array of syllogisms, appeared in arms and in a threatening attitude, it was the crushing weight of the authority of all the churches in the world, morally united to repel the Declaration drawn up by the Bishop of Meaux in the name of his colleagues, and forcibly imposed by Louis XIV as a fundamental law of the State.

23. Had Bossuet reflected with a serious and unbiassed mind upon this unanimity of sentiment, which, after the example of St. Augustine, he turned to such account against heresy, he would not have hesitated to disavow an act in which passion played so prominent a part; at least he would have observed a prudent silence. But the pride of his intellect revolted against the censure of the Catholic world; and the Bishop of Meaux undertook to defend his work. He devoted the labor of thirty years to the celebrated *Defence of the Declaration of the Clergy of France*, written in a style worthy of the purest Latin antiquity; but the form, however faultless, cannot justify the matter. "To give a full and clear view of the doctrine," says Bossuet, "we shall proceed, after the manner of geometers, to establish, as clearly as we are able, five propositions linked together, and communicating light and strength to each other: 1. The temporal sovereignty is lawful, from the beginning, even among the infidels. 2. That sovereignty, even among the infidels, comes from God. 3. Sove-

reignty was, from the beginning, even among infide. nations, so constituted of God, that after Him it is supreme; and God established none other to depose it or bring it to order. 4. By the institution of the legal priesthood, God made no change in the condition of the temporal sovereignty; on the contrary, He declared more expressly that after God it is supreme in its order. 5. The institution of the Christian priesthood likewise made no change in sovereignty; on the contrary, the New Testament and the tradition of the Fathers clearly teach us that Jesus Christ gave no power to His ministers to regulate temporal concerns or to bestow and take away the power of any ruler whatever." Such are the principles which Bossuet seeks to establish in order to confirm the first article of the Declaration. The legitimacy and the divine origin of sovereignty among infidel nations are admitted on all hands, and are out of the question. But it is false, in a historical point of view, that among the unbelievers the temporal sovereignty was not made subject to the spiritual power in matters of worship affecting the conscience of the people. Lycurgus. appealed for the sanction of his laws to the oracle of Delphi; Numa claimed for his the inspiration of the nymph Egeria. The annals of the human race, with which no one was more perfectly acquainted than Bossuet, formally disproved his third proposition. It is equally false to say that "by the institution of the legal priesthood, God made no change in the condition of the temporal sovereignty; but that, on the contrary. He declared that it is the first in its order." The whole history of the Jewish race presents the kings subject to the authority of the prophets. Samuel appoints Saul; Samuel deposes Saul, when that prince proves false to his trust, and gives his place to a poor shepherd-boy, the youngest of the sons of Isai. David, the anointed of the Lord, founds a dynasty; but it is a prophet who confirms, in the person of Solomon, the right of succession to the throne; it is by the ministry of the prophets that God takes away ten tribes from the son of Solomon to constitute a second kingdom under the rule of Jéroboam.

Bossuet's fourth proposition is thus likewise contradicted by history. The fifth and last proposition, the only truly important one, is not more tenable in the strict sense in which Bossuet would have it taken. That the Sovereign Pontiffs should have received from Christ no power to regulate temporal concerns is of little importance. The submission due to sovereigns is a matter of conscience which concerns the moral order, and involves the question of eternal salvation. Nobody, we think, will deny this. But the Catholic Pontificate is the only spiritual authority instituted of God to regulate matters concerning salvation, to decide questions in the moral order, which interest the conscience. Therefore, it belongs to the head of the Catholic Church, the Vicar of Jesus Christ, to define, without appeal, all doubtful cases which may arise touching the submission due to the sovereign. That the Church should have directly received no authority from Christ *to bestow or to take away the power of any ruler*, makes but little difference. It is certain that a Catholic, in a case of doubt concerning a contested sovereignty, will consult the authority established by Christ to direct his conscience. He questions the Church to learn whom, and how far, he can and must obey. And in order that, in such a case, the conscience of the faithful may be free from all scruple, from all anxiety, Jesus Christ gave to His Church what was not given to the synagogue—the power of binding and loosing all the ties of the soul, when He said to His Vicar: " Whatsoever thou shalt bind upon earth, it shall be bound also in Heaven ; and whatsoever thou shalt loose on earth, it shall be loosed also in Heaven." Here, then, we see the Church brought, by the force of circumstances, into the temporal domain, and brought in as a sovereign power. Bossuet objects, with all the other Gallican writers, that, during the first ages, the Church did not decide cases of conscience arising between kings and their subjects. The fact is true enough ; but the reason of the fact is easily found. There was as yet no society constituted upon Christian principles. Thus, all Bossuet's reasoning to prove the independence of the temporal power, falls to the ground. The first article of the *Declaration of the Clergy of France* cannot stand the test of sound criticism.* As to the three others, Fénelon, in a Latin treatise—*De Auctoritate Summi Pontificis*—censures them as entirely opposed to tradi tion, and declares himself in favor of the opinion more common among Catholics, maintaining, with Bellarmine, the following proposition : " The Sovereign Pontiff, even though he should fall into error or heresy as an individual, cannot in any way define, as of faith, a heretical doctrine, in a decree addressed to the whole Church." We prefer to side with Bellarmine and Fénelon, to adopt the opinion most commonly held among Catholics and supported by testimonies constantly recurring throughout the whole course of tradition. If it be allowable to indulge a feeling of pride at being a member of the clergy of France, it is certainly not allowable to form a Gallican church, with a doctrine different from that of the Roman Church, the mother and the mistress of all the others.

24. Innocent XI. had not quailed in the struggle, so pain ful to his heart, in which the bishops of a nation that gloried in the title of "Eldest Daughter of the Church," gave a disgrace ful example of insubordination and revolt against the Holy See. He was not yet without weapons to defend himself and to meet the invasion of French absolutism. While the king bestowed the highest favor and preferment on the authors of the Declara tion—the members of the Assembly of 1682—Innocent refused to grant them canonical institution and the necessary bulls. The Pope's refusal was a natural and a necessary result of circum stances. The king, by his edict of March 23, A. D. 1682, made it binding upon all the bishops and doctors to recognize the Declaration of the clergy, and he presented to the Holy See, for promotion to the episcopate, only such ecclesiastics as had sub scribed it. The Pope, on the other hand, said to the candidates

---

* It is well known that, at the close of his life, Bossuet, enlightened, doubtless, by the lengthy discussions to which the controversy had given rise, thus wrote of his work: " Whatever may become of the ' Declaration,' we shall not undertake to defend it here.' -*Gallia Orthodoxa.*

thus presented: "Write that you do not recognize the Decla-ration, and I will confirm your election." In this state of things, Louis, by a royal edict, forbade that any application should be made to the court of Rome for bulls of episcopal institution He directed the respective chapters to bestow upon those ap-pointed by him, the title of spiritual administrators, in con-tempt of the canons of the fourteenth general council, the second of Lyons, which expressly forbade it. In fine, through his solicitor-general in the parliament of Paris, he appealed to the next council from all that the Pope "had done, and might yet do, to the prejudice of the king of France, and of his subjects, as well as of the rights of his crown."

25. It seemed impossible that any thing could add to the intensity of the crisis. Thirty-five bishops named by the Most Christian King to various episcopal sees, were without canonical institution; and this abnormal position continued during the whole Pontificate of Innocent XI. A fresh difficulty and equally animated discussions, in a matter utterly foreign to all dogmatic questions, added a new degree of animosity to these lamentable contests. It related to the *Franchises* which the ambassadors of the various powers, at the court of Rome, had arrogated to themselves, not only for their residence, but for all the neigh-boring quarter. They would admit within those limits no judi-cial or financial officer of the Pope; hence they had become the asylum of all the bad characters and plunderers of the country They not only took refuge there from the pursuit of the law, but even sallied forth to commit crimes in the neighborhood; these asylums were also made the depositories of contraband goods. Popes Julius III., Pius IV., Gregory XIII., and Sixtus V., had issued several decrees to abolish this right of asylum; the ambassadors had never been willing to submit to the decrees, and their attendants had always repulsed the Pontifical officers who came to enforce them. Innocent, who had never learned to flinch from what he deemed a duty, and relying, at the same time upon the respect and love of his people, whose affection he had won by his virtue, his modesty and disinterestedness,

determined, at length to abolish an abuse which had become intolerable. He announced that he would require no change in the customs of the ambassadors already established at his court, but that he would no longer receive any who would not consent, beforehand, to renounce the assumed right of asylum. This new measure at first met with some opposition; the court of Spain, rather than submit, abstained for a time from sending an ambassador to Rome; the republic of Venice recalled its representative; but at length all—the emperor, the king of Spain, the king of Poland, James II. of England, and the other powers ---yielded to the just demands of the Sovereign Pontiff.

26. Louis XIV had allowed the Duke of Estrées to remain, until his death (A. D. 1687), at the court of Rome, to avoid the necessity of a decision. At the death of the ambassador, the nuncio, Ranuzzi, earnestly requested Louis to direct the duke's successor to make the renunciation subscribed by the other ambassadors, and thus to contribute to the return of peace and security to the capital of the Christian world. The king haughtily replied: "I have never regulated my actions by those of others; God has placed me here to give example to others, not to receive it." He appointed the Marquis of Lavardin to succeed the late Duke of Estrées, and expressly ordered him to maintain the right of asylum which had been enjoyed by his predecessors. Lavardin accordingly set out with a retinue of eight hundred well-armed men. On the 7th of May, 1687, Innocent issued a bull excommunicating any one who should attempt to maintain the right of asylum or offer any resistance to the officers of the law He declared that he did not recognize Lavardin as an ambassador, forbidding the legates of Bologna and the other governors of his provinces to show him any marks of honor when he should enter the States of the Church. Notwithstanding this protest, Lavardin entered Rome on the 16th of November, at the head of his armed and threatening escort; the Pope renewed his prohibition to the cardinals to hold any intercourse with him, refused him an audience, and laid an interdict upon the church of San Luigi, in which the marquis had received communion.

When this last measure was reported to the court of Versailles, the king's solicitor-general Harlay appealed, as against an abuse of power, from the bull of excommunication issued by the Pope. " He did not admit," such are his words, " that the Sovereign Pontiff ever had the right to include in his excommunications the ambassadors whom the king might choose to send him. He attributed this sign of mental aberration in the Pope, to old age, which was weakening his powers." The attorney-general, Talon, was still more violent; he represented the Pope as a heretic, and reproached him with " affecting to give France a disgust for the things which would be most advantageous to religion."

27 This overbearing conduct toward the common Father of the faithful, showed how far Louis allowed himself to be blinded by his pride and by the splendid successes which had crowned the first years of his reign. It was now twenty-seven years since he had taken the reins of government into his own hands, and in this long career of power he had marched from success to success, from victory to victory ; he had extended the bounds of France in all directions ; he had humbled every rival, every enemy   From the hour when he began his proud struggle with the Holy See, victory forsook his banners, and Europe, which had been humbled by so many triumphs, now stood aghast at his reverses. At the death of the Archbishop-elector of Cologne, the votes of the chapter were divided between Cardinal Furstenburg, bishop of Strasburg, a creature of France, and the young Prince Clement of Bavaria, bishop of Ratisbon. The Pope declared in favor of the latter candidate. Louis, in his vexation, addressed a manifesto to the Pope and the cardinals, closing with the announcement that, to obtain the justice which was due to him, he should seize the city of Avignon, uphold the rights and liberties of the chapter of Cologne, and send troops into Italy to enforce the respect to which he was entitled (September 6, A. D. 1688). Mean-while, the Archbishop of Paris had assembled the bishops then in the capital, the parish priests, the heads of chapters and

communities, and addressed them in vindication of the course adopted by the government toward the court of Rome. The University of Paris had, on its part, appealed from the Pope to a general council; all the French clergy seemed to be animated by the same zeal in the struggle against the head of the Church, thus displaying in the name of the " Gallican Liberties," much more servility and fear of the king, than real independence. On the 7th of October, the French troops took quiet possession of the Comtat-Venaissin, while the Dauphin set out at the head of twenty-five thousand men, to attack Philipsburg, without any previous declaration of war. But the same moment witnessed the beginning of the revolution in England and Holland, which was to place William of Nassau, prince of Orange, the bitter rival of Louis XIV., upon a powerful throne; which was to arm Europe for its independence, and inaugurate a fearful struggle against the Great King. Louis, made wiser by misfortune, will yet renounce his insolent pretensions, and display, in the midst of disasters, a greatness of soul, the more admirable as it is free from the reproach of pride and ambition.

28. Innocent XI. did not live to witness this happy change. The preceding years had been signalized by a measure of extreme importance on the part of Louis XIV.—the *Revocation of the Edict of Nantes*, which edict, it will be remembered, was granted by Henry IV in favor of the Huguenots. Richelieu had annihilated the Protestants as a political party; but he had allowed them to keep their places in the parliaments, their synods, in a word, a part of their internal organization. Louis XIV determined to put an end, by force, to a state of things which stood in the way of his designs for the unity of France. It has been said that the court of Rome was a party to the design. The majority of histories, even those which are called classical, assert the fact. But it is wholly false. The Edict of Nantes was revoked in 1685, at which time Louis XIV., far from going to the Holy See for counsels to guide his administration, was holding his kingdom in a kind of schism,

and was preparing the contest of the *Franchises* against Innocent XI. It is well known that the Sovereign Pontiff openly disapproved of the violence exercised against the Calvinists It was this very censure that provoked the expression we have already quoted from Talon : " The Pope affects to give France a disgust for the very things which would be profitable to religion." The "Revocation of the Edict of Nantes" was, therefore, a measure altogether political, in which the Holy See had no share, and which comes rather within the province of profane than of ecclesiastical history France, limited in her conquests by Holland, found within her own bounds another Holland, which rejoiced at the reverses of the Great King. This consideration determined the course of Louis XIV Beside the state of public opinion was favorable to his designs. On the 22d of October, A. D. 1685, the edict of revocation appeared. It had been drawn up by Le Tellier, and Louvois, his son. The first article withdrew all the privileges granted to the Calvinists by Henry IV and Louis XIII; the next two forbade the exercise of their religion throughout the kingdom ; the fourth required all the reformed ministers to quit France within fifteen days ; the fifth and sixth offered rewards to all who should renounce their religion ; the ninth and tenth promised an entire amnesty and the integral restitution of their property to those who should return within four months ; finally the eleventh decreed bodily punishment against all who might relapse, yet permitting the Calvinists to remain in their homes, to enjoy their goods and property, to transact their business, without any danger of persecution, on the grounds of religious belief, provided they did not assemble for purposes of public worship. The last concession promised a kind of freedom of conscience ; but it was violated by the excessive zeal of the officers intrusted with the execution of the edict. The dragoons of Louvois were a strange class of missionaries. Politically speaking, Louis XIV was right in seeking to restore unity of faith in his kingdom, but, in a Christian point of view, he should have sent priests instead of soldiers to do the work. Such was the judgment of Fénelon, and even of Madame de Maintenon, who was then bound to the king by the closest ties. Still, "the French people," it is Sismondi himself who makes the avowal, "applauded these measures. The Parisians, especially, hurried madly to Charenton, where they tore down the temple in which the Protestants of the capital met for public worship; not a trace of the building was left to mark the spot." At a later period (1701–1704), the Cévennes were made the scene of bloody contests by the insurgent peasants known as the *Camisards*. Supported by fanaticism, and protected by their rocky mountain fastnesses, they maintained a long resistance against the regular troops sent to subdue them. France was obliged to employ against them three of her marshals, in succession,—Montrevel, Villars and Berwick,—and yet they were finally reduced more by negotiations than by force of arms. It must be said, moreover, that writers have nearly always given a singularly exaggerated account of the period styled the *Dragonnades;* just as some historians have quintupled the number of Calvinists who then quitted France. The most scrupulous research limits the number to sixty-six or sixty-eight thousand of all ages and of both sexes, instead of six hundred thousand, the number given by the school of Voltaire and by Protestant writers. Again, the measure was instrumental in repairing a number of injuries suffered by Catholics, in recalling to the true faith a multitude of people who had been misled, in clearing the kingdom of the most obstinate advocates of error, in a word, in taking from the sect all the means of disturbing the peace and tranquillity of the nation. Such results would fully compensate for the material injury that might have resulted to France from the expulsion of the Calvinists, even supposing them as real as these exaggerated accounts would make them.

29. While Louis XIV was persecuting the Huguenots in France, his policy led him to enter into terms with Islamism. The immense changes which had taken place in the situation of Europe, since the beginning of the sixteenth century, had

assigned a new part to France. France, which at the time of the Crusades had struck such powerful blows at the crescent, seemed now to wield the same power only against Christian nations, and look for allies among the Turks. The treaty of peace concluded between the Emperor Leopold I. and Mahomet IV., after the battle of St. Gothard (A. D. 1664), had been violated by the Porte, which raised a Hungarian nobleman named Tekeli to the royal dignity, by conferring upon him, as a vassal of the Sultan, the government of that portion of Hungary belonging to Austria. The court of Vienna remonstrated with the Divan, which answered by sending ten thousand Ottoman troops to Tekeli, and by ravaging, with fire and sword, the Austrian possessions in Hungary Mahomet IV., who was ruled by his grand-vizier, Kara-Mustapha, renewed the vow of his predecessors—" to feed his horse with a measure of oats on the altar of St. Peter at Rome." The less aspiring vizier was thinking of another European-Turkey, with Vienna for its capital. A force of three hundred thousand Turks assembled at Belgrade, under the command of Mustapha. In the Ottoman council, the necessity of reducing the fortified cities on the army's route was discussed. " Austria," said the vizier, " is an immense tree, of which Vienna is the trunk ; the branches will fall of themselves if the trunk is once cut down." The immense army accordingly began its march toward Vienna, in the month of April, 1683. On learning the approach of the enemy, the emperor quitted his capital, and withdrew to Lintz with his court. The cabinet of Versailles secretly rejoiced at an invasion which would help to crush the house of Austria. But Pope Innocent XI. kept a watchful eye upon the interests of Europe ; he was the Urban II. of the seventeenth century His nuncios succeeded in effecting an alliance, offensive and defensive, between the emperor and the king of Poland, the heroic John Sobieski. Sobieski had twice already saved his kingdom from the tide of Mussulman invasion. He was now a third time to save Christendom, before the walls of Vienna. The Sovereign Pontiff gave Sobieski the hope of an alliance between James, the hero's son, who was then sixteen years old, and an Austrian archduchess; he promised to use all his power to make the Polish crown hereditary in his family—a wise forethought, which, if realized, might perhaps have saved Poland. Innocent then ordered public prayers at Rome for the success of the Christian arms. He sent a hundred thousand crowns to the emperor, and an equal sum to the king of Poland. The Sacred College had helped to make up this holy alms; Livio, the Pontiff's nephew, had alone contributed ten thousand crowns from his patrimonial estate. Once more the Papacy was the salvation of the Christian world.

30. The Austrian army under Duke Charles of Lorraine, numbered hardly forty thousand warriors. Ten thousand men, under the Count of Starenberg, garrisoned the threatened capital. The duke made a vain effort to check the march of the Mussulman host on the banks of the Raab. The Austrians, repulsed by the Turks, before they could effect a junction with the forces of Sobieski, were obliged to fall back upon the Danube, in the direction of Vienna. The Turkish camp was at length pitched before the walls of the city on the 14th of July, A. D. 1683. Vienna was completely invested. The vizier summoned the garrison to surrender; he was answered by a formidable discharge of artillery The enemy began the work of intrenchment; and a fire of shells which shook the ramparts, had, in a few days, laid in ashes twenty convents with a number of churches and dwellings. The monasteries and churches without the walls and a great part of the extensive suburbs, were given to the flames by the Mussulmans. All the bells in Vienna were silent during the siege, save one, the bell of St. Stephen's, called *Angstern* (anguish) By order of the Count of Starenberg, the signal of the combat was given from the belfry of St. Stephen's, on the 6th of July The sound of the tocsin was mingled with the great war cry which burst from the lips of the whole population. Citizens and students, and even women flew to arms. All swore to conquer or to die. Sleep and rest were unknown. The days were spent in fighting, the nights

in repairing the breaches in the walls and in burying the dead. This fearful work had lasted forty-five days; eighteen times the Turks had stormed the walls, and the beleaguered Christians had made twenty-four sallies; one-half of their feeble garrison had fallen. The Duke of Lorraine could not attack the Turks, without exposing his army to certain destruction; he had encamped behind the mountain of Cayenberg to await the King of Poland. The Count of Starenberg, driven to the last extremity, succeeded in communicating with him by a short note. "There is no time to lose! We are undone unless you come!" Suddenly the sight of several rockets ascending from the heights of Cayenberg, announced the arrival of Sobieski with his twenty thousand Polish warriors; and hope returned to the sinking hearts of the defenders of Vienna. The King of Poland had come by forced marches. On his route, triumphal arches met him at every step bearing the words which were also written in every heart and uttered by every tongue, "Salvatorem expectamus." He had crossed the Danube on a triple bridge hastily thrown across the stream by the Duke of Lorraine, near Tuln; and now he joined his forces to those of the duke, and of the Electors of Bavaria and Saxony. The chief command of the combined Christian armies, numbering seventy thousand men, was immediately given to Sobieski. The Poles were ill-clad and poorly equipped; some of the German princes expressed their surprise at the fact. "Do you see those men?" said Sobieski, "they are invincible; they have sworn to clothe themselves only with the spoils of the enemy" "If these words," says a biographer, "did not clothe the troops of the King of Poland, they mailed them." The sight of Sobieski sent a thrill of enthusiasm through the Christian ranks. As he passed along the lines, he was greeted with repeated cries of "Long live King John!" On the 12th of September, 1683, at daybreak, Sobieski with the chief officers of the army repaired to a chapel situated on the height of Leopoldberg. The Papal nuncio, Marco d'Aviano, celebrated the Mass served by the Polish hero himself, who knelt with his arms extended in the form of a cross. After the sacrifice, Sobieski called his son James and knighted him as he knelt at the foot of the altar He then directed him to mount his horse, sword in hand, and not to quit his side. The young prince, who proved himself worthy of his name on that immortal day, obeyed with joy Sobieski, though not without great difficulty, drew out his army in order of battle, along the thickly wooded hills about Vienna. The command of the right wing was intrusted to the Grand Hetman Jablonowski; the left was led by the Duke of Lorraine; he himself took charge of the centre. He gave the appointed signal, and from every point of the line, a heavy discharge of artillery poured death and destruction upon the besiegers. The disastrous fire lasted from ten o'clock in the morning until one in the afternoon. At that moment, the watchful eye of Sobieski caught sight of a long file of camels moving in the direction of Hungary The Turks were preparing to retreat. The King of Poland ordered his army to charge the enemy The Christian warriors, led by the gallant Sobieski, poured down like a torrent upon the troops of Kara Mustapha, and a fearful hand to hand contest followed. At five o'clock the Turks broke and fled in utter rout; and at nightfall, of all the immense besieging army, but twenty thousand Moslem corpses were left to guard the walls of Vienna. The Polish king sent to the Pope the standards taken from the enemy, with the words of Cæsar to which the hero gave a character of Christian modesty: " *Veni, vidi, Deus vicit*—I came, I saw, God conquered." On the day after the battle Sobieski, riding at the head of the allied forces, made his entry into Vienna. The people knelt as he passed, shedding tears of joy, and hailed him as their savior. Mothers held up their little ones that they might look upon the hero Sobieski's eyes were filled with tears. "It is God Who has done all, my friends," he said to the multitude that pressed around him. "Let us go and return thanks to Him who gave us victory" He was followed by the throng into the church f the Augustinians, knelt before the altar in the chapel of Loreto, and himself intoned the Te Deum. And the anthem of the

God of battles, chanted by a whole people, rolled through the trembling arches of the basilica. A priest then entered the pulpit and made a discourse on the rescue of Vienna, taking for his text the words which Pius V., of glorious memory, applied to Don John of Austria, after the victory of Lepanto: "Fuit homo missus a Deo, cui nomen erat Joannes." And all eyes were at once turned upon John Sobieski. The deliverance of Vienna is one of the greatest events of modern history; Innocent XI., by the sword of the Polish hero, had forever turned back the tide of Moslem invasion from Christian Europe. Through the intervention of the glorious Pontiff, a triple alliance was formed between Austria, Poland and Venice, against the Turks, who were forced successively to yield all their conquests.*

31. While Innocent XI. was thus struggling against enemies from without, his untiring watchfulness was exercised within, against the heresies which threatened the domestic peace of the Church. He condemned the New Testament of Mons and several other Jansenistic works lately published. He also anathematized sixty-five propositions drawn from works of modern casuists, and by a bull of November 19, A. D. 1687, confirmed the sentence of the Spanish Inquisition against the person and the writings of Molinos, the author of a. work entitled the "Spiritual Guide." Molinos taught a system of *quietude* and contemplation, as absurd as it was dangerous, and which obtained for his followers the name of *Quietists*. This heresy made Christian perfection consist in a state in which man no longer reasons on his own actions, remaining in a state of utter inaction. "The perfect man," says Molinos, "reflects neither on God nor on himself; he desires nothing, not even his salvation; he fears nothing, not even hell; he so identifies himself with the will of God, that nothing can disturb him; neither impure thoughts, nor blasphemies, nor unbelief; in a

---

* For the history of the siege of Vienna and the war against the Turks, vid. *Histoire de Constantinople*, by M. BAPTISTIN POUJOULAT, from which we have borrowed this interesting episode

word, none of the temptations to which he may yield ; on the contrary, they are, in his eyes, the means which God uses to purify the soul ; when the soul is once purified, when it is intimately united with God by the perfect state of the prayer of *quietude*, it is no longer accountable to God for the most criminal *actions*, it no longer takes part with what goes on in this tabernacle of flesh ; fornication, adultery, even despair, which are horrible crimes in those who have not yet reached the state of *quietude*, become indifferent actions in the true contemplatives, who receive no stain from them." Molinos, in the garb of a penitent and before the whole court and people of Rome, solemnly abjured his errors. We shall yet find his doctrine seducing one of the most beautiful minds of modern times, who atoned for his momentary illusion by a noble example of submission to the Holy See.

32. This was the last act of the laborious Pontificate of Innocent XI. The great Pontiff died, full of years and glory, on the 12th of August, A. D. 1689, after a reign of thirteen years. The people invoked him as a saint, and contended for his relics.

§ III. Pontificate of Alexander VIII. (October 6, A. D. 1689—February 1, 1691).

33. Cardinal Ottoboni was seventy years old when he was chosen to succeed Innocent XI.; he took the name of Alexander VIII. The advanced age of the new Pontiff had not impaired his strength; he was well known as a man of rare prudence, perspicuity, thorough knowledge of business, great sweetness and moderation of character, to which he knew how to join a prudent and reasonable firmness. Louis XIV thought that he might now easily end to his own advantage, the difficulty existing between the Holy See and the court of France. He gave up the right of asylum, which had caused so much disorder. The Duke of Chaulnes, envoy of France at the Roman court, signed the renunciation in his master's name.

and Louis restored Avignon and the Comtat-Venaissin to the Pope (A. D. 1690). Alexander, in return, granted to the king of France the right of naming the bishops of Metz, Toul, Verdun, Arras and Perpignan; a right not included in the concordat between Leo X. and Francis I.

34. But these concessions could not secure a final peace so long as the king persisted in exercising the right of *regale* in France, and in enforcing, as a State law, the Declaration of 1682. Alexander VIII. made repeated but fruitless efforts to induce the king to renounce this claim. He then began to prepare the bull *Inter multiplices*, which may be called the great work of his Pontificate. "Appointed by the Lord," says the Pope, " to defend the rights of His Church, thinking day and night, with bitterness of heart, on the duties of Our office, with tears and sighs We have raised up Our hands to the Lord, and besought Him, with all the fervor of Our heart, to send Us the help of His powerful grace, that We may worthily discharge the Apostolic ministry intrusted to Us. Therefore, after having consulted most of Our venerable brethren, the cardinals of the Holy Roman Church; after having received the opinions of many doctors in theology and canon law, who, being specially appointed by Us to investigate the question, have examined it with all possible care; following in the footsteps of Innocent XI., Our predecessor, of happy memory, who *condemned*, *annulled* and *abrogated* all the acts of the Assembly of the clergy of France, in the matter of the *regale*, with *all that followed from it;* desirous, moreover, that this should be regarded as expressly relating to the acts of the Assembly of 1682, touching both the extension of the right of *regale*, and the *Declaration on the ecclesiastical power,* as well as all decrees, judgments and edicts therewith connected. We declare, after mature deliberation, and in virtue of the fulness of the Apostolic authority, that *each and every one of the acts done in the above-mentioned Assembly of the clergy of France in* 1682, touching both the extension of the right of *regale* and the *Declaration on the ecclesiastical power,* and *the four propositions therein contained,*

were of right, *null, invalid, illusory*, wholly and entirely without force from *the beginning; that they are still so, and shall be so forever, and that no one is bound to observe them, or to observe any one of them, even though he should have bound himself to them by an oath.* We, moreover, declare that they are to be deemed null and void, and as if they had never existed; and still, by way of greater precaution, and in so far as need may be, We, of Our own accord and certain knowledge, after serious reflection, in the fulness of Our authority, *condemn, abrogate, invalidate, annul, and wholly and utterly deprive of all force and effect, the said acts and dispositions, and all the other above-mentioned things, and before God, We protest against them, and declare their nullity.*"

35. This bull was drawn up and signed on the 4th of August, A. D. 1690. Yet the Pope delayed its publication, hoping that Louis XIV would submit without obliging him to have recourse to this extreme measure. But on the 30th of January, 1691, feeling the approach of death, and that he was about to appear at the bar of the Sovereign Judge, Alexander VIII. summoned the cardinals, and made them acquainted with the tenor of the bull, which thus became as the testament of the dying Pontiff. Ten days later he gave up his soul to God. There is certainly something solemn and imposing in this condemnation of Gallicanism, pronounced by Alexander VIII. from his bed of death! Several French writers have seized this occasion to assail the memory of the pious Pontiff; nor is it astonishing. Few are the guilty that bless and approve the sentence of the judge who condemns them! With us, this act of firmness on the part of Alexander VIII., makes his brief Pontificate one of the most important in the history of the Church.

CHAPTER III.

§ I. Pontificate of Innocent XII. (July 12, a. d. 1691—July 12, 1700).

1 Election of Innocent XII. Bull *Romanum Decet Pontificem* against nepotism.—2. State of England and of France, at the accession of Innocent XII. Peace of Ryswick.—3. Letter of Louis XIV to Innocent XII., disavowing the acts of the Assembly of 1682, and declaring that the necessary orders have been issued for the revocation of the royal edict which followed the declaration.—4. Letter of the French bishops to Innocent XII., declaring the decrees of 1682 null and void.—5. Innocent XII. grants canonical institution to the thirty-five bishops appointed by Louis XIV., and consents to the extension of the right of *regale* to the whole kingdom.—6. François de Salignac de la Motte Fénelon.—7. Madame Guyon.—8. The *Maximes des Saints* of Fénelon. State of the question agitated between Bossuet and Fénelon. Disgrace of Fénelon.—9. Sentence of the Pope. Fénelon's work condemned.—10. Submission of Fénelon.—11. Death of Innocent XII.—12. Victory of Temesvar or Zentha, won by Prince Eugene of Savoy over the Turks.

§ II. Pontificate of Clement XI. (November 23, a. d. 1700—March 19, 1721).

13. Character of the eighteenth century.—14. The question of the succession of Charles II. of Spain.—15. Antecedents of Cardinal Albani.—16. Election of Cardinal Albani as Clement XI.—17. The Duke of Anjou, grandson of Louis XIV., is proclaimed king of Spain, in virtue of the will of Charles II., and takes the name of Philip V.—18. War of succession in Spain, from 1700 to 1713. Reverses of Louis XIV Prince Eugene defeated by Marshal Villars at Denain. Treaty of Utrecht. Treaty of Rastadt.—19. The investiture of the kingdom of the Two Sicilies claimed at the same time by by Philip V of Spain and Leopold I. of Austria.—20. Political concessions wrung from Clement XI. by the Imperial forces.—21. Encroachments of the secular power in Savoy upon ecclesiastical privileges.—22. Abolition of the Tribunal of "The Sicilian Monarchy."—23. The "Case of Conscience."—24. Quesnel. The *Réflexions Morales.* Quesnel's pamphlets against Cardinal De Noailles, archbishop of Paris.—25. Bull of Clement XI., *Unigen*

Domini Sabaoth.—26. The *Problème Ecclésiastique* relative to the work, *Réflexions Morales.* Critical situation of Cardinal De Noailles. Ineffectual attempt of Bossuet in his favor. Decree of Pope Clement XI.—27. The bull *Unigenitus*, condemning the *R flexions Morales.*—28. Reception of the bull *Unigenitus* in France.—29. Death of Louis XIV.—30. Death of Bossuet. Leibnitz.—31. Philip of Orleans, regent of France. The Sorbonne. Cardinal De Noailles and other prelates appeal from the bull *Unigenitus* to the "Pope better informed." The bull *Pastoralis.* Edict of Philip of Orleans, making the bull *Unigenitus* binding in France.—32 Question of the *Chinese Rites.* The bull *Ex Illa Die.*—33. A glance at Protestant England. The Episcopalians. The Presbyterians.—34. The Quakers and Methodists.—35. Collins. Condemnation of his work on " Freedom of Opinion.—36. The Sultan Achmed III. violates the treaty of Carlowitz. The Turks defeated by Prince Eugene at Peterwaradin and Belgrade. Peace of Passarowitz.—37. Mechitarists.—38. The Plague in Marseilles in 1720. Belzunce. Clement XI. sends three ship-loads of corn to the city of Marseilles.—39. Death of Clement XI.—40. Saints and learned men at the close of the seventeenth and the opening of the eighteenth centuries.

§ III. Pontificate of Innocent XIII. (May 15, a. d. 1721—March 7, 1724).

41. Incident in the conclave concerning Cardinal Paolucci. Privilege of exclusion enjoyed by the crowns.—42. Leading events of the short Pontificate of Innocent XIII.—43. Death of Innocent XIII.

§ I. Pontificate of Innocent XII. (July 12, a. d. 1691—July 12, 1700).

1. Cardinal Antonio Pignatelli was raised to the chair of St. Peter, July 12, a. d. 1691, and took the name of Innocent XII. His first act was one which filled the court of Rome with joy, while it showed the noble heart and upright intentions of the new Pontiff. Many of the Popes, yielding to a family affection natural to the human heart, had intrusted some of the highest government offices to their kindred. Special titles, such as the generalship of the Church and of the Pontifical galleys, were usually bestowed upon relations of the Pope. A cardinal-nephew too often appeared the born minister of his uncle, the Sovereign Pontiff. It is true that some great and

illustrious examples at times protested against this abuse ; and we have mentioned them in their proper place. But no general measure had yet definitively proscribed its recurrence. The glory of abolishing nepotism forever was reserved to Innocent XII. After preparing the way for the blow he was about to strike, the Pope, on the 23d of June, 1692, published the bull *Romanum Decet Pontificem*, which he required all the cardinals to subscribe. The titles reserved for the relatives of the Sovereign Pontiffs, and other dignities to which extraordinary salaries had been annexed, were abolished. This reform effected an economy of eighty thousand crowns in favor of the Apostolic chamber. It was strictly forbidden that Pontiffs should, in future, enrich their relatives with the property of the Church, or grant to their nephews the great authority and unbounded power which had hitherto been enjoyed by certain cardinal-nephews. To insure the lasting observance and force of the bull, Innocent required all the cardinals to bind themselves by oath to secure its execution, and that in future the same oath should be renewed in every conclave. True to this principle, he forbade all the members of his family to come to Rome during his Pontificate, and distributed among the poor, whom he called his *nephews,* all the wealth which some of his predecessors had but too lavishly squandered upon their kindred. At the same time, by his close attention to the repression of all disorders, by his strict care in the choice of ecclesiastics, by the vigilance with which he detected and punished the cupidity of judges, by his economy, personal frugality and liberal alms, the new Pontiff won the esteem of his contemporaries and a just right to the admiration of posterity

2. One of the first cares of Innocent XII. was to take up the negotiations pending with France on the declaration of 1682. As always happens when discussions are complicated by new incidents, the *regale*, the first cause of the troubles was nearly forgotten; all attention was absorbed by the *Four Articles*. Louis XIV had already ceased to appear as the victorious monarch whose will was the law of all Europe. A new

revolution had just broken out, in spite of him, in England.
After the murder of Charles I. that country had borne the yoke
of the regicide Cromwell, who ruled with absolute power until
his death (A. D. 1658).   By the devoted energy of General Monk,
the throne was restored to the lawful heir of the unfortunate
Charles I., who reigned as Charles II.   But he had not the
strong and steady hand required to hold the reins of government among a still phrensied people.*   Charles II. died, leaving no legitimate heir to the throne, and the sceptre passed
into the hands of James II., his brother, and second son of
Charles I.   During life, Charles II. had concealed his real sentiments in favor of the Roman communion, but on his death-
bed, he had secretly abjured Anglicanism.   James II. was
unwilling to compound with his conscience; he ascended the
throne of a Protestant nation, openly professing the faith which
was in his heart.   A discontented faction began, at the very
outset to undermine his authority.   William of Nassau, prince
of Orange, the son-in-law of James II., placed himself at the
head of the rebels, dethroned his father-in-law (1688), and was
base enough to encircle his brow with a usurped diadem.   Louis
XIV received the royal fugitive with great magnificence and
took his cause in hand.   But his noble efforts to restore him to
the English throne were ineffectual.   France lost the empire
of the ocean, and the gallant Tourville had the grief, in losing
the naval battle of La Hogue, to see that England was henceforth mistress of the seas (1692).   These reverses gave a disastrous blow to the power of Louis XIV.   But the victories of
Fleurus, Steinkerk, and Nerwinden, which won for the great
Marshal Luxembourg the heroic surname of *Tapissier de Notre-
Dame*†—" Upholsterer of Notre-Dame"—those of Catinat in

---

* It was during the reign of Charles II. that the names *Whig* and *Tory*, as designations
of party principles, first came into use.   The Whigs represent the liberal, democratic party,
opposed to the crown.   The tories, on the contrary, profess the deepest regard for the
monarchical idea and principles, of which they are the zealous champions.   They form the
Conservative party.

† When, at the close of the campaign of 1693, a solemn service of thanksgiving was
celebrated at Notre-Dame, the cathedral was lined with the standards taken from the ene

Italy and Flanders, and of the Duke of Vendôme, in Spain, nobly indemnified Louis for his losses, and led to the celebrated peace of Ryswick, in which the monarch showed himself even above his success, sacrificing, by a single stroke of the pen, nearly all his former conquests.

3. Europe was astonished at this display of moderation. Some historians represent it as a mere political manœuvre. We firmly believe it to have been inspired by a deep conviction, by that kind of presentiment which seldom deceives great minds, and which warns them at the critical moment, that they may tempt fortune no further with impunity The conduct of Louis XIV. toward Pope Innocent XII. is a proof of this On the 14th of September, A. D. 1693, Louis XIV wrote to the Sovereign Pontiff from Versailles : " Most Holy Father, I have always entertained great hopes of the exaltation of Your Holiness to the Pontificate, for the good of the Church and the advancement of our Holy Religion. I now experience its effects with great joy, in all the noble and beneficial meas- ures adopted by Your Holiness for both these objects. This redoubles my filial respect, and, as I am desirous to show it by the strongest proofs in my power, I am most happy to make known to Your Holiness that I have given the orders necessary for the revocation of my edict of March 23, 1682, touching the Declaration of the Clergy of France—to which I was obliged by existing circumstances. As I am desirous not only that Your Holiness should be acquainted with these my sentiments, but that the whole world also may know, by a special mark, how great is my reverence for the high and saintly qualities of Your Holiness, I doubt not that You will deign, in return, to grant me proofs and evidences of a paternal affec- tion. In the mean time I pray that God may grant Your Holi- ness many years of such happiness as is the sincere wish, Most

---

my. Marshal Luxembourg found himself hemmed in by a multitude eager to see the hero of so many glorious fields. Nor was he released until a prince of the blood, taking him by the hand, introduced him by calling out—"Room, room for the Upholsterer of Notre Dame." This was the surname bestowed by the popular enthusiasm

Holy Father, of your devoted son." These noble and beautiful sentiments might well efface the scandals of the past!

4. This retraction was purely voluntary and spontaneous on the part of Louis; Innocent XII. had courted it by no concession. After the example of his two immediate predecessors, he formally refused to grant canonical institution to the thirty-five bishops appointed by the king, and openly showed his determination to repel every attempt that might be made to abate any thing of the dignity of the Papal See. The French clergy were convinced that a longer resistance was impossible. Innocent rejected several formulas submitted to him by the clergy, as not being sufficiently explicit. At length a commission, chosen from among the bishops who had taken part in the Assembly of 1682, addressed to the Sovereign Pontiff a letter expressive of the most sincere repentance: " Prostrate at the feet of Your Holiness, we acknowledge the inexpressibly bitter grief that fills our hearts, by reason of the proceedings of the Assembly, which have highly displeased Your Holiness as well as your predecessors. Therefore, if any articles may heretofore have been considered as decreed, in that Assembly, on the ecclesiastical power and the Pontifical authority, we consider them as not having been decreed, and declare that they are to be so considered." Bossuet at the same time uttered, in his *Gallia Orthodoxa*, the words already quoted: " Whatever may become of the 'Declaration,' we do not undertake to defend it here." Such was, then, after ten years of ceaseless discussions, the end of the great contest arising from the Declaration of 1682 and the " Four Articles" which it contained. The Declaration has no longer any force, either with the Popes who have always anathematized it, nor with the prelates who had signed and who now disown it, nor with the king who revokes the edict enforcing its observance, nor with Bossuet who had drawn it up and who now dismisses it almost with ignominy With these facts in view, it seems to us that history and truth are strangely abused, when it is openly asserted that the doctrines of Gallicanism, properly so called, have never been positively condemned by

the Holy See, and that they have remained, on theological grounds, in the Church, open to discussion.

5. Rome once more maintained her prerogatives, even in the teeth of the most powerful monarch of Christendom. The perilous situation of France, for ten years tottering on the brink of schism, had no longer any reason to remain so. Innocent XII. opened the arms of mercy to his children who had strayed for a moment, but who now returned to the bosom of their father. The bishops appointed by the king signed an act of submission to the Holy See and a retraction of all the acts of the Assembly; it was not until after this absolute recantation, that Innocent granted them canonical institution. To give fuller expression to the joy that filled his heart at this unlooked-for return, Innocent XII., in the fulness of his Apostolic authority, and waiving, in virtue of his sovereign power, the question of discipline which had given rise to such lengthened discussions, granted the right of extending the *regale* to the whole kingdom of France. From that time, the Sovereign Pontiff showed himself a faithful ally of Louis XIV., and the closest union was maintained between the supreme head of the Church and the Most Christian King.

6. Side by side with Bossuet, and under his auspices, a name destined to become the admiration of the world, the love of every feeling heart and the *delight of the human race*, was illustrating the ranks of the French clergy François de Salignac de la Motte Fénelon, descended from an old and illustrious family of Périgord, had entered the service of the sanctuary at an early age. His birth and high mental qualities pointed out the way to the highest honors; but his modesty and virtue led him into silence and retirement. He had, in the beginning, aspired to the office of the zealous missionaries whose part it was to bear the light of faith to distant countries, and whose generous self-devotion he has so eloquently portrayed in his beautiful sermon for the Epiphany The entreaties of his family, the affectionate pleading of his uncle, the bishop of Sarlat, detained him in his native land, of which he was to become one

of the brightest ornaments. Disappointed in his desire for foreign missions to which his ardent soul would have led him, he devoted himself to an apostolate which he deemed no less profitable, the care of the *Nouvelles Catholiques*.* The duties and cares of this office, the simple direction of a community of women, for ten years absorbed the admirable faculties of his mind and prepared him for the composition of his first work, the " *Traité de l'éducation des filles*—Treatise on the education of young girls"—a master-piece of delicacy and reasoning, which, in a single little volume, presents more correct and useful ideas, more refined and deep observations, more practical truths and sound morality, than many long works since written upon the same subject. Fénelon had contracted with Bossuet ties of friendship which promised to be lasting. Admitted to familiar intercourse with that great mind, his mild and winning disposition tempered the sharp and domineering spirit of the Eagle of Meaux. It was at this time that Fénelon wrote his treatise on the " Ministry of Pastors"—*Du Ministère des Pasteurs*. It was the aim of this work to show that the great majority of men being unable to decide for themselves in every question of dogma, divine wisdom could give them nothing more sure to keep them from going astray than an *external authority*, which, deriving its origin from the Apostles and from Christ Himself, displays an unbroken succession of pastors All the proofs, all the authorities and all the arguments, brought together by Fénelon in his " Treatise," are but the natural consequence of that principle, which is set forth with so masterly a hand that the Protestants themselves could make no serious attack upon it. The qualities of the man himself, the merits of the work, and the all-powerful recommendation of Bossuet, determined Louis XIV to intrust the author with a mission in Poitou, shortly after the revocation of the Edict of Nantes. The monarch attached the greatest importance to the conver-

---

* This was a society of religious established in Paris for the purpose of bringing up and instructing, in the principles of the Catholic faith, young girls belonging to Calvinist or Lutheran families.

sion of the Calvinists, as it would greatly help to smooth the difficulties which hindered the execution of the edict. Fénelon accepted the duty, which was not without its dangers; but he absolutely refused the armed force generally given to the other missionaries. He asked to choose the colleagues who were to share with him a ministry of persuasion and mercy. He converted without persecuting, and won affection for the faith of which he was the apostle. This success brought the young missionary into greater notice than ever. On his return, Fénelon was appointed preceptor to the grandson of Louis XIV., the Duke of Burgundy, of whom he made an accomplished prince, and from whom France looked for long years of glory and happiness. Bossuet had held the same office in relation to the Dauphin. But the two teachings were as different in their results as were the respective characters of the two illustrious preceptors. Bossuet knew not how to bend his great mind to a level with the weakness of a child. He spoke to the Dauphin in a language which held France and Europe in admiration, by its loftiness, its erudition, majesty and eloquence. He thus succeeded in inspiring the young prince only with an insurmountable aversion to every kind of study. To this want in the mind of the prince were joined an intractable character, a gloomy and morose disposition, the fear of not appearing to advantage, as he was interiorly convinced of his own mediocrity. The premature death of the Dauphin was a family grief; but France, which had looked for nothing great from him, gave him no tears. The Duke of Burgundy, his son, was hardly entering upon the term of boyhood, when he was placed in the hands of Fénelon. Then followed a contest worthy of the deepest attention of thinking minds. A struggle was going on between the defects of a young prince, haughty, quick-tempered, disdainful and proud, and the affectionate and winning gentleness, the yielding and pliant genius, the charming and resistless grace of Fénelon. It was—to use an image naturally suggested by the subject—Minerva, under the form of Mentor, teaching Telemachus the way to wisdom. In a few years the triumph of Fénelon was so remarkable that it was universally celebrated as a public victory   The member appointed to reply to Fénelon's discourse, on the day of his admission to the Academy, thus addressed the illustrious abbé : " The young prince intrusted to your care, and so worthy of his lineage, the most august in the world, has advanced in the knowledge of those things which it becomes him to know, far beyond our most sanguine expectations; he is already the honor of his age, the hope of the State and the terror of our foes."   Animated by the consoling hope of one day realizing his ideal upon the throne, and viewing the welfare of France in the education of its king, he carefully rooted out every dangerous impression that nature and a premature consciousness of power might have planted in the heart of the young prince, and instead of the defects of an intractable disposition, he displayed in his pupil the habit of the most salutary virtues.   This education, of which we have immortal remains, in some of Fénelon's writings, seemed the master-piece of a genius devoted to the happiness of mankind. When death snatched the Duke of Burgundy from the love of France, he carried to his untimely grave the hopes and the tears of a whole century   Fénelon, in the midst of the court, and in a position that drew all eyes upon him, won universal esteem and affection by the charms of a brilliant and graceful mind, of a refined and eloquent conversation.   His beautiful imagination and his genius displayed themselves in spite of him, and he easily won forgiveness for the resistless ascendant gained through personal superiority, by his pleasing manner, his perfect politeness and a modesty even greater than his worth. Louis XIV nominated him to the archbishopric of Cambrai. The whole court applauded the choice; and Bossuet desired to be the consecrating prelate (June 10, A. D. 1695).

7 Thus far these two great men had been bound together by a feeling of mutual confidence. A father and his son, a kind master and a docile scholar, could not have been held by a connection more intimate, more constant, more sweet and affectionate. A question of *spirituality*, raised at this period,

soon changed this situation, and changed the two friends into two rivals, we had almost said into two enemies; but the soul of Fénelon never knew the sentiments of violence, hostility and bitterness, which it is painful to record of Bossuet, in his regard. A woman, Mme. Guyon, had brought into France the *quietism* of Molinos. Misled by the visions of a disordered imagination, Mme. Guyon also fancied a state of the soul in which divine love so entirely absorbs all the human faculties, that it reigns ever pure, disinterested, free from all relapse or any other feeling; and constitutes, in perfect repose, a true impeccability Under the influence of these ideas, Mme. Guyon thought herself called to the exercise of an extraordinary ministry in the Church; during the whole course of her life she seemed to be haunted by the idea that she was to form a kind of mystical association according to her doctrines. She accordingly wrote on grace and pure love with an enthusiasm which she succeeded in communicating to others. Besides, her life and conduct were utterly irreproachable. She was arrested on account of the boldness and eccentricity of her opinions, but was afterward admitted to the society of the Duke of Beauvilliers, favored by Mme. de Maintenon, and allowed to disseminate her opinions in the female seminary of St. Cyr. It was here that Fénelon first met her. Naturally inclined to a tender and affectionate piety, he allowed himself to be influenced by the charms of a doctrine in which the most extreme ideas of spirituality seemed to open the heart to all the inspirations of divine love. That was his illusion; " he sinned through excess of divine love, whereas those who attacked him sinned through lack of love for their neighbor."

8. The correct judgment, the sound logic, the eagle glance of Bossuet, saved him from falling into any such error. He soon saw, through all the circumlocutions of mystical language, the ʼangerous tendencies of Mme. Guyon's doctrine. He exposed all the errors of *quietism*, with his usual eloquence, in the celebrated *Instruction pastorale sur les états d'oraison* (A. D. 1695). Fénelon undertook to answer this work, and in 1697 he pub-

lished his *Maximes des Saints*, in which he endeavored to support his system by texts of the Fathers and Doctors of the Church The question at issue between the two great athletes of France was delicate and subtle enough to allow both to err. It was to be decided whether there can be a love of God, pure, disinterested, perfectly free from all idea of reward and all thought of self. Now, it seems certain that, for some moments at least, a soul, meditating on the perfections of God, may love Him without a thought of the reward promised for that love; that it may love the goodness of God toward creatures, without adverting to the fact that it is itself the object of that sovereign goodness. But this is only a momentary abstraction, which can by no means constitute an habitual state of the soul. To maintain the contrary, to assert that this impulse of sublime perfection can become the very foundation of Christian life; that the soul may, without guilt, carry disinterestedness so far as no longer to desire salvation and to be indifferent to eternal loss, is the extreme doctrine condemned in *quietism*. However, Bossuet, as soon as he had read the work of Fénelon, hastened to throw himself at the feet of Louis XIV., begged forgiveness for not having sooner made known to him the *fanaticism* of his colleague, and entreated him to prevent, by prompt action, *the excesses of this second Montanus, of another Priscilla.* Such a proceeding, such insulting and cruel words, against a prelate, the preceptor of the Dauphin, beloved by the whole court, caused a profound sensation; for they received immense weight from the credit of Bossuet, whom Louis XIV had styled a "Father of the Church." Fénelon a second Montanus! We cannot persuade ourself that Bossuet would not have later disowned the comparison which was made in the heat of passion. Posterity deplores such a display of violence. Bossuet urged the king to denounce the "Maximes" to the Pope, assuring him that "the errors of the Archbishop of Cambrai would be anathematized by the Holy See, as soon as they reached the ears of the Vicar of Christ." Fénelon asked leave to plead his own cause at Rome. Louis refused it, and removed him from the court, notwithstanding the tearful pleadings of the young Duke of Burgundy, who ever cherished for his Mentor a gratitude that outlived every disgrace. Meanwhile, all the friends and relatives of Fénelon were banished, and Mme. Guyon was thrown into a dungeon of the Bastile.

9. The Bishop of Meaux sent to Rome his nephew, the Abbé Bossuet, afterward bishop of Troyes, to urge the condemnation of the archbishop's work. While, in France, the uncle attacked Fénelon's doctrine by a multitude of writings, in which we too often find the impress of passion accompanying that of genius, the unworthy nephew of the great prelate assailed it in Rome with the weapons of calumny and bad faith. Innocent XII. appointed a commission to examine the "Maximes." After a year's investigation, and sixty-four sessions of six or seven hours each, the ten commissioners stood divided; five had always pronounced in favor of the work; the other five agreed that by means of a second edition it might easily be made irreproachable. To the urgent solicitations of Louis XIV., that he would pronounce a definitive sentence, the Pope replied that "the matter was not sufficiently elucidated." The King of France seized the occasion to redouble his severity toward the friends of the Archbishop of Cambrai, and he again wrote to Innocent XII., urging him at length to pronounce an express condemnation, "threatening, otherwise, to have recourse to extreme measures." When these threats of schism reached Rome, the Pope had already pronounced sentence. In a brief dated March 12, A. D. 1699, Innocent XII. says: "After consulting several cardinals and Doctors in theology, We condemn and censure, of Our own accord, the work entitled *Maximes des Saints*, in whatever language or edition it may appear. By the reading and the use of this book, the faithful might be insensibly led into errors already condemned by the Church." The brief then censures twenty-three propositions drawn from the "Maximes," as respectively rash, mischievous in practice, and erroneous; but not one was styled heretical.*

* It is worth while to remark, that the brief condemns the propositions which suppose an

10. On the feast of the Annunciation, March 25th, A. ɪ 1699, Fénelon was about to enter the pulpit of his cathedral to preach on the solemnity of the day, when his brother brought him the first tidings of the condemnation. The archbishop recollected himself for a moment, then, without betraying the least sign of emotion, he began a discourse on the perfect sub- mission due to authority The news of the condemnation had already been rapidly circulating in the numerous assemblage that pressed about the archbishop. The admirable presence of mind, the sublime bearing, and religious serenity which fore- told the submission of the illustrious prelate, and was, in some sort, a solemn pledge of its sincerity, bathed every countenance with tears of emotion, pain, respect and admiration. On the 9th of April, the very day after that on which he had received the royal permission, Fénelon, greater a thousand times in his defeat than his enemies in their proud triumph, issued a charge to the regular and secular clergy of his diocese. "At length," says the archbishop, "our Holy Father the Pope has condemned the book entitled *Explanation of the Maxims of the Saints*, with the twenty-three propositions taken from it; the brief has already been seen by you all. We submit to this brief, dearly beloved brethren, both as to the text of the book and the twenty-three propositions, simply, absolutely and without a shadow of qualification. We forbid all the faithful of this diocese to read the work or to have it in their possession. We shall be consoled in our humiliation, beloved brethren, if the ministry of the word, which we have received from our Lord for your sanctification, be not weakened, and if, notwith- standing the humiliation of the shepherd, the flock still grow in grace before God.—God forbid that we be ever mentioned, unless to recall that the shepherd deemed it his part to be more docile than the least of his flock, and that he placed no limit to his submission." As a lasting monument of his humble retrac- tion, he ordered, for the exposition of the Blessed Sacrament,

habitual state, in this life, but not those which suppose simply *acts* or a *transitory state* of pure love, without any relation to our supernatural happiness.

a golden monstrance, supported by two angels; one of them was represented trampling under foot several heretical books, one of which bore the title of his own work, though none of the condemned propositions had been branded with heresy This example of perfect submission was a subject of admiration to the whole world. Innocent XII. sent a brief to the immortal prelate, commending his courage with all the affectionate tenderness of a father. Fénelon's disgrace did not end with the question of *quietism*, which had resulted so much to his honor. The publication of his "Telemachus," that admirable work, always more relished the more it is read, destroyed every hope of reconciliation with Louis XIV. The death of his royal pupil soon took away his last hope; and Fénelon died of a broken heart, mourned by his diocese, by France, and by all Europe.

11. Innocent XII. had gone before him to the grave. The Pontiff died on the 7th of September, A. D. 1700, after a reign of nine years. His election had been a time of joy to the Roman people; his death was an occasion of general mourning.

12. The last years of the Pontificate of Innocent XII. were signalized by new triumphs against the Turks. The Sultan Mustapha had sworn to revenge the disgrace of the siege of Vienna. He led an army of one hundred and thirty thousand men against Belgrade (May, A. D. 1697). The armies of Leopold I. were commanded by a hero who could well oppose even this formidable invasion. Prince Eugene of Savoy was by birth a Frenchman; Louis XIV., generally so correct in his judgment of men, failed to discern his talents, and the prince offered to Austria the services of a sword which was to place France on the very brink of ruin.* He made his first campaign

* Eugène de Savoie Carignan was the son of Eugène Maurice, count of Soissons, a grandson of Charles Emanuel I., duke of Savoy, and Olympia Mancini, one of the nieces of Cardinal Mazarin. He was known at Versailles as the "little abbé of Savoy," being then engaged in ecclesiastical studies. He was refused an abbacy by Louis XIV., and having soon after abandoned theology for military reading, he was refused the command of a regiment, as he had been the abbacy. The young soldier was stung to the quick, left his native land, and offered his services to Leopold I. of Austria, who accepted them. Louis XIV., on learning the circumstance, asked some of his courtiers: "Do you not think, gen

under Sobieski, before Vienna; further service led to rapid promotion, and he was soon one of the greatest captains of the seventeenth century, that age so rich in illustrious warriors. Leopold I. made him commander-in-chief of the Austrian forces, and sent him against Mustapha. Eugene pitched his camp near Sigedin. Having learned from a Turkish prisoner that the sultan intended to cross the Theiss by a bridge near the village of Zentha, for the purpose of laying siege to Temesvar, Prince Eugene, without losing a moment, marched his army along the left bank of the Theiss, and, two hours after noon, drew up his forces on the plain of Zentha (September 11, 1697). More than one-half of the Mussulman army had already crossed the stream. The Christian leader determined to attack the enemy before they could bring their whole force upon the field. With the eagle eye of genius and the spring of the threatened lion, dividing his army into twelve columns, six of cavalry and six of infantry, he enfolded the Ottoman camp on all sides, and sent a force to the bridge of Zentha, to prevent the remainder of the Turkish force from joining Mustapha. When these dispositions had all been made, the day was within two hours of its close. But there was time enough for the hero to win a most brilliant victory. The Turks had surrounded their camp with a ditch and palisades, as if to resist a siege. Prince Eugene gives the signal for the combat. The cross-fire of his batteries thunders with deadly precision upon the Turks in their intrenchments. They make but a feeble reply. The fire of small arms soon begins, and at length the order is given to charge the Mussulmans, and a fierce hand-to-hand struggle ensues. At seven o'clock twenty thousand Turkish corpses strew the plain. The sultan, almost alone, disguised as a private soldier, stripped of every attribute of imperial sovereignty, fled toward Temesvar. The victor spent the night awake upon the bloody field. "The combat," he wrote to the emperor, in his official report, "ended with the day, as if the

tiemen, that I have suffered a great loss?" He did not know then that he was losing the fortune of France, the future hero of Oudenard and Malplaquet.

sun would light with his latest rays the most brilliant victory
won by the imperial arms." Europe applauded the triumph of
the hero. The Pope sent him a string of brilliants and a sword
with a golden scabbard, as to the liberator of Christendom. The
peace of Carlowitz (1699), between Austria and Turkey, a result
of the victory of Temesvar, inaugurated the downfall of the
Ottoman Empire.

§ II. Pontificate of Clement XI. (November 23, a. d. 1700— March 19, 1721).

13. The eighteenth century opens with the Pontificate of
Clement XI. Each period of the Church's history, through
which we have now passed, has had its contest, its characteristic struggle. The spirit of the world and the spirit of
God, ever in opposition, have from the beginning contended for
the history of mankind. But no other period presents a series
of events more varied, more numerous assaults, more violent
shocks. The birth and growth of unbelief, which denies at
once all dogmas, which assumes the mission of annihilating the
Church, by the heresy of Jansenism, the most persevering, if
not the most perverse, of all; the storms of a revolution which
shook all Europe, and which still lasts, will bring out, more
triumphantly than all arguments, more eloquently than studied
discourses, more convincingly than any syllogisms—by facts,
evident, repeated, resplendent, incontestable, because almost
contemporaneous—the divinity, the immortality of that Church
which alone stands against all the leagued powers of passion,
anger, revenge, disorder and violence; which outlives revolution and ruin; breaks every hostile power, heals every sorrow,
and is ever the first to restore her throne amid the fragments
of crumbling empires.

14. Clement XI. was worthy to inaugurate the period of
which his stormy reign was a representation in miniature. At
the time when the conclave was assembling to elect a successor
to Innocent XII., the attention of Europe was called to a ques-

tion which seemed to concentrate the interests, the welfare, the destinies of the world. The sovereign of a monarchy upon which the sun never set, the sovereign of the Catholic Nether lands, of the Milanese, of the kingdoms of Naples and of Sicily, of the kingdom of Spain, of the empires of Mexico, Peru, the Philippines—the king of Spain, Charles II., the last direct scion of Charles V., was sinking under a lingering illness; he was dying without leaving an heir of his race. Who should now gather up the reins of such a formidable power? All minds were filled with dread of fearful wars. Charles II. wished to prevent them by a testament. Controlled by a true spirit of religion, rendered deeper by the near approach of death, he wished especially to be just, and not to load his conscience with any guilt of partiality His long struggles with France were forgotten; he felt that, at his last hour, he could no longer be a relative of the Austrians or an enemy of the Bourbons, but a soul before God, detached from the things of this world, and called to judge with justice according to law, if he would find a merciful Judge in Heaven. To enlighten his conscience, he determined to consult the supreme Pastor of Christendom, the Vicar of Jesus Christ; and he sent to Rome the first lord of his bedchamber. Pope Innocent XII., who had reached an extreme old age, intrusted the examination of the matter to Cardinal Albani, who drew up the brief in reply to the question of Charles II. "Being Ourself," said the Pope, " on the point of appearing before God, We turn away from all personal affection, and re-commend to Your Majesty to look only to the peace of the Christian world, the interest of Europe, and the greater good of your subjects." He then showed that the two acts of re-nunciation to the Spanish throne, made, before their respective marriages, by Anne and Maria Theresa, of Austria, queens of France, could be of no force; this decision was grounded upon the principle that those renunciations having been made in favor of Spain, to preserve the peace and equilibrium of the world, Spain had a right to annul them when she could more efficiently secure her independence and integrity, as well as the peace and the equilibrium of the other states; which end would be gained if both Austria and France could be prevented from uniting the two crowns. The twofold object would be effected by choosing a prince of either house, who could never bear both sceptres at once. In consequence of this decision, Charles II. signed a will, on the 2d of October, A. D. 1700, leaving his whole domination to the Duke of Anjou, second grandson of Louis XIV., and, in the event of the refusal of France, to the Archduke Charles of Austria; he died on the 1st of November, with a quiet mind, and happy in the consciousness of having provided for the welfare of his people.

15. The account of the death and testament of Charles II. reached Rome as the cardinals were assembling in conclave They felt the necessity of speedily filling the vacancy in the Holy See, in view of the great events to which the Spanish succession would soon give rise in Europe. Cardinal Albani, who had drafted the brief of Innocent relative to that question, was naturally a prominent candidate. But he had other equally important claims to the choice of his colleagues. As secretary of the late Pontiff, he had likewise drawn up the bull against nepotism. His modesty was eminently displayed on the occasion of his promotion to the cardinalate. Alexander VIII., wishing to create twelve cardinals in the next consistory, directed Albani, his secretary, to prepare the discourse for the occasion, which was to contain the names of the new dignitaries. After binding him to strict silence on the subject, the Pope began to dictate the names. Having named eleven, he began to pace the floor in silence, as if trying to call the twelfth to mind. Then suddenly turning to his secretary, as though astonished at his not writing: "Continue," said he, "write down the twelfth." "But who is he?" asked Albani. "What," rejoined the Pope, "can you not write your own name?" Albani, throwing himself at the feet of the Pope, begged him to choose in his place a more worthy subject. The Pontiff replied: "We have made several changes in the names of the others whom we designed to raise to the cardinalate, but it never

once occurred to Us to change yours." The humble secretary had no alternative but to submit with resignation. Such were the antecedents of the cardinal whom the Sacred College was about to raise to the Sovereign Pontificate.

16. After a deliberation of four hours, the votes were unanimous in his favor. But Albani, in great pain and confusion, protested that he felt too unworthy of such an honor, and declared that he would positively refuse to sit upon the Apostolic throne. This was a return to the days of St. Gregory, when the humility of the saints led them to fly the highest dignities with all the earnestness displayed by the ambitious in their pursuit. The cardinals thought, at first, that it would be easy to overcome this refusal of the first moment of surprise. It was quite the contrary Albani's emotion subsided a little only to allow of deeper reflection, and so keen was his grief that he became seriously ill. He was even obliged to keep his bed, " where," says his biographer, " he seemed deaf to all consolation except that which could not be granted." All Rome was astir to force his consent; kindred, friends and citizens of all classes crowded, some to the doors of the conclave, others before the altars, to ask of God and of men the means to move Albani. The cardinals came one by one to the cell of the Pope-elect, to overcome his resistance. At length Cardinal Le Camus, bishop of Belley, undertook to convince him in due form, and to prove to him that he could not longer resist the Sacred College without resisting God Himself. Arming himself with the " Pastoral of St. Gregory the Great," he entered the cell of Albani, who could not repress a smile when he saw the ponderous folio under the arm of his colleague. Struck by the unanimity with which all, both old and young, strove to overcome his opposition, Albani listened patiently while the Cardinal read the passage of the " Pastoral," which states that while refusing the highest honor through humility, yet he ceases to be humble who does not obey the voice of God which speaks in the unanimity of the votes. " All these reasons," replied Albani, "would be good had I the necessary qualifica-

tions." He announced to the cardinals that he summoned them all before the tribunal of the Sovereign Judge, and that if they did not desist from their attempt, they should answer on the day of judgment for the unavoidable faults into which his inability would certainly betray him in the discharge of the sublime functions of the Pontificate. After two days and two nights spent in prayers and tears, and having received the declaration of four learned Doctors of Rome, whom he consulted, that further opposition would be a manifest resistance to the will of God, he finally yielded the much-desired consent and took the name of Clement XI.

The family of the new Pontiff appeared before him after his accession. "Remember," said the Pontiff to his brother, "that you have lost your natural relative; you have in me now but a father, in common with all the rest of the faithful." He forbade all his relatives to meddle with public business, to aspire to any office, or to assume the title of prince; in a word, to pass the bounds of private citizenship. This prohibition was punctually enforced. For his own conduct, Clement XI. made it a rule to confess and to celebrate the Holy Sacrifice every day He gave little time to sleep, and lived so simply that the daily expense of his table did not exceed the value of fifteen cents, French currency Every hour of the day was strictly and exclusively divided between prayer and the duties of the Pontificate. When motives of health obliged him to take the air, which, however, seldom happened, his exercise consisted in visiting some church, where his chief relaxation was found in acts of charity and devotion. Such was the Pontiff whom God seated upon the throne of St. Peter, at the opening of a century in which the Church was to be assailed by the most furious storms. In its actual state, the Christian world needed a Head in the vigor of age—a Head equal to every kind of labor. God seemed to have placed Clement XI. upon the Apostolic chair, that he might there show himself superior to all assaults and disgraces, always the same in prosperity, in sickness, in sufferings, in struggle and in rest. The number, the importance, and the danger of the events which signalized his Pontificate, have caused it to be compared with that of St. Gregory the Great. The political complications into which he was thrown, though often seemingly inextricable, never terrified him. They only served, on the contrary, to bring out in bolder relief his prudence, his genius and his greatness of soul.

17 When the testamentary disposition of Charles II became known in France, Louis XIV called an extraordinary council, to which only four persons were admitted—the Dauphin, the Duke of Beauvilliers, the Marquis De Torcy, minister of foreign affairs, and the Chancellor Pontchartrain. One voice pronounced against the acceptance of the bequest; one remained undecided; the other two were in favor of accepting it. Louis XIV after a long silence made known his decision; it remained for three days a secret. He at length announced it in these terms, to the Duke of Anjou: " The King of Spain has made you king, the lords ask for you, the people desire you, and 1 consent. Be a good Spaniard; that must henceforth be your first duty; but remember that you were born a Frenchman." He then presented him to the court with the words: " My lords, here is the King of Spain." A few days later, the Duke of Anjou, who then assumed the name of Philip V., took leave of his royal grandfather before setting out for his new realm " My son," said Louis, as a last farewell, " remember that the Pyrenees no longer exist." The Cardinal of Porto-Carrero, who was at the head of the council of regency appointed by Charles II., hastened to proclaim the accession of the young prince, who was also acknowledged at Brussels by the Elector of Bavaria, governor of the Netherlands for Spain, and at Milan by the prince of Vaudémont. Clement XI., true to the policy pointed out by the brief of Innocent XII., of which he had drawn up the plan, while a cardinal, addressed congratulatory letters to Philip V., and tendered him subsidies. Many writers have blamed Louis XIV for what they call his ambition in regard to the Spanish succession. What would they not have said had

he refused to receive the bequest of Charles II. ? There are situations which compel. The King of France could not, without prejudice to the nation of which he was the sovereign, reject the throne bequeathed to a son of France. The cordial and ready concurrence given on this occasion to the cabinet of Versailles by a Pope of the character of Clement XI., is a weighty consideration, perhaps too much overlooked. It is true that the accession of Philip V was the signal of fearful disasters for France; but great men are such, not so much in knowing how to avail themselves of success, as in knowing how to rise above misfortune; and in this light, Louis XIV won the admiration of his very enemies.

18. Meanwhile, all Europe, alarmed at the prodigious growth of French influence, and excited by the emperor Leopold I., to support the claim of his son, the Archduke Charles, against Philip V., had leagued against Louis XIV Austria, England, Holland, Portugal, and the Elector of Brandenburg, to whom Leopold then gave the title of King of Prussia, notwithstanding the protests of Clement XI.,* joined the league against France and Spain. Then began the great war against France, which lasted until 1713, and continued between Spain and Austria until 1725. Louis XIV was sixty-three years old when hostilities began, and seventy-five when they ended. During this interval he had witnessed the death of his son, the Dauphin, of his grandson, the Duke of Burgandy, and of his daughter-in-law, Adelaide of Savoy Of all his legitimate descendants, there remained but a weak and sickly child of five years. After some successes against united Europe, he suffered the successive reverses of Hochstett, Ra-

---

* The title of King of Prussia, granted by Leopold to the Elector of Brandenburg, was an infringement upon the ancient rights acquired over that province by the religious and military order of the Teutonic Knights. It was in vain that the Pope brought forward the oldest and most authentic documents, and protested, by every means in his power, against an innovation which violated long-standing rights. He issued several briefs, requesting the Catholic sovereigns not to recognize the royalty of the house of Brandenburg. In spite of his opposition, Frederick was acknowledged as King of Prussia, in the treaty of Utrecht (1713), though the Holy See admitted the title only in 1787, in the Pontificate of Pius VI.

millies, Turin, Oudenarde, and Malplaquet. "We must humble ourselves under the hand of God," said Madame de Maintenon, when she brought him the tidings that at Hochstett the French, under Marshal Tallard, had lost forty thousand men, including prisoners. The king's only generals now were the men known as *the small change of the great Luxembourg*. His enemies, on the contrary, had two able and successful leaders, Prince Eugene of Savoy, the hero of Temesvar, and the English Duke of Marlborough. The Huguenots of the Cevennes, who had taken up arms on the revocation of the Edict of Nantes, seconded the efforts of foreign enemies by arousing the spirit of civil war at home, under the name of Camisards and of house-burners: to crown all other misfortunes, the crops were ruined by the frost in 1709, and France became a prey to the horrors of famine. Already Marlborough and Prince Eugene spoke of passing through Paris to attack Spain, where Philip V., more fortunate than Louis, saw his throne restored by the Duke of Vendôme on the brilliant field of Villaviciosa. Louis was never more truly great or Christian than in these fearful trials. Deeply touched by the sufferings of his people, by the humiliation of his arms and of his children, by the bloody losses of his nobility, by the wretched condition of all France, which was like a man reeling under the fatal blow, who still stands, but totters to his fall, he did not harden his heart against these strokes of fortune, but received them as a judgment of Providence, as a punishment for his faults. He sincerely wished for peace, nor did he hesitate to ask it, declaring that he was ready to purchase it even at the price of immense sacrifices. The allies (A. D. 1700) carried their harshness to the extent of requiring, as a preliminary condition, that Louis XIV should himself dethrone his grandson, Philip V "If I must have war," replied Louis, "I would rather wage it against my enemies than against my children." Then acquainting the nation with the position of affairs, he requested the bishops, by their prayers, to call down the Divine assistance upon France. He sent for Marshal Villars to Versailles. "You see to what

a state we are brought," said the king to him; " we must conquer or perish, and end all by a glorious blow. Seek the
enemy and give him battle." " But, sire," replied the marshal,
" this is your majesty's last army " " Be it so," returned
Louis : " I do not require you to defeat the enemy, but to attack him. If you are unfortunate, write to me privately I
will ride through Paris with your letter in my hand. I know
the French people : I will bring you four hundred thousand
men. We will conquer, or I will bury myself with them beneath the ruins of the monarchy " Villars departed. Three
months later, the victory of Denain, over Prince Eugene, forty
Austrian divisions captured, five fortified places carried, a
trophy of a hundred pieces of cannon and of four hundred
thousand pounds of powder, answered the heroic resolution of
Louis XIV., saved France, and closed that celebrated campaign, the *ornament and the crown* of Villars (1712). On the
11th of April, 1713, England, Holland, Savoy and Prussia
signed, with France, the treaty of Utrecht, recognizing Philip
V as king of Spain. The duke of Savoy, Victor Amedeus I.,
obtained the investiture of the Sicilian States; he was soon,
however, forced to abandon them, and to content himself with
the erection of his hereditary domain into a kingdom, which
changed his ducal coronet into a royal crown. Louis XIV
gave up a portion of his conquests, but his grandson was on
the Spanish throne, and France enjoyed an honorable peace.
Since the year 1700, two emperors had reigned in Germany.
After Leopold (1705), Joseph I. ascended the throne; his
death (1711) left it to the same archduke Charles whose
claim to the Spanish throne had caused the late war, and who
took the title of Charles VI. It might have been expected
that the elevation of Philip's rival to the imperial throne would
put an end to all these troubles, since under no circumstances
would Europe allow the reconstruction of a power like that of
Charles V., which would have been a standing threat to all the
other States. Still Charles VI., unable or unwilling to understand the situation, refused to accede to the treaty of Utrecht.

Villars undertook to make him repent his resolution. Within
a year the emperor was obliged to sign the treaty of Rastadt
(1714), which secured to France Strasbourg, Landau, Huningen,
New Brisach and the whole of Alsatia. This particular treaty
did not hinder Charles from continuing hostilities against Philip,
which lasted until 1725.

19. We have here given this rapid sketch of the war of the
" Spanish Succession," to explain the difficult position of Clement XI. That Pontiff had, in the very beginning of his reign,
shown himself favorable to France ; each new disaster of the
French arms caused a bitter pang in his heart. Philip V.,
whose accession to the Spanish throne had been spontaneously
recognized by the Sovereign Pontiff, used every means in his
power to obtain from the Roman Court the investiture of the
kingdom of the Two Sicilies, which had always been looked upon
as a fief of the Holy See. Leopold at the same time made the
same request. Clement XI., having submitted the question to
several congregations of cardinals, at length pronounced his
decision. He declared that, as the common Father of the faithful, his first desire was the peace of the Christian world ; that,
consequently, he had determined to observe a strict neutrality
between the two belligerent powers, though recognizing Philip
V as lawful sovereign of Spain. He then asked the powers to
respect the Italian territory His petitions were useless ;
Lombardy was first made the scene of hostilities between the
two competitors ; and the Imperial troops took possession of
Ferrara, a city of the Pontifical States. It seems to be the singular destiny of Italy, that the nations must in turn choose it
as the field on which to settle their disputes by arms ! On the
eve of St. Peter's day (A. D. 1701), the ministers of Spain and
those of the Empire offered, on behalf of their respective
sovereigns, the yearly tribute for the Two Sicilies, with the
palfrey Clement stood unmoved between the two parties,
refused the rival offerings, and, on St. Peter's day, declared
that this refusal of the tribute of Naples, after the war begun
by the Emperor of Austria, in league with England, Holland,

Portugal, and the Duke of Savoy, against Spain and France, in no way prejudiced the supreme dominion of the Roman Church over the Two Sicilies, that is, over the island of Sicily and the whole kingdom of Naples.

20. Joseph I., the successor of Leopold, showed no less disposition than his predecessor to use force toward the Sovereign Pontiff. By his orders, the Austrian troops in the territory of Ferrara attacked the fortress of Commacchio, a Pontifical fief. This unjustifiable aggression drew from Clement XI. an energetic protest. In the brief *Hactenus Lenitatis* (July 17, A. D. 1705), the Pope asks the youthful monarch whether he pretends to set himself up as the judge of the cause of Jesus Christ and of His Vicar on earth. He exhorts him to give up his pretensions, and to show, in his conduct, the respect due to the Head of the Church. On these conditions the Pope will forget his past injustice, and embrace him as his *first-born* (*primo-genito*); but if the prince continues his course of violence, the Pope will lay aside the mercy of the father to punish his rebellious son by excommunication and even by arms, if needs be. "Know," added Clement, "that though you be not ashamed to war against the Church and against God Himself; though you forsake the ancient reverence of the Austrian throne for the Holy See; know that the same God Who bestows kingdoms can also destroy them." The protest of the courageous Pontiff was fruitless; he must wait till some favorable solution of the difficulty should be offered by the turn of events. Europe, in arms, presented multiplied cases of serious violation of international law. There are periods so shaken by political storms, that the voice of justice is unheard amid the general din.

Clement XI. was doomed to experience, to the end of his Pontificate, the difficulties raised by the Spanish succession against the Holy See. The forces of Charles VI., victorious over France, joined the Prussian troops and rolled like a torrent over the Italian territory   They were little disposed to spare a Pope who had, on many occasions, shown an undisguised sympathy with the cause of Louis XIV and Philip V.; the old pretensions of the Empire to the sovereignty of Italy were again revived. The imperial party appointed a limited time within which the Pope must decide on the acceptance or rejection of their offers of peace; among the conditions of which, the recognition of the Austrian pretender to the Spanish throne was the most important; meanwhile they invested the city of Rome. The situation was one of the most critical recorded in the history of the Papacy. For eighteen years, Clement XI. had been striving to secure the triumph of the opposite policy In this extremity, he determined to put off the decision as long as possible, hoping that events might send him some unlooked for help. He was disappointed. He waited till the appointed day, after which, if he were still undecided, the imperialists had threatened to overrun his capital and his dominions; it was at eleven at night, the last hour of the last day, that he gave his signature to an act against which the violence that extorted it should be a sufficient protest. Hostile writers have represented this as a mark of versatility which, say they, "dishonored the character of the Pontiff." We may here be permitted to remark, in the first place, that there was no question of a dogmatical decision. Clement XI. yielded to armed constraint a consent which saved Rome and the Holy See His signature, under the circumstances, spared the world a deluge of evils. If the Pope found it necessary to yield, if he was compelled to deviate from the line of conduct which experience had until then taught him to be the best; it is not to fickleness in his political opinions that his conduct must be ascribed, but to one of those fatal combinations of events by which God is wont to work out His own hidden and marvellous designs. Moreover, the Pope's signature exercised no marked influence upon the general result; the Austrian arms were unable to insure its ratification, and the house of Bourbon continued to rule over Spain and a great part of Italy.

21. Independently of these political complications which troubled his Pontificate, others of no less moment claimed his serious attention. The court of Turin had just then sanctioned

a practice which, had it prevailed, would have constituted a serious encroachment of the secular power upon ecclesiastical authority. An edict, issued in 1697, decreed that the governors should grant to no one the *placet* necessary for obtaining the clerical habit, or for promotion to Holy Orders, until previous information, called a *general patrimonial*, had been taken by the minister, as to the number of priests then in the country, the qualifications of the candidate, his habits, his talents, birth-place, &c. Innocent XII., who was the reigning Pontiff at that time, wrote to the Archbishop of Turin, urging him to use all his influence to have the edict revoked; but it was renewed in 1698, with the addition of an aggravating clause. It prescribed that parish churches should have only a limited number of clerics for their service; and their patrimony was limited to a rate which none might exceed. The archbishop felt bound to proclaim the nullity of such a decree. Another was published, first at Ivrea, then in Piedmont, ordering that all ecclesiastical property, persons, communities and colleges, though until then exempt, should now be subject to a yearly tax, and that this provision should be enforced, if necessary, by means of sequestration. Such was the position of affairs at the accession of Clement XI. A congregation of cardinals was named to examine the matter, and an Apostolic decree enjoined the bishops to proceed against the ministers of Savoy by every means which the canons placed in their hands. Notwithstanding this solemn decision, the difficulty remained in the same state during the whole of Clement's Pontificate, and was settled only in the reign of his successor, Innocent XIII.

22. In 1715, Clement XI. was again called to intervene in a debate of no little importance. He abolished the right of hereditary legation in Sicily, and also the tribunal " of the Monarchy " The existence of this tribunal dated from the eleventh century. Urban II., it was said, bestowed upon Roger, count of Sicily, and his successors, the rights of Papal legates in that island. From this concession came the tribunal

"of the Sicilian Monarchy," which claimed the privilege of pronouncing the final decision in all the ecclesiastical affairs of the island. The historical fact of the concession made to Count Roger has more than once occupied learned pens. Baronius discusses it at considerable length, and denies the existence of the alleged bull. Be this as it may, St. Pius V made several efforts to abolish the tribunal. It seemed to him inadmissible that a lay sovereign should exercise the functions of a legate, should pronounce and withdraw censures, and, in short, perform all the acts of a purely ecclesiastical jurisdiction. But the kings of Sicily succeeded in holding their prerogative, strange as it seemed, when an incident of no great importance in itself renewed the dispute. Tedeschi, bishop of Lipari, having been compelled by the officers of the treasury to pay some taxes from which he was exempt, laid a protest before the Sicilian government; justice was refused him, and he excommunicated the two officers who had committed the arbitrary act. They applied to the tribunal "of the Sicilian Monarchy," which gave them absolution, and sent a deputy to Lipari to enforce its decree. The deputy was guilty of acts of censurable violence in Lipari. The Pope intervened, and declared the absolution pronounced by the tribunal null and of no effect. The irritation was now at its height; two dioceses were laid under interdict; the tribunal wished to annul this interdict; Clement maintained it. An open persecution was then begun in Sicily against the members of the clergy, and even against laymen who took sides with Rome. While things were in this state, the treaty of Utrecht, as we have seen, gave Sicily to the Duke of Savoy. The officers of the Spanish monarch, who had until then most warmly defended the pretensions of their royal master, now adopted a directly opposite line of conduct. The viceroy, the president of the *tribunal* and his assessors would not quit the island until they had explicitly retracted all the acts of their administration hostile to the Holy See, and received from the Pope absolution from the censures incurred. The new King of Sicily, on the contrary, openly announced

his intention of holding to the privileges enjoyed by his predecessors. Clement XI. redoubled his firmness; he ordered
on pain of the most rigorous penalties, the strict observance of
the interdict, and annulled, by another bull, the first ordinance
issued by the Spanish officers in the beginning of the dispute.
Victor Amedeus, on the other hand, forbade all his subjects
to obey any foreign decree whatever, without his sanction.
Negotiations were carried on to settle the difficulty; but all
proving fruitless, Clement XI. published a bull on the 11th of January, A. D. 1715, against the last edict of the king, and a month
later abolished the right of hereditary legation and the tribunal
" of the Sicilian Monarchy." The bull was signed by thirty
three cardinals. An appeal was made for the King of Sicily
and the contest continued. When Philip V again became
master of the island, in 1718, he endeavored to restore peace.
An arrangement was in process, but the condition of Europe
delayed its conclusion. Clement XI., through his whole Pontificate, was doomed to wage ceaseless wars without ever seeing
his efforts crowned with final success. The Sicilian question
was not definitely settled until the reign of Benedict XIII.,
when Charles VI. was in possession of Sicily; the tribunal
was then finally abolished.

23. These struggles occupied but the least part of the reign
of Clement XI. It was mostly taken up by the Jansenist question, revived in the beginning of the eighteenth century with
more ardor than ever. In 1701, all the old disputes were renewed, by the appearance in France of the celebrated " Case of
Conscience." This name was given to a moral decision which
seemed to concern only some private individual, and which really
aimed at destroying all the decisions of the Church against the
errors of the day A provincial confessor was represented in a
state of perplexity concerning the conduct he was to adopt
toward an ecclesiastic whom he had always looked upon as a
good man, but who was now represented to him as unsound in
his belief. He said, that having questioned him on certain
points, he had received the following answers : " I condemn the

five propositions of the 'Augustinus,' in all the acceptations in which the Church has condemned them; but in the question of *fact*, I think it sufficient to show the submission of silence and respect; and, so long as I cannot be judicially convicted of having maintained any of these propositions, my faith cannot be suspected. I believe that, since we are required to love God above all things, and in all things, as our last end, all actions which are not referred to him, at least virtually, and which are not performed through some impulse of love, are so many sins.—I hold that he who is present at Mass with a will and an affection for mortal sin, without any feeling of repentance, commits a new sin.—I do not believe that devotion to the saints, and especially to the Blessed Virgin, consists in all the vain formulas and idle practices found in certain authors," &c. Forty Doctors of the theological Faculty of Paris answered, that the views of the ecclesiastic in question were neither new nor singular, nor condemned by the Church; that they were not such in fact, that he might not receive absolution without renouncing them. This decision was kept secret for a whole year; after which it was given to the light, and countless numbers of the pamphlet were printed in Paris. The greatness of the scandal was equal to that of the insidious attack, which aimed at the utter overthrow of the whole authority of the Apostolic Constitutions, and of all that had been done against the late heresies. The forty Doctors who had implicated themselves prevented their personal condemnation by a humble retraction, thanks to the efforts made by the Bishops of Chartres and of Meaux. Cardinal de Noailles, archbishop of Paris, then published an ordinance condemning the decision of the consulters, as opposed to the Pontifical Constitutions; as tending to bring in debate questions already decided, and to perpetuate disturbances; in fine, as favoring the practice of equivocation, of mental reservation, and even of perjury (A. D. 1703). The bishops of the several dioceses issued similar ordinances.

24. At this period, the history of religious polemics presents a name clothed with the melancholy renown of heresy,

and almost eclipsing that of Jansenius himself. Pasquier Quesnel, a priest of the Oratory, had early shown himself one of the warmest defenders of the new sect. The death of Arnauld left him at its head. His first work, which made so deep an impression, and rendered the author's after-life so stormy, was the *Réflexions Morales*. It would seem that the work was begun with very good intentions, and contained nothing reprehensible. It consisted of short maxims and pious thoughts on the words of the Saviour, designed by Quesnel for the use of the young priests of the Oratory, with whose instruction and direction he had been intrusted. Deeply versed in the knowledge of the sacred Scripture and of the Fathers, the author displayed in this work great learning and sound criticism. The minister of State, Loménie de Brienne, the Marquis de Laigne, and other pious persons, who had been edified by reading the book, urged Quesnel to write a similar one on the four gospels. The high encomiums which they bestowed upon this work, in a conversation with Mgr. Vialart, bishop of Châlons-sur-Marne, induced that prelate, who was highly esteemed for wisdom and virtue, to examine it himself. Having read and examined the book with care, the bishop approved it in a pastoral letter, dated September 5, A. D. 1671, recommending it to the use of the clergy and faithful of his diocese. Meantime, Quesnel had openly embraced Jansenism, and was banished to Brussels, with the Superior of the Oratory, Fr. Abel de Sainte-Marthe, a friend and partisan of Arnauld. During his exile, Quesnel finished his book, revised the first part, published in 1671, seasoning it with Jansenistic principles to make it conformable with his last additions, and the work, thus refitted, was presented in 1691 to M. de Noailles, who had succeeded M. Vialart in the See of Châlons-sur-Marne. On learning that the work had been approved by his predecessor, and that it was read with pleasure and profit in his diocese, the bishop, without further examination, gave his sanction to the new edition. In the course of the same year, M. de Noailles was transferred to the metropolitan See of Paris. Here he displayed the greatest

zeal against the Jansenists In 1696, he condemned a work
by the Abbé Barcos, a nephew of Duvergier de Hauranne.
This book, containing all the teaching of Port Royal, bore the
title of "Exposition of the faith of the Church touching grace
and predestination." We have mentioned the condemnation of
the "Case of Conscience," by the same prelate, in 1703.

Quesnel now turned his attacks upon the archbishop of
Paris. He could not restrain his tears when, in his retreat at
Brussels, he beheld the "Case of Conscience," the great hope
of the sect, suddenly overthrown by a general rising of the Catholics. His tears were soon changed into a torrent of gall
which spared no one. He wrote to Cardinal de Noailles, accu
sing him of having struck a fatal blow at the peace of the Church,
and reproaching the forty Doctors who had retracted their first
decision, with the "scandal of a cowardly, forced submission,
in opposition to the light of conscience and of truth." This
letter was soon followed by another of the same kind, entitled,
'Letter of a bishop to a bishop." Quesnel repeats the same
sentiments, but this time with more schismatical insolence and
glaring impropriety Clement XI. speedily branded the decision of the "Case of Conscience," and opposed his solemn sen
tence to the audacious efforts of the sectary. He addressed
two briefs respectively to the king and to the Archbishop of
Paris. These briefs were the signal for a storm of new insults
from the Jansenists. Some of their writers did not blush to
say that the brief to the king "showed the heart of a tiger."
The Pope determined to promulgate his sentence in a still more
explicit and irrefragable manner. He defined, with equal precision and authority, how far true Catholics are to carry their
obedience to the Pontifical Constitutions received by the whole
Church.

25. This was the object of the celebrated bull, *Vineam Domini Sabaoth.* After quoting the decrees of Innocent X. and
Alexander VII. on the same subject, Clement XI. laments the
obstinacy of those hypocritical sectaries who, not satisfied with
not receiving the truth, seek to avoid it by every possible subter-

fuge. They do not blush, says the Pope, to use, in defence of their errors, the very decrees promulgated against them by the Holy Apostolic See. Such has been their conduct especially, respecting the. letter of Clement IX., in the form of a brief, to the four refractory bishops of France, and the two letters of Innocent XII. to the bishops of the Netherlands; as if Clement IX., while requiring by this brief an absolute and perfect obedience from the four prelates, and expressing his will that they should sign the *Formula* of Alexander VII., could really have admitted any exception whatever, since he protested that he would never receive any; as if Innocent XII., while formally declaring that the five propositions taken from the book of Jansenius, were condemned in the sense which they naturally convey to the reader, meant to speak not of the sense which they form in the book, or which Jansenius expressed, but of some other different sense; as if that Pontiff had wished to modify, restrict, or change, in any way, the Constitutions of Innocent X. or of Alexander VII., in the very brief in which he declared, in express terms, that they had been and were still more than ever in force, and that he would maintain their decisions by all the means in his power. The Pontiff then directly attacks what the Jansenists had agreed to call the *respectful silence*. "Under this subterfuge," said the Pope, "by which they dispense themselves from an inward adherence to an external retraction of the doctrine of Jansenius, they do not reject, they only hide, their error; they irritate instead of curing the wound; far from obeying, they deride the Church; they open to the children of rebellion a large field for the propagation of heresy Some have gone to such a pitch of impudence, that, forgetting the rules, not only of Christian sincerity, but even of common honesty, they have not hesitated to assert that it is lawful to sign the *Formula* prescribed by Alexander VII., even though not intentionally judging the work of Jansenius to be heretical. This is making sport of the Apostolic Constitutions, and not submitting to them as a Christian." It would be hard to make this declaration more clear, precise and manifest; but these very qualities were so many additional motives to make it pernicious and detestable in the eyes of the Jansenists. The Catholics received it with respect; to them it was the word of Peter confirming his brethren in the faith; the sectaries themselves were obliged to confess that Rome no longer left them the resource of the distinctions, the mental reservations and subterfuges which they had so long abused.

26. Quesnel, far from submitting to the bull of Clement XI., chose the moment of its appearance to hurl at Cardinal de Noailles a treacherous weapon which he had long been whetting in secret. We have seen that the prelate, while bishop of Châlons, imprudently gave his sanction to the second edition of the "Moral Reflections." He was not aware that the work contained all the poison of the Jansenist doctrines, which he afterward condemned in the "Exposition of the faith of the Church," by Barcos. Paris, and indeed all France, was suddenly flooded with copies of a pamphlet, entitled "Problème Ecclésiastique," in which the anonymous author opposes Louis-Antoine de Noailles, bishop of Châlons in 1695, approving those doctrines in the "Moral Reflections," to Louis-Antoine de Noailles, archbishop of Paris in 1696, condemning the same doctrines in the "Exposition of the faith of the Church." The sensation caused by this pamphlet, at a moment when all minds were attentive to the debate, was immense. The simple statement of a fact would have vindicated the Archbishop of Paris. The approbation of the "Moral Reflections" had been given on the testimony of another, without a second examination, without any idea of the heretical additions made to a work previously authorized by the bishop's predecessor. But this statement might have argued a culpable carelessness on the part of the prelate, in a matter so serious as the approval of a dogmatic work. The statement, therefore, was not made. The "Problème Ecclesiastique" was condemned to the flames by a decree of the Parliament of Paris. Quesnel was, by order of Philip V., arrested at Malines and thrown into prison. Some of his friends succeeded in releasing him, by piercing through one of

the walls. After some time again spent in concealment and wandering about the Netherlands, he at length settled in Amsterdam, where Codde, bishop of Sebaste and Vicar Apostolic in Holland, who had lately been deposed for his attachment to the same doctrines, invited him to make his abode. Here he began to write again in favor of the "Ecclesiastical Problem." The Archbishop of Paris was still in the same embarrassing dilemma; the only possible means of freeing himself from it was the only means he was unwilling to use. Accusations were fast multiplying; Bossuet took the field, and endeavored to justify the cardinal by showing that there were points of essential difference between the doctrines contained in the "Moral Reflections," and those of the "Exposition." But the thesis was untenable even for the genius of the Eagle of Meaux. This system of defence only aggravated the position of the cardinal. The Jansenists published the work of Bossuet, with the title, "Vindication of the Moral Reflections, by Bossuet." Clement XI., hoping to put an end to discussions which only multiplied scandals, issued a decree on the 13th of July, A. D. 1708, in which he most severely censured and condemned the "Moral Reflections" of Quesnel.*

27. This measure was not productive of the effects that might have been expected from it. The Jansenists continued to defend the work of Quesnel and the "Ecclesiastical Problem." Louis XIV., weary of seeing France thus torn by endless discussions, asked the Pope for a clear and explicit Constitution, to put an end to all these debates. Never had a heresy thus persistently made a mockery of the thunders of the Church, or with greater insincerity eluded the anathemas of her Pontiffs. For half a century, France and the Netherlands had been made a religious arena in which the Jansenists carried on their obstinate struggle. Clement XI. was as truly alive as Louis XIV to the necessity of restoring peace. He had thus far

---

* The real title of this work was, *Le Nouveau Testament en français, avec des réflexions morales sur chaque verset, ou Abrégé de la morale de l'Evangile, des Actes des Apôtres, des Epîtres de Saint Paul par le P. PASQUIER QUESNEL*, prêtre de l'Oratoire.

shown no want of zeal in the discharge of his duties as Pontiff.
He had the grief to see all his efforts fail before the hypocrisy
of the sect; but his was one of those heroic natures that never
sink under reverses. A congregation of cardinals, appointed
by him, entered upon a careful examination of the "Moral
Reflections." A hundred and one propositions, drawn from the
work, were submitted, with various qualifications, to the Pontifical censure. Clement then ordered public prayers in all the
churches in Rome, to implore the light of the Holy Ghost. At
length, on the 8th of September, A. D. 1713, the celebrated Constitution, *Unigenitus Dei Filius*, was promulgated. It condemns
the work of Quesnel as containing a hundred and one propositions respectively false, captious, offensive to pious ears, tainted
with heresy, erroneous, in a word, heretical, and renewing various errors, especially those contained in the celebrated propositions of Jansenius. All the faithful are forbidden to hold or to
teach the said propositions, or to speak of them in any other
sense than that conveyed by this Constitution. "Moreover,"
continues the Pope, " by the express and particular condemnation of the hundred and one propositions, We would by no
means be understood to approve what is contained in the rest
of the book. In the course of the examination made of it, We
have noticed several other propositions bearing a close relation
and affinity to those just condemned, and filled with the same
errors. We have also remarked many others, calculated to
breed disobedience and rebellion against authority, civil and
ecclesiastical. In fine, what is still more intolerable, We have
found the text of the New Testament altered in a most censurable manner, and agreeing, in many places, with the French
translation of Mons, long since condemned. Bad faith has been
daring enough to wrest the text from its true sense, to give it
a false and dangerous meaning. For these reasons, in virtue
of the Apostolic authority in Us vested, We forbid and condemn the book of 'Moral Reflections,' under whatever title
and in whatever language it has been or may hereafter be
printed,—in whatever edition or whatever version it has

appeared or may yet appear,—as eminently calculated to mislead the faithful by the false appearance of instruction full of piety. We likewise condemn all other books and pamphlets, in manuscript or in print, or—which God forbid—that may hereafter be printed, in defence of this work. We forbid every one of the faithful to read, to copy, to keep, or to use them, on pain of excommunication incurred by the very act."

28. The first appearance of the bull fulminated against the work with which the very fate of Jansenism was, in some sort, closely linked, threw the whole sect into deep consternation. The bull *Unigenitus*, sent by Clement XI. to Louis XIV., was laid before the assembly of the clergy Forty of the prelates received it; only seven hesitated and joined Cardinal de Noailles in refusing to sign it. The cardinal, still in the awkward position in which the Ecclesiastical Problem had placed him, thought it inconsistent with his honor to acknowledge the condemnation of a book published with his approbation. This was an ill-timed delicacy; but, to those who know the human heart and the windings of self-love, this conduct, however afflicting, cannot seem wonderful. Still, more than a hundred bishops published the bull *Unigenitus* throughout the kingdom. Louis XIV openly proclaimed his firm determination to support it, even by force if necessary The convent of Port Royal,* of which the nuns had always refused to subscribe the *Formula*, was closed by a royal edict (October 29th, A. D. 1709), and the buildings razed to the ground. Jansenism had no longer a legal existence. Its spirit still survived, and took refuge in the parliaments. That of Paris, encouraged in its opposition by Cardinal de Noailles, long refused to register the bull *Unigenitus;* but Louis XIV declaring that he would, in case of necessity, hold a bed of justice, the bull was registered on the 14th of February, 1714, notwithstanding the protest of the

---

* Some of the nuns of the Order, who had remained in the convent in Paris, on showing themselves more docile and subscribing the *Formula*, were allowed to remain. Their community lasted until the time of the "National Convention." The convent has since been transformed into the "Hospice de la Maternité" (A. D. 1814).

president, Ménard. Several prelates, however, still held out in their resistance. The Archbishop of Tours publicly attacked the bull in a pastoral letter; Cardinal de Noailles, in contempt of all propriety, did the same. These isolated protests were far more than balanced by the applause of the Catholic world, which had readily submitted to the voice of Christ's Vicar upon earth. Clement XI. could have silenced the detractors of his bull; the royal government was prepared to support him with energy, but the Pope, animated by the true spirit of religion, which never punishes until every expedient of mildness and mercy has been exhausted, moderated the absolute determination of the king, and advised him to wait until events should offer the means of a more peaceful solution.

29. The reign of Louis XIV. was drawing near to its end; the health of the great prince was sinking under the infirmities of age. On the 29th of August, A. D. 1715, he said to the cardinals De Rohan and De Bissy: " I die in the faith and obedience of the Church; I am not informed of the questions which trouble her; I have only followed your counsels; I have done only what you wished; if I have done wrong, you shall answer for it before God, whom I call to witness." He then sent for the Dauphin, afterward Louis XV., then five years old. " My dear child," said the dying monarch to him, " you will soon be the king of a great realm; what I most earnestly recommend to you is, never to forget your duty to God; try to remain at peace with your neighbors. I have been too fond of war; do not imitate me in this, nor in my great expenses. In all things take advice, and seek to know the best, that you may follow it always; relieve the burdens of your people as soon as you can, and do what I have had the misfortune not to be able to do myself." He closed this touching interview by these words to the young Dauphin: " My dear child, I give you my blessing with all my heart." After which he kissed him twice with the greatest tenderness; then turning to the members of his court, he said to them: " Gentlemen, I entreat your forgiveness for the bad example I have given you; I owe you

many thanks for the manner in which you have always served me, for the fidelity and attachment you have always shown me. I beg for my grandson the same unvarying fidelity you have always displayed in my regard. It is my hope that you will all concur in maintaining union, and that if any one goes astray, you will help to bring him back." Until his last breath, he showed the courage of great souls. "Why do you weep?" he asked his attendants; "did you think me immortal?" Thus died, at the age of seventy-seven years, one of the greatest kings that ever governed men. He seemed to have lived just long enough to preside at the obsequies of the age, of which he had concentrated all the splendor and glory about himself. The Duke of Orleans was proclaimed regent for the young king, Louis XV

30. Louis XIV had been preceded to the grave by Bossuet. On the 12th of April, A. D. 1704, that great light of the Church of France was extinguished in death. The friends of the illustrious bishop, prostrate at the foot of his bed, begged his last blessing. One of them, at the same time, expressed his deep gratitude for all the goodness the bishop had shown him, entreating him to think sometimes of the friends he was leaving on earth, and who had been so devoted to his service and his *glory*. At the word *glory*, Bossuet, who already felt the shadows of death falling about him, who was now a stranger to earth, seized with a holy terror in the presence of the Supreme Judge, whose sentence he was about to receive, raising himself from his bed of pain, and animated by a holy indignation, found strength to exclaim distinctly: "Cease such discourses; pray to God to forgive me my sins." In the last years of life, Bossuet had conceived the project of bringing back the Protestants to the Catholic faith. With this view, he maintained a regular correspondence with the great Leibnitz, the deepest philosopher of Germany The esteem in which the distinguished philosopher held Catholicity, is shown by his " theological system," in which he admits nearly every article of our faith.

31. The regent of France, Philip of Orleans, was a frivo

lous prince of more than loose morality, and gave the example of that deplorable license into which the nobility plunged without a second thought, and dragged the kingdom to speedy destruction. The man whom he placed at the head of his administration, and whom he afterward made the Cardinal Dubois, was even more worthless than his master. The regent did not follow the policy inaugurated by Louis XIV., respecting the Jansenists. He took no pains to hide the fact that the *Unigenitus* was personally offensive to him. Those who had been banished during the preceding reign, for disobedience to the Pontifical decisions, were now recalled. The Sorbonne, which had first received the Constitution, now began to assail it. Clement XI., indignant at such a proof of bad faith, suspended the privileges of that institution, and forbade it to confer ecclesiastical degrees. The Sorbonne did not cease its hostile demonstrations, and, in 1717, joined those who had appealed, at the same time revoking the decree by which it had, in 1715, excluded from the doctorate all its members who had, by word or writing, attacked the bull. On the 5th of March, A.D. 1717, an instrument appeared, signed by Cardinal de Noailles, the bishops of Mirepoix, Montpellier, Boulogne and Senez, and by a number of ecclesiastics of the second order; it was entitled, "An Appeal from the bull Unigenitus to the Pope better informed, or to the next General Council." In order to gain the signatures of as many adherents as possible, these prelates did not hesitate to offer sums of money to all who consented to sign the paper. But the body of the French episcopate lamented these disorders. Languet, formerly bishop of Soissons, but at that time archbishop of Sens, especially signalized himself by his zeal in defending the outraged rights of the Apostolic See. The Duke of Orleans wanted scandal; he was gratified beyond his wish. He was beginning to be alarmed at the turn taken by the debate. By an edict published in 1717, he imposed silence upon both parties; but he found it easier to unchain the winds than to check them in their mad career. The edict of the regent was unheeded. Meanwhile, Clement XI.

had condemned the appeal of Cardinal de Noailles and of the four bishops. On the 25th of March, 1718, he wrote an autograph letter in Italian, to the Archbishop of Paris, conjuring him to give the example of submission, and to return to the path of obedience. This affectionate and conciliatory measure was likewise fruitless. At length, on the 27th of August, 1718, by the bull *Pastoralis*, the Sovereign Pontiff declared that, in future, he should not recognize as sons of the Church those who refused to obey the bull *Unigenitus*, though adorned with the honors of the episcopate or of the cardinalate. The regent and the refractory bishops, alarmed at the unshaken constancy of Clement XI., proposed to receive the bull if the Pope would add some explanations. But the Pontiff refused this concession as injurious to the Apostolic See. Several French bishops, with a view to facilitate the restoration of peace, tried to present these explanations, though in terms most honorable to the Holy See. Clement XI., while commending their zeal, still declined any mediation. There was no alternative but to submit. An edict of the Duke of Orleans (1718), ordered that throughout all France the bull *Unigenitus* should be faithfully received and observed, forbidding any appeal to a future council, and annulling all those which had already been made. Notwithstanding all these motives for desisting from a lamentable opposition, Cardinal de Noailles and the four refractory bishops would not yet submit. They contented themselves with observing what they called the *respectful silence*. The Pope might have used strong measures, but he would not " quench the smoking flax," and history, which has commended the firmness of Clement XI., has also recorded the memory of his merciful and exhaustless clemency. It was enough for the Pope that the legal observance of the *Unigenitus* was required in France ; the rest was a mere matter of time.

32. In the year 1715, by the bull *Ex illa die*, Clement XI. had closed a celebrated controversy known as the *question of the Chinese rites*. The first missionaries in China were the Jesuits. Thoroughly conversant with the literature and history

of that country, their attention was naturally attracted to the study of the civil and religious ceremonies of the Chinese. The rites paid to their ancestors and the honors given to Confucius constituted the two leading features of their ceremonial. The people were so deeply attached to these practices, which were, in some sort, identified with the history and manners of the nation, that to abolish them seemed sure to close all hearts, in the Celestial Empire, against the Catholic faith. After a mature examination, most of the missionaries thought that the Chinese ceremonies were safe from the charge of superstition and idolatry. Their great desire to facilitate the conversion of the Chinese, especially of the learned, whose example might lead the rest of the people, " their charity and their zeal," says M. Crétineau-Joly, " misled them." They laid the question before the Congregation of the Propaganda, in the light in which it appeared to them, and they on several occasions, received answers which authorized them to allow the neophytes to continue their ceremonies as they had been represented. But some Dominican religious who had come to evangelize the country, in their turn, viewed the matter in a different light They exposed their doubts to the Holy See. The difficulty grew with the vehemence displayed by both parties in the defence of their respective views. To put an end to these lamentable discussions, Clement XI. decided that the Chinese ceremonies should thenceforth be forbidden among the new Christians of the Celestial Empire. Such was the object of the bull *Ex illa die*. " The suppression of the Chinese ceremonies," says a late writer, " was a measure of great wisdom. The least motive to suspect them of idolatry ; the animosity which diversity of opinion daily embittered among the missionaries ; the epithets of ' abettors of idolatry' and ' flatterers of idolatrous kings;' the display of scandalous divisions before the eyes of the idolaters, thus making Christianity a by-word among them ; —all this was doubtless the greatest evil that could befall the Gospel; to put an end to it, there were no considerations that might not be disregarded."

33. England now irresistibly demands the attention of the historian. The nation had been divided in two since the schism of Henry VIII. From that moment Protestant England persecutes Catholic England without rest or interval. The heads of Mary Stuart and of Charles I. fall beneath the axe of Anglicanism. Protestant England proscribes James II. and his son; she excludes from the throne whoever professes the ancestral faith; the crown is bestowed upon the Dutch Calvinist, William of Nassau, with his wife, Mary Henrietta, the heretical daughter of the dethroned Catholic king, and afterward upon another daughter of the same king, Anne, with her Lutheran husband, George of Denmark (A. D. 1702-1714); finally upon a German Lutheran, George of Hanover (1714-1727), to the prejudice of more than fifty princes who had better claims to the throne, but who professed the religion of old England, the religion of the great and saintly kings, Edward and Alfred. To justify the apostasy, at least in its own eyes, Protestant England wields the pens of its writers to calumniate Catholic England, the Isle of Saints. Such are the aim and spirit of the histories of Burnet, of Rapin, Thoyras, of Hume, and, in fact, of nearly all the historical publications produced in England. Meanwhile, Anglicanism is crumbling into an infinity of sects, which, according to their governmental form, may be comprised in two classes—the Episcopalians, who recognize an episcopal authority; and the Presbyterians, who do not. The Episcopalians—the Established Church—have kept the hierarchy of bishops, priests, and deacons; but the Roman Church looks upon their ordinations as utterly null, on two grounds: one of fact, the other of right :— 1. Matthew Parker, the so-called Archbishop of Canterbury, and the stock of the whole Anglican episcopate, since 1559, was never validly ordained bishop, nor even priest, since his consecrator, Barlow, was not himself ordained. 2. The form of ordination prescribed by the ritual of Edward VI., according to which Parker was consecrated bishop by a man who was not properly in that Order himself, is null and insufficient; it excludes the very idea of sacrifice and priesthood; so that the

Episcopal Church of England possesses only a civil hierarchy, without any sacred character. Thus the Episcopalians have but the shadow of a hierarchy, while the Presbyterians have not even that shadow. The Presbyterians are so called, not because they have, or recognize, priests, in the Christian sense, but because they consult the elders of their assemblies, who are called *presbyteri*, in the pagan sense of the Greeks. From their ranks most of the dissenting sects have sprung. One of the most remarkable among them is that of the Quakers. They derive their name from the trembling and contortions which they exhibit in their assemblies, when they believe themselves moved by the Spirit of God. Their founder was George Fox, an illiterate shoemaker, of a gloomy and melancholy disposition. In 1647, under Charles I., amid the troubles of civil war, he went about preaching against the Episcopal clergy, war, taxes, luxury, the use of oaths, &c. The fundamental articles of his doctrine are: 1. The perfect equality of all men; consequently, the abolition of all social distinctions, of all outward signs of respect, of all ranks. 2. God gives to all men an inward light, sufficient to lead them to eternal salvation; consequently, there is no need of priests, nor of pastors, nor even of the Holy Scriptures; any individual, man or woman, is entitled to preach and to teach, when moved by the Spirit. 3. To gain eternal life, it is enough to avoid sin and to do good works; there is no need of sacraments, of ceremonies, or of external worship. 4. The principal virtues of a Christian are temperance and modesty; all superfluity of ornament and dress must, therefore, be discarded. 5. It is morally wrong to swear or to take an oath for any cause whatever, to carry on a suit at law, to bear arms, to make war, &c. "The quakers and even the quakeresses," says Mosheim, "went about through cities and villages, like madmen and Bacchanalians, declaiming against Episcopacy, against Presbyterianism, against every established form of religion. They made a mockery of public worship, insulted priests during the celebration of the holy offices, trampled upon the laws and the authority of magistrates, all under the pretext that they were obeying the inspiration of the Holy Spirit." One of the sect, William Penn, having received from the English government a large tract of territory in America, brought over a numerous colony of Quakers to cultivate it, and named his new province Pennsylvania. The opening of the eighteenth century saw the rise of another sect, that of the Methodists (1729). Its birthplace was the University of Oxford. Several students, who had devoted much time to reading the Bible, formed themselves into a small society under the direction of two brothers, John and Charles Wesley They strictly regulated all their actions, and devoted their whole time to study, prayer, and good works. This exact regularity attracted general attention, and obtained for them the name of Methodists. John Wesley, who aspired to the leadership of a sect, assumed the power of appointing bishops and priests, though he was neither himself. The new religion soon gained celebrity by the extravagant excesses of its members. Cornwall, where the sect was most numerous, was literally invaded by a convulsive epidemic. Like the Quakers, the Methodists sent a colony to the New World.

34. License in religious opinions is the shortest road to unbelief. England was at this time the seat of doctrines which were but the prelude of the system of universal scepticism, whose standard was to be raised within half a century, by the schools of false philosophy Anthony Collins, an English philosophical and sceptical writer, in 1707, published a " Treatise concerning the use of reason in propositions depending on human testimony," in which he establishes an opposition between the certitude afforded by revelation and the evidence given by reason. In the same year, he engaged in the controversy between Dodwell and Dr. Samuel Clarke, concerning the immateriality and immortality of the soul; he opposed the immortality and spirituality of the soul. It was not to be expected that Collins should have any very exact notions on the liberty of man after having reasoned so incorrectly concerning the nature of the soul. He placed liberty in the will alone, only excluding con-

straint or physical necessity   Clarke maintained the contrary opinion, with that clear reasoning which characterizes his writings.   Collins replied by his " Discourse on Free-thinking," in which he openly attacks all revelation.   It was written, as the title shows, at the time of the rise and progress of a society of free-thinkers, who, under the pretext of an attack upon superstition and *Popery*, were really sapping the foundation of all religion.   " The want of justice and sincerity displayed by Collins, in the whole course of this work," says Leland, " has given rise to very just complaints."   He continually reasons on the supposition that the defenders of revelation are opposed to a reasonable freedom of thought.   Whatever evil has been done by any Christian, he deems an argument against Christianity, and every thing that has ever formed a subject of controversy must, in his system, be looked upon as doubtful.   In the issue, the work tended to Deism.   To the credit of the English clergy be it said, they rose up in a body against the bold innovations of Collins, who removed to Holland.   Here, under his personal superintendence, was published a French translation of his " Discourse on Free-thinking" (A. D. 1714).   Clement XI. submitted the work to the examination of a commission, and condemned it by a solemn decree.   Collins led the advanced guard of the Voltairian school, which was at a later period repeatedly to draw upon its writings the thunders of the Holy See.

35. The care bestowed by Clement XI. upon the work of repressing heresies and mischievous doctrines did not withdraw the attention of the great Pope from the general interests of Christendom.   The Sultan, Achmet III., successor to Mustapha II., violated the treaty of Carlowitz, by attacking the Venetians in the Morea, in the beginning of the year 1715.   Betrayed by the Greeks of the Peloponnesus, who, like the Greeks of the Lower Empire, preferred the Mussulman yoke to a Catholic government, the Venetians were forced to abandon the Morea, conquered fifteen years before by the illustrious Morosini.   This war was marked by fearful slaughter on the part of the Turks; the few Venetians who escaped the Ottoman scimetar, were

nearly all reduced to slavery The atrocities perpetrated by
the Turks in the Morea aroused all Christendom. A general
cry of horror and revenge was heard from one extremity of
Europe to the other. The Holy See, which had so often before
armed nations and kings, in the name of religion and civilization, against Islam, once more raised its mighty voice. Clement
XI. now displayed a zeal equal to that of Urban II., of Pius
V., or of Innocent XII. To every European court he sent his
legates and his apostolic briefs to arouse the Christians, and he
made an immense outlay from his own treasury to support the
holy war. "If it becomes necessary," said the Pontiff, "I
shall purchase the success of this undertaking by the sale of
every chalice and ciborium in Italy" At his call, Spain,
Portugal, Genoa, Tuscany, the Knights of Malta, equipped their
squadrons, and the combined fleet rode the waters of the archi-
pelago under the Pontifical banner. On the Continent, the
hero of Temesvar, Prince Eugene of Savoy, prime minister of
Austria and commander-in-chief of the imperial armies, called
upon the Divan, in the name of Charles VI., to return to the
observance of the violated treaty of Carlowitz, and to restore
the Morea to the Venetians, from whom it had been unjustly
wrested. The Divan replied by a declaration of war. At the
head of sixty thousand men, the invincible Eugene crushed the
Turks at Peterwardein (August 5, A. D. 1716), just as he had
crushed them nineteen years before, near Temesvar, on the plains
of Zentha. Six thousand Mussulmans were left upon the field ;
one hundred and fifteen pieces of cannon, fifty standards, and
a considerable amount of money, fell into the hands of the
Christians. A few days later, the city of Temesvar, the last
bulwark of Islamism in Hungary, was once more under the
Austrian flag. One year afterward, Belgrade, defended by one
hundred and fifty thousand Turks, after a siege of three weeks
by Prince Eugene, surrendered to the Christians (August 1,
1717). These two brilliant campaigns resulted in the treaty
of Passarowitz. Here again the Turks were forced to receive
terms from the Christians. This peace, one of the most glori-

ous and advantageous ever contracted between Austria and the
Ottoman Empire, took from the Porte, Peterwardein, Belgrade,
Temesvar, Semendria, with a great portion of Wallachia and
Servia.   Important places in Dalmatia and the Ionian Islands
were restored to Venice.   The Porte kept the Morea, but the
possession of that peninsula did not counterbalance the great
territorial losses of Turkey in the Danubian provinces.   The
treaty of Passarowitz was solemnly signed on the 21st of July,
1718.   It was the crowning glory of Prince Eugene, who displayed as much statesmanship on this occasion, as he did genius
and heroism at the head of his armies.   The conqueror of the
Turks sent to Clement XI., whose noble zeal had so greatly
contributed to the success of the Christian arms, several standards taken from the enemy   The Pope, accompanied by the
Sacred College, went to the Church of St. Mary Major to return
thanks to the God of armies; with his own hands he laid the
captured standards upon the altar of the Blessed Virgin, whose
help he had implored, and then intoned the Te Deum.   It is
evident that Prince Eugene could have taken Constantinople,
after the victories of Peterwardein, Temesvar, and Belgrade, and
such, it is said, was his design.   But France, Holland, England
and Russia, the mediating powers in the congress of Passarowitz,
checked the warlike projects of the hero.   They were alarmed
at the power, the prodigious development daily acquired by
Austria.   The European balance of power would have been
looked upon as destroyed, had the Germans marched as conquerors into the capital of the Turkish Empire.   In later times,
the great question of European equilibrium, relative to the
much coveted possession of Constantinople by a powerful nation,
has again saved the Turks, who, no longer their own masters,
owe their presence on the shores of the Bosphorus, only to the
rivalry—natural in such a case—of the Christian powers.*

36. The political vicissitudes of the Morea, by turns under
the domination of the Venetians and of the Turks, gave occasion to the return of a great number of Armenians to the

* POUJOULAT, *Histoire de Constantinople*, t II., pp. 306, 307, 308.

Catholic faith. This happy event was in great part due to Peter Mekhitar, a native of Sebaste, in Cappadocia (A. D. 1676). Having completed his studies in the patriarchal monastery of Echmiadzin, he received the title of *vertabied,* or doctor. In the year 1700 he removed to Constantinople, where he devoted himself for some time to the ministry of preaching. The Armenians of that city were then divided in their obedience between two rival Patriarchs. Mekhitar made fruitless efforts to re-unite them. Then, turning to the Roman Church, he had the courage openly to preach submission to the Pope. This step exposed him to the full hatred of the schismatics. The mufti ordered his arrest; but the courageous missionary succeeded in eluding all their pursuits: by the help of some devoted friends, he embarked, under the disguise of a merchant, and reached Smyrna in safety (1702). A decree of the Grand Turk followed him even there; again he was obliged to conceal himself, and in a few days sailed in a Venetian ship, bound for the Morea, where he was joined by several of his disciples. The Morea was then in the hands of the Venetians. The Venetian governor allotted Mekhitar a suburban town with the neigh boring territory Here the illustrious fugitive built a church and a monastery, in which he dwelt until 1717, when the Turks once more gained possession of the Morea, Mekhitar was obliged to fly with his community. On the 8th of September, 1717, the Republic granted him the island of St. Lazarus, where he built another church and monastery, which became the residence of the Armenian religious, who still retain it under the name of the Mekhitarists. To his monastery Mekhitar added a printing establishment, for the publication of such books as might be necessary for the instruction of his countrymen, and to introduce among them the true doctrine of the Roman Church. The progressive influence of Christian Europe has now put a stop to persecutions in Constantinople. The Armenian Catholics have a Patriarch who depends immediately upon the Holy See, thus reviving and representing the Armenian nationality up to St Gregory the Illuminator.

37 France was edified at the heroic charity and self-devo-tion displayed by the holy bishop, Belzunce. In 1720, a young princess of Orleans, a daughter of the regent, had passed through the kingdom, amid feasts and rejoicings, on her way to marry the Duke of Modena. The French lords who had ac-companied her in this festive journey returned to Marseilles on ships decked with wreaths of flowers, and accompanied by the harmonious strains of musical choirs. Suddenly Marseilles was startled by the report of an unlooked for apparition, a formida-ble apparition which carries terror in every age, to all countries, which always moves about accompanied by dismay and death, riding in triumph over heaps of victims. A ship from Sidon had brought the plague. This was the eighteenth time, since the days of Julius Cæsar, that it visited Marseilles. At the fearful tidings, the noble, the rich, the magistrates, all fled be-fore the contagion. The lazaretto was without attendants, the hospitals without wardens, the tribunals without judges, the revenue without collectors. The city was deprived of pur-veyors, of police, of indispensable laborers. The tide of emi-gration was checked only when the Parliament of Provence drew a line, including Marseilles and its vicinity, pronouncing sentence of death upon all who should cross the boundary And the parliament forthwith took to flight, thus first violating the law it prescribed to others. But the desolate city still had its bishop left. When urged to follow the example of the magistrates, " God forbid," he replied, " that I should for-sake the people to whom I am bound to be a father! I owe them my care and my life, since I am their pastor." We bor-row from the account of the generous prelate some particulars of the scenes of horror amid which he moved during the two years that the plague ravaged the fated city. " All our public squares, all our streets," says he, " were piled up with great heaps of dead bodies, left unburied often two or three whole weeks, in many parts of the city, affording food for famished dogs. The fear of contagion soon seized all minds; every natural sentiment yielding to the instinct of self-preservation,

nearly all the sick were pitilessly turned out of their houses, children by their own parents, and parents by their children, and they were left, almost without help, amid the corpses which had changed the streets into infectious hospitals and fearful cemeteries.   The inhabitants, sinking under fear and horror, vainly took the precaution to shut themselves up in their houses, or to seek their safety and preservation in the country ; the plague followed them even there.   Then, amid the harrowing pain which filled my heart, I had the unspeakable consolation to see the greater part of the secular and regular clergy of the city and country hastening with emulous zeal to the relief of our plague-stricken brethren.   The most impetuous rivers were but a weak obstacle to the zeal of some of the religious of Provence, who, finding every avenue closed, fearlessly swam the rapid streams to come to my help and end their days in the practice of the most heroic charity   Their memory should be handed down as an example to the most remote posterity "   Belzunce himself was worthy to lead that band of heroes and of martyrs. All his attendants were carried off in the beginning ; alone, poor, because he has given all, always on foot, the early dawn finds him in the dark and infected dens of misery, night comes down upon him amid the heaps of dead in the public places ; he slakes their thirst, he consoles them like a father, exhorts them like an apostle, and bends over their diseased forms to catch the last dying confession.   Europe learned the heroic bearing of Belzunce with a cry of admiration.   Clement XI., in two special briefs, congratulated him on his devoted charity, granted a plenary indulgence to all those of his flock stricken down by the plague, as well as to all those who ministered to them, and announced that he had shipped him about two thousand bushels of corn, at the expense of the Roman Church. The Pope, in fact, dispatched three ships loaded with wheat ; one was wrecked, the other two were taken by African corsairs.   But when these barbarians learned whence they came and for what purpose they were designed, seized with a feeling of reverence, they faithfully sent them to the unfortu-

nate city On the 1st of November, 1720, Belzunce consecrated his diocese to the adorable Heart of Jesus, in order to
touch the Saviour of the world with pity for his desolated flock.
The sound of all the bells gave notice, early in the morning, of
this august ceremony An altar was raised at the end of the
Cours, the principal street of Marseilles. The holy bishop,
attended by the scanty remnant of his clergy, barefooted
and bareheaded, with a rope about his neck and a crucifix in
his hands, walked in procession to the place. The sight drew
tears from every eye. Belzunce made a most touching discourse,
broken at every moment by the sobs of both the speaker and
the hearers. Then followed the act of reparation and the con
secration of the diocese to the Heart of Jesus; the ceremony
was closed by the Holy Sacrifice of the Mass. The people,
prostrate in that immense square, and in the streets from which
a view could be had of the altar, were bathed in tears, and
joined their petitions to those of their pastor, in the firm
confidence that Heaven would now hear them with favor. Nor
was their hope vain; from that day of benediction the plague
began to disappear, and Marseilles seemed to revive. Louis
XV afterward named Belzunce to the peerage and bishopric
of Laon, and to the archbishopric of Bordeaux; but the conduct
of the saintly prelate was of that kind for which earth has no
fitting reward. He refused both dignities, to remain with his
beloved flock at Marseilles. Popes Clement XI., Benedict
XIII., Clement XII., and Benedict XIV loaded him with marks
of esteem and affection; Clement XII. honored him with the
pallium.

38. Meanwhile Clement XI. had closed his Pontificate, one
of the longest, stormiest and most glorious in the history of the
Church (March 19, A. D. 1721). Jansenism has vainly done
its best to dim the aureola of glory which encircles the name of
the illustrious Pontiff. The Lutheran city of Nuremberg struck
medals in his honor; and the Pacha of Egypt, on hearing of
his death, declared that he could have wished the glory of the
Koran such a chief as Clement XI.

39. We have been compelled, in order to give proper attention to the great events which marked the decline of the seventeenth and the opening of the eighteenth century, to pass
lightly over the biographies of the saints and learned doctors
who consoled the Church in her struggles against heresy within
and enemies without. The Blessed Cardinal Barbadigo, bishop
of Padua; B. Francis de Posadas, of St. Domingo; B. Nicholas
de Longobardi, of the Order of St. Francis of Paula; St. Francis
Hieronymo, and the two Frs. Segneri, of the Society of Jesus;
St. Joseph of Cupertino; BB. Bernard de Corleone, d'Offida,
Bonaventura de Potenza, Thomas de Cora, Pacifico de San
Severino, and St. Veronica Giulani, all of the Order of St. Francis of Assissium; B. Joseph Oriol, a priest of Barcelona; B.
Sebastian Valafré, a priest of Savoy—presented, in every rank
and condition of life, the high example of those virtues of which
the Roman Church has ever been the model and the mother.
France admired the austere life of the Abbé de Rancé, the
reformer of La Trappe. A host of scholars, theologians and
philosophers, such as Bianchini, Fontanini, Vignole, Laderchi,
Ughelli, Coleti, Fabretti, Zacagni, Cardinals Ciampini and Quirini,
the Benedictines Banduri, Magliabecchi, in Italy; Fathers Sir-
mond, Petau, Labbe, De Marca, Morin and Lecointe; Combefis,
a Dominican; Mabillon, Lenain de Tillemont, d'Acheri, Benedictines; Leo Allatius and Thomasin, the Oratorian—proved
that the Church was as truly the queen of science as of virtue;
and this testimony is borne in her favor by the illustrious
Newton, who lacked only the true faith to make him the
greatest man of that brilliant age. The Venerable John Baptist de la Salle, a canon of Rheims, founded, in 1681, the
institute of the Christian Schools, for poor children, which still
continues through succeeding ages to display the same modest
devotedness and heroic charity. The Church, like her Divine
Founder, always went about *doing good.*

§ III. PONTIFICATE OF INNOCENT XIII. (May 15, A. D. 1721–
March 7, 1724).

40. The Constitutions for the election of the Pope prescribe
that, to make the election lawful, all the absent cardinals must
have been summoned, even such cardinals as may have been
excommunicated; the Cardinals de Noailles and Alberoni were
accordingly invited to attend the conclave; the former excused
himself on the plea of his advanced age; Alberoni, who, after
ruling Spain as prime minister of Philip V., had fallen into disgrace and retired to Parma, answered the call of his colleagues.
Fifty cardinals had met; when the name of Cardinal Paolucci
was pronounced, by those who were counting the ballots, as
having received a great number of votes, Cardinal Althan,
minister of the emperor of Germany, Charles VI., to the great
astonishment of the Sacred College, rose up, and, in his master's name, pronounced exclusion against Paolucci. With
admirable modesty and humility, Cardinal Paolucci asked to be
heard, and praised the justice of the prince who, knowing his
incapacity, excluded him from the Pontificate, of which he
declared himself unworthy. Meanwhile the examiners continued to count the ballots, and three votes were wanting to
make the required two-thirds in favor of Paolucci. "Most
assuredly," says Ottieri, "had the cardinal received the required
number of votes, he would have been proclaimed, for the exclusions pronounced by the courts of Austria, France and
Spain are admitted, not as a definitive compact, but by way
of *prudent consideration*, in order to avoid a schism in the
Church, in case the princes should refuse to acknowledge a
Pope whose election had been displeasing to them." This
incident naturally brought the question of exclusions before the
Sacred College. Some writers assert that the privilege of exclusion enjoyed, in the conclaves, by the three courts of Vienna,
Paris and Madrid, took its rise in the Council of St. John Late-
ran, held by Pope Nicholas II. in 1059. But the question

debated in that council was the coronation of the Sovereign Pontiffs, for which the emperor's consent was necessary, and not their election.   The right of exclusion which we have just seen exercised in the name of Austria, against Cardinal Paolucci, dated no farther back than one century   It sprung, as Ottieri perfectly expressed it, from a kind of provident connivance, from a prudent deference, which would not have the Sovereign Pontiff personally disagreeable to the great Catholic powers, for the Pope is the Father and Pastor of them all.   There have been nearly thirty schisms, all occasioned and fomented by the spirit of distrust existing between the Pontiffs and the secular rulers It is proper, then, to have some regard for the repugnances of certain courts; otherwise the peace of the Church is jeoparded, the Pontiff is deprived of the respect and friendship of the most powerful princes.   Such were the reasons alleged in 1644, by the learned Cardinal de Lugo, in favor of maintaining the exclusions.   The conclave of 1721 respected the considerations; it expressed to Paolucci its deep and sincere regret, and on the 15th of May, A. D. 1721, elected Cardinal Conti, who took the name of Innocent XIII.

41. The house of Conti had already given to the Church seven Popes, among whom were St. Leo the Great, St. Gregory the Great, Innocent III., Gregory IX., and Alexander III. The new Pontiff gave promise of walking in their glorious footsteps.   But the shortness of his reign did not allow the realization of the hopes excited by his election.   He did, however, immortalize his name by the virtues which placed him in benediction among the Roman people.   In his desire to settle the Jansenist controversy in France, he addressed two briefs respectively to Louis XV., and to the Regent, assuring them that the only possible means of reconciliation was a frank and sincere submission, without reserve or equivocation.   He complained of the difficulty experienced in bringing the opposing prelates to recall their appeal, earnestly inveighed against a letter written to him by some among them, and declared that " to intrust the lambs of the flock to such shepherds was to

injure those lambs rather than to give them guardians." In fine, to meet the objections of different parties, he repeated that the constitution *Unigenitus* condemned only errors, and attacked neither the sentiments of the Fathers nor the opinions of the schools. The regent caused these briefs to be printed at the Louvre; but he did not succeed in obtaining the submission of Cardinal de Noailles and the four appealing prelates. The cabinet of Versailles was then soliciting from the Roman Court the appointment of Dubois to the cardinalate. Dubois was the son of an apothecary of Brives-la-Gaillarde, in which town he was born, in 1656. Having acted as preceptor to the Duke of Chartres, son of the Duke of Orleans, brother of Louis XIV., he obtained several rich benefices through the influence of his pupil. At the death of Louis XIV., Dubois, by his servile compliance, won the confidence of the regent, and became successively, Councillor of State, Secretary of the cabinet, and Envoy extraordinary to England (A. D. 1715), to watch over the league of Great Britain and Holland with France. He had negotiated a peace at Hanover and the Hague. The regent appointed him minister of State (1718), and archbishop of Cambrai (1720). In these various diplomatic missions, Dubois, it must be confessed, displayed a degree of talent which could hardly have been expected in a man of his corrupt morals. The Regent now redoubled his urgent entreaties to Innocent XIII. to raise his favorite to the purple, and had them seconded by those of *nearly all the sovereigns.* The Pope made a long resistance, but the importunities were renewed; at length he yielded, and the appointment, which so much astonishes us at this time, was then what might be termed a European appointment Massillon consented to take part in the consecration of the new prelate. With the bulls of canonical institution, Pope Innocent sent him a brief, exhorting him thenceforth to live more conformably to his high dignity Dubois promised; God grant he may have kept his word!—Meanwhile, the Turks were preparing for war and revenge. Villena, Grand Master of Malta, fearing that the Mussulman attack might fall upon that island, asked help from the Pope. Innocent XIII. immediately sent all the means at his command. The cardinals contributed according to their respective fortunes. Cardinal Salerno, a Jesuit, was asked what he had to offer. " I have neither lands nor income," he replied, " but King Augustus, of Poland, has just sent me a cross set with gems, that I will cheerfully sacrifice." It was sold for a thousand Spanish *doppie,* and this sum was added to the other voluntary contributions, amounting to a hundred thousand Roman crowns.

42. The strength of the Pope was failing from day to day He had been compelled, for the benefit of his shattered health, to spend some time at a neighboring country seat. On his return to his capital, the nobility and the people came forth spontaneously to meet him. It was like the return of a beloved father to the bosom of his family The multitude followed him even into the apartments of the palace, where he thus gave an *audience of love and affection* to nearly the whole city of Rome. The Pontifical guards lowered their arms and gave free entrance to the throng, in which nobles, magistrates, porters and sailors, pressed forward in one indiscriminate mass. Innocent XIII. deserved these marks of love and veneration. " He was," says Lalande, " the best sovereign known to this day The Romans have continued for many years to proclaim his praise and to deplore the short duration of his Pontificate. Under his reign universal plenty prevailed, the police were efficient, the nobles and the people were equally happy " He died on the 7th of March, A. D. 1724, at the age of sixty-nine years. When urged, in his last moments, to fill the vacancies in the Sacred College, " I am no longer of this world," he replied, and with these words he expired.

CHAPTER IV.

§ I. Pontificate of Benedict XIII. (May 29, a. d. 1724—February 21 1730).

1. Sketch of the progress of Jansenism by Fénelon.—2. Council held by Benedict XIII. in the church of St. John Lateran.—3. Schism of Holland. —4. Council of Embrun. Deposition of Soanen, bishop of Senez.—5. Sub mission of Cardinal de Noailles, archbishop of Paris.—6. M. de Vintimille, archbishop of Paris. Submission of the Sorbonne.—7. The parliament forbids the celebration of the feast of St. Gregory VII.—8. Liturgical revolution in France.—9. Authors of the different particular liturgies of France.—10. Death of Benedict XIII.

§ II. Pontificate of Clement XII. (July 12, a. d. 1730—February 6, 1740).

11. Election of Clement XII. Case of Cardinal Coscia.—12. Affair of Bichi, Apostolic Nuncio at Lisbon.—13. Death of the Regent. Ministry of Cardinal Fleury. War for Stanislaus Leczinski, king of Poland. Peace of Vienna. —14. Conduct of Clement XII. during the war. Corsica and the republic of San Marino place themselves under the protection of the Pope. Cardinal Alberoni is made Legate of the Holy See, in the Romagna.—15. The deacon Paris. Convulsions in the cemetery of St. Médard.—16. Canonization of St. Vincent de Paul.—17. View of the conduct of the parliament respecting the Gallican Liberties.—18. Refusal of the Sacraments.—19. Voltaire. His *Lettres philosophiques* or *Lettres sur les Anglais*, condemned by the theological Faculty of Paris.—21. Freemasonry condemned by Clement XII.—22. The rules of the Maronite and Melchite religious approved by the Pope. Joseph Assemani.—23. Death of Clement XII. Success of the Turks against the Austrians.

§ III. Pontificate of Benedict XIV (August 17, a. d. 1740—May 3, 1758).

24. Antecedents and election of Benedict XIV.—25. The succession to Charles VI., emperor of Germany.—26. Frederick the Great, king of Prussia.— 27. Alliance between France and Prussia, to lower the house of Austria.— 28. Maria Theresa defended by the devotedness of the Hungarian nobles. Reverses of the French arms. Death of Cardinal Fleury.—29. Illness and

death of Louis XV. Successes of the French arms. Treaty of Aix-la
Chapelle. Accession of the house of Lorraine to the imperial throne of
Austria.—30. Conduct of Benedict XIV during the continuance of the
hostilities.—31. Charles Edward.—32. Scandalous conduct of the parliament of Paris in the affair of the refusal of the Sacraments. *Representation*
of the bishops to Louis XV.—33. Banishment of the parliament of Paris.
—34. Recall of the parliament. Fresh acts of violence. Pastoral letter of
Christopher de Beaumont, archbishop of Paris. Brief of Benedict XIV.
Declaration of Louis XV. against the attempts of the parliament.—35
Damiens.—36. Death of Benedict XIV. Analysis of his Bullary. Treatise
on the *Diocesan Synod.*

§ I. PONTIFICATE OF BENEDICT XIII. (May 29, A. D. 1724— February 21, 1730).

1. IN a private memorial to Clement XI. (A. D. 1705), Fénelon thus spoke: " The experience of sixty-five years clearly
proves that the Jansenist sect is not to be brought back by
gentle means Unless vigorous measures are used, there is no
danger that the Church may not fear. Never, not even in the
hour of its most rapid growth, had Calvinism so many partisans
and defenders. Belgium and Holland are deeply infected with
the poison of the new errors. The Duke of Medina-Cœli favors
the introduction of Jansenistic works into Naples. The doctrine
has reached as far as Spain; even in Rome, Cardinal Casanate
is suspected of having some connection with the sect. In France,
Cardinal de Noailles is so completely in the power of its leaders
that, for the past ten years, it has been impossible to free him
from their snares. Many bishops follow his example; there
are still some who would confirm the rest in the right way, if
the multitude were not drawn into the wrong path by these
leaders. What shall I say of the religious orders? Nearly all
the Dominicans go beyond the limits assigned by the Congregation *De Auxiliis*, and conspire with the Jansenists to maintain
the theory of compulsory grace. The Barefooted Carmelites
obstinately preach the same doctrine. The Augustinians,
misled by the illustrious name of their holy patron, insensibly
adhere to the Augustin of Ypres. The regular canons of St
Geneviève are animated by the same sentiment. The Benedic-

tines of St. Maur and of St. Vannes unite all their efforts to
secure the triumph of Jansenism. The Premonstrants have
so openly displayed their partisanship, that, fiom the very
beginning of the contest, they have been known in Belgium as
the *White Jansenists*. The Oratorians of M. de Bérulle inculcate
the same errors, not only by their dogmatic writings, as in the
theology of Juénin, but by academic theses and in the spiritual
direction of the ladies of the Court. The most learned among
the Belgian Capuchins have taken so little trouble to hide their
real sentiments, that the superiors have been obliged to remove
the lectors and guardians from their charges. The Recollets
present the same example. Even the missionaries of St. Lazarus, so far removed from that faction, while they remembered
the teachings of St. Vincent de Paul, are becoming cold and
yielding, and seem to incline by degrees in the same direction.
I know one seminary in which the professor is spreading the
poison of Jansenism. The members of St. Sulpice alone have
the courage to battle against the contagion. The cardinal
archbishop accordingly esteems and loves them very little."
What a fearful picture! The desolated and tottering Church
found her enemies in her own children, who did not blush to
rend the bosom of their common mother. No more eloquent
proof could be presented than these lines of the illustrious archbishop of Cambrai, of the necessity of a strong, unchangeable,
infallible authority, to recall the wandering, to repress scandals,
repair errors, and confirm all the brethren in unity and faith.

2. Cardinal Orsini, on ascending the throne of St. Peter, as
Benedict XIII. (May 29, A. D. 1724), gave his first care to the
dangerous progress of Jansenism. He convoked a council for
the following year, at Rome. This assemblage coincided with
the period of the Jubilee, and held its sessions in the church
of St. John Lateran. The Pope made an opening address, in
which he dwelt particularly upon the motives which should induce the Popes and bishops to hold frequent synods, and upon
the benefits accruing from them to the Church. The council
held seven sessions. The principal ordinances concern the

duties of bishops and other pastors, Christian education, residence, ordinations, the holding of synods, the good example
which pastors should give to their people, the solemnizing of
feasts, and various other matters of ecclesiastical discipline.
At the head of these decrees the council placed two more important ones : the first required bishops, beneficiaries, preachers and
confessors, before entering upon their respective charges, to subscribe the profession of faith of Pius IV ; the second was
worded as follows : " As, to maintain the profession of Catholic
faith in its purity and integrity, it is very necessary that all
the faithful most carefully avoid and sincerely detest the errors
which, in these latter times, have risen against the same faith,
all bishops and pastors of souls shall take the most exact care.
as heretofore, that the constitution *Unigenitus*, promulgated by
Clement XI., of holy memory, and which we recognize as the
rule of our faith, be observed and executed by all, of what rank
or condition soever, with the unreserved obedience due to it.
If, then, they learn that any one (of their own diocese, or province, or even a stranger), residing within their jurisdiction, does
not receive this constitution, let them not fail to take measures
against him, according to their power and the extent of their
pastoral jurisdiction. And if they deem a more efficient remedy
necessary, let them denounce these stubborn and rebellious
children of the Church to the Apostolic See. Let them also
institute a strict search for the works published against this
constitution, or which support the false doctrines condemned
by it, and let them obtain possession of them, that they may
afterward be referred to Us and to the Holy See."

3. The revolt of Jansenism was multiplying scandals. On
the 27th of April, A. D. 1723, seven Dutch priests, on their own
authority, appointed a Jansenistic archbishop at Utrecht. The
see had been vacant since the death of Codde (1710), who was
deposed by the Holy See because of his connection with the
sect. The Apostolic vicars afterward sent to Holland were
forced to abandon their mission ; the spiritual government of
the country was intrusted to the nuncios of Cologne and

Brussels.   But the partisans of Codde and of Quesnel had never
been willing to submit to their authority, and acknowledged
only the vicars general appointed by Codde, or by the Chapter
of Utrecht, which claimed the right of governing during the
vacancy of the See.   It appointed pastors, gave dimissorial
letters, and exercised all the other functions of ecclesiastical
administration.   The Roman Court, on the contrary, judged that
the Chapter of Utrecht having ceased to exist since the change
of religion in Holland, the priests who assumed the title of
canons of Utrecht could not be considered as forming the metropolitan Chapter.   How could seven priests, followed by hardly
sixty others, represent the clergy of Holland, while the sound
majority remained true to the authority of the Holy See?   A
schism was therefore established in Holland, and held out against
all the efforts of the Sovereign Pontiffs, until the end of the
eighteenth century   The United Provinces thenceforth became
the refuge for all Jansenists whose position had become too
dangerous in France.

4. The appealing bishops had not withdrawn their opposition to the Apostolic Constitutions.   Soanen, bishop of Senez,
was the most obstinate of all.   The archbishop of Embrun,
Pierre de Tencin, as metropolitan of Senez, called a council in
his archiepiscopal city, to try his rebellious suffragan.   The
council consisted of the bishops of the province, who were
joined by the Archbishops of Lyons, Vienne, Besançon, Aix,
and Arles.   According to the last Apostolic ordinance published by Benedict XIII. in the Council of St. John Lateran,
all ecclesiastical superiors were charged to follow up the Jansenists within their respective provinces or dioceses.   Soanen
refused to submit to the authority of his metropolitan, and left
the council.   The Fathers at first endeavored to recall him by
friendly entreaties and canonical warnings; but in vain.   At
length, on the 20th of September, A. D. 1727, when the promoter had stated his conclusions, the doctrines of the bishop of
Senez were condemned as rash, scandalous, seditious, injurious
to the Church, to the bishops, and to the royal authority, schis-

matical, full of errors, heretical, and tending to foment heresies. It was decreed that Soanen should be suspended from all ecclesiastical power and jurisdiction, from the exercise of his functions as bishop and priest. The council provided for the government of the diocese, by appointing a vicar-general charged to govern that church, and to secure respect for the constitutions of the Holy See. The sentence was confirmed by the suffrage of a great number of bishops, who, at the same time, issued a special decree in support of the bull *Unigenitus*. The decisions of the council were ratified by Benedict XIII., and subscribed by thirty-one French bishops; but Soanen was supported by fifty advocates of the parliament, a host of pamphleteers, and twelve Jansenist bishops, with Cardinal de Noailles, archbishop of Paris, at their head.

5. This was one more scandal added to all those into which that prelate, through a mistaken idea of honor and a lamentable obstinacy, had allowed himself to be drawn since the appearance of the famous "Ecclesiastical Problem." And yet Cardinal de Noailles was, in disposition, gentle, pious, and gifted with most estimable qualities. A want of discernment in the choice of those to whom he gave his confidence, and a too great readiness to receive the impressions of others, caused all his mistakes. So true it is, that weakness in rulers is the most dangerous of all defects. Men of sound mind interested themselves in the abnormal position into which the Archbishop of Paris had thus drawn himself; every thing was done to bring him to retract his unpardonable conduct. The Pope secured the efforts of devoted men about the person of the Cardinal, while the Jansenists, on the other hand, left nothing undone to keep in their ranks a prelate whose name was to them a safeguard and a buckler. When the cardinal consented to sign the letters written to the king against the Council of Embrun, as well as a protest to the parliament against the registering of any edict in favor of the council, the sect, through all its organs, praised the archbishop's courage to the skies, and placed his name among those of the Fathers of the Church. The cardinal enjoyed these scandalous

honors for a while, but the hour of repentance came. The
Spirit of God, more powerful than all intrigues, touched his
heart and enlightened his understanding.   He saw the trouble,
the rebellion and disorder which were desolating the Church,
since the bishops openly resisted the decrees of the Holy See.
He shed tears of grief over actions of which he would have
wished to blot out the memory.   From that moment his resolve
was fixed, irrevocable.   On the 19th of May, A. D. 1728, he wrote,
with his own hand, a retraction of his protest against the Council of Embrun, and made the solicitor-general sign his recantation.   On the 19th of July, he wrote to the Pope the most
touching apology : " Warned," said he, " by my gray hairs, of
the account I must soon give at the tribunal of God, I throw
myself at the feet of Your Holiness, entreating you to open to
me the arms of your mercy   I submit to the decisions of the
Holy See, and sincerely receive the bull *Unigenitus*."   It remained to make the world acquainted with the glorious retraction, and the cardinal did not falter in the discharge of this
duty   On the 11th of October, he sent to every part of his
diocese a pastoral letter which filled the true friends of the
Church with joy, but carried mourning and despair into the
Jansenist camp.   "We condemn," said the aged and noble
prelate, " the book of ' Moral Reflections,' in the same terms as
those used by the Pope against that work ; and we declare it
unlawful to hold other sentiments than those defined by the
bull *Unigenitus*.   Therefore we forbid any one to have or to
read the book of ' Moral Reflections,' as well as all other works
written in its support; we revoke, in mind and heart, our pastoral instruction of 1719, and all that may have been published
under our name, contrary to this present ordinance."   The cardinal was ending where he should have begun ; but the generous
courage of such a recantation compensated for the long delay.
The Jansenists revenged themselves by publishing various acts
coming, as they alleged, from the cardinal, and in which he was
made to declare that he still held to his appeal.   But the prelate rejected the authorship of these apocryphal documents, in

a circular to the bishops of France, and in a letter to the Pope, accompanied by his pastoral. Benedict XIII., in a solemn consistory, publicly testified to the cardinals the joy he felt at the submission of the Archbishop of Paris, to whom he dispatched the brief *Sapientissimum consilium*, highly commending his conduct, and granting the Jubilee which he asked for his diocese, excluding from that spiritual favor those who had opposed the bull *Unigenitus*.

6. The retraction of the archbishop was not productive of as much good as his resistance had done harm. The Jansenist bishops did not follow the cardinal in his obedience as they had in his opposition. The bishops of Montpellier, Auxerre, Troyes, Metz, Mâcon, Tréguier, Pamiers, and Castres, continued to defend a sect so often anathematized. But, however deplorable this conduct, what is the moral force of that limited number of prelates against the Pope, supported by the whole episcopal body? M. de Vintimille, archbishop of Aix, succeeded Cardinal de Noailles in the See of Paris in 1729. He found himself at the head of a diocese which his predecessor's weakness and religious bias had filled with confusion, troubles and discord. His patience, gentleness and moderation triumphed over most of his opponents. The Metropolitan Chapter, by a solemn act, conformed to the pastoral letter of Cardinal de Noailles; at the same time, twenty-eight parish priests of Paris wrote to M. De Vintimille, insolently complaining of his conduct, and acquainting him with the fears which they entertained, as they said, on his behalf. The archbishop took no notice of the insult, but on the 29th of September, A. D. 1729, published his ordinance and pastoral instruction in regard to the bull *Unigenitus*. He assured the faithful that the bull, far from injuring the purity of faith and morals, and *striking at the Gallican liberties*, on the contrary, condemned capital errors in dogma. He pointed out the sad effects of resistance to that law of the Church—the docility of the faithful destroyed, the Vicar of Jesus Christ calumniated, the authority of the bishops slighted, all subordination swept away, and the appearance of a flood of

seditious writings calculated to sow abroad the spirit of hatred, revolt and independence; but too many of these willingly misguided wanderers remained deaf to the prelate's warning. On the 8th of November, 1729, the theological Faculty of Paris declared its definitive acceptance of the bull *Unigenitus*, decreed that all the Doctors who refused to sign it should be excluded from their body, and that whatever had been already done against the authority of that constitution deserved to be buried in the deepest silence and in endless oblivion. The Doctors of the provinces conformed to this decree, which received seven hundred and seven signatures; thirty-nine of these were of bishops.

7   This return warranted cheering hopes, but other events of a character equally hostile to the Holy See soon made their appearance, showing that the leaven of Gallicanism and the poison of Jansenism had not yet ceased to work in France. Benedict had just published the Office of St. Gregory VII., and made it obligatory for the whole Church. The parliament of Paris thought itself justified in overruling the Pontifical decree, in virtue of the abuse existing in France, which made the publication of the Sovereign Pontiff's decrees depend upon their previous registration by the parliament. The Doctors and civilians of France accordingly issued a decree prohibiting the Office of St. Gregory VII., and forbidding all the ecclesiastics of the kingdom to recite it. The parliaments of Metz, Toulouse, and Rheims imitated that of Paris, declared that Gregory VII. was not a saint, and forbade the celebration of his feast. The bishops of Verdun, Montpellier, Troyes, Auxerre, and Castres issued pastoral letters, written in the same spirit as the parliamentary decrees. It will not be necessary to explain the motives on which the Gallican magistrates and bishops thus assailed the memory of one of the greatest Popes that ever ruled the Church. The whole life of St. Gregory VII. was one unceasing struggle with the temporal powers in armed revolt against the Holy See. The *so-called Gallican liberties* did not grant to the Pope the liberty of upholding the rights of the Apostolic chair. It seems to us that, in this case, the

conduct of the parliaments was not only scandalous but ab urd. Benedict XIII. was, with reason, astonished to learn that men of law, supported by a few bishops, dared to forbid the celebration of the feast of a saint recognized by the Church; he issued a brief annulling the parliamentary decrees and the charges of the Jansenist bishops. The parliament of Paris suppressed the Papal brief; but it could not suppress the immutable, infallible authority, always respected by every true Catholic, of that Roman Church which has received the deposit of faith, the rule of belief, the guidance of souls, the government of the spiritual world.

8. The encroachments of Gallicanism upon the field of liturgy was not to end here. Notwithstanding the regulations of the Council of Trent, and the clear, formal and explicit constitution of St. Pius V., the French bishops assumed the power of giving to their dioceses new missals, new offices, and new breviaries. Unity in prayer, that imposing and magnificent harmony of the universal Church, sending up to God, on the same day, at the same hour, from every quarter of the globe, the same vows, in the same words and in the same tongue; that form of prayer which should be, according to the Holy Fathers, the rule of faith—all would now be destroyed. The heretics of every age had striven to alter the liturgy of the Church of God, as a means to insinuate their errors. The Jansenists could not neglect this system of proselytism; they were the real authors of the liturgical revolution, under the cloak of the archbishops of Paris—Harlai, Noailles, and even Vintimille, who did not see at once the full import of the new tendencies. It was the Popes who formed the whole divine office; they made its rubrics, regulated its ceremonials, composed its prayers, reformed the calendar, compiled the martyrology; they have appointed a special Congregation of Cardinals to explain all its difficulties. St. Damasus caused the psalms to be sung in choir by day and by night, with the addition to each one of the doxology or *Gloria Patri.* St. Gregory the Great composed prayers, antiphons, homilies, regulated the office in all its parts, and

gave his name to the grave, imposing and majestic Gregorian chant. Pope St. Stephen, during his sojourn in France, whither he had come to seek assistance against the Lombards, reformed the office and the chant, which had undergone some changes in that country Pepin and Charlemagne, to draw closer the ties which bound their subjects to the Roman Church, caused the Roman office and chant to be received throughout their kingdom, and, thus restored by their efforts, it subsisted during a thousand years, until the invasion of Jansenism. The new liturgical reforms which followed the labors of the Council of Trent and of St. Pius V were received in France as in the other Catholic countries. Such had been the perpetual succession of pious labors and holy efforts of the Church, ever living and ever animated by the Holy Ghost, to regulate the prayers which she addresses to God the Father, through our Lord Jesus Christ. In the eighteenth century, Jansenism made a great effort to destroy in France this unity of prayer and adoration, and, by perfidious insinuations, skilfully inserted into the public office, to turn away the faithful from the frequentation of the sacraments, from their devotion to the Blessed Virgin and the saints, from confidence in the Divine goodness, to darken the holy joy of the children of God by the gloomy terrors of the doctrines of insufficient grace.

9. The first defacers of the Catholic liturgy were Nicholas Letourneux and the Jansenist Benedictine, Claude de Vert, whose joint labors manufactured the new Breviary of Cluny, the boldest and the most hostile to the Sovereign Pontiff, which equally degrades the worship of the Blessed Virgin and the authority of the Apostolic See. The Order of Cluny, once so true to the head of the Church, thus disowned the brightest pages in its annals. After them the Jansenist Foinard propagated liturgical novelties, and drew up for them a kind of creed in his well-known work, "Plan of a new Breviary, in which the Divine office is to be especially made up from the pages of Holy Writ."* The very title, " *New* Breviary," is a sufficent

---

* " *Projet d'un nouveau Bréviaire dans lequel l'office divin serait particulièrement composé de l'Écriture Sainte* "

evidence that antiquity, tradition, authority, the living prayer of the Church, were contemptuously set aside to make way for the views of a private individual, who, like all other sectaries, would cut up texts, isolate or combine them to suit his own fancy, in order to turn them from their true meaning, and wrest them to the support of his errors. The idea of Foinard was realized in the Paris Breviary, published by Cardinal de Noailles, and composed by the Jansenist Duguet. Vigier, Mésenguy and Coffin, carried out the work of Duguet with even greater boldness; they compiled a new Paris Breviary, published by Charles De Vintimille, which was received with so much dissatisfaction that, in order to insure its adoption, it was necessary to make repeated corrections of errors not concealed with sufficient care. Orleans and Nevers had their particular Breviaries (A. D. 1730), composed by the Jansenist Lebrun Desmarets, who had been condemned to the galleys, and died impenitent. Charles De Coislin, bishop of Metz; Caylus, bishop of Auxerre; Bossuet, the unworthy bishop of Troyes; Colbert, bishop of Montpellier; and Montazet, bishop of Lyons, forcibly introduced the same novelties into their respective dioceses. This revolution was prolonged until 1770. Charles Loménie De Brienne, whose name was to be known in a connection so unfortunate for the Church, was the last bishop in France to bring a new liturgy into his diocese. The religious orders, forgetting their traditional respect for the sacred customs of the past, allowed themselves to be drawn into the current of innovation. The congregation of St. Vannes adopted a Breviary and a Missal, modeled upon the Parisian. The order of Prémontré laid aside its Roman Breviary to take up a new one, compiled by one of the monks of the order, who afterward took the oath of the *civil constitution* of the clergy The Congregation of St. Maur also had a particular Breviary, drawn up by an apostate Benedictine, Nicholas Foulon. " All these new Breviaries," says the Abbé Bertrand de la Tour, " profess to follow the pattern set in the Paris Breviary; *it is the centre of Gallican unity,* instead of Rome, which name is now hardly ever uttered, and which is *only the centre of Catholic unity*. The Pope may reign in the Vatican, but here his laws, his censures, his rubrics, his prayers, his Breviary, his Missal, and his Ritual will be despised. Thus sapped in her very foundations, shaken at every joint, France is astonished to find herself almost schismatical."

10. Meanwhile, Benedict XIII. was closing his Pontificate. He died on the 22d of February, A. D. 1730, at the age of eighty-one years. Such was his virtue, says the learned Muratori, that he was universally looked upon as a saint. In his incomparable humility, he esteemed his title of Theatine religious far beyond all the glory and majesty of the Sovereign Pontificate. To a perfect disinterestedness he joined a boundless tenderness for the poor. He was often known to embrace them, seeing in them Him whose Vicar he was on earth. His penances and fasts were extraordinary; his mildness proverbial, and Rome still quotes the expression of Benedict XIV: "I love the modesty of Benedict XIII., that gentle Pontiff, who caused his own coach to draw back in the very midst of Rome, to avoid a difficulty with a Roman noble." There is but one serious charge to be made against Benedict XIII.—he was not always careful enough to keep his ministers within the strict limits of duty and justice. He had given his confidence to Cardinal Coscia, who abused the Pontiff's goodness, and by his exactions drew upon himself the hatred of the Roman people.

§ II. Pontificate of Clement XII. (July 12, A. D. 1730— February 6, 1740).

11. Cardinal Corsini, a member of one of the first families of Florence, was almost unanimously elected to succeed Benedict XIII., and took the name of Clement XII. On the day after his coronation, the people crowded around the Vatican with cries of "Long live Pope Clement XII.! Justice upon the justice of the last minister!" Cardinal Coscia, against whom these cries were directed, had fled from Rome immedi-

ately after the death of Benedict XIII.; but the Sacred College had sent him a safe-conduct, that he might take his place in the conclave. Now the excited people seemed eager for his head. To appease the sedition, Clement XII. promised that a strict investigation should be made into the administration of all the officers who had abused the confidence of the late Pope. Cosria was first deprived of active and passive voice in the Congregations; a Pontifical decree required his presence in the Roman States until the end of his trial; and he was informed that he must give up all spiritual jurisdiction in his diocese of Beneventum. Coscia refused obedience, and a special Congregation was appointed to carry on the trial. The cardinal was condemned to refund to the treasury the sum of two hundred thousand Roman crowns, which he had fraudulently obtained during the term of his ministry. The cardinal asked the favor of not being imprisoned in the castle of St. Angelo; Clement generously granted it; but Coscia, fearful for the future, took advantage of his freedom to fly to Naples. His disobedience was punished by an interdict, and his property was sold for the benefit of the Apostolic Chamber, which he had so shamefully plundered.

12. These acts of rigorous justice announced a firm and vigilant Pontiff, who would never flinch from duty, however painful its performance. The court of Lisbon soon had occasion to learn this. The kings of Portugal began to claim that the nuncios sent to the court of Lisbon should enjoy the same privilege as those who were sent to the great powers; which consisted in promotion to the cardinalate at the end of their nunciature. The court of Lisbon was especially desirous to obtain this favor, as it would have been a more solemn recognition, on the part of the Sovereign Pontiffs, of the recent kingdom of Portugal. But the other European sovereigns opposed the pretensions of Lisbon; and Rome, always prudent, did not deem that the fitting time had yet come. John V of Portugal was a man of violent temper, and could brook no contradiction. He thought to gain by force what he had asked as a favor; accordingly, under the Pontificate of Benedict XIII.. he de-

manded the cardinal's hat for Bichi, then nuncio at Lisbon ; the request was not granted and Bichi was even recalled. But the king forbade him to quit the court, refused to receive the successor sent in his stead, openly broke with Rome, and forbade all his subjects, under the most severe penalties, to hold any communication with the Pontifical court. Such was the state of things at the accession of Clement XII. This Pope was nearly related to Bichi ; the King of Portugal hoped that this circumstance would facilitate an accommodation, and negotiations were opened with the new Pontiff. Clement XII. declared that the nuncio must at once withdraw from Lisbon. Obedience was now a necessity ; Bichi returned to Rome, was succeeded by the prelate already appointed ; and, later, the Pope, to show that firmness is always allied to gentleness in the heart of the Vicar of Jesus Christ, raised Bichi to the dignity of cardinal.

13. Meanwhile, important events had taken place in France. The regent, Philip of Orleans, died, the victim of his own unbridled passions (August 10, A. D. 1723), shortly after his unworthy minister, Cardinal Dubois. The young king, Louis XV., had been freed from wardship and crowned in the preceding year. After the brief ministry of the Duke of Bourbon, Louis intrusted the government of the kingdom, with the title of prime-minister, to his former preceptor, Cardinal Fleury, bishop of Fréjus. The cardinal had already reached the advanced age of seventy years, but he set vigorously to work to repair, by a mild and prudent administration, the scandals and disorders caused by the Regent and his court. The marriage of Louis XV with Mary Leczinski, daughter of Stanislaus, ex-king of Poland, placed upon the French throne the charms of virtue and amiable graces. But this reaction against the vices of the regency was not powerful enough to restore the lost morality of France. Philip of Orleans had surrounded himself with all that made open profession of license, libertinism, and impiety The court of the Regent corrupted society ; society corrupted the young king, virtue was but a name, duty a word, religion a bugbear, fit for the people ;

and gold, with all the pleasures it can buy, became the idol of France.   The accession of Cardinal Fleury to power was like a moment of rest between two storms.   He loved peace ; and peace was a necessity for France.   He allowed the kingdom to repair its losses, and to enrich itself by an extensive commerce, without attempting any innovation, treating the State as an immense and robust body that recuperates itself ; he lowered the taxes, fixed the value of the currency, and brought into the Court an example of exactness and economy   In a political point of view, this was a happy period for all nations, which forgot the past in a noble rivalry of commerce and art.   All was peace from Russia to Spain, when the death of Augustus II., king of Poland, who had dethroned Stanislaus Leczinski, the father-in-law of Louis XV., once more threw Europe into a state of war.   The Poles offered the crown to Stanislans, who was proclaimed king in the most lawful and solemn manner, by the Assembly of the Estates (September 12, A. D. 1733)   But the Emperor of Austria, Charles VI., managed another election, supported by his arms and by those of Russia, and another assembly of Polish lords offered the crown to the son of Augustus II. (October 5, 1733.)   Stanislaus repaired to Dantzic to support his claim in person.   He was worthy to wear a crown, and nothing, perhaps, better shows the defect of the elective system, than the sight of the best of kings, of that Stanislaus, whose name and virtue still live in the memory of grateful Lorraine, twice driven from Poland, which he would have made the happiest of nations.   The nobles who had elected Leczinski, now shamefully forsook his cause.   Ten thousand Russians, under the Count of Munich, besieged Dantzic ; Stanislaus, too weakly supported by France, was unable to hold out against them   The city was taken ; a price was set upon the head of the lawful king, and it was only after running the greatest risks in the disguise of a sailor, that he succeeded in escaping.   The French ministry would have been disgraced before all Europe, had it not avenged the insult received in Poland.   France joined Spain and Sardinia against Austria.

If Stanislaus could not be restored, he could be avenged. A French army marched into Germany, under Marshal Berwick, who was killed before Philipsburg. His loss alone was a sad reverse. The Duke of Noailles and the Marquis of Asfeld, his successors, took the city; this was a great exploit, especially as the enemy's forces were under the command of Prince Eugene. Another French army, sent into Italy, under Villars and the Duke of Savoy, took possession of Milan. The Marquis of Coigny, Villars' successor (1734), defeated the Count of Merci, in the brilliant actions of Parma and Guastalla, while Don Carlos, the son of Philip V., with the Duke of Montémar, the victor of Bitonto, expelled Visconti, viceroy of Naples for Charles VI., and made themselves masters of Sicily by taking Messina and Syracuse. The Emperor of Austria was but too glad to sign the terms of peace proposed by victorious France. Cardinal Fleury, who had the wisdom to prevent England and Holland from taking part in this war, was also able to bring it to a happy close without their intervention. By the " Treaty of Vienna " (October 3, 1735), Stanislaus received the government of Lorraine and made the happiness of that province during a reign of twenty-eight years;* Don Carlos was recognized as King of the Two Sicilies; the King of Sardinia received a portion of the Milanese, the other remaining in the hands of Charles VI.; in fine, Francis, Duke of Lorraine, who was dispossessed in favor of Stanislaus, received the expectancy of Tuscany, whose Grand Duke, the last of the Medici, was dying without heirs. The Treaty of Vienna was the masterpiece of Fleury's able and prudent policy

14. Amid these formidable military operations, the greater part of which had, as usual, been carried on in the Italian territory, the bearing of Clement XII. was that of a Pope; all his efforts were directed to one end—that of making the scourge of war as light as possible for the suffering people. The suc-

---

* It was agreed, in the terms of tho Treaty, that, at the death of Stanislaus, Lorraine and the duchy of Bar should pass to France   Cardinal Fleury thus secured to the crown one of its fairest and richest provinces.

:essive arrival and sojourn of the imperial and the Spanish
'orces loaded the inhabitants of Bologna, Ferrara, and Ravenna
with forced contributions. The Sovereign Pontiff indemnified
them out of his private purse. When the treaty of Vienna had
given the kingdom of the Two Sicilies to Don Carlos, Clement
conferred upon him the investiture of the Neapolitan States,
which depended upon the Holy See, and exerted all his influence to allay the feelings of discord and hatred secretly working in the midst of a people so often conquered, and by so many
different masters. The Papacy was always the refuge of oppressed nationalities, and the natural defender of every acquired
right. The Corsicans revolted against the tyranny of the
Genoese republic, expelled the governor imposed upon them,
and sent, as their deputy to Clement XII., Paul Otticoni, with
the mission to request the Pope to restore the Pontifical
authority in their island. Had the Holy See been possessed
of that ambitious and grasping policy so unjustly charged upon
it by the enemies of the Church, the Sovereign Pontiff would
have eagerly seized the occasion of regaining possession of
an island which had for several centuries formed part of the
patrimony of St. Peter, and had passed into the hands of the
Genoese only by a flagrant usurpation. Yet, spite of the titles
which justified the offer made by the Corsicans to Clement
XII., the Pope, far from accepting it, thought it more worthy
of him to offer himself as a mediator of peace. He accordingly
sent a brief to the Archbishop of Genoa, requesting him to
communicate his proposition to the Senate. It was rejected;
the Pontiff protested in vain against this display of haughtiness; he had the grief to see Corsica bend once more beneath a hated yoke. But he had at least the consolation of
having acted as became the true Father of all the faithful, whose
only ambition is to heal all dissensions, to appease all quarrels,
without ever seeking to make his own profit of any   Another
case of the same kind soon followed. At a distance of four
leagues from Rimini, and five from Urbino, stands the small
city of San Marino, whose inhabitants, together with those of

seven neighboring villages, constitute a little republic. This little State was for a long time under the protection of the dukes of Urbino; but that house having passed away about the middle of the seventeenth century, the republic of San Marino placed itself under the patronage of the Holy See, which thus acquired a kind of suzerainty over it. During the Pontificate of Clement XII. some of the inhabitants of San Marino complained of violent and arbitrary acts committed by some of the officers of the republic, and earnestly besought the Pontiff to receive them under the mild and beneficent government of the Roman Church. Receiving no answer to their petition, they applied to Cardinal Alberoni, who, after his disgrace in Spain, was happy to receive the appointment of Apostolic legate in the Romagna. The lust of power never dies in an ambitious heart. Alberoni communicated the request of the inhabitants of San Marino to the Roman Court, and asked the Pope for positive instructions on the subject. Clement XII. answered the cardinal, through the Secretary of State, directing him to repair to the frontier of the republic, and there to wait until the inhabitants should voluntarily come to renew their first request. " Should the majority of the responsible inhabitants," said the Pope, " still desire the incorporation into the Pontifical States, the cardinal may take possession of the city; should it be otherwise, he shall by no means urge the matter, but at once return to the seat of his legation." This prudent moderation was not to Alberoni's taste. The impetuous cardinal, who had failed in Spain, in the attempt to place his master, Philip V upon the French throne, thought to cover himself with glory in Italy, by giving to the Pope the republic of San Marino. Without waiting for a manifestation of consent, as the Pope had formally prescribed, he entered San Marino, took possession of the republic, established a governor, and made various laws for the government of the State, notwithstanding the refusal of a great number of the citizens to swear allegiance Clement XII., learning this abuse of power, disavowed the action of his unfaithful legate, annulled all his proceedings, and

by a Pontifical decree, restored to the republic all the rights
and privileges before granted to it by Popes Martin V., Urban
IV., Clement VIII., and Leo X. Europe applauded this noble
disinterestedness, and Alberoni gained, by his rash attempt,
only the shame of having failed in an undertaking as injudi-
ciously planned as it was unfortunately carried out.

15. The first years of the Pontificate of Clement XII. were
marked by new scandals on the part of the Jansenists in
France. Francois Pâris, a deacon of the diocese of Paris, died
on the 1st of January, A. D. 1727, after a life spent in obscurity,
and could have had no suspicion of the celebrity that awaited
his tomb. He had remained in the deaconship, conformably
to a common practice of the Jansenists, and spent two years at
a time, without receiving the Holy Eucharist, even at Easter.
This omission of a formal precept was, in the eyes of the sect,
a mark of the highest perfection. The teaching of Arnauld,
on " Frequent Communion," had borne its fruit. Other examples of the same kind are found among the Jansenists; the
most striking is that of Father de Gennes, an ex-Oratorian,
who was " so holy," says his biographer, "as to abstain from
communion during fifteen years." Alas! such examples of
holiness have since become but too common! The deacon Pâris
was buried in the little cemetery of the parish of St. Médard,
where he might have slumbered in the most perfect oblivion, had
not the sect felt the necessity of some excitement to raise its
daily decreasing credit. It was accordingly imagined to trans
form the obscure deacon into another Thaumaturgus. The secta
ries met in a body about his grave, with convulsive writhings and
contortions, renewing in the eighteenth century, in the midst of
France, the most enlightened nation in the world, the extravagances of the Quakers of Cromwell's day in England. At the
same time, the country was flooded with apocryphal accounts
of pretended miracles wrought through the intercession of the
new saint; the lame had suddenly recovered the use of their
limbs, paralytics were suddenly cured amid strange convulsions.
The bait of novelty, the love of the marvellous, the success of

interested views, soon drew to the cemetery of St. Médard
superstitious crowds, ready, at the slightest appearances, to
believe whatever they were told. " The authority of the bull
Unigenitus," said a coryphæus of Jansenism, " is such that we
need miracles to counterbalance it." The most striking feature
of the scenes enacted in the cemetery of St. Médard, were the
convulsions of the energumens. These convulsions, often attended with pain, obliged the sufferers to seek what the sect called
" the greater and the lesser helps," (*les grands et les petits
secours*) ; these consisted in violent blows inflicted upon different
parts of the body, with stones, hammers, or even with swords.
Indecency vied with absurdity in this scandalous jugglery.
Women were seen, writhing with strange gestures and movements, and preaching against the bull *Unigenitus*. The partisans
of these ridiculous prodigies must have been struck with a deep
blindness not to see their falseness. Some of these wretched
women seriously announced to the public that, on a given day,
and at a certain hour, they would give themselves to be crucified for the greater glory of Jansenism. It was time for
authority to interfere, and to put a stop to these mischievous
follies. M. De Vintimille issued a pastoral letter, vehemently
inveighing against the pretended miracles of the deacon Pâris,
against the disgraceful convulsions, forbidding the dissemina-
tion of relations of them, or the admission of their reality,
and condemning whatever had already been done in the matter.
Clement XII. confirmed the Archbishop's pastoral; unhappily,
two bishops, De Colbert and De Caylus, sided with the convulsionists and issued pastorals in their support. Languet,
Archbishop of Sens, whose zeal against Jansenism we have
already had occasion to mention, took in hand the cause of
truth, good sense and religion. The sect never forgave the
eloquent writings which he then published and in which he
lashed the convulsionists and their apologists, with as much
spirit as sound reasoning. The Benedictine La Tasts, afterward bishop of Bethlehem, joined his efforts to those of the
illustrious prelate. The charges of the two opposing bishop

were condemned at Rome and suppressed by a decree of the
council.   The chief agent of the apocryphal miracles, the
advocate La Barre, was sent to the Bastille with four wretches
whom he used as tools to cheat the public credulity   The
cemetery of St. Médard was closed by order of the king.   Even
these severe measures did not put a final stop to the convul-
sionary scenes; they were carried on in the dark, and have
found believers even up to a very recent date.   The birth of
a New Messiah, in 1792, was solemnly proclaimed by the Jansenists of Lyons.   This child of prodigy, named *Elie Dieu*, was
to begin his mission in 1813.   The heretical prophecy met the
fate of so many of its fellows.

16. Overcome on the ground of miracles, Jansenism intrenched itself in the parliaments, all more or less infected with
its spirit.   A mysterious fund*, well supplied by the offerings
of the sect, supported the *Gazette Ecclésiastique*, the official organ
of the Jansenists, as well as the gratuitous printing and dis-
semination of libels against the Pope and the bishops; it also
served to maintain monks and nuns who had abandoned the
cloisters, and to pay the expenses of the agents sent in different directions to rekindle the zeal of the lukewarm, to spur
on the ardent, and to make new proselytes.   A circumstance
analagous to that of the Office of St. Gregory VII. renewed the
old difficulties, and proved to the world that none of the great
glories of religion could escape the censures of Jansenism.
Clement XII., by a bull of June 16, A. D. 1737, canonized St.
Vincent de Paul, the benefactor of France and of Europe, an
undying honor to the human race.   On the 4th of January,
1738, by an edict which history might well desire to bury in
eternal night, the whole French magistracy, represented by
the parliament of Paris, suppressed the bull of canonization

* This fund was known by the name of *boite à Perrette;* it was so called from the name
ot Nicole's housekeeper, Nicole himself having left a first deposit of forty thousand livres
for the support of the cause.   In 1728 the abbe Dorsanne, vicar-general of Cardinal de
Noailles, added a bequest of one hundred and sixty-four thousand livres.   The stock soon
amounted to the immense sum of a million and a half.

The pretext for this unspeakably disgraceful conduct was a passage of the Pontifical bull, in which Clement XII. commends the Christian hero for his zeal against the Jansenistic error. Several parish priests in Paris joined their protests to the parliamentary decree, and ten of the most distinguished barristers of that time supported the manifesto of these unworthy priests by a written opinion, "in which they declared that the defects which abounded in the bull authorized the curates to protest against its being registered, which would not prevent them from appealing at a more fitting time, as against an abuse." It will not be hard to conceive the intense pain inflicted upon the heart of the Sovereign Pontiff by such a scandal given by the priests and magistrates of a nation styling itself the "Eldest Daughter of the Church," and respecting a saint who was the brightest glory of France. Still he did not deem it best to act under the circumstances with a rigor which would have given more publicity and force to a lamentable opposition. He contented himself with dealing by negotiation with the court of France. His complaints found an organ and a powerful defender in the queen, Mary Leczinski. At her petition, Louis XV ordered that the parliamentary decree should be suppressed, and the memorial of the curates considered null and void. He at the same time checked another false step of the magistrates, who had forbidden the title of ecumenical to be given to the fifth Lateran council; as if it belonged to secular judges to decide the ecumenicalness of councils. The king annulled their decree, but they still persisted in maintaining the principle it contained.

17 Had we no other guide than the first principles of the Catechism, or even the most ordinary common sense, we must pronounce the conduct of the parliament of Paris, in this case, absurd; but we must change our opinion if we would square it with the "Liberties of the Gallican Church." Fleury, treating of these celebrated "Liberties," speaks thus: "The *ancient* doctrine has been left to doctors often less pious and less exemplary in their morals than those who teach the *new*

Sometimes, also, those who have opposed the *novelties* were profane and licentious jurists or politicians who have outraged truth and made it odious. It is wonderful that the ancient and sound doctrine should have been able to exist amid so many obstacles." What Fleury here styles the *ancient and sound* doctrine is the doctrine of the parliaments, of the jurists, or of the *profane and licentious* politicians; his *novelties* are the sentiments of the Roman Church, of the most illustrious doctors and saints, such as St. Vincent de Paul, St. Francis of Sales, St. Thomas Aquinas. Now if the parliaments, the jurists, the profane and licentious politicians have preserved the ancient and sound doctrine against the scandalous *novelties* introduced by the Popes and the saints, it cannot be denied that it also belongs to them to examine and to pass final judgment upon bulls of canonization and even councils called ecumenical, in order to point out and to brand the *corrupting* tendencies of the saints and of the Roman Church. The consequence is strictly logical.

18. The parliament soon showed that it had no idea of leaving the principle in the state of a theory, but meant to apply it in practice. Since the promulgation of the bull *Unigenitus*, when a sick Jansenist called for the holy Viaticum, the Catholic bishops and priests required that the patient should first submit to the decisions of the Church concerning the errors he had held, and that he should confess to an approved priest. The last clause was the more necessary, as Jansenist priests secretly visited every quarter of Paris, and even all the provincial cities, ready to give unconditional absolution to any heretic who requested the help of their ministry. The Jansenists in fact held the principle that a suspended priest could licitly hear confessions, nor would they admit that any ecclesiastical authority had the power to withdraw that right. The conduct of the orthodox bishops and clergy was displeasing to the magistrates who composed the parliaments; they looked upon it as an equally unjust and arbitrary act of violence. The magistrates soon began to issue decrees enjoining the pastors of souls to

give the holy Viaticum, without conditions, to every Jansenis
on pain of fine, imprisonment, and exile.   This persecution of
the French parliaments against the Catholic Church began
openly in 1731.   On the 28th of April, the parliament of Paris
gave judgment against the Bishop of Orleans, in favor of a
Jansenist woman who had been refused the sacraments.   The
king annulled the decree, as an abuse, because it laid an injunction upon a bishop in spiritual matters.   The parliament presented remonstrances to which the king replied, that he persisted in supporting the decree of his council and forbade the
magistrates to give any contrary decision; his orders were not
respected.   The conflicts were but the harbingers of that spirit
of revolt and independence, whose withering breath was to
sweep away the monarchy amid bloodshed and ruin.   But
Louis asserted his mastery   He abrogated the decree of the
parliament, made it null, and pronounced it void and of no
effect.   He ordered that the minute of it should be erased, and
the ordinance of suppression inscribed in the margin.   This
display of rigor checked the boldness of the parliament for a
season, but it revenged the shame of its defeat by suppressing
a decree and a brief lately issued by Clement XII. against a
" Life of the deacon Pâris," against the pretended miracles of
the cemetery of St. Médard, and against a pastoral letter of the
Jansenist bishop of Montpellier.   This new attempt against the
authority of the Holy See passed unnoticed.

19. This period is signalized by the appearance of a man
who was to join the immortality of genius to that of scandal,
who seemed to have received from hell the power of destruction
and deep hatred against all civil and ecclesiastical hierarchies,
who astonished his age by the nobility of his character and the
prestige of his talent, equally hypocritical and corrupt; who
seemed to have collected, as into a focus, every idea of unbelief,
of license, of universal negation, of hostility to the Church and to
Christ; who assumed the mission of branding the holiest articles of belief, of calumniating the purest glories, of denying the
existence of God, of the soul, of conscience, of religion, of

sapping the foundations of all social institutions, consolidated by centuries of benefits and of victories; who succeeded in hurling the oldest monarchy of Europe into an abyss of blood. amid the enthusiastic applause of all Europe; in a word, of Voltaire, who was just entering upon his long career of literary and immoral triumphs, by so much corruption and glory, by so much greatness and infamy Compelled to withdraw to England in 1726, in consequence of an imprudent challenge, the youthful Aroult de Voltaire bore with him in his exile a deep and bitter resentment. In this frame of mind he was strongly impressed by the government, the laws and the customs of that nation. The freedom, of which the British institutions presented rather the image than the reality, captivated that superficial mind already seduced by false theories of independence. The speculations of Collins, Tindal, Wollaston, Morgan, and Chubb, which aimed at raising deism upon the ruins of faith, made a deep impression upon the mind of the fugitive; and he then resolved to carry back to France a religious system which flattered every passion, consecrated every form of belief, and realized, in its widest acceptation, that freedom of opinion which had been the dream of Luther, was now the aim of philosophy, and afterward became the favorite weapon of every revolution. From his retreat in England, Voltaire sent forth his *Lettres philosophiques* or *Lettres sur les Anglais*. They touch upon every subject—theology, metaphysics, history, literature, science, and manners. The lively, keen, and dogmatic style, the delicate derision and irony, the biting epigrams, all the collection of literary qualities and defects which made the fortune of Voltaire, were found in this work from an author not yet thirty years old. Religion was treated, in these letters, in the same sarcastic style; he scoffed at the Catholic clergy and at our religious rites, while heaping praises upon the then illiterate and extravagant sect of Quakers. " I am a body, and I think; that is all I know; I deem it impossible to demonstrate the immortality of the soul." France had been overstocked with scandalous works of every description; but she had never before heard the language of impiety uttered in a manner so clear, so absolute, so formal. Bossuet, the great Bossuet, was no longer in the field to scatter with his invincible eloquence these sophisms of foreign birth. The Theological Faculty of Paris condemned the *Lettres sur les Anglais;* but the decree was powerless to check the invasion of philosophism, which had now a head, a guide, an apostle. Voltaire was allowed to return to France, where he was received with enthusiasm by the lords of the court of Louis XV., who blindly rushed to the precipice on a path strewn with flowers.

20. The Theological Faculty of Paris at the same time condemned a Jansenistic work entitled, " Opinion on the jurisdiction and approbation necessary for a confessor* " The author, whose name was Travers, gloried in being one of those who had appealed and refused to sign the " Formula," or to receive the bull *Unigenitus.* The object of his work was to prove dogmatically that any priest, though not approved, could validly and licitly absolve any penitent that might come to him. This was the thesis of the Jansenists and the parliaments in the cases of the refusal of the sacraments. Travers agreed that the usage of the Church was against him, but he was by no means afraid of it. The decision of the Council of Trent, declaring the nullity of any absolution given by a priest without jurisdiction, either ordinary or delegated, was of no more importance in his eyes. "That decree," said the Jansenist doctor, "applies only to priests contemporary with the Council. Beside, I find in it another error. The approval of confessors by the bishop to the exclusion of the curates, might pass for a judgment against the latter who have not been called; it may be viewed as a judgment pronounced by those who, though seeming to be parties in the case, are not to be its advocates and judges, and against which, therefore, the curates have a right to provide themselves when they may have the liberty to do so." Such is his style of treating a decree universally re-

---

* *Consultation sur la juridiction et sur "approbation nécessaires pour confesser.*

ceived and a council respected by the whole Church. It is plain that while the Jansenists did not spare the authority of the Holy See, they showed no more respect for that of the ecumenical councils, to which, however, they continually appealed. The Sorbonne condemned the work of the innovator; Languet, whose name is heard wherever there is a Jansenist to be met, and Cardinal Tencin, archbishop of Embrun, joined their condemnation to that of the Sorbonne.

21. Voltaire had sworn to disseminate the deism of England; at the same epoch another importation of the same stock was spreading in France, in Germany, and in Italy Under the name of Freemasonry, a secret society, claiming to have inherited the traditions of the Templars, gathered together, undei the pretext of the public good, men of the highest wealth, rank, and intelligence. All the emblems of the society related to the fundamental idea of the building of a temple. In the idea of the founders, the temple was, doubtless, to be a new world freed from all religious belief, hierarchical subordination, or regular form of government. Freemasonry thus concentrated within itself all the germs of destruction, all the hidden poisons, that were to break forth at the appointed time for the ruin of the social body The members were admitted only after a mysterious and fearful ordeal; they were bound to strict secrecy concerning all that they might see or hear in the lodges, as they called their assemblies. The real object of the institution was known to a few leaders, and never intrusted to the private members, who were amused with vain formulas and mysterious symbols, true children's toys. It was enough to have gathered together a secret army, perfectly disciplined, ready to rise at the first signal against the Church and society By the bull *In Eminenti* (April 28, A. D. 1737), Clement XII. condemned Freemasonry, forbade the faithful to take part in it on any pretext whatever, or to contribute to its progress in any man ner. This solemn anathema against the Freemasons has nevei been revoked. The revolution of 1789, that volcano whose lava had long been boiling in the breasts of the secret societies,

should have sufficiently enlightened every honest mind as to the real aim of those dangerous associations; yet Freemasonry lives even in our own day, and governments, by a fatal want of foresight, think it enough for their safety to place at the head of the sect some well-known or devoted names. It is a cloak thrown upon the billows of the sea.

22. The vigilance of the Sovereign Pontiff reached the farthest regions of the globe. On Lebanon, the ancient retreat of Elias and his disciples, there were a great number of monasteries, some composed of Maronites, or native Syrians, others of Melchite Greeks. Each had a community in Rome, where their best subjects were perfected in knowledge and piety and then sent back to their native land as apostolic missionaries. With the exception of a few monasteries, independent of each other, the Maronite religious constituted two Congregations; the older that of St. Eliseus, or of Mt. Lebanon, the other of St. Isaias, both under the rule of St. Anthony, the patriarch of the monastic life in Egypt. These religious were cordially united and obedient to the authority of the Roman Church. The Abbot-General of the congregation of Mt. Lebanon or of St. Eliseus, applied to the Pope for a confirmation of their rules and constitutions. Clement XII. granted the request by a bull of March 31, A. D. 1732. The Congregation of St. Isaias followed substantially the same rule, but a national council having decreed that all the Maronites should have their statutes approved by the Holy See, the Congregation applied to Clement XII. for a special confirmation, which was granted by a brief of the 17th of January, 1740. In the preceding year the Pope had approved the rules of the Melchite monks of the congregation of St. John the Baptist, on Mt. Lebanon, especially for their monastery in Rome. At the same time the learned Orientalist, Joseph Assemani, visited all the monasteries in Syria, by order of the Pope, and returned, after an absence of three years, with a large collection of medals and manuscripts to enrich the Vatican library

23. Clement XII. died on the 6th of February, A. D. 1740.

after a reign of nine years. The death of Prince Eugene, at Vienna (April 27, 1737), revived the fallen courage of the Turks. They defeated the Austrians and retook Belgrade and Temesvar; the Hungarian prince, Rakoczy, who held secret communications with the Mussulmans, and whose ravages in Hungary obliged Austria to conclude a peace on unfavorable terms, was the chief cause of these misfortunes; he was ex communicated by Clement XII.

§ III. Pontificate of Benedict XIV (August 17, A. D. 1740—May 3, 1758.)

24. Among the cardinals created by Clement XII., the most illustrious was undoubtedly the theologian Prospero Lambertini, a Bolognese, whose learning even surpassed that of the most distinguished Benedictines of that period, so rich in illustrious names. His education had been remarkable; his rapid progress soon brought him far beyond all the students of his own age. The most serious studies could not tire his ardor for work, or dull the vivacity of his mind. St. Thomas was his favorite author in theology He applied himself with equal success to the study of canon and civil law, and was early appointed consistorial advocate. Being afterward made Promoter of the Faith, he had occasion to take part in the usual processes for the beatification and canonization of Saints; and to this circumstance we are indebted for an admirable work on this subject; it is his masterpiece. Passionately devoted to the sciences, to historical researches and monuments of art, Lambertini was connected with all the great men of his time. He had the highest esteem for F. Montfaucon, with whom he had become acquainted at Rome. Successively canon of St. Peter's, consultor of the Holy Office, a member of the Congregation of Rites, canonist of the Penitentiary, archbishop of Bologna, and finally cardinal, Lambertini always reflected honor upon the high dignities to which the confidence of the Popes

had raised him. Such was the man for whom the highest
destinies were in store; on the 17th of August, A. D. 1740, a
unanimous vote called him to the Sovereign Pontificate. He
was asked, according to the established usage, whether he accepted the eminent dignity "I accept it," he replied, "for
three reasons; I am unwilling to oppose the manifest will of
God, which I recognize in this election, since I have never desired the Sovereign Pontificate; I will not, by refusing, seem
to despise your favor; in fine, I think it time to close a conclave which has already lasted too long."

25. Each year of the Pontificate of Benedict XIV was
marked by some important bulls, sometimes to preserve the
purity of sound doctrine against the attacks of error, sometimes
to reform abuses; at times, also, for the introduction of useful customs. One only political event—but one which left a
long and baneful mark upon the after history of Europe—
troubled the Pontiff's reign. It was the war for the Austrian
succession, which broke out at the death of Charles VI. (Octo
ber 20, A. D. 1740). As the last scion of the house of Aus
tria, that prince had sacrificed all to secure to his family the
succession to the imperial crown, by a Constitution known as
the Pragmatic Sanction. This measure formed the main object
of all his political transactions for a period of twenty years;
and when he sunk into the grave, he thought that he had left
the way to the throne open for his eldest daughter, the Archduchess Maria Theresa, who had married the Grand Duke of
Tuscany Nearly all the European powers had promised to
observe the "Pragmatic Sanction;" but, as Prince Eugene
wisely remarked, "an army of a hundred thousand men would
have enforced it better than a hundred thousand treaties."
Events proved the hero's foresight. Scarcely, however, had
Charles closed his eyes, when claimant after claimant appeared
to dispute the succession. Beside Francis of Lorraine, the
husband of Maria Theresa, came the electors of Bavaria and
Saxony—the former, Charles Albert, on the ground of descent
from a daughter of the emperor Ferdinand I. the latter, Augus-

tus III., as the husband of the eldest daughter of the emperor
Joseph I. From another quarter Philip V of Spain, and
Charles Emmanuel of Sardinia, claimed the succession on different grounds. The king of France, sprung from the eldest
branch of the house of Austria, through the mother, and the
queen of Louis XIV could have proved a better claim than
any of the various competitors; but he preferred to act as arbiter rather than as rival, and this resolve showed as much disinterestedness as wisdom and moderation. The cause of so many
crowned heads was pleaded throughout the whole Christian
world by public memorials; a general war seemed unavoidable; the storm broke out in a direction in which no one had
thought of looking for it.

26. We here venture to remark, that in the middle ages a
question of this nature would have been solved by more peaceable means; recourse would have been had to the arbitrament of
the Sovereign Pontiff, and so much the more justly in this case,
that the German Empire was created by the Popes. But in the
eighteenth century the parts seemed to have been reversed;
the great powers seemed to have banished the Papacy to the
exclusive domain of its spiritual jurisdiction, and we shall soon
find them even questioning its right to exist. Ducal Prussia,
lately erected, as we have seen, into a hereditary kingdom, had
been ruled for thirty years (A. D. 1713–1740) by Frederick
William I., elector of Brandenburg, a Protestant prince, a stern
and fierce soldier. This military founder of Prussia looked
upon the State as upon a regiment. Fearing lest his son
might not carry out his plans, he felt strongly tempted to cut
off his head. This son, afterward Frederick II., was not pleasing to a father who could esteem and appreciate only physical
strength. The prince was small in stature, with broad shoulders,
a hard and piercing eye, and a strange physiognomy. He was
a wit, a poet, a musician, but especially a philosopher, imbued
with all the new ideas, in politics and religion, which the Voltairian school was to raise to honor; his tastes were depraved,
his instincts immoral; he had a passion for writing wretched

French verses, which Voltaire was cringing enough to praise as masterpieces; he knew no Latin, and despised his mother tongue, the German. But he had one quality which gained him the title of " Great;" *he willed*. He would be brave; he would make Prussia one of the first States of Europe; he would be a legislator; he would have the deserts of his country inhabited—and he succeeded. He did for Prussia what Peter the Great had just done for Russia. When the question of the Austrian succession first arose, he foresaw the general confusion that must follow, and hastened to turn it to his profit He could claim from Maria Theresa, in her capacity of sovereign of Hungary, four duchies in Silesia. His ancestors had renounced their claim because they were weak; he felt himself strong, and he revived them. He accordingly demanded of Maria Theresa the possession of Lower Silesia, in return for which he promised to help her to the imperial throne by his credit, arms, and money   But the blood of a long line of emperors flowed in the veins of the heroic princess; she could not think of dismembering the patrimony of her ancestors; she preferred war. Frederick invaded the province to which he laid claim, in the month of December, 1740; and the victory of Molwitz (1741), the forerunner of greater triumphs, crowned his first campaign.

27 The King of Prussia had foreseen that his success would win him allies, and that France would not miss so favorable an opportunity of helping to the downfall of her ancient rival, the house of Austria. Still, Cardinal Fleury wished to remain true to the faith of treaties; in the councils of the French monarch, he pleaded the cause of Maria Theresa, in the name of honor, of justice, and perhaps of prudence. This steady opposition to the current of opinion will ever be an honor to the character of that prudent minister. But Louis XV was now surrounded by youthful nobles, who were eager for combats; their opinion prevailed; the king no longer heeded the voice of his old preceptor; an alliance offensive and defensive between France and Prussia against Austria was signed, and

the octogenarian minister undertook the direction of an enterprise to which he was opposed.

28. Charles Albert, elector of Bavaria, was recognized by the cabinet of Versailles as lawful heir to the imperial throne; Louis XV gave him an army commanded by Maurice de Saxe and Chevert; and the army gave him a crown. Charles Albert invaded Bohemia, made himself master of Prague, and was crowned at Frankfort as Charles VII. (January 24, A. D. 1742). It was something to have grasped the sceptre, but it was necessary to hold it. Circumstances seemed to favor him, while the situation of Maria Theresa was desperate in the extreme. The peril itself furnished resources. A fugitive among the Hungarians, she called together the four Orders of the State at Presburg, appeared before them, holding in her arms her eldest child, afterward Joseph II., and addressed them in Latin, a language which she spoke with ease and elegance: " Forsaken by my friends, persecuted by my enemies, attacked by my nearest relatives, I have no hope but in your fidelity, in your courage, and in my constancy; to your care I intrust the daughter and the son of your kings; their hope is in you." The nobles, deeply affected, drew their swords, exclaiming with enthusiasm: " *Moriamur pro rege nostro Maria Theresia !*"—"Let us die for *our king* Maria Theresa!" Never did princess better deserve this sincere devotedness. They could not withhold their tears as they uttered their oath to defend her; she alone restrained hers; misfortune needs firmness to command sympathy England and Holland, foreseeing that the state of things would soon change, sent pecuniary assistance to the princess, whom the popular enthusiasm ·had just proclaimed *king* of Hungary. The King of Sardinia, won over by important concessions, broke off from the league, and embraced the cause against which he had lately taken up arms. The enemies of Maria Theresa served her still better by their faults. Discord entered among them, breaking up the harmony, and consequently the success of all their measures. Prince Charles, brother of the Grand Duke, harassed the allies with his pandoors,

his tolpachs. Croatians, and hussars, a fearfully destructive scourge for troops dispersed and easily surprised. At length the Franco-Bavarian army was almost annihilated without a single action of importance. Meanwhile the King of Prussia, victorious at Czaslaw, and much more deeply concerned for his personal interests than for the collective advantage of the league, had on his own account, concluded, with Maria Theresa the treaty of Breslaw, which left him in possession of Silesia. The Elector of Saxony was included in this convention, so that the French, seeing no prospect of a diversion, were soon forced to evacuate the city of Prague. Marshal Belle-Isle retreated with thirteen thousand men, the shattered remnant of a once formidable army; and, from the extremity of Germany, which they had reached by victorious marches they were compelled to fall back on the Rhine to defend themselves. Charles VII. was driven out of Bavaria, and his present losses equalled his past success (1742). Cardinal Fleury did not outlive these disasters, which his prudence could not avert, but which his able administration energetically strove to repair (January 20, 1743) On the death of his minister, Louis XV., like his great grandfather, took the reins of government into his own hands. His mildness and affability had won all hearts, and if the latter part of his reign had been in keeping with its happy beginning, posterity would have ratified the beautiful title of *le Bien-Aimé*—the Well Beloved— bestowed on a memorable occasion by the gratitude of his people.

29. Louis XV felt bound to avenge the reverses of his arms. The English had just entered into a definitive alliance with Maria Theresa. Their army, commanded by King George II. in person, was surrounded near Dettingen by the skillful tactics of Marshal de Noailles. The position was that of Poitiers and Crécy; the result was the same; the precipitate haste of the French was their own ruin, and the name of Dettingen was added to the list of fatal days in the history of France. In this critical situation Louis did not hesitate; he thought

that the post of the King of France was where the danger was greatest. He hastened to Flanders (A. D. 1744), with his best generals, De Noailles and Saxe, took Courtrai, Menin, Ypres, Furnes and La Knoque. Suddenly he learned that Charles of Lorraine had crossed the Rhine, at Spires, with sixty thousand men; that he was advancing through Alsatia, and even reconnoitering Lorraine. Louis, leaving the field of his triumphs to the care of Marshal Saxe, hurried to the rescue of his threatened provinces. At Metz he was prostrated by a malignant fever which, in a few days, brought him to the gates of death. This intelligence, borne with the speed of the wind, from province to province, from city to city, was everywhere received with tears and lamentations. The churches, open day and night for public prayers, were always crowded. Louis, thinking his last hour at hand, said to his Minister of War, Count d'Argenson: "Write in my name to Marshal de Noailles, that while Louis XIII. was carried to the grave, the Prince of Condé was gaining a victory" On the next day the king was out of danger. The courier who brought the news to Paris was embraced and nearly smothered by the people; wild with joy, they even kissed his horse and led him through the city in triumph; the streets resounded with the joyful cry: "The king is safe! Long live Louis XV the Well-Beloved!" Louis, by his courage, showed himself worthy of this enthusiastic affection. The victories of Fontenoy, Lawfeldt and Rocoux, the capture of Tournai, Ghent, Oudenarde, Ostend, Brussels, Mons, Namur, Bergen-op-Zoom, and Maestricht, forced the enemies of France to sue for peace (1748); and beside, there had long ceased to be any motive for continuing hostilities. In 1745, the emperor Charles VII., whose destiny was becoming daily more uncertain, died in his capital, Munich, rather of grief than of disease. Maria Theresa succeeded in obtaining the votes of the Diet in favor of her consort, and the imperial crown thus passed to the house of Lorraine, in the person of Francis I. His accession was confirmed by the peace of Aix-la-Chapelle, in which the victorious Louis XV treated, to use his own words, "not like a trader but like a king." Frederick the Great kept his Silesian possessions. All the other claimants restored the territory they had conquered. Never had a war so formidable caused so few changes; it was a second treaty of Ryswick (October 17, 1748).

30. During this long period of hostilities Benedict XIV observed the strictest neutrality toward all the belligerent powers. Italy had also been the scene of bloody combats. A strong French force under Marshal Maillebois was sent to restore, in the Duchy of Milan and Parma, Don Philip, son-in-law of Louis XV., and son of Philip V and Queen Elizabeth Farnese. Like Moses on Mt. Horeb, the Pope prayed for the success of the right. The Austrian, Spanish and Neapolitan troops established themselves indiscriminately in the Pontifical States. The officers passing through Rome made it a duty to respect the throne of religion and the abode of peace. The armies of Charles of Lorraine and of Lobknowitz met before the gates of the city, without in the least troubling the security of the Romans. After the peace of Aix-la-Chapelle Benedict XIV received a just indemnity for the sojourn of the troops in his dominions; and the European powers, while thus discharging their obligations toward him, strengthened their respective alliances by the sacred bond of universal concord.

31. It was now two years since the final settlement of a question in which the Papacy had always been deeply interested. The proscribed members of the house of Stuart had found in Rome a noble and generous hospitality The Sovereign Pontiffs could not forget that the attachment of that family to the faith, was the sole cause of all their misfortunes; the capital of the Christian world was, for the illustrious exiles, as a second home, in which they found, if not the power, at least the respect, due to their rank and to their birth. In 1745, Charles Edward, grandson of the unfortunate James II., seizing the occasion offered by the contest between France and England, determined to try the fortune of war. A fishing boat landed him on the coast of Scotland that boat was bearing back Catholicity to the "Isle

of Saints," in the person of the heir of so many kings. When the young prince made himself known to some of the inhabitants of Moidart, they threw themselves at his feet and said to him: " What can we do? we have no arms, we are poor, we live on oaten bread and till a barren soil." " I will till this soil with you," replied the prince; " I will eat of your bread, I will share your want; and I bring you arms." They swore to restore the son of their kings to the throne of his fathers, and the prince was soon surrounded by a little band of faithful highlanders with a few French auxiliaries. The English government set a price upon the head of Charles Edward, and offered thirty thousand pounds sterling to any one who should give him up. The young prince, true to the teaching of his Church, acted more generously, and issued an order forbidding his adherents to make any attempt upon the life of George II. or of any member of the royal family The victory of Preston Pans over General Cope, was the reward of this generous order. Charles Edward marched into England, as far as Derby, about one hundred and twenty miles from London. Everything promised success to the Pretender, when the Scottish chiefs, in a moment of doubt as to their fortune, decided upon a retreat. The prince vehemently opposed the measure and followed the retiring army, mad with indignation. The English, under the Duke of Cumberland, the greatest of the British commanders of his time, took the offensive and followed the Scotch into their own country. Victory once more crowned the cause of justice at Falkirk, but the Duke of Cumberland was victorious at Culloden (April 27, A. D. 1746), and completed the destruction of the Jacobite party by executions which won for him the surname of the " Butcher." Charles Edward, after almost miraculously escaping the dangers that threatened his life, died in Florence. His brother, the Duke of York, was raised to the cardinalate by Benedict XIV in 1747, and died, Dean of the Sacred College, in 1807 With him perished the glorious but unfortunate race of the Stuarts.

32. The importance of the war for the Austrian succession had, for a moment, calmed the fury of Jansenism; but it arose

with new life after the treaty of Aix-la-Chapelle. The refusal of
the sacraments to the sectaries, without a certificate of confession attesting that the patient had received absolution from an
approved priest, was still the object of their recriminations.
On the 29th of December, A. D. 1750, a councillor denounced
an act of this nature to the parliament of Paris. The priest
who had made the refusal was instantly summoned. When
questioned as to the motive of his conduct, he answered that
he was accountable for it only to his archbishop, whose orders
he would strictly obey. The offended magistrates committed
the priest to prison, while the procurators and advocates of the
parliament waited on the archbishop, the intrepid Christopher
de Beaumont. The prelate replied that, having found the custom of requiring certificates of confession established in his
diocese, nothing should induce him to depart from it. Public
indignation was aroused by the arbitrary conduct of the parliament; the priest was released, but the magistrates revenged
themselves by issuing a decree "forbidding all ecclesiastics to
do anything tending to create a schism, especially by any
public refusal of sacraments, on the ground of the absence of
certificate of confession, or of a declaration of the name of the
confessor or of receiving the bull *Unigenitus.*" This scandalously
bold decree was ever afterward the foundation of every measure
taken by the tribunals against the Catholic clergy. Thousands of
copies were scattered in all directions. They bore an allegorical
stamp, representing the magistracy under the form of justice,
with the pompous legend : "Custos Unitatis, Schismatis Ultrix."
Alarmed by these anarchical symptoms, twenty-one prelates
met in Paris and addressed a letter to the king under the name
of "Representations," in which they strongly expressed all
their grief and indignation. The parliament had dared, by a
decree of May 5, 1752, to accuse the venerable Languet,
Archbishop of Sens, of favoring schism. On this subject the
bishops presented another memorial to Louis XV "Magistrates," said they, "who can authentically learn only from us
what really constitutes schism, do not hesitate to bring that

odious charge against their pastor; and as a proof of the blindness with which prejudice has stricken them, they accuse the
prelate of being a schismatic, at the very time when, by a
special decree, they forbid that the insulting epithet should be
applied to the least of your Majesty's subjects."

33. The parliament had nothing solid to oppose to this logic,
as clear and simple as good sense and truth could make it.   It
had recourse to new acts of violence.   On the 4th of January,
A. D. 1753, the Bishop of Orleans was condemned to pay a fine
of six thousand livres, and a curate of his diocese to perpetual
banishment, for refusing the sacraments.   The king, tired of
these repeated scandals, thought to prevent their renewal by a
decree requiring them to "abstain until further order, from all
prosecution and procedure for refusal of the sacraments."   The
order, stamped with the royal seal, was sent to the parliament,
which refused to register it, continued its tyrannical acts of
violence, and decreed that, in default of all other business, it
should continue its sittings to judge ecclesiastics guilty of
refusing the sacraments.   Louis sent a command to the rebellious magistrates to register the royal edict on pain of disobedience and of incurring the indignation of the king.   The parliament declared that it could not obey, and continued, in the
same session, to try several cases of refusal of sacraments.
What a strange confusion of the simplest notions of law and
justice!   Royal officers, appointed by the king to administer
justice to the people, teach the people, by their example, to
condemn the king; they devote all their energies to persecuting
the Catholic Church in the name of a hypocritical, restless, and
dangerous sect, which rejects all authority, repudiates all
powers, and intrenches itself in insubordination as in an inex-
pugnable fortress!   The struggle is now between the king and
the magistrates; the time is at hand when it will be between
the king and the people.   The body of French society thus
showed symptoms of a near and irremediable decline.   Louis
XV could not yield.   All the members of the parliament were
banished to Bourges, Poitiers, and Pontoise, and particular

courts were instituted, by a royal edict, for the administration of justice (1753).

34. Louis XV might have believed that this severe measure would put an end to the disorders. Severity was always painful to his kind heart; in the month of August, A. D. 1754, he consented to sign the recall of the parliament. " After the punishment of its resistance and its refusal to do justice," said the king in his edict, " we have yielded to the voice of clemency, hoping that the parliament will fulfill our wishes by an unreserved fidelity and submission." If the magistrates made the promise, they did not keep it long. The pastoral letters of the Catholic bishops were, by order of the parliament, thrown into the flames. Nothing was now heard but summons, sentences, fines, seizures, imprisonment, and exile decreed against the pastors who refused to administer the sacraments to the Jansenists. Some apostate and suspended priests took advantage of the disorder to multiply scandals, and, escorted by the sergeants of the parliament, to take the holy Viaticum to impenitent heretics. Christopher de Beaumont, archbishop of Paris, was banished, first to Conflans, afterward to Lagny. The Bishop of Orleans, M. de Montmorency, a name linked with all the glories of France, was banished from his diocese, and his chapter was subjected to a real persecution. M. Poncet, Bishop of Troyes, the noble successor of the unworthy Bossuet, was condemned to pay an enormous fine; his property was seized and confiscated. M. de Brancas, archbishop of Aix, was exiled by the parliament of Provence. The bishops of Vannes and of Nantes suffered the same fate. M. de Belzunce, whose name was uttered by the city of Marseilles only as that of a hero and a saint, found no more favor than his colleagues, in the eyes of the guilty magistracy, which took to itself the odious mission of assailing the most venerable members of a clergy whose virtue was the admiration of all Europe. These monstrous outrages were crowned by a decree of the parliament of Paris, in which it was stated that " they incidentally received the attorney-general, appealing from the execution of

the bull *Unigenitus* as an abuse, especially inasmuch as certain ecclesiastics claimed for it the character or the effects of a rule of faith." It was consequently decreed that "there existed an abuse," and the order was issued, "that every ecclesiastic, of what dignity soever, should preserve, in regard to the bull, a general, respective, and absolute silence." The Archbishop of Paris, the illustrious De Beaumont, could not allow such an attempt to go unpunished. From the place of his exile he published a celebrated "Pastoral Instruction," treating of the authority of the Church, the teaching of faith, the administration of the sacraments, and the submission due to the bull *Unigenitus*. On the 4th of November, 1756, the parliament ordered the archbishop's pastoral to be burnt by the hangman on the Place de Grève. Benedict XIV now sent forth the voice of the Head of the Church, that voice once so revered in France. After expressing his heartfelt grief for the series of disorders which that unhappy country was now made to witness, he paid a well-deserved homage to the generous firmness of the faithful bishops. He announced that the *Unigenitus* was a rule of faith, certain, formal, irrefragable; "that no one can withhold the submission due to it without risking his eternal salvation. Hence it follows that the holy Viaticum should be refused to the refractory, by the general rule which forbids the admission of a public and notorious sinner to the Holy Eucharist." Peter had spoken by the mouth of Benedict XIV ; the magistrates, still rebellious, suppressed the Pontifical brief. At length, on the 10th of December, 1756, Louis XV issued an edict which was thought calculated to restore peace. He required respect and submission to the bull *Unigenitus*. He declared that the silence prescribed by the former declarations could not impair the right of the bishops to teach their people. He decided that priests could not be prosecuted for refusing the sacraments to notorious heretics. The king held a bed of justice, and had this new edict registered in his own presence, which so enraged the members of the parliament that most of them sent in their resignation.

35. Deaf to the voice of its archbishop, of its king, of the Sovereign Pontiff, the parliament was about to feel one of those thunder-strokes with which Heaven sometimes smites the guilty. On the 4th of January, A. D. 1757, Louis XV received an anonymous letter warning him to " take the part of his people, not to be so indulgent toward the clergy, and to order that the sacraments should be administered to the dying ; that otherwise his life was not safe." On the following day the knife of a regicide signed the mysterious note. At seven o'clock in the evening, as the king was entering his carriage, he was stabbed by Damiens, the servant of a parliamentary councillor. The murderer was arrested on the spot, and confessed that " he had learned his hatred to the king in the hall of the parliament of Paris; that he had heard it said there, that the murder of the king would put an end to all the refusals of the sacraments and would be a meritorious action." He moreover asserted, in every interrogatory, that he had no accomplices ; but public opinion was not deceived ; it assigned as his collective accomplice—parliamentary Jansenism. This fearful result of its disobedience brought the magistracy, for a season, to its senses. But party spirit had soon again drawn it beyond the bounds of a moderation which was not its natural temper. This was soon experienced by the archbishop of Paris, whose unshaken firmness aroused all the fury of his obstinate enemies ; he was a third time banished to Périgord.

36. In the following year, Benedict XIV. ended his Pontificate (May 3, A. D. 1758). The Bullary of the learned Pontiff is an analysis of the labors of his reign. In the first years after his accession, he decided a question concerning the Malabar rites, somewhat analogous to that which had arisen concerning the Chinese ceremonial. Particular briefs were issued for the regulation of the various jurisdictions of Maronite, Coptic and Melchite Christians, as also for the Catholics of Albania and Servia. The vigilant Pontiff wrote many letters to the Polish bishops concerning an abuse which had crept into that country, and which all the repeated endeavors of the Popes have not yet

succeeded in completely rooting out. It was the deplorable facility with which the bishops of Poland, without sufficient canonical investigation, pronounced the nullity and dissolution of marriages. On this subject, Benedict XIV. recalls the teaching of the Church on the indissolubility of the sacred tie and the wise regulations issued on the matter by the Council of Trent. Among the decrees relating to America, one of the most remarkable is that in which he pleads the cause of the wretched natives reduced to bondage by their pitiless conquerors. The same tender charity finds expression in his briefs in favor of the poor in the Pontifical States. It clearly shows the father's heart aching for the sufferings of his children. Benedict XIV crowned his Pontifical career by the publication of his magnificent treatise on the *Diocesan Synod*, of which it has been said that it should be the *Manual of Bishops*.

CHAPTER V

§ I. Pontificate of Clement XIII. (July 6, a. d. 1758—February 2, 1769).

1. Conspiracy of the philosophy of the eighteenth century against the Church.
—2. Jean Jacques Rousseau.—3. Character of Clement XIII. and of his
minister, Cardinal Torregiani.—4. Political state of Europe at the accession
of Clement XIII.—5. Expulsion of the Jesuits from the kingdom of Portugal.—6. Persecution of the Society of Jesus in France.—7. Suppression of
the Society by a decree of the parliament of Paris.—8. Clement XIII., in a
secret consistory, annuls the decree of the parliament.—9. The Seven Years
War ; Treaty of Paris.—10. The Bull *Apostolicum* in favor of the Jesuits.
—11. Clement XIII. condemns the *Catechism* of Mésenguy ; the *History
of the People of God*, by the Jesuit, Berruyer ; the work of Helvetius ; the
Encyclopædia ; and the work of Felvonius.—12. The Jesuits expelled from
Spain, Naples, Parma and Malta.—13. Brief of Clement XIII. to the King
of Spain.—14. Death of Clement XIII.

§ II. Pontificate of Clement XIV. (May 9, a. d. 1769—September 22, 1774)

15. Election of Clement XIV.—16. Position of the Papacy in respect to the
European Powers.—17. Suppression of the Society of Jesus by Clement
XIV.—18. Death of Clement XIV.—19. Death of Louis XV Accession
of Louis XVI.—20. St. Alphonsus Maria de Liguori.

§ I. Pontificate of Clement XIII. (July 6, a. d. 1758—February 2, 1769).

1. We are entering upon a lamentable period of the Church's
history Hatred of Catholicity had passed over from England
into France ; the new race of unbelievers showed their hostility,
at first, in a less general and pointed form ; they began only by
allusions more or less transparent. Thus the " Persian Letters," by Montesquieu, and the " Life of Mahomet," by Count
Henry de Bouillon-Villers, were evidently designed, under a

skillful disguise, to show the superiority of Mahometanism over the religion of Jesus Christ. After these isolated attacks, comes a real league; with a formidable agreement it is organized and maintained in the state of a standing conspiracy Toward the year 1757 Voltaire's correspondence assumes that character of violence and excitement, that appearance of battle array, which adopted as its password, *Ecraser l'Infâme*, by which term was meant the Christian religion. By raising this standard and motto of destruction, Voltaire announced the aim and placed himself at the head of the party " He had sworn," says his panegyrist, Condorcet, " to devote his life to the ruin of the Church and of all positive religion." He kept his oath, and his principal theme, repeated under a thousand forms during his long and checkered career, was that Christianity was a human invention, sustained by priests and imposed by kings, as the best curb for the people. His accomplices were many and various. First among them stand the parliaments. " They think," wrote d'Alembert, " to serve religion by their zeal in combating the refusal of the sacraments, but they are serving *reason* without suspecting it. They are the executioners of philosophism, whose orders they receive without knowing it." Next to the faithless magistracy which placed at the service of the enemies of the State and of the Church an authority it had received to protect Church and State, the number of unbelievers and demolishers was very great. It will be enough to mention the most widely-known of those fatal celebrities. They were the skeptical Bayle, who maintained that a society can flourish only on condition of annihilating within itself every religious ideas and belief; d'Alembert, a mathematician of fine mind, who wished to preserve some academic forms, even amid the revolutionary storm of which he was one of the most influential movers; Diderot, that fastidious writer who tried to supply the want of talent by impudence, and who openly declared in favor of Atheism; Damilaville, of whom Voltaire said: " He does not deny God, but he hates Him;" in fine, Baron Holbach, Condillac, Helvetius and the infamous La Mettrie, made their works the organs of the most positive materialism. Their chief work against Christianity was the "Encyclopædia," directed by d'Alembert and Diderot. It contributed, more than any other, to propagate anti-religious opinions; it is an immense monument of confusion and of false philosophy; a real Tower of Babel reared by the genius of hell against God and His Christ. In that work, nature took the place of God, the mind was but a transformation of matter, and all religion was looked upon as a political invention of the priests. They do not blush to teach that it is only by chance that the life of man differs from that of the animal. The Encyclopædia was the great arsenal in which the unbelievers found the arms they wielded so fiercely against the faith. Its appearance was announced to Europe as an event that should regenerate the world. The age of light was dawning; the era of darkness, of fanaticism, of ignorance and superstition was now at an end; reason and philosophy were to endow mankind with a brilliant future, with unknown joys and splendors. Every adventurous mind eagerly plunged into this newly opened way Even the great Buffon, in his Natural History, too often confounds God and nature, Providence and matter. La Lande, while studying the heavens, did not read there the name of their author, and his many works do not once speak the name of God. All, together with Volney and Dupuis, denied the existence of the Scriptural personages, and only saw in the Gospel narrative an astronomical dream.

2. Among these names we have not classed the one which, with that of Voltaire, embodies the whole philosophical movement of the eighteenth century Jean Jacques Rousseau belongs to no school, entered into no league, kept aloof from every party A deep and inveterate hatred, springing from daily rivalry, separated him from Voltaire. He was a man of paradoxical and independent mind, passionately given to chimeras; of a corrupt heart, which made vice its ideal and disguised corruption under the coloring of innocence; of an unsettled disposition, without nobleness or dignity, and so fickle that he passed in an instant from one extreme to the other; hu-

capable of forming a habit of virtue, he could momentarily feel its attraction; a prose-writer, in our opinion, far superior to Voltaire, possessed of a persuasive, pathetic and captivating eloquence, he hid, under the appearance of benevolence and philanthrophy, doctrines perverse in morality, impious in religion, subversive in politics, destructive of social order, of all hierarchy, principle, worship and authority. Rousseau presents this singular contrast, that he can always be refuted by himself; he attacks the Gospel miracles, and yet no man ever wrote a more sublime page on the character of that divine book; he boasts the majesty, the grandeur and pomp of the Catholic worship, with the same pen that wrote the famous *Profession de foi du Vicaire Savoyard* and the pedagogical Utopia, *Emile*, which the author had placed, in his dreams, above Telemachus, and in which he taught that his pupil should not hear of God until he had reached the age of twenty years. The work in which Rousseau shows most hostility to religion, is the " Social Contract," which accuses Christianity of having broken the unity of the State, destroyed love of country, favored tyrants, and annihilated manly virtues. Such were the enemies who arose against the Church in the eighteenth century, and who were preparing, by their united efforts, to raise the most fearful storm that had ever threatened its existence. " The unbridled freedom of opinion, the ravings of party spirit, found another faithful ally It was that policy, in some sort hereditary among a certain class of statesmen, magistrates, and jurists; a system by which the secular power always aimed more or less at enslaving the Church and subjecting it to their hostile pretensions. In that hour of mournful memory, it became the duty of every man to choose his standard. The line of battle was drawn, the object of the war proclaimed, the order of attack arranged with fearful unanimity. It is before this array that Clement XIII. ascends the Pontifical Chair." (July 6, A. D. 1758.)*

RAVIGNAN, *Clément XIII. et Clément XIV.* pp. 24-26. We have made extensive use of this remarkable work of the illustrious Christian orator, in treating this period of Church history; we have no fear of going astray with genius and virtue for our guides.

3. Raised, in spite of himself, to the summit of spiritual power, he was to meet but hostile and leagued opposition there where the Apostolic See might justly have looked for defense and support. In the day of these memorable struggles, Heaven at least gave to the holy Pontiff a minister worthy of himself, in the person of Cardinal Torregiani. "He is an upright man," says Duclos, "a hard worker, and thoroughly conversant with business. Since he cannot deny that the Court of Rome is daily losing authority in Catholic Europe, he looks upon those losses as passing clouds, and says: 'We have the word of Jesus Christ, the Church is indestructible.' He does not seem to suspect that there can be a difference between the Church and the Court of Rome." What the levity of Duclos censures, we seriously deem a eulogy Torregiani was right in admitting no distinction between the Church and the Holy See: they are one and the same. And this conviction is, in the soul, the expression of true faith and of Christian firmness. Thus Clement XIII. and his minister were bound together by deep and conscientious views of faith, by a sound appreciation of the struggle at hand, by generous firmness and constancy—all devoted to the defense of the sacred interests of religion.

4. Their opponents—at first successively, but afterward in a body—were the cabinets of all the Catholic powers. Foremost appears Pombal, minister of Joseph I., king of Portugal. That weak and voluptuous prince governed only in name; his kingdom was under the despotic rule of Pombal. Naturally bold and tyrannical, he preferred the influence of foreign and destructive opinions to the stability of Christian and national traditions; he accordingly plunged, without reserve, headlong into the career of innovations; overthrew every obstacle that stood in the way of his designs; declared war against the Church, whose authority was burdensome to him; and, by incredible exactions, which it is hard to explain, of a country until then peaceable and religious, he made a state convulsed by agitation and disorder. Pombal was all-powerful at Lisbon; Choiseul, in France, with the title of prime minister, had less

power. He was often forced to receive laws from the philosophic league, the parliaments, Madame de Pompadour and
Jansenism. Louis XV was no longer the virtuous monarch
who triumphed in the affections of his people; wholly given up
to the gratification of his passions, he left the reins of government in the hands of inferiors. The Countess du Barry, who
succeeded Madame de Pompadour in the king's favor, was for
twenty years the shame of France and the scandal of the
world. Louis was sometimes momentarily aroused from this
lethargy of disorders and vices, but only long enough to
exclaim: "Well, it will last quite as long as myself;" and he
again turned to his infamous pleasures. Meanwhile, all the
royal family made constant efforts to recall him to his duty by
practicing, before his eyes, the highest virtues. The queen,
Maria Leczinski, and the two princesses-royal, were types of
the Christian woman; his only son, the Dauphin, father of
the Duke of Berry (Louis XVI.), of the Count of Provence
(Louis XVIII.), and of the Count of Artois (Charles X.), was
snatched away, by an untimely death, bearing with him to the
grave the hopes of France and the fortune of his illustrious
house; his grandson and presumptive heir (Louis XVI.); his
daughter, Madame Louise of France, who exchanged the splendor of Versailles for the humble cell of a Carmelite; his grand-
daughters, Madame Elizabeth, called the "Angel of the Court,"
and Madame Clotilde, queen of Sardinia, the process of whose
beatification is now before the Roman Court—presented, in
their conduct, a striking contrast with the vices of the age and
the scandalous life of the king. But their virtuous examples
produced no effect upon a society so deeply corrupted. Choiseul, minister of France from 1758 to 1770, the period of his
disgrace, was a skillful, restless and daring politician. Justly
regarded by the philosophers of the age as the worthy promoter of their ideas, he actively sought their approbation and
support; by this means he reached a certain degree of popularity; and, in the presumptuous confidence which it gave him
of accomplishing his designs, he went beyond all bounds   In

Spain, Charles III., successor of Philip V., placed himself in a singular position, by his lamentable contest with the Church. Austere in his morals, sincerely attached to religion, upright, honest, but easily deceived on account of his very honesty, he had not learned how to bestow his confidence. Wall, Grimaldi, d'Aranda, Campomanez, Monino, Manuel de Roda, were his ministers or chief agents. Roda was rather a Jansenist than a skeptical philosopher, but, in that very character, he was the most bitter enemy of the Holy See and of the liberties of the Church. Campomanez, solicitor-general of the council of Castile, and minister of state, brought to the struggle the learning and the disposition of a hostile jurist. He attacked the bishops with the weapons of polemical discussion and judicial proceedings. D'Aranda, loaded with the officious praises of the French philosophers, to whom he was a devoted friend, placed his talents at the service of the enemies of the Church. With the addition of Tanucci, the minister who ruled Naples under Ferdinand IV., and a violent adversary of the Holy See, we have about a complete list of the statesmen who swayed the destinies of the Catholic powers during the Pontificate of Clement XIII. Catholic Germany, Austria in particular, seemed for a moment to stand aloof from the anti-religious movement. Maria Theresa was a princess unsurpassed in piety, goodness of heart and love for her people. But she was unwittingly ruled by the influence of Jansenistic advisers. Van Swieten and De Haën, chief physicians to the empress, belonged to Dutch families attached to the schismatical archbishop of Utrecht. They used their influence at the court of Vienna to spread their doctrines, and persuaded Maria Theresa to appoint a commission for the reform of theological studies. This commission perfectly carried out the views of the innovators. Ambrose de Stock, a friend of the two physicians, was made president of the Theoogical Faculty of Vienna in 1753; the Jesuits were removed from the chairs of theology and canon law; the new professors, mostly laymen, were exclusively appointed by the secular power, in contempt of the rights of the bishops. From that late Germany was successively invaded and ruled by schismatical doctrines, which claimed to subject the Church and its authority to the secular power. At about this time, Nicholas of Hontheim, suffragan bishop of Treves, better known by the name of Febronius, was preparing the way, by secret attacks, for his bold treatise on "The State of the Church and the legitimate power of the Sovereign Pontiff." Everything was ready for the reign of Joseph I. The universities of Münster and Bonn were established to propagate schismatical teachings. Such were the elements of the religious and social revolution about to burst upon Europe.

5. The Jesuits had the distinguished honor of being the first victims immolated to the hatred of the sectaries, the philosophers, and the leagued politicians. The first blow at that illustrious Order was struck by Pombal. In 1757 he had already sent positive instructions to Don Francis d'Almada, the Portuguese ambassador at Rome, to request of Benedict XIV the suppression of the Society This memorial closed with these words : " The extreme corruption of these sons of so holy a religion has reached the lamentable point, in the kingdom of Portugal, and still more in its transatlantic possessions, that there are few of the Jesuits who do not live more like merchants, soldiers, or tyrants, than like religious." The charge was as unjust as it was unmeasured. The Jesuits at the head of the Reductions in Paraguay, were at once the fathers and the rulers of their Indians. Forming a considerable body, they had necessarily extensive business relations ; but they were neither merchants, nor warriors, nor tyrants. The case of Father Lavallette, which occurred about this time, and which was so eagerly seized upon by the enemies of the Jesuits, to calumniate the Society, was but an isolated, personal error, to be regretted certainly, but altogether unconnected with the Society itself. When Benedict XIV received Pombal's request, he was suffering from the illness of which he died. The Pontiff had shown himself to be one of the most zealous defenders of the Society of Jesus ; he thought that he might grant to the

Portuguese minister, one concession which could only end in bringing clearly to light the innocence of the Jesuits. By a brief of April 1, A. D. 1758, he appointed Cardinal Saldanha, Archbishop of Lisbon, Apostolic visitor of all the Jesuit estab lishments in Portugal, directing him to draw up a report of all the charges brought against them. He at the same time recom- mended the Cardinal-visitor to proceed with the greatest consi- deration toward a Society " which has," said he, " deserved so well of the Church; which has, at the price of its sweat and blood, borne the light of faith to the ends of the earth." He moreover forbade him to issue any decree without the previous approval of the Holy See. This was all that Pombal desired. Taking advantage of the weakness and advanced age of the archbishop, he wrung from him an ordinance of interdiction against all the Jesuits in Portugal. In vain did Clement XIII. exert all his firmness in their favor; he wrote to Joseph I. a letter in which the goodness, wisdom, and moderation of the Pontiff were joined to the apostolic vigor hereditary on the throne of St. Peter. All was useless. On the 3d of September, 1758, the report was spread in Lisbon that an attempt had been made upon the life of the king; this was a scheme of Pombal's. Joseph I. withdrew from the public gaze; Pombal plotted in the dark. After some surprising delays Pombal caused the arrest and imprisonment of two hundred and twenty-one Jesuits, one-half of whom died in their dungeons; the Society was suppressed by a royal edict, its members were driven out of the kingdom, declared traitors and rebels and their property confiscated. The Jesuits were seized in all directions, crowded into several ships, and insultingly thrown upon the shores of the Pontifical States. Pombal kept three of the religious, whom he accused of sharing in the pretended attempt against the king: Fathers Malagrida, Alexander and De Mathos. They were handed over to the Inquisition; but the Inquisitor- General, Don Joseph of Braganza, a brother of the king, refused to condemn them. Pombal created an extraordinary tribunal for the prosecution of this singular trial. Malagrida, a venera ble old man of seventy-five years, was condemned to the stake as a false prophet, and he suffered the barbarous punishment. " Thus," says Voltaire, " was the extreme of absurdity added to the extreme of horror."

6. The enemies of the Society, in France, profited by this event to further their own designs. They had already long been striving to crush the Jesuits by hatred and ridicule. The kingdom was flooded with calumnious pamphlets against the Society The most abominable of all these libels was the one entitled : " An extract of the dangerous and pernicious asser- tions of all kinds, which the self-styled Jesuits have at all times persistently maintained, taught and published."* Calumny and malice are stamped upon every page of this work; there is no crime that the Jesuits must not be represented as hav- ing taught and of which they are not accused. Never had bad faith been carried to a greater extreme. By a decree of the parliament of Paris, a copy of the work was sent to every bishop in France ; this was a gross insult. The immortal Christopher de Beaumont, Archbishop of Paris, in a pastoral letter, refuted all the calumnious charges heaped by the magis- trates upon the institute of the Society of Jesus. He closes his letter with these words : " We are convinced that this insti- tute is *pious*, as the Council of Trent has declared; that it is *venerable*, as it was styled by the illustrious Bossuet. We know that the doctrine of the whole body has never been corrupted, and we are very far from looking upon the ' Collection of Asser- tions ' as the summary and result of the teaching proper to the Jesuits." This courageous protest brought upon the new Athanasius the thunders of the parliament and the punishment of exile. Louis XV. had no personal motives of dislike toward the Jesuits, but Madame de Pompadour hated them because of the frank expression of their opinion in her regard ; she had sworn against them the hatred which vice always bears to virtue. All historians, without exception, have borne witness

---

* *Extrait des assertions dangereuses et pernicieuses en tous genres, que les soi-disant Jésuites ont dans tous les temps et persévéramment soutenues, enseignées et publiées.*

to the vindictive hatred of the royal courtezan; and Choiseul wholly devoted to his own greatness and power, was careful not to oppose the favorite; the suppression of the Jesuits was resolved. Public opinion, so unhappily misguided, displayed itself in the most clamorous demonstrations against the Jesuits, on the 8th of May, A. D. 1760, the day on which the parliament pronounced judgment against Father Lavallette, a member of the Society, in Martinique. He had signed a bill of exchange upon his colleague, Father De Sacy, then in Paris. The bill was protested; the case, at any other time, would have been a mere commercial affair; it was now made a State offense, the parliament took cognizance of it, and the sentence was pronounced amid the frantic applause of the multitude. The Jesuits were condemned to meet the bill of exchange, and to pay, besides, fifty thousand livres, interest and costs. We do not undertake to discuss the merits of this sentence. Father Lavallette was guilty, at least, of great imprudence; but it is reasonable to believe that, at no other time would the whole Society have been made responsible for the rashness of a single member. The new philosophers, now so earnestly toiling to overthrow the whole fabric of religion, judged that the destruction of the religious orders was one of the first measures to be secured. They thought it necessary to sacrifice the Jesuits first, and they accordingly leagued against them. The French episcopate, on the other hand, exerted its whole strength in support of the Society Only three prelates made common cause with the parliaments in rebellion against the Church. Fitz-James, Bishop of Soissons, the leader of the Jansenist party in France; De Beauteville, Bishop of Alais, a weak minded but obstinate man, entirely ruled by the sectaries; and De Vaugiraud, Bishop of Angers, until then a friend to the Society of Jesus; but he had, in pastoral letters, approved the "Extract of Assertions" published by order of the parliament of Paris. Fitz-James issued a pastoral letter of the same tenor, which Clement XIII. condemned by a decree of the 13th of April, 1763. The Pope knew how to temper firmness with sweetness and indulgence   After this warning blow at the Bishop of Soissons, he wished to use gentle· means with the other two prelates, less obstinate and less guilty; his letters to them are models of Apostolic spirit and zeal, joined to the sweetest inspirations of charity

7 Louis XV was petitioned in favor of the Jesuits by the queen, the Dauphin, and by all the virtuous members of his court; but the hatred of the parliaments triumphed. On the 6th of August, A. D. 1762, a definitive decree suppressed the Society of Jesus in France. The decree asserted that there was an abuse in their institute; that it was inadmissible by its very nature in any civilized State, as contrary to the natural law, dangerous to the spiritual and the temporal authority   It pronounced the vows and oaths made by the religious, null and void, and all affiliations to the Society, abuses. All the Jesuits were ordered to quit their houses; they were forbidden to follow the institute and its rules, to wear its habit, to live in community, or to hold communication with one another; finally, they were declared incapable of holding any office, unless they had sworn to teach the " Four Articles." This crowned the triumph of the enemies of the illustrious sons of Loyola; the example of the capital was followed with wonderful readiness by the provinces, while the sound portion of the nation wept over the deplorable attack upon the dearest interests of Catholicity   " The decree of the parliament," says the Protestant Schall, " is too clearly stamped with passion and injustice to gain the approval of any honest, unprejudiced mind; the attempt to force the Jesuits to condemn the principles of their Order, was to pronounce an arbitrary decision upon a fact of history evidently false, and made up for the occasion. But in such diseases of the human mind as those which affected the generation then on earth, reason is silent, the judgment is clouded by prejudice." The four thousand Fathers then in France were obliged to seek another home.

8. The Head of the Church could not view with an indifferent eye the heavy blow thus struck at religion. Clement XIII.

felt bound to express his sentiments on the inconceivable sentence of the parliament of Paris; he thus spoke of it in an allocution pronounced before a secret consistory of cardinals, held
on the 3d of September, A. D. 1762: " Secular magistrates," exclaimed the Sovereign Pontiff, with sorrow and indignation,
" usurp the doctrinal teaching which was intrusted only to the
pastors of Israel, to the watchful shepherds of the flock.   They
usurp it in contempt of that Divine oracle : ' The lips of the
priest shall keep knowledge, and they shall seek the law at his
mouth.'   Imputations and calumnies are heaped upon the institute of the regular clergy of the Society of Jesus, a pious
institute, useful to the Church, long approved by the Apostolic
See, honored by the Roman Pontiffs and the Council of Trent
with imperishable praise.   The rules of the Society are assailed
with opprobrium ; they are represented as contrary to all law,
divine and human ; they are proscribed and condemned to the
flames.   In fine, though I shudder when I say it, the members
of that religious body, who have vowed to follow its rules, and
who, at the foot of the altar, have called upon Almighty God to
be the witness and the guardian of their most solemn pledge,
are now by violence dispensed from their observance ; nay,
even an execrable despotism, hitherto unparalleled, forbids them,
under the severest penalties, to fulfill the vows uttered by their
lips, and received by Almighty God.   Their property is sold
in contempt of ecclesiastical immunities ; they are stripped of
their habit and their name ; they are denied all intercourse with
their brethren ; they are deprived of every hope of obtaining any ecclesiastical benefice, of temporal employment, unless,
among other engagements, they first swear to support and defend the four too well-known propositions of the Assembly of
the French Clergy of 1682, propositions which Our predecessor
Alexander VIII. condemned and annulled."   Clement XIII.
accordingly condemned the decree of the parliament, and declared it null and of no force.   Motives of prudence forbade
that this Pontifical act should then receive the final character
of publicity   He still hoped that, under the influence of some

better inspiration, the government of Louis XV. would return to a more moderate course of action.

9. The hopes of the Holy Pontiff were not to be realized. As if Providence had wished to punish France, that kingdom was suffering from a disastrous war, known as the "Seven Years' War." The English, regardless of the treaty of Aix-la-Chapelle, seized the French possessions in Canada, and attacked the merchant vessels of France, as they sailed in unsuspecting confidence on the high seas; more than three hundred fell into the hands of these unscrupulous spoilers. In spite of his peaceful intentions, Louis XV found himself compelled to take up arms (A. D. 1754). France and Austria, after a hostile separation of three centuries, were united; Russia, Poland, and Sweden, likewise divided among themselves, now joined together in favor of Louis XV ; Spain, Holland, and Sardinia remained neutral; so that, in all Europe, England found no other ally than Prussia, still ruled by the great Frederick. The genius of that sovereign was worth ten alliances. The bloody defeat of Marshal de Soubise at Rosbach, raised Frederick's glory to its zenith. The English, notwithstanding the celebrated "family compact," negotiated by Choiseul between the various branches of the Bourbon family—France, Spain, Naples, and Parma— seized the French establishments in the Indies, in America, and in Senegal, with the rich Spanish colonies of Cuba and the Philippines, destroying Havana and Manilla. Louis XV and Spain were forced to sign the treaty of Paris, one of the most disgraceful, but, at the same time, one of the most necessary in her history In that disastrous war France lost the flower of her youth, one-half of her treasure, her navy, her trade, her credit, and her glory The kingdom of Louis XIV was no longer recognizable (1763).

10. In the evils under which France was groaning, Clement XIII. saw a punishment from Heaven. In the Pontiff's judgment, the Lord was thus avenging the unjust expulsion of the Jesuits, the abuse of the sacraments, and especially the violent and sacrilegious administration of the Eucharist, which, by order

of the parliaments, was so often repeated in that unhappy
country, in favor of refractory and impenitent Jansenists. Clement, therefore, issued the bull *Apostolicum,* as a solemn warning to France He begins by declaring that no earthly consideration can limit the exercise of the Apostolic mission
intrusted to him by God Himself; that he must, that he will,
fulfil it to its fullest extent. He shows how solicitous the
Holy See has been at all times in regard to the religious Orders; he reviews the whole series of the solemn acts by which
his predecessors have constantly approved, confirmed, commended, and encourgaged the Society of Jesus. While that
Society is made the object of so many attacks, he should look
upon himself as recreant to a sacred duty if he did not rise up
in its defence; "so much the more," adds the bull, "since its enemies most shamelessly insult the Church of God, by the implied
assertion that she has erred, so far as to judge and solemnly
declare pious and agreeable to God, what is in itself impious
and irreligious; and that she has thus fallen into an error the
more criminal that she has so long—for a space of more than
two centuries—to the great prejudice of souls, allowed her
bosom to be soiled by a stain so blighting." The heart of the
common Father is then pleased to pour itself out in praise of
the persecuted Society; he consoles, animates, and raises it by
the most touching encouragements. Finally, *in deference,* said
the Pontiff, *to the just petitions of Our Venerable Brethren, the
bishops of all parts of the Catholic world,* he once more approved
and confirmed the Institute. The bull *Apostolicum,* a solemn
decree of the sovereign power of the Church, was sent to every
Catholic kingdom; but the spirit of philosophy which ruled Europe, showed as little respect for the voice of the Holy See, as it
had paid to that of justice and innocence, respecting the Jesuits.
In France, Portugal, and Naples, it was condemned by the government, and prohibited in the most insulting and ridiculous
forms and language. The order of the Jesuits thus remained suppressed in unhappy France; it received its disgrace with a noble and touching resignation. Its only protest was an apology by

Father Cerutti, a masterpiece of eloquence, logic, elegance, spirit, and dignity History has received it in a serious light, and time has undertaken to bring justice upon the unjust persecutors.

11. The melancholy and intricate concerns of the Society of Jesus did not alone enlist the attention of the Sovereign Pontiff, or turn his mind and heart from the grave and countless preoccupations inseparably attached to the Government of the Universal Church. Jansenism especially offered to his zeal repeated occasions of exercising the power of supreme judge which the Popes held from God. Hardly any of his letters to the bishops of France close without a lament upon that plague-spot so full of danger for the faith of Christ. He pronounced a solemn sentence of condemnation against the Catechism of Mésenguy ; this was a severe blow to the sectaries, since they saw, in the proscription of that work, a renewal of all the anathemas hurled against Quesnel and his partisans. And to show that he could brand the guilty as well as vindicate the innocent, even while he so energetically defended the Society of Jesus against the assault of philosophism, he censured, as infected with a scandalous and profane levity, the " History of the People of God," by Father Berruyer. " You need not ask Us," he wrote to Henri de Montesquiou, bishop of Sarlat, " what We think of Jansenism. We have already anticipated what you could desire from Us in that respect, in Our replies to several French bishops who were lamenting the woes of your Church. We have expressed Ourself so clearly and at such length that no one should now have any doubt of Our firmness nor of the constancy of the Roman Church in her decisions." The same zeal was applied, with the same truth and the same energy, to combat all the other errors of that lamentable period. Dangerous books appeared in swarms ; the most impious and shamefully perverse doctrines were spread in profusion. Clement XIII. could not fail in one of the most important duties of the Supreme Apostolate. In the very beginning of his reign, he had condemned the work of the materialist Helvetius, and the " Encyclopædia," into which anti-Christian philosophy had

gathered a confused mixture of all errors, as a means of fighting against the truth. Ecclesiastical discipline, the divine and unchangeable principles of the sacred hierarchy, were closely attacked by daring innovators. De Hontheim, a suffragan of Trèves, had lately published, under the assumed name of Febronius, his work on the " State of the Church and the lawful authority of the Sovereign Pontiff" (A. D. 1763). This work, which denied the most generally acknowledged and incontestable rights of the Pope, gave great scandal to the Christian world. The brothers Ballerini, of Verona; Father Zaccharia, a Jesuit, in his "Anti-Febronius;" Father Zech, also a Jesuit, and Thomas Mamachi, a Dominican, met the work with their learned refutations. Clement XIII. solemnly condemned it by a decree of February 27, 1764. On the 14th of March following he warned the Bishop of Wurtzburg and the Archbishop of Mentz to guard their flocks, both pastors and people, against the dangerous teaching of this book. " That artful writer," said he, "hides his perfidy under the cloak of piety, he diminishes, as he claims, or rather he utterly destroys the authority of the Sovereign Pontiff, in order, by this condescension, to bring back heretics to Catholic unity; a wonderful condescension, indeed, which, instead of converting the heretics, perverts the Catholics." The Doctors of the University of Cologne also published a learned and bold refutation of the work of Febronius; they received the congratulations of the Pope. " It is the part of Christian heroes," said the Pontiff, " to rush at once into the fray and vigorously repel the assaults of the Church's foes. We love you the better for it, We are grateful to you." This holy war filled the Pontificate of Clement XIII., and, toward the close of his toilsome career, gathering up all his failing strength, he wished to bequeath to the world a last token of his heroic courage, by arousing the zeal of the episcopate against the torrent of dangerous books and evil teaching which threatened to ingulf the world. In an encyclical letter addressed to all the patriarchs, primates, archbishops, and bishops of the Christian world, the Supreme Pastor reminds them of this grave and solemn obligation. " You, who have been made dispensers of the mysteries of God and armed with His almighty power to break down the bulwarks of error, work with courage and constancy to turn away from poisoned pastures the lambs intrusted to your care, and redeemed by the blood of Jesus Christ."

12. Charles III. of Spain was, as we have already re-marked, a sincerely Christian and virtuous prince, and truly desirous to do good. But the principal persons by whom he was surrounded, exerted all their power of counsel and action to ruin the Society of Jesus in his estimation and to banish it from his dominions. It was sought to throw an impenetrable vail over the motives which determined Charles III. to order the expulsion of the Jesuits from Spain. The decree of expulsion, called the Pragmatic Sanction, says of these motives that the king *kept them inclosed in his royal heart.* No official instru-ment, no written document, no deposit in the archives, has ever revealed the mysterious reason. Evidently, and designedly, an absolute royal order caused the least traces of it to be des-troyed. Still, a tradition, bearing all the evidences of authen-ticity and of truth, has handed down that State secret. One day, as the community of the first Jesuit establishment in Madrid was at dinner, a package of letters, one of which bore the post-mark of Rome, was handed to the Superior, who sent them all, unopened, to his room. Hardly had they been placed there when an officer from d'Aranda appeared with an order from the king of Spain to search all the papers of the Jesuits. The letters were seized. The one bearing the stamp of Rome was opened by the king himself, when he read with equal sur-prise and indignation that rumors were rife in Rome, grounded on the illegitimacy of his birth, that a revolution was probably imminent in Spain, in which the Court of Rome would take an active share, to place the crown upon the head of the lawful heir. The Father Rector was instructed to prepare the minds of his religious for the event, and to give notice of it to the Superiors of the other houses "This letter," says the Prot-

estant writer Schall, " was written by order of the Duke of Choiseul, by a skillful forger who succeeded in perfectly imitating the writing of the General; it was directed to the Rector in Madrid and mailed at Rome. D'Aranda was on the watch for the moment of its arrival, and held himself in readiness to seize it before it could even be read." The devilish plot succeeded admirably Charles III. suspected nothing; wounded in the tenderest spot, he fell into the snare, and prepared to hurl at the Jesuits the sentence so long and vainly solicited. He secretly consulted several Doctors and theologians to know whether a sovereign, for reasons which he cannot make public and *which he keeps secreted in his royal heart,* can, in conscience, banish a religious Order from his dominions. The Doctors answered in the negative, but the courtiers and royal councillors were strong in the affirmative. " On the 2d of April, A. D. 1767," says Count Alexis de Saint-Priest, " on the same day, at the same hour, in the north and in the south of Africa, in Asia, in America, in every island that owned the Spanish sway, the governors of the provinces, the alcaldes of the cities, broke the triple seal that guarded the royal orders. They were identical in substance ; under the severest penalties, even, it is said, on pain of death, they were enjoined to proceed at once with an armed force to the houses of the Jesuits, to surround them, to remove the religious from their dwellings and to transport them as prisoners, within twenty-four hours, to a certain place mentioned. The prisoners were to embark at once, leaving their papers under government seal, and taking with them only their Breviaries. It must be confessed that this arrest and shipment of the Jesuits was conducted with barbarous haste. Nearly six thousand priests of all ages, many of illustrious birth, distinguished scholars, aged men bowed down by infirmities, deprived of the most indispensable necessaries, were crowded into the holds of ships and turned adrift upon the sea, without any determined course or term for their exile." The edict was put into execution in every land subject to the crown of Spain, not even excepting Paraguay and those flourishing Reductions into which the Jesuits had brought the light of civilization with that of faith.

13. But the voice of the Sovereign Pontiff was raised to utter the language of the most warrantable grief and the most justifiable remonstrances. "Of all the calamities which have befallen Us during the nine unhappy years of Our Pontificate, the most afflicting to Our paternal heart is that which Your Majesty has just inflicted by the expulsion of the members of the Society of Jesus. Thou, too, my son: *tu quoque, Fili mi!* So, Our beloved son Charles III., the Catholic king, is he who is to fill the cup of Our bitterness, and to hurry Our wretched old age, amid tears and sufferings, to the grave." The king thus answered the Pontiff's letter: "To spare the world a great scandal, I must ever keep within my own breast the fearful secret which has necessitated these rigors. Your Holiness must believe me on my word; the safety of my life requires of me a profound silence on this matter." The secret which the misguided monarch could not reveal to Clement XII. is known to history, and its infamy falls upon the authors of the deed of darkness and iniquity. The example of the King of Spain was quickly followed in his family His son, the King of Naples, or rather Tanucci, the minister to whom Charles III. had intrusted the government of Naples during the prince's minority, followed the impulse given by the court of Madrid; all the Jesuits of the six houses in Naples were seized in the same night and conveyed to Pozzuoli, whence they were removed from the kingdom. In the following year the Duke of Parma and the Grand Master of Malta also expelled every member of the family of Loyola (A. D. 1768).

14. Under the repeated blows of so many assaults, under the crushing weight of such fierce storms, Clement XIII. sunk at last, broken-hearted to the grave. He fell suddenly, at the hour when Providence had decreed to give him the rest and the crown so dearly bought. He died on the 2d of February, A. D. 1769, at the age of seventy-five years.

§ II. Pontificate of Clement XIV (May 19, a. d. 1769—September 22, 1774).

15. " The struggle kept in suspense by Clement XIII," says the Count de Saint-Priest, "and decided by his death, was one of the gravest importance."—" The suppression of the Society of Jesus* was now the unfortunate centre around which gravitated all the interests of the Church. As a condition of the restitution of the rights in part questioned, and in part torn from her, it was demanded that she should sacrifice the Jesuits, in whose defence she has lost those rights, during the holy contest undertaken for them under the pontificate of Clement XIII." " In the state of affairs at this period," adds the Count de Saint-Priest, "there was no longer any hope of an accommodation. The pride of the Bourbons forbade their relinquishing anything they had once begun. After having banished the Jesuits from their own dominions, they deemed it a point of honor to sweep them from the face of the earth. But the sacrifice must be wrung from the Holy See itself; it belonged to that power to disband the army which had sprung up before the eyes of the sixteenth century, ready-armed to combat the new spirit that was overthrowing the order of Europe. Should it be allowed to fall under the blows of a lying philosophy? Was it absolutely necessary to acknowledge the claims of that offspring of the Reformation, more dangerous than its parent?" Now, the necessary step in this matter could be taken in one of two ways : either openly, by requiring the conclave to pass a resolution by which the future Pope should be bound to the cardinals to suppress the Jesuits; or secretly, by obtaining from the Pope-elect a written promise to suppress the Society Both plans were rejected by the cardinals attached to the various crowns, as not only dangerous but even unlawful. There was, therefore, no compact, either public or private, between

* History of the Pontificate of Clement XIV, v. i, p. 175.—Theiner.

the Powers and the Pope-elect.   The cardinals simply exercised their right of exclusion, in behalf of their respective sovereigns, against the unsatisfactory candidates.   At length, on the 19th of May, A. D. 1769, Cardinal Ganganelli received all the votes except that of Cardinal Orsini, who cried out in vain that Ganganelli was a Jesuit in disguise.   His protest was unheeded; the new Pontiff was proclaimed and took the name of Clement XIV   His election was attended by none of the irregularities alleged against it.   It was the work of a few hours, preceded by no promise, written or secret.   The political intrigues at work during the conclave, were in no way prejudicial to the liberty of suffrage.   The candidates proposed by the crowns were all successively rejected.   The Spirit of God, which baffles all stratagems, and works out its own hidden designs by means of the interests and passions of men, was watching over the destinies of the Church.   The promotion of Clement XIV to the Apostolic Chair, has every quality of validity and soundness.   Novaes ascribes to a marvellous disposition of Providence the fact that, to the exclusion of the Roman princes, of even the sons of kings, who then took part in the conclave, the cardinals raised to the Pontifical throne the only religious then in the Sacred College; "at a time," he adds, "when religious were generally so little in favor, when, in nearly every European court, they were made the victims of the persecutions and sarcasms of ministers, of kings, and of philosophers."

16. The situation of Europe was fearful.   "Never, perhaps in modern times," says Schall, "has the Pontifical See found itself in a crisis so fearful as at the accession of Clement XIV   The anti-religious party ruled in every court.   It is certain that the various States meditated projects of schism, as appears in the creation of national Patriarchs independent of the Roman court.   The prudence of Clement XIV dispelled the danger." Though seated upon the Pontifical throne, Ganganelli made no change in the simplicity of his life and manners.   Gentle, kind, affable, always even-tempered, never hasty in his judgments, and never allowing himself to be misled by the heat of an in

considerate zeal, he might have had a most glorious Pontificate, in better times, But the storm was raging; the winds were let loose upon the bark of Peter, and threatened, unless the hand of God was stretched out to save, to bear away the pilot in its rage. France, Spain, Naples, Parma, and Venice were at open war with the Holy See; Portugal, already on the threshold of schism, was its determined enemy The first question to be solved, therefore, was that of the Jesuits. "How suppress them, and yet how save them?" asks the Count de Saint-Priest. "Must the Pope brave the anger of the most powerful princes of Europe, drive them into schism, and perhaps even into heresy ? Must the Holy See be exposed to the risk of losing not only Beneventum and the Comtat-Venaissin, but even the filial obedience of Portugal 'Most Faithful,' of France 'Most Christian,' of Spain 'Most Catholic?' How, on the other hand, could he strike out from the land of the living an Order approved by so many Popes, looked upon as the bulwark of Europe, the buckler of the faith !"

17 Clement XIV inaugurated his Pontificate by an act which raised a violent storm. In the bull *Cœlestium munerum thesauros* he thus speaks : "It is with joy and happiness that We bestow of the abundance of heavenly treasures upon those who earnestly seek the good of souls. As we reckon among those faithful laborers in the field of the Lord, the religious of the Society of Jesus, We most assuredly desire to nourish and increase, by spiritual favors, the enterprising and active piety and zeal of those religious." This brief drew lively and bitter complaints from the courts of France, Spain, and Naples. They demanded the suppression of the Jesuits as an indispensable condition of the repose of Europe, the tranquillity of the Church, and the peace of the world. For two years the Pope resisted all solicitations, all petitions, all manner of violence even; but Charles III. had made the question a personal matter; he de-⁺ermined to constrain the Holy See by every means in his power, and it was he who hounded on the other European courts in that fierce and truceless persecution of the Society

At his instigation, France had already seized the Comtat-Venaissin, and Naples took possession of the Principality of Beneventum. Clement XIV still held out. Charles III. sent to Rome his minister Monino, the most fierce and bitter enemy of the Jesuits. From that moment the august Pontiff was hourly beset by a ceaseless, unrelenting obsession. The Spanish minister one day urged an interested argument; he pledged himself to the Pope for the restitution of Avignon and Beneventum on the very day on which the Pope should sign the brief of suppression. But he received from the Vicar of Him who drove the buyers and sellers out of the temple, the courageous reply: " Know that a Pope governs, but does not barter souls." With these words he broke off the conference and withdrew in indignation; when he reached his own apartment, his grief found vent in tears, and he sorrowfully exclaimed "May God forgive the Catholic King!" Clement had long hoped in the piety of Maria Theresa of Austria. That princess, a daily witness of the good done by the Jesuits, and foreseeing the evils that must follow their ruin, made a strong resistance to the importunate solicitations of the King of Spain. The Pontiff had placed his hope in that resistance. Happy in having found an opposition which agreed so well with his plan and his views, he made it a rampart under the protection of which he hoped, for a time at least, to escape the cruel demands of the courts. But even this last hope was to betray him; the last barrier was soon to fall. Maria Theresa, with a weakness characteristic of all mothers, had given to her son and unworthy heir, the title of emperor. Joseph II. left, even from his earliest years, in the hands of the philosophers, had imbibed all their hatred for the Church, he was destined to inaugurate a reign most deplorable for Germany. This restless, captious prince, always meddling in ecclesiastical concerns, and whom his brother, the great Frederick, always mentioned by the ironi cal epithet of "My brother the Sacristan," spared neither worship nor churches, nor convents, in his pretentious claims and ordinances. At length he prevailed upon his mother to consent to the suppression of the Jesuits.   Maria Theresa was a great queen, a heroic princess, an honor to her sex, and an ornament to the time in which she lived, but she had no longer a will when her son had spoken; she consented to the suppression of the Jesuits on condition that the young emperor should have the disposal of their property   But cupidity proved stronger than prudence.   Thus was the last hope plucked from the breast of Clement XIV   Yet, left to himself, deprived of all support, he still hesitated.   But delay was no longer possible for the unhappy Pontiff.   On the 21st of July, A. D. 1773, he pronounced the final sentence; the Pope was like the master who, to save the ship, sacrifices his most precious goods to the storm.   By the bull *Dominus ac Redemptor*, the Society of Jesus was suppressed. "Inspired, as we humbly trust, by the Divine Spirit," said the Pope," urged by the duty of restoring unanimity to the Church, convinced that the Society of Jesus can no longer render those services for which it was instituted, and moved by other reasons of prudence and State policy, which We hold locked in Our own breast, We abolish and annul the Society of Jesus, its functions, houses, and institutions."   The sense of this brief is by no means doubtful; the punishment inflicted by the Pontiff is not a chastisement, but a sacrifice, made with a hope of peace; the sentence was not called for by justice; it was an administrative measure, advisable on account of the complications of the moment.   "Was it lawful?" asks Father Cahour.   "Yes," he continues; "for the Holy See had the right to suppress what it had itself established.   Was it prudent and opportune?   Many say that it was not.   But I respect the critical situation in which the Vicar of Jesus Christ found himself placed, and my only regret is, that this time, the sacrifice of Jonas, granted to the fury of the waves, has only given new boldness to the storm."

18. This was the last Pontifical act of Clement XIV ; he died on the 22d of September, A. D. 1774, miraculously assisted in his last moments by St. Alphonsus Liguori.   Clement XIV. has been variously judged even by his own contemporaries.

Some have greatly exalted him; and these were generally men who felt but little friendship for the Church, its liberties and its rights. Others have too much depreciated him; these were Catholics, but men who did not sufficiently reflect upon the critical circumstances in which the Pontiff was placed. Caraccioli has contributed more than any other, to the calumnies uttered against this Pope, by the apocryphal collection of letters known under the name of *Letters of Ganganelli:* " Authentic history will sufficiently vindicate the memory of Clement XIV ; his election was free and without simony, notwithstanding the simoniacal intentions and external pressure of the courts ; the extreme difficulty of the times; the moral violence constantly exercised by the Powers to constrain Clement XIV ; the uselessness of the half measures and lengthened compromises with which he opposed them; the threats, the fears of a schism which beset a Pope naturally mild and conciliating, are so many extenuating circumstances. Clement XIV might well, then, persuade himself that the good of peace required him to stifle his affection and esteem for the Society and to sacrifice it to the cruel exigencies of that unhappy epoch."

19. The death of Clement XIV was closely preceded by that of Louis XV That prince who had, during life, given so much scandal, when his last hour drew near felt a return of those feelings of faith which his heart had cherished in youth, and which were hereditary in his august family He humbled himself beneath the invisible hand that smote him, made a public acknowledgment of his long continued wanderings, asked pardon for them from his people, and died with tears of compunction at the age of sixty-four years (May 10, A. D. 1774). He left the crown to his grandson, the virtuous and unfortunate Louis XVI. Had a love of what is good, high qualities of mind and heart, the most humane sentiments, a spirit of justice, disinterestedness, and probity, been sufficient titles to insure the fortune of a prince, Louis XVI. would have been the happiest of kings. But they who are called to the fearful mission of governing men, have more need of firmness than of other virtues. Louis

XVI. was too kind not to be weak.   His whole life was a long struggle against crime and wickedness ; and in the struggle Louis was always defeated.   Crime and wickedness triumphed, as a lesson at once to kings and to people.

20. In speaking of the death of Clement XIV we men tioned the name of St. Alphonsus Liguori, that great bishop, the wonder of his age and the glory of Italy   He had devoted seventy years to instructing the poor inhabitants of the Neapolitan country, when, on the 9th of May, A. D. 1762, he received a letter from the Apostolic Nuncio at Naples, announcing to him that Pope Clement XIII. had appointed him Bishop of St. Agatha of the Goths.   The announcement came upon him like a thunder-stroke, he was lost in confusion, struck dumb; he was found in deep agitation and bathed in tears. The pious Congregation of missionaries, founded by him, shared his grief and dreaded the thought of losing its father and guide. He immediately wrote a letter of renunciation, thanking the Pope for his good-will, and alleging his incapacity, his advanced age and infirmities, his vow never to accept any dignity and the scandal which would therefore be given to his Congregation. The protest of his humility was useless ; he was obliged to bend his will to that of the Sovereign Pontiff, or rather to that of God.   His congregation of *Redemptorists* likewise bowed to the decree of Providence which required the painful sacrifice.   Liguori, while a bishop, continued to lead the poor and penitential life of a missionary   During the thirteen years of his after life he consecrated every instant to the glory of God and the service of the Church.   Having inherited the pious traditions of the mystic school, he succeeded in communicating them to the daily practice of the faithful.   The first work which we have from his heart, rather than from his pen, was the " Visits to the Blessed Sacrament and to the Blessed Virgin," a delightful little volume which has furnished meditations to many pious souls at the foot of the altar.   A number of other works of the same kind—*Practice of the love of Jesus Christ ; Motives for loving Jesus Christ ; Meditations on the Mysteries of the Childhood of*

Jesus; The Way of the Cross; Meditations and devout practices on the Passion of Christ; Seven Tracts on the Religious State; Advice concerning a Religious Vocation; Meditations on the same subject; Advice to Novices to urge them to per everance; the *Selva* or *Forest,* in which he furnishes priests with a fund of matter for meditations *on the dignity, the virtues, and the duties of the priesthood; Advice to persons of all conditions; Eternal truths or Maxims;* and the *Preparation for Death*—recall the style, the unction, the persuasive and touching grace of St. Francis of Sales. But the work which has conferred immortal glory on St. Liguori, and has been most useful to the Church, is unquestionably his " Moral Theology," published in 1753. It was a providential remedy for the incalculable evils which the late heresies had not failed to produce in the direction of souls. Jansenius made the use of the sacraments impracticable by the exaggerated dispositions he requires in penitents and especially by the spirit of harshness with which he inspires confessors. St. Liguori wrote his Theology on a diametrically opposite principle. He brought back the moral rule of the Gospel and of the Church to its first character of gentleness, sweetness, and charity Much has been said of the holy bishop's opinion on probabilism. The substance of his teaching on the subject may be stated in a few words. Of two probable opinions on which the Church has not pronounced, we are not bound to follow the more severe, either for ourselves or for others; for ourselves, we *may,* but we are not *obliged* to follow it; for others, we neither may nor can make it obligatory upon them. Thus a pastor, a confessor, who, of two probable and free opinions, makes an obligation of the more severe, even so far as to refuse absolution to those who will not submit to it, lays upon souls a burden which neither God nor His Church ever intended to make them bear; he commits a real sin, and must answer before God for all the souls he may have turned away from salvation by his tyrannical rigorism. Such is the substance of what St. Alphonsus teaches on probable opinions; we believe the same with him, with the Roman Church which has several times approved his theology, and we do not believe a different manner of teaching or action admi.-- ,le. St. Alphonsus Liguori, by an incontestable and well authenticated miracle. consoled the last moments of Pope Clement XIV from whom he was separated by a space of more than forty leagues. God permitted that the soul of the Saint, in an ecstasy, should be transported tc the bedside of the dying Pontiff. St. Liguori died on the 1st of August, 1787.

CHAPTER VI.

PONTIFICATE OF PIUS VI. (February 15, A. D. 1775–August 29, 1799).

PONTIFICATE OF PIUS VI. (February 15, A. D. 1775—August 29, 1799).

1. We come at last to the great social catastrophe toward which Europe has been so long driven by the madness of Protestantism, by the hatred and violence of Jansenism, by impiety, the license of the new philosophy, the improvidence of kings, the scandals of the courts, the insubordination of the people, and the simultaneous triumph of unsound doctrines in all the States of Christian Europe. The hour of revolution was at hand, and the world was about to be disturbed by the most fearful political and religious calamities. Until then, many tempests, many storms had threatened the bark of Peter; but, if we may so speak, these dangers bore a character only of momentary violence. When passions had once been allayed,

the Papacy found its empire re-established over souls which had remained sincerely faithful and obedient; the former heresies attacked only particular dogmas; the persecuting princes died and left their thrones to less hostile successors. Now it was not a prince, nor a heresiarch, nor a persecuter that raised the fearful storm; it was the radical, universal, unsparing denial of every belief, the destruction of every institution, the fall of thrones and of altars, the rise of popular sovereignty, inaugurated amid general ruin and torrents of blood, denying God, Jesus Christ, His worship, His vicars, His priests; and, in the name of reason, forcing upon the world the ravings of the wildest delirium. Had not the enemies of the Church, the great lords, wits, poet-philosophers and elegant Atheists of the eighteenth century, been themselves the first victims of the revolution, they might have applauded their work and enjoyed their triumph—for the triumph seemed complete; they had pro· claimed their philosophy Queen of the universe, and the people raised up altars to Reason and danced before them upon the ruins of downfallen royalty, to show, after its own fashion, that they were worthy of their masters and had understood their teaching. But the Church has promises of immortality stronger than all the powers of hell. She was the first to rise up from the dark abyss, greater, more glorious, more heroic than ever. The Revolution only added another name to the martyr-roll of the Papacy

2. Cardinal Giovan-Angelo Braschi was elected to succeed Clement XIV and took the ever-immortal name of Pius VI. On learning his election, he prostrated himself, in tears, before the altar, and after some moments of fervent prayer, said to the cardinals: "Venerable Fathers, the conclave is ended, but how unhappily for me!" With these words, so sadly prophetic, Pius VI. began one of the longest and most unfortunate Pontificates recorded in the annals of the Church. One of the first acts of the new Pontiff was to order a distribution of alms among the poor. He next stopped several pensions which he deemed unnecessary, required a strict account of the public

funds, conferred ecclesiastical dignities and civil offices only upon candidates fully worthy of his confidence ; he showed himself humane, affable, laborious, and beneficent ; his whole time was divided between the discharge of his religious duties, his public functions, his Museum, and the Vatican library It was he, indeed, who originated the idea of establishing that Museum, single in its kind in the world, to which masterpieces of all the arts and the most precious relics of antiquity, were yet to draw admirers from every civilized nation of the world. The actions of Pius VI. had a character of high generosity that displayed his whole soul. We shall only mention the works undertaken in the port of Ancona, the only one in the Papal States in which commerce could be protected; the restoration of the Quirinal palace, in which he caused the famous obelisk to be raised; the herculean task of draining the Pontine marshes; the repairing of the Appian way and of the aqueduct of Terracina; the construction of the canal of Soligna, with many others equally useful and magnificent. The great undertakings of his Pontificate did not withdraw the attention of Pius VI. from his tender care for the poor. He founded and endowed hospitals ; he erected houses of refuge for poor young girls ; he established in Rome, the Brothers of the Christian schools, to whom he intrusted the education of the poor children ; and grateful Rome inscribed upon the façade of their institution the eulogy so sublime in its simplicity : " Pius VI., Father of the Poor."

3. Suppressed by a Pontifical bull, banished by the Catholic princes, the Jesuits found a home where they could least have looked for it. Frederick the Great, a Protestant king and a philosopher, and Catherine I., empress of Russia, had written to the Pope to inform him that, knowing no better teachers of youth than the Jesuits, they meant to keep them in their dominions. The situation was a delicate one. By the brief of suppression, the Jesuits were forbidden to continue living in communities, to receive novices, and consequently to perpetuate their Order. The General, Ricci, had solemnly sworn to the

Pope to renounce all power and jurisdiction as Superior. The other Jesuits, faithful, as ever, to the decree of Rome, even when that decree was their own death-warrant, refused the generous offers of Catherine and Frederick, so long as the Pope did not authorize their acceptance. Pius VI. was, on the other hand, divided between the feelings of esteem and affection which he openly professed toward the Jesuits, and the well grounded fear of arousing, by an untimely manifestation, the hardly appeased hatred and hostility of the Catholic Powers. He met the difficulty concerning the European courts with the noble frankness that always appears as the distinctive trait of his character. He laid before them the propositions made by the Empress of Russia and the King of Prussia. He was told that, in this matter, he might follow the promptings of his own heart, provided he did not give to the expression of his will a character of too great publicity Pius VI. accordingly authorized the Jesuits in Russia and Prussia to open their educational institutions, to establish novitiates, in a word, to confer upon the north of Europe those blessings of which the nations of the south had so blindly deprived themselves.

4. While Pius VI. ascended the throne of St. Peter, France was enjoying the festivities celebrated at Paris on the accession of Louis XVI. Never did a reign begin with brighter promise ; never, indeed, had a prince mounted the steps of the throne with better intentions or with a deeper sense of the greatness of his mission. The virtues of the youthful monarch were so pure, so sincere, so brilliant, that the very schools of philosophy could not withhold their share of praise ; but, as if his very virtue had been given him only to hurry the hapless prince more swiftly to his ruin, he allowed himself to be allured by views of humanity, of public good, of philanthropy, under which the modern innovators cloaked their subversive theories and revolutionary doctrines. His ministers, Turgot, the Count of St. Germain, and Necker, were men whose faith was in systems, who thought that political economy might answer the purposes of religious principles in a nation. Still, some

beneficial reforms were effected in the government, but Louis spoiled everything, when he inaugurated his reign by the recall of the parliament banished by Louis XV It has been said that men, taken individually, are seldom capable of gratitude; in bodies, never. The first act of the parliament, after its restoration, was to oppose the registry of the edicts published by Louis XVI. This was a source of new intrigues, cabals, and even of riots; for the people were already learning this in France, while the young nobility, intoxicated by visions of a far-off independence, hastened to the battle-fields of America to fight for its republican institutions and to conquer the order of Cincinnatus. This was truly a period of blindness, in which all the parts were confused, in which the disorder of ideas was equalled only by the enthusiasm with which men plunged into untried paths! The American Revolution brought upon France two disastrous results; it brought the financial crisis, the prelude of the revolution, and the spirit of independence by which that revolution was consummated.

5. Though farther removed from social dissolution, Germany, under Joseph II., seemed to be verging upon schism. What appeared under the name of Gallicanism in France was seen as Josephism in Germany Errors change their name in accordance with times and countries, but they do not change their nature. The work of Febronius was the theological hand-book of Joseph II. Imbued with its principles, so favorable, beside, to the ambition of sovereigns, he assumed the mission of opposing the rights, the authority, and the jurisdiction of the Holy See; he was ambitious to be the universal bishop, the general council of his kingdom. Without even consulting the Sovereign Pontiff; generally, indeed, in contempt of his formal protests, Joseph settled, by arbitrary decisions, all ecclesiastical questions, deprived bishops of their revenues, expelled them from the Orders of their provinces, or abolished their sees. An imperial decree subjected all Pontifical bulls to the ratification or *placet* of the monarch. This was an importation into Germany of the purely French invention of subjecting

Pontifical bulls to the necessity of parliamentary registration Other edicts interdicted, throughout the whole extent of the empire, the teaching of the bull *Unigenitus ;* it was ordered that the very text of the bull should be removed from any theological work in which it might be found ; and that professors should speak of it only as a purely historical document, without any religious value. Bishops were forbidden to confer orders without the previous consent of the emperor ; one-half of the diocesan seminaries were closed ; of the two thousand religious communities scattered .over the whole face of the Empire, he left only seven hundred in existence ; confraternities were abolished, and processions suppressed. He went so far as to fix the number of priests for each church. It was in allusion to all these regulations, so foreign to the usual legislation of a sovereign, that Frederick spoke of the emperor as. " My brother the Sacristan."

6. The Roman Court had fruitlessly exhausted all diplomatic means to recall Joseph II. to a line of conduct more worthy of himself, more worthy especially of the memory of his illustrious and pious mother. Pius VI. was the Apostolic Pastor whom no consideration could turn aside from the path of duty It had long been an unheard of thing for a Pope to leave the Pontifical States ; yet Pius VI. suddenly formed the resolution of undertaking a journey to Vienna, in the hope that his presence and his words would be more effectual than letters, with the youthful Cæsar. The news of this journey was an event in Europe ; the Sacred College, fearful of the results of such a step, made the most earnest entreaties to withdraw the Pope from his courageous project. " We shall go," replied Pius, " where duty calls, just as We should go to martyrdom for the interests of religion ; happy to defend it, the successors of St. Peter have not feared to risk their lives. We may not desert the bark of the Church even amid the most violent storms." The effect of the Pope's presence in Vienna was prodigious ; his journey had been like a popular triumph. On the 22d of March, A. D. 1782, Pius VI. entered the capital of Aus-

tria, surrounded by more than fifty thousand of its inhabitants.
So great was the number of people who hastened from all
parts of the Empire, that serious alarm was felt, for a time, lest
a scarcity of provisions should ensue. It must be confessed
that Joseph II. showed dispositions far less favorable than
those of his subjects. He observed toward the Pope the formalities required by ordinary politeness, but he would moderate
none of his schismatical pretensions. His prime minister,
Kaunitz, afforded to the whole court the scandalous spectacle
of a Christian refusing to show to a Pope even the least possible marks of the deference due to so many titles. Pius VI.
quitted Vienna, touched by the display of affectionate devotion
on the part of the people, but deeply grieved at the attitude
persistently maintained by the emperor. By an unparalleled
want of even decent consideration, the Austrian police, so strict
on all other occasions, had allowed the circulation in Vienna,
during the Pope's sojourn in that capital, of an insulting
pamphlet, entitled " Quid est Papa !" Its author, the Protestant
Eybel, openly denied the Pontifical supremacy and loaded the
Papacy with the coarsest calumnies. This shameless assault,
it should be told, met with eloquent antagonists in the very
midst of German Protestantism. The distinguished historian,
Johannes Müller, then a young man, answered Eybel, in the
admirable work, " The Journeys of the Popes," in which he
triumphantly vindicated the insulted honor of the Papacy
Eybel's pamphlet afterward drew upon its author the thunders
of the Church. Joseph II. meanwhile continued his course of
schismatical innovations. In the month of August, 1786,
the so-called council of Ems, convoked by the emperor, drew
up a decree in twenty-three articles, intended to consecrate the
erroneous doctrines of Josephism. It was first stated that
Jesus Christ had given to the apostles and to the bishops, their
successors, an *unlimited* power of binding and of loosing in all
cases and for all persons, and that, therefore, no further recourse
to Rome was necessary The exemptions granted to religious
were annulled, excepting those confirmed by the emperor—

strange inconsistency, which refused to the Pope, in an ecclesiastical matter, an authority granted to the civil power. After
other similar innovations, it was stipulated that all dispensations sought from any other source than the bishop's tribunal,
should be null; that the Papal bulls should not be binding if
they were received only by the bishop, and that nunciatures
should no longer exist. The abolition of the oath made by the
bishops to the Pope, was decreed. Should the Pope, they
said, refuse to confirm the bishops on these new terms, they
would find, in the rules of primitive discipline, some way of retaining possession of their office under the protection of the
emperor. Leopold, grand duke of Tuscany, followed the
example of his brother, Joseph II. He had given himself up
to the influence of Ricci, bishop of Pistoja, an ambitious and inconsiderate prelate, utterly perverted by Jansenistic opinions,
who published pastoral instructions styling Soanen, the deposed
Bishop of Senez, "a saintly and pious man;" Mésenguy he
called "the light of the Church," and Quesnel a "martyr."
He had caused an Italian translation to be made of the "Moral
Reflections," and presented copies to his priests urging them to
make use of that *golden book*. Ricci called a Synod at Pistoja
(September 19, 1788), for the more solemn promulgation of the
errors which he was spreading. Fearing that he might not find,
in his own diocese, a sufficient number of priests disposed to favor
his intentions, he summoned several Jansenist Doctors from
various places, especially from the University of Paris, where
Natalis, Tamburini, and other theologians were displaying
those sentiments. The bishop appointed Tamburini promoter
of the synod, though, being a stranger, he had in truth no right
even to a seat in it. The synod lasted ten days and was composed of two hundred and thirty-four priests, to whom Ricci
promised that the *Holy Ghost would come down upon them, and
that their oracles should become those of God Himself.* The doctrine contained in the bull *Unigenitus* was rejected as impious.
The Constitution of the schismatical province of Utrecht was
proclaimed the very type of the true discipline of the Church

The devotion to the Sacred Heart of Jesus, which the predecessors of Pius VI. had endeavored to propagate in the Church,
was condemned; sacred images were made the object of a
sacrilegious contempt; condemnation was pronounced against
the multiplicity of religious Orders which Ricci wished to reduce
to one; he also called for the suppression of perpetual vows
and admitted only the rule of Port Royal. Pius VI., in the
bull *Auctorem Fidei*, condemned the synod of Pistoja.

7 The scourge of revolutions was sent to teach Joseph
II., and his imitators, what it costs princes to tear themselves
violently away from the Holy See, and to encroach upon its
jurisdiction. The Estates of Belgium refused to submit to the
schismatical exactions of Joseph II.; the professors to whom
he would have given the chairs in the Universities of Louvain
and Luxembourg, then filled by those who taught doctrines
favorable to Rome, were driven out by the students and the
people; the Estates of Brabant and of Hainault refused the
accustomed subsidies. Joseph thought to check the evil by
severe measures, and he abrogated the privileges of Brabant.
The troubles increased, the emperor suppressed the diocesan
seminaries and in their stead substituted a general seminary to
which the bishops of the two provinces were ordered to send
their students. None of them obeyed, and the Cardinal of
Mechlin issued a pastoral letter declaring that the teaching of
the Josephist professors was opposed to the Catholic belief.
The cardinal was arrested by the emperor's order, with the
Bishop of Antwerp, who had taken the same stand. The insurrection now broke out in all directions; Belgium was up in arms;
the war was actually begun. Joseph II., wholly unprepared for
such an event, proposed an armistice, which was disdainfully
rejected, and the imperialists were forced to quit the Netherlands.
The emperor, who had brought upon himself this disgrace
by so many acts of violence and injustice, now entreated the
Pope to remedy the evil. The merciful Pius VI. wrote to the
bishops of Belgium with that intention (January 23, A. D. 1790).
It was too late; the Belgian insurrection had taken too deep

root; beside, the French revolution was looming up in the hori
zon with constantly growing proportions, threatening to ingulf
all the others.   Joseph II. died during the first shocks of that
fearful convulsion (February 20, 1790).   Had he lived longer,
circumstances would have brought him to a more prudent and
moderate course, and his minister, Kaunitz, converted too late
to wiser principles of government, often repeated to him : "The
French revolution will last long; perhaps, even, for all time."

8. The great storm which has been called the French Revolution, refused to be turned away by all the efforts, all the
sacrifices, all the endeavors of Louis XVI.   To remedy the
financial crisis which served as its pretext, the unfortunate mon
arch had successively called to the head of his councils De
Calonne, De Brienne, Necker, and others.   De Calonne, a man
of superficial mind and narrow views, without business experience, found no other means of satisfying the debts of the
kingdom than to contract new ones.   The real amount of the
national debt in 1788, the gulf which swallowed up the French
monarchy, has been greatly exaggerated; it did not amount to
more than one hundred and ten millions.   There is not one of
the least Powers of Europe, whose actual debt is not propor-
tionately four times as great.   But at that period the financial
system upon which national credit is now based, had not yet
been discovered.   De Calonne was succeeded by the cardinal-
archbishop of Toulouse, Loménie de Brienne, an ambitious prelate, who saw in this new dignity only the additional renown it
was to give to his name ; he dreamed himself the head of
another ministry, like that of Mazarin : as for serious and
practical ideas, he brought to the king only incomplete systems
of political economy, gathered from the various authors who
then treated of that science as a matter of taste.   Yet, the
cardinal has, in our estimation, one merit which has been too
much overlooked; he offered to rid the king of the rebellious
parliament and to replace it by a " cour plenière "—of which all
the members—to be chosen by the government—should be
irremovable.   But Louis XVI. was a man of half-measures;

the cardinal's plan alarmed him; the ministry was changed; taking with it, perhaps, the last hope of safety Necker gave the death-blow to the tottering monarchy by suggesting to Louis the fatal plan of assembling the States-General, to lay before them the disastrous state of the finances, and to rely upon their wisdom for the remedy

9. The Estates met at Versailles on the 5th of May, A. D. 1789; on that day Revolution made its entry into the palace of the kings. Hardly a month had elapsed since their first session, when the States-General, changing their name, their object, their mission and their charge, called themselves the National Assembly, swearing not to part until they had given a Constitution to France, and through Mirabeau, answering the royal officer who ordered them to cease their sittings : " Go and tell your master that we sit here by the will of the people, and that we are only to be driven out by the bayonet." The people now rose up, the only, the great, the absolute power Sixty thousand men, after carrying terror and pillage to every quarter of Paris, laid siege to the Bastille, on the 14th of July, 1789. They searched the dungeons, which were said to swarm with the victims of tyranny—they found two prisoners. One of the heroes of the republican expedition to America, a man without means, without courage, whose whole merit consisted in a groundless popularity—Lafayette—organized a national militia, a standing insult to the army, a meaningless institution, ruinous alike to the State and to individuals, and secured for himself the title of commander-in-chief of the National Guard of the kingdom. On the 4th of August, 1789, the National Assembly abolished all titles of nobility, at the request and with the applause of the greatest lords themselves. Without debate, without deliberation, the work of ten centuries was destroyed in three hours. We cannot attempt to describe the shocking scenes of the 5th of October, 1789, and those of other days of mournful memory, written with an indelible stain of blood upon that page of the annals of France. A prisoner in his own capital, insulted in his most legitimate affections, trembling

for the life of the august princess with whose destinies he had linked his own, and whose love the French people now repaid with outrages, her virtue and benefits with the most revolting calamities, Louis XVI. knew how to ennoble himself, in heroic resignation, by the very greatness of his misfortunes.

10. It was impossible in the general confusion, that the history of the Church and its Constitution should escape without insult.   On the 13th of February, A. D. 1790, a decree of the Constituent Assembly suppressed religious Orders and monastic vows, and declared the property of the clergy at the disposal of the nation ; at length the celebrated decree known as the " Civil Constitution of the Clergy," ordered that thenceforth the bishops should be appointed by the electors, and invested by the metropolitan, who was to be chosen in the same manner; they would be allowed to write a letter of etiquette to the Pope, acquainting him with their appointment.   The same decree abolished the hundred and thirty-five bishoprics then existing in France, and replaced them by eighty-three *civil* sees, to correspond with the number of the new departments lately substituted by the assembly in the place of the old and popular division into *provinces*.   It was attempted to force Louis XVI. to ratify this tyrannical decree; the king refused, and referred it to the Sovereign Pontiff.   Pius VI. perfectly understood the position of the unhappy monarch; his letter seems more like an address to a prisoner than to a king.   " Let us put our trust in Providence," he writes, " and by an unshaken attachment to the faith of our fathers, let us deserve from Him the help of which we stand so much in need."   The Pope then referred the king for the solution of his question to the two archbishops of Vienne and Bordeaux, De Pompignan and De Cicé.   The two prelates had the deplorable weakness to advise the pure and simple acceptance of the measure.   De Pompignan afterward died of a broken heart at his own scandalous weakness, and De Cicé published a retraction equally humble and explicit.   Louis XVI. gave his signature to the " Civil Constitution of the

Clergy," and thus sanctioned a schism in the kingdom which had until then gloried in the title of Most Christian.

11. Louis XVI. wrote to the Pope, requesting him to confirm, at least provisionally, some of the articles of the "Civil Constitution of the Clergy" The Pontiff called a Congregation of Cardinals to consider the request, and by their advice determined to consult the French bishops, since they were in a better position to judge of the spirit and connection of the decrees, and also of the measures suited to the difficult situation. On the 30th of October, A. D. 1790, thirty French bishops signed a profession of faith known as the "Exposition of Principles on the Civil Constitution of the Clergy." The author, Mgr. de Boisgelin, archbishop of Aix, who also signed it, defended in it the true principles of the Church, without recrimination or bitterness, with a moderation and solidity that would have recalled less prejudiced minds. The *Exposition* defended the essential jurisdiction of the Church, the right to decide on discipline, to make regulations, to institute bishops, and to give them a mission; which rights were wholly denied by the new decrees. It also complained of the suppression of so many monasteries; of the violence which claimed to annul promises made to God, and to tear down sacred barriers set by no human hand. The bishops concluded with the request that the cooperation of the Holy See should be admitted to legalize all the changes that might be made; that due force should be given to the authority of the Pope, *without whom nothing of importance should be undertaken in the Church.*

These considerations made no impression on the public mind. On the 27th of November, A. D. 1790, the Constituent Assembly decreed that all the bishops and priests, who should not within eight days, have sworn to observe the "Civil Constitution," should be looked upon as having given up their charge A special clause announced that, in the event of the refusal of the metropolitan, or the oldest bishop in the province, to consecrate the bishops chosen in accordance with the revolutionary forms, the consecration should be performed by any other bishop whatever ; and that, for the confirmation and canonical institution, the civil administration would point out to the candidate a bishop of its own choice, to whom he should apply

The 4th of January, A. D. 1791, was the day appointed for the ecclesiastical members of the National Assembly to take the oath of defection and schism. Amid the loud cries of a phrensied mob crowding about the doors with shouts of " Death to the priests who will not take the oath !" the president called upon M. de Bonnac, bishop of Agen. " Gentlemen," said the prelate, " the sacrifice of wealth is of little moment to me ; but there is one sacrifice which I cannot make, that of your respect and my faith ; I should be too sure of losing both did I take the oath required of me." M. de Saint-Aulaire, bishop of Poitiers, ascended to the tribune. " Gentlemen," he said, " I am seventy years old ; I have spent thirty-three in the episcopate, and I shall not now disgrace my gray hairs by taking the oath required by your decrees ; I will not swear." At these words the clergy on the right rose up in a body, applauded the words of the venerable prelate and proclaimed that they all shared the same sentiments. But Henri Grégoire, pastor of Embermenil, in the diocese of Nancy, a man notorious for his exaggerated revolutionary principles, gave the example of defection. He appeared in the tribune and endeavored to persuade the clergy on the right that the Assembly had no intention of touching religion or the spiritual authority, and that in taking the oath they bound themselves to nothing at variance with the Catholic faith. The Assembly then decreed that instead of individual summons, a general call should be made. The president made the call : " Let those ecclesiastics who have not yet taken the oath, rise and come forward to swear." Not one answered the schismatical appeal, and yet the cries of death were growing fiercer at the doors of the hall. All honor to the clergy of France ! There is no nobler page in the history of the Church. The Assembly at once decreed that the king should name new bishops and pastors to take the places of those who had refused to swear. Of the three hundred ecclesiastics sent as deputies to the National Assembly, not more than twenty adhered to the schismatical Constitution of the clergy The bishops of the various provinces followed the example of their colleagues in Paris, and out of one hundred and thirty-five French bishops, only four were found under the standard of schism. They were—Cardinal de Brienne, archbishop of Sens, and the Bishops of Viviers, Orleans, and Autun. The after career of these prelates was ill-calculated to vindicate their conduct on this occasion. De Brienne, who was already well known and understood, sent back the cardinal's hat, obtained a short time before by means of intrigue, was deposed from his dignity by the Pope, and died miserably in 1794. The bishops of Orleans and Autun, Jarente and Talleyrand, unhappily placed in a state of life for which they were so ill-suited, renounced it to enter into civil offices and even contracted marriage ties. M. de Savines, bishop of Viviers, who gave in his resignation and was elected according to the new form, afterward entered upon so extravagant a course that it is questioned whether his defection was not an effect of insanity. Among the pastors and vicars of the provinces, the great majority, at least fifty out of sixty thousand, refused to take the oath prescribed by the " Civil Constitution." Of the remainder, the greater number swore only with reservations for all that was contrary to the Catholic faith; a very weak minority swore absolutely and without reserve. In a word, nearly the whole French episcopate and the great majority of the secular clergy, proved true in the hour of trial.

12. On the 10th of March and on the 13th of April, A. D. 1791, Pius VI. addressed two briefs respectively to the bishops of Constituent Assembly and to the clergy and faithful of France, declaring the radical nullity of the " Civil Constitution of the Clergy " The appointment of the new bishops was, in his eyes, unlawful, sacrilegious, and contrary to the canons. He commanded all the ecclesiastics who had taken the oath to recall it within forty days, on pain of suspension from all clerical orders, and of irregularity if they continued to discharge their

functions. Notwithstanding these decrees of the successor of St. Peter, of the Vicar of Jesus Christ, the schismatical Villar had himself consecrated in Paris as Bishop of the department of Mayenne. But the diocese of Laval did not hearken to the voice of the hireling; the false pastor everywhere met only shame and contempt.

13. In ordinary times, these violent proceedings of the National Assembly would have constituted a deplorable schism; but at this period of strange confusion it was only an episode which was soon to pass away with every institution, every right, every principle, in a fearful deluge of blood. On the 1st of October, A. D. 1791, the Legislative took the place of the Constituent Assembly. All the efforts of Louis XVI. to avert the catastrophe had been vain. His flight to Varennes only gave another triumph to his enemies. The Legislative Assembly, composed of the most ardent partisans of Paris and the provinces, conceived the design of abolishing royalty, which stood in the way of those bloodthirsty innovators. On the very day on which Louis appeared in their midst they decreed that he should no longer enjoy the titles of "king" and "majesty" and that the obligation to uncover in his presence had ceased to exist. The nobles and princes of the blood, foreseeing the excesses to which the revolutionists would soon give themselves up, hastened to fly the land that was preparing to devour its own children. The Legislative Assembly pronounced sentence of forfeiture against the absent princes, of death against every refugee who should not have returned to his home before the 1st of January, 1792, and of banishment against all priests who refused to take the oath of the Civil Constitution. Indignation restored to Louis XVI. all his native energy; he wished to use, in turn, the Constitution so much abused by his enemies, and answered the two baneful decrees by a veto. Then came forth from the Masonic lodges the odious society of *Jacobins*, so named from their place of meeting in Paris. This vile herd of abandoned men, plotting in open day against all religion, against all order, against every throne, and every government,

spread like a foul contagion through the provinces, infected the cities, and ravaged even the country districts, proscribing all that possessed a name, a fortune, talent and virtue. The last vestige of principle was whelmed in the torrent, the shameless mob crowned itself with the emblem of infamy, with the odious *red cap* worn by convicts. Clubs of Girondists and Cordeliers were formed in Paris on the model of those of the Jacobins; while Pétion and Santerre inaugurated the "Rein of Terror." Louis XVI. was forced, with tears in his eyes, to sign a declaration of war against Austria; the 20th of June and the 10th of August are dates written in letters of blood on the annals of France; the Legislative Assembly made way for the Convention, and the first act of the new Assembly was to declare Louis XVI. deposed from the royal dignity He was at first kept a prisoner in the Luxembourg, but three days later was sent to the Temple with the queen, Marie Antoinette, his sister, Madame Elizabeth, the Dauphin, his son, a child of seven years and a half, Madame Royale, his daughter, the Marchioness of Tourzel, the governess of the royal children, whose devotedness outlived their misfortune, and three devoted attendants, whose names have been preserved by history as models of fidelity —they were, Hue, Chamilly, and Cléry It was a day of mourning and of shame for France. On the 2d of September, simultaneously with the tidings that the Prussians were already in Champagne, the streets rang with the fierce cry, "To the prisons! Let us kill the prisoners!" A kind of phrensy seemed to have seized upon the multitude; a great number of priests and aged men, crowded together in the monasteries of the "Carmes," of St. Firmin, of La Force, and of St. Germain at Bicêtre, were butchered with unparalleled barbarity; the horrible massacre lasted four days, and cost the lives of more than eight thousand French citizens in Paris alone. In those scenes of sad and bloody memory, the brutal murderers were seen singing and dancing around their palpitating victims, tearing out their entrails, and even drinking their blood. Some of the proscribed escaped by means of bribes. Manuel received fifty thousand crowns for the ransom of the Princess de Lamballe, the daughter-in-law of the virtuous Duke of Penthiévre. He had hardly received the money, when he sent to La Force a band of assassins, who brought him back upon a pike the head and heart of the unfortunate princess, after having paraded it for some time before the windows of the Temple, in the sight of the unfortunate Marie Antoinette, a bosom friend of the princess. Two days later, standing in the tribune of the Jacobins, and wearing the red cap for a diadem, d'Orleans solemnly foreswore his fathers, and, at his own request, the Commune declared that he should thenceforth bear the name of Egalité.

14. The Convention was formed under the influence of the reign of terror. The trembling electors voted according to the wishes of the *Septembriseurs*—Septembrists—as the most furious Democrats were called. Paris and all France threw their refuse into the mass—the two Robespierres, Danton, Collot d'Herbois, Billaud-Varennes, Camille Desmoulins, Couthon, St. Just, Brissot, Marat, Legendre, Panis, Sergent, Fabre d'Eglantine, and even Philip Egalité. These men, whose memory is forever doomed to the execration of posterity, took in the Convention a place which they called "the Mountain"—*La Montagne*—they were themselves, in consequence, styled the Mountaineers—*Montagnards*. On the 3d of December, A. D. 1792, after a discussion which betrayed the incapacity of St. Just, the ridiculous sophisms of Condorcet, and the hypocritical pity of Robespierre, the Convention announced that it would proceed to the trial of *Louis Capet*, as the infamous rabble styled their king. On the 11th, Louis XVI. was brought before the Assembly by Santerre. He heard, without emotion, the fifty seven charges to which he was called upon to answer. His reply was characterized by a force and precision only equalled by its moderation and simplicity The president, Barrère, charged him with having made his alms and benefits a means of seducing the people "Ah! sir," replied the august prisoner with emotion, "I have never tasted a sweeter satisfaction than

that of giving to the needy." When arraigned at the bar Louis XVI. asked the Assembly to allow him a counsel and defence On his return to the Temple he was separated from his family The king was allowed to choose his counsel; he intrusted his cause to Tronchet and Target, both members of the late Constituent Assembly The latter declined the honorable task. Malesherbes, though seventy years old, offered himself to take the place of the cowardly Target. " In his prosperity," said he, "the king honored me with his favor; I cannot forsake him in his adversity." Malesherbes afterward received his reward upon the scaffold. M. de Sèze was added to these courageous pleaders. The fate of the defence had been anticipated; the judges hardly listened to it. " Remember," said De Sèze, "that history will judge your sentence, and its judgment will be that of ages." History has pronounced; it has glorified the victim, and finds no words to brand the executioners. Louis XVI. was condemned to death. When Philip Egalité, who sat in the Convention, was called upon for his vote, he uttered from the tribune this shocking speech: " Wholly absorbed in the thought of duty, convinced that all those who have been, or in future may be, guilty of injuring the sovereignty of the people, deserve death, I vote for *Death*." Such a word, from those lips, drew a cry of horror even from the men who were thought dead to every feeling of humanity; and the Assembly, with one voice, uttered the exclamation: " The Monster!"

15. On the 30th of December the sentence was made known to the royal victim by the person styled "the minister of jus tice." Louis XVI. received it with the calm serenity of innocence. He was allowed to see his unhappy family for the las time, and to receive the consolations of religion from M. Edge worth de Firmont, an Irish clergyman. Louis lengthened th interview with the queen, his daughter, his son, and his sister, as long as he could bear up against his emotion. At the end of two hours, feeling that he could hold out no longer, he gave his last blessing to these worthy objects of his tenderest affections, and hastened back in silence to his own apartment, with

his face buried in his hands. He then spent some time in private communication with the Abbé Edgeworth; the hours seemed too short for his piety; it was necessary to force him to seek some rest. He slept soundly until five o'clock. The sacrifice of life had been offered up; he was now a Christian martyr going forth to die by the regicide steel of the Convention, as the martyrs of the early Church died by the orders of Nero and Diocletian. When the king had received communion, Cléry threw himself at his feet: "Ah, my master! ah, my king!" he exclaimed, "if my devotedness and my services can have been pleasing to you, the only reward I ask is your blessing; do not refuse it to the last Frenchman who has remained true to you!" The king gave his blessing to the faithful attendant with the same composure as if he had still inhabited the palace of his fathers. Santerre had placed a hundred thousand National Guards under arms; he appeared before the august captive; the fatal hour had come: "Let us go," said Louis, "I am ready" He was seated in a carriage with two gendarmes who had orders to kill him at once if any attempt was made in his favor: the barbarous precaution was useless. Among so many thousands of men, most of whom abhorred the parricidal act about to be perpetrated, not one was found to raise his voice in favor of his king. A deadly stupor seemed to have fallen upon all minds. Louis XVI., untroubled by the various passions that moved the spectators, prayed during the whole journey to the scaffold, and nothing could ruffle the peace of his soul no longer bound to earth. When the executioner approached to bind his hands, Louis, who was not prepared for this new act of violence, was on the point of ordering him back. "Sire," said the abbé, "this humiliation will constitute one more feature of resemblance between your Majesty and the God who is to be its reward." Louis then held out his own hands, and with a firm step approached the instrument of death, while his confessor exclaimed with enthusiasm: "Son of St. Louis, ascend to Heaven." Before laying his head upon the block, the king turned to the people

and began to address them : " Frenchmen, I die guiltless of the
crimes imputed to me ; I forgive my enemies "—the fierce Santerre here interrupted him with the words, " I brought you here,
not to harangue the people, but to die ;" and he ordered the
drums to beat, thus drowning the voice of the victim. The
head of the King of France, of the most virtuous and best of
kings, rolled from under the fatal knife ; an attendant of the
executioner* held it up before the people, with the words : " It
is the head of a tyrant" (January 21, A. D. 1793). On the day
before his trial, Louis XVI. had drawn up his testament, immortal as the religion by which it was inspired.

16. The effect produced in all Europe by this tragic event
is beyond description. At Rome, Pius VI. ordered a solemn
service for the repose of the soul of the unfortunate monarch ;
he addressed the cardinals assembled in a consistory : "Why
are not Our words broken by sobs and tears ? Should We not,
in sighs and groans, rather than in words, pour out the overwhelming grief with which We are obliged to make known to
you the fearful crime of the 21st of January ? But from such an
array of wicked and ferocious judges, from so many extorted
votes, what could We look for but deeds that must win infamy,
horror, and execration from all coming ages ! The imprisonment and death of Louis XVI. were attended by circumstances
so lamentable, that no man, who still retains a feeling of humanity, can hear them without shuddering, especially when We
remember the character of Louis, mild, affable, generous, an
enemy of rigor and severity, filled with love for his people,

---

* Samson, the man who presided over the execution of Louis XVI., took no active part
in the deed. Born in 1740, of a family which had for two centuries held the office of executioner, his gentle and pious disposition was in strange contrast with the terrible functions
of his office ; it was necessary to use force to bring him to the execution of Louis XVI. The
fearful sight made so deep an impression upon him that he died of it within six months,
expressing the most bitter grief at having taken a part, though indirect, in a deed so atrocious. He left a sum of money to defray the expenses of a yearly mass of expiation, to be
said on the 21st of January, for the repose of the soul of Louis XVI. His pious intention
was faithfully complied with, in the church of St. Lawrence, until 1840, the period of his
son's death. For a space of twenty years, there was no other expiatory ceremony in
France ; the first protest was that of the executioner.

gentle and indulgent toward all. Had Our exhortations been
heeded, We should not to-day be called on to lament the ruin
now fallen upon France, and threatening kings and kingdoms.
O France! styled by our predecessors *the mirror of Christianity,
the unshaken support of the faith*, thou whose Christian fervor
and devotion to the Apostolic See was unequalled among nations, how hast thou fallen into this gulf of disorder, of license
and impiety? Thou hast heaped upon thyself but dishonor,
infamy, the indignation of nations and kings, of the little
and the great, of the present and the future!" The solemn
Mass of requiem for the soul of Louis was celebrated in the
Pontifical chapel; among those present were the Princesses
Victoria and Adelaide, aunts of the late king. During the
panegyric of Louis XVI., the Pope was several times seen to
shed abundant tears on hearing the praise pronounced upon the
virtues of a prince, who had fallen under the weight of such
undeserved misfortunes. The death of the king was but a prelude to that of the other royal prisoners in the Temple. Marie
Antoinette, the daughter of the Cæsars, who had brought to
the throne of France virtues shamefully calumniated by her
enemies, a deep and true love for her adopted country, which
was never taken into account, Marie Antoinette was doomed
to share the fate of her royal consort. She was kept during
seventy-four days in an unwholesome dungeon of the Concier-
gerie, without other food than a scanty allowance of bread and
water. The queen was dragged before the revolutionary tribunal and loaded with calumnious accusations, to which she
replied with equal energy and propriety Chauveau-Lagarde
illustrated his name by his heroic defence of the unhappy
queen; but of what avail are the pleadings of eloquence, misfortune, and courage, with such ferocious judges? "I was a
queen," said Marie Antoinette to them, "and you have put my
consort to death; I was a mother, and you have torn me from
my children; there is nothing left but my blood; take it, and
do not prolong my sufferings." In a few hours she was passing
through the streets in the fatal cart, amid the jeers of a vile rabble

paid to insult her. The queen turned a last look upon the Tuileries, the sight of which moved her to an extent which she could
not hide. The priest in attendance reminded her that then was
the time to show her courage. "It is not when my woes are
about to end," answered the queen, "that I shall be seen to fail."
On reaching the scaffold, she threw herself upon her knees, and
raising her eyes to heaven, "O God," she exclaimed, "enlighten
and touch my executioners." Thus perished, at the age of thirty-
eight years, a princess who deserved all the love of her people,
and who ended her royal life upon a scaffold. Madame Elizabeth met the same fate. The Dauphin died in prison under
the cruel treatment of the infamous Simon. Madame Royale,
reserved by Providence for a life of little sunshine and many
tears, escaped almost miraculously from the hands of her executioners; she was afterward exchanged. *Terror* was now the
political system of France. Four millions of victims, of every
age, and rank, and condition, were sacrificed to the ambition of
Robespierre, the abortive Cromwell of the French Revolution,
possessing the cruelty, without the talent, of the English republican. Orders were given for the plunder of all the churches,
and the suppression of the Catholic worship in France. The
churches contained wealth to the amount of eight hundred
millions, in sacred vessels and costly vestments; the public
treasury did not receive two hundred, all the rest became the
booty of the spoilers. In the midst of one of the regular sessions of the Convention, a number of soldiers entered the hall
wearing Pontifical vestments; they were followed by a double
line of men of the lowest class, clothed with copes, chasubles,
and dalmatics; behind them were borne on handbarrows great
heaps of chalices, ciboriums and monstrances of gold and silver.
The procession filed past to the air of republican songs, and the
actors in the sacrilegious scene concluded by publicly renouncing
all worship other than that of liberty Every street was lighted up by the flames which consumed the sacred books, pulpits,
confessionals, sacred vestments, pictures, and relics of saints.
Around these flaming piles, the populace, drunk with wine and

impiety, danced and blasphemed the God of its fathers. The
statues of saints were mutilated, crosses were broken, iron railings were removed, the bells were melted, and some of the
steeples were even torn down, on the pretext that by their elevation they were in opposition to republican equality Even
tombs were not respected; the royal ashes that rested in
St. Denis were scattered to the winds, the patroness of Paris
found no favor in the eyes of these madmen, and the shrine of
St. Geneviève was burnt in the Place de Grève. The new
divinity of this senseless people was Reason, who received in
the temples of the true God, under the form of living statues,
the incense of brutalized worshippers. The priests were banished to Guiana and to the hulks. Most of them died martyrs
to their fidelity, their devotedness, and their faith. A number
of the bishops and priests of the Constitutional Church then
resigned their functions, apostatized and married. The exiled
clergy everywhere, but especially in England, received a most
touching welcome, which they repaid by an edification that
afterward bore good fruit. The death of Robespierre (July
28, A. D. 1794—9th Thermidor, year III.) put an end to this
series of horrors.

17 The Convention was followed by the Directory Of
her ancient traditions, France had kept but one—her warlike
courage. All the powers of Europe—Germany, Prussia, Holland, England, Spain, and Sardinia—had declared war against
the Convention. Generals of an hour, soldiers without food or
clothing, repulsed combined Europe. The Vendean war, in
which a *people of giants* took in hand the outraged cause of justice and the monarchy, was not more successful in turning
France from the path of crime, disgrace, and infamy At that
hour, from amid the heap of ruins, from the very bosom of
these disorders, arose a name which history was yet to place
beside the names of Alexander, of Hannibal, and of Cæsar. A
young Corsican, trained in the military school of Brienne, was
about to cut himself an imperial mantle out of the fragments of
crumbled monarchies and to extend his glory from the Pyramids

to Mt. Thabor, from the Nile to the Black Sea.　Bonaparte, who had already displayed his genius at the siege of Toulon, was made commander-in-chief of the army of Italy (March. A. D. 1796).

18. Pius had opposed this series of revolutionary outrages with a truly apostolic courage.　He had strongly protested against the confiscation of ecclesiastical property; against the seizure of the Comtat-Venaissin, in the name of the republic ; against the scandalous emancipation of religious orders, the law of divorce, the marriage of priests, the massacre and banishment of the faithful members of the clergy　Against these unparalleled outrages, he had used only spiritual weapons, and had moreover observed, in his political relations, a strict neutrality which the weakened temporal power of the Holy See rendered indispensable.　At the very moment when the republican troops invaded the Italian territory, the Pope, wholly devoted to the care of governing souls, was publishing his bull *Auctorem fidei*, in which he condemned the synod of Pistoja, as renewing the repeatedly condemned errors of Wycliffe, Luther, Baius, Jansenius, Quesnel, and the schismatical tendencies of the " Declaration of the Clergy of France," of 1682.　Such was the attitude of the Sovereign Pontiff in the spring of 1796, when, from the summit of the Alps, Napoleon Bonaparte made his first address to his troops : " Soldiers, you are naked, ill-fed. The Directory owes you much and can give you nothing.　Look upon this fair land; it is yours.　Here you shall find glory, wealth, and honors."　The victories of Montenotte, Lodi, Castiglione, Rivoli, and Arcola, answered this appeal of military eloquence, which the student of Brienne had drawn from the deep study of Plutarch, Tacitus, and Livy　Bonaparte proved himself as able in the cabinet as in the field.　The treaty of Rastadt (November, A. D. 1797), in which the youthful conqueror dictated terms of peace, created and organized the Cisalpine republic, while it brought Austria and Sardinia to a pacification disadvantageous to themselves.

19. The negotiations with the Pope were doomed to a less

happy end. It was in vain that the hero of Arcola sent to Pius VI. a messenger with these words: " Tell Pius VI. that Bonaparte is not an Attila, and that, though he were one, the Pope should remember that he is the successor of St. Leo." The Directory named thirty million crowns as the sum which the Holy See must pay unless it would witness the loss of all its Italian possessions. Moreover, the Legations of Urbino were seized. The terms were hard, but submission was a necessity All the orders of the State vied in generosity and zeal to make up the enormous sum which the insolence of triumph required of the Roman States. Pius VI. sent all his plate to the mint, and the generous example was followed by all his people. Meanwhile, the commissioners sent by the Directory came to Rome, and announced in the name of Talleyrand, the unworthy bishop of Autun, who had been appointed Minister of Foreign Affairs by the Republic, that, as a preliminary condition of peace, the Pope was required to recall the briefs by which he condemned the " Civil Constitution of the Clergy " The cardinals, convoked by the Pope, declared that such a demand could not be complied with, as it would overthrow the whole doctrine of the Church. No decision could have been more conformable to the intentions of Pius VI. and to his sentiments of piety " We look upon the crown of martyrdom," he exclaimed, " as far more glorious than that which We now wear." This apostolic speech was a prophecy; it became the rule of conduct of the heroic Pontiff.

20. On the 12th of February, A. D. 1798, the French troops entered Rome under the command of Berthier; they erected a liberty tree on the square before St. Peter's, and on the 15th, General Cervoni appeared in the Vatican before the Vicar of Jesus Christ, to tell him that he was no longer a temporal sovereign. As he seemed to be somewhat confused in his exordium, the Pope said to him: " Well, sir, make known your business without a preface; We are prepared for the worst." Cervoni then proceeded to state that the continuance of the Catholic worship should be solemnly guaranteed, and that the spiritual author-

ity of the Head of the Universal Church should be preserved in ts fulness and integrity   The Pope here remarked : " Sir, that authority We hold from God, and no earthly power can wrest it from Us."   The general endeavored to justify what had been done in regard to the temporal power.   The Pope took up each article in turn, quoted facts, sufficiently proving his fidelity and the unjust violence of the Directory; after which he courteously dismissed the general.   The Pope was to have a guard of five hundred men; on the 16th of February it was suddenly disbanded and Pius VI. was a prisoner in his own palace. They wished to reduce the august Pontiff to request his own removal from Rome ; but all their efforts were fruitless, and, on the 17th of February, he received a positive order to repair to Tuscany, with a threat, in the event of his refusal, that he should be taken away by force.   " But I am hardly convalescent," said the martyr ; " I cannot forsake my people and my duty ; I wish to die here."   " You can die anywhere," brutally replied Haller, the commissioner of the Directory ; " if gentle means cannot move you, force will perhaps be more eloquent." Left alone with a few faithful attendants, Pius VI. for the first time seemed broken down by grief.   Entering his oratory, he recollected himself for a moment in the presence of God, and soon returned with his usual serenity   " It is the will of God," he said, " it is the will of God !   We must be ready to bear whatever it may please Providence to send."   And during the forty-eight remaining hours which he spent in Rome, he did not cease to attend to the business of the Church.   On the very night of his departure (February 20, 1798), the French Commissioner, who had anticipated the dawn, found Pius VI. absorbed in prayer before his crucifix.   " Be quick !" cried the impatient minister of that sacrilegious violence; and hurrying his victim down the staircase of the Vatican, he did not lose sight of him until he had entered the carriage in waiting.   Thus was the venerable Pontiff dragged from his palace and hurried to the uncertain place of his exile and execution, in the thick darkness of a stormy night.

21. On the 25th of the same month, the Pope reached Sienna, where he was lodged, during three months, in an Augustinian monastery   On the 2d of June he was removed to a Carthusian monastery, near Florence.   Still, as his presence in Italy was disagreeable to the Directory, it was determined to bring him into France.   On the 1st of April, A. D. 1799, he was forced to set out for Parma; but here his condition became so alarming that the physicians protested strongly against another removal.   The French officer entered the chamber of the august patient, uncovered the Pope's bed, looked for a moment at the Pontiff with that fierce brutality which so well suited his mission, left the room, and returned almost immediately with the words : "Dead or alive, he must start."   The Duke of Parma had the baseness to furnish a troop of satellites to escort Pius VI. as far as Turin.   As he was trying to justify his conduct to the Pope, by alleging the constraint put upon him, the martyr answered : "Your Royal Highness uses the same argument as did the Jews when deliberating upon the course to be taken in regard to Christ. They said : 'The Romans will come and take away our place and nation.'   Your Royal Highness will allow me to quote the comment of St. Augustine upon the passage : 'They feared the loss of their power, wholly forgetful of everlasting life; and so they lost both.'"   Pius VI. reached the capital of Piedmont on the 22d of April, and learned, on the following day, that France was to be the land of his exile.   "I will go wherever they wish," said the dying Pontiff, raising his hands and eyes to heaven.   On the 26th, he was removed during the night, and taken across the Alps on a rough litter.   During whole hours he found himself hanging over deep abysses and pierced by a cold wind.   At Briançon he was separated from the faithful companions of his martyrdom, and, after displaying a heroic endurance of suffering, at length reached Valence on the 14th of July   "My bodily pains," said he, " are nothing in comparison with the anguish of my heart.   The cardinals and the bishops dispersed !   Rome ! my people ! the Church ! ah. that is the

thought which tortures me night and day In what a state do I leave them!" To these bitter reflections, to this poignant grief, were added new .persecutions. The Directory ordered that the Pope should be removed to Dijon, expressly forbidding any halt at Lyons. But the Pontiff's illness had meanwhile made such rapid progress, that the least exertion might hasten the fatal hour. They were forced to leave him at Valence. On the 13th of August, a deceptive appearance of improvement was visible in the state of the august patient; an immense multitude thronged about the dwelling, earnestly entreating the favor of a last blessing. The officers tried to disperse the crowd, but fearing an insurrection, they begged the Pope to show himself to the people. Pius VI., trusting more to humble submission than to his strength, had himself carried to the balcony, in his Pontifical dress; standing up in the presence of a multitude moved to tears, he exclaimed, in a loud and distinct voice : *Ecce homo,* and with affectionate tenderness gave them his last blessing. On the 29th of August, 1799, Pius VI. expired, breathing a prayer for France. " In truth," says Ranke, " it seemed as if the Papal power was forever at an end." So it might appear to human judgments ; but, amid the most disastrous and threatening events, God was watching, according to His unfailing promise, over the immortal destinies of His Church ; the bark of Peter is never nearer to the harbor than when it seems about to sink beneath the waves.

CHAPTER VII

§ 1. Pontificate of Pius VII. (March 14, a. d. 1800—September 20, 1823).

1 Election of Pope Pius VII.—2. The Concordat.—3. The bull *Ecclesia Christi.* Schism of the " Little Church." Bull *Qui Christi Domini.*—4. Cardinal Caprara in France. Translation of the body of Pius VI. to Rome. Ratification of the Concordat by the *Corps Législatif.* Ceremony at the reopening of the churches in France.—5. Murder of the Duke of Enghien.— 6. Letter of the emperor to Pius VII. Solemnization of the marriage of Napoleon and Josephine.—7 Coronation of the emperor. Sojourn of Pius VII. in Paris. His return to Rome.—8. Memorial of the Pope to Napoleon. The emperor's reply.—9. The marriage of Jerome Bonaparte. Firmness of the Pope. Benevento and Ponte-Corvo retaken from the Holy See. Military occupation of Pesaro, Faro, Sinigaglia, and Civita-Vecchia, by order of the emperor.—10. Peace of Tilsit. Fresh attack of Napoleon upon the Holy See.—11. Occupation of Rome by the French troops under General Miollis.—12. Bull of excommunication *Quum memoranda die.*—13. The Pope removed to Savona.—14. The emperor appoints an ecclesiastical commission. Letter to the captive Pope. The Pope's reply.—15. Divorce of Napoleon and Josephine. The case of the second marriage with Marie Louise.—16. The emperor's interview with the Abbé Emery.—17. A deputation of four bishops sent to the Pope. Concessions wrung from Pius VII.—18. First sessions of the Council of Paris. Arrest of the prelates De Boulogne, Hirn, and De Broglie.—19. Second period of the Council of Paris. Decree of the council. Its confirmation by Pius VII.—20. Campaign of Moscow.—21. The Concordat of 1813, wrung by violence from the Pope.—22. Pius VII. revokes the Concordat of 1813.— 23. The Restoration.—24. Return of Pius VII. to Rome. Restoration of the Jesuits.—25. The " Hundred-Days."—26. Last acts and death of Pius VII.

§ II. Pontificate of Leo XII. (September 28, a. d. 1823—February 10, 1829).

27. Election of Leo XII. His first allocution to the cardinals.—28. Liberal ism in Europe.—29. Count Joseph de Maistre.—30. The Viscount de Bonald.—31. Gallican tendencies in France. The Abbé de Lamennais -

32. Concordat with Hanover. Death of Louis XVIII.—33. Feutrier.--
34. Death of Leo XII.

§ III. PONTIFICATE OF PIUS VIII. (March 31, A. D. 1829—November 30,
1830).

35. Election of Pius VIII. Encyclical letter to all the bishops of the Catholic
world.—36. Conquest of Algiers. Revolution of 1830.—37. Interview
between Mgr. de Quélen and Louis Philippe.—38. Death of Pius VIII.

§ IV. PONTIFICATE OF GREGORY XVI. (February 2, A. D. 1831—June 1, 1846)

39. Election of Gregory XVI. First acts of his Pontificate.—40. Domestic
administration of Gregory XVI.—41. Plunder of St. Germain l'Auxerrois
and of the archiepiscopal residence in Paris.—42. The cholera in 1832.—
43. Spread of dangerous doctrines in France. Condemnation of De
Lamennais.—44. The reign of Louis Philippe.—45. Symptoms of religious
restoration in France. Death of Gregory XVI. Election of His Holiness
Pius IX.—46. Conclusion.

§ I. PONTIFICATE OF PIUS VII. (March 14, A. D. 1800—September 29, 1823).

1. THE Revolution had not yet overcome all Catholic
Europe; the death of the martyr-Pope happened precisely at
the moment when the European coalition was winning new
triumphs over the French Republic. This circumstance enabled the cardinals to meet in Venice, and a few months later
France and the world learned, with astonishment, the election
of a Pope. Unbelief, schism, and heresy, exultingly proclaimed
that the Papacy had lived out its time, and that Pius VI. would
have no successor. And yet, amid the turmoil and confusion of
revolutions, wars, hatred, and rivalry, Cardinal Chiaramonti,
bishop of Imola, was unanimously elected and took the name,
which he bore with so much glory, of Pius VII. Two months
later, the new Pope entered Ancona amid salvos of artillery.
The Russian men-of-war, then in the harbor, fired an imperial
salute, by a special order of Paul I. Six hundred citizens of
Ancona, continually relieving each other, having taken the
horses from his carriage, drew it by long ropes, decked with

ribbons of various colors, to the palace of the cardinal-arch-bishop. On the 3d of July, A. D. 1800, amid indescribable transports of joy on the part of the Roman people, Pius VII. solemnly took possession of the capital of the Christian world.

2. The French reverses in Italy were owing to the absence of a man who held the world in admiration of his splendid exploits on the battle-fields of the East. Egypt, the land of ancient glories, seemed to Bonaparte a fit pedestal for his name, a field worthy of his glory On his return to France, crowned with victorious laurels, but with triumphs fruitless, except of renown, the youthful conqueror was made first consul. He wished to deck this republican dignity with fresh laurels. Italy, the field on which his genius was first displayed, again called for his arms; on the 27th of April, A. D. 1800, he led his army across Mount St. Bernard, and on the 14th of June the celebrated battle of Marengo once more gave him a right to dictate terms of peace to Europe. France received her returning hero with unspeakable enthusiasm. No one could mistake; Bonaparte was to be the restorer of order. Two ways lay open before him for the fulfilment of his mission—the Monk of legitimacy, he could with his victorious sword, rebuild the French Monarchy for the benefit of the Bourbons; or he could take to himself a power which placed itself in his hands. Bonaparte chose the latter course. The history of France was adorned in his reign with brilliant pages; but not one of them, perhaps, is half so glorious as would have been the record that the hero of Arcola, of the Pyramids, and of Marengo, had seated upon the throne of his fathers the heir of Louis XVI. Bonaparte saw that he must first prepare the materials for the edifice he was about to rebuild. It was then that, with the help of the most enlightened men, he drew up those collections of laws, those codes, better suited to immortalize his name, if possible, than even his brilliant victories. Every department of the administration, every public office, underwent a thorough reorganization, more powerful, more central, and easier of control. These improvements brought with them a return of confidence and

credit, insuring to the new government strength for the present and security for the future. In the midst of these labors for the legislative and administrative resurrection of France, Bonaparte was meditating a work that was to crown them all, and open a new era in the history of the Catholic Church It was the peace, the reconciliation of France with the centre of unity, the successor of St. Peter, by the Concordat of 1801. The first proposal was made on the day after the battle of Marengo, by the victor himself. This declaration was so spontaneous, so clear, so precise, that on the very day a cardinal was instructed to communicate it to His Holiness. Pius VII. had just entered Rome. " Tell the first consul," he replied, "that We shall be happy to enter into an arrangement which promises an issue so honorable, so well suited to Our Apostolic ministry, so agreeable to tho desire of Our heart." Consalvi, a prelate toward whom Napoleon seemed to be very favorably disposed, was immediately made cardinal, and charged by Pius VII. to arrange the terms of the Concordat. The French general at the same time sent to the court of His Holiness a man whose name is still dear to the Catholics of France—M. Cacault, whose moderation, conciliatory disposition, wise and prudent diplomacy, won the highest admiration. On taking leave of the first consul, M. Cacault asked how he should treat the Pope. " Treat him," answered the warrior, "as if he had two hundred thousand men." Notwithstanding the display of good will on both sides, the negotiations proceeded slowly. Pius VII. determined to send to Paris Cardinal Consalvi, who was called *the Syren of Rome*, in the hope that the able prelate might succeed better with the first consul. Pius VII. did not overrate the ability of his Nuncio Extraordinary On the 16th of July, 1801, the Concordat was signed in Paris by the first consul, and ratified in Rome a month later by the Pope. The most important articles are substantially as follows :—The religion of the Roman Catholic and Apostolic Church shall be freely practised in France.—The Holy See, in concert with the government, shall determine new limits for the French dioceses.—His Holiness

will announce to the titularies of the old dioceses, that he, with
firm confidence, expects from them, for the good of peace and
unity, every sacrifice, even the resignation of their sees.   If
they refuse, the new dioceses shall be provided ~~by the govern-
ment~~ with new incumbents.—The nominations to vacant bishoprics shall be made by the first consul, and the canonical institution given by the Holy See.—The bishops shall appoint
pastors; but their choice must be limited to persons not objec-
tionable to the government.—For the good of peace and the
happy re-establishment of the Catholic religion, His Holiness
declares that neither he nor his successors will, in any manner,
disturb the holders of ecclesiastical property, and that consequently the ownership of the said property, the rights and
revenues attached to it shall remain in the hands of the actual
holders or of their assigns.—The government shall insure a
proper salary to bishops and pastors.—His Holiness recognizes
in the first consul all the rights and prerogatives enjoyed at
his court by the old government.

3. The bull *Ecclesia Christi* acquainted the Catholic world
with the happy conclusion of the Concordat (August 15, A. D.
1801).   On the same day, Pius VII. dispatched a brief to the
French bishops, telling them that the preservation of unity and
the general good of the Church required of them the pure and
simple renunciation of their sees.   " We are compelled," he
wrote, " by the necessity of the times, which wreaks its violence upon Us too, to announce to you that your reply must be
forwarded to Us within ten days, and that the reply must be
definitive, so that, if it be not such as We look for from your
devotion, We shall be obliged to consider you as having refused
to comply with Our request."   Of one hundred and thirty-five
episcopal sees existing in France, in 1789, fifty-one titularies
were dead, three had already handed in their resignation.
Among the eighty-one remaining bishops, forty-one acceded to
the request of the Pope and offered their resignation.   The
oldest among them, Mgr. de Belloy, bishop of Marseilles, a
venerable man of ninety-two years, the immediate successor of

Belzunce, wrote to Mgr. Spina: "Filled with veneration and obedience for the decrees of the Sovereign Pontiff, I do not hesitate to place in his hands my resignation of the bishopric of Marseilles. It is enough for me that His Holiness deems the measure necessary for the preservation of religion in France, to insure my submission." These words breathe the truly apostolic spirit which animated the three hundred bishops of Africa, under the presidence of St. Augustine, when they offered to yield their sees to the Donatist bishops if they would but renounce the schism. The French bishops did not display the same edifying unanimity Thirty-six of them stood apart from their forty-five noble colleagues and refused the Pope's request, not absolutely, but by their delays. Their protestations amounted to a complaint that the Holy See had never before undertaken to exercise a like authority, and that the measure should have been concerted with the bishops. The reply was easily found ; it was necessary to save France from shipwreck, and Bossuet himself has said that in case of necessity, or even of manifest utility, the Pope has all power and is above the canons. The result of this opposition of the thirty-six bishops to the Concordat was a kind of sect or schism known as that of the *Anticoncordatists* or the *Little Church,* a sect which seemed to place its merit in decrying the Pope and his authority ; a schism in which M. de Thémines, former bishop of Blois, appears to have died. Without allowing himself to be troubled by this resistance, Pius VII, on the 29th of November, 1801, published the bull *Qu. Christi Domini,* to require the observance of the Concordat. He announced that, in virtue of his Apostolic authority, he should disregard the opposition of the refractory bishops and chapters. He suspended them from the exercise of their jurisdiction and declared all their administrative acts null and void. He abolished all the episcopal sees then existing in France, and, in their stead, created sixty new bishoprics, divided into ten provinces. This division was made in accordance with that of the Departments, so that each diocese comprised one, two, or even sometimes three Departments. and the sixty sees included the whole territory of France. The bull *Qui Christi Domini* makes no mention of the dioceses established by the Civil Constitution of the clergy That division was looked upon as never having existed, and the Pope had no need to take away the jurisdiction of those who held none.

4. Immediately after the ratification of the Concordat, Pius VII. sent a legate *à latere* to watch and direct its observance. The legate was Cardinal Caprara, who had already acted as nuncio at Cologne, at Lucerne and Vienna. Consalvi returned to Rome, and was made prime minister. One of the first requests made by the legate was to have the remains of Pius VI. brought from Valence to Rome. The posthumous return of the martyr-Pontiff was a real triumphal progress through all Italy, especially at his approach and entrance to Rome. The whole city, and even all Europe, in the persons of its ambassadors, formed part of the funeral escort. On the 18th of February, A. D. 1802, in the basilica of St. Peter, the solemn Mass, the funeral oration and obsequies were celebrated by Pius VII. in person, in the presence of the ambassadors of all the Christian Powers. It was a kind of reparation of honor on the part of all Europe, to a Pontiff who had so cruelly suffered from the violence or the neglect of all Europe. But the Concordat did not advance so successfully in Paris. Napoleon had to contend with more than one opposing influence. To those who wanted no religion, he was obliged to point out the necessity of religion for the order of all human societies. To those who spoke of Protestantism, he replied that the great interest, the great power of France, was her unity He was repeatedly urged to declare himself head of the Church, as had been done in England, and to set aside the Pope. As he was one day more than usually pressed on this point, he cut short his interlocutor with the exclamation : " Enough, sir, enough : do you also wish me to have myself crucified ?" and as the man of expedients looked at him in astonishment, evidently at a loss to understand his meaning, " That is not your idea," said the consul, " nor is it

mine. Well, sir, that is what must be undergone for the true religion. And beside that one, I neither know, nor wish to know, any other." At length the *Corps Législatif* adopted the Concordat as a law of the State, on the 5th of April, 1802. The councillor of State, Portalis, before reading it, made a remarkable discourse, showing the advantages of the new measure. But he at the same time caused the adoption of several *organic articles*, tending to place the clergy under the absolute control of the government, and of which no mention had been made in the preliminary arrangements for the Concordat. This was a remnant of Jansenistic duplicity by which certain influential men were still ruled. The Pope earnestly protested against these surreptitious additions, which, in time, were abrogated, either expressly or tacitly by being allowed to pass into a state of desuetude. On the 9th of April, Cardinal Caprara entered upon the discharge of his functions. Bonaparte then named the incumbents for the new bishoprics, and the legate gave them the canonical institution in the name of the Holy See. Eighteen of the former prelates were called to govern the new dioceses. Unhappily, a minister of some influence obtained the appointment of twelve of the constitutional bishops : some of them had been, or afterward were, sincerely reconciled with the Holy See; but three or four of them did no more honor to the government or good to their flocks than they displayed true submission to the Pope. The most remarkable nomination was that of the venerable bishop of Marseilles, De Belloy, to the Metropolitan see of Paris. He was then ninety-two years old; he survived his promotion eight years, and died at the age of a hundred, crowned with the loving veneration of all his flock. At length, on the festival of Easter, April 18, 1802, in the Cathedral of Notre Dame at Paris, the new Church of France, re-established by the grace of God and the authority of the Holy Apostolic See, celebrated its own resurrection, amid the triumphal chant and joyful tears of the faithful. The cardinal-legate officiated pontifically before the first consul and his legion of heroes, astonished at the splendors of a ceremonial to which their eyes had long been unaccustomed. A solemn Te Deum sent up to the throne of the God of mercies the expression of the gladness and gratitude of a great people restored to the faith.

5. Great events were crowding upon Bonaparte, greater than in the days of Louis XIV France, in 1802, stretched from the Ocean to the Alps and to the Rhine ; the Ligurian Republic, with its capital, Genoa ; the Cisalpine Republic, its head, Milan, with other Italian States, were its appendices. This wide-spread influence and stretch of territory were the work of the conqueror of Egypt and Italy Misled by perfidious counsels, he had the misfortune to tarnish his glory by the murder of the Duke of Enghien, a crime without reason, without cause, without precedent, a reminder of the days of Terror, under a government whose very existence was a protest against that Terror. But the power of him who was to be known to the world as Napoleon, was so formidable, that no Frenchman dared to brand the crime, instigated by ambition and policy—we mistake: a young man, who was to become, who was, indeed, already the greatest literary glory of his age, M. de Châteaubriand, the author of the " Genius of Christianity," that immortal work so instrumental in preparing the way for the religious restoration in France, was then Secretary of the French embassy in Rome. He at once sent his resignation to the first consul, saying that " he willingly served a government of glory, but that he could not bring himself to serve a government of blood."

6. The assassination of the heir of the house of Condé threw a gulf between the past and the future. On the 14th of September, A. D. 1804, Bonaparte, who had changed his title of Consul for life, to that of Emperor, and his Corsican name for that of Napoleon, wrote the following autograph letter to Pius VII. : " Most Holy Father, the happy change wrought in the character and morals of my people, by the restoration of the Christian religion, leads me to beg Your Holiness to give me a fresh proof of your interest in my welfare and in that of the

great nation which I govern, in one of the most important
events recorded in the annals of the world.   I entreat Your
Holiness to confer, in its highest expression, the sanction of
religion upon the anointing and coronation of the first emperor
of the French.   The ceremony will receive new lustre if performed by Your Holiness in person.   It will draw down upon us
and upon our people the blessing of God, in Whose hands are
the destinies of empires and of families.   Your Holiness well
knows my long-cherished sentiments of affection, and may
gather from them the happiness with which I shall seize this
occasion to give new proofs of it."   As an earnest of his sincerity, Napoleon had restored to the Holy See the principalities
of Benevento and Ponte-Corvo; he had presented to Pius
VII. two ships of war, to protect his commerce, and sent to
Rome, as ambassador, his uncle, Cardinal Fesch.   On the 25th
of November, 1804, Pius VII. reached Fontainebleau, where
he was met by Napoleon; they affectionately embraced and
entered the carriage together.   The minister of police asked
the Pope, "How he had found France?"   Pius replied, "All
thanks to Heaven, we passed through it amid a whole people on
their knees!   We were far from believing it to be in such a
state."   On his arrival in Paris, he received the deputations from
the senate, the legislative body, and the tribunate.   It was like
a national reparation of the outrages heaped by the Revolution
upon the successor of St. Peter.   Four constitutional bishops,
Lecoz of Besançon, Lacombe of Angoulême, Saurine of Strasburg, and Raymond of Dijon, insisted upon being present at the
coronation without subscribing the conditions stipulated by the
Pope in their regard.   Pius was inflexible.   The bishops submitted, threw themselves at the Pontiff's feet, and assured him
of their perfect obedience.   Another, and a still more delicate
obstacle stood in the way of the coronation.   Napoleon had
contracted a civil marriage, in 1796, with Josephine de la
Pagerie, widow of the Viscount de Beauharnais; but the union
had never received the nuptial blessing of the Church.   The
Pope required that the marriage should be solemnized accord-

ing to the Catholic ritual; Napoleon, fearful of the scandal that might arise, refused; but Pius VII. declared that, though he had been ready to make every possible concession in civil matters, he could not disregard the doctrines of the Church. Still, he wished to save all susceptibilities. Consequently, on the eve of the coronation, at eleven o'clock at night, a chapel was prepared in the emperor's apartments and at midnight Cardinal Fesch gave the nuptial benediction to the emperor and empress. The witnesses were Portalis, and Duroc, Grand Marshal of the palace; nothing was made public. When Cardinal Fesch returned to the Pope, Pius simply asked: "My dear son, has the marriage been solemnized?" "Yes, Holy Father." replied the cardinal. "Then," said the Pontiff, "We no longer oppose the coronation of the august empress."

7 The ceremony took place on the 2d of December, in the Church of Notre Dame. "Do you promise," asked the Pope, "to maintain the peace of the Church of God?" "I do promise," answered the conqueror, with a firm voice. He too soon forgot his solemn pledge. The Pope devoted the remaining days of his sojourn in Paris to the interests of religion, which was the main object of his journey. He presented a list of requests relating to the necessities of the Church, to the freedom of the pastoral ministry, and to the abrogation of some of *the organic articles.* Some cardinals thought this a favorable opportunity to demand the restoration of the three Legations, but the disinterested Pontiff would not hamper with temporal concerns the more urgent claims of spiritual matters; and, solely bent upon furthering the interests of religion, he urged, by word and writing, the adoption of measures calculated to repair past evils, to restore to the Church and to France their past glory and the institutions destroyed by the Revolution. The people were never tired of looking upon the venerable Pontiff, whose noble dignity was so much enhanced by a winning sweetness, whose deep piety increased the respect felt for his august character. Accessible to all, he loved to satisfy all and to reiterate his blessings. He bestowed them with especial

tenderness upon children, and, like Him Whose Vicar he was, seemed to delight in being surrounded by the innocent and attractive charms of that guileless age. The presence, the virtues, the charity of the Head of the Church contributed to dispel many prejudices, to recall many wanderers to the fold, and to excite the admiration of the very enemies of the faith. At length Pius VII. set out on his return to Italy, and entered Rome on the 16th of May, A. D. 1805. In this visit, while all seemed outwardly to smile upon him, the Pontiff had occasion to show his apostolic courage and firmness. Napoleon was already planning a universal monarchy; he wished to have the Pope under his hand. With this view, he caused an offer to be privately made to the Pontiff, of a palace in Paris, thrice the size of the Vatican; the Pope might fix his residence there, and from Paris, Pius VII. and Napoleon would together rule the world. "All has been foreseen," replied the Vicar of Jesus Christ. "Before leaving Rome, We signed a formal abdication, to take effect in the event of Our being deprived of Our freedom; the deed is without the reach of the French power; it is in the hands of Cardinal Pignatelli at Palermo, and when the intended project shall have been put into execution, you will hold the person only of a wretched monk called Barnabo Chiaramonti." On the very night of this sublime reply, more glorious than the victory of Marengo, the emperor signed the orders for the departure. On the Pontiff's arrival at Rome, the last of the Stuarts, the Cardinal of York, a venerable prelate of eighty years, in his capacity of Dean of the Sacred College, received Pius VII. at the door of St. Peter's basilica, and congratulated him on the happy issue of his journey *

8. The Pope addressed to Napoleon a memorial on the situation of the Holy See and of the Pontifical States. "As it is necessary for the general good of Christendom," wrote the Pontiff, "that its Head should not want the means to discharge the duties imposed upon him, for his own preservation, the

---

* During his sojourn in Paris, Pius VII. obtained from Napoleon the re-establishment of the Seminary of Foreign Missions, as also of those of the Holy Ghost and of the Lazarists.

Pope cannot be indifferent to the use of those means. His Holiness, therefore, asks the emperor to repair, as far as possible, the losses experienced by the Holy See, and thus to imitate the generosity of Charlemagne." Napoleon himself dictated the answer to the memorial. " Should God grant us the length of days common to men, we hope to find opportunities in which we may extend and consolidate the domain of the Holy See ; even now we are able and willing to stretch out a helping hand, to withdraw it from the confusion and distress into which it has been plunged by the shocks of the late wars, thus giving to the world a proof of our veneration for the Holy Father, of our protection over the capital of Christendom, and in fine of our constant desire to see our religion unsurpassed in the pomp of its ceremonial, the splendor of its temples, and in all that can win the respect and veneration of the world."

9. Napoleon now appealed to the Pope to annul the marriage which his brother Joseph, still a minor, had contracted in the United States with Miss Patterson. The Pope's reply to this request will always stand as a systematic explanation of the teaching of the Church on the indissolubility of the marriage tie. This letter may be looked upon as the personal work of the Pope, for we recognize in it his powerful logic, his mild urbanity, his usual system of revision ; and he moreover declares himself its author. " Your Majesty," says the Pontiff in conclusion, " will understand that, upon the information thus far received by Us, it is not in Our power to pronounce a sentence of nullity We cannot utter a judgment in opposition to the rules of the Church, and we could not, without laying aside those rules, decree the invalidity of a union which, according to the word of God, no human power can sunder." The emperor was not to be stopped by this refusal. He caused the civil tribunals to annul the marriage of his brother, who afterward married a princess of Wurtemberg. The emperor at the same time ordered the military occupation of Ancona, a city belonging to the Holy See (A. D. 1805). The Pope wrote to him on the subject: " The order lately given by Your

Majesty to General St. Cyr, to take military possession of a
city of Our domain, caused Us no less surprise than grief. We
cannot forbear expressing the pain We feel at this treatment,
which We think so entirely undeserved." Napoleon returned
a bitter reply to the Pope's complaint: "I am not only," he
said with insolent haughtiness, "the soldier of the age; were I
a little more its master, I should declare myself Supreme Pontiff, and *I* should not *allow souls to perish*." The emperor's
irritation grew with time. He recalled Cardinal Fesch from
the Roman Embassy, and sent in his stead Alquier, a Protestant and a regicide. The motive of these new rigors was the
Pope's refusal to take part in the continental blockade. The
principalities of Benevento and Ponte-Corvo were seized
and incorporated in the kingdom of Naples. Napoleon gave
Benevento to his Minister of foreign affairs, Talleyrand, formerly bishop of Autun, upon whom he might bestow rank and
wealth, but whom no one could restore to a good name in public opinion. Ponte-Corvo was given to the Protestant general
Bernadotte, afterward king of Sweden. Almost simultaneous
orders were received by General Lemarrois to occupy Pesaro,
Fano, Sinigaglia, and the whole Adriatic coast within the jurisdiction of the Holy See. A body of French troops marched
from the kingdom of Naples upon Civita-Vecchia, and took
possession of the fort and citadel. One of the officers in charge
demanded of the French commander by what right he made the
seizure. The officer replied: "You serve a petty prince and I
a great monarch—that is my warrant." Pius VII. on this occasion said to the ambassador Alquier: "We warn you that, if
any attempt is made to take Rome, We shall refuse entrance to
the Castle of St. Angelo. We intend to make no resistance,
but your troops must break the doors with their cannon.
Europe shall see how We are treated, and We shall at least
have acted in a manner conformable to Our honor and Our conscience." On the 17th of June, 1806, Cardinal Consalvi resigned his office, and was succeeded by Cardinal Casoni, an old
man of seventy-four. The Pontifical government, deeply hurt

by the enfeoffment of Benevento and Ponte-Corvo, ceased to send instructions to Cardinal Caprara, the legate in Paris, and regulated all the business of the Holy See in Rome itself.

10. The glory with which Napoleon was crowning his arms left Europe no leisure to note these acts of violence. Ulm, Austerlitz, Jena, Eylau, Freidland, those immortal triumphs crowned by the treaty of Tilsit (July 8, A. D. 1807), gave to Eugene Beauharnais the vice-royalty of Milan and Northern Italy; to Jerome, the kingdom of Westphalia. During the conferences at Tilsit, Alexander, emperor of Russia, and the king of Prussia, Frederick III., urged Napoleon to declare himself the head of a national religion in France. He refused; yet, if he did not imitate the sovereigns of Northern Europe in their sacrilegious encroachments upon the religion and the conscience of their subjects, if he maintained the Sovereign Pontiff as spiritual Head of the Church, he meant to make him a docile instrument of his policy, and thus to seduce all the Catholics in the world. We shall yet see what it cost him to have raised his hand against that Church of which it is written " The gates of hell shall not prevail against it." In pursuance of his plan of intimidation toward the Holy See, Napoleon sent the following message to Pius VII. : " All Italy is ·mine by right of conquest. If the Pope will not, at my demand, expel all English citizens from his States, close his ports against them, and place his fortresses in the hands of my troops, in the event of a war between France and England, I shall take away his temporal authority, I shall appoint a king of Rome, or send a senator to rule the State." " What can Pius VII. effect by denouncing me to all Christendom?" wrote Napoleon to Eugene Beauharnais. " He can lay an interdict upon my throne; he can excommunicate me. *Does he think this will make the muskets fall from the hands of my soldiers ?* He would have nothing left to do then but to cut my hair and shut me up in a monastery " At the same time the court of France sent official notice to the Holy See of the marriage of Jerome Bonaparte with a princess of Wurtemberg. In the reply

which he was expected to make, the Pope must either refer to the former marriage or not. His silence would approve the new alliance. " We still hope," he wrote, " that, after the examination made by Us of the reasons alleged for the nullity of the first alliance, contracted by the Prince, in Baltimore, new and just motives, not yet made known to Us, may appear, by the force of which the second union, now notified to Us by Your Majesty, may prove valid. This hope sustains Us in the sorrow and anxiety which We cannot banish, when We remember what We formerly wrote to Your Majesty, after mature deliberation, on the matter."

11. On the 2d of February, A. D. 1808, a French army under General Miollis entered Rome; on that very night the Pope directed the following protest to be posted upon the doors of every church in the Eternal City : " Pope Pius VII. finding himself unable to accede to all the demands made of him by the French government, since conscience and the voice of sacred duty forbid, deems it necessary to undergo the disastrous consequences with which he was threatened in case of refusal, even to the military occupation of his capital. Resigned, in humility of heart, to the unsearchable judgment of Heaven, he places his cause in the hands of God ; yet, not to fail in the essential obligation of guarding the rights of his sovereignty, he formally protests, in his own name, and in that of his successors, against any usurpation of his domains ; it being his will that the rights of the Holy See be, and remain, perfectly untouched." The Pontifical Guard was disarmed, and General Miollis held the Castle of St. Angelo. Pius VII. announced to Alquier that, so long as the French troops remained in Rome, he should look upon himself as a prisoner, and that consequently negotiations would be impossible. The cardinals were exiled and taken by armed force to the various countries from which they came By a decree of April 2d, Napoleon took possession of the prov inces of Urbino, Ancona, and Macerata. Among the motives for the sacrilegious usurpation, it was alleged : " The gift made by our illustrious predecessor Charlemagne, of the territory com-

prised in the Pontifical States, was made for the benefit of
Christendom, and not for the advantage of the enemies of our
holy religion." These enemies of the holy religion were the
English, to whom the Pope gave free entrance into his ports;
beside, Napoleon's likeness to Charlemagne was the likeness
that exists between the spoiler and the giver.

12. Pius VII. had made the illustrious Cardinal Pacca his
prime minister. He calmly administered his authority while
awaiting the last blow meditated by imperial violence. On the
6th of September, A. D. 1808, a major named Muzio came to the
secretary's office on Monte Cavallo, and communicated an order
for the exile of Cardinal Pacca. But the Pope, who had
hastened to the apartment on learning the officer's business,
directed him to tell the general that he was weary of suffering
so many outrages and insults from a man calling himself a
Catholic; that he commanded Cardinal Pacca not to obey the
general's orders, and that he intended to keep him as the companion of his captivity   The close of the year 1808 was a long
series of violations of the law of nations, of protests and of
threats of fresh violence. On the 10th of June, 1809, amid
thunders of artillery from the Castle of St. Angelo, the Pontifical banner was lowered and the French flag raised in its place,
while a decree of Napoleon, published by proclamation in every
quarter of the city, announced that what remained of the
Roman States was thenceforth to form a part of the French
Empire. Cardinal Pacca hastened to the apartment of the Holy
Father. As they met, the same thought was expressed by
both at once as they simultaneously uttered the words of Jesus
Christ: *Consummatum est.* On the morrow the celebrated bull,
Quum memoranda illa die, was found posted upon the doors of
every church in Rome. "By the authority of Almighty God,"
said the Pope, "by that of the holy Apostles Peter and Paul,
and by Our own, We declare that all those who, in Rome, or in
the territories of the Church, have been guilty of sacrilegious
attempts upon the temporal rights of the Holy See, with all
their principals, abettors, advisers, and adherents; those **who**

have helped to the perpetration of those deeds of violence, or have themselves perpetrated them, have incurred *major excommunication ;* and if necessary, We *excommunicate and anathematize* them anew." Napoleon was not expressly named in the bull; but it was impossible to mistake the meaning of the words of Pius VII. On the 6th of July, 1809, a detachment of gendarmes, under General Radet, surrounded the Vatican. The Pope was attended by Cardinals Pacca and Despuig, with several prelates and ecclesiastics of his court. Radet appeared before the Vicar of Jesus Christ, telling him that he was ordered to arrest and to take him to General Miollis. "If you think yourself bound to carry out such orders from the emperor," replied the Pope, "because you have sworn fidelity to him, consider how much more We are bound to uphold the rights of the Holy See, to which We are pledged by so many oaths." He then asked the general if he must go alone; he was told that he might take with him his minister, Cardinal Pacca. At the gate of the palace, a carriage was in waiting; when the Pontiff and the cardinal had entered, a gendarme locked the door; Pius VII. was not taken to the quarters of General Miollis; he was now on his way to éxile.

13. The Pope asked the cardinal whether he had brought any money with him. The two illustrious fugitives then examined their purses; in that of Pius VII. were twenty-two cents of French money, and sixteen were found in that of his minister. "Thus," says the cardinal in his memoirs, "they were setting out on their journey *in Apostolic style.*" The Pope showed these remains of his fortune to General Radet, and remarked with a smile : " Of all Our principality, this is what remains to Us." They journeyed through northern Italy, amid populations in tears, who threw themselves on their knees as the carriage passed, in spite of all the efforts made by the guards to drive them off. The Pope entered France by way of Grenoble. There he was separated from Cardinal Pacca, who was taken to Fenestrelle, a stronghold on one of the highest points of the Alps, between Piedmont and Dauphiny, where he ex-

piated, by three years and a half of strict confinement, the crime
of having been true to his sovereign. Pius was taken to Savona, and kept in the prefecture under a guard of gendarmes; no
one was allowed to speak to him alone. Napoleon offered His
Holiness a monthly allowance of a hundred thousand francs,
to meet his expenses. The Pontiff refused all, kept himself
within his apartments, and only appeared at intervals to give
his blessing to the people. He was allowed neither to read nor
to write, except under the eyes of one of his guards. The
cardinals could not escape the persecution directed against
their Head. Napoleon brought them all to Paris, in order to
control their votes more directly, in the event of a vacancy in the
Holy See. Those only were allowed to remain in Rome, whose
age and infirmities made it impossible for them to undertake so
long a journey. Napoleon seemed to delight in parading them
before the eyes of his capital, and in forcing them to appear at
his court.

14. Napoleon's conduct was the beginning of a fall into
schism. "It is very strange," said the emperor one day to the
Abbé Emery, "that you, who have studied theology all your
life, you and all the bishops in France, should be able to find
no canonical way of settling my difficulty with the Pope.
Had I studied theology only six months, I should soon unravel
the whole difficulty, because God has given me understanding."
The emperor assembled an ecclesiastical commission to provide
for the wants of the churches, and especially to find a method
of doing without the Pope in the institution of bishops. The
result of this commission was a letter addressed to the Pope by
Cardinal Maury, a great orator, but a man of low ambition, who
proved himself unworthy of the Roman purple. Maury asked
the Pope to grant the canonical institution to the bishops named
by the emperor. "After so many innovations," answered the
Pontiff, "made by the emperor to the great detriment of religion, and against which We so repeatedly, but so vainly, protested; after the banishment of so many bishops, and of the
greater number of Our cardinals; after the imprisonment of

Cardinal Pacca, at Fenestrelle; after the usurpation of the Patrimony of St. Peter; after seeing Ourself assailed by armed men in Our own palace, dragged from city to city, so closely guarded that even the bishops of the places through which We passed could not approach Our person; after these multiplied outrages, how can We now communicate with their author?" The energy of the reply disconcerted the emperor, as it set all his calculations at fault. But the commission, composed of court prelates, laid before Napoleon a memorial, in which it had the assurance to lavish praises upon the religion, the justice, the Catholic zeal of a sovereign who had just usurped the Patrimony of St. Peter, and who held the Head of the Church in captivity; it insinuated the calumnious accusation brought against the Pope, of sacrificing the interests of religion to considerations of a purely temporal nature. This monument of cringing servility is one of the infamous stains on the annals of the Gallican Church.

15. The conduct of the same bishops was equally disgraceful on another occasion. The victories of Eckmuhl, Essling, Raab, and Wagram, conquered the peace of Vienna (October 13, A. D. 1809). While the emperor sent his brother Joseph into Spain to seek a crown which cost the blood of so many Frenchmen, and placed his brother-in-law, Murat, upon the throne of Naples, he was preparing, for himself, to repudiate Josephine Beauharnais. The soldier of fortune would mingle his blood with that of the Cæsars. The emperor of Austria, Francis II., consented to give to Napoleon the hand of his daughter, Marie Louise. But it was necessary first to annul a marriage, legitimate, valid, consecrated by the Church, and which an ambitious caprice now sought to break, after a union of fifteen years. The episcopal Commission, when consulted in the matter, decided that recourse to the Pope was impossible, the case must be laid before the diocesan officialty, with recourse to the Metropolitan officialty, and finally to the primatial officialty of Lyons. None of these tribunals was in existence; they were all immediately established. As the see of Paris was vacant,

Cardinal Fesch was appointed to fill it, and he thus became judge of the case in all three capacities—as first superior of the diocesan officialty, as Metropolitan of Paris, and as Archbishop of Lyons, Primate of Gaul. The sentence was such as might have been expected. On the 2d of April, 1810, Napoleon married the Archduchess Marie Louise; the cardinals were invited to attend the nuptial solemnity, but thirteen of them failed to appear, " for the reason," they declared, " that the Pope had had no part in the dissolution of the first marriage." Napoleon put no bounds to his anger against these courageous prelates; he no longer allowed them to wear the distinctive color of their rank, and made them dress in black. This was the origin of the well-known distinction between the red cardinals and the black cardinals. The emperor then banished the black cardinals to various provincial towns, and deprived them of their income. On the 20th of March, 1811, Napoleon became the father of a son, who received at his birth the title of King of Rome; the usurped title was not destined to be a harbinger of good to the imperial infant.

16. The heart of the great emperor was not gladdened by the joys of domestic life. He laid before the ecclesiastical Commission, always in session, propositions wholly subversive of the authority of the Holy See. Cardinal Fesch, urged this time by the influence of the Abbé Emery, ventured to remark to his formidable nephew: " Sire, all the bishops will resist, you are going to make martyrs." That word made the emperor shudder. Sending for the Abbé Emery, he asked him in a tone of furious anger: " What is the Pope ?" The venerable octogenarian had already offered up the sacrifice of his life; " Sire," he replied, " I can hold no other opinion, on that point, than that which is contained in the Catechism taught by Your Majesty's orders in all the churches of France. *The Pope is the Head of the Church, the Vicar of Jesus Christ, to whom all Christians owe obedience.* Can a body exist without its Head; without him to whom, by divine right, it owes obedience ?" " Well," rejoined the emperor, " I grant the spiritual power. But the

temporal power was given to the Pope by Charlemagne, and I, as Charlemagne's successor, feel bound to take it back from him, because he does not know how to use it and it hinders him in the discharge of his spiritual functions." Emery was prepared for this attack. "Your Majesty," he said, "honors the great Bossuet. Bossuet, Sire, speaks thus: 'We are well aware that the Roman Pontiffs and the priestly order have received, by the grant of kings, and do lawfully hold, property, rights, and principalities, as other men do, on very good titles. We know that these possessions, inasmuch as they are dedicated to God, should be sacred, and that no one can, without sacrilege, invade or seize them, or give them away to seculars. To the Apostolic See has been given the sovereignty of the city of Rome and of other possessions, that the Holy See might more freely and securely exercise its power throughout the whole world. On this we sincerely congratulate, not only the Apostolic See, but also the universal Church, and we pray, with all the fervor of our heart, that, in every way, that *sacred principle* may remain safe and untouched.'" The Abbé Emery delivered from memory this passage of the "Defence of the Declaration of the Clergy," which he had carefully studied. Napoleon broke off the conference. "The Abbé Emery," said he, "spoke like a man who is thoroughly master of his subject; I like to be talked to in that way" "The emperor," says Cardinal Pacca, on this subject, "would, perhaps, never have been a persecutor, if, in the beginning, he had found in the bishops of France the firmness, the learning, and the courage of the Abbé Emery"

17 These parleys amounted to nothing. The emperor thought that he should meet with more success by calling a national council, for the 9th of June, A. D. 1811. He hoped, by this measure, to intimidate the Pope, and to force him into compliance. He made a show of granting the request of the cardinals and bishops assembled at Paris, that they might be allowed to send a deputation to Savona; but he himself named the prelates who were to compose the deputation; appointed a

day for their return to Paris, and dictated the fundamental articles of the new treaty they were to conclude, if they found the Pope disposed to negotiate. The three prelates named were: M. de Barral, archbishop of Tours; M. Duvoisin, bishop of Nantes, and M. Mannay, bishop of Trèves, all learned prelates and skilful in the transaction of business, but of a servile compliance toward the secular power. The terms dictated by Napoleon were as follows:—The emperor agreed to abide by the Concordat of 1801, but on two conditions: 1. That the Pope grant canonical institution to the bishops already presented; 2. That in future, he send the bulls, within three months after the presentation, that otherwise the Metropolitan be allowed to confer the institution upon the suffragan.—Pius VII. at first rejected the propositions of the deputies, with energy, but at length, at the last hour, he yielded; and, availing themselves of a momentary weakness, the negotiators at once drew up, under his eyes, a promise which it would have been impossible for him afterward to disavow, though it did not bear his signature. Pius VII. consented to grant canonical institution to the bishops named, in the hope, as he said, that the concession might restore peace and order in the Church. Hardly had the deputies withdrawn, when Pius VII., realizing the gravity of the concessions wrung from him by surprise, fell into a deep melancholy and wept most bitterly; with deep groans he accused himself in terms of heartfelt repentance. The bishops, meanwhile, returned to the emperor with a report of their mission; but the Pope's promise was for the time kept secret.

18. The imperial council, or the Assembly of French bishops called by Napoleon, met on the 17th of June, A. D. 1811. It consisted of ninety-five prelates, of whom six were cardinals, nine archbishops, and eighty bishops. It was an imposing assemblage, but, in a canonical point of view, it was not a council. In fact, the first condition necessary was, that the bishops should be allowed to come freely and of their own accord; but Napoleon had arbitrarily summoned those

whom he deemed favorable to his views, to the exclusion of
the others whom he held in prison or in exile. Cardinal Fesch
began by taking upon himself the office of president; he officiated Pontifically at the opening ceremony, when Mgr. de
Boulogne, bishop of Troyes, a rival of Maury in eloquence, but
of a far more noble character, made a discourse which insured
his disgrace with the emperor. "Never," said he, "shall we
forget all that we owe of love and respect to that Roman Church
by which we were begotten to Jesus Christ and nourished with
the milk of doctrine; to that august Chair which the Fathers
call the citadel of the truth, and to that supreme Head of the
Episcopate, without whom the whole Episcopate would destroy
itself and could only wither away like a branch torn from the
parent stock. That See may be displaced, it cannot be destroyed; its splendor may for a time be taken from it—its power
never! Wherever that See may be placed, there shall all the
others be gathered around it; wherever that See may be moved,
there shall it be followed by all Catholics; for wherever it
stands, there shall be the root of succession, the centre of
government, and the sacred deposit of the Apostolic traditions."
These words made a deep impression, but caused no change in
the result of the Assembly Only one general session was
held; after that there were only congregations held at the
archiepiscopal palace. The serious, the difficult question for
which Napoleon had called the prelates together was, to find
a satisfactory substitute for the Pontifical bulls in the canonical
institution of bishops. The Bishop of Nantes asked whether,
in a case of extreme necessity, the bulls might not be dispensed
with. But the Commission refused to accept the question
put in this form, and wished that it should be first discussed whether the council had the authority to appoint another
way of instituting bishops. The question gave rise to long debates; at length the majority of the bishops, to their honor be
it said, decided that it would be necessary to refer the matter
to the Pope by a solemn deputation. Napoleon, irritated by
this turn of affairs, signed a decree dissolving the council, on

the 18th of July, 1811. The bishop of Ghent, Mgr. de Broglie; the bishop of Tournay, Mgr. Hirn; and the bishop of Troyes, Mgr. de Boulogne, who had displayed a truly apostolic firmness in the course of the debate, were arrested at night and thrown into the dungeons of Vincennes. Napoleon was fairly started in the way of persecution.

19. The Council of Paris, dissolved in a fit of anger, was reopened by a new whim of the emperor. Napoleon ordered the Ministers of worship, in France and Italy, to summon successively each of the bishops of their respective nations then in Paris, in order to force them, in the personal interview of the closet, to sign a promise, in conformity with that signed by the four deputies, under the eyes of Pius VII. The caresses, the intimidation, used individually upon the various prelates, succeeded admirably. Assured of having the majority of the votes in his favor, the emperor once more summoned the council (August 5, A. D. 1811), which, on the motion of M. de Barral, passed the following decree: "Article 1. Agreeably to the spirit of the canons, archbishoprics and bishoprics shall not remain vacant more than one year, at the furthest; within that space of time, the nomination, institution, and consecration must be completed. 2. The emperor shall be requested to nominate to the vacant sees, in conformity with the Concordats; and the candidates appointed by the emperor shall apply to our Holy Father the Pope for canonical institution. 3. Within six months after the notification of said nomination, made to the Pope, by the usual means, the Pope will grant canonical institution, according to the Concordats. 4. Should the Pope have failed to grant the institution within the stated six months, the metropolitan, or, in his default, the oldest bishop of the ecclesiastical province, shall proceed to the institution of the bishop nominated; and, if the institution be that of a Metropolitan, the oldest bishop shall confer the institution." This decree was presented to the Pope for confirmation, by five cardinals and nine bishops deputed to wait upon the august prisoner at Savona. Pius VII., already fettered by the promise made to

the first deputation, surrounded by cardinals solemnly pledged to favor the designs of his persecutor, terrified by the fearful picture of the evils which, it was represented to him, would burst upon the Church in the event of his refusal, yielding at length to the importunities with which he was beset, consented to grant the bulls to the bishops named by the emperor, approved and confirmed the decree of the council by a brief, drawn up by Cardinal Rovarella, one of the deputies.

20. The report of this triumph reached Paris as Napoleon was preparing to set out on his Russian campaign. On the 9th of May, A. D. 1812, the emperor, always hitherto triumphant, quitted a place to which he was doomed to return only with the shame of defeat. He was followed by six hundred and fifty thousand men; he had under his orders eight monarchs, who came to pay their court to the emperor as he passed through Dresden. This is the hour which God has chosen to show His judgments. The *muskets are about to fall from the hands of his soldiers*. Heaven will now confirm the excommunication launched against the conqueror by the august Pontiff of the Vatican. On the 9th of June, while Napoleon is passing through Prussia, Pius VII., by his order, is rudely transported from Savona to Fontainebleau. We know the history—Moscow, Smolensk, the Beresino, the Niemen. The French were no longer fighting against enemies; they were battling with the elements. " All turned against them," says an eye-witness of those fearful scenes, " even their weapons. They seemed an insupportable weight to their numbed and frozen arms. In their repeated falls, *the muskets fell from their hands*, were broken or lost in the snow When they rose, it was without their arms; *for they did not throw them away, hunger and cold snatched them from their grasp.* The fingers of many of the men froze upon their pieces, and thus deprived them of the motion necessary to preserve a little remnant of heat and life."

21. The Pope had been five months a prisoner at Fontaine-

blcau,* when Napoleon reached Paris, the herald of his own
terrible defeat. The *Grande Armée* was reduced to twenty
thousand men, wandering, needy, starving, without clothes and
without arms. While busied in repairing the immense disaster,
with his usual incredible activity, he understood how useful it
would be for his success to effect a real or at least an apparent
reconciliation with the Holy See. He accordingly visited Fontainebleau. The Pope and the emperor had not met since the
day of the coronation. How changed was all since then! Napoleon was, by turns, caressing, hostile, cold, impetuous, and
threatening. He laid before the Pope a new Concordat,
"which," he said, "would smoothe all difficulties." Pius VII.
was seventy-one years old. His health, shattered by grief and
fatigue; his feelings, excited by the desire of seeing the cardinals held in captivity; the importunate solicitations of the
prelate Bertozzoli, who urged him to make every concession;
the entreaties of the two Italian cardinals intrusted with the
negotiation of the important matter, and who continually
harassed him with threatening anticipations; the total absence
of any wise, noble, friendly voice to arouse that soul weighed
down by suffering; in fine, the prospect of approaching death—
all combined to dishearten the Pontiff. Pius VII. was now
left with little more than the faculty of making that mechanical
motion of the hand necessary to write a name. That name was
affixed, on the 25th of January, A. D. 1813, to a paper which the
emperor signed at once. The Pope bound himself to give the
canonical institution within six months to the bishops named,
after which delay the institution might be conferred by the
Metropolitan or the oldest suffragan. He renounced the sovereignty of Rome and agreed to reside wherever it might please
Napoleon. The emperor commanded that the conclusion of
this Concordat, wrung from the Pope by a shameful abuse of

* While Pius VII. was forsaken or betrayed by cardinals and bishops, whose first duty
was fidelity to the Head of the Church, several families, equally illustrious by their rank
and their sincere religious sentiments, among others, those of Montmorency-Laval and of
the Marchioness de la Riandrie, consoled the august captive by testimonials of their unal-
terable devotion.

power, should be solemnly announced to the empire, and a *Te Deum* sung in all the churches. On these terms the cardinals saw the end of their captivity or their exile; they hastened to meet the Pope. Pius VII. was especially anxious to see Cardinal Pacca, his consoling angel.

22. The interview between the Pontiff and his old friend was most touching. " Pius VII.," says the illustrious cardinal, " was bent, pale, haggard, his sunken eyes almost dark and lifeless." The remembrance of the concession lately wrung from him weighed upon him as a gnawing remorse. Pacca assured him that, helped by the counsel of the faithful cardinals, " he could repair the evil that had been done." These words seemed to recall the august Pontiff to his senses; his countenance lighted up as he asked : " Do you then think that there is any remedy ?" " Yes, Holy Father," replied the cardinal; " with a will, there is no evil that cannot be remedied." On the 24th of March the Pope sent an autograph letter to Napoleon, most formally and explicitly retracting his concessions of the 25th of January " In the presence of God," wrote the Pontiff. " before Whom We shall soon be called to give an account of the power intrusted to Us as Vicar of Jesus Christ, for the government of the Church, We declare, in all Apostolic sincerity, that Our conscience invincibly opposes the execution of the articles contained in Our deed of the 25th of January. We acknowledge with grief and confusion that We should be using Our authority, not to *build up*, but to *destroy*, had We the misfortune to execute what We imprudently promised, not, as God is Our witness, with any evil intention, but through pure weakness, for We are but dust and ashes. We can only address Your Majesty in the words spoken by Our predecessor Pascal II. to the Emperor Henry V : ' Our conscience recognizing the evil of Our writing, We confess it to have been evil, and, with the help of God, We wish it to be completely annulled, that no harm may come from it to the Church, nor any prejudice to Our soul.' " Napoleon was not touched by this sublime humility; he uttered threats of death

against the faithful cardinals; but events, more swift than his will, were pressing upon him on all sides and left him no time to commit new deeds of violence. The forced resignation of the Bishops of Ghent, Tournay, and Troyes, and the usurpation of their sees by intruded imperialists, were the last religious acts of the reign of Napoleon.

23. The eagles, once borne on victorious pinions through all the capitals of Europe, now driven back to the very heart of France, had lost their proud flight and their scream of triumph. Brienne, Montereau, Montmirail, Toulouse, Champaubert, Vauchamp, Nangis, and Paris, were the last gigantic struggles of an exhausted nation, of a genius forsaken by fortune and falling amid the ruins of its own glory   On the 23d of January, A. D. 1814, Pius VII. was once more removed, by the emperor's orders, and taken toward the south of France. Napoleon feared that the allied powers might set his prisoner at liberty   But Fontainebleau had hardly lost sight of the Sovereign Pontiff, when it received another great personage, who was destined to give the astonished world a lesson on the emptiness of human glory   Napoleon, beaten back by the allied armies, in that palace where the Pope had so long lingered in captivity, learned that the Emperors of Russia and of Austria, the King of Prussia, and the Duke of Wellington, his conqueror, had entered Paris, that his deposition had been decreed on the 1st of April, by the senate, through the influence of Talley-- rand,* his former minister, a man loaded with his favors.   On the 4th of April, urged, constrained by his most intimate confidants, Marshals Ney and Berthier, of whom he had made princes, he signed his own abdication to satisfy the demands of his father-in-law, Francis of Austria, and of the Emperor Alexander, who had said to him, six years before, at Tilsit: "The

---

* On their meeting in Paris, the allied sovereigns were still undecided as to the use they should make of their victory. Some spoke of the regency of Marie Louise. for the benefit of the young King of Rome; the name of the Duke of Orleans was suggested by others , Talleyrand, in that tone of a political oracle, which was respected by victory itself. remarked: "The legitimist rule can alone save France." His advice prevailed, and the Bourbons, whom he was afterward to betray, owed him their return.

friendship of a great man is a gift of Heaven." In the court-
yard of Fontainebleau he embraces his eagles for the last time,
and starts for the island of Elba, that narrow sovereignty
allowed by his conquerors to him, the conqueror of the world.
—Amid the tears and joyful acclamations of a whole people,
Louis XVIII, now took possession of the throne of France,
upon which his predecessor, Louis XVII., had never reigned ;
Mme. Royale, now Duchess of Angouleme, was at his side,
a memory of past storms and a pledge of present forgiveness.
France was in ruins, but the return of her sovereign restored
her in the eyes of the allied sovereigns. Peace was concluded
on the 30th of May, 1814. France kept her boundary as it
existed in 1792, and even gained some slight extent of territory on the north and east. The Bourbons would return only
as respected sovereigns, and armed Europe appreciated this
noble and generous sensitiveness. Louis XVIII., before entering into his capital, stopped at St. Ouen to sign the Constitutional Charter, the spontaneous concession of a magnanimous
heart, which proved that the past was all forgotten, but which
was not powerful enough to secure the future. Weary of a
despotism of fifteen years, France welcomed, with enthusiasm,
a system which gave her a national representation, freedom of
the press, an equilibrium of the powers, through the two Chambers of Peers and Deputies. Three articles of this charter concerned religion; they were as follows : " Every individual may
profess his own religion with equal freedom, and obtain equal
protection for his worship. Still the religion of the Catholic,
Apostolic and Roman Church is the religion of the State. The
ministers of the Catholic, Apostolic and Roman Church, and of
the other Christian denominations, shall alone receive salaries
from the royal treasury."

24. Pius VII. reached Ancona on the 12th of May. The
enthusiasm excited among the people, by the return of the venerable Pontiff, bordered on delirium. The Pope's carriage was
drawn by the inhabitants, amid shouts of triumph, salutes of
artillery, and the joyous sound of all the bells. On the fol-

lowing day, the venerable Pontiff, bathed in tears, crowned, in the cathedral, the statue of the Blessed Virgin under the title of "Regina Sanctorum Omnium;" a guard of honor escorted him as far as Loretto. During his journey he gave orders that the kindness and respect due to misfortune should be shown to Mme. Lætitia, the mother of Napoleon, and to Cardinal Fesch, who came to Rome, seeking that hospitality which Rome never withholds from the unfortunate. On the 24th of May, Pius VII. made his solemn entrance into the capital of the Christian world. At his side was Cardinal Pacca, the faithful companion of his exile, who shed tears of joy at the unlooked-for happiness of a Pope he loved so well. On the next day several Roman noblemen, who had been implicated in the late disturbances, came to ask forgiveness of the Pope. "And do you think," asked the Vicar of Jesus Christ, with sublime humility, "that We have no faults to atone for Ourself? Let us join in forgetting the past and in thanking God for the present." What was said of St. Vincent de Paul may also be said of Pius VII. "When he conversed, he took away the soul of his hearer and put his own in its place." As soon as he was again seated upon his throne, the Pope determined to repair the injury done by the times to the Jesuits. He was convinced that a cruel experience of twenty-five years had at length taught the Christian rulers the true character of the Revolution and the hidden aim of the simultaneous outcry raised in Europe against the Society of Jesus. On the 7th of August, A. D. 1814, the bull *Sollicitudo* officially restored the Society of Jesus throughout the Christian world, and the decree was hailed with joy by all the true friends of the Church and of religion.

25. On the 26th of February, A. D. 1815, a man attended by a few fellow-fugitives landed at Cannes; twenty days afterward Napoleon was in the Tuileries; he had cut his way through the troops sent against him. Marshal Ney, whose double treason is recorded in history, accompanied with a regret that a character so weak should ever have been allied to such heroic daring on the field of battle, promised to seize and

bring back in an iron cage the man whose very presence was a revolution;—he was the first to give the example of defection. and Napoleon once more found himself at the head of an extemporaneous Empire. His reign lasted a hundred days and overturned the order of Europe. Pius VII. displayed all his native firmness amid the storm. " M. l'Ambassadeur," said he to the minister of Louis XVIII., " fear nothing, this is a visit which will last but three months." Wellington and Waterloo undertook to realize the prophecy of Pius VII. Napoleon, beaten for the first time in a pitched battle, showed himself great in his misfortune. Like Themistocles, he sought hospitality from the nation against which he had fought so long. England had not the generosity to appreciate such greatness of soul; she replied by an act of dastardly meanness. But she was the unwitting instrument of Providence, punishing, in the prisoner of St. Helena, the persecutor of Pius VII.

26. The situation of the Church of France once more called for the attention of the Pope. On the 11th of June, A. D. 1817, a new Concordat was signed by the Holy See and Louis XVIII., to restore that of Leo X. and Francis I., and to abolish the " organic articles" in so far as they were contrary to the doctrine and laws of the Church. All the episcopal and archiepiscopal sees erected in the year 1801 were to be maintained with their actual incumbents; forty-seven new sees were to be erected. The principal dispositions of the Concordat could not be carried out, because the Chambers refused to ratify them. The tribune was already beginning to take its stand in opposition to the throne. It was at this time that Mgr. Frayssinous, so well known for his *Conferences* of Notre Dame, wrote his work on the " True Principles of the Gallican Church," in which doctrines hostile to the Holy See were set forth with the same assurance as if, since 1682, men had neither learned nor forgotten any thing. Mgr. d'Aviau, the illustrious and holy archbishop of Bordeaux, wrote to the author these beautiful words : " Yes, old French bishop as I am, I could sincerely wish that a reputation so well deserved as yours had not been abused to

display the deplorable theories of Gallicanism." Pius VII
exerted all his moderation and inexhaustible kindness to soothe
the excited minds and extinguish these fatal discussions. On
the 5th of June, 1817, he concluded a Concordat with Maximilian, king of Bavaria, to regulate the ecclesiastical affairs of
that kingdom. In 1818 a similar treaty was signed by the Pope
and the King of the Two Sicilies. In 1819, a brief, addressed
to all the bishops of France, put an end to the difficulties
caused by the Concordat of 1817 The tireless vigilance of the
illustrious Pontiff seemed to gain strength with years. On the
13th of September, 1821, a bull, stamped with a truly Apostolic
energy, was launched against the Carbonari who threatened the
peace of Italy On the 5th of May, in the same year, Napoleon breathed his last on the rock of St. Helena, and Pius VII.,
forgetting all his wrongs, remembering only his benefits, prayed
for his persecutor. Europe was proud of its Pontiff, whose
reign was the longest since St. Peter's. But his shattered
health sunk under multiplied labors. On the 20th of September, 1823, Pius VII. slept peacefully in the Lord, and went
to receive, in a better life, the reward of his toils and his virtues. A few moments before his death, an ecclesiastic addressing him by the title of " Your Holiness," he said with a sigh :
" How! *Holiness!* I am but a poor sinner." Thus died one of
the greatest Pontiffs of modern times.

§ II. PONTIFICATE OF LEO XII. (September 28, A. D. 1823—
February 10, 1829).

27 Cardinal Della Genga was elected to succeed Pius VII.
on the chair of St. Peter and took the name of Leo XII. Infirmities and the labors of his various nunciatures, in Germany
and in France, had broken him down before his time—he was
but sixty-three years old. On learning his election, he said to
the cardinals : " Why make a Pope of a skeleton ?" The sincere piety, the pure morals and amiable qualities of the new
Pontiff speedily won the admiration of the world. Leo XII.

did not shrink from the thought of the difficulties to be met in the government of the Church. His first allocution to the cardinals disclosed his whole mind. "You are not ignorant, Venerable Brethren, of the cruel wounds lately inflicted upon the Church of Jesus Christ; what enemies fight against the true faith; what a looseness of morals everywhere prevails; what clogs, difficulties, and stumbling-blocks, are everywhere thrown in the way of the Church. It shall be Our care, Our labor, day and night, to stem this fearful torrent of evils."

28. The new enemy now threatening Christian Europe and the Church was the so-called *liberalism,* an offshoot of the spirit of revolution. While the iron hand of Napoleon weighed upon the world, there was but one despotism—his own. The Restoration was the epoch of the awakening of liberty; then arose a despotism more threatening, more terrible, perhaps—the despotism of the masses, the despotism of popular sovereignty The press, so long restrained, now poured out upon the multitudes floods of the most impious, licentious, and anarchical ideas. Then France and Europe wondered at the multiplied editions of the philosophers of the eighteenth century; the Voltaire of the hovel rose up beside the monumental Voltaire of the great libraries. A misguided generation still thirsted for those poisoned springs; so true is it that, if history is indeed the great school of experience for individuals, yet its lessons are almost invariably lost upon the masses. They preserve the memory neither of the mind nor of the heart. Leo XII. struggled with noble energy on the new field in which the enemies of Catholicism had set their standard. He found faithful allies in the clergy of Europe. In France, the illustrious orator, Mgr. de Boulogne, that confessor of the faith, attacked the evil emanations of the press in eloquent pastoral letters, which were translated into every language as fast as they fell from his inspired pen. But his courageous efforts could not wholly check the fearful tide of opinions. The press had, in the tribune, a staunch ally, a constant echo, a devoted power.

29. In the hour of danger, the hand of God ever prepares and

holds in readiness, for the defence of His Church, men whose talents, energy, and character, are equal to the call of events. Two illustrious names now showed forth, in full splendor, the great apologetic glories of Catholicism. They were those of two laymen, Joseph de Maistre and De Bonald. Joseph de Maistre was born at Chambéry, on the 1st of April, A. D. 1753, of a family of French origin; one branch still subsists in Languedoc. He received his first lessons of piety in the arms of his mother, Christine de Motz, who afterward intrusted the care of his education to the Jesuits. When the French forces invaded Savoy, in 1793, he went to Lausanne, where he was engaged by the king of Sardinia, Victor Amadeus, in an important correspondence with the Department of foreign affairs. His residence on the frontier of France, in a free country, the common asylum of refugees from all parties, afforded him opportunities of making himself thoroughly acquainted with the events which interested all Europe; his deep historical studies, his foresight and his penetrating mind gave an immense value, not only for his master, but for all the European cabinets, to his notes on men and on the real situation of affairs. Bonaparte found this correspondence, whole and entire, in the archives at Venice; he read with surprise and admiration the accurate and able judgments, the political prophecies realized by himself. With this practical knowledge of things, M. de Maistre could safely treat great religious questions, and he did it with resistless brilliancy, spirit, and logic, in his immortal works, *du Pape* and the *Soirées de St. Pétersbourg*. Under the pen of this illustrious writer, history is no longer a narrative of the past, it is a prophecy of the future; the law of religion is not only a means of salvation for individuals, it is the necessary, the indispensable condition upon which depends the existence of society.

30. His contemporary, the Viscount de Bonald, whose son now so ably graces the Roman purple in one of the most illustrious sees of Gaul, was educated by the Oratorians at Juilly. When the "Civil Constitution of the Clergy" was forced

upon the weakness of Louis XVI., M. de Bonald was president
of the administration in the department of Aveyron. He wrote
to his colleagues a letter, afterward made public, in which he
most energetically branded the conduct of the Assembly, and,
fearless of the thunders he might be invoking upon his head,
dared to uphold the necessity of referring the whole matter to
the judgment of the Pope. " The National Assembly," he
wrote, " has decreed changes in ecclesiastical discipline and in
the Constitution of the clergy; it has imposed upon pastors the
oath of observing and maintaining them. And could I, who am
commanded to believe, not to decide; I, who know that a disregard for the Holy See and for the authority of the chief pastors has been the main-spring of all the religious dissensions
that have desolated the Church and the State; I, who can not
separate the respect I owe to my religion from the respect it
requires for its ministers—could I venture to anticipate the
decision of the Head of the Church, brave the unanimous opin·
ion of my pastors, and dishonor my religion, by putting its
priests in the alternative of sacrificing conscience or interest;
between perjury and degradation. Could I say to them :
Swear, or give up your office, your means of subsistence, as
men were once told, *Believe or die !* No, no, gentlemen, no!
humanity, no less than religion, revolts at the thought!" After
this splendid resignation, M. de Bonald was soon on his way
to exile. This manly eloquence was recognized in the author
of so many religious works, in which the highest philosophy
becomes a willing handmaid to the science of the sanctuary
His " Theory of Political and Religious Authority, in Civil Society, demonstrated by reasoning and history," placed M. de
Bonald, at the very outset, among the most distinguished thinkers and writers. The first edition of that work which marked an
epoch, was seized by the police of the Directory and destroyed
The author answered the outrage by a new masterpiece. In
1802, appeared the work entitled " Primitive Legislation viewed
in later times by the sole light of reason." This is the capital
work of the Christian philosopher. In 1818, he published his

"Philosophical Inquiries on the first Objects of Moral Perceptions."

31. The spirit of these two illustrious writers was in strong contrast with the symptoms of Gallican resuscitation shown by some members of the clergy   M. de Frayssinous, not content with publishing writings showing a spirit of hostility to the Holy See, stood up in the Parliamentary Tribune, against the spread of Ultramontane doctrines.   Mgr. de la Luzerne, cardinal-bishop of Langres, in his numerous writings, upheld the old ideas of Gallicanism which had resisted so many revolutions, outlived so many falls, and seemed to have impregnated the heart of the French clergy, like the oil soaked into a vessel.   It was then that a priest, hitherto unknown, entered the lists and gave his name, destined at a later period to win a renown so widely different, to the applause of the Catholic world. The first volume of the " Essay on Indifference in matters of religion" had just appeared (A. D. 1818), signed by M. l'abbé de Lamennais. Within a year that name had gained the celebrity attached to those of Châteaubriand, De Bonald, and De Maistre. Logic and eloquence, vigor and grace of style, bold thoughts, sublime imagery, that majestic flow of language which recalled the traditions of the Golden Age, the new manner, the captivating turn, the choice of subject—all was beautiful in this work. Its effect was immense ; its author was already styled a second Tertullian ; alas! he was destined to bear too close a likeness, by his errors, to that great character of the first ages of the Church ; but then nothing foretold the coming defection.   An escort of young and brilliant minds, devoured by zeal for the truth and thirst for learning, gathered around the new teacher, and the Church applauded the triumph of one of her children. The second volume of the " Essay on Indifference " appeared soon after ; De Lamennais was now but a bold declaimer. Misled, doubtless, by the generous illusion that he might do away with all the old systems of philosophy and compel the unbelieving to bow to the yoke of faith, he claimed to make the common consent of men an infallible criterion of truth.   The

liscussions to which this celebrated thesis gave rise, in the
religious world, are well known. It is known, too, that they
ended in a lamentable apostasy. God doubtless wished to give
another example of the impotence of genius when it strays
from the path of obedience.

32. Leo XII. had, in the meantime, published the bull
Impensa Romanorum Pontificum sollicitudo (March 26, A. D
1824), to secure, by a Concordat, the interests of the Catholic
Church in Hanover. The Pontifical decree created two bishoprics in that kingdom, Hildesheim and Osnabrück. The Pope
provided for the observance of the decrees of the Council of
Trent, endeavored to recall the dissident members of the " Little Church," in France ; condemned the schism of the Jansenists at Utrecht; expressed the solicitude of the Church for the
Irish and Belgian Catholics; restored to the Jesuits the direction of the Roman College and prepared the way for a Concordat
between the Holy See and the Grand Duchies of Baden and
Nassau. By the bull *Etsi Filius Dei*, he approved the Congregation of Oblates of the Blessed Virgin, founded by two Pied-
montese priests, to preach the gospel to the people and to give
missions. He likewise succeeded in settling the difficulties
which opposed the re-establishment of the episcopal sees in the
province of the Upper Rhine. Less successful in France, where
de Frayssinous was at the head of the Department of public
education, Leo XII. had the grief to see that prelate endeavoring to establish a new Sorbonne, *to be the guardian of French
principles.* This gave occasion to the youthful archbishop of
Paris, Mgr. Hyacinthe de Quélen, to give the first proofs of
that episcopal vigor which he was at a later period to display
with so much glory He expressly announced to the minister
that he should refuse all faculties to the priests intrusted with
the chairs in the new Sorbonne. The most pressing solicitations
failed to change his determination, and the project of de Frayssinous failed. Such was the situation of affairs in France at
the death of Louis XVIII. (September 16, 1824.) A disputed question of jurisdiction kept the clergy of Paris from fol-

lowing the remains of the king to St. Denis; the evil-disposed gave a different meaning to this circumstance, and stated that the king had died without having accepted the last consolations of religion. But Louis XVIII. died a Christian death. On the eve of his decease, as the curé of St. Germain was reciting the last prayers, in a low tone, by his bedside : " M. le curé," said the dying monarch, " pray aloud and do not fear that you will frighten me. I am not afraid of death; only bad kings do not know how to die." The throne of France passed to the Count of Artois, brother of Louis XVI., who took the name of Charles X. He inaugurated his reign by a measure which proved the goodness of his heart while it betrayed the weakness of his character; he abolished the censorship of the press; this was disarming himself in the presence of the enemy.

33. Charles X. removed De Frayssinous from the ministry of public education, and gave his place to M. Feutrier, bishop of Beauvais. The administration of this prelate was signalized by an open hostility to the true principles of ecclesiastical discipline. Several bishops had intrusted their seminaries to members of the Society of Jesus. Many French families availed themselves of this circumstance to obtain for their children a Christian education, and to avoid the obligation of sending them to the University institutions, already beginning to excite suspicion by their teaching. On the 16th of June, A. D. 1828, two ordinances of Charles X., the one countersigned Portalis, the other Feutrier, forbade the bishops to employ members of a religious order in the ecclesiastical schools, to receive any externs or even boarders, beyond a limited number. This decree placed Christian families in the painful alternative, either of exposing their children to the dreaded contagion of the government schools, or of sending them abroad for the safety of their faith and morals. The French bishops protested against the decrees in a memorial addressed to Charles X., and declared that they could not in conscience observe their prescriptions. Leo XII. was consulted; his answer was addressed to M. Feutrier, who did not think proper to make it public. Several

of the prelates published a circular, in which they granted to the government only a right of *inspection—surveillance*—over seminaries. The Pope condemned this doctrine. " The expression *inspection*," said he, " in the wide sense in which it may be taken, should not certainly be admitted in the Church of Jesus Christ ; it has been unanimously rejected by several councils." Notwithstanding these significant words—in spite of their own convictions, the bishops were forced to bow to the power of the minister. To make the submission easier, certain subsidies were voted to their preparatory seminaries, and the state of servitude was thus organized.

34. Leo XII. ended his Pontificate on the 10th of February, A. D. 1829, wept by his own people and by all Christendom. The year of his death was signalized by the Catholic *Emancipation* in England. The efforts of the celebrated O'Connell, whose eloquent appeals have not yet died away, and whose death was an occasion of general mourning in Europe, effected that act of strict justice, which gave at length to a considerable portion of the population of the United Kingdom the rights so long withheld by the most revolting intolerance. The Pontificate of Leo XII. was marked by the apparition of the cross of Meigné ; the sign of man's redemption, soaring in the heavens, had once again, as in the days of Calvary, been the scandal of the impious—the consolation, the hope, and the strength of the faithful.

§ III. PONTIFICATE OF PIUS VIII. (March 31, A. D. 1829— November 30, 1830).

35. Cardinal Castiglione, elected on the 31st of March, A. D. 1829, under the name of Pius VIII., inaugurated a reign which was destined to be but short, by the publication of the celebrated encyclical letter, *Traditi humilitati nostræ.* Like a watchful sentinel set upon the mountain to give warning of approaching danger, the Holy Pontiff raised the cry of alarm, amid a society corrupted by false philosophy, misled by the deceitful shadow of liberty, perverted by the press, seduced by

the sophistry of the tribune; an imprudent and blind society, hurrying to snatch the fruit from the tree of the knowledge of good and evil, and exulting in its very madness. Pius VIII. pointed out to the reprobation of the world—1st, the endeavors of a multitude of men, hidden under the cloak of false philosophy, to overturn the chair of St. Peter, the centre of truth, the depository of tradition, the guardian of faith and morals; 2d, the lamentable tendency toward a spirit of indifference in religious matters, as if the multiplied religious systems could all insure salvation; 3d, the spread of Bible Societies; 4th, that of the secret societies already condemned by Popes Clement XIII., Benedict XIV., Pius VII., and Leo XII.; in fine, the Pope called the attention of bishops to the evil of mixed marriages, a source of most serious disorders, and of the loss of so many souls.

36. The apprehensions of the Sovereign Pontiff were too soon justified by the event. The Dey of Algiers had insulted the French consul. Charles X. said to M. de Bourmont: "Algiers has insulted France; go and take Algiers. All the soldiers I place under your orders are my children; be sparing of their blood, see that all their wants are satisfied; you shall answer to me for all." Two months later, the white flag floated over the Algerian rock that had so long threatened the freedom of the seas. These were noble words and great deeds (July 5, A. D. 1830); but it was the legacy of the legitimate monarchy; its testament was to be a victory. While the French soldiers were covering themselves with glory, abroad, the government was preparing for a fearful struggle at home. The charter of Louis XVIII. had borne but bitter fruit;—disorders in the administration, a spirit of insurrection in the masses, an organized system of insult against every thing beautiful, holy, and respectable; in a word, anarchy everywhere. It was time to break that network that enveloped the monarchy At least so it was then believed. On the 25th of July, 1830, appeared the celebrated *Ordinances*, suspending the freedom of the press, changing the mode of election, and dissolving the ancient Chamber.

Were such ordinances issued to-day, after the personal experience of thirty years added to the experience of our fathers, only one fault would be found with them—that they are not absolute enough. The reason is, that, weary now of an unbridled freedom, barren in its results, ruinous in its excesses, unpopular by its ceaseless harping upon the miseries of the people, without the slightest attempt to relieve them, we feel an immense want of authority In 1830, the deceitful mirage was still trusted; the Ordinances caused a revolution. Charles X. trod the path of exile, bearing with him, in the folds of his glorious banner, three generations of kings. There was a man in readiness to gather. up the fragments of that great fall, which he had, perhaps, provoked, but of which he certainly hastened to profit; from the midst of the barricades he raised up a throne destined to be no stronger, and took the name of Louis Philippe I., king of the French.

37 The courageous archbishop of Paris, Mgr. de Quélen, was urged, in an interview with the new monarch, to lead the way in taking the oath in the Chamber of Peers, since his example, it was alleged, would determine all the inferior clergy to imitate him. " That is a mistaken notion," answered the prelate. " The government that should thus receive my oath would have M. de Quélen dishonored, it would not have the Church of France. The Pope is the only one who can settle the question. If he sanctions the oath and the prayers for the actual head of the State, the oath will be taken and the prayers will be recited everywhere; should he forbid them, I shall be the first to obey him; and the public prayers, which I have thought proper to sanction provisionally, shall be stopped, if he forbid them, as soon as his will is known." Pius VIII. was consulted, and replied by a sanction which he could not refuse. The Papacy, according to the public law of modern Europe, has no share in the making or unmaking of governments; but it saves souls and consolidates peace under all governments. The noble reply of Mgr. de Quélen was not forgotten.

38. Amid the storms excited by the new revolution in

France, Pius VIII. closed his short Pontificate.   Borne down by years and infirmities, he died on the 30th of November, A. D. 1830. As temporal ruler, he gave special attention to improvements in the condition of the poorer classes; he lessened the taxes and furnished work for the people.   As Head of the Universal Church, he intervened, after the capture of Adrianople and the treaty of peace concluded between the Russians and the Porte, in favor of the Armenian Catholics who had been driven from their homes ; he obtained for them the erection of an Armenian archbishopric in Constantinople itself, the recall of the exiled, the recognition of their rights, and the restitution of their property.   He strongly urged the Emperor of Brazil to abolish slavery in his States, and Don Pedro respected the voice of the common Father of Christendom.   The tidings of the Irish Emancipation, under the ministry of Sir Robert Peel (April 12, 1829), gladdened the heart of Pius VIII., in the beginning of his Pontificate ; and the conquest of Algiers, destroying the piratical dens in which thousands of Christian victims had been pining away for centuries, soothed, in his last hours, the grief caused by the spirit of revolt then breaking out in all directions.

§ IV PONTIFICATE OF GREGORY XVI. (February 2, A. D. 1831— June 1, 1846).

39. On the 2d of February, A. D. 1831, from the balcony over the main entrance of the Quirinal, Cardinal Albani announced to an immense multitude the name of the new Pontiff. " I make known to you tidings of great joy ; we have for Pope, His Eminence Mauro, Cardinal Cappellari, who has taken the name of Gregory XVI." The moment was a solemn one.   At the death of Pius VIII., Europe was fearfully convulsed by the shock of the revolution of July, which had spread in all directions.   France is as the great heart of the world ; each of its pulsations is felt to the ends of the earth ; it is the political thermometer of nations.   Italy, divided into so many petty

sovereignties, agitated by secret societies, and especially by the *Carbonari;* Italy, which has preserved but the memories of its ancient glories, amid the shameful weakness of its enervated characters, was stirred up by the breath of French liberalism. The rebellion already extended from Bologna to the gates of Rome. But the storm was stilled under the hand of St. Peter's successor; a cry of universal joy hailed the accession of Gregory XVI., who inaugurated his Pontificate by acts of bounty and firmness. " What strengthens Us most," said the Pontiff, in the encyclical letter published three days after his enthronization, " is the thought that the Heavenly Father will not allow the trials he sends Us to exceed Our strength." With the help of Austria, he put down the symptoms of revolt in the Pontifical States. If it pained the fatherly heart of Gregory XVI. to use such means for the pacification of the States of the Church, he suffered no less keenly at the sight of the anarchy and disorder breaking out in many other lands; and it was for this reason that he so strongly urged the bishops of Poland and of Belgium to stand aloof from all share in political matters, by reminding them of their ministry of peace, and of the duties of subjects toward their rulers. Liberalism vainly poured out all its wrathful venom against a Sovereign Pontiff who dared to proclaim, in the full light of the nineteenth century, the principle of St. Paul, that " all power is from God." The abuses of the temporal power in Poland, soon after, afforded the enemies of the Church ample matter for their malicious attacks ; it was proclaimed from every tribune, it was written in every public organ, that all was over with the Papal grandeur and dignity. Gregory XVI. deceived these ill-boding prophecies. In his circular letter to all the bishops of the Catholic world (August 15, 1832), while openly declaring himself the adversary of a false and dangerous spirit of innovation, he solemnly proclaimed his firm resolve to preserve and to defend the ancient Apostolic traditions.

40. As soon as peace was completely restored to the Pontifical States, the Pope at once turned all his energies to the

reformation of old abuses, and to the exclusion of new ones. The universities, closed during the revolution, were reorganized; a system of greater economy introduced into every department of the administration; officers in high places removed for dishonesty or oppression; the receipts and expenses, since 1817, subjected to a necessary investigation, to determine the lawfulness of the privileges, pensions, and subsidies granted since that date; a new body of laws promulgated; a new penal code submitted to the judgment of all the presidents of tribunals; a more equitable assessment of the land tax proposed to the deputies convoked from all parts of the Pontifical States; Chambers of Commerce established in Rome, and in the cities and seaports of the provinces; the courts of appeal and the criminal courts thenceforth to be presided over by lay judges; the most rigorous justice exercised toward all; arts and sciences patronized with equal taste and magnificence; the Etruscan Museum founded in the Vatican; the Basilica of St. Paul raised up from the ruins of the conflagration of July 15, A. D. 1823. Such were the domestic labors which marked the Pontificate of Gregory XVI. The Pope continued to live like a simple monk, according to the austere rule of the Camalduli, sleeping upon the ground, abstemious in his diet, watching far into the night, working with untiring zeal, praying always. He loved to gather about him and to make use of the great men of his time; he appointed the learned Cardinal Lambruschini, Secretary of State; restored the nunciature in France, after an interruption of twelve years, intrusting it to a prelate, whose name is dear to every Catholic heart, whose faithful services were afterward rewarded with the Roman purple, and whose recent loss was an occasion of general mourning—Mgr. Fornari; he brought into the Sacred College—as, formerly, Leo X. had introduced Bembo and Sadolet—the finished scholar Angelo Mai,* and the philologist Mezzofanti.

---

* Since the writing of these lines, H. E. Cardinal Mai has ceased to exist. His death is an irreparable loss to ecclesiastical science, of which he was one of the most learned and successful restorers; it has thrown a veil of deep mourning over all who had the happi

41. The most furious among the revolutionary leaders in France did not hide their desire and their intention of destroying the Catholic worship; the politicians who now held the power in their own hands wished to put a curb on the spirit of anarchy, even while giving pledges to the spirit of revolution. The first acts of Louis Philippe gave expression to this twofold tendency The church of St. Geneviève was deprived of its sacred character of worship, and turned into a heathen temple, with its heathen name of Pantheon; the modified charter no longer recognized the Catholic religion as the religion of the State, but only declared that it was that of the majority of the French people. Still Louis Philippe imperiously required the oath of the clergy for his new power, and the insertion of his name in the public prayers sung in all the Catholic churches. Mgr. de Quélen gave the example of this act of official submission; but his heart and his sympathies were with another cause. Gregory XVI. knew it well; he understood and admired that noble self-devotion; more than once, words of kindly sympathy fell from the chair of St. Peter to console the heart of the afflicted prelate. The work of irreligious violence still went on in Paris. The church of St. Germain l'Auxerrois was sacked; the archiepiscopal residence was plundered and utterly destroyed.

42. Mgr. de Quélen, to avoid the fury of the persecution, was obliged to seek shelter among faithful friends, and lived like an exile in the midst of his diocese. The hand of God, more powerful than the hatred of men, was soon to draw him forth again into the light. A scourge hitherto unknown in Europe, the plague of modern times, perhaps the same as that of earlier ages, with a mere change of name—the cholera, crossing the bounds of Asia, after ravaging the north of Germany, had now reached the soil of France, heralded by the terror and dismay that goes before its every step. Suddenly apprehensions become a reality; the cholera is in Paris; the

ness to know and to admire the affability, the sweetness, and the modesty of the learned cardinal

hospitals are filled; the additional ones opened in every direc
tion are unequal to the demand; all business ceases; all better
instincts are changed and weakened ; families shut themselves
up in solitude ; the infant dies at the breast of the mother, who
sinks in turn, to be closely followed by the other members of the
household ; the scholar is seized in his study, the mechanic in
his workshop ; the wealthy in their sumptuous apartments, the
poor in their dens of squalid misery   One single day records
eighteen hundred deaths (April 10, A. D. 1832).   It was as the
funeral of a whole people ; the Belzunce of the nineteenth century, Mgr. de Quélen came forth from his retreat at the call of
the plague, which was to him as the voice of God.   He appeared
more majestic than in the hour of his greatest prosperity, more
calm than in the day of peace ; he feared neither the storms
lately unchained against him, nor the scythe of the pitiless
reaper who swept away, at random, virtue and vice, without
distinction of age or rank.   He hastened to the hospitals,
crowded with dying sufferers, where each instant was marked
by a sigh of death.   Every heart was moved, every eye was
filled with tears.   At the bedside of fathers and mothers, who
left their children to his care, soothing the sharp pang of agony,
pressing the icy hands of the agonized victims, receiving their
last aspirations, Mgr. de Quélen promised to be a father to so
many orphans.*   On the 28th of December, 1832, he appeared in public for the first time since the plunder of his
residence.   The church of St. Roch, in which the heroic prelate
was to preach, was besieged, from an early hour, by dense
masses of people, who crowded every approach to the holy sanctuary   Every eye was fixed upon the pulpit, awaiting the
approach of the prelate.   At the sight of the noble countenance,
wan with grief, prematurely wrinkled by suffering, but ever

---

* Several of these wretches acknowledged to Mgr. de Quélen, with many tears, that they
had taken part in the plunder of the archiepiscopal palace and in the scenes of horror by
which it was attended. " We did not know you then," they exclaimed, bursting into tears,
' we were deceived by our leaders." The heroic prelate comforted them, allayed their remorse by repeated assurances of his forgiveness, and soothed their agony by his paternal
consolations. He revenged himself only by redoubled zeal and tenderness.

mild and majestic, a unanimous feeling of deep emotion thrilled the whole assembly ; at the sight of the immense concourse of the faithful, who had come together to see him once more, to hear his voice again, he could not restrain his own tears. His voice, tremulous at first, gained firmness as he proceeded, without losing any of its unction ; not a word of reproach, not a reminder of the past, escaped his lips ; like St. Vincent de Paul, he came to plead the cause of the orphans, and he gave his whole attention to that duty As the holy archbishop quitted the pulpit, he saw that vast multitude, in tears, pressing around, almost smothering him, kneeling to receive his blessing. Eighty thousand francs, the fruit of the collection, were placed, on the evening of that glorious day, in the hands of the prelate, to begin the work of charity for the cholera orphans, a work which has since poured over a million into the bosom of the poor.*

43. The cholera was but a momentary check to the torrent of evil doctrine in France. It has been said that the government did not favor the spread of these doctrines, but it at least tolerated them ; or rather, devoted to all the political vicissitudes of the majority, it had enough to do to provide itself with ministers ever ready to recompose a cabinet continually changing. Born of revolution, the new power supported itself by means of intrigue, of flattering all revolutionary passions, repressing riots, eluding the efforts of assassins, destroying men by means of each other, and continually renewing this sisyphian toil, which seems to be the character of every parliamentary administration in France. To exist amid so many elements of ruin was already an achievement. Saint Simonianism, Fourierism, phalansterism, the French Rite of the Abbé Chatel, an apostate priest, by turns misled the public mind and drew down upon their authors the thunders of the Church. But the clamors of the liberal press deafened the ears of the people to

---

* " General returns made by the officers of the fund for the cholera orphans." *Historical Notice*, by M. Sylvain Caubert. The return is confirmed by the accounts of the Princess de Beauffremont, treasuress of the fund.

the once revered voice of the successor of St. Peter. The grossest instincts of materialism, protected by unbelieving ministers, and represented, in the meanest hamlets, by those whom the Government placed at the head of the communes, came upon the nation like an incurable leprosy Once, indeed, the voice of the Vicar of Jesus Christ silenced the general din. It was when it spoke to condemn M. de Lamennais. Then, thirty-three million French Catholics bent in obedience. But the man who might, by an act of docility, have won a right to rank forever with the immortal Fénelon, met this deserved censure with the scandal of the *Paroles d'un Croyant*, of which Europe soon destroyed the incendiary pages.

44. The governments of Germany were not more favorable to religion. Pius VII. had forbidden the bishops of Rhenish Prussia to solemnize mixed marriages, except on certain conditions expressly specified. Gregory XVI. renewed the prohibition. The king of Prussia, Frederick-William III., urgently solicited the bishops to disregard the order They refused. On the 20th of November, A. D. 1837, Mgr. Augustus Droste-Vischering, archbishop of Cologne, was seized, like a criminal, by an armed force, and thrown into a dungeon. His imprisonment caused an immense sensation. It was afterward the salvation of the Orthodox Church in Germany At a later period, Switzerland showed equal intolerance, and an open persecution was begun against the illustrious bishop of Lausanne and Geneva, Mgr. Marilley France then witnessed the famous struggles concerning the University monopolies and the freedom of teaching, as well as that of the councils. Mgr. de Quélen died in 1840, wept by all France. The men in power thought that they might gain more from a new archbishop who should be indebted to them for his election. They erred. Mgr. Affre ascended that throne which he was to illustrate by his glorious martyrdom. The last words that passed between him and Louis Philippe were the following: " Remember, archbishop, that more than one mitre has been broken !" " True, Sire ; but God preserve the king's crown, for we have seen many crowns

brɔken, too." The tragical end of his heir, the Duke of Orleans, the multiplied attempts upon his own life, the periodical convulsions of France at the approach of the elections, the symptoms of discontent daily expressed by local insurrections, the corruption which stood even upon the steps of his throne and devoted some of his ministers to public contempt, were lessons lost upon Louis Philippe. He was doomed to fall, as he had risen, in the midst of the barricades.

45. Yet, amid these threatening signs of approaching storms, the Church had her consolations and her glories. The admirable work of the Propagation of the Faith, which had sprung, all armed, from a noble and pious heart, sent its missionaries to the farthest shores. The Arch-Confraternity of Notre-Dame-des-Victoires multiplied miracles and conversions, wrought through the intercession of the Mother of Mercy; the clergy of France won the admiration of the world by its learning, zeal, and piety; may we not be permitted to inscribe here the names dear to our gratitude, and enshrined in the veneration of the whole Catholic world—H. E. Mgr. Gousset, archbishop of Rheims, and of Mgr. Parisis, then bishop of Langres. The pulpit of Notre-Dame was then filled by those two princes of sacred oratory, Fathers Ravignan and Lacordaire. The Catholic tribune had the illustrious Count de Montalembert. The science of history, recalled by Thierry and Guizot, though in spite of themselves, to a spirit less hostile to Catholicity, was beginning to do justice to the names of St. Gregory VII., of Innocent III., and of St. Pius V Such were the various elements at work in European society at the death of Pope Gregory XVI. (June 1, A. D. 1846). His wisdom, firmness, and constancy, unshaken by the fiercest storms, have won him an immortal name in history Fifteen days later (June 16, 1846), Cardinal Mastai Ferretti, bishop of Imola, ascended the Pontifical throne, under the glorious name of Pius IX., amid the glad and triumphal anthems of Italy and of the world. Heir to the name of Pius VI. and of Pius VII., like them, he has triumphed over the storm; he is loved and venerated as they were.

46. We have now given a complete view of the various phases through which the Church has passed during the eighteen centuries of its existence. Religion, the daughter of Heaven, the noble ally of society, the mother of civilization, the protectress of science, the benefactress of the human race, has remained pure and unchanged, while all around her has undergone ceaseless variations The Roman Empire has fallen; the Jews have been scattered over the face of the earth; Paganism has disappeared from Europe; she alone stands, as the funeral processions of nations pass by, raising her majestic brow amid revolutions and ruins. What has become of Arianism? Where are the Nestorians, the Eutychians, the Monothelites, the Pelagians, the Manicheans? What has become of that swarm of heretics by whom she was so often assailed? Their names, indeed, still live in the records of history, but their works have perished; the offspring of passion and of lies, time has scattered them to the winds; and that Roman Church, whose glory they would have dimmed, whose name they even dared at times to usurp, has outlived them; she has dared their efforts, she laughs at their threats and their impotent attacks; because she is built upon the imperishable rock against which the powers of hell shall never prevail

APPENDIX

SKETCH OF THE ORIGIN AND PROGRESS

OF THE

CATHOLIC CHURCH

IN THE UNITED STATES OF AMERICA.

BY REV. C. I. WHITE, D. D.

I.

WHEN the divine Founder of Christianity threatened the Jewish people with the forfeiture of the high privileges that had been conferred upon them, declaring that the kingdom of God would be taken from them, that many would come from the east and the west, and would sit down with Abraham, Isaac, and Jacob in the kingdom of heaven, but that the children of the kingdom would be cast out into the exterior darkness,* He only affirmed that general law which Divine Providence observes in the government of the world, by which the blessings or graces bestowed upon one nation or individual, if rejected or abused, are transferred to another who will make a better use of them. This law of the translation or substitution of graces was fulfilled, not only in regard to the posterity of Abraham who opposed the teachings of Christ, and even put Him to death; it has been illustrated throughout the whole history of the Christian Church. The recognition of this law may be termed the philosophy of ecclesiastical history. It is the great practical lesson or wisdom to be derived from the contemplation, on the one hand, of the power and mercy of God for the salvation of souls, and, on the other, of the rigorous justice which will be meted out to those who reject the offers of His goodness. We behold prov-

Matth. viii.

inces and kingdoms, where the true faith once flourished in all its splendor, deprived of this rich inheritance; while, at the same time, the glad tidings of salvation are borne to other regions of the globe seated in darkness and in the shadow of death. If Luther and his fellow-reformers in the sixteenth century succeeded in wresting from the Church a large portion of her children, the providence of God had already prepared a fruitful field for the precious seed of truth in the new world discovered by the genius and enterprise of Columbus, where all the losses sustained by Catholicism in Europe were more than compensated by its widely-extended and enduring conquests in America. In Mexico and in the southern portion of the continent, the true faith soon rallied under its banners millions of souls that had been grovelling in the darkness of barbarism and infidelity. The light of revealed truth was not to penetrate so easily, or with such rapid march, into that territory which is now embraced within the limits of the United States. Here it was destined to encounter obstructions of every kind, which would delay indeed, but could not prevent ultimately the triumph of the faith. Although the successes which it has achieved commenced at a later period than those in other portions of the continent, they are not the less to be considered as a part of that Providential scheme, by which the Church is to repair on American soil the losses which it has suffered in other regions of the world.

According to this view of the subject, or even considering it in its purely historical facts and developments, it is a matter of surprise that the more recent writers on ecclesiastical history have not attached a greater importance to the establishment and progress of Catholicity in the United States. There is scarcely a history of the Church published within the last thirty years in which any thing more than a brief allusion is made to the state of religion in this country. The work of the Abbé Darras, a translation of which is now presented to the public, seems to ignore altogether the important fact that in the United States of America the Catholic Church has a wider field of operation than in Europe; that it counts its millions of children, united under the government of a numerous, zealous, and learned hierarchy, and exhibits in its political and social condition the amplest facilities for the propagation of the true faith and the most favorable circumstances for its diffusion among men. For this reason it has been thought advisable to append to the history of Darras a sketch of the establishment and progress of Catholicism in the United States, not merely to supply a vacuum in that work, but particularly to give its readers on this side of the Atlantic some insight into that series of events which must necessarily be for them a subject of peculiar interest. Many excellent publications on our Church history have appeared within the last thirty years; but they are limited in their scope, touching only upon particular branches of the subject. We shall refer to them more especially in the sequel. In the historical sketch here presented to the public, we shall draw freely from those sources of information, without overlooking those original documents which may render the narrative more interesting and instructive.

.II.

In the territory now comprised within the limits of the United States, Catholicity, from its earliest introduction, had but a temporary, fluctuating, sporadic existence. In this respect, however, it only presented those features which have been almost universally exhibited upon the announcement of the gospel among barbarous and superstitious nations, or the preaching of the true faith in the midst of a neterodox people. From the year 1512, when Florida was discovered, down to the year 1776, when the American Colonies declared their independence of the British government, we behold but an alternation of triumphs and trials, in which the zeal of the apostle, the courage of the confessor, and the heroism of the martyr displayed themselves as in the purest ages of the faith, and laid the solid foundation of that spiritual edifice which is now presented to our admiration in the American Church.

During the period of which we are speaking, the theatre of missionary zeal embraced the Spanish colonies of the South, New Mexico, Florida, and California; in the North and West, Maine, New York, and the Valley of the Mississippi; and in the East, the colonies of Maryland and Pennsylvania. In the first-mentioned region, the blood of the martyr flowed from the very outset. In 1542, Father Padilla, a Franciscan priest, and a lay-brother were both pierced with arrows by the Indians whom they sought to evangelize. After an interval of forty years, however, missionaries of the same order succeeded in converting whole tribes to the faith; and although the result of their labors was considerably impaired by the incursions of hostile nations, the inhabitants in general remained steadfast in their religious principles. About the same time, the Dominican Fathers, aided by the Jesuits and Franciscans, were pursuing their apostolic labors in Florida; but,

not until several generations of martyrs had shed their blood in vindication of the faith, did the natives of that region embrace Christianity.
The zeal of the devoted missionary was at length crowned with success. Communities of neophytes gathered round the Spanish posts,
and this happy state of things continued until the middle of the
eighteenth century, when the country was invaded by the hostile
colonists of Carolina, the missions were destroyed, and the Indians
driven back to their wandering life.* Toward the close of the
seventeenth century, flourishing missions were established at different
points in Texas, by the Franciscan Fathers, who also, in 1768, visited
Upper California, where, in the course of fifty years, they had not less
than seventy-five thousand converted Indians under their spiritual
charge. These splendid results of their labors, however, almost totally
disappeared when the political revolution of 1825 drove the missionaries from that country.

In the North, the field was occupied chiefly by the sons of St. Ignatius. As early as 1612 they succeeded in evangelizing the Indians
of Mount Desert Island, off the coast of Maine; but this good work
was soon checked by the assaults of a piratical crew from the shores
of Virginia. Some years after, in 1646, a mission was commenced by
Father Druillettes among the Abnakis (now the Penobscots and Pas-
samaquoddis) within the State of Maine, which resulted in the conversion of the whole tribe. Their most illustrious missionary was
Father Rasle, who lived among them for thirty-two years, until 1724,
when he fell a victim to the cruelty of the English settlers, who at the
same time did their utmost to obliterate every trace of Catholicity
among the Indians. To this day, however, they persevere in the faith
of their fathers. In the State of New York, the Jesuits were equally
successful, after the severest trials, and even that of martyrdom itself,
in converting to the faith the powerful nation of the Iroquois. But,
by the machinations of the English, the missionaries were at last compelled to abandon their Catholic cantons, the people of which emigrated to Canada, where they still preserve their nationality and their
religion.

In the seventeenth century, the Jesuits extended their labors to different parts of the West, in the vicinity of the great lakes, while Father
Marquette, after having discovered and explored the Mississippi in
1673, opened all that country to the enterprising zeal of his brethren.
Flourishing missions soon sprang up among the various tribes that

* Shea's *Catholic Missions;* Henrion, *Histoire des Missions.*

stretched from the head waters of the Mississippi to the Gulf of Mexico; but, after a century of indefatigable toil, these Catholic settlements became, to a great extent, destitute of pastors, owing chiefly to the suppression of the Society of Jesus, and, as a necessary conse· quence, the faith was destined to languish and, in some localities, to be extinguished. It is worthy of note that, in 1727, soon after the permanent colonization of Louisiana by the French, an Ursuline community was founded at New Orleans, under the auspices of the Jesuits, which has continued its work of charity and education without interruption to the present day. This is the first religious community of women established within the actual territory of the United States.

As early as 1570, the soil of Maryland was bedewed with the martyrs' blood, when Jesuit Fathers from Florida visited the country in the hope of evangelizing the natives, but were put to death through the treachery of their Indian guide. In 1634, a more successful effort was made to plant the true faith in that part of America. Sir George Calvert, an English nobleman and a convert to the Catholic faith, having obtained from the British king a charter for the settlement of Maryland, a colony of two hundred English families, chiefly Catholic, landed on the shores of the Chesapeake Bay, on the 25th of March of the above-mentioned year, accompanied by two priests, Fathers Andrew White and J Altham, with two lay-brothers, all of the Society of Jesus. On the same day, after having offered up the holy sacrifice of the Mass, they carried in procession a large cross to a place marked out for it, the Governor, commissioners, and other Catholics bearing part in the ceremony, and "raised it a trophy to Christ the Saviour, humbly chanting, on bended knees and with deep emotion, the Litany of the cross." The missionaries, on their arrival, lost no time in commencing their apostolic labors. The site for a city having been selected on St. Mary's River, an Indian hut of the larger size was obtained, which was the first chapel in Maryland. "Besides attending to the spiritual wants of the settlers, the pious missionaries visited the different Indian tribes. Father White resided for some time among the Patuxent tribe, some of whom joined the Church." In 1639, a priest was stationed on Kent Island in the Chesapeake Bay, and the same year Father White "took up his abode among the Piscataway Indians, about fifteen miles south of Washington City The fruits of his labors were seen in the conversion of the king, Chilomacon, his family, and many of the tribe." Soon after, the young queen and nearly all the natives of Potopaco (Port Tobacco) were added to the Church, making about one hundred and thirty converts. The Jesuit missionaries continued their labors successfully for ten years, having been assisted toward the end of that period by some Capuchin friars. In 1644, however, a rebellion broke out in the province, which resulted the following year in the expulsion of the Governor and the overthrow of his authority, and in suspending the work of the mission. " A body of soldiers, or rather lawless brigands, who arrived in 1645, laid waste, destroyed, and fired the whole colony. Having driven the Governor into exile, they carried off the priests and reduced them to a miserable slavery." Although the missioners returned in the course of a few years, they were soon destined to encounter the most serious obstacles in evangelizing the natives, and to suffer the most painful restrictions even in exercising the holy ministry among the settlers. The Catholic colonists still retained, in 1649, an ascendency in the legislature, and passed an act which provided, that no Christian believer should be disturbed on account of his religious opinions. The wisdom or prudence of this legislation has been questioned: but it is difficult to understand how a different course could have been pursued under existing circumstances; for, if the Maryland charter did not require the proprietary to tolerate the Protestant sects, he was at least compelled by the increasing anti-Catholic spirit and influence in the mother-country, to manifest the most liberal policy. At all events, the Catholic population were now doomed to persecution in the very land where they had erected the standard of civil liberty. By successive acts of the provincial assembly, they were denied the right of openly practising their religion, were compelled to pay a tax for the support of the Anglican clergy, were forbidden to teach, and were disqualified for holding civil employments, unless they took an oath which amounted to a denial of their faith. This system of oppression led a portion of them, and even the proprietary himself, to renounce Catholicity, while the great majority persevered in their adherence to the Church, and many among the wealthier class sought beyond the sea those advantages for education which they could not enjoy in their own country. The erection of Catholic churches being prohibited, divine worship was confined to private residences, or to chapels contiguous to them, and this state of things continued until 1770, when a more liberal spirit began to manifest itself, the result alike of a growing opposition to the oppressive laws in favor of the Anglican establishment, and to the obnoxious policy of the British government.

While the Catholics of Maryland were objects of persecution those of Pennsylvania enjoyed comparative freedom. From the

foundation of the latter colony, in 1682, they were at least tolerated, and as early as 1686 we find a priest among the inhabitants.
In 1730, Father Greaton, a Jesuit, was sent from Maryland to Phila
delphia, and founded the church of St. Joseph. Eleven years after,
missions were established at Goshenhoppen, Conewago and Lancaster,
which have ever since been flourishing centres of Catholicity. About
the same time, the military station at Fort Duquesne (now Pittsburg),
while the territory was occupied by the French, was served by Catholic chaplains. As we have stated above, from 1642, for a period of
about sixty years, the Jesuits were occupied in the arduous work of
evangelizing the aborigines in the interior of the State of New York:
but in the city of that name there were few Catholics, and owing to
the persecuting policy of the Colonial government, except under
Governor Dongan, they enjoyed but temporarily, during the last
quarter of the seventeenth century, the ministry of a Catholic priest.
Such indeed was the intolerance of the government that, in 1741, a
man by the name of John Ury, supposed to be a Catholic priest, was
publicly executed, chiefly on the ground of his being a clergyman
of the Catholic faith.

Such was the state of religion in the Colonies when they deter
mined to throw off the British yoke, and to establish an independent
government. This revolution in the political world naturally led to
a change of public sentiment, at least practically, in regard to differences of religion. The convention of 1774 made the following
appeal: "As an opposition to the settled plan of the British administration to enslave America will be strengthened by a union of all
ranks of men within this province, we do most earnestly recommend
that all former differences about religion or politics, and all private
animosities and quarrels of every kind, from henceforth cease and be
forever buried in oblivion; and we entreat, we conjure every man by his
duty to God, his country, and his posterity, cordially to unite in defence
of our common rights and liberties." Although motives of expediency,
rather than a spirit of toleration, dictated this proclamation, it could
not but conduce in the long run to the advantage of the true faith.
Before the provinces had thrown off the British yoke, the Catholic religion had not penetrated into any but Maryland and Pennsylvania.
"The laws were most rigorous against the exercise of it. A priest
was subject to death for only entering within their territories. Catholics were subject to the most grievous penalties for adhering to the
worship which their consciences approved; and were not only ex
cluded from every office under government, but would hardly have

been suffered to remain in any of the other provinces, if known to profess the faith of Rome. In this situation of things, few Catholics settled in other States; or, if they did, dissembled their religion, and either attached themselves to some other, or intermarried with Protestants, and suffered their children to be educated in error. Even in Maryland and Pennsylvania, the condition of Catholics, as was noticed before, was a state of oppression. The few Jesuits who could be spared from the English mission were insufficient even to answer the exigences of the two provinces in which they first settled; and no other clergymen undertook the perilous task of carrying the true faith into the other provinces. Such was the state of things when a general revolt from England took place.

"Having renounced subjection to England, the American States found it necessary to form new constitutions for their future government, and, happily, a free toleration of religions was made a fundamental point in all these new constitutions; and, in many of them, not only a toleration was decreed, but likewise a perfect equality of civil rights for persons of every Christian profession. In some, indeed, the yet unextinguished spirit of prejudice and intolerance excluded Catholics from this equality.

"Many reasons concurred to produce this happy and just article in the new constitutions: First. Some of the leading characters in the direction of American councils were, by principle, averse to all religious oppression; and, having been much acquainted with the manners and doctrines of Roman Catholics, represented strongly the injustice of excluding them from any civil right. Secondly. Catholics concurred as generally, and with equal zeal, in repelling that oppression which first produced the hostilities with Great Britain; and it would have been impolitic, as well as unjust, to deprive them of a common share of advantages purchased with common danger and by united exertions. Thirdly. The assistance, or at least the neutrality of Canada, was deemed necessary to the success of the United States; and to give equal rights to Roman Catholics might tend to dispose the Canadians favorably toward the American cause. Lastly, France began to show a disposition to befriend the United States; and it was conceived to be very impolitic to disgust that powerful kingdom by unjust severities against the religion which it professed." *

It cannot be doubted that the political events of the times were

---

* Manuscript relation of Bishop Carroll in regard to the origin and condition of Catholicity in the United States.

preparing the way for an important change in the religious condition of the country. Sectarian prejudice and rancor were sensibly diminishing, and a wider field was opened to the Catholic missionary. As an instance of this, may be mentioned the application made by the Congress of the Confederation to the Rev. John Carroll, an ex-Jesuit of Maryland, to co-operate with a committee of laymen in 1776,* for the purpose of conciliating the Canadians in favor of their cause. Rev. Mr. Carroll, a native of Maryland, was educated in Europe, and became a member of the Society of Jesus. After the suppression of the order, in 1773, he returned to America, and devoted himself to the duties of the holy ministry. It was not long, however, before his dignity of character, and his connection with one of the most illustrious families in Maryland, gave him a considerable prominence in political and ecclesiastical affairs. He was an ardent patriot; and, so far as prudence and propriety would permit, he supported with all his influence the cause of independence.' Though much occupied with missionary duty at this time, he found leisure for the composition of an able defence of the Church against her enemies. One of these, the Rev. Chas. Wharton, had until recently been a fellow-member of Dr. Carroll in the Society of Jesus, and in apostatizing from the faith he addressed a letter to his former parishioners in England as an apology for his conduct. This pamphlet was held up as unanswerable by the adversaries of Catholicity, "whom the elegance of its language and their own ignorance in religious controversy equally contributed to deceive." The answer of Dr. Carroll, entitled "Address to the Roman Catholics of the United States," was much admired for its learning, close reasoning, and courteous style both in Europe and America.†

"Notwithstanding the happy change in the government and laws of the different States, still religion reaped little advantage from it before the close of the war. The priests were too few; many of them were worn down with age and hardships. Besides which, during the whole war there was not the least communication between the Catholics of America and their bishop, who was the vicar apostolic of the London district. To his spiritual jurisdiction were subject the United States. But, whether he would hold no correspondence with a country which he perhaps considered as in a state of rebellion, or

---

* Benjamin Franklin, Charles Carroll, of Carrollton, and Mr. Chase.

† Wharton was twice married, and died a Protestant minister at Burlington, New Jersey, at the age of 86.

whether a natural indolence and irresolution restrained him, the fact is that he held no kind of intercourse with priest or layman in this part of his charge. Before the breaking out of the war, his predecessor had appointed a vicar, the Rev. Mr. Lewis, and he governed the mission of America during the bishop's silence. Soon after the termination of the war, the clergy of Maryland and Pennsylvania, being sensible that, to derive all advantage from the new state of things in America, it would be proper to have an ecclesiastical superior in the country itself; and knowing the jealousy prevailing in the American governments against the right of jurisdiction vesting in a person residing in Great Britain, addressed themselves to the Holy See, praying that a superior might be allowed, and that he might be chosen by the clergy, subject to the approbation and confirmation of his Holiness."[*] Dr. Carroll, in stating this, remarks, in a letter to Rev. Mr. Thorpe at Rome :[†] "We think it not only advisable in us, but, in a manner obligatory, to solicit the Holy See to place the episcopal powers, at least such as are most essential, in the hands of one amongst us, whose virtue, knowledge, and integrity of faith shall be certified by ourselves."

The wisdom of this proceeding among the American clergy is clearly shown from the remarkable fact, that an arrangement to the same effect was at that very time under consideration at Rome. In deference to the views of the clergy, who petitioned simply for a superior invested with the necessary faculties (deeming it premature to have a bishop), the Holy See appointed the Rev. Mr. Carroll to that office, empowering him, among other things, to bless the holy oils, and to administer the sacrament of confirmation, a sacrament which had never yet been conferred in the United States.[‡] The form of spiritual administration thus established was not altogether palatable to the American clergy, as they feared lest their dependence on the Congregation of the Propaganda might excite the jealousy of the authorities in many of the States, where Catholics were still excluded from civil employments, and even that of the Federal government itself, in the Constitution of which it was declared, that no person should be eligible to office who was a subject of a foreign Power. This objection was plainly and frankly intimated by Dr. Carroll to Cardinal Antonelli, Prefect of the Propaganda. " Your Eminence," he says, " may rest assured that the clergy and faithful in this country would

[*] *Relation* cited above.   [†] Nov. 10, 1783.

[‡] The official letters announcing this appointment were dated June 9 and 16, 1784, but were not received by Dr. Carroll until Nov. 26th of that year.

endure every suffering rather than reject the divine authority of the Holy See; but, at the same time, they request that no pretext be given to the adversaries of our holy religion to censure us, as if depending more than is necessary upon a foreign Power; and that the mode of appointing the ecclesiastical superior be such as to accord with the spiritual jurisdiction of the Holy See, and to remove all occasion of imputing to the Catholic body any opposition to their civil government."*

Though, at the time that an ecclesiastical superior was appointed, the clergy deemed it unnecessary and even inexpedient to have a bishop, their objections were soon overruled by a mature consideration of the subject. They found by experience that religion would be exposed to great injury in the United States, if the refractory spirit of many among the immigrant priests of that time did not receive a proper check by the exercise of the highest spiritual authority. In this they only coincided with the policy which Rome was inclined to adopt. A committee of three was therefore named by the American clergy to present a petition to Rome for the erection of an episcopal see in the United States, and for the privilege of nominating, themselves (at least for this time), a fit person to occupy it.

While these proceedings were in progress, Dr. Carroll was busily engaged in the discharge of his functions as superior of the American Church. After visiting Philadelphia, New York, and other parts of his extensive charge for the purpose of administering confirmation, he applied himself vigorously to the establishment of an academy at Georgetown, D. C., as an institution which would not only "unite the means of communicating science with an effectual provision for guarding and improving the morals of youth," but would also serve as a nursery for encouraging the vocation of young men to the ecclesiastical state. With the assistance of the faithful in America and of his friends in Europe, he was enabled to accomplish this important object, and a building was soon commenced on the banks of the Potomac, "on one of the most lovely situations that imagination can frame."†

One of the most laborious and most painful duties of Dr. Carroll's office at this time was, to insure the progress of religion against the unhappy influence exerted by a schismatical spirit both among clergy and laity. "Every day," he says, "furnishes me with new reflections, and almost every day produces new events, to alarm my conscience

* Feb. 27, 1785.
† Letter to Rev Charles Plowden, 1788.

and excite fresh solicitude at the prospect before me. You cannot con ceive the trouble I suffer already, and still greater which I foresee, from the medley of clerical characters coming from different quarters, and various educations, and seeking employment here. I cannot avoid employing some of them, and they begin soon to create disturbances. As soon as this happens, they proceed to bring in Jesuitism, and to suggest that every thing is calculated by me for its restoration : but of all classes of such persons who have been yet amongst us, I have found the Capuchins, both German and Irish, most intolerable. To a great deal of ignorance they join most consummate assurance ; add, that they seem to have no principle of a religious life. We have some German Recollects and Irish Dominicans, and some secular priests, who behave properly and even commendably."* In New York, Boston, and Philadelphia, all the firmness and prudence of Dr. Carroll were called into requisition by ambitious and insubordinate priests, who, instead of promoting union and charity among the people, only sowed the seeds of discord and scandal. This was notoriously the case at New York, during the schism excited by Rev. Mr. Nugent, who officiated in opposition to the order of Dr. Carroll, and who, with his party, was guilty of such violence as to compel the ecclesiastical superior to leave the church, whither he had gone to instruct the people in their duty. On the other hand, the majority of the clergy acquitted themselves zealously of their duties. In 1785, when Dr. Carroll submitted to the Propaganda a statement of the condition of things in the Church of the United States, the number of Catholics was computed to be about twenty-five thousand—sixteen thousand in Maryland, seven thousand in Pennsylvania, and two thousand in New York and the other States.† The number of priests in Maryland was nineteen, in Pennsylvania five ; but this force was soon increased by the appointment of pastors in New York, Kentucky, Charleston, and other places.

The period of Dr. Carroll's jurisdiction as prefect-apostolic (from 1784 to 1790) was simultaneous with the great political events which followed closely upon the American Revolution. and resulted in the adoption of the Constitution of the United States. When the Catholics of that day called to mind the trials and persecutions of former times, they could not but feel a deep interest in the framing of the organic law, which was in future to characterize the legislation of the

---

* Letter to Plowden, 1789.

† This enumeration, afterwards found too low, did not include the Canadian French and others, living west of the Ohio and on the borders of the Mississippi.

republic, and having united with their fellow-citizens of all religious denominations in achieving the independence of their country, they did not hesitate to use their influence in giving to the fundamental law of the land that form and spirit which would secure the civil liberty they so much valued, and for which they had so bravely fought. For this purpose, some of the leading members of their body, among whom was Rev. Dr. Carroll, drew up a memorial to Congress, representing the necessity of adopting some constitutional provision for the protection and maintenance of the civil and religious freedom, the purchase of which had cost so much blood and treasure among all classes of citizens. Through the influence of General Washington, this memorial was favorably received, and it resulted in the enactment of the third article of the *Amendments* to the Constitution, which declares that " Congress shall make no law respecting an establishment of religion, or prohibiting the free exercise thereof." As this amend ment was adopted by a congress of all the States, it was a solemn recognition of the principle which should in future govern their respective legislative acts, and since that period it has been happily incorporated into their fundamental law. The importance of this Constitutional enactment, which was due chiefly to the far-reaching wisdom and enlightened patriotism of some among the more distin guished Catholics of the time, can not be overestimated. It was the most effectual barrier that could be raised against the revival of the persecuting spirit which had disgraced nearly all the colonies, and which would most probably have again lifted its hydra head, if the States had not in solemn convention repudiated it as incompatible with the essential character of the American government. But, an open field and a fair fight with error, this was all that Catholicity required to develop its power and to march on to victory."*

* We can not at this moment quote any official document, to prove that the above-mentioned Catholic memorial was presented to Congress. We have made the statement upon what we consider equally reliable authority, a letter of the late Bishop Fenwick, of Boston, who mentions Rev. Dr. Carroll, Charles Carroll of Carrollton, George Meade (father of General Meade of the United States army), Thomas Fitzsimmons, and Dominick Lynch, as framers of the memorial. From this and other circumstances, we are led to the opinion that Crétineau-Joly, in his history of the Society of Jesus, is for the most part correct in the portraiture which he has drawn of the Rev. Dr. Carroll. That he was a friend of Washington, in the vulgar sense of the word, can not be asserted; but we think that the historian of the Jesuits wished merely to intimate, that Dr. Carroll and Washington were friends in the higher and more excellent meaning of the word; that they entertained a profound regard for each other, manifesting it on all befitting occasions, and mutually co-operating in such measures as tended to the public weal. In a letter to the writer, the late Hon. Geo. Washington Parke Custis, a nephew of the illustrious Washington, referring to Rev. Dr

III.

The request of the American clergy, in regard to the erection of an episcopal see, having been granted at Rome, they lost no time in determining its location and in the selection of a candidate for the mitre. They fixed upon Baltimore, "this being," says Dr. Carroll, "the principal town of Maryland, and that State being the oldest and still the most numerous residence of true religion in America. So far all was right. We then proceeded to the election, the event of which was such as deprives me of all expectation of rest or pleasure henceforward, and fills me with terror with respect to eternity. I am so stunned with the issue of this business, that I truly hate the hearing or the mention of it, and therefore will say only, that, since my brethren—whom in this case I consider as the interpreters of the Divine will—say I must obey, I will even do it; but, by obeying, shall sacrifice henceforward every moment of peace and satisfaction." Though 't appears from these words of Dr. Carroll that he acquiesced in the choice which had been made, he did so with the most unaffected humility. "My own knowledge of myself informs me, better than a thousand voices to the contrary, that I am entirely unfit for a station, in which I can have no hopes of rendering service but through His help and continual direction who has called me to it, when I was doing all in my power to prevent it."*

Upon the reception at Rome of the proceedings of the clergy, by which Baltimore was designated as the episcopal see, and the V Rev. Dr. Carroll nominated as bishop, the official documents were immediately dispatched to him, appointing him to the new see, and containing the most flattering testimonials of the high esteem in which he was held, and of the joy which his election had awakened in the capital of the Christian world. "It is a splendid and glorious office," says Cardinal Antonelli, "to offer to God, as it were, the first fruits of that portion of the Lord's vineyard. Enjoy, therefore, so great a blessing, not only for the salvation of yourself, but for that of others, and for

Carroll, says: "From his exalted worth as a minister of God, his stainless character as a man, and, above all, his distinguished services as a patriot of the Revolution, Dr. Carroll stood high, very high, in the esteem and affections of the Pater Patriæ." From the same source we learn, that in the days of the first Presidency, when Washington passed through Baltimore to and from the seat of government, a band of Revolutionary worthies always assembled to do him honor, and among them Dr. Carroll ever held the most conspicuous post, and received the first grasp of Washington's hand.

* Letters to his friend Plowden.

the increase of the Catholic faith, which we trust will become more and more widely established in that distant region." *

Soon after the reception of his bulls from Rome, Dr. Carroll repaired to England, where his person and merit were well known, and presented himself for consecration to the Rt. Rev. Dr. Walmesley, bishop of Rama and senior vicar apostolic in that kingdom. By invitation of Thomas Weld, Esq., the ceremony of consecration took place, during a solemn high mass, in the elegant chapel at Lulworth Castle, on Sunday, the 15th day of August, A. D. 1790, feast of the Assumption of the B. Virgin Mary, and the munificence of that gentleman omitted no arrangement that could possibly add dignity to so august a ceremony. A discourse was delivered on the occasion by the Rev. Chas. Plowden, who thus alluded to the rising Church in America: "Never, perhaps was this truth (that the formation of the kingdom of Christ is the ultimate object of the whole dispensation of Providence in the government of this world) more sensibly evinced, than in th late violent convulsions by which the hand of the Almighty has dismembered the great British empire in the Western world, the destinies of which, we trust, are founded in His tenderest mercies. For, although this great event may appear to us to have been the work—the sport of human passions, yet the earliest and most precious fruit of it has been the extension of the kingdom of Christ, the propa gation of the Catholic religion, which, heretofore fettered by restrain ing laws, is now enlarged from bondage, and is left at liberty to exert the full energy of divine truth. Already is Catholicity extended to the utmost boundaries of the immense continent of America; thousands are there earnestly demanding Catholic instructors, and all, penetrated with reverence for the Apostolical See of St. Peter, have concurred to demand from his successor a Catholic prelate, whose knowledge and whose zeal may establish the faith of Peter upon the rains of those errors which the first inhabitants carried forth with them from this country. But, if Britain infected them with error, we have the consolation to know that their Catholicity is also derived immediately from us; and as we in former ages received the faith of Rome from the great St. Gregory and our apostle, St. Austin, so now, at the interval of twelve hundred years, our venerable prelate, the heir of the virtues and labors of our apostle, will this day, by commission from the successor of St. Gregory, consecrate the first father and bishop of the new church, destined, as we confide, to inherit those

* Nov. 14, 1789. The bulls for the new see were dated Nov. 6.

benedictions which the first called have ungratefully rejected. Glorious is this day, my brethren, for the Church of God, which sees new nations crowding into her bosom; glorious for the prelate-elect, who goes forth to conquer those nations for Jesus Christ, not by the efforts of human power, but in the might of those weapons which have ever triumphed in this divine warfare: he is not armed with the strength of this world, but he is powerful in piety, powerful in zeal, powerful in evangelical poverty, and firm reliance on the protection of that God who sends him."

These remarks have all been substantially verified in the history of the Catholic Church in the United States. While Divine Providence was preparing on the Western Continent a new and grateful field for the seed of truth, it was disposing events in Europe and other countries for supplying that field with zealous and active laborers, who would bring forth fruit in good season. The revolution in France was now beginning to wear a threatening aspect for religion as well as for the throne, and the Abbé Emery, superior-general of the Sulpitian Society in France, fearing its ultimate suppression in that country, entered into a correspondence with Bishop Carroll, still in Europe, with a view to the establishment of an ecclesiastical seminary in the United States. Alluding to this negotiation, Dr. Carroll says: "We have settled that two or three gentlemen, selected by Mr. Emery, shall come over to Baltimore next spring. They are furnished with the means of purchasing ground for building, and, I hope, of endowing a seminary for young ecclesiastics. I believe they will bring three or four seminarians with them, who either are English, or know it, professors of philosophy and divinity. They will be amply provided with books, apparatus for the altar, church, &c. I propose fixing these very near my own house and the cathedral of Baltimore, that they may be, as it were, the clergy of the church, and contribute to the dignity of divine worship. This is a great and auspicious event for our new diocess; but it is a melancholy reflection that we owe so great a blessing to the lamentable catastrophe in France." *

Having arranged this important business, and collected considerable funds from his friends in England for the academy at Georgetown, Bishop Carroll set sail for America.† He could not leave

---

* Letter to F. Plowden, London, Sep., 25, 1790.

† About this time, a French colony was established in Ohio, about the place now called Gallipolis, and an effort had been made by its founders to have a bishop appointed for their spiritual benefit. The project, however, failed, owing probably to the creation of the new see of Baltimore: but Dom. Didier, a Benedictine of St. Maur and Chaplain of the

England, however, so soon without a feeling of regret that he left behind him so many valuable men, his dearest friends, and the friends of religion and models of virtue. " Long shall I retain the impression made on me at Lulworth, by the goodness, the charity, the loveliness of every branch of that most respectable family, and I am sure my heart will be full of the gratefulest emotions when I shall sail abreast of the Castle."*

On landing at Baltimore, December 7 Bishop Carroll was wel comed by a large body of Catholics and others, with every demon stration of joy, and on the following Sunday he was installed in his episcopal see, according to the rites of the Roman Pontifi cal. On that occasion he addressed his people in the following words :—

" This day, my dear brethren, impresses deeply on my mind a lively sense of the new relation in which I stand now before you. You have often heard my voice within these walls ; and often have I used my feeble endeavors to rouse you from the sleep of sin, and to awake in you the sentiments of virtue and practical piety. But when I thus addressed you, I considered it indeed as my obligation to admonish and instruct you ; but I did not view it as an indissoluble obligation. My superintendence over your spiritual concerns was of such a nature that I could relinquish it, or be removed from it at pleasure. But now the hand of Providence (ah, may I hope that it is not an angry,

colony, was invested with ample powers, to be exercised in obedience to and with the approbation of Dr. Carroll. (Letter of Father Thorpe, July 21, 1790.)

The late Bishop Bruté, in his memoranda, alludes to the same fact, stating that the Abbé, Boisnantier, of St. Roch, Paris, was appointed at Rome in 1789 bishop of Scioto (Gallipolis). " I knew Mr. Boisnantier well: he spoke to me of his nomination, and undertook to look for his papers, but not finding them readily, I only learned *ex auditu* this remarkable fact of a see having been established in Ohio as early as that period. I have no doubt but Mr. Emery was aware of this, which shows how soon the *papists* had their eye on the Valley of the Mississippi."

* This language of Dr. Carroll was fully justified by the admirable qualities of the Weld family. Mr. Weld, who died in 1811, was the beau-ideal of a truly Christian nobleman. Though living in the midst of honor and affluence, his habits were those of a fervent religious Mental prayer, attendance at Mass, spiritual reading, recitation of the breviary, were for him daily exercises of piety, while he approached the sacrament of penance weekly and the holy communion every two or three days. The rosary and spiritual reading were exer cises performed in common with his family. He always made an annual retreat. He was the first, after the act of Catholic emancipation, to build a separate chapel for the worship of God. His charities were boundless. Besides founding an establishment of Trap pists and the Jesuit college at Stonyhurst, he built several chapels, either wholly or in part, and provided for their support. Five or six communities of religious women owed to him a good part of their subsistence.—*Letter of Father Corbe, S. J.*

but a Providence merciful to you and me)—the hand of Providence has formed an indissoluble tie—has bound me by an obligation which I can never renounce—an obligation of ever attending to your eternal interests; of watching perpetually over your conduct; of stemming, to the utmost of my power, the torrent of vice and irreligion; of conducting you in the ways of virtue, and leading you to the haven of eternal bliss. The shade of retirement and solitude must no longer be my hope and prospect of consolation. Often have I flattered myself that my declining years would be indulged in such a state of rest from labor and solicitude for others, as would leave me the best opportunity of attending to the great concern of my own salvation, and of confining myself to remember my past years in the bitterness of compunction. But it has pleased God to order otherwise; and though my duty commands submission, it can not allay my fears—those fears which I feel for you and for myself. For, my God! how much reason have I not to fear for myself when I view the extent of my duties, on the one hand; and on the other, my weakness and natural inability to fulfil them. In this, my new station, if my life be not one continued instruction and example of virtue to the people committed to my charge, it will become, in the sight of God, a life not only useless, but even pernicious.

"It is no longer enough for me to be inoffensive in my conduct and regular in my manners. God now imposes a severer duty upon me. I shall incur the guilt of violating my pastoral office, if all my endeavors be not directed to bring your lives and all your actions to a conformity with the laws of God; to exhort, to conjure, to reprove, to enter into all your sentiments; to feel all your infirmities; to be all things to all, that I may gain all to Christ; to be superior to human respects; to have nothing in view but God and your salvation; to sacrifice to these, health, peace, reputation, and even life itself; to hate sin, and yet love the sinner; to repress the turbulent; to encourage the timid; to watch over the conduct of even the ministers of religion; to be patient and meek; to embrace all kinds of persons;—these are now my duties—extensive, pressing, and indispensable duties;—these are the duties of all my brethren in the episcopacy, and surely important enough to fill us with terror. But there are others still more burdensome to be borne by me in this particular portion of Christ's Church, which is committed to my charge, and where every thing is to be raised, as it were, from its foundation: to establish ecclesiastical discipline; to devise means for the religious education of Catholic youth—that precious portion of pastoral solicitude; to provide an

establishment for training up ministers for the sanctuary and the ser
vices of religion, that we may no longer depend on foreign and uncer
tain coadjutors; not to leave unassisted any of the faithful who are scat
tered through this immense continent; to preserve their faith untainted
amidst the contagion of error surrounding them on all sides; to preserve
in their hearts a warm charity and forbearance toward every other
denomination of Christians; and, at the same time, to preserve them
from that fatal and prevailing indifference which views all religions
as equally acceptable to God and salutary to men. Ah! when I consider these additional duties, my heart sinks almost under the impression of terror which comes upon it. In God alone can I find any
consolation. He knows by what steps I have been conducted to this
important station, and how much I have always dreaded it. He will
not abandon me unless I first draw down His malediction by my
unfaithfulness to my charge. Pray, dear brethren, pray incessantly,
that I may not incur so dreadful a punishment. Alas! the punishment would fall on you as well as on myself—my unfaithfulness would
redound on you, and deprive you of some of the means of salvation.

"The fears which trouble me, on my own account, would receive
some abatement, if I could be assured of your steady adherence to the
duties of your holy religion. But how can I be assured of this, when
I recollect what experience has taught me, and that worldly contagion, example, influence, and respect, together with impetuous passions, seek perpetually to plunge you into habits of vice, and afterward into everlasting misery; and when I know that not one soul will
perish from amongst you, of which God will not demand of me, as its
shepherd, a most severe account. Unhappily, at this time, a spirit of
infidelity is prevalent, and dares to attempt the subversion of even the
first principles of religion and morality, and to break down all the
fences which guard virtue and purity of body and mind. Licentiousness of discourse and the arts of seduction are practised without
shame, and, it would seem, without remorse. Ah! will it be in my
power to oppose these fatal engines of vice and immorality? Dear
brethren, allow me to appeal to your consciences; question them with
candor and truth. Can I say more to bring you back to the simplicity
of faith, to the humble docility of a disciple of Jesus, to the fervent
practice of Christian duties, than I have said to you heretofore? But
what reformation followed then my earnest entreaties and exhorta
tions? Was prayer more used? Were parents more assiduous in the
instruction of their children? Were their examples more edifying?
Was swearing and blaspheming diminished? Was drunkenness

suppressed? Was idleness extirpated? Was injustice abolished? May I hope that on this occasion God will shower down more abundant graces; that your hearts will be turned from the love of the world to the love of Him! If I could be so happy as to see prevailing among you such exercises of piety as evidenced your attachment to religion and your zeal for your salvation, I should myself be relieved from much of my solicitude—prayer; attendance on holy mass; frequentation of the holy sacraments; humble docility to the advice and admonitions of your pastor. 'Obey,' says St. Paul, 'those who are put over you, as having to render to God an account for your souls.'"

He concluded his address by exhorting his hearers to cultivate a true devotion to the mother of God, under whose special protection he had placed the extensive diocese with whose interests he was charged.

Alluding to the general situation of the Church at this time, Dr. Carroll says: "It has its successes and disappointments. The capuchin Whelan left his numerous congregation of Kentucky, composed of emigrants from Maryland, whilst I was in England. They are now without a priest, except a rambling Irish one, to whom I refused faculties some years ago. * * * I am anxious to obtain a good one for the poor souls there, who in general are virtuous, and some of them eminently so. At Boston there has been much offence given to Catholics and Protestants by the disagreement of the two priests* and their abettors. * * * In other places we gain ground; and several new settlements for extending religion are in prospect, as in Virginia, N. Carolina, and Georgia. In S. Carolina we have one already."†

Soon after his arrival in his diocess, Dr. Carroll visited Boston for the purpose of composing the differences in the congregation of that city. "It is wonderful," he writes, "to tell what great civilities have been done to me in this town, where, a few years ago, a Popish priest was thought to be the greatest monster in the creation. Many here, even of their principal people, have acknowledged to me that they would have crossed to the opposite side of the street rather than meet a Roman Catholic some time ago. The horror which was associated with the idea of a papist is incredible; and the scandalous misrepresentations by their ministers increased the horror every Sunday. If

* Revs. Messrs. Rousselet and Thayer, who had been preceded by a Mr. De la Poterie, a most abandoned character. Mr. Thayer was a convert, a pious and zealous priest: but his zeal not being "unto sobriety," he got himself into various difficulties.

† Rev. Mr. Ryan

all the Catholics here were united, their number would be about one hundred and twenty." On his return from Boston, where his presence had produced at least a temporary calm, he had the happiness of welcoming the band of clergymen and students who had come from France to found an ecclesiastical seminary in Baltimore.* It was a source of indescribable joy to the new bishop to witness the accession of such distinguished priests to the ranks of the American clergy. They were to assist him by their counsels, to strengthen the missionary force of his immense diocess, and to establish a nursery of learned and devoted laborers for this interesting portion of the Lord's vineyard.

In obedience to the laws of the Church, and to provide more effectually for the welfare of the flock committed to his care, Dr. Carroll convoked a diocesan synod as soon as circumstances would permit. In the circular which was issued to the clergy on this occasion, we read as follows : " The necessity of consulting together on the means of continuing the episcopacy of the United States, for the decent ordering of divine worship, and uniformity in the administration of the sacraments, and discipline of the diocess and clergy, and devising means, if possible, for the support of the ministers of religion ; these are the principal objects which will engage your attention." The synod was convened for the 7th of November, 1791, when twenty-two clergymen assembled, under the presidency of their venerable bishop, to deliberate upon the important matters regarding the interests of religion in the United States. The meeting of such a number of priests was a novel and impressive spectacle in this part of the world. The four first sessions of the synod were occupied with the consideration of the statutes relative to the sacraments. In the fifth and last session, the most salutary regulations were adopted in regard to the celebration of festivals, the support of the clergy and other matters, and a petition was adopted praying the Holy See to establish a new episcopal see, or at least to appoint a coadjutor to the Bishop of Baltimore. The spirit which characterized the enactments of the first diocesan synod in the United States, the importance of the subjects treated, and the wisdom and zeal of the chief pastor who presided over its deliberations, are so admirably set forth in a pastoral letter which he shortly after addressed to his flock, that the reader will excuse us for presenting it at length in the present sketch.

---

* The Rev. gentlemen were, Messrs. Nagot, *superior ;* Levadoux, *procurator ;* Garnier and Tessier, *professors ;* also a Mr. Delavau, canon of Tours.

JOHN,

By DIVINE PERMISSION, AND WITH THE APPROBATION OF THE HOLY SEE, BISHOP OF BALTIMORE—

To my dearly beloved Brethren, the Members of the Catholic Church in this Diocess, Health and Blessing, Grace to you, and Peace from God our Father and from the Lord Jesus Christ:

The great extent of my diocess, and the necessity of ordering many things concerning its government, at the beginning of my episcopacy have not yet permitted me, my dear brethren, to enjoy the consolation, for which I most earnestly pray, of seeing you all, and of leaving with you, according to the nature of my duty, some words of exhortation, by which you may be strengthened in faith and encouraged in the exercises of a Christian life. Esteeming myself as a debtor to all, and knowing the rigorous account which I must render for your souls to the Shepherd of Shepherds, our Lord and Saviour Jesus Christ, I shall have cause to tremble while I leave any thing undone by which religion and true piety may be promoted, and the means of salvation multiplied for you.

In compliance with the obligation, resulting from the relation in which I stand to you, my endeavors have been turned toward obtaining and applying, for the preservation and extension of faith, and for the sanctification of souls, means calculated to produce lasting effects, not only on the present, but on future generations. I thought that Almighty God would make the ministers of His sanctuary, and myself particularly, accountable to Him if we did not avail ourselves of the liberty enjoyed under our equitable government and just laws, to attempt establishments in which you, dear brethren, may find permanent resources, suited to your greatest exigencies.

Knowing, therefore, that the principles instilled in the course of a Christian education are generally preserved through life, and that *a young man according to his way, even when he is old, will not depart from it* (Prov. xxii. 6), I have considered the virtuous and Christian instruction of youth as a principal object of pastoral solicitude. Now who can contribute so much to lighten this burden which weighs so heavy on the shoulders of the pastors of souls, and who have so great an interest and special duty in the forming of youthful minds to habits of virtue and religion, as their parents themselves, especially while their children retain their native docility and their hearts are uncorrupted by vice?

How many motives of reason and religion require that parents should be unwearied in their endeavors to inspire into them the love and fear of God, docility and submission to his doctrines, and a careful attention to fulfill his commandments! *Fathers, bring up your children in the discipline and correction of the Lord* (Ephes iv. 4). If all to whom God has given sons and daughters were assiduous in the discharge of this important obligation, a foundation would be laid for, and great progress made in, the work of establishing a prevailing purity of manners. The same habits of obedience to the will of God; the same principles of a reverential love and fear of Him, and of continual respect for His holy name; the same practices of morning and evening prayer, and of frequentation of the sacraments; the same dread of cursing and swearing, of fraud and duplicity, of lewdness and drunkenness; the same respectful and dutiful behavior to their fathers and mothers; in a word, the remembrance and influence of the parental counsels and examples received in their youth, would continue with them during life; and, if ever the frailty of nature or worldly seduction should cause them to offend God, they would be brought back again to His service and to true repentance by the efficacy of the religious instruction received in their early age. Wherefore, fathers and mothers, be mindful of the words of the apostle, *and bring up your children in the discipline and correction of the Lord*. In doing this, you not only render an acceptable service to God, and acquit yourselves of a most important duty, but you labor for the preservation and increase of true religion; for the benefit of our common country, whose welfare depends on the morals of its citizens; and for your own happiness here as well as hereafter, since you may be assured of finding, in those sons and daughters whom you shall train up to virtue and piety by your instructions and examples, support and consolation in sickness and old age. They will remember with gratitude, and repay with religious duty, your solicitude for them in their infancy and youth. These being the advantages of a religious education, I was solicitous for the attainment of a blessing so desirable to that precious portion of my flock—the growing generation. A school has been instituted at Georgetown, which will continue to be under the superintendence and government of some of my Reverend Brethren—that is, of men devoted by principle and profession to instruct all who resort to them in useful learning, and those of our own religion, in its principles and duties. I earnestly wish, dear brethren, that as many of you as are able would send your sons to this school of letters and virtue. I know and lament that the expense will be too great for many families, and that their children must be deprived of the *immediate* benefit of this institution. But, indirectly, they will receive it; at least, it may be reasonably expected that some, after being educated at Georgetown, and having returned into their own neighborhood, will become, in their turn, the instructors of the youths who cannot be sent from home; and by pursuing the same system of uniting much attention to religion with a solicitude for other improvements, the general result will be a great increase of piety, the necessary consequence of a careful instruction in the principles of faith and Christian morality.

This school, dear brethren, if aided by your benevolence and favored with your confidence, will be the foundation of an additional advantage to true religion in this our country. Many amongst you have experienced inconvenience and disadvantage from the want of spiritual assistance in your greatest necessities, in sickness, in troubles of conscience, and for want of opportunity to avail yourselves of the counsels and offices of the ministers of religion. It is notorious to you all, that the present clergymen are insufficient for the exigencies of the faithful, and that they will be more and more, so as the population of our country increases so rapidly, unless by the Providence of our good and merciful God, a constant supply of zealous and able pastors can be formed amongst ourselves—that is, of men accustomed to our climate, and acquainted with the tempers, manners and government of the people to whom they are to dispense the ministry of salvation. Now, may we not reasonably hope that one of the effects of a virtuous course of education will be, the preparing the minds of some, whom Providence may select, to receive and cherish a call from God to an ecclesiastical state?

Should such be the designs of Infinite mercy on this portion of His flock, all of us, dear brethren, will have new cause to return God thanks for having conducted to our assistance a number of learned and exemplary clergymen, devoted by choice and formed by experience to the important function of training young ecclesiastics to all the duties of the ministry. This essential service is already begun by these, my respectable brethren. An ecclesiastical seminary, under their immediate direction and episcopal superintendence, has entered on the important function of raising pastors for your future consolation and improvement, and I cannot forbear recommending their undertaking to your patronage and charitable encouragement. How great and lasting a benefit will they confer on this and future generations, who shall contribute to endow it with some portion of those goods which themselves have received from a benevolent Providence, and for the use of which they must account to Him from whom they received them! What a consolation will it be to them in this life, and source of happiness in the next, if, through their benefactions, the seminary be enabled not only to support its directors and professors, but likewise some young men, candidates for holy orders, whose virtues and abilities may be far superior to their worldly fortunes! By endowments, such as I now recommend, great services have been rendered to religion and morality. If donations for objects of piety have ever been excessive, as some have pretended, the particular one now recommended to your charity, and the temper of our times and laws, leave no cause to apprehend the renewal of such an abuse.

Other objects besides those already mentioned claim our common solicitude. It will be of little use to prepare ministers for the work of the ministry, if afterwards they cannot be employed, for want of a necessary maintenance, in the laborious discharge of pastoral functions. Whilst the offices of our religion were performed only in two of the United States, and even in them the number of Catholics was much less than at present, fewer laborers were wanted, and there were funds sufficient for their subsistence, independent of any contributions from the justice or the charity of the respective congregations. But our holy faith being now spread through other States, and the number of Catholics being much increased in those where it existed before, it becomes absolutely necessary to recur to the means of supporting public worship and instruction, which is prescribed not only by natural equity, but likewise by the positive ordinances of divine wisdom, both in Jewish and Gospel dispensations. *Know you not*, says St. Paul, 1 Cor. v. 13, *that they who work in the holy place, and they that serve the altar, partake with the altar? so also the Lord ordained that they who preach the Gospel should live by the Gospel.*

In obedience to this divine ordinance, primitive Christians, when they went to the celebration of the sacred offices of religion, presented their offerings on the altar of the Lord, signifying by this act that they were not intended so much for their pastors as consecrated to God himself. And, indeed, the Church regarded them in this light, and decreed in her canons, that the religious obligations of the faithful should be employed, first, for the maintenance of the ministers of the sanctuary, which being provided for, the remainder should be applied towards the relief of the poor, and the building and repairing of churches and places of worship, necessary for public convenience, and the decent ordering of divine service.

God has made it our duty to join in the solemn rites of sacrifice and prayer, and in receiving the sacraments instituted for our benefit and the improvement of our souls in piety and grace. The administration of these requires men set apart for and consecrated to so sacred a function; men not assuming of themselves, but receiving their authority from God, through His Church, and their succession from the Apostles, through the Bishops, by whom they are ordained.

Now it is evident, that, since God has imposed on all an obligation of joining in these acts of religion, He requires likewise, that all should use the necessary means for acquitting themselves of that obligation; and, consequently, that each one bear his proportion of common and necessary expense for the support of public worship. This duty has been insisted on so little amongst us, as long as the assistance of the faithful was unnecessary for the maintenance of their pastors, that many will hardly conceive it to be a duty. Hence they are often without pastors; of course they become remiss in their religious duties, and finally regardless of them. Their offspring, uninstructed and ignorant of the principles of faith, are led astray by false doctrines, and seduced by corrupt examples. Hence, likewise, churches for the celebration of divine service, and the great Eucharistic sacrifice of the law of grace, are not built at all, or are suffered to fall into decay.

They are without chalices, without the decent and necessary furniture of the altars, without vestments suited to the different services of the Church, in a word, without those sacred utensils its ordinances require, and which contribute to impress the mind with a becoming sense of the majesty of religion, and conciliate respect for its august ceremonies. Hence, finally, results the great evil, and source of many other disorders, that, by failing to make provision for the necessary support of pastors, and the maintenance of public worship, you fail likewise of fulfilling the obligation of being present at mass on every Sunday and holiday; you lose the opportunity of receiving necessary and salutary instruction; and, finally, an habitual disregard for the sanctification of the Lord's Day and for the exercises of prayer and religion becomes prevalent.

In this matter, I recommend earnestly to you, my dear brethren, not to be too indulgent to yourselves, in forming principles which indeed may satisfy an erroneous conscience, and suit your attachment to your ease, and your worldly interests, but cannot afford you a reasonable assurance of having fulfilled your necessary and essential duty to Almighty God. Every inconvenience is not sufficient to exempt you from the obligation of attending at mass, on Sundays and ither days prescribed by the church. The obstacle must be grievous and weighty, amounting almost to an impossibility, moral or physical. Has such an obstacle or inconvenience existed with respect to all those who hear mass perhaps not more than once in a month, or seldomer? Are there not congregations, where now divine service is performed only once a month, which are fully competent to the expense of keeping a clergyman to reside amidst them, and to administer to them continually in all holy things; to offer every day for them, and in the presence of some at least of them, the great sacrifice of the law of grace? to teach, to admonish and reprove them? to instruct their children and servants in the doctrines and exercises of religion, and thus to make lighter the burden, which rests on parents and heads of families? to watch perpetually over the morals of all, and to prevent the contagion of error or evil example? to be ready, and near at hand, to administer to all, in times of sickness, the spiritual succors committed to his dispensation? I cannot, dear brethren, enumerate the advantages which will result from so desirable a situation, as that of having constantly amongst you your pastor and spiritual guide; and I exhort you with great earnestness to use much industry. and with thankfulness to Almighty God, for the temporal blessings received from His hand, generously to devote a part of them to the obtaining a benefit, from which such important consequences will be derived. The sacrifice of property which you make for a purpose so useful and religious, is a kind of restitution to Him who first gave it to you, and besides being an act of the virtue of religion, because it is suggested by the desire of encouraging and supporting divine worship, it is moreover an act of exalted charity toward the poor and ignorant, who will be enabled to obtain essential instruction, relief in all their spiritual necessities, through the means and contributions of the rich and middle classes of life; tand these will hus become partakers in the merit and rewards promised in these words of the Prophet Daniel, *they who instruct many to justice, shall shine as stars for all eternity.* (Ch. xii. v. 3.)

I will venture to add, that even with respect to this world you will find it to be no loss to concur toward the regular support of the ministry and services of religion. Habits of temperance and frugality are generally the effects of evangelical instruction. The lessons and duty of industry are frequently inculcated by virtuous and careful pastors: your children and servants will be admonished perpetual'y to shun idleness, dishonesty, dissipations, and that train of expense which always follows them. These, by their effect on domestic economy, will make abundant compensation for the charges in support of religion. Besides, you have a divine promise, that God will use a more special Providence for your subsistence, when you make it your first care to fulfil His holy law. *Seek first the kingdom of God, and His justice, and all those things shall be added unto you* (Mat. vi. 34).

Amongst all obstructions to the due celebration of divine services, and the regular attendance on the sacred functions of religion, this backwardness of the faithful to contribute for its support is one of the greatest, as was generally agreed and represented by my venerable brethren, the Clergy of the Diocess, in a synod held some months ago. When I convoked them, I formed some statutes of general concern which will be communicated to you, and amongst them are the following relative to the matter of which I have just now treated, and enforcing the same observations.

Extract from the Statutes of the Diocesan Synod, held at Baltimore, from the 7th to the 10th of November, 1791.

STATUTE V That the Holy Eucharistic Sacrifice may be celebrated with all reverence and becoming respect; and that the faithful may be excited more and more to a lively devotion toward this singular pledge of divine mercy, it is decreed that the congregation be reminded frequently how disrespectful it is, that any thing used for the Holy Sacrifice should be of the meanest materials, or not kept cleanly and entire, and that suitable vessels and utensils for the altar, as chalices, ciboriums, and cruets, decent vestments and linen for the ministry of the altar, wax candles and wine fit for mass be not provided. Let the Christian people be told with minute attention that God Himself was pleased to ordain every thing relating to his service in the Jewish law and temple. How much more care, therefore, should Christians use, for the decency of divine worship, since they possess not the shadow of future blessings, as the Jews, but the substance and reality of them! Let them be admonished likewise of the offerings made by primitive Christians at the time of mass, and let them know that such must be very regardless of the honor of God, as refuse or neglect to contribute for these things, without which the functions of religion seem to lose their dignity and authority, and the devotion and veneration for the Blessed Eucharist is greatly diminished.

VI. It is decreed, therefore, that in every congregation two or three persons of approved virtue and respectability be chosen by the congregation, or appointed by the pastor, to be church-wardens or guardians;

and that the person so appointed, on Sundays and other festivals, after the reading of the first gospel at Mass, or after the sermon, shall collect the offerings of the faithful.

VII. The offerings, according to the ancient practice of the Church, are to be divided into three parts, so that one may be applied to the maintenance of the pastor; another to the relief of the poor; and a third to the procuring of all things requisite for divine worship, and for building and repairing the church. But if provision be made otherwise for the maintenance of the pastor and the poor, all offerings are to be appropriated to the fabric of the church, or furnishing it with proper utensils and ornaments for the more dignified celebration of divine worship.

VIII. The offerings made by the faithful, to render God propitious to themselves or others, through the efficacy of the Holy Sacrifice of mass, should be accepted by the ministers of the altar in such manner as to afford no room for suspicions of avarice or simony; let them be contented therefore with such an acknowledgment of their services as cannot be burdensome to the bestowers of it; nor yet so insignificant as to render the priestly ministry despicable in the opinion of inconsiderate men.

XXIII. The number of Catholics having increased, and being dispersed through the different States, and at great distances from each other, it is become necessary to have likewise a greater number of spiritual laborers; but these cannot be brought from foreign countries or maintained unless the faithful concur toward bearing that expense, as they are bound by the law of God, and according to the testimony of St. Paul, who says, *If we have sown unto you spiritual things is it a great matter if we reap your carnal things?* (1 Cor. ix. 11). The faithful, therefore, are to be reminded often of this duty, with which if they neglect to comply, they will omit, through their own fault, hearing mass on Sundays and festivals, and receiving the sacraments at those seasons in which they need them most, the seasons of sickness, of Easter, and when, through the prevalence of sinful passions, or long habits of vice, a speedy reconciliation with God becomes indispensably necessary. Wherefore, as long as they refuse to contribute for the ministry of salvation, according to the measure of worldly fortune given to them by a beneficent God, and thus violate the divine and ecclesiastical laws, they are to know that they are in a state of sin, and incapable of receiving forgiveness in the tribunal of Confession; and that they will be answerable to God, not only for their own non-compliance with duties so sacred, but likewise for the ignorance and vices of the poor people that remain destitute of Christian instruction, on account of the sordid avarice of those who are more favored with the gifts of fortune. To begin, then, in this diocess that which is practised in other Christian countries, the preceding regulations were formed, relative to the oblations of the faithful, and others will be added hereafter.

I trust that you, my dear brethren, will consider these statutes with the same candor and in the same spirit in which they were formed. It was not in the spirit of avarice, but of real solicitude for the preservation of faith, and for your increase in godliness and heavenly knowledge. They were suggested by the desire of seeing you assisted with the same means of salvation as your Catholic brethren in all other countries, and with the hope that you would use the same endeavor as they, to appropriate to yourselves the blessings of a regular instruction and uninterrupted ministration of divine worship. To accomplish this salutary purpose more effectually, and render more certain the subsistence of the ministers of religion, they are directed to require at marriages, and funeral services a certain very moderate compensation, to which they whom God has blessed with abundance may add according to their benevolence; and which my reverend brethren are hereby charged not to require from those to whom, on account of their great poverty, any compensation would be burdensome.

On this occasion I cannot forbear mentioning an abuse, or rather a prevalent neglect and indifference with respect to your departed parents and relations. When death has removed them from your sight, you seem to forget that doctrine of our divine religion, which ought to call forth all your tenderness, I mean the doctrine, that *it is a holy and salutary thought to pray for the dead, that they may be delivered from their sins* (2 Maccabees xii. 46). How different is your behavior, when such events happen, from that of your Catholic brethren all over the world! Their sensibility is not confined to the unprofitable tears and lamentations of a few days; their faith follows their deceased friends into the mansions of another life, and enkindles all their charity; they procure prayers and sacrifices to be offered to God for the repose of their souls; the exercises of charity to the poor, and all the works of mercy and religion are employed for their relief, as long as there remains a reasonable ground to fear that they may want it. Thus St. Augustin testified his sensibility, after the death of his holy mother, St. Monica; thus, as Tertullian, St. Cyprian, and other primitive Fathers teach us, children expressed their duty and veneration for their parents, and surviving Christian spouses for them to whom they had been united by the ties and duties of a virtuous marriage.

When it pleases God to call your friends out of this world, do you, my dear brethren, give such proofs of your affection for them? You attend them to the grave, you shed over it a few tears, and there is the term of your care and solicitude.

If a charitable priest offer up to the throne of mercy, for their sake, the Blood of the Lamb of God, who takes away the sins of the world, he does it generally unsolicited and unthanked by you. You make no sacrifice of interest or enjoyments to charity and religion, that the deceased may find speedy mercy and an anticipated enjoyment of everlasting bliss. I earnestly beseech you to deserve no longer this reproach on your charity and sensibility. Follow your departed brethren into the regions of eternity with your prayers, and all the assistance which is suggested by the principles of faith and piety. Let the great sacrifice of propitiation be offered for all who die in the unity of the Catholic Church and in due submission to her wholesome precepts. Where it is possible, let a funeral service be performed. And I recommend it strongly to the pastors of all congregations, and to the faithful themselves, to promote the forming of pious associations, whose special object shall be to bestow on the dead, and especially on those who die poor and friendless, the best offices of religion, that is, to procure for them a decent interment accompanied with the prayers and sacred rites ordained by the Church.

In this my address to you, my dear brethren, I have been chiefly solicitous to recommend to your attention those things which will be of general advantage to the preservation and increase of true religion. I have no doubt but that your immediate pastors will give you caution frequently against the prevailing and most dangerous vices; and will instruct you how to walk in the observance of all Christian duties. I shall only add this, my earnest request, that to the exercise of the sublimest virtues, Faith, Hope, and Charity, you will join a fervent and well-regulated devotion to the Holy Mother of our Lord and Saviour Jesus Christ, that you will place great confidence in her intercession, and have recourse to her in all your necessities, but more especially your spiritual necessities. Having chosen her to be the special patroness of this diocess, you are placed, of course, under her powerful protection, and it becomes your duty to be careful to deserve its continuance by a zealous imitation of her virtues and reliance on her motherly superintendence.

The Sunday immediately following the feast of her glorious assumption into Heaven, or the feast itself, whenever it happens to fall on a Sunday, is to be celebrated as a principal solemnity of this diocese, on which we are to unite with one heart and in one earnest supplication to the Father of all mercies and the Giver of every good gift, through the intercession of the Blessed Virgin, that he may be graciously pleased to preserve, increase, and diffuse a sincere and well-grounded attachment to the principles of our holy religion, to avert from us the seduction of error and pestilential infidelity, to awake and renew in us the spirit of solid piety and of watchfulness over our unruly passions, to animate us to the fulfilling of all the commandments, to pour down on our country blessings spiritual and temporal, and to receive our grateful and humble thanks for the innumerable favors which we continually receive from a bountiful Providence.

That these acts of religion may be more acceptable, by being offered with purified hearts, I earnestly exhort and recommend to all who shall join in the celebration of this great festival, to expiate their offences by sincere compunction in the sacrament of penance, and to enrich their souls by those abundant graces which are annexed to a worthy participation of Christ's Body and Blood. I have solicited, for your sake, my dear brethren, from the Holy See, special spiritual favors for this solemnity, and have no doubt but the fatherly solicitude which his Holiness the Vicar of Jesus Christ has always shown hitherto for your improvement in every Christian virtue, will induce him to grant the favors requested, of which, in due time, you shall receive proper notice.

What may not be hoped, if to other means of salvation, such as are always to be found in the salutary institutions of the Church, you will add every year this, likewise, that is now suggested? if you recur to God, the fountain of mercy and grace, through the intercession of the Queen of Angels? if you honor her greatest festival with peculiar and fervent exercises of piety, and with a determined will of making the precepts of the Gospel the rule of your lives? The Church bears her this honorable testimony, that it is often owing to her patronage that nations preserve or recover the integrity of Christian faith and morality. Let this be exemplified in our own country. *Walk worthy of the vocation in which you are called* (Eph. iv. 1). Give no cause of its being said of any one of you, *thou that makest thy boast of the law, by transgression of the law dishonorest God* (Rom. ii. 23). On the contrary, endeavor continually, *that you may declare His virtues who has called you out of darkness into His admirable light*, that they among whom is *your conversation, considering you by your good works, may give glory to God in the day of visitation* (1 Pet. ii. 9, 12) *For this cause I bow my knees to the Father of our Lord Jesus Christ, that he would grant you, according to the riches of His glory, that Christ may dwell by faith in your hearts; that, being rooted and founded in charity, you may be able to know also the charity of Christ, which surpasseth knowledge, that you may be filled unto all the fulness of God. Now to Him who is able to do all things more abundantly than we desire or understand, to Him be glory in the Church, and in Christ Jesus, unto all generations, world without end. Amen.* (Eph. iv. 16 *et seq.*).

JOHN,

Bishop of Baltimore

BALTIMORE, *May* 28, 1792.

To accomplish the good which he contemplated, Bishop Carroll had the happiness of witnessing the frequent arrival in America of clergymen who were endowed with all the qualities for the missionary life. The Dubois, the Flagets, the Dubourgs, the Cheverus, and many others of the same eminent character, were gathering around him to consolidate the excellent institutions which he had commenced, and to spread far and wide the blessings of religion by instruction and the administration of the sacraments. The academy at Georgetown had been set on foot, and was acquiring reputation; while the seminary at Baltimore flourished in the spirit of piety and regularity. The missionary field, while it was supplied with additional laborers, also presented a more abundant harvest in the numbers of the faithful, which began sensibly to increase under the favorable circumstances which the new political *régime* offered for immigration, and for the more out-spoken profession of Catholicity. Charleston and Savannah, in the South; West Pennsylvania; the old French missions of Illinois, Indiana, and Michigan; and the churches of Boston, New York, Albany, Kentucky, and other places, felt the beneficial influence of the providential dispensation which had conducted so many worthy ecclesiastics to the shores of America. The Rev. Stephen T. Badin, the first priest ordained in the United States, was sent to Kentucky, in 1794, and for many years was the principal, and for some time the only missionary in that region. One of the most consoling incidents of Dr. Carroll's administration, was to supply with zealous pastors the Indian tribes in the northeast and northwestern part of the United States. Having appealed to his pastoral solicitude, in their

·arnest desire to enjoy the blessings of religion, he complied with their wishes as soon as circumstances would enable him to do so. The Rev. Messrs. Ciquard, Cheverus, and Romagné, successively attended the Penobscot and Passamaquoddy tribes in Maine, while Rev. Messrs. Levadoux, Richard, and Rivet, labored among the Catholic settlements and Indians of the Northwest. These missions were supported, to some extent, by an appropriation from the United States government, through the instrumentality of Bishop Carroll.

The progress of religion in these early times was promoted, in no small degree, by the communities of the devout female sex, which were successfully introduced into the country. In 1790, the Carmel· ites of St. Theresa's reform established a convent in Charles County. Maryland. A few years after, a community of *Poor Clares* was founded in Georgetown, D. C., which, however, had no permanent existence. It was succeeded, in the same town, by a society of pious ladies, who subsequently, under the direction of the Rt. Rev. Leonard Neale, adopted the rules of the Visitation of St. Francis de Sales, and now have many flourishing institutions in different parts of the country.* At a later period, Mrs. Seton, a convert to Catholicity in New York, commenced an academy at Baltimore, in 1808, for the educa tion of young persons of her sex, which resulted, the following year, in the establishment, at Emmetsburg, Maryland, of the Sisters or Daughters of Charity, whose benevolent administrations in orphan· asylums, hospitals, and poor-schools, are now the theme of universal praise throughout the land.

Contemporary with these increased resources for female education, both secular and religious, was the progress of institutions for the literary and ecclesiastical training of young men. The Hermits of St. Augustin were introduced, at Philadelphia, by Father Carr, as early as 1790, and the church of St. Augustin and a flourishing college, near that city, are now under their direction. The Sulpitians, at Baltimore, commenced the collegiate institution of St. Mary's, in 1799, which soon rose to a highly prosperous condition.† A few years after, a preparatory seminary, under the charge of the same clerical congregation, was founded at Pigeon Hills, near Hanover, Pennsylvania, but was soon transferred to the vicinity of Emmetsburg, Maryland, and resulted in the excellent institution of Mt. St. Mary's

---

* Rev. Father Neale, an ex-Jesuit, was appointed Bishop of Gortyna, *in part*, and coadjutor of Bishop Carroll, in 1795; but the bulls having been delayed, he was not consecrated till 1800.

† Discontinued, unfortunately, in 1850.

College and Seminary, which was first conducted by the Rev. John Dubois, and which still renders the most important services to religion and education.

Among the events which contributed materially, at this period, to promote the interests of the Church, was the restoration, in the United States, of the Society of Jesus. This had always been a cherished object with Dr. Carroll and the other ex-members of the society; and when they had received positive information that it had continued without interruption in Russia, and that the general in that country had authority to aggregate others, at least *in foro conscientiæ*, Bishop Carroll and his coadjutor, Dr. Neale, applied to the general, Father Gruber, requesting to be made acquainted with the real state of things, and, if practicable, to be allowed a participation in the privi leges accorded to the society in Russia. Upon the receipt of Father Gruber's answer, * authorizing a renewal of vows and the appoint- ment of a superior, Dr. Carroll held a meeting, May 10, 1805, at which six of the former fathers of the company were readmitted ; and, on the 21st of June following, the Rev. Robert Molyneux was named by Dr. Carroll to the charge of the renascent society There soon arrived from Europe other members, to give vigor and efficacy to the college at Georgetown, and to various missions in Maryland and Penn- sylvania. In the spring of 1806, another important establishment for the American Church was commenced in Washington County, Ken- tucky, by Rev. Edward Fenwick and other members of the Order of St. Dominic. A novitiate was soon opened for the instruction of can- didates for the priesthood, while the fathers of the convent labored zealously in the performance of missionary duty.†

These numerous accessions to the ranks of the clergy, afforded Dr. Carroll more ample means of supplying the wants of the faithful; but, considering the extent of the harvest, the laborers were comparatively few. The jurisdiction of the Bishop of Baltimore embraced not only the thirteen original States, but all the territory belonging to them, which now included Upper and Lower Louisiana, and all the country west of the Mississippi River.‡ New Orleans had been made an episcopal see, in 1793, and the Rt. Rev. Dr. Penalver had charge of

* March 12, 1804.

† In 1804, Rev. Michael Egan, of Lancaster, Pennsylvania, was empowered to establish a province of Franciscan Minors in the United States; but the project had no favorable result. At the same time, a community of Trappists, from Val-Sainte, Switzerland, arrived in Baltimore, and, after successive fruitless attempts in various parts of the country to es tablish their order, they returned to Europe.

‡ He was also charged, in 1809, with the care of the missions in severa. of the West

the diocese until the country was ceded to the French. Another bishop was appointed to succeed him, after his departure for Santa Fé, the Rt. Rev. Dr. Porro, who, however, never reached his see; and the absence of episcopal authority, or the contentions which arose on the subject of jurisdiction, gave birth to the most lamentable discords in that part of the Church, which continued for many years, and were productive of the greatest scandals. Louisiana being now within the domain of the United States (having been purchased in 1803), the Holy See directed Dr. Carroll to administer its ecclesiastical affairs, and he appointed successively Rev. Messrs. Olivier and Dubourg his vicars, with full powers for that mission.

The schism at New Orleans was, unfortunately, not the only one that saddened the heart of the chief pastor and aggravated the burden of his administration. While the people found an occasion of scandal at Charleston, S. C., and in Westmoreland County, Pa., in the irregular conduct of the priest, at Philadelphia and Baltimore they encouraged ambitious and insubordinate clergymen to rebel against episcopal authority, and to exercise faculties which did not belong to them. The cases of Rev. Francis From, in West Pennsylvania, and of Rev. Cæsarius Reuter, in Baltimore, are worthy of special notice, inasmuch as they were brought before the civil tribunals, and led to the declaration of a principle which has subsequently governed the decision of our courts. From had taken possession of the church property near Youngstown (left by Rev. Mr. Brauers), against the positive prohibition of Bishop Carroll, who refused to employ him as pastor; and Reuter, at Baltimore, with the aid of a party, occupied the German church, to the exclusion of a large part of the congregation, who would not join him because he officiated without any faculties from the bishop. In the latter instance the court decided that the church should be restored to the pastor appointed by the bishop;* in the former case, the judge gave a similar opinion, thus recognizing the principle, that a congregation professing to be united with the Roman Catholic Church, must be governed, in the tenure and administration of the church property, by the rules or canons of said church.†

During this early period, when the number of Catholics was small

India Islands—St. Croix, St. Thomas, and St. John, belonging to Denmark—the Dutch Island of St. Eustatia, and the neighboring ones of St. Kitts, Antigua, and Barbouda.

* Father Brosius was the legitimate pastor, and the case was Brosius v. Reuter.—GEN. HARPER'S *Manuscript Notes.*

† Executors of Brauers v. From, cited by De Courcy.

and sparsely settled, the clergy in many instances were subject to the greatest hardships, and it may not be either uninteresting or uninstructive for the present generation to learn, from the most authentic sources, the trials which some of the missionaries had to endure, as well as the rude state of society which existed in some parts of the country, and the eccentric character of some among the clergy themselves. At the risk of being charged with a deviation from the dignity of historical narration, we feel bound to present the following extracts from original documents:

Oct. 17, 1795, Rev. L. S. Phelan writes to Bishop Carroll, from West Pennsylvania. A log church had been commenced near Greensburg, but not completed. " Your reverence can have no conception of my distress here, even for the necessaries of life, for really I have not any thing like a sufficiency of food such as I get, and indeed poor and filthy it is. Most of the Irish, who, though poor, were by far the most generous, have now quit this settlement; five or six German families alone remain, whose chaplain I may call myself, since I cannot pretend to travel for want of a horse, and these people, indeed—abstraction made of religion—are the last of all mankind for sentiments of humanity. The poor man I live with is not paid what was promised for my board, and, whether he intends it or not, he treats me accordingly. Perhaps he can't help it. Bread is the sole support of his family. Morning, noon, and night, flour and water, or bread and water, with a little burnt grease thrown over, is the support of his starved and almost perfectly naked large family. Since my arrival, the only meat they had was a little pig about twenty or thirty pounds, and a calf ten days old, of which we have eat this whole week, till it became musty and green for want of salt. When I arrived first, they had about a dozen of hens, of which I must have eat eight, as they still have four. . . Thus have I spent five months of a very rigorous Lent, that threw me into a diarrhœa, that, in such wretchedness and cold, made me pass a most penitential winter."

The following will show what singular characters were occasionally met with in those days, and what a rough set of people the priest had sometimes to encounter. A clergyman offers his services to Dr. Carroll, from Naples, February, 1797: " The purport of my troubling your lordship is no other than that, as being informed there is a scarcity of horses, in your new found world, to cultivate the vineyard of the Lord, should your lordship be under the deplorable necessity of supplying the defect by employing even asses, I should most humbly offer myself for one, though I can boast of nothing to recommend me for so sublime a function," &c.

Another priest, writing from Milltown, Pa., in January, 1799, informs Bishop Carroll that he had a large tract of land about twenty miles from there, had placed his sister, *a nun*, on it, allotting her and her Order five hundred acres. He requests the bishop to send him, in the spring, "twenty Munster or Connaught men, and, if they are poor, I'll pay them as much a year or a day as any other gentleman in the country, provided they are Catholics, because there are plenty of other descriptions here already; but I don't approve of it. Thus you'll free me from a reprobated clan of infamous Scotch-Irish, superior in all kinds of wickedness, only in a superlative degree, to the most vile celebrated convicts.   What a holy relief it is for me to be so soon reprieved from such a degraded, dragooning group of infectious reptiles! This before I would not mention to you, until I could be settled, in dread you might suppose interested views might oblige me to exaggerate in my reports. It's as good as a farce to hear, that since I came back, in consequence of the cold, I am dislodged from my spring-house, and obliged to turn into the pig-sty, that is, the poor, honest man's own house, which is worse than can be described in the old German style, where cats, young dogs, and young fowls, both men and their wives, sons and daughters, we all in one stove-room comfortably kennel together; but what is more humorous is, that I am kept in pledge, in this sweet-scented situation, for my quarter's diet and lodging." We shall conclude this part of the subject with a portraiture drawn by the pen of Father Whelan, who had many years before been a missionary in Kentucky. Writing from White Clay Creek, Pa., January 7, 1805, he says: "As to Thos. Maguire and his wife, a priest might as well go and lodge in a wolf-pen as with them—he being a wild Irish savage, she being either of the Sambo or Shawnee breed, though some say that she is a Hottentot. But, let the case be as it may, she is one whose exterior appearance and interior disposition differ totally from any woman I ever conversed with. At the second word she will give me the lie to my face. Her husband, though present, would say nothing to all this.   .   No man in Bedlam suffers more than I do, in the company of four wolves. I hope it is a temporal purgatory. and will atone for some of my sins."

IV

In 1808, the number of Catholics had so much increased, in the Eastern States and in the country west of the Allegheny Mountains, that the Sovereign Pontiff deemed it expedient to raise Baltimore to the dignity of an archiepiscopal see, with four suffragan bishopries, Philadelphia, New York, Boston, and Bardstown. The Rev. Michael Egan was appointed to Philadelphia; Rev. John Cheverus, to Boston; and Rev. Benedict Flaget to Bardstown, who were all consecrated by Archbishop Carroll at Baltimore, in the autumn of 1810. The Rev. Luke Concanen, of the Order of Preachers, appointed for New York, was consecrated at Rome; but he died at Naples on the eve of embarking for his diocess. At this time there were about seventy priests and eighty churches in the United States, with a Catholic population of probably one hundred and fifty thousand. As an evidence of the progress of the Church, it may be stated that in 1808 six priests were ordained on one day, and as Dr. Carroll remarks in a letter to his coad jutor, it was "a happy day for the diocess." Before the bishops separated for their respective sees, they adopted various points of disci pline, and addressed a letter to the Sovereign Pontiff, in which they pray him to aid them with such instructions, as the welfare of the Church in general and of the United States in particular might require; to appoint chief pastors to the sees of New York and New Or leans, and to indicate the future mode of providing for vacant bishop rics. They also issued a brief pastoral on a few matters of immediate moment, reserving for another occasion a general review of the ecclesiastical discipline observed throughout the country. Pastors of the different churches were admonished not to allow strange priests to say mass, without the permission of the ordinary; they were also informed that the sacrament of baptism should be administered in the church, in those towns which had one, unless necessity should otherwise dictate; that the people should be advised to have the ceremony of marriage performed in the church, when it could be done without great inconvenience; and that they should be dissuaded from an attachment to entertainments and diversions dangerous to morals, such as frequenting the theatre, a fondness for dancing assemblies, reading books injurious to faith and morality, and the promiscuous reading of all kinds of novels.

The extensive correspondence which these important matters required, occupied the earnest attention of Archbishop Carroll, especially as the see of Philadelphia soon became vacant by the demise of Dr. Egan, in 1814, "whose few years of administration," as Bishop England remarks, "were years of difficulty." He was a pious, zealous, and learned prelate, but deficient in that firmness which was necessary to cope with the machinations of evil-disposed men. The Rev. Lewis

Debarth was appointed administrator of the diocess during the vacancy of the see, and, soon after he entered upon the charge, he had the happiness of welcoming to the city of Philadelphia a band of Sisters of Charity from Emmetsburg, to take the direction of an orphan asylum and school. This was the first colony sent by Mother Seton to extend the work of charity. The efforts of Bishop Flaget, in his new field of labor, were soon crowned with the most gratifying results. In a few years he had established an ecclesiastical seminary under the direction of Rev. John B. David, who had accompanied him to Kentucky, and two institutions of religious women, the Lorettines and the Sisters of Charity of Nazareth, who, in aspiring to the practice of Christian perfection, would devote themselves to the education of young persons of their sex.* In the diocess of New York, the affairs of the Church had assumed an aspect of decided improvement, owing to the zeal of the learned and exemplary clergymen whom Archbishop Carroll had stationed in that city—Fathers Anthony Kohlman and Benedict Fenwick, of the Society of Jesus, the former of whom was invested with the powers of vicar-general. They established in New York City a literary institution for young men, which did much good. To their efforts, also, was due the erection of the Cathedral, which was dedicated in 1815. Some time before this, a remarkable case was decided by the civil tribunal of New York, in which Father Kohlman was a prominent actor, and which resulted in determining an important principle of law. It was a case of restitution ; and the question having arisen, whether a priest was bound to give evidence as to matters disclosed to him under the seal of the confessional, it was decided that a priest could not be compelled to answer in such cases.†

On witnessing these evident manifestations of progress in the cause of religion, the Most Rev. Dr. Carroll could congratulate himself, that his labor and solicitude had not been vainly bestowed upon the rising Church of the United States. He had conducted it, under the providence of God, from a state of poverty, persecution, and distress, to a condition of comparative prosperity. He beheld it an ecclesiastical province, with its bishops, an increasing body of clergy, its convents, colleges, ecclesiastical seminaries, and with a bright prospect of still further extension for the glory of God and the salvation

---

* The Lorettines were instituted by Rev. Charles Nerincks, of Kentucky, one of the most laborious and saintly priests that have labored in the missions of America.

† A full report of this case was published by Counsellor Sampson, including a treatise by Father Kohlman on the Catholic doctrine touching the sacrament of Penance. The volume is entitled *The Catholic Question,* N. Y., 1813

of souls. Under these consoling circumstances was he called to the reward of the faithful servant, on the 3d of December, 1815, in the eighty-first year of his age. During his last illness, he displayed the same greatness of character which had distinguished him during life. As he drew nearer to his end, the glow of religious hope seemed to increase within him—the effect of his strong and lively faith in the cross of Christ, and of his filial trust in the protection of the mother of God. These two sentiments were dominant in his last moments, and led him to express the wish that he should be laid on the floor, that he might expire in the posture of the deepest humility, and to remark to his confessor, that the greatest consolation he experienced in that awful hour, was the reflection that he had placed his diocess under the patronage of the Blessed Virgin Mary.*

Archbishop Carroll, though of low stature, had a commanding and dignified appearance. "The configuration of his head, his whole mien," says one of his friends, "bespoke the metropolite." While his superior faculties and acquirements, with his great personal consideration and influence, inspired universal respect, his courteous and affable manners and the benignity of his nature attracted and delighted all who approached him. His conversational powers were of the highest order, derived from his extensive reading and his well-improved opportunities of information, at home and abroad. As a scholar his attainments were varied and extensive, and his writings exhibit in general a model of classical style. But the eminent qualities of Dr. Carroll shone forth most conspicuously as a prelate. His sound judgment and great prudence, combined with equal zeal, firmness, and mildness, gave him a peculiar fitness for the administration of affairs. His letters to clergymen, whose errors of conduct and whose scandals he was forced to condemn, breathed at the same time a spirit of charity and condescension which rarely failed to bring them to a sense of their obligations. In private as in public life he was the model of all. His piety was of the most tender and exemplary character. Although constantly receiving visitors, and frequently at the close of evening, he never omitted, at the appointed hour for night-prayer, to retire gracefully from the company, and, with the few colored servants of his household, to recite with them the customary devotions. In a word, Archbishop Carroll exhibited in his person the truly episcopal character as portrayed by St. Peter: "Feed the flock of God which is among you; overseeing not by constraint, but willingly, according to God; not for filthy lucre, but cheerfully: nor as

* Ego mater pulchræ dilectionis et agnitionis et *sanctæ spei*. Eccli. 24.

lording it over the portions, but as becoming a pattern of the flock from the heart."*

The Right Rev. Leonard Neale, coadjutor of the late archbishop, succeeded him in the metropolitan see. Dr. Neale had, for twenty-five years, zealously co-operated with his illustrious predecessor, in promoting the interests of the Church, rendering the most efficient services as pastor at Philadelphia, president of the college at George-town, and director of the Visitation convent in the latter city, when he assumed the charge of the archdiocess. The burden, however, was too great for his years and infirmities. Eighteen months after his accession to the see of Baltimore, he died at Georgetown, having, during his short administration, exhibited in a high degree the firm-ness of a truly Christian prelate, in opposing the irregular proceedings of two schismatical and scandalous priests at Charleston, South Caro-lina. Before his demise, the Rev. Ambrose Maréchal, professor at St. Mary's Seminary, in Baltimore, had been appointed his coadjutor, but he was not consecrated until December, 1817. Like his venerable predecessor, he had a thorny path to travel in the earlier period of his episcopacy. Besides the troubles at Charleston, which were eventually composed through the exemplary zeal and prudence of Rev. Messrs. Cloriviere and Ben. Fenwick, the pacification of the Church at Norfolk, Virginia, was an object of his earnest solicitude and most active exertions. In that city, the spirit of insubordination among some of the laity, abetted by a most unscrupulous clergyman, Rev. Thomas Carbery, threatened the Church with the most lamentable evils. The party who were opposed to the duly appointed pastor, Rev. James Lucas, went so far as to apply to the schismatical Bishop of Utrecht, for the purpose of having a certain priest consecrated bishop of Norfolk, who was afterward to consecrate bishops for all the States of the Union, and to establish in this country an " Independent Catholic Church of the United States." But this diabolical project failed, by the refusal of the priest in question to enter into the design.†

---

* 1 Peter, v.—The funeral oration of Archbishop Carroll was delivered by the Rev. Dr. Gallagher, who applied to him, in a very happy manner, those words of Scripture: " Ecce sacerdos magnus qui in diebus suis placuit Deo et inventus est justus, et in tempore ira-cundiæ factus est reconciliatio." Eccli. 44.

† Carbery officiated as a priest at Norfolk, without faculties, and he openly cautioned the civil authorities in Virginia to beware of the spiritual power of the Pope. It was providential for the Church, that the true character of this man, who had a few years before been nominated by the Bishop of New York as a fit person to fill the see of Charles-ton, was discovered in time

These unfortunate disturbances, which had their chief source in the antagonism or conflict of nationalities, were a sufficient motive for the Holy See to create a bishopric in Virginia, while the great distance of the Carolinas and Georgia led to the creation of an episcopal see at Charleston. In 1820, the Rt. Rev. Dr. England, formerly parish-priest of Bandon, in Ireland, took possession of the latter diocess, and Rt. Rev. Patrick Kelly, a native of the same country, arrived in Norfolk, Va., where he found it more convenient to reside than in his see at Richmond. When Dr. England arrived in his diocess, it could count only five or six small churches (one in Charleston, three in Georgia, and one in North Carolina), with only two clergymen in the field. He soon succeeded in establishing a seminary, where young men could have an opportunity of receiving a good secular and ecclesiastical education. At a later period, he introduced a community of Sisters of Mercy, who have rendered important service to the diocess. At the time of which we are speaking, there were not more than two or three churches in Virginia, and only one priest. The stay of Dr. Kelly in America was not of long duration, it having been discovered at Rome, upon a further consideration of the subject, that the appointment of a bishop for Virginia had been premature.* In admitting this to Arch bishop Maréchal, who had protested against the measure, Cardinal Fontana informed him also that the circumstance was a matter of profound regret at Rome, and that the Sovereign Pontiff, wishing to give him some pledge of his apostolic kindness, would soon send him a gold chalice of exquisite workmanship, to be a perpetual memorial of the distinguished favor which he bore toward the Archbishop of Baltimore and the church under his care.† Another mark of the particular regard of his Holiness for the American Church, was the institution of the Marian Theological Faculty in the University of St. Mary's at Baltimore. This grant was made, as the official decree states, " that young men, instructed in the various branches of knowledge, and particularly in the sacred sciences, should be qualified to conduct others in the right way, and by the combat of error to promote the progress of true religion."‡ The Rev. Messrs. Whitfield, Deluol, and Damphoux, were the first recipients of the doctoral honors, in accordance with the afore-mentioned decree.

* After laboring with great zeal for the welfare of his people, during his brief administration in America, Dr. Kelly was transferred to the see of Waterford, in Ireland, in 1822.
† This chalice is used only on grand occasions in the Metropolitan Church.
‡ March, 1822.

One year after the creation of the new diocesses in the South, Cincin nati was erected into an episcopal see, and the Rev. Edward Fenwick, O. P., appointed to fill it. This diocess embraced Ohio, Michigan, and Northwest Territory. Father Fenwick had made several mission ary visits to Ohio; but in 1818, he and Rev. Nicholas D. Young, O. P., settled permanently in Perry County, where the first chapel in that State was erected. Religion soon exhibited the signs of a rapid prog ress. In two years after his appointment, he computed the number of Catholics in Ohio at eight thousand, and about twelve thousand in Michigan; there were twenty-two congregations, and seven priests to attend them. In a short time the diocess was blessed with establish ments of Sisters of Charity from Emmetsburg, and of the Nuns of St. Dominic, for the cause of charity and education.

While the progress of the faith was promoted by the creation of new episcopal sees, it was equally advanced by the appointment of bishops to those which had become vacant. New Orleans was now provided with a chief pastor, Rt. Rev. Dr. Dubourg, who on his re turn from Europe, in 1817, brought with him a zealous band of mis sionaries to aid him in his arduous labors. Deeming it inexpedient to ettle in the capital of Louisiana, he made Missouri the more immedi ate theatre of his apostolic zeal. Here he established a seminary and college under the Lazarists, or priests of the congregation of the Mis sion; another college at St. Louis, under the Jesuits, who also com menced a novitiate of their order at Florissant. The Ladies of the Sacred Heart, and the Lorettines from Kentucky, with the Ursulines at New Orleans, were his resources for the education of young ladies and the gratuitous instruction of the poor and the people of color. In 1823, the removal of Bishop Dubourg to New Orleans made it neces sary that he should have the aid of a coadjutor in Upper Louisiana, and Rev. Joseph Rosati was appointed to this responsible office. Shortly after this, Rev. Michael Portier, who conducted a college at New Orleans, was named vicar apostolic of the territory embracing Alabama and Florida, and subsequently he became Bishop of Mobile, when the same country was formed into a diocess. Owing to intoler able annoyances and oppositions from clergy and laity, Bishop Dubourg resigned his see in 1826, and returned to his native country. He was succeeded at New Orleans by Rev. Leo de Nekere, the city of St. Louis being now an episcopal see, of which Dr. Rosati was the incum bent.

The see of New York, vacant by the death of Dr. Concanen, was filled toward the close of 1815 by the Rt. Rev. Dr. Conolly, of the Order of St. Dominic. He was a zealous and laborious prelate, and had to contend with many difficulties in his episcopal administration. He had the happiness of welcoming to the city of New York a colony of Sisters of Charity from Emmetsburg, for the care of orphans and the instruction of the poor—which was the second foundation of that excellent society in the United States. On the death of Dr. Conolly, in 1825, the diocess was wisely administered for two years by Very Rev. John Power, a learned, eloquent, and amiable clergyman, when the Rev. John Dubois, president of Mount St. Mary's College, was appointed bishop of New York. At that time he computed the number of Catholics in his diocess at one hundred and eighty-five thousand, with fourteen churches and about the same number of priests.

In the diocese of Bardstown, religion was advancing with rapid strides. A new and elegant cathedral was consecrated in 1819, and the same year Dr. Flaget had the happiness of conferring the episcopal character on the Rev. Father David, who had been appointed his coadjutor, and was his right arm in promoting the interests of the Church in that region. Shortly after, the colleges of St. Mary's and St. Joseph's were founded in the diocess; the former by Rev. William Byrne, the latter by Rev. George A. Elder, both distinguished by their zeal and piety. A convent of religious women, under the rule of St. Dominic, was also commenced in this diocess about the year 1819.

The spiritual vineyard embracing the New England States, of which the see of Boston was the centre, had also borne its fruits. In 1818, a convent of Ursulines was established in that city, and subsequently transferred to Charlestown, where it became a flourishing house of education for young ladies.* Soon after this foundation, the diocess was deprived, by the death of Rev. Dr. Matignon, of a missionary who had given the first impulse to the prosperity of the Church in New England, and who was universally respected for his eminent abilities and virtues. But the Church was to suffer an equal, if not greater loss, by the departure of Dr. Cheverus, bishop of Boston, for his native country. He had long resisted the urgent appeals of his family to return among them; but the solicitations renewed from still higher authority appeared to him an indication of the divine will, and he left America in the autumn of 1823, to take possession of the see of Montauban, in France.† He was succeeded by the Right Rev. Bene-

---

* Rev. Mr. Thayer, to whom we have already alluded, was the originator of this religious house, after his final departure from the United States to fix his residence in Ireland.

† Afterwards transferred to the archiepiscopal see of Bordeaux. and invested with the purple

dict J. Fenwick, who in entering upon his new field of labor found only three priests and nine churches or chapels in the immense district placed under his charge. The number of Catholics was about fifteen thousand, the one-half of whom were in Boston and its vicinity.

The see of Philadelphia, after a vacancy of six years, during which it was ably administered by Father Debarth, was filled by the Right Rev. Henry Conwell, who had been previously vicar-general of Armagh, in Ireland. The mitre for him was truly a crown of thorns. The whole period of his administration (about eight years) was an open and deplorable conflict with an unprincipled clergyman, the Rev. William Hogan, pastor of St. Mary's Church, Philadelphia, and his party. This priest, whose faculties had been withdrawn by the bishop, continued to exercise the ministry, and was upheld in his scandalous proceedings by the trustees of the church. He would probably have recanted and returned to a sense of duty, if his false friends among the laity, who were totally destitute of the spirit of religion, had not encouraged him in his wicked course. At length, this unhappy man quitted the scene of his scandals, went South, took a wife, published several infamous attacks upon the Catholic Church, and died without giving any sign of repentance, verifying the words of Scripture, " the wicked man, when he is come into the depth of sins, contemneth; but ignominy and reproach follow him."* The departure of Hogan, however, did not quell the storm.† Such was the excitement created by the schismatical party, that the good bishop, anxious to restore peace to his distracted flock, entered into a compromise with the trustees, relative to the appointment of pastors. This arrangement was condemned by the Holy See as an infringement of the ecclesiastical authority, and Dr. Conwell was summoned to Rome, ostensibly for the purpose of presenting a full exposition of the state of things in his diocess, while the Rev. William Matthews, of Washington City, was appointed to administer its affairs. Soon after this, the spirit of discord began to subside, but not without leaving behind it a scene of desolation— many lost to the Church by a total extinction of the faith, and a still greater number become obdurate in refusing to avail themselves of its consoling ministrations.

Amidst the scandals which a portion of the Church in Philadelphia exhibited, Archbishop Maréchal witnessed with joy the progress of religion in other parts of the United States; and among the events

---

* Prov. xviii.

† Rev. Messrs. O'Meally, Harold, and Ryan, figured very unreputably in this schism.

which justly claimed his gratitude to Heaven, was the manifestation of a supernatural power in confirmation of the true faith. The gift of miracles resides in the Church, in virtue of the promises of her divine Founder, and He displays this extraordinary intervention of His power as times and circumstances may require. An event of this kind, beyond all question miraculous, occurred in the case of Mrs. Ann Mattingly, of Washington City, sister of the Hon. Thomas Carbery, then chief magistrate of the national metropolis. After a sickness of several years' duration, which subjected her to the most intense sufferings, and which had resulted in the formation of external tumors and ulcers, she was at length reduced to the point of death, and her physicians pronounced her situation beyond the reach of medical skill. In this condition she was advised to resort to the prayers of Rev. Prince Hohenlohe, canon of Olmutz, who was renowned for his sanctity, and who had the reputation of obtaining the most extraordinary favors from God. She accordingly performed a novena, or nine days' devotion, in union with some of her pious friends, as the prince had directed, and on the 10th of March, 1824, immediately after the reception of the Holy Communion, she was instantly restored to health. The tumor had disappeared, the ulcers on her back were healed, and, rising from her bed, she spent some time in prayer and thanksgiving, and during the day received hundreds of visitors who crowded to see her. Various miracles of the same kind were wrought at the Visitation convent, Georgetown, D. C., at St. Joseph's Sisterhood, Emmetsburg, and other places, which aroused the attention of many persons outside of the Church to this brilliant evidence of her claim to their respect and submission.*

While miracles of this kind attested the truth of Catholic doctrine, other supernatural events had many years previously been permitted by the Almighty within the present limits of the United States, which are worthy of record, inasmuch as they tend to confirm and illustrate the famous saying of St. Thomas Aquinas, that God would send an angel, if necessary, to instruct in the faith those who sincerely seek after it by making a right use of the gifts of nature. The grounds on which this opinion of the angelical Doctor was based, were not of a purely speculative nature. It rested equally upon the experience of the Christian Church; and it is a source of gratification to know that this experimental evidence has been witnessed in this country, as in other

---

* See a full report of the evidence in regard to these facts, by Dr. England, bishop of Charleston in the third volume of his works, p. 393.

parts of the world. About the commencement of the present century there lived in Jefferson County, Virginia, a man named Adam Livingston, a Pennsylvanian by birth, and a Lutheran in religion. A short time after his settlement in Virginia, he was much disturbed by invisible beings that haunted his house. His property was destroyed, his barn was burnt, his cattle all died, his clothes were cut in pieces. Chunks of fire were thrown or thrust into the beds, the crockeryware was scattered upon the floor, and (what was most astonishing) articles of clothing were cut in the form of a half-moon, while boots, saddles, and other things were all demolished in the same way. Three men came from Winchester, in order to free the house from its annoyances: but they no sooner entered it, than a huge stone was seen to issue from the fire-place, and whirl round upon the floor for more than fifteen minutes, when the gentlemen sneaked away. Livingston applied also to three conjurers, who gave him some herbs, a book (common prayer), and a riddle, by way of catching the devil; but the first night, the book and herbs were found in a very ignominious piece of chamber-furniture, which was covered with the riddle. After some time, Mr. Livingston had a dream: he seemed to be climbing a high mountain, with great difficulty, catching at roots and bushes to effect the ascent; and, after reaching the summit, he saw a man dressed in a peculiar costume, and heard a voice, saying to him, "That is the man who can relieve you." He immediately inquired about the neighborhood, to ascertain what kind of a man this could be; and having been informed that Catholic priests wore the sort of dress which he had seen, and that one of them would officiate on the following Sunday at Shepherdstown, he determined to be there on that day. As soon as the priest came to the altar, for the celebration of mass, Mr. L. was so much overcome that he burst into tears, and said, "That is the very man whom I saw in my dream—that is the one to relieve me." The service ended, Livingston related his sad story to the clergyman, the Rev. Dennis Cahill, who at first looked upon it as a mere delusion; but having been persuaded to visit the residence of the Livingston family, and after investigating the matter, he sprinkled the premises with holy water; and before he left, a sum of money, which had been taken away, was found at the door. He afterward celebrated mass in the house, when the work of destruction ceased. Mr. Livingston joined the Catholic Church, and after this event he and his family were frequently favored with the visits of an invisible person, whose voice instructed them in the different points of Catholic doctrine and practice, recited the rosary with them, and exhorted them to prayer and penitential works. Fourteen persons were converted to the true faith in one season by these extraordinary revelations, while Catholics themselves were inspired with more religious sentiments. Mr. Livingston afterward removed to Loretto, in Pennsylvania, and some of his family are said to have died in the odor of sanctity.*

It may not be out of place, although not strictly in the chronological order, to mention another supernatural fact, which took place within the present limits of the United States, in the first quarter of the seventeenth century. The Sons of St. Francis were then evangelizing the Territory of New Mexico, and Father Benavides, superior of the mission, was applied to by a distant tribe of Indians, who had not yet been visited, and who wished to be baptized. These Indians stated that they had been instructed in the Christian faith by a lady, who frequently visited them, and then disappeared, without their knowing anything further about her. Missionaries were, however, sent to this Indian tribe, who were found to be well acquainted with the doctrines of the Church, and were at once admitted to the sacraments. Some years after, Father Benavides, on a visit to Spain, related this circumstance to the general of the Franciscans, who was at once reminded of the supernatural favors accorded to Mary of Agreda, a nun of the same religious institute. Upon a careful investigation of the subject, it was discovered that she was perfectly acquainted with all the details of the missionary enterprise among the above-mentioned tribe of Indians: she described the localities, stated the precise day and hour when certain events took place, so that Father Benavides was fully convinced of her having been the chosen instrument in the hands of God for bringing that portion of the Mexican Indians to a knowledge of the Christian religion.† However extraordinary such a fact may appear, it is by no means incredible to those who know that the very life and substance of the Christian Church lies in the supernatural order.

Within the period of Dr. Maréchal's administration as archbishop of Baltimore, Catholic charity gave birth to an institution, the origin and benefits of which, being largely connected with the Church on this side of the Atlantic, deserves particular notice. In 1815, Bishop Du-

---

* Letters of Rev. Demetrius A. Gallitzin, in St. Louis *Leader*. December, 1855—Dr Gallitzin's work on Holy Scripture, where he cites the above-mentioned facts as an evidence of the supernatural power residing in the Church of Christ.—Also manuscript narratives of Mrs. Dr. McSherry, an eye-witness to the circumstances which are here related.

† Görres, *La Mystique*. tom. 2, p. 341.—Also Memorial of Father Benavides, 1630.

bourg, of New Orleans, occupied with the wants of his dioeess, made an urgent appeal to his friends in Lyons, in behalf of that object, and suggested the formation of a society for the aid of the Church in Louisiana. A similar project was started about the same time for the benefit of the missions in the East. A few years after, a new impulse was given to this charitable work by the proposal, on the part of a clergyman from New Orleans, to make it universal or *catholic* in its operation, by assisting the labors of the apostleship throughout the world. This idea prevailed, and on the 3d of May, 1822, feast of the Finding of the Holy Cross, was organized the " Association for the Propagation of the Faith," which received the approbation of the Supreme Pontiff of Christendom, and was enriched by him with the spiritual treasures of the Church. Subsequently, all the bishops of France encouraged it by their official recommendation, and it has since been established in every part of Europe, in Asia, and in different parts of North and South America. The institution has for its object, to assist, by prayers an alms, the labors of Catholic missionaries throughout the world. One member receives the subscriptions (one cent a week) of ten others the amount of which he hands over to another member, who receives ten such collections, or one hundred subscriptions, which are placed in the hands of the treasurer. Two committees, one at Paris and the other at Lyons, administer the affairs of the association and distribute the funds. An account of the receipts and expenditures is published annually in the *Annals of the Propagation of the Faith*—a *brochure* which appears every two months, containing a variety of missionary intelligence, especially as communicated in letters of missionaries, from different parts of the world. Over 227,000 copies of the Annals are published every second month—in French, 145,000 ; Breton, 2,600 ; English, 20,000 ; German, 20,500 ; Spanish, 2,000 ; Flemish, 6,200 ; Italian, 26,000 ; Portuguese, 2,500 ; Dutch, 2,000 ; Polish 500. The receipts of the association, for the year 1864, amounted to $1,000,000 about $130,000 of which were sent to the United States.

While this truly Catholic institution was increasing in usefulness, Archbishop Maréchal, of Baltimore, was ealled to the reward of his many virtues, on the 29th of January, 1828. In his person were blended the most extensive learning and most aetive zeal, with a sweetness of temper and affability of manner which made him universally respected and beloved. Before his death, he had secured the appointment of the Very Reverend James Whitfield as his successor in the metropolitan see, who was consecrated on the 25th of May of the same year. One of the earliest aets of Dr. Whitfield's administration was to sanction the establishment at Baltimore of the Oblates Sisters of Providence—a society of colored women, formed by the zeal of Rev. H. Joubert, of St. Mary's College. This community was subsequently recognized at Rome, and it has done much good in the religious education of colored children, chiefly in Baltimore, as only one foundation of the institute has been elsewhere made. But the most important event of this period, was the holding of the first Provincial Council of Baltimore, which was opened on the 4th of October, 1829. There were present, the Archbishop of Baltimore, and the Bishops of Bardstown, Charleston, Cincinnati, St. Louis, and Boston; also, twelve priests, as theologians or superiors of different religious communities. Four prelates were absent, the Bishop of New York, the coadjutor Bishop of Bardstown, the Bishop of Mobile, and the Bishop of Philadelphia, who was represented by the administrator, Very Reverend William Matthews.* The Fathers of the Council published thirty-eight decrees, conducive to a better observance of ecclesiastical discipline, which were confirmed by the Holy See, and the spirit of which was embodied in an admirable pastoral letter,† from which we must quote at least the following words: "When we look around us, and behold how, within a few years, our churches have multiplied and our numbers increased, we feel deeply grateful to Him who, being able 'from the very stones to raise up children to Abraham,' has allured them to the paths of salvation." There was certainly just ground for these words of congratulation, when we consider the progress of the Church from 1800 to that time. We then see Bishop Carroll, with his coadjutor, charged literally with "the solicitude of all the churches," Catholics scattered in every direction to the number of sixty thousand, and but few clergymen, perhaps not more than forty, to supply the wants of this increasing population. For the higher education of young men there were but two institutions, while there was but one academy for young ladies. The Carmelite and Ursuline convents alone offered a retreat to female piety, that aspired to the practice of the evangelical counsels. Such was the numerical force of the Church thirty years before the opening of the first provincial council. Now, there were eleven diocesses, ten bishops, two hundred and thirty-two priests, two hundred and thirty churches, nine ecclesiastical seminaries, eight colleges, twenty female academies, and a Catholic population of at least half a million. The number of priests

* Rev. Leo de Nekere still hesitated to accept the mitre.
† Drawn up by the Right Reverend Dr. England.

was distributed as follows: in the dioceses of Baltimore and Rich mond, fifty-two; in New Orleans and St. Louis, eighty; in New York, twenty; in Boston, eight; in Philadelphia, eighteen; in Bardstown, twenty-one; in Charleston, ten; in Cincinnati, eighteen; in Mobile, five. These figures show a decided and rapid progress of the Church, considering the various obstacles it had to contend with; and although the Catholic population would have been much greater if there had existed, from the beginning, every facility for the instruction and spiritual assistance of those who belonged to the household of the faith, it cannot be denied that Catholicity had advanced, in spite of the numerous difficulties it encountered, much in the same way that its triumphs have been effected in every part of the world.

V.

In glancing at the subsequent history of the Church in the United States, we are compelled, by various reasons, to avoid entering into details, and we shall, therefore, merely refer to the more prominent events that have taken place. Of these, the principal are the different councils that have been held, and the multiplication of dioceses.

The second provincial council of Baltimore was convened in October, 1833, under the presidency of Archbishop Whitfield. Five other bishops assisted at it, among whom were the Rt. Rev. Francis P Kenrick, coadjutor of Philadelphia, Rt. Rev. John B. Purcell, of Cincinnati, and Rt. Rev. Frederick Rézé, of Detroit.* On this occasion the Fathers of the council adopted a regular mode of nominating bishops to vacant sees, and proposed that the Indian tribes in the far West, and the Catholic negroes in the colony of Liberia, should be confided to the care of the Society of Jesus. As early as 1823, Dr. Dubourg, of New Orleans, had taken steps for providing the Indians of Missouri Territory with spiritual assistance, and Fathers Vanquickenborn, Hoecken, and other Jesuits, labored with the most signal success among the Kickapoos, Potowatomies, Osages, and different other tribes, until 1850, when the Indian Territory was made an apostolic vicariate, and the Rt. Rev. F. B. Miège, S. J., was appointed to that field. There are two principal missions for the Indians in this district, that of the Potowatomies, on Sugar Creek, and that of the Osages, on the Neosho River, both in the State of Kansas. Schools

* Bishop Fenwick, of Cincinnati, and Bishop de Nekere, of New Orleans, had died—the former in 1832, and the latter only one month preceding the meeting of the prelates. Detroit had been made an episcopal see, embracing Michigan and the Northwest Territory

are conducted for their benefit by Ladies of the Sacred Heart and the Sisters of Loretto. There are several thousand Indians belonging to this mission. Repeated deputations having been sent to St. Louis, from the Flat-heads, west of the Rocky Mountains, who had been drawn to the faith, many years before, by some Catholic Iroquois from Canada, and who earnestly solicited the aid of the Black-gowns for their spiritual wants, Father de Smet set out for their distant country in 1840, and in the course of a few years established flourishing missions among that and other tribes. A few years before the Jesuits had commenced their labors in the eastern part of Oregon, the Rev. Francis N. Blanchet and Rev. Modest Demers, priests from Canada, had penetrated to the western portion of the territory, where they formed missionary stations among the Chinouks, the Nez-Percés, and among other sections of the aborigines. At a later period, Dr. Blanchet was appointed archbishop of Oregon City, with several suffragan bishops. To the Rev. Magloire Blanchet, his brother, was assigned the diocess of Walla-Walla (now Nesqualy), and that of Vancouver's Island, in British territory, was confided to the charge of Rev. Mr. Demers. The number of converted Indians in this region is about six thousand. In Michigan and the surrounding country, the missions among the Indians have been eminently successful. The Rev. Gabriel Richard, Vincent Badin, and Samuel Mazzuchelli, were among the earlier laborers in this interesting field.* They were succeeded by Rev. Messrs. Déjean and Baraga, the latter of whom is now bishop of Marquette, Michigan, and has the superintendence of all the Indian missions in that region, which number several thousand souls. Bishop Baraga has published different works in the Indian dialects, such as catechisms, prayer-books, meditations, bible-history, etc., which form an admirable collection for the instruction and edification of this interesting portion of his flock. We have already alluded to the Penobscot and Passamaquoddy Indians, at Old Town and Pleasant Point, in Maine. This mission was commenced by the Jesuits more than two hundred years ago, and Father Rasle, after laboring among the tribe for many years, was murdered by the New Englanders, at Norridgewalk, in 1724. "Just one hundred and ten years after," says Bishop Fenwick, "on the 23d of August, 1834, I erected a beautiful monument over his grave, and

---

* Mr. Richard was one of the most laborious and devoted missionaries of the North-west, where he spent forty years. He established at Detroit the first printing-press in that part of the United States, started the first paper, the *Michigan Essay*, and in 1823 was sent to Congress to represent the interests of the territory.

delivered a discourse to upward of twelve thousand persons assembled on the occasion."* After Dr. Carroll had become bishop of Baltimore, these Indians, who had long been deprived of a resident pastor, were attended more regularly, chiefly by Father Romagné, who was eighteen or twenty years among them. Since 1848 they have been confided to the care of the Jesuits.

In conformity to the recommendation of the prelates of the second council, an attempt was made to establish a Catholic mission among the blacks of Liberia. The Jesuits being unprepared to furnish laborers for this field, two priests of Irish birth, Rev. Edward Barron and Rev. John Kelly, offered their services for this arduous enterprise. They embarked for Africa in 1841, and, after a partial success, Dr. Barron was appointed vicar apostolic of Upper Guinea; but the climate proving fatal to most of the missionaries associated with him, the good work was eventually abandoned.†

The third provincial council of Baltimore was held in April, 1837. A few years previously, upon the death of Archbishop Whitfield, Rev. Samuel Eccleston, a native of Maryland and a convert to the Catholic Church, succeeded to the metropolitan see. At the council over which he was now called to preside, there assisted eight other prelates. In compliance with their request, new episcopal sees were created at Nashville, Natchez, and Dubuque—the first being assigned to the care of Rev. Richard P. Miles, O. P., the second to Rev. John J. Chanche, Sulpitian, and the third to Rev. Matthias Loras, vicar-general of Mobile.‡ The pastoral letter which the prelates addressed to their flocks on this occasion, contained a vigorous protest against the misrepresentation and persecuting spirit which had resulted in the destruction of the Ursuline Convent, at Charlestown, Mass., in 1834, by a fanatical mob.§ The faithful were also exhorted "to sustain with better efforts those journals which," the Fathers say, "though not officially sanctioned by us, still are most useful to explain our tenets, to defend our rights, and to vindicate our conduct." Catholic

* Manus. Letter to B. U. Campbell, Jan., 1844.

† Dr. Barron died in 1854, at Savannah, Ga., victim of his charity during the prevalence of yellow fever.

‡ Rev. Thomas Heyden, of Bedford, Pa., had declined the appointment to Natchez.

§ The same spirit has led to acts of violence, pillage, and destruction in other places, as in Baltimore, where the Carmelite Convent was threatened by a mob, in August, 1839; at Philadelphia, where, in 1844, St. Michael's Church was burned. But fanaticism rose to its highest pitch during the *Know-Nothing* movement, especially in 1854, when several churches were destroyed, and a priest tarred and feathered. Most of these outrages occurred in New England.

journalism was then in its infancy. There were five weekly papers—
the *United States Catholic Miscellany*, of Charleston, the *Truth-Teller*,
of New York, the *Catholic Telegraph*, of Cincinnati, the *Catholic
Herald*, of Philadelphia, the *Catholic Advocate*, of Bardstown, and
the *Wahreits Freund*, a German paper, of Cincinnati. Several other
periodicals had been started within a few years previous, but they had
only a brief career.* The *Miscellany*, at Charleston, was the first
champion in the field, having been introduced in 1822, under the auspices of the illustrious Dr. England, whose genius, erudition, and untiring zeal supplied its pages for many years with the most able and
interesting articles. This journal was continued until the breaking out
of the late civil war, and its series of volumes constitutes one of the
most valuable repertories of information of which our Catholic literature can boast. During the last thirty years our periodicals have had
a very fluctuating existence—frequent undertakings succeeded by
equally frequent failures. Among the monthlies, the *United States
Catholic Magazine*, followed by the *Metropolitan*, the *Catholic Cabinet*,
and the *Expositor*, did good service to the cause of religion, while *Brown-
son's Review*, the only quarterly that Catholicity has produced in this
country, from 1844 to 1861, was, with some exceptional articles, a lucid
exponent and vigorous defender of Catholic principles. The Catholic
Tract Society of Baltimore, which commenced its monthly publications
in 1839, and continued them for five or six years, deserves honorable
mention, as having produced some of the best essays that we possess in
vindication of the true faith.† The "Catholic Almanac and Laity's
Directory," from 1833 to the present time, is a most useful publication,
and abounds with articles of the greatest historical interest.‡ Of the
three or four monthlies now in existence, the principal is *The Catholic
World*, the contents of which are chiefly selections, which are judi-
ciously made, furnishing a great variety of interesting and instructive
reading. We have now ten Catholic weeklies, with several published
in the German language, the respective merits of all which are justly
appreciated by the public. Among them is the *Ave Maria*, which is
devoted to subjects more particularly connected with the honor of Our

---

* The *Metropolitan*, a monthly, and the following hebdomadals: the *Jesuit*, the *Catholic*,
the *Shepherd of the Valley*, the *Green Banner*, the *New York Weekly Register and Catholic Diary*.

† A similar undertaking has been started in New York.

‡ A Laity's Directory was published in New York, in 1817 and 1822, but the work mentioned above is the only one of the kind that has appeared in a regular series. Even in
this there was an interruption for two years during the late war, which was the cause also
of some defects in the more recent numbers.

Blessed Lady.   The *Annals* of the Propagation of the Faith, already alluded to, are also republished at Baltimore.

It is much to be regretted, that our Catholic journals, with a few exceptions, have had so ephemeral an existence, because there is no country, perhaps, where they could accomplish more good than in the United States, if they were established on a solid footing and conducted in a proper spirit.   There always has been, but never so much so as at the present time, a disposition on the part of those who are outside of the Church, to accept the truth when proposed to them with its numerous and invincible evidences, while the Catholic population, from the many dangers to which they are exposed by the peculiar state of society in this country, have need of all the light and information that Catholic genius and learning can impart, to make them duly sensible of the inestimable blessing of faith and of the obligations which it imposes.   The causes of the frequent failures in Catholic journalism may be reduced to one—the want of sufficient funds to carry on the work. If these funds existed, they would enable publishers to employ competent editors, and an ample corps of writers could be obtained, to supply the pages of a periodical with articles which, by their variety and interest, would command public attention.   No Catholic journal can live long in this country, as experience has proved, unless it force itself as it were upon the popular favor.   The great mass of our population read little more than the newspapers.   Political, commercial, and business journals are the great sources of their information, because they are filled with matters which interest them.   If religion, the Church, with their grand and elevating truths, their historical interest, their ennobling and beneficent influence upon society, are not presented in our Catholic journals with an indisputable claim to be the successful rivals of the world, these journals cannot accomplish their mission permanently.   Those of our weekly papers that have been in existence for fifteen or twenty years, owe their continuance only to the great talent and extraordinary efforts that have been exerted in the cause.   But it is a question, perhaps not unworthy of consideration, whether the ends of Catholic journalism could not be more effectually promoted, by adopting some system or organization similar to that of the non-Catholic sects in this country, who have their weekly and quarterly publications, the recognized exponents of their peculiar opinions, and who sustain their periodicals by a common fund levied upon all their members.   Why could not some arrangement of this kind be effected for our own purposes ?   If each diocess in the Union would furnish on an average three hundred subscribers, at three or four dollars annually, to the work of Catholic publication, a fund of over fifty thousand dollars would be realized, which would be sufficient to meet the expense of several weekly papers and a quarterly review, on the most enlarged, respectable, and influential scale. While the great mass of the people would be satisfied with a weekly journal, there is a certain class, both in and out of the Church, who would require the more dignified and more elaborate form of the quarterly. In fact, for the more intelligent and the better educated class among outsiders, the quarterly is the only means of reaching their intellect and conscience. Every phase of error in this country has its organ; why should not Catholicity, which numbers at least one-seventh of the population, have a periodical which, by its ability in treating the great social questions of the day, as well as by its variety of theological, philosophical, literary, and scientific essays, and a well-digested summary of general intelligence from all parts of the world, would force itself upon the attention of thinking men, and dart some rays of light into the darkness and confusion of mind, which are misleading so many thousands of our countrymen? We want for America what the *Civilta Cattolica* is for Italy, what the *Dublin Review* is for Great Britain; a periodical which will exhibit the Catholic sentiment in regard to the questions which are of special interest to the people of this country; and until we have supplied this desideratum, we can scarcely be said to have made the best investment of the talent and resources which God in his infinite goodness has vouchsafed to our Church.

After alluding to our periodical literature, it may not be out of place here to notice briefly the other productions of Catholic genius and learning in this country. Archbishop Carroll, prior to his receiving the mitre, was the first to lead the way in theological discussion with the adversaries of the Church. We have already referred to his able controversy with the apostate Wharton. Father Anthony Kohlman next distinguished himself by his lucid exposition of the *Catholic question* in regard to the Sacrament of Penance, and by his *Unitarianism Examined*, a profound and unanswerable argument against the Anti-Trinitarians. Dr. Gallitzin has left us his *Defence* of Catholic principles and *Letters* on the Holy Scripture, which are well suited to the wants of inquirers into the grounds of Catholic faith. Besides these works, the principal publications of a doctrinal and controversial character are, the *Discussion* between Hughes and Breckinridge, the *Debate* between Purcell and Campbell, the work of Dr. England on the *Roman Chancery*, that on the *Ceremonies* of the Mass and Holy Week, and other writings of the same distinguished author;* the volume of Dr. Pise on *Christian ity* and *the Church*, Fredet's *Defence* of the Eucharist, Bishop M'Gill's *Our Faith, the Victory*, and Weninger's Protestantism and Infidelity. But the most important publication on Catholic theology is that of Archbishop Kenrick, in five volumes, 8vo, which has been adopted as a text-book in several of our ecclesiastical seminaries. His other works, *Primacy* of the Apostolic See, *Vindication* of the Catholic Church, and his treatises on Baptism and Justification, with the revised transla- tion of the Bible, are all indicative of the most varied and extensive learning. The *Evidences of Catholicity*, by the Most Rev. Dr. Spald- ing, is also a finished specimen of theological argument in a popular form, while his *D'Aubigné Reviewed* is a full and victorious refutation of that arch-perverter of history. The *Miscellanea* of the same author is a collection of the most able polemical and other essays. Rev. Father Hecker has supplied a great want for this country, in his *Ques- tions of the Soul* and *Aspirations of Nature*, which are admirably adapted to the necessities of those who have yet to learn the first prin- ciples of religious inquiry, and of whom the number is legion.

In the domain of ecclesiastical history, including biography, our literature can boast of Dr. Pise's *History* of the Church, not completed and not well digested, and his *Biography* of St. Ignatius and his com- panions, which is a much better constructed work. Archbishop Spald- ing's *Sketches of Kentucky* and *Life of Bishop Flaget* are full of interest, and written in an attractive style. Besides these, we have the *Life of Mrs. Seton ;* Bishop Bayley's *Catholic Church* in New York, and his *Life of Bishop Bruté ;* Father de Smet's *Indian Sketches* and *Oregon Missions ; Catholic Missions*, by John G. Shea, a most valuable compilation ; HISTORY of the Catholic Church in the United States, by Shea and De Courcy, containing many facts and evidencing much research, but incomplete, and, as a history, devoid of method. The articles published in the United States Catholic Magazine, on the Life and Times of Archbishop Carroll, by the late B. U. Campbell, of Baltimore, are valuable contributions to our Catholic history.

It would be unpardonable in us not to state, before dismissing this subject, that several of our Catholic authors have earned for themselves a well-deserved reputation in the field of fiction. The names of Dr. Pise, Mrs. Anna Dorsey, Mrs. Sadlier, Messrs. McLeod, Huntington, McSherry, Cannon, Bryant, and Rev. Mr. Boyce, are conspicuous in this particular branch of writing, which is not without its influence in producing the most salutary impressions. As to poetry, we shall

* His works have been published in five large volumes, 8vo

confine ourselves to the remark, that the sweetest effusions of the muse that have graced the pages of our *Magazines*, are from the pens of two ladies in the West, "Moina" and "S. R. T."

The brief exposition which we have given of the principal publications, bearing immediately upon Catholic interests, is sufficient to show that our literature is steadily advancing. According to the progress of the Church Catholic genius, learning, and piety, must find their expression in works which circumstances will call forth, and it is gratifying to note particularly that the present period is developing one of the most important branches of Catholic science, the history of the constitution, trials, and triumphs of the Church.*

In the month of May, 1840, was convened the fourth council of Baltimore, at which thirteen bishops assisted. At the request of the prelates, the see of Bardstown was transferred to Louisville, and that of Richmond was provided with a chief pastor in the person of the Right Rev. Richard V Whelan, a native of Baltimore. One of the most important decrees of this council was in relation to the security of church property, a subject which, in the present condition of our civil law, is of a very perplexing nature.

At the fifth council, which met in May, 1843, sixteen bishops were present, and upon their application to Rome the new sees of Little Rock, Chicago, Hartford, Milwaukee, and Pittsburg, were erected. Among the other wise regulations adopted by the prelates, was that which requires the pastors of congregations to keep a distinct record of the property, real or personal, which belongs to the church, so that in case of removal, by death or otherwise, the rights of the church may be properly guarded and secured.

The sixth council was held in May, 1846, and twenty-three bishops took part in its deliberations. By their action " the Blessed Virgin Mary conceived without sin was chosen as the Patroness of the Church in the United States," and at their request new sees were established at Buffalo and Albany, in the State of New York, and at Cleveland, in Ohio. Texas, before an apostolic vicariate, was made a diocess, with Galveston as the see.

In May, 1849, the seventh council of Baltimore was assembled, and attended by twenty-five bishops. The Fathers signified that they would hail with pleasure the definition of the Immaculate Conception of the Blessed Virgin Mary, as a doctrine of the Catholic Church, if

---

* Darras' *History* of the Church, now published by Mr. P. O'Shea, New York, and *Artaud's Lives of the Popes*, under press by Sadlier & Co., will supply a great want, and one which has been long felt in the United States.

the Holy See deemed it expedient to proclaim the dogma.   By another decree, they strictly enjoined upon pastors not to officiate at marriages already performed by non-Catholic ministers, nor at those in which any such ministers would be subsequently resorted to.   At the recommendation of the prelates, new episcopal sees were erected at Wheeling, Virginia ; Savannah, Georgia ; and St. Paul, Minnesota.   The territory of New Mexico was made an apostolic vicariate, and Monterey, in Upper California, was provided with a bishop.*   The see of St. Louis had been raised to the metropolitan rank in 1847, and at the request of the seventh council, other metropolitan churches were created in 1850 ; at New Orleans, with Mobile, Natchez, Galveston, and Little Rock, as suffragans ; at Cincinnati, having for suffragans Louisville, Detroit, Vincennes, and Cleveland; at New York, with Boston, Hartford, Albany, and Buffalo, as suffragans.   There were now six ecclesiastical provinces, that of St. Louis embracing the sees of Dubuque, St. Paul, Chicago, Milwaukee, and Nashville ; and that of Baltimore retaining those of Philadelphia, Pittsburg, Richmond, Wheeling, Charleston, and Savannah.   Soon after these arrangements, Archbishop Eccleston was called to his reward, in April, 1851.   He was of a tall and commanding figure, and remarkable for his fine manners and ease in conversation.   Gifted with talents of a high order, he had cultivated them with diligence, and as a preacher he was eloquent, graceful, and persuasive.   He was succeeded in the course of a few months by the Right Rev. Dr. Kenrick, bishop of Philadelphia, who was transferred from that see to Baltimore, and was also appointed apostolic delegate, to preside at the plenary council of the episcopate of the United States.   At this council, which was held in May, 1852, there were present six archbishops, and twenty-six bishops.   By their recommendation eight new sees were created, viz.: Erie, Pa.; Burlington, Vermont ; Portland, Maine ; Brooklyn, New York ; Newark, New Jersey ; Covington, Kentucky ; Quincy, Illinois ;† and Natchitoches, Louisiana.   San Francisco was made an archiepiscopal see, with Monterey as its suffragan, and Upper Michigan became an apostolic vicariate.   Since this great expansion of the Catholic hierarchy in the United States, councils have been held in several of the new provinces,

* California and New Mexico were ceded to the United States in 1848.   Monterey had been made an episcopal see in 1840, and a bishop appointed.   The see becoming vacant, Rev. J. S. Alemany, O. P., became its second bishop in 1850.   At that time there were about fourteen priests in Upper California, and thirty in New Mexico   Rev. John Lamy, of Ohio, was appointed vicar apostolic of the latter country.

† Now Alton, Illinois.

and additional sees have been created. Archbishop Kenrick, who presided over that of Baltimore for nearly thirteen years, had the proud satisfaction of witnessing before his demise this increasing development of the Church, and the steady and rapid multiplication of its resources for the accomplishment of its divine mission. His name will always be conspicuous among the most distinguished prelates, for piety and learning, and for the many excellent works with which he has enriched our literature. By a decree of July 25, 1858, the prerogative of place was granted to the see of Baltimore, so that in councils, assemblies, and meetings of every kind, precedency is given to the Archbishop of Baltimore for the time being, and the seat of honor above any archbishops of these provinces that may be present, without regard to the order of promotion or consecration. In 1864, the Right Rev. Dr. Spalding, bishop of Louisville, was transferred from that see to the Metropolitan Church of Baltimore, and the eminent qualities which he possesses warrant the assurance, that his administration of ecclesiastical affairs will add another bright chapter to the history of Catholicity in the United States.

Within the period now under consideration, some of the most distinguished prelates of the American Church, besides those already mentioned, passed from the scene of their labors. The names of Bruté, David, Dubois, England, Rosati, the two Fenwicks of Cincinnati and Boston, Flaget, Hughes, and others, will ever be cherished with grateful recollection, for they were " men of renown, and our fathers in their generation."* Like St. Paul, they would willingly " spend and be spent "† themselves for the souls committed to their care. " In the midst of the Church they opened their mouth, and the Lord filled them with the spirit of wisdom and understanding."‡ " When they went up to the holy altar, they honored the vesture of holiness."§ They strove with zeal for the glory of God. and He made them " honorable in their labors, and accomplished their labors."¶ In a word, they labored " as good soldiers of Christ Jesus " " they preached the good; they were instant in season and out of season, reproving, entreating, rebuking, in all patience and doctrine."‖ Hence, " nations shall declare their wisdom, and the Church shall shew forth their praise."**

The Church in this country now counts seven archbishoprics. thirty-six bishoprics, and four apostolic vicariates. The religious

* Eccli. xliv., 1. † 2 Cor. xii., 15. ‡ Eccli. xv., 5; Offic. Doct. § Eccli. l., 12. ¶ Wisdom x, 10 ‖ 2 Tim. ii., iv. ** Eccl· xxxix., 14.

orders and congregations, both of men and women, have also greatly increased in number and in the sphere of their operation, while the Trappists in Kentucky, the Benedictines in Pennsylvania, and the Cistercians in Iowa, have their mitred abbots. According to the last issue of the *Catholic Almanac*, there are two thousand five hundred and seventy-eight priests, and about the same number of churches. There are thirty ecclesiastical seminaries, and about three hundred literary institutions of the higher class, for youth of both sexes, conducted for the most part by members of religious congregations.* In recording this consoling advancement of Catholicity throughout the United States, especially in the North and West, justice requires us to state, that it is owing in a great measure to the faith, zeal, and generosity of the Irish people, who have emigrated to these shores, and their descendants. We are far from wishing to detract from the merit of other nationalities :† but the vast influence which the Irish population have exerted in extending the domain of the Church is well deserving of notice, because it conveys a very instructive lesson. The wonderful history of the Irish nation has always forced upon us the conviction, that, like the chosen generation of Abraham, they were destined in the designs of Providence to a special mission for the preservation and propagation of the true faith. This faith, so pure, so lively, so generous, displays itself in every region of the globe. To its vitality and energy must we attribute, to a very great extent, the rapid increase in the number of churches and other institutions which have sprung up and are still springing up in the United States, and to the same source are the clergy mainly indebted for their support in the exercise of their pastoral ministry. It cannot be denied, and we bear a cheerful testimony to the fact, that hundreds of clergymen who are laboring for the salvation of souls, would starve, and their efforts for the cause of religion would be in vain, but for the generous aid which they receive from the children of Erin, who know, for the most part, how to appreciate the benefits of religion, and who therefore joyfully contribute of their worldly means to purchase the spiritual blessings which the Church dispenses.

As to the parish-schools throughout the country, we can only form a conjectural estimate of them. Probably not one-sixth of the congregations that are served by the clergy, enjoy the benefits of a

---

* About one-third of these are for the education of young men.

† The Catholic Germans have shown great zeal and energy in our large cities, and particularly in the region of the Northwest. Some of the largest and most tasteful edifices for divine worship have been erected by their active and liberal efforts.

parochial school: and when we take into consideration the important facts, that most of the parochial schools for boys are under the charge of teachers who are but very imperfectly qualified for this important office, and that the onus of supporting these schools falls upon the clergy, whose only reliance is the charity of the faithful, we cannot wonder at the earnest attention which was given to this subject by the prelates of the Plenary Council. "We exhort the bishops," they say, "and, considering the very serious evils which commonly follow from a defective training of youth, we beseech them, through the bowels of the divine mercy, to see that schools be established in each of the churches in their dioceses; and should necessity require it, and cir cumstances permit, to provide for the employment of competent instructors from the revenues of the churches to which the schools are attached."* A similar decree had been enacted in the first Provincial Council of Baltimore. This legislation of the bishops in the United States was but an expression of the Catholic sentiment universal throughout the world, that the religious education of youth is the very life and substance of the Church, for the preservation of the true faith, and its development in the order of Providence, for the welfare of society and the salvation of souls. There is no country, perhaps, in which these considerations should have more weight than in the United States of America. The general mixture of Catholics with errorists of every description in social and political life, the inter- marrying with the sects, the gigantic efforts made by the State for the support of schools, in which religion is ignored, and which by the completeness of their outward arrangements present every attraction to the poorer class of people, are serious obstacles which Catholicity has to contend with. For this reason, there was nothing that so en- grossed the attention of the first bishop of Baltimore, as the establish- ment of a Catholic institution for the religious education of youth; and his successors, with their collaborators in the episcopal charge, have always exhibited the same solicitude. During the administration of Archbishop Maréchal, the Holy See urged upon him, with peculiar emphasis, the obligation of having such schools, in order to oppose the efforts and influence of heterodox combinations; and it may not be amiss to quote the words of Cardinal de Somaglia, in his circular of August 5, 1820. After alluding to the efforts of the sects to mislead the people, he says: "You therefore see how solicitous and energetic the pastors of the Church should be, to guard their flocks against the

* Decree 13 of Plenary Council—No. 90 in the general collection.

assaults of wolves who come to them in the clothing of sheep. If the shepherds sleep, the enemy will come, and soon the cockle will grow up in the midst of the wheat. Hence it is necessary to make every effort to withdraw children from these sectarian schools, and to admonish parents of their duty in this respect. The most effectual means for this purpose, would be to establish schools in which the poorer class could be properly instructed. Will the necessary funds for this be wanting? A useful lesson on this point may be learned from the heterodox societies themselves; for, as we are informed, they support their schools by a penny contribution levied upon all the members. Why should not Catholics do the same? We therefore exhort you, and through the bowels of our Lord Jesus Christ beseech you, to adopt the most effectual means of guarding your flock against the attacks of those who would lead it astray, and that, mindful of the words of the apostle, 'there shall be false teachers, who shall bring in sects of perdition,' you exert every effort to prevent Catholic youth from being perverted." The only means of counteracting the evil influences above mentioned, and others which lead to the same result, is the more general establishment of parish-schools, in which Catholic youth will be trained to the knowledge and practice of their religion, and a more enlarged and earnest attention to the sacred sciences in our higher institutions of learning, by which the faith will acquire a more solid and influential character. Thus will the Church and the momentous objects of its existence acquire gradually a greater importance in the eyes of the Catholic population: thus will innumerable vocations to the priesthood and the religious life be secured, while they are now lost amidst the worldliness and materialism of the age. It is not for us to suggest the ways and means of effecting these happy results: but the wisdom of the chief pastors, "who have been appointed to govern the Church of God," who from the beginning until now have so nobly struggled against all difficulties in extending the kingdom of Jesus Christ in this part of the world, and whose labors have been crowned with such glorious results, will judge how to combine the various resources which Catholic piety and generosity present, both here and from the admirable association for the propagation of the faith, for insuring the great victory of faith in this hemisphere. " This is the victory which overcometh the world, our faith."*

* The following is a list of the archbishops and bishops, who constitute the present hierarchy of the Church in the United States:—

Name.	Residence.
Mt. Rev. Alemany, Joseph S	San Francisco, California.

APPENDIX.

Name.	Residence.
Rt. Rev. Amat, Thaddeus	Los Angeles, California.
Bacon, David W	Portland, Maine.
Baraga, Frederick	Marquette, Michigan.
Bayley, James R	Newark, New Jersey.
Mt. Rev. Blanchet, Francis N	Portland, Oregon.
Rt. Rev. Blanchet, A. A. M	Ft. Vancouver, Washington Territory.
Carroll, George A	Covington, Kentucky.
Conroy, John J	Albany, New York.
de Goesbriand, Louis	Burlington, Vermont
de St. Palais, Maurice	Vincennes, Indiana.
Domenec, Michael	Pittsburg, Pennsylvania.
Dubuis, M	Galveston, Texas.
Duggan, James	Chicago, Illinois.
Elder, W. H	Natchez, Mississippi.
Feehan, John P. A.	Nashville, Tennessee.
Grace, Thomas L	St. Paul, Minnesota
Hennessy, John	Dubuque, Iowa.
Henni, John M	Milwaukee, Wisconsin
Juncker, H. D	Alton, Illinois.
Mt. Rev. Kenrick, Peter R	St. Louis, Missouri.
Rt. Rev. Lamy, John	Santa Fé, New Mexico.
Lavialle, Peter J	Louisville, Kentucky.
Lefevere, Peter P	Detroit, Michigan.
Loughlin, John	Brooklyn, New York.
Luers, John H	Fort Wayne, Indiana.
Lynch, P. N	Charleston, South Carolina.
Martin, Augustus	Natchitoches, Louisiana.
Mt. Rev. McCloskey, John	New York.
Rt. Rev. McFarland, Francis P	Providence, Rhode Island.
McGill, John	Richmond, Virginia.
Miege, John P	Leavenworth, Kansas (Vic. Apost)
O'Connell, Eugene	Marysville, California (Vic. Apost)
Mt. Rev. Odin, J. M	New Orleans, Louisiana.
Rt. Rev. O'Gorman, James M	Omaha, Nebraska (Vic. Apost.)
Mt. Rev. Purcell, John B	Cincinnati, Ohio.
Rt. Rev. Williams, John J	Boston, Massachusetts.
Quinlan, John	Mobile, Alabama.
Rappe, Amadeus	Cleveland, Ohio.
Rosecrans, Sylvester H.	Cincinnati, Ohio.
Mt. Rev. Spalding, Martin John.	Baltimore, Maryland.
Rt. Rev. Timon, John	Buffalo, New York.
Vérot, A	Savannah, Georgia.
Whelan, Richard V	Wheeling, Virginia.
Wood, James F	Philadelphia, Pennsylvania.

The sees of Little Rock and Erie, and the apostolic vicariate of Florida, are vacant.

INDEX.

INDEX TO APPENDIX.